WARFARE in the CLASSICAL WORLD

WARFARE in the CLASSICAL WORLD

An illustrated encyclopedia of weapons, warriors and warfare
in the ancient civilisations of Greece and Rome

John Warry

St. Martin's Press
New York

A Salamander Book

© Salamander Books Ltd 1980

For information, write:
St. Martin's Press Inc.
175 5th Avenue,
New York,
N.Y. 10010, USA

Manufactured in Belgium

ISBN 0-312-85614-8

Library of Congress 80-54639

Credits

Editor: Philip de Ste. Croix
Designer: Nick Buzzard
Editorial research: Paul McDonnell-Staff
Picture research: Caroline Lucas

Color figures:
Jeff Burn © Salamander Books Ltd
Black and white figures:
Clive Spong © Salamander Books Ltd
Color equipment drawings:
Peter Sarson and Tony Bryan
© Salamander Books Ltd
Black and white equipment drawings:
Mike Craig © Salamander Books Ltd
Battle plans:
Stonecastle Graphics
© Salamander Books Ltd
Tactical diagrams:
Jamie Courtier
Alan Hollingbery
Ralph Stobart
Stonecastle Graphics
© Salamander Books Ltd
Maps:
Ralph Stobart
Jamie Courtier
Base map © George Philip & Sons Ltd
Historical information
© Salamander Books Ltd

Filmset:
Modern Text Typesetting Ltd, England
Color and monochrome reproduction:
Bantam Litho Ltd
Culver Graphics Ltd
Photosummit Ltd
Scansets Ltd
Tenreck Ltd, England

Printed in Belgium:
Henri Proost et Cie, Turnhout

Editor's Acknowledgements

A large number of people have assisted in the preparation of this book, as a brief glance at the list of credits opposite and the author's acknowledgements overleaf will testify. In addition to thanking all the artists who have contributed so notably, and the individuals and institutions who have generously answered our requests for pictures and information, I would particularly like to thank the editorial researcher, Paul McDonnell-Staff, for his untiring efforts. It was his task to produce reference material for virtually all the artwork included, and in addition he has written the captions for most of the artwork panels as a corollary of this research. I am very grateful for his help. I would also like to thank Phil Barker, the President of the Society of Ancients, for the assistance and advice that he generously offered me.

A brief note about the battle-plans may avoid confusion in the minds of some readers. It will be noticed that our plans frequently differ from those of earlier researchers; nor do they always accept the army strengths recorded in ancient texts. As contemporary accounts of war still illustrate, numbers of combatants and casualties are often distorted in the furtherance of propaganda. Paul McDonnell-Staff has studied all the extant accounts of each battle in this book and related them to the physical geography of the battlefield, and probable frontages of units involved in order to build up an overall picture which we trust is as accurate as any previously published.

The maps in the book are intended as illustrations of the general historical trends within each period considered. Some contemporary place names have been included in conjunction with the less familiar ancient names. In this, the usage corresponds with that adopted in each chapter, the intention being to make cross-reference between map and text as easy for the reader as possible.

Philip de Ste. Croix

Contents

Author's Foreword

A few words about the structure and design of this book may help the reader. Each of the fourteen chapters begins with notes on ancient literary sources and the political background of warfare during the period treated. The periods allotted to the several chapters are by no means equal in time, ranging from the 13 years of Chapter 12 (The Wars of the Triumvirate) to the three-century Imperial epoch of Chapter 13 (The Military Task of Imperial Rome). The criterion that determines the time-span of a chapter is in every case political, for in the history of warfare political circumstances determine the combatants; or according to the well-known dictum of Clausewitz, "war is nothing but a continuation of political intercourse with an admixture of different means". However, most sections in each chapter are devoted to brief studies of military art, weapons, fortifications, navies, siegecraft, individual battles, leadership, etc.

Having regard to the above plan, Chapter One is a special case. We need not apologise for trying to extract history from Homer. We have assumed that a long oral tradition, perhaps five centuries old, separates Homer from his "primary sources". Verse is an older art than prose. In early illiterate epochs, its function was mnemonic, its poetry a by-product. Priam's Troy and the voices which originally commemorated it may therefore have preceded Homer by as many years as Alexander the Great and Ptolemy, his contemporary witness, preceded Arrian. The existence of such oral sources would account for those features of Mycenaean civilisation which are strikingly reflected in the Homeric poems, as would the intervening letterless centuries for many interpolations and omissions.

Throughout the book, it should be noted that the artists' reconstructions with their appended explanations are mostly based on research independent of that which underlies the text of the fourteen chapters. Consistency has everywhere been a prior aim, but if an acute critic here and there detects divergent trends of opinion, this will neither surprise nor dismay anyone who recognizes the essentially controversial nature of the subject. In some places, for sheer lack of space, the authors and illustrators have settled on a division of labour. Chapter 12, for instance, sets out the meagre historical facts which have been handed down to us in connection with the battle of Actium, while the battle plans and subjoined commentary offer a controversial modern interpretation of events.

The book is of course avowedly a summary. In summarising one is bound to generalise, and in generalisation many significant details and variant interpretations of evidence are unavoidably omitted. Moreover, although the subject is fascinating, detailed study often raises more questions than it answers. In these circumstances, wishing to spare the reader a tiresome style hedged by continual provisos, the author and illustrators may sometimes appear rashly dogmatic, but they have nevertheless, wherever uncertainty arises, always paid attention to other views before adopting their own. For example, it was agreed to illustrate a trireme with a central deck and a hatch for the insertion of a mast. This does not mean that we are unfamiliar with the theory of side-decks and a central well, such as originated in Germany and, as early as 1949, enjoyed the formidable advocacy of Professor G.S. Kirk. However, it is clear, on literary evidence alone, that the structure of triremes differed with time and place, and as many varieties of them may have been known to the ancient world as there are conjectures about them among modern scholars.

Artists' reconstructions apart, illustrations include photographs of ancient representations, the ruins of fortifications and the remains of weapons. There are also maps, plans, and tabulated displays of statistics and events. The table of dates which runs horizontally across the foot of each page is meant to correlate Mediterranean and Western Asiatic events with those which occurred in centres of civilisation further east. But the fact remains that most recorded history during our period is Graeco-Roman, and the dates given will also usefully supplement the chapters, in which the appearance of a chronicle has been deliberately avoided in order to make way for a series of separate and self-contained military studies. Nevertheless, the attempt to trace development, cause and effect in any subject implies some sort of history, and the fourteen chapters are designed to illustrate a story of continuous evolution. At all events, it is hoped not to leave the impression sometimes unfortunately created by a school syllabus, that Ancient History halted abruptly at the death of Alexander the Great, then drew a deep breath before recommencing in Italy with Romulus and Remus and the Wolf.

Apart from our deep indebtedness to Dr Graham Webster of the University of Birmingham for reading proofs of Chapters 7 to 14 and for advising on matters in which he is a widely recognized authority, grateful acknowledgements are due to Mr Edward O'Donoghue of St John's College, Cambridge, for reading Chapters 1 to 6 and to a number of institutions and individuals who have assisted in various ways. These include notably the staff of the Joint Library of the Society for the Promotion of Hellenic Studies and the Roman Society, whose services have on several occasions included a willingness to quote Greek over the telephone—even on Saturday mornings. A great deal of advice and help has also been obtained from the staff of the Central Library of the Royal Military Academy, Sandhurst, the Libraries of the University of London and its Archaeological Institute, and of the Royal Holloway College, while in addition to facilities enjoyed as a reader in the British Museum, the author has welcomed the opportunity of discussion and correspondence with authorities in the Museum's Department of Greek and Roman Antiquities and the Department of Western Asiatic Antiquities. He is also grateful for help received from the press and information services and cultural attachés of the Greek, Italian and Spanish Embassies in London, for advice concerning replicas and reproductions of reliefs on Trajan's Column from the Victoria and Albert Museum, for information about surviving early chariots from the School of African and Oriental Studies of the University of London, for prompt attention to enquiries about Scythian bows by the Museum of Archaeology and Anthropology in Cambridge, and for ample material on the construction of ancient ships offered by the Department of Transport of the Science Museum, London. Thanks is also owing to Professor Francesco Roncalli of the Museo Gregoriano Etrusco in the Vatican for details of ancient shields preserved in Italy and to Professor A.M. Snodgrass of the University of Cambridge, whose name is always closely associated with the study of Greek arms and armour, for valuable guidance to photographs and their interpretation in periodical publications. However, it goes without saying that the author, researcher and illustrators take full responsibility for all that occurs in or is omitted from their respective contributions.

John Warry
Camberley, Surrey, England 1980

The Pronunciation of Ancient Languages

It is possible to form some idea of the way in which Greek and Latin were pronounced in ancient times. Evidence is to be found in the spellings of ancient languages as we have received them in manuscripts and inscriptions, in the comments of grammarians, and in the pronunciation of derived modern languages. In practice, however, a modern student tends to compromise between an inferred ancient pronunciation and the habits of his own tongue as conditioned by his own language.

The Italian pronunciation of Latin, widespread as a result of ecclesiastical use, may be regarded as international property. However, the letters "c" and "g" in classical Latin were pronounced hard, even when followed by the soft vowels "e" and "i". Moreover, Latin, like Greek, distinguished between long and short vowels. Modern scholars whose languages preserve the same difference (cf English *beat* and *bit*), try to draw the distinction in their pronunciation of the ancient languages.

Long before Greek began to be taught in western Europe, words borrowed from Greek, not to mention many Greek proper names, had appeared transliterated in Latin and received a Latin pronunciation. Not surprisingly, after the Renaissance, the pronunciation of Greek in western schools and universities was influenced by Latin traditions, particularly in the matter of accentuation.

If one is able to recognize long or short syllables, the rules of Latin accentuation are extremely simple. Dissyllables (with minimal exceptions) are accented on the first syllable. Polysyllables are accented on the penultimate when this is long, otherwise on the antepenultimate. Unfortunately, long and short syllables cannot be recognized without knowledge of Latin. Diphthongs are always long, but Latin sometimes transliterates Greek diphthongs as single vowels, and these must be treated as diphthongs for purposes of accentuation (eg in *Coronea*, formed from Greek *Koroneia*). Apart from all such considerations, familiarity with derived words in modern languages, particularly Italian, often suggests the correct Latin stress.

The principles of Greek pronunciation are quite different. The accentuation of polysyllables is most frequently determined by the quantity (length) of the final syllable, not the penultimate, and many words—as hardly ever in Latin—are accented on the final syllable.

Considering the long history of Latin and Greek, first as languages of common speech, and subsequently as pronounced in schools, universities, and churches, it is inevitable that their pronunciation should have undergone many changes in the course of more than two millenia, quite apart from local differences. It is therefore impossible to define a "right" pronunciation. But Western Europeans, without experience of the classical languages, will probably make themselves most easily intelligible to other Western Europeans if they pronounce Latin as though it were Italian, and Greek as though it were Latin.

If, however, one wishes to be understood among Greeks, Greek words must receive the Greek accent. This is made much easier by the fact that since the third century BC, Greek accents have been marked on words as part of the spelling (except where block capitals are used). Greek accents, as written, take three different forms: acute, circumflex and grave. These originally indicated differences of musical pitch. Indeed, the phonetic difference between a stress and a pitch accent is not always clear cut, since higher tones make a sharper impact on the ear. In any case, the Greek accents as used to-day all call for a similar stress in pronunciation and are distinct only in the manner of their writing.

Another important change in post-classical Greek has been brought about the process of itacism, which has equated the pronunciation of no less than three Greek vowels and as many diphthongs with an Italian "i". Many consonant sounds have also undergone change. Although post-classical, the so-called "modern" pronunciation of Greek is in fact very ancient and probably dates from early Byzantine times.

In Western Europe, vernacular forms of both Latin and Greek names are another source of confusion. For instance, Horatius Flaccus the poet (but not Horatius Cocles who defended the bridge) is written both in English and French as "Horace" and pronounced as linguistic habits dictate. The mute "e" at the end of a French or English word is often especially confusing because a Greek final "e", when retained in transliteration, is pronounced. Thus *Lade* is a dissyllable and *Ithome* a trisyllable. Also compare the modern vernacular dissyllable form "hoplite"

Above: *A military discharge certificate found at Malpas in England, dating from AD 103, the time of Trajan. It was issued to Reburrus of the 1st (Tampius') Pannonian Cavalry and conferred citizen's rights on him as a time-expired auxiliary.*

(plural: "hoplites") with the Greek trisyllable *hoplites* (plural: *hoplitai*). The difficulty occurs in English and French, but the German plural "Hopliten" happily invites no such confusion with the Greek singular.

In this connection, one should perhaps notice a few principles of transliteration as they apply in different European languages. German renders the Greek letter "kappa" as "k", but the Romance languages Latinise to "c". English usually Latinises, but sometimes writes "k". Latin rendered the Greek letter "upsilon" by a letter "y", which was reserved specially for this purpose. But Italian uses no such letter and replaces every Latin "y" with "i".

A reader with no background of classical study may pardonably conclude that if he adopts whatever pronunciation first comes to mind he cannot be very far from one phonetic norm or the other. However, if more than one word is to be pronounced in the same context, consistency is obviously to be considered desirable.

Consistency is admittedly a sore point when it comes to rendering ancient proper names, and most writers on classical themes find that it must often be sacrificed to usage and readability, especially where one is concerned with transliteration from the Greek alphabet. For the spelling of the name Boudica (Boadicea) the reader is referred to the book of this title by Graham Webster, whose reasons for adopting such a usage are fully explained therein.

Homeric and Mycenaean Warfare

Over one thousand years before the beginning of the Christian era, a Greek expeditionary force laid siege to the city of Troy in Asia Minor. Homer's epic account of this gives a graphic, if fragmentary, picture of warfare in the early classical world.

Ancient Authorities

Homer's *Iliad* is not history, but it is historical fiction, and it is the most obvious point at which to begin an account of ancient Greek warfare. The Homeric poems were composed in the 8th or 9th century BC, but the events which they describe echo a much earlier past. The theme of the *Iliad* is announced in its opening lines. It concerns a quarrel between two Greek leaders in their war against the city of Troy and it traces the grave and far-reaching military consequences of this quarrel. Achilles, the young Greek commander with whose attitudes and behaviour the *Iliad* is chiefly concerned, could be courteous and even generous but, when roused, he abandoned himself to violent and implacable fury. The first victims of his wrath were the Greeks themselves. After quarreling with the commander-in-chief of the Greek allied forces, he withdrew his support from the common war effort. Later, when his dearest friend, Patroclus, had been killed as the result of his behaviour, Achilles' anger was turned against Hector, the enemy leader at whose hands Patroclus had met his death. Achilles avenged Patroclus and, in his usual implacable manner, barbarously outraged the corpse of his conquered foeman. But the *Iliad* ends on a conciliatory note; Achilles overcame his anger and restored Hector's body to the Trojans for decent cremation.

In military terms, the story of Achilles' anger means that phase of the Trojan War in which the Greek army, deprived of its full complement, was fighting, sometimes desperately, on the defensive. The Greek counter-offensive against the Trojans began only when Achilles' bitterness was diverted from his own commander and focused once more upon the enemy. The *Iliad* is, therefore, concerned with only one phase of the whole Trojan War.

The other great epic said to be "by Homer" is the *Odyssey*. It tells of the return of one of the Greek leaders, Odysseus, to his island home of Ithaca, off the north-west coast of Greece. One might describe it as a "sequel" to the *Iliad*, and it contains many references to the events of the Trojan War. It has been observed that the *Iliad* describes the Homeric world at war, while the *Odyssey* is an account of that same world at peace; though peace in this context means—as perhaps it has come to mean in our own times—a period of disorganized as distinct from organized violence.

Other poems, now lost, seem to have aimed at completing the history of the early Greek world. These "Cyclic" epics, as they were termed, are summarized in prose synopses on some manuscripts of Homer's poems. The causes and early events of the Trojan War were recorded in a verse narrative generally known as the *Cypria*—perhaps because the poet who composed it was a native of Cyprus.

The story of other incidents in the Trojan War was told in the *Little Iliad* and *The Sack of Troy*. The first relates the death of Paris, the Trojan prince whose abduction of Helen from Greece had been the occasion of the war. The second poem contains the well-known story of the Wooden Horse and of the capture of Troy by the Greeks after a ten-year siege. The Trojan hero Aeneas and his followers, in this account, escape furtively from the city, aghast at warning omens, before the fatal night of its capture and sack. But there are representations in early Greek art of Aeneas carrying his aged father to safety, as later described by Virgil.

Another of the Cyclic epics was called, alternatively, the *Aethiopis* or the *Amazonia*. It told how the Trojans were aided by Penthesilea, the queen of those legendary women warriors the Amazons. But Penthesilea was killed by Achilles in battle. The same fate awaited Memnon, king of the Ethiopians, who also led a relief force to

| BC The chronology of the early historic period is necessarily approximate: | 1600 Early Mycenaean culture (as revealed by excavation at sites indicated in the Homeric poems): | The shaft graves at Mycenae: evidence of boar's-tooth caps (cf. Iliad Book X) | Mycenaean weapons: Cyclopaean walls: representation of chariots: | Writing tablets with records in linear scripts | 1570-1425 Cretan palaces at Knossos and other centres flourish despite disasters |

Troy. The *Aethiopis* went on to describe the subsequent death of Achilles himself, who fell when storming one of the city gates, the victim of inspired archery.

Throughout antiquity, poets, dramatists, painters and sculptors treated and developed the themes of the Cyclic epics; but this treatment necessarily interpolated the standards and usages of later times into the ancient background. The main literary evidence for our subject must remain the *Iliad* of Homer. Archaeological evidence is of course another question. We shall discuss it later.

Political Background

The commander-in-chief with whom Achilles quarrelled was Agamemnon. A consideration of the role which he plays in the *Iliad* suggests that his apparent military and political supremacy was as much a question of honour as of jurisdiction. He was entitled to a special prize out of any booty taken. At the beginning of the *Iliad*, he had sacrilegiously helped himself to a priest's daughter, but when the god Apollo marked his displeasure with a visitation of plague (as in unhygienic siege conditions he must frequently

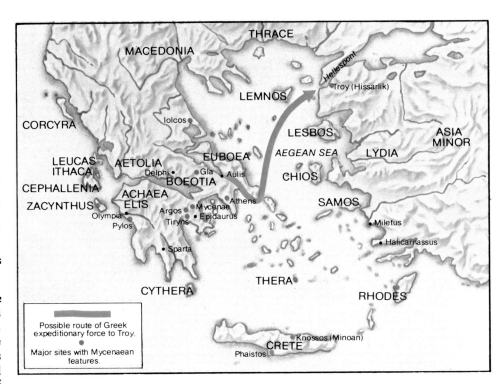

Above: *This map illustrates the major archaeological sites at which Mycenaean features have been found. The culture flourished during the latter half of the 2nd millenium BC.*

Above: *According to legend, King Priam fled for sanctuary when Troy was sacked but died at Zeus' altar by the hand of Neoptolemus. Later artists introduced the arms and armour of their own day into the scene.*

Left: *As the inscribed names reveal, Hector and Menelaus are fighting over the fallen Trojan, Euphorbus, an incident in the* Iliad. *This Rhodian plate dates from the late 7th century BC, as do the arms shown.*

have done) Agamemnon was obliged to return his favourite concubine to her father without ransom. We should notice at this point that the general assembly of the Greeks, which met to discuss the plague situation, had been convened by Achilles, not by Agamemnon; Agamemnon, resenting this, compensated himself by impounding one of Achilles' concubines.

There is a kind of democracy here. It is not a democracy based either on the rights of man or of the citizen. The concept of human rights was unknown in the ancient world, founded as its civilization was on the institution of slavery. As for citizens' rights, they certainly had no place in the Homeric world. But one can see that there was a nicely balanced separation of powers among the Greek leaders. Agamemnon could not afford to flout the opinion of his assembled army, especially when it was backed by Achilles' armed resources. On the other hand, Achilles felt unable to withold his own captive concubine when Agamemnon sent heralds to collect her. Agamemnon was, after all, nominally in command, and he had the right to a prize.

It was, moreover, Achilles' turn, for all his ungovernable temper, to respect public opinion. Agamemnon originally claimed in the assembly to be compensated by what, in the absence of any public fund, would have amounted to a capital levy on the whole army. Achilles countered with the more popular suggestion that the army should compensate Agamemnon later, when more booty was available. The

politics of the amendment were irresistible, but Agamemnon retaliated angrily with an amendment of his own. He would be compensated not by a levy on the rank and file, but by one of the leaders, preferably Achilles himself. Thus the Homeric lords, for all their lofty aristocratic style, could not dispense with the subtleties of demagogy.

Like others among Homer's heroes, Agamemnon is the subject of divergent traditions. According to one account, his position as supreme commander was a purely *ad hoc* appointment, the result of general consensus, since he and his brother, the wronged Menelaus, had carried out a recruiting drive throughout Greece to raise forces to restore Helen and avenge her abduction. In this case, the widespread sympathy which they enlisted for their cause must have been linked with the hope of gain and honour on the part of the other Greek rulers. There is, however, another story, according to which Helen's father* had exacted a vow from her assembled suitors that they would support her chosen husband against any challenge to his married rights. The existence of this oath suggests some kind of feudal allegiance, owed by the other Greek lords to Agamem-

*Her putative father, to be mythologically precise.

| | 1500 | | | 1480 | | BC |
| Epoch of Cretan wealth, culture and sea-power | Queen Hatsheput in Egypt (18th dynasty) | Evidence of destruction in Crete | Mycenaean culture spreads to Cyprus | Hatsheput succeeded by her son Thutmosis III | Period of greatest Egyptian expansion (4th Nile cataract to Euphrates) | |

11

non's family; this probability is strengthened by the further story that Odysseus feigned madness in order to evade service in the Trojan expedition: something he need not have attempted if he were free from obligation.

In contrast with the Greek leadership, the authority of the Trojan royal family was unequivocal. Its members were generally united and worked as a team. King Priam and his sons commanded the allegiance not only of adjacent communities in the Troad, but of a far-flung empire which straddled the Hellespont (Dardanelles), extending both into south-east Europe and Asia Minor. Certainly, there was no question of purely war-substantive command such as Agamemnon's position sometimes seems to have entailed.

Hector, Priam's eldest son by Hecuba, the current queen consort, was both commander-in-chief and Troy's most formidable fighting man. Again, this contrasts happily with the Greek situation, in which Agamemnon and Achilles were rivals for military prestige. The Trojan government, comparable perhaps with some dynastic governments in the Middle East today, had supported and ratified Paris' abduction of Helen. Troy's wealth, derived from its command of Black Sea trade routes, made it a target for predators. Yet we should not dismiss the story of Paris and Helen as lacking all historical basis. By Homeric usage—for which parallels can easily be found—he who married a queen was entitled not only to her dowry in the form of gold, silver and moveables, but to territory and jurisdiction as well. Paris, having eloped with Helen, married her. She did not live with him in Troy as his mistress. Even in the modern world it is possible, as a result of differing national marriage laws, for a woman to have different husbands in different countries. When Paris was killed in action, his brother Deiphobus married Helen. The Trojan royal family seems to have been determined not to relinquish its claim to a kingdom in mainland Greece.

There is, perhaps, in this harmonious family government, one discordant note, which could have resulted in a palace revolution had Troy survived the war. Aeneas, who, at the end of Book Two of the *Iliad*, seems to have ranked second in command to Hector, was descended from a cadet branch of the Trojan royal house. In Book Thirteen it is made clear that he was dissatisfied with the meagre honours which he had received at Priam's hands. Later, Achilles taunted him

with having an eye to the royal succession, and indeed we hear of a divine prophecy according to which Aeneas was destined one day to rule over the Trojans. The *Sack of Troy*, as has already been noted, records his premature and surreptitious flight from the doomed city, and among late authors there are even some who accuse him of having sold Troy to the Greeks. However, the portrait in the Roman poet Virgil's *Aeneid* of an honest man, attentive both to his domestic and religious duties, is the tradition which has reached us, and perhaps this is the picture which would in any case have persisted, even if it had not been admirably in accord with Virgil's political commitments.

In reading the *Iliad*, it is easy to form the impression that the Trojans themselves were of Greek extraction. For the most part, they had Greek names. They conversed easily enough with their Greek foemen, now negotiating a truce, now exchanging boasts and threats. The assumption of a common

language may of course be regarded as a poetic convenience, but such convenience is denied by Homer to the Trojans when he describes their relations with their allies. At the end of Book Two, Iris, the messenger of the gods, impersonating a Trojan sentinel, advised Hector to obviate the language difficulty by delegating authority to the leaders of the national contingents.

In this connection, it should be recalled that Homer has no word applicable to all the Greek-speaking peoples. He usually refers to those who served under Agamemnon as Achaeans*—sometimes as Argives or Danaans. But although these local designations are extended to mean much more than

---

*The name has been thought to occur on Hittite inscribed tablets in the form *Achehijawa* (late 14th to end 13th century), and, in an Egyptian inscription of c 1225, the Akawash are mentioned as raiders of the Nile Delta. Interesting attempts have been made to supplement our knowledge of Greek history with these Hittite and Egyptian records.

The Dendra Panoply c1400 BC
This unusual suit of armour was found at Dendra near Mycenae. It has many advanced features such as the articulated shoulder pieces and skirt. The helmet is made of pieces of boar's tusk on a base of leather thongs. The drawing shows how such armour may have been worn. Such a panoply would not have required a shield and seems rather heavy for a foot soldier. It may have been worn by a chariot-warrior unable to manipulate a large shield in the confines of the vehicle. Fragments of arm guards and greaves were also found at Dendra, but it is not known if they also belong to this panoply.

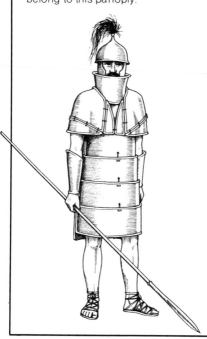

BC	1450	1425	1400	1390
	Hittites establish empire in Anatolia (Indo-European language)	The use of bronze plate armour at Mycenae (discovery at Dendra, May 1960)	The use of bronze helmets in Crete (discovery at Knossos)	In Mesopotamia, emergence of Assyrians as independent power

Above: *This mid-6th century warrior invites comparison with a 5th century hoplite, but there are important differences. His shield is of "Boeotian" design and his weapon a javelin.*

the inhabitants of Achaea or the city of Argos—once ruled by king Danaus—they do not necessarily include all persons of Greek language and culture. Apart from other peoples of Asia who supported Priam, there were allies from Lycia, led by the prince Sarpedon, who, despite some chronological confusion, was said to have come originally from Crete. Glaucus, his lieutenant, was also a Lycian. Homer describes how, during a lull in the fighting, Glaucus had a few friendly words with the Greek hero, Diomedes. The Lycian explained how his family came originally from Argos and Diomedes immediately discovered that they were bound by ties of hereditary friendship; their grandfathers had in the past, as host and guest respectively, exchanged gifts in Argos. Accordingly, the two men, now fighting on different sides, vowed to avoid each other in battle and themselves exchanged armour in token of friendship. Sadly, it is implied that Diomedes had an ulterior motive; Glaucus'

armour was of gold, worth more than ten times as much as Diomedes' bronze panoply was valued.

Arms and Armour

Homer refers elsewhere to gold armour, but seems to despise it. The usual material for weapons was bronze. Iron is well known in Homer, but is used for making implements, not weapons—though iron arrowheads existed. Methods of producing iron were presumably still primitive and it appears to be valued as a substitute for bronze rather than as an improvement upon that particular material.

The characteristic offensive weapon in the *Iliad* was the spear. It was made of ash wood and was for throwing rather than thrusting—though Achilles killed Hector with a thrust of his spear. Hector's own spear is recorded as being 11 cubits long (about 18ft, 5·5m).

Swords are referred to as being large and sometimes two-edged. When not in

---

Early Greek Arms

The Body Shield (below)
The most common type of Mycenaean shield was apparently the figure-of-eight shield shown. It is seen on wall-paintings and described in detail by Homer. The reconstruction below is based on these sources. The frame consists of two bow-shaped pieces of wood fastened to form a cross. The horizontal has a short reinforcing piece which acts as a grip. The shield is made of several layers of toughened bull's hide glued and stitched to a wicker core. The rim, as described by Homer, is of leather.

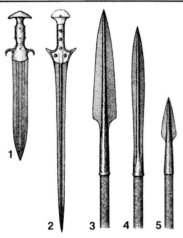

Mycenaean Weapons 1500-1200 BC
1 shows a type of short bronze sword which became popular c1400 BC, and remained in use until the end of the Mycenaean period c1100 BC. This reconstruction is based on an example said to have been found in Ithaca, the home of Odysseus. **2** shows the earlier long sword, in use from c1500 BC but declining in popularity c1300 BC. This one is based on an example found at Mount Olympus. The three spearheads (**3**, **4**, **5**) are from Ialysos on Rhodes and date from roughly the same period. They were excavated a few years before Schliemann discovered Troy. They are remarkable for their large size—up to 2ft (·65m) long. Such heads can only have been attached to a thrusting spear, not a throwing weapon. They may have been wielded two-handed by a warrior mounted aboard a war-chariot.

The Argos Panoply c750 BC
The arms and armour of the Indo-European peoples who swamped Mycenaean culture in the 12th and 11th centuries were quite new. Bronze helmets such as that shown, with either integral or hinged cheek-pieces became almost universal. The corslet is an early example of the well-known "Bell" type which evolved into the "muscled" cuirass. It consisted of front and back plates joined by leather straps. The open right had two tubes which were locked by a central pin passing through.

Early Hoplite c600 BC
Around the 8th century BC the classic *hoplon* shield with its characteristic grip evolved (see p 35). A particularly well-equipped warrior is shown here; most would not be as well armed. The "Bell" corslet has now reached its classic form while the exposed right arm, legs and groin have additional armour. The helmet, of a type known as "Illyrian", has a crest that lies along the crown of the bowl. This reinforced the line along which the two halves were joined.

1380
Final destruction of the Palace at Knossos

1377-1358
In Egypt, Ahmenhotep IV (Akhnaton) introduces monotheistic form of sun-worship

1300
Destruction of sixth city at Hissarlik (Troy VI) previously identified as Homeric Troy

Construction of "beehive" (*tholos*) tombs at Mycenaean sites

BC

13

use, they were slung in a sheath from a baldric. They seem to have been used for cutting rather than for thrusting.

Shields were bodylength. They were suspended from a strap round the neck and knocked against a warrior's ankles as he walked. They were made of bull's hide and were plated with bronze. The shield of Ajax had seven layers of bull's hide; of these, the spear of Hector penetrated six, but was arrested by the seventh. Ajax' shield is also described as being like a tower; he was a man of enormous stature, who both needed and could manage such a shield. But the use of smaller, round shields may be inferred, notably from the wearing of greaves. Achilles' greaves, which were loaned to Patroclus, were fastened with a silver clasp. Greaves were possibly more like gaiters, not necessarily of metal, though there is a reference to the Achaeans as wearing bronze greaves.

A Homeric hero's helmet was characteristically of bronze, though leather caps were also in use and must have been more common with the rank and file. The bronze helmet was surmounted by a horse-hair plume which nodded in the air with awe-inspiring effect. The helmet itself was effectively resistant and a sword sometimes shattered on encountering it.

Protective metal armour seems to have been mainly the privilege of the leaders, and for this reason it required a leader to defy a leader in battle. Otherwise, the situation was that of infantry thrown against tanks. Armour was very precious, and when a hero had fallen there was usually a fierce fight for possession of his arms and armour. However, subject to these limitations, the rank and file were not necessarily ill-equipped. They are frequently mentioned as being adept with the spear. Achilles' Myrmidons, who were something of a local *corps d'élite,* wore some kind of breastplate or corslet, probably not of metal. Diomedes' followers are mentioned as being equipped with shields, which they used at night as pillows, while their spears stood upright, thrust into the ground on their spiked butts. Diomedes himself had a carpet for a pillow rather than such a shield.

On the Trojan side, shields were also standard equipment in the archer Pandarus' contingent; these shields were used to screen him while he let fly a treacherous arrow during a time of solemnly sworn truce.

Homeric arms and armour, it must be remarked, are the subject of much controversy. In the present context, we

must limit ourselves to generalizations; but even so it is difficult to avoid statements which are open to challenge.

Chariots

Apart from weapons and panoply, both the Greek and Trojan chiefs were sufficiently wealthy to maintain horses and chariots. These were essential to their way of fighting. The normal purpose of a chariot was to carry a fully armed warrior to the battlefield, where he would dismount and fight on foot while his charioteer waited at a discreet distance with the horses and vehicle. If the warrior survived, he would eventually retire from the fight, remount his chariot and be driven back to his own lines.

In practice, chariots often became more deeply involved in the fighting. They were frequently within bowshot,

War-Chariots

It is not easy to reconstruct a war-chariot such as was used in the Greek Bronze Age from the few highly stylised and archaic representations which have survived. Bronze Age chariots from Egyptian tombs of the 15th century BC provide an analogy, and the two-horse racing chariots depicted by Greek artists of the historical period do not differ essentially from these.

Literary Evidence
The type of chariot described in the *Iliad* was drawn by two horses. Exceptionally, four horses are allocated by Homer to Hector's chariot and he gives their names. Ancient scholars considered on grammatical grounds that Homer's text was corrupt at this point, but in any case anachronistic artists of classical times introduced four-horse war-chariots into their

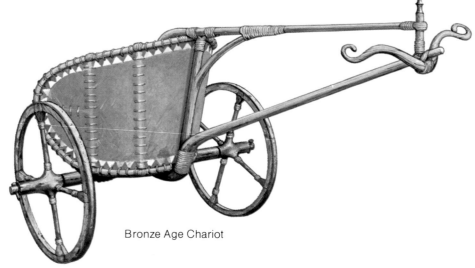

Bronze Age Chariot

spear throw—or even stone's throw—of the enemy. Homer describes how an arrow missed Hector in his chariot and killed his charioteer. Another charioteer was later killed by a stone flung by Patroclus. In the thick of battle, horses and chariots ploughed their way through the wreckage of enemy chariots, trampling and crushing the bodies of fallen men, while they themselves were spattered with blood. Patroclus, with a thrust of his spear, impaled an enemy warrior in his chariot and hauled him out, over the rim of the chariot, still impaled, like an angler hauling a fish to land. The chariot needed smooth terrain for efficient performance; on difficult ground the pole that connected the yoke with the car itself could easily break, allowing the horses to bolt. This happened to many Trojan chariots as their drivers tried in vain to negotiate the ditch round the Greek camp.

BC	1250			1200			
	Lion gate at Mycenae constructed (comparable with Hittite architecture)	Destruction of seventh city at Hissarlik (Troy VII a) now generally identified as Homeric Troy		Migration and expansion of Dorian Greeks	Destruction of Mycenaean Pylos	The use of non-metallic armour at Mycenae (evidence of the Warrior Vase)	In Asia, the collapse of the Hittite empire

14

representations of the deeds of the heroic past.

In the 16th book of the *Iliad*, the Trojans in their chariots are forced to withdraw across the ditch outside the Greek camp. In this process the yoke-poles of many chariots are broken and the liberated horses career away, leaving their unfortunate masters stranded. The junction of the pole with the chariot was a weak point, vulnerable to shock. On the Egyptian chariots the pole was extended backward under the car as far as the axle to ensure maximum solidarity, but ideograms on Cretan tablets of the 14th century BC suggest that Bronze Age chariots were sometimes strengthened by a horizontal strut projecting from the rim of the car and linking with the pole above the yoke. Such a design is illustrated in this reconstruction.

Vase Paintings
The pitcher (top left) is from Cyprus: the work of a Bronze Age potter and artist. The Greek black-figure vase, with its chariot scenes, is to be found in the Archaelogical Museum in Madrid.

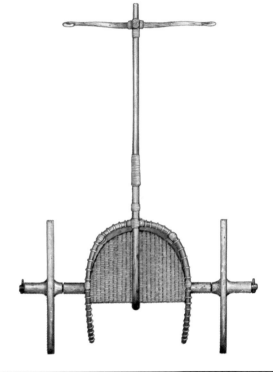

Homeric chariots were drawn by two horses and carried two persons, the warrior and the charioteer. There is a detailed description of the chariot of the goddess Hera. This is instructive, though a chariot owned by a goddess must be presumed more luxurious than those available to mortal men. Hera's chariot had an iron axle-tree. Her horses had gold frontlets. The circumference of the wheels was of gold, with bronze tyres, and the centre was of silver. The wheels themselves had eight spokes, though in early artistic representations of chariots four spokes are characteristic. In contrast, the axle-tree of Diomedes' chariot was of oak, not metal.

The highly ornamental turn-out of Hera's chariot is possibly fanciful, just as the shield of Achilles, fashioned by Hephaestus, the smith of the gods, can be in no way regarded as typical. Yet we may have here the faithful description of a ceremonial chariot, resembling in some respects those of Tutankhamun's tomb with their rich gold and inlay. These too were products of a world in which iron artefacts were making their first appearance.

Methods of Fighting

In normal circumstances, as we have observed, the Homeric warrior chieftain dismounted from his chariot and approached the enemy on foot. He carried either one or two spears, which he launched against his opponent. If the enemy remained unscathed, he then protected himself with his shield against the inevitable retaliatory shafts. If the spears of both parties were thrown in vain, the two champions might immediately set about each other with swords or, before resorting to these weapons, they might hurl heavy stones or small rocks at each other. With these ready-to-hand missiles the Trojan plain seems to have been extremely well provided.

There was a good deal of opportunism in such fights. When Menelaus and Paris tried to decide the issue of the war in single combat, Menelaus' sword broke in three or four pieces against the crest of Paris' helmet. Menelaus, however, despite his disappointment, seized Paris by the helmet crest and began to drag him

Left: *The Warrior Vase (c 1200 BC). These regimented soldiers in leather (?) armour, though nearer than Golden Age Mycenae to Homer's date, are further from the epic tradition.*

1197-1165
Ramses III of Egypt repels attacks by northern invaders (the "Sea-Peoples")

1112-1074
Flagging Assyrian power restored under Tiglath-Pileser I

1050
The latest direct evidence of Mycenaean culture

1006
King David reigns at Jerusalem

BC

15

towards the Greek lines. Paris was thus nearly strangled by his helmet strap, and no doubt would have been but for the attention of his goddess mother, who arranged for the strap to break. Menelaus was left holding the helmet while Paris made good his escape.

Most descriptions of fighting centre in the heavily armed leaders themselves, but attention is drawn to the large numbers of the Greek army and the Trojans are sustained by one contingent after another of loyal allies. In scenes of violent fighting, not only are we made aware of anonymous casualties but of many flying spears and arrows sped by anonymous hands. The rank and file of the army is described as fighting in formations (*phalanges*). Both sides were marshalled by their leaders in good order, but after battle was joined the scene was confused and sanguinary. The enemy ranks were more easily broken when one of their leaders was killed. This might lead to full-scale rout, when chariots were useful in pursuit. It does not, however, seem that the word *phalanges*—Homer only once uses the singular *phalanx*—denoted the closely packed formations with which it was associated in the fighting of a later epoch. Quite certainly the Homeric *phalanx* did not rely on the spear as a thrusting weapon as the classical *phalanx* did.

Discipline in the Greek army was on the whole good. The Greeks marched in silence, unlike the Trojans who chattered volubly, perhaps because of their language and liaison difficulty. One notably insubordinate character on the Greek side should, however, be mentioned in this context. Homer is very

contemptuous of Thersites, who was a thorn in the flesh of the Greek leadership. His demagogy was not of the subtle kind which we have noticed in Agamemnon and Achilles, but consisted in raising laughs at the expense of the commanders: something which, in the circumstances, cannot have been difficult. Odysseus at last beat him and reduced him to tears. In the *Aethiopis,* Achilles grows sentimental over the Amazon queen whom he has killed in battle. Thersites accuses him of having been in love with her. But Achilles is unamused, and kills Thersites.

In the *Iliad*, there are frequent allusions to arrows, though as a weapon the bow seems to have been secondary to the spear. Some of the leaders on both sides were good archers, notably Paris and Pandarus among the Trojans. Of the Greeks, Teucer was the best archer, shooting down nine of the enemy in the course of the *Iliad*. But

Above: *Phoenician silver bowl from Cyprus (7th century BC). As a siege picture perhaps contemporary with the first written versions of the* Iliad, *it is of particular interest to us. A Phoenician city is seen under attack.*

like other aristocratic archers, he was also able to fight hand-to-hand with spear and shield; when his bow string broke he was quick to arm himself with other weapons. Odysseus, according to the *Odyssey*, was conspicuous for his archery, but he did not use a bow in the Trojan War except on a very special commando mission, which we shall describe shortly. Odysseus, in fact, left his bow at home when he came to Troy.

Generally speaking, in Homer, "a good spearman" is synonymous with "a good fighter". Yet archery was a crucial factor in the Trojan War. Both Achilles and Paris met their deaths from enemy arrows. It had been

prophesied that Troy could not be taken without the bow of Philoctetes, the unfortunate Greek leader who languished long in the island of Lemnos, *hors de combat* and suffering from a festering snake-bite. Only when his services were re-enlisted was Paris killed and Troy taken.

Not only Philoctetes himself but his whole contingent were noted for proficiency in archery, while on the Trojan side the Paeonians, who came from Macedonia, constituted a corps of archers. Apart from this, the presence of massed bowmen may be inferred from the frequent reference to arrows, not all of which were launched by the bows of the aristocracy. It should perhaps be noted that the bows described by Homer were not of the most efficient kind. Nor were they used in the most efficient way. The bows themselves were composite, made of two curved horns joined at the centre. The string was drawn by the archer only to the breast, not to the ear as was done with the English longbow of the Middle Ages. The effective range of an arrow was possibly not much greater than that of a well-thrown spear.

Greek Strategy and Siege Warfare

The prose summary of the Cyclic epic narrative tells us that, after the death of the Trojans' ally Eurypolus, the Greeks "besieged Troy". Whatever this implies, it is not recorded that during the first nine years of the war any attempt was made to starve Troy into surrender. Indeed, the arrival of successive relief forces proves that any such attempt would have had little prospect of success. There were no walls or trenches of circumvallation. On the contrary, the Greeks were obliged to dig a ditch and build a rampart on the shore to protect their own camp and beached ships. After the withdrawal of Achilles and his troops from the war, Hector led a heavy attack on the Greek camp and penetrated the ramparts in an almost successful

Left: *Greek sailing ships are seen on this vase (c 520 BC). Unlike war galleys, merchantmen relied on sail. Manoeuvre was not required of them and rowers would occupy cargo space.*

Right: *A Phoenician warship from a frieze showing Sennacherib's visit to Phoenicia in 702 BC. The empires of Assyria and Persia in turn recruited navies from Phoenician cities.*

attempt to burn the ships. The situation was at last saved by Patroclus, commanding Achilles' troops and wearing Achilles' armour.

After Achilles' own return to the war, the Greeks were able once more to take the offensive. According to one tradition an argument took place between Achilles and Odysseus as to whether Troy could best be captured by force or fraud, each of the two heroes making recommendations in accordance with his own character and abilities. Achilles, in pursuit of his policy, led a violent attack on the Scaean gate (ie, the West Gate) of the city and died fighting there. Odysseus' counsels were vindicated when Troy was eventually captured through the stratagem of the Wooden Horse.

Not only was no attempt made to starve Troy into surrender, but no assault was made upon the walls. It should be stressed that Achilles' final attack was launched against one of the city's gates; and this in turn should remind us that the Trojans, in making their earlier attack on the Greek camp, broke in through the camp gates. Hector himself smashed the gates in with a heavy stone, breaking the hinges and the long bar which held them. At the same time, he had ordered that chariots should be left temporarily at the edge of the ditch and assault made against the rampart on foot. One commander disregarded his orders and attempted to pursue the flying enemy through an open gate on the left flank of the beached ships. But the gate was well defended and the assault came to no good. Meanwhile, the outcome of the fight on the ramparts remained in

doubt, though the Lycian leader Sarpedon succeeded in dismantling some of the battlements. When the attackers were eventually driven out of the camp, they poured back over the ditch, many of their chariots—which had previously entered the enclosure —coming to grief in the process.

The inference to be drawn from these facts is that the Greeks of the Homeric period knew virtually nothing of siegecraft. By contrast, the eastern peoples of whom we hear in the Old Testament were capable of both reducing cities by starvation and of attacking fortifications. It might be possible to draw the further inference that the Trojans were more skilful than the Greeks in assailing fortified positions— something which they had perhaps learnt from their oriental contacts— though it seems unfair to compare the ramparts of a military camp with the permanent walls of a city.

Homeric Ships

The ships which were the target of Hector's attack in the *Iliad* were lightly built, easily launched, easily beached and easily relaunched again. To protect the Greek ships from Trojan assault, Agamemnon was in favour of hurriedly rowing them out to sea. He was dissuaded by Odysseus, but the physical possibility of such an emergency manoeuvre was not in question.

The Homeric ships carried a single sail on a yard suspended from halyards. The prow and the stern were decked, but the intervening space amidships was occupied by rowers'

858-824
Shalmanezer III rules an Assyrian empire extending from the Tigris to the Mediterranean

850
Date suggested for the composition of the Iliad (on internal and archaeological evidence)

814
Carthage founded by colonists from Tyre (traditional date)

776
The first Olympiad

BC

17

benches. Odysseus, as a passenger in a Phaeacian vessel, slept in the stern, on the flat surface of the deck—not under it. There was no lower deck.

Already, in Homeric times, the construction of a merchantman differed from that of a war galley. References to merchant ships prove that they were comparatively broadbuilt, and they apparently had a normal complement of 20 rowers. Fighting ships, which were also troopships, carried considerably more men. The rowers must, for the most part, have been fighters themselves, and there does not usually seem to have been any distinction between oarsmen and marines, such as existed on Greek warships in classical times. We learn that the rowers in Philoctetes' seven ships were

all skilled archers—like their leader. On the other hand, Agamemnon provided ships for the contingent from Arcadia—an inland territory—since the Arcadians were not a seafaring people and did not possess ships of their own. The context suggests that the Arcadians were not called upon to do the rowing either.

Achilles sailed with 50 ships to Troy, and each ship carried 50 men. The Homeric narrative does not specify 50 rowers. Ships of the Boeotian contingent carried 120 men each. One cannot assume that all of them were rowers; if they were, they must have relieved each other at the oar. In any case, the number of rowers cannot always have coincided with a ship's full complement. Odysseus lost six men out of each of his

Above: *About 1500 BC the island of Thera was destroyed by an earthquake. The excavated ruins have yielded these wall-paintings of ancient ships reminiscent of Nile boats.*

ships in his fight with the Cicones, those old Thracian allies of Troy, not to mention other casualties incurred at later stages in his voyage. If the rowers were all fighting men, casualties were to be expected; thus, the same ship cannot always have been propelled by the same number of oars.

Warships seem to have been chiefly used for assaulting coastal cities and raiding littoral areas. There is no description of any naval engagement, properly speaking, between Greeks and Trojans. Sea fights, however, certainly

Early Greek Ships

The Pentekonter
Length: c65ft (c20m)
Beam: c3·5ft (c1m)
Draught: c2·5ft (c·8m)
Crew: Captain, *keulestes* (time-beater), 50 rowers, helmsman, 4-5 deck crew.
The "50-oared vessels" to which Homer refers are not necessarily contemporary with the fall of Troy, but may date from his own period c800 BC.

Their ancestors are large war-canoes and Bronze Age skin-covered boats, but these ships are quite advanced. They are mainly constructed of pinewood and consist of several long-itudinal members covered by a stressed carvel-built (smooth) skin, with ribs inserted afterwards. Two frames are carried above the gunwales to support the oars and create more leverage. A mast and sail were used for long distance voyaging but

these were left ashore on going into battle, as the extra weight slowed the vessel and made it less stable and so less manoeuvrable and more vulnerable to ramming. Two large oars or paddles lashed to the stern were used for steering. Later these became asymmetrical and thus easier to turn (see trireme on pp 30-31). As they were little more than open boats packed with rowers with little room for provisions and

water, they normally were beached each night and never ventured far from shore. In battle ships attempted to inflict mortal wounds on one another with their rams or else board one another. Naturally a large vessel held an advantage, hence the rapid growth of warships from 20- and 30- to 50-oared galleys. With these the practical limit in size for ships with one bank of oars had been reached.

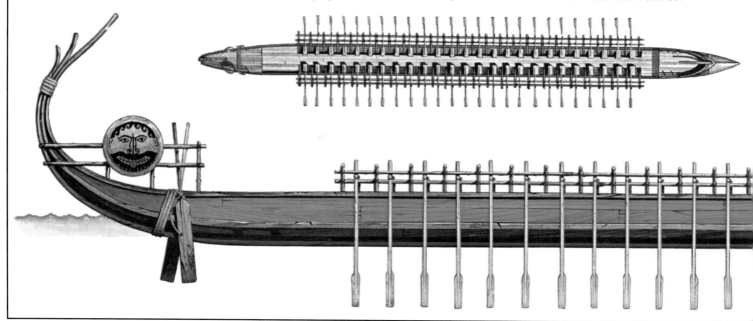

753
Traditional date of foundation of Rome

About the same time Cumae, first Greek colony in Italy, founded

745-727
Tiglath-Pileser III further extends Assyrian power

Greek lyric poet Terpander recites Homer at Sparta

735
Beginning of Greek colonisation in Sicily

took place in Homeric times, and the Greek ships were equipped for such fighting. When the Trojans attacked the ships on the beach, the Greeks met them with long, jointed boarding pikes, of a type used in sea fights. The pike wielded by Ajax was 22 cubits (about 36ft, 11m) long.

The Trojans do not seem to have maintained a standing navy of any importance. When Paris sailed for Greece in search of the world's most beautiful bride, a special shipbuilding programme was inaugurated for the purpose. Such at least was the story of the Cyclic poet. Presumably the coastal allies of the Trojans had navies to equal those of mainland Greece. At any rate, ships must have ferried their Thracian supporters across the Hellespont.

Intelligence and Commando Operations

The Thracian expedition in defence of Troy, to which we have just referred, was singularly ill-fated. Its leader, King Rhesus, did not survive his first night on the Trojan plain. The story is told in the Tenth Book of the *Iliad*.

On the night in question, the Trojans were deployed on the plain before their city, poised to strike at the Greek camp. They were now under no pressure to retreat within their walls and their watch fires were everywhere visible. The Greeks were tense and anxious. If possible, some suitably communicative prisoner was required, from whom the enemy's immediate intentions might be

learned. In order to gain intelligence of this sort, Odysseus and Diomedes volunteered for a highly perilous night reconnaissance.

By good luck, Hector had also sent out a Trojan spy called Dolon, to bring back information about the state of affairs in the Greek camp. Odysseus and Diomedes encountered Dolon in the darkness. After a brief chase, they captured him, induced him to talk and then killed him. Apart from other useful information, they learnt the position of Rhesus and the newly-arrived Thracian allies. These became their target. The Trojans, according to Dolon's information, were keeping watch while their allies slept. His information proved correct. Odysseus and Diomedes slaughtered 12 of the Thracians who sur-

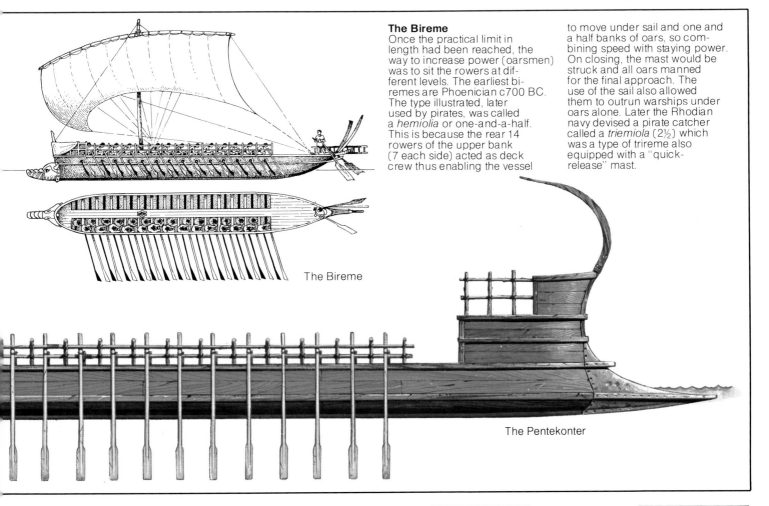

The Bireme
Once the practical limit in length had been reached, the way to increase power (oarsmen) was to sit the rowers at different levels. The earliest biremes are Phoenician c700 BC. The type illustrated, later used by pirates, was called a *hemiolia* or one-and-a-half. This is because the rear 14 rowers of the upper bank (7 each side) acted as deck crew thus enabling the vessel to move under sail and one and a half banks of oars, so combining speed with staying power. On closing, the mast would be struck and all oars manned for the final approach. The use of the sail also allowed them to outrun warships under oars alone. Later the Rhodian navy devised a pirate catcher called a *triemiola* (2½) which was a type of trireme also equipped with a "quick-release" mast.

The Bireme

The Pentekonter

Semi-legendary leader, Aristodemus, vainly champions Messenian independence against the Spartans

701
Sennacherib, king of Assyria, unsuccessfully besieges Jerusalem

About this date in Greece, Boeotian poet Hesiod born

680-669
Esarhaddon, king of Assyria, conquers Egypt: greatest extent of Assyrian empire

BC

19

rounded Rhesus and finally killed the king himself, driving away his fine Thracian horses. On the way back to the camp, they stopped to collect the bloodstained arms and equipment of Dolon, which they had hung on a clump of tamarisk to mark their route.

The differences of arms and equipment described in Book Ten from those which feature elsewhere in the *Iliad* have led some scholars to regard the episode of Dolon and Rhesus as an interpolation. For the purposes of the night raid, Diomedes wore a leather helmet without a crest, while Odysseus borrowed a bow and quiver of arrows, setting on his head a leather-and-felt cap overlaid with boar's tusks. It must be remembered, however, that the occasion was exceptional. For a night operation of this kind, it was only natural to avoid the use of brazen armour which would gleam in the light of the Trojan watch fires.

Information about chariots and their use may also be gleaned from the episode. Not only Rhesus, but also all his henchmen possessed chariots. Diomedes at one point considered dragging Rhesus' chariot by hand or even lifting it in his arms with the valuable armour inside it. This, even when one allows for Diomedes' heroic strength, suggests that the Thracian chariots were very lightly constructed. Dolon's information related not only to the Thracians but to other allies of Troy, and he described the Phrygians and Maeonians in words which can

Below: *This inlaid dagger from Mycenae shows lion hunters with vast shields. Descriptions of such shields in the* Iliad *seem to link Homer by oral tradition with the Mycenaean past.*

Right: *An ornamental miniature shield. The Mycenaean figure-of-eight shield supplied a motif for various forms of design and decoration.*

most naturally be interpreted as meaning that they were chariot-fighters and chariot-owners. Among the Trojan allies, chariots were perhaps not always a purely aristocratic prerogative. One gains the impression that in some contingents a chariot and two horses amounted to standard equipment. There is no hint of this in the account of the Trojan allied forces given at the end of Book Two, but such an interpretation accords well with the prominent part later played by chariots in the attack on the Greek camp.

Archaeological Evidence

Evidence for the existence of leather-and-felt caps overlaid with boar's tusks, such as Odysseus wore in the night operations just described, has been strikingly furnished by archaeological discoveries. Felt and leather are, of course, perishable materials, but vanished caps have left their residue of boar's tusks.

The whole question of archaeological corroboration must now be raised. In the second half of the nineteenth century, first Schliemann and then others excavated many localities which had been celebrated in the Homeric poems. As a result, there came to light the relics of ancient civilizations which corresponded impressively with descriptions given in the *Iliad* and *Odyssey*. Apart from sensational gold treasure, Schliemann recovered bronze weapons which had been deposited in

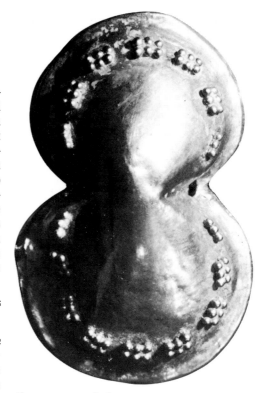

the graves of their warrior owners at Mycenae. Characteristic of these Mycenaean weapons was a long, rapier-like sword blade. It had a tang for insertion in a hilt of some other material, but the tang was too frail for the weapon and it must easily have broken on impact. Some such tangs have, in fact, been discovered broken. But breakage in a sword of this kind, occurring at the hilt, would save it from shattering into several pieces, like that of Menelaus in the *Iliad*. However, another type of shorter sword has also been found in the tombs of the same period. The tang here has been developed into a substantial flanged hilt and represents an improvement in design. Archaeologists assign these

BC

663-610
Egyptian king, Psamtik (26th dynasty) expels Assyrians

657-585
Cypselus and his son Periander, autocrats of Corinth, promote trade, culture and colonisation

650
Beginning of Second Messenian War about this time

Aristomenes traditional Messenian hero wins battle at Stenyclerus against Spartans but is eventually defeated

Spartans inspired by their warrior poet Tyrtaeus

20

weapons to an epoch spanning the 17th to 15th centuries BC, at least 300 years earlier than the destruction of the ancient city at Hissarlik in Asia Minor which is commonly identified as Homer's Troy.

Spearheads are less common than swords in early Mycenaean graves. Perhaps they were so precious to the living that they could not easily be spared for the dead. The spearheads which survive are of different sizes. The large ones are massive and must have belonged to thrusting weapons, but the smaller ones could well have been fitted to javelin shafts.

Schliemann found fragments of boar's tusks but no metal helmets at Mycenae. The Mycenaean gold breast-plates, though beautiful, were frail and obviously intended for ornamental purposes. Excavations at Mycenae yielded a large number of arrowheads made of flint and obsidian. The material, not common in mainland Greece, suggests that they were imported. Representations of shields were discovered, notably on an inlaid Mycenaean dagger blade. Such shields appear to have been made from bull's hide and two designs are conspicuous: the oblong, tower-like shield and the narrow-waisted, figure-of-eight shield. Both are large, long shields, capable of covering the user from chin to ankle. The former readily suggests the shield of Ajax described in the *Iliad*. Even the figure-of-eight type might qualify for that epithet of "circular" or "well-rounded" which Homer commonly applies to shields. After all, its form is that of two adjacent convex circles.

Mycenae and Crete

Later developments in Mycenaean culture were revealed by the excavations of Sir Arthur Evans in Crete. This phase is generally known as the "Palace Period" and its weapons often represent a structural improvement on those of the earlier epoch, correcting original weaknesses in design. The tombs from which the weapons have been recovered seem to be those of aristocratic warriors, with whom it is easy to associate the heroes of the *Iliad*. But one notable change exhibited in this period is the development of bronze armour and bronze helmets. Arrowheads remain common, being made of flint, of obsidian and of bronze. One entire panoply of plate armour and fragmentary evidence of other panoplies, such as are associated with the Cretan Palace culture, have also been dis-

covered in mainland Greece. They featured bronze shoulder pieces and gorgets which anticipate the plate armour of a medieval knight. Such panoplies are heavy and must have considerably restricted the mobility of the wearer. The agility displayed by the heroes of the *Iliad* is quite inconsistent with their use, and they may be dated 1450-1350 BC.

Archaeologists also recognize a later period of Mycenaean civilization which is distinguished by an abundance of less splendid, smaller weapons. One has the impression that the heroic age has passed and that the armourers are concerned to produce weapons for a great many commoners rather than for a few aristocrats. At the same time, Mycenaean civilization seems more widespread and its characteristic culture is detected westward as far as Sicily and the Lipari islands and eastward as far as Cyprus and the Syrian coast. For the tendency to produce more and worse, economizing on raw materials and cutting costs, we perhaps have an analogy in the industries of our own day. But the weapons produced were perhaps more efficient, if less splendid. The whole Mycenaean period covers roughly the latter half of the second millenium BC.

Pictures and Writing

When archaeologists discover and decipher an ancient writing, they extend the period of history backward into an era which was previously prehistoric. This has happened in connection with Mycenaean civilization. Written records of the period have been discovered at many sites in

association with Mycenaean cultures. The language of these records is Greek, though the Greek is not written in the letters of the Greek alphabet. The archaic script used is that which archaeologists have classified under the title of "Linear B".

Following up the work of Schliemann, Sir Arthur Evans discovered at Knossos in Crete a multitude of baked clay tablets impressed with Linear B writing, though the script was not then deciphered and was not thought to be Greek. In addition to the writing, these tablets often carried pictographs, comparable to the diagrammatic pictures which advertise the amenities of our motorway parking areas. These pictographs supplement the written records and thus helped in the complicated process of their decipherment.

Unfortunately, no *historical* records have so far been discovered. The clay tablets are largely records of accounts and inventories. But it is of present interest that many of these refer to the contents of the Palace armoury or ordnance depot at Knossos. The number of chariots stored for use in time of war ran into hundreds. Chariots also appear on sculptured bas-reliefs at Mycenae, apparently in battle scenes. There is no evidence that the Mycenaeans ever rode on horseback; another circumstance which connects them with the people described in Homer. It is interesting, also, to find evidence of chariots which seem to have been a standard issue to troops,

Below: *The walls of Troy and the base of a tower. At Hissarlik, on the traditional site of Homeric Troy, successive cities have been built on the ruins of their predecessors.*

| 630 | | 625 | | | 600 | | BC |
Cyrene founded by colonists from Thera — Assyrian power crumbles — Babylonians and Medes become first independent, then dominant in Mesopotamia — The lyric poetess Sappho and poet Alcaeus flourish in Lesbos — Marseille and Tartessus in Spain colonised by Greeks from Phocaea in Asia Minor

21

Above: *Mycenae, like other fortified sites of the late Aegean Bronze Age, was defended by Cyclopean walls surmounting a rocky eminence. In Homer, Mycenae was the city of Agamemnon.*

not merely the personal property of aristocratic leaders. The method of storing chariots was evidently systematic; records are interpreted to mean that the car of a chariot was normally stacked separately from its wheels, or even dismantled into smaller components. One certainly gains the impression that chariot-fighting as practised by the Knossos regime was a much more highly organized form of combat than it appears to have been in Homer. At the same time, armies in peacetime normally present a more organized appearance than they do when examined in the heat of battle.

Chariots apart, the clay tablets provide information about arms and armour of various kinds. Some of the pictographs are more realistic than others; but even with these, difficulties of interpretation arise. Swords, for instance, cannot be easily distinguished from daggers. Even the Greek word which in Homer normally means a sword is suspected in its Mycenaean context of indicating specifically thrusting weapons, which would include daggers. Objects which are more difficult to represent, such as protective body-covering, present even greater problems to the archaeologists.

Fortifications

The ruined city now identified as Priam's Troy was first excavated by Schliemann on the hillock at Hissarlik in north-west Asia Minor, where ancient Troy is traditionally supposed to have stood. It shows signs of having been destroyed by fire and violence and stands on the ruins of earlier cities, one of which appears to have been shattered by an earthquake. Greek legend also tells of an earlier Troy which was destroyed by Heracles. According to the story, the god Poseidon, who presided over earthquakes as well as the sea, contributed to the disaster. Archaeology confirms the existence of massive walls on this site—a further endorsement of the ancient tradition.

According to archaeological evidence, also, the burnt city at Troy must have flourished at the same time as did Mycenae in mainland Greece. Like

Right: *The massive gatehouse fortifications at Tiryns. Homeric poetry offers further evidence that in the Aegean Bronze Age gateways were an attacker's main target.*

Far right: *The famous Lion Gate of Mycenae. The square blocks of the wall around the gateway contrast typically with the rough polygonal blocks used in other parts of the fortifications.*

Mycenae, other Mycenaean sites are characterized by the massive construction of their walls. These are built in a style known as "Cyclopean"; for the Greeks of later antiquity believed that they were the work of the Cyclopes, a legendary race of giants. Cyclopean walls are constructed of huge roughhewn rocks piled one upon another, with smaller stones inserted to fill the interstices which were inevitably left by their irregular contours. Near a gateway, however, blocks are often squared and laid in horizontal courses.

In distinguishing the gate areas thus, the Mycenaean builders may have had an eye merely to appearance; but they may also have been providing a more

BC

598
Nebuchadnezzar II of Babylon destroys Jerusalem and deports the Jews (who were allied with Egypt)

574
Nebuchadnezzar besieges and destroys Tyre

569-525
Amasis of Egypt allies himself with Lydia, Cyrene and the Greek autocrat of Samos, Polycrates

Amasis concentrates a Greek trading community at Naucratis (in Nile Delta)

22

tactics. In the Theban War, which reputedly took place a generation earlier than the Trojan War (to cite the story on which the Greek dramatists based their works), each of the seven commanders who led the assault on Thebes selected one of the city's seven gates for attack. All seven leaders were unsuccessful, and six were killed.

Conclusion

When we compare archaeological with literary and traditional accounts of the Homeric world, we are faced with notable points of resemblance, as well as points of difference. Our assignment, therefore, of the Homeric epics to the realm of historical fiction seems justified. One cannot claim for these poems the status of history. Outstanding poetic merit is in itself an obstacle to the historian. For a poet tries to breathe the life of his own day into the dry bones of the remembered or recorded past. In striving to fuse the past with the world of his own immediate experience, he is inevitably hard put to avoid producing anachronisms.

In our own literature, the romances of King Arthur and the Knights of the Round Table afford a comparable instance. They are purportedly based on the exploits of a Romano-British king whose legend dates from the European Dark Ages, but Arthur and his paladins wear the armour and assume the behaviour of French knights in the medieval age of chivalry. In addition to these diverse ingredients, it is also easy to detect in the Arthurian romances elements which derive from the history and religion of the pagan Celts of pre-Roman times. Such syncretism is often to be expected in traditional epic compositions.

solid defence. In the ancient legends, an attempt to storm a city meant an attempt to storm a city gate. At Mycenae, a bastion projects near the main gate, from which missiles could be launched obliquely against an enemy in the gateway. Achilles, according to the testimony of the Cyclic poet, was killed while attacking the Scaean gate of Troy. A later legend had it that he was hit in the heel. Those who told the story obviously envisaged the fatal arrow as coming either from the flank or the rear.

Bastions flanking gateways can be found elsewhere in Mycenaean fortifications. This is wholly consistent with the literary evidence on early storming

Even in the drama of a historic period, much the same process may be detected. We do not condemn Shakespeare for alluding in *Julius Caesar* to a doublet, a clock and a book with pages; and in our own century, T. S. Eliot, as if to vindicate a poet's freedom in this respect, deliberately introduced anachronisms into his treatment of a historic subject.

To expect Homer or any other poet who portrays a past epoch to provide us with history is to misunderstand the nature of literary art. However, the situation remains tantalising. There may often be elements of history in epic compositions, for the poet has neither the time nor the patience to invent his own history. But without the aid of external evidence it is impossible to distinguish history from fiction, even though we are certain that both are present. The difficulty arises wherever epic works have survived their sources; and archaeology, though in some ways its testimony is uniquely vivid, only becomes a substitute for documentary tradition when it can point to history in the form of inscriptions or writing on some durable material.

Scholars are perennially tempted to relate Homeric descriptions to archaeological discoveries in Greece and the Aegean area, because in many instances literary and archaeological evidence closely correspond. In other instances, however, they are strikingly discrepant.

Archaeology apart, discussion as to the date of the composition of the Homeric poems encounters a semantic difficulty. What is meant by composition? From a poetic point of view, Shakespeare's description of Antony's meeting with Cleopatra on the River Cydnus is Shakespeare's composition, and Plutarch's description of the same scene is the raw material with which he worked. But if our interests were entirely historical, we might claim with equal truth that Plutarch, or even one of the earlier writers on whom Plutarch based himself, was the composer of this record and that Shakespeare merely adapted it.

Our esteem for the Homeric poems of course derives from their poetic merit, and it is natural to adopt the language of literary criticism when discussing them. However, if we attempt to extract history from Homer, then this terminology may well prove misleading. At least, the meaning of the word "composition" must change, and when we talk of the date of a composition our meaning will change correspondingly. Not a poet, but his source lies closer to the contemporary accounts on which history is ultimately based.

The Persian Wars

In the 5th century BC, successive rulers of the mighty Persian Empire sought to expand their dominions westward. In a series of engagements vital to the future of western civilization, the Greek allies withstood and repulsed the invaders.

Ancient Authorities

The history of the Persian invasion of Greece is narrated in continuous and connected form by Herodotus, who was born about 484 BC in the Greek city of Halicarnassus on the south-west coast of Asia Minor. An Ionian Greek himself, he wrote in his own dialect, but he travelled widely and resided for a time at Athens before settling in the Greek colony of Thurii in southern Italy, where he died about 424 BC. The first Persian invasion thus took place shortly before his birth and the second during his infancy.

The Athenian, Thucydides, who chose for his theme the history of later wars, lived and wrote in the second half of the fifth century BC and his references to the Persian Wars sometimes supplement knowledge gained from Herodotus. But we have in Aeschylus' play the *Persae* an account of the second Persian invasion and the battle of Salamis by one who had perhaps fought in that battle—as he had at Marathon ten years earlier. His brother was, in fact, killed in action at Marathon. Aeschylus was, of course, a poet and a dramatist and his purpose was not to write history. But no modern

historian is likely to overlook the importance of Aeschylus' play as a source of knowledge.

Apart from that, there remains the fragmentary evidence of Greek lyric poets who lived a century before the Persian Wars and who refer to the political situation in the eastern Aegean which preceded Persian power in that area. Their inadvertent historiography may usefully be added to Herodotus' account of the same period. Nor should we

despise the relevant biographies of Plutarch, which were written some six centuries after the events with which we are concerned. Plutarch was a serious and scholarly writer and he had access to many books, monuments and inscriptions which have long since been destroyed. Monuments and inscriptions, of course, have, particularly in the last century and a half, been frequently recovered by the spade of the archaeologist, and our knowledge has been further supplemented by the deciphering of mutilated Greek papyrus manuscripts found in Egypt. Even so, the writers and commentators of late antiquity have a very great advantage over us.

The Events of the Persian Wars

The Persian Empire was brought into existence suddenly by the victories of Cyrus the Great—almost as suddenly as it was to be destroyed a little more than 200 years later by the victories of Alexander the Great. In the early sixth century BC, the Persians occupied territory round Susa, just eastward of what we still habitually call the Persian Gulf. Cyrus overwhelmed the Medes to the north of his kingdom and then, before any grand alliance could be formed against him, turned his attention

Left: The routes of the two Persian forces of Darius I and Xerxes.

Below: The Persian Empire at its greatest extent. Darius' conquests and the revolt of the Ionians soon led him to confrontation with Greece.

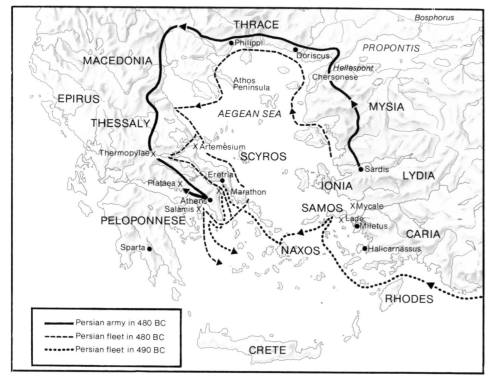

Persian army in 480 BC
Persian fleet in 480 BC
Persian fleet in 490 BC

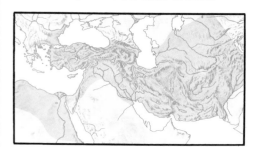

BC	549	546		539
	Cyrus the Great occupies the Median capital of Ecbatana and founds the Persian Empire	Cyrus defeats Croesus, king of Lydia, on the Halys river and captures Sardis	The Persians soon conquer Greek states on the Ionian coast	Cyrus captures Babylon and resettles its deported Jewish community in Palestine

Battle of Marathon 490 BC

Persians	Greeks
Infantry	
20000	Athens 9000 (hoplites)
	Plataea 600 (hoplites)
Cavalry	
5000	None
Fleet	
Triremes 200	None
Transports 400	
Seamen 40000	

General Situation The Persian Expedition lands at Marathon Bay. The Athenians and Plataeans hold the high ground covering the coast road to Athens. The outnumbered Greeks expect Spartan reinforcements delayed by religious observance. Both sides await developments and as the full moon draws near, so does the promise of the arrival of the Spartans.
1 The Persians act, sending a strike force of all their cavalry and some infantry by sea towards Athens. The remaining infantry advances to prevent the Athenians returning to their city. The Greeks' only chance is to defeat the Persians and reach Athens before the naval force arrives. To match the Persian front they must stretch their line. They form up deeply on the wings but only thinly in the centre. The Plataeans hold the left; Callimachus (the Athenian War Archon) commands the right.
2 The Greeks advance rapidly across the plain, running at a charge when within archery range. The Persians are astounded by such temerity. The Greek wings overpower the Persian tribal levies and unenthusiastic Ionian Greek conscripts, but their weak centre gives way and is broken. At this crucial point in the battle, Athenian discipline pre-

vails. The troops on the flanks refrain from pursuing their foes and instead turn on the Persian centre in a classic pincer move. The Persian centre crumbles but many men manage to board their ships safely. Others are pursued and slain in the marshes nearby. The Greeks attempt to capture the ships, seizing seven of them.
Aftermath The Athenians leave a force guarding the battlefield and make a forced march back to Athens. They arrive about an hour before the Persian fleet which can only sail back to Asia empty handed. The Persian casualties amount to some 6400 dead, many of them drowned while attempting to escape. The Athenians, incredibly, have lost only 192 men, among them however their Archon Callimachus.

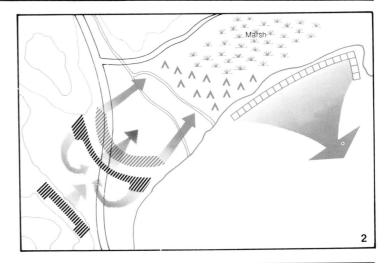

westward to the Lydian power in Asia Minor. He conquered Croesus, the Lydian king, and took Sardis, the Lydian capital. Croesus may be described as a "Philhellene". He was on terms of friendly co-existence not only with the Greek cities of the eastern Aegean, which he dominated, but with those of mainland Greece. It is easy to believe that most Greeks regarded his fall with dismay. On the other hand, the Greek ideal of freedom, involving the preservation of small, independent city states, implied at some stage a certain clash with any large imperial power that extended over the peninsula of Asia Minor.

Cyrus divided his empire into provinces under the rule of governors or "satraps" —to use a Persian word which we have inherited in its Greek form. The subjugation of the Aegean coast was completed by his general Harpagus, while Cyrus himself returned eastwards to capture Babylon—the event recorded in the Old Testament—before meeting his death in

an obscure war amid northern tribes. His son Cambyses, despite some evidence of mental instability, added Egypt to the empire, and after an interlude in which a usurper ruled, the imperial throne was occupied by Darius, another scion of the royal (Achaemenid) family.

Darius organized the empire into 20 satrapies and sought to extend his empire into south-east Europe. He led his armies beyond the Bosphorus and even beyond the Danube. In the last campaign, against the Scythians, he fared ill; the Persian force would probably have been surrounded and annihilated if it had not been for the loyalty of Darius' Ionian Greek contingent, which guarded the Danube bridgehead. From the events of this campaign, both Darius and the Ionian Greeks drew mistaken conclusions. Darius assumed that in future he could rely on the unswerving loyalty of the Ionians, and the Ionian Greeks, conscious that the Persians had been worsted by the Scythians, judged that the time was

close when they themselves might with impunity and fair prospects raise a revolt against their Persian overlord.

From Miletus, the chief city of the Ionians, an embassy* came to mainland Greece canvassing armed aid from compatriot states. The Spartans, cautious diplomats as ever, hesitated and at last refused to help. The Athenians, impulsive as ever, contributed 20 ships to the cause of Greek independence in the East; the city of Eretria, on the big island of Euboea, also contributed five ships.

At first, the Ionian revolt met with success. The Greeks marched inland and burned Sardis, the old capital of Croesus, to which a Persian satrap had succeeded. But retribution followed. The Greek fleet was destroyed at the battle of Lade in 494 BC. Miletus was

---

*The ambassador was Aristagoras, the Greek autocrat who then ruled Miletus, subject to the authority of the Persian king.

also destroyed by the Persians, its inhabitants being massacred or enslaved. This news came as a shock to the Athenians. They rightly suspected that worse was to follow. Darius, aware of the naval help which had been given to the Ionians, was preparing a punitive expedition against the Greek mainland. His armada, commanded by his son-in-law, set sail in 492 BC and hugged the northern Aegean coastline. (Ancient Mediterranean ships preferred to keep within sight of land if possible). A storm badly damaged the Persian fleet off the promontory of Mount Athos, so Darius was obliged to try again.

Another fleet was sent, under other commanders, by way of Naxos across the central Aegean. Eretria, the weaker of the two guilty cities, was quickly captured and burnt. The Persians now disembarked on the north-west coast of Attica, in the plain of Marathon, from which the road ran, skirting Mount Pentelicus on the south, straight to Athens. But an Athenian army opposed the landing and gloriously routed the Persian forces in a battle on the plain. The Persians who survived or had not been committed to the battle were then transported by their fleet round Cape Sunium, to approach Athens from the Saronic Gulf. But the victorious Athenian army hastened back from Marathon along the Athens road and confronted the Persians once more when their ships arrived. No second landing was attempted by the Persians.

Darius died in 486 BC, having avenged himself against Eretria, but not against Athens. Athens had, in fact, incurred new guilt from the Persian point of view. The outstanding punitive task was inherited by Darius' son, Xerxes. In 480 BC, ten years after his father's final expedition, Xerxes crossed the Hellespont with an army whose size was to become legendary and began his march through Thrace into northern Greece. The Persian fleet accompanied the march of the land forces, sailing along those northern Aegean shores on which Darius' navy had previously suffered wreck. But before setting out, Xerxes had had a canal cut through the neck of the Athos peninsula: a three years' task. His armada was thus spared the hazards of rounding the cape.

On this occasion, Sparta had been persuaded to participate in the Greek national effort. One of her kings, with what amounted to a suicide squad and such allies as he could muster, made a glorious stand at Thermopylae, while a Greek fleet fought a delaying action against the Persian ships off Artemisium, the northerly headland of Euboea. But

the resistance was overcome and the Persians were soon masters of northern Greece. The Athenian population had been evacuated to the island of Salamis and other neighbouring coasts; the Persians entered Athens, burnt its citadel and killed the few defenders. At Salamis, a decisive battle was fought with the Greek fleet. The Persian armada was routed with crucial losses, and Xerxes, perhaps anxious about the repercussions of his defeat further east, bitterly retraced his steps, with much of his army, towards the Hellespont, leaving his general Mardonius with other land forces to complete the conquest of Greece. In the following year, however, Mardonius' forces were crushed at the battle of Plataea; those who survived followed Xerxes back to Asia.

While the battle of Plataea was being fought, a new situation had developed in the eastern Aegean. The surviving ships of Xerxes' fleet were beached, with a

Left: *The tomb of Darius I of Persia who died in 486 BC. In the course of his 35 year reign he created the Persian Empire, extending it from Egypt to the Indus valley.*

Below left: *A coin of Xerxes, Darius' son. He pursued his father's retaliatory war against Athens, but his fleet was destroyed at Salamis and his army defeated at Plataea.*

palisade round them, at Mycale on the Asiatic mainland, while the Greeks, who had cautiously followed by sea, watched from the coast of Samos. Taking courage at last, the Greeks sailed across the straits which separated them from the mainland and destroyed both the enemy camp and fleet. One may guess that they were spurred into action by news of the victory at Plataea. Herodotus says that the victories of Plataea and Mycale occurred on the same day, but perhaps we need not take him too literally.

Mycale anticipated another Greek triumph on the banks of the Eurymedon river in southern Asia Minor. But Greek successes were not uninterrupted, and an expedition subsequently dispatched to assist Egyptian rebels against their Persian overlord came to grief. Not until 449 BC was it possible to reach an agreement by which Persia recognized the independence of Greek cities in the eastern Aegean.

The Persian High Command

The Persian numbers in the two invasions were so overwhelmingly superior that one naturally tends to blame the Persian commanders for the startling lack of success. The initiative for both enterprises came from the Great Kings themselves and there seems to have been no question of any significant "power behind the throne". Yet there is nothing particularly blame-worthy in their conduct of the two operations — apart from the undertaking itself. There comes a time in the history of every empire when expansion has gone far enough and stability and consolidation, if not retrenchment, are needed. The handful of Athenian and Eretrian ships that had abetted the Ionian revolt was a poor pretext for such a massive military and naval effort.

If we turn to Aeschylus' play, we find some contrast between the characters of Darius and Xerxes. The *Persae* presents the story of Xerxes' crestfallen return to Persia after his defeat at Salamis. Darius' ghost appears and denounces the folly which has led to the recent débâcle.

Darius is stern and dignified; in contrast, Xerxes is petulant and ineffective. At first sight, Herodotus' narrative might seem to confirm this estimate. One recalls the incident when high winds destroyed the first bridge which Xerxes had constructed over the Hellespont, whereupon Xerxes ordered that the rebellious waters should be whipped as a punishment for the outrage. But perhaps this was not mere childishness on his part. In his multi-national host there were many simple tribesmen who knew nothing of the enlightened Zoroastrian religion of the Persians; thus, to restore morale, it was no doubt necessary to demonstrate that even the gods of the winds and the waves were subject to the Great Kings of Persia.

Again, we are inclined to regard Xerxes' return to Susa, his remote capital, after the disaster of Salamis, as weak and cowardly. Mardonius, his general, seems to have been left callously to his fate in Greece. But the matter may be viewed quite differently. The success of the Persian kings lay very largely in their ability to delegate power. Cyrus, when he conquered Lydia, had delegated the completion of his conquest

Right: *A bronze helmet of the Corinthian type, dated c460 BC. Taken from the Corinthians by the Argives, as the inscription shows, it was dedicated to the god, Zeus.*

Below: *This vase painting by Exekias shows Homeric heroes engrossed in a boardgame. Their arms and armour, however, are typical of the hoplite panoply of the 6th century BC.*

to his general Harpagus, and probably Mardonius was expected to complete the conquest of Greece in the same way. However, when all has been said, the delineation of character in Aeschylus' play should not be lightly dismissed. Aeschylus was, after all, writing at a time very close to the events which he described and he cannot altogether have overlooked the reputations which Darius and Xerxes respectively had earned for themselves among their contemporaries.

As for Mardonius, he was Darius' son-in-law, and had commanded the Persian fleet when it met with disaster on the rocks of Mount Athos. Darius' dissatisfaction with him is clear, for in the subsequent expedition which that monarch launched against Greece, Mardonius was not in command. Datis and Artaphernes were in charge of the fleet which sailed across the central Aegean to Eretria and Marathon. However, Mardonius was a man of no mean ability

and his later reinstatement proves that he enjoyed Xerxes' confidence. After Xerxes' return to Persia, Mardonius tried by sensible diplomacy to divide the Greek states against one another before deciding to engage in battle with them. His chances of success in this diplomatic initiative were very good and with a little more perseverance he might have succeeded. But, cut off from supplies by sea, he perhaps had difficulty in feeding his large army and was accordingly under pressure to reach a decision with the utmost possible speed.

The Athenian Leadership

Among the Persian kings' misfortunes must be counted the brilliance and resolution of individual Greek leaders pitted against them. Miltiades, whose courage and judgment won the battle of Marathon, was a colourful and adventurous character, whose uncle—of the same name—had in fascinating circumstances become king of a barbarian people in the Thracian Chersonese (the Gallipoli peninsula). By fair means and foul the younger Miltiades contrived to inherit his uncle's dominion, but after the Ionian revolt there was no place for him in Persian-controlled Thrace and he took refuge in Athens. Here he was elected one of the ten generals who were responsible for the city's policies, and in the crisis of 490 BC he persuaded Callimachus the *polemarch,* or commander-in-chief, to use his casting vote in favour of prompt military action. After this, the other generals were content to vest their powers in Miltiades.

Persian strategy, it would seem, aimed at keeping options open. A seaborne attack might be made on Athens from the south while the defenders were engaged at Marathon. Alternatively, the Greek army might be destroyed, thus opening up the land route. It might even have been possible, in view of the invaders' numerical superiority, to combine the two. Miltiades seems to have sensed the Persians' indecision and to have made a lightning attack at a psychological moment. The wings of his army had been reinforced, no doubt as a precaution against Persian cavalry. But cavalry was not used, probably because it was embarked on the ships when the Greek attack was made. The effect of Miltiades' formation, however, was to roll up the opposed Persian wings and encircle the enemy centre, which had been temporarily victorious.

Carried forward by their enthusiasm, the Greeks now attacked the Persian ships. In doing this, they perhaps

516
Darius campaigns unsuccessfully against Scythians on the Danube

510
Hippias, expelled from Athens with Spartan help, takes refuge with Darius

At Rome, expulsion of last King Tarquinius Superbus (traditional date)

c505
Aristodemus, popular autocrat of Cumae, defeats the Etruscans at Aricia

BC

27

Artemisium and Thermopylae 480 BC

Persians	Greeks
Foot soldiers	
130000	7000
Cavalry	
20000	None
Fleet	
Triremes 1200	Triremes 271
Many supply ships	

General situation In 481/480 Xerxes prepares for a massive invasion of Greece. A simultaneous Punic invasion of Sicily is to prevent reinforcement of the mainland. The Greeks plan two actions north of Athens to stem the Persian advance.
1 The Greek fleet under the Spartan Eurybiades and Athenian Themistocles positions itself in a channel between Euboea and mainland Greece. A Persian force attempting to skirt Euboea is wrecked by a storm. The whole fleet cannot sail as the army requires supplies from them. A frontal assault on the Greeks is repulsed and the Persian ships have to ride out the storm over-

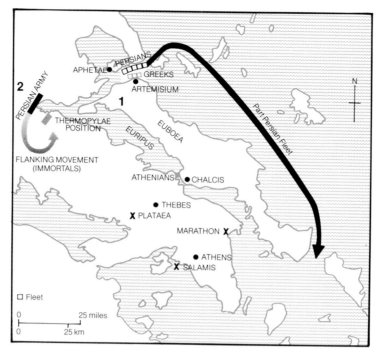

night. A second attack two days later is again held.
2 7000 Greek troops led by Leonidas make a stand in a narrow pass—the middle gate— between the mountains and the sea at Thermopylae. A further 1000 Phocians are stationed to guard the most vulnerable of the flanking routes around the mountains. The engagement at Artemisium prevents Xerxes from landing troops behind the Greeks. An all-out frontal assault on successive days is repulsed with heavy Persian losses. 10000 Immortals under Hydarnes, guided by a Greek traitor, make an outflanking march. When the Phocians retire to high ground, the Persians bypass them. Leonidas learns of this and orders all but 2000 of his men to withdraw before they are cut off. The remaining hoplites are surrounded, and in a violent clash Leonidas is killed. The Spartans retire to a small hill where they are killed to a man.
Outcome Xerxes marches south to occupy Athens, whose inhabitants take refuge on Salamis.

---

attempted too much and at this point Callimachus himself was killed. So Miltiades emerged as the hero of the hour. His strategy and tactics were no doubt inspired by a strong element of self-interest, for he wished to recover his power in the Thracian Chersonese. Certainly, when he obtained command of the Athenian fleet after the victory at Marathon he used his authority for personal ends in a campaign against supposed Persian sympathizers in Paros. He was prosecuted at Athens for this abuse and died in prison in 489 BC, of wounds received at Paros.

When Xerxes launched his invasion in 480 BC, Greece was again saved from Persian domination by a man of unusual character. Themistocles had been something of a rake when young, but he took to politics and placed his natural disingenuity at the service of the state. Like Miltiades before him, he had complete confidence in his own judgment and was able to compel the confidence of others. Like Miltiades, also, he was not nominally in command at the great victory of which he was the architect.

Themistocles was determined that a sea battle should be fought in the narrow straits between the island of Salamis and the main coast of Attica. But, dismayed by Persian success on land, his allies would gladly have dispersed, each to defend his own territories. The Greek leaders disputed bitterly among themselves and tempers were lost, until the Spartan admiral raised his staff in a threatening gesture. "Strike," said Themistocles calmly, "but hear me." The Spartan heard him.

Even so, Themistocles mistrusted his allies and secretly planted an informer on the Persians with the intelligence that the Greek ships intended to make their escape from Salamis before it was too late. Xerxes promptly dispatched a naval force to block all exit from the straits. Dispersal was no longer possible and the Greek fleet in its entirety was obliged to fight where Themistocles wished it to make its stand.

Miltiades and Themistocles must for ever be remembered as the respective saviours of Greece in the two Persian invasions. But the Persian concession of freedom to the Ionian islands was in fact won by Cimon, the son of Miltiades. The question of Ionian liberty had, after all, been the original cause of war, even if later Athenian campaigns in the east were more obviously motivated by thoughts of the corn supply from Egypt and Cyprus.

Cimon was the victorious admiral in the battle off the mouth of the Eurymedon river in 466 BC. Previously, he had attacked Persian positions in Thrace and successfully eliminated a pirate stronghold in the island of Scyros. He died on active service in Cyprus a few years before the honourable and advantageous peace with Persia was reached. Unlike his father, he seems to have been incorruptible. His enemies, it is true,

Right: *Themistocles the Athenian statesman. His shipbuilding programme enabled Athens to defeat the Persians at Salamis and emerge as a dominant Greek city state despite the opposition of Sparta.*

accused him of taking bribes from the Macedonian king, but he was acquitted of the charge. He cherished the ideal of a united Greece, which made him friendly towards Sparta. But the Spartans would not trust an Athenian and Cimon's pro-Spartan sympathies made him unpopular in Athens, where he was a target for political attack.

499			498
Histiaeus, autocrat of Miletus, is detained by Darius at Susa	Aristagoras, his son-in-law, incites revolt among the Ionian Greeks	The revolt is not supported by Sparta, but Athens contributes 20 ships and Eretria 5	Ionian Greeks revolt and burn Sardis

The Spartan Heroes

In a glowing passage, Herodotus hails Athens as the champion and vindicator of Greek liberty. Indeed, Spartan hesitancy at crucial moments very nearly proved disastrous. Yet we must underestimate neither the Spartan war effort nor the Spartan leadership. Leonidas' action at Thermopylae remained a model of heroism for Greece and for the world. Moreover, Leonidas was not only a hero; he was a thoughtful strategist. Reconnaissance soon proved that it would be futile to meet Xerxes in the comparatively open country north of Thessaly, so Leonidas chose Thermopylae as the strategic point at which Greek lives could be sold most dearly. The coastline has changed in the course of nearly two and a half millennia; in 490 BC the defile between the cliffs and the sea was very narrow and the road ran through this defile. Xerxes pressed forward on that narrow front against 7,000 Greek heavy infantrymen, committing at this point his *corps d'élite*, the "Immortals": so called because previously selected men waited to fill the place of casualties. Eventually, the Persians were shown a mountain path by which the Greek flank could be turned. Leonidas saw that he must either retreat to a hopeless position farther south or meet death at Thermopylae. He accordingly decided to send back the allies, while he and a few other Peloponnesians and 1,100 Boeotians continued their delaying action with a counter-attack. At last, overwhelmed by sheer numbers, Leonidas and his force

perished to a man, thus putting Spartan military ideals quite literally into practice.

Leonidas, when he marched north, had not expected to return and had taken with him only those Spartans who had children to succeed them. In the nature of things, the children of fighting men in their prime are young, and Leonidas himself left a young child, Pleistarchus. The Spartan constitution recognized a curious dual kingship, but in practice one of their two kings was usually the dominant partner. Leonidas' nephew Pausanias was appointed to act as regent during the minority of Pleistarchus; in this capacity Pausanias led the combined Greek forces to victory at the battle of Plataea, a year after Thermopylae. Pausanias' triumph, following the victory at Salamis, contrasts with the events of the previous summer, when the Persian advance seemed irresistible. But, sadly, Pausanias' character also contrasted with that of the selfless Leonidas. After the victory at Plataea, Pausanias aimed at personal domination throughout Greece. To this end, he intrigued with the Persians, his former enemies, and when the intrigue was detected by the Spartans he came to a miserable and inglorious end.

The Persian Fleet

No one who reads Herodotus' narrative can underestimate the importance of the naval factor in the two Persian invasions. The Persians were an inland power and possessed no fleet of their own. It says all the more for the organizing ability of the

Great Kings—of Xerxes in particular—that they were able to muster such vast armadas. It also suggests that their knowledge of Greek seamanship and fighting power was such that they by no means despised the enemy with whom they had to deal.

The largest contingent of the Persian fleet consisted of Phoenician vessels, manned by Phoenician crews. Rather surprisingly, the Persians relied also upon ships and crews from the Greek Ionian cities which they had subjugated. Inevitably, they must have felt some doubts about the loyalty of the Greek contingents of their own fleet. On several occasions during the campaigns, the Ionian effort seems to have been half-hearted, and at the battle of Mycale the Ionian Greeks at last deserted their Persian overlords to aid their compatriots.

Artemisia, the Greek princess who ruled Halicarnassus (subject to Persian goodwill), was present herself on shipboard at the battle of Salamis, fighting on the Persian side. However, she seems to have joined either fleet as circumstances dictated at any particular moment, for when pursued by an Athenian vessel she deliberately rammed and sank another galley of her own contingent. The Athenian, thinking that she had changed sides, abandoned the pursuit and Artemisia made good her escape without further impediment.

The truth is possibly that Xerxes found it less risky to take the Ionian fleet with him than to leave it in his rear. On every ship there was a force of soldiers, either Persians, Medes or others whose loyalty was to be trusted. Persian commanders often took the place of local captains and Xerxes probably kept the leaders of the subject communities under his personal surveillance. Their position very closely resembled that of hostages to the Persians.

Apart from the Phoenician and Greek naval contingents, there was in Xerxes' fleet an Egyptian squadron which was to distinguish itself in the course of the fighting. We hear also of ships from Cyprus and Cilicia. Cyprus contained both Greek and Phoenician cities and the people of Cilicia were largely of Greek extraction. Whether the Cilicians felt any bond of sympathy with the Greeks of the mainland is another question, but only the links of empire united them with the Persians. The proportion of the total naval strength to that of the land army is

Ionian fleet defeated at Lade
   The capture of Miletus by the Persians causes dismay at Athens and the revolt collapses
   Darius plans punitive expedition against mainland Greek participants
   In Peloponnese, Sparta by defeating Argos becomes supreme

Themistocles, in office, directs the fortification of the harbour at Piraeus

recorded: the land forces, when counted by Xerxes at Doriscus in Thrace, were, according to Herodotus, 1,700,000 strong; the strength of the fleet is given with some precision as 1,207 vessels, not including transports.

The Structure of Ancient Ships

At this point something must be said of the construction of ancient ships in general and of ancient warships in particular. Mercantile and transport vessels were comparatively broad-beamed and correspondingly capacious. They had to depend on sails rather than oars if room was to be left for the cargo. The Greeks sometimes referred to them as "round ships". By contrast, it may be remembered that the Latin for a warship was *navis longa*—a long ship. Throughout the ancient period which we are considering, warships were comparatively long and streamlined. They were built for speed and relied upon oars rather than sails. The Persians, in their two invasions, naturally needed both transports and warships.

The characteristic warship which developed about the time of the Persian Wars, and which was used in the battles with which we are concerned, was the trireme. This word is formed from the Latin; the Greek is *trieres*. The meaning is literally three-oared or triply furnished, but the reference is apparently to three *banks* of oars, which were ranged one above the other. At an earlier date biremes, vessels of two oar-banks, were built. More common was the pentaconter,

Naval tactics

There were two main methods of fighting which placed contradictory demands on warship design. The first was ramming. This called for the smallest possible ship built around the largest possible number of rowers. The Athenian navy with its small number of marines followed this philosophy. The other was boarding. This called for larger ships able to carry the maximum number of boarders. The boarding school of thought eventually prevailed, since, in order to ram, a vessel had to make contact, which was just what the boarders wanted. Hence the development of large ships with full decks. (see chapter six). The manoeuvre-and-ram school relied on two main tactics—the *diekplus* and the *periplus*. The *periplus* was a simple extension of the fighting line to outflank an enemy and ram his vulnerable sides (see

right). The *diekplus* was more complex and called for skilful rowing and excellent timing, and was a favourite of the manoeuvre-and-ram school (far right). The counter, to form more than one line, was quickly adopted. A defensive tactic was the *kyklos*. To aid boarders, grappling hooks and boarding planks were used. As ships got larger, more complex devices were developed: catapults to cause casualties and clear the decks before boarding; the *corvus*, (a kind of swing bridge); towers to give a height advantage, and finally the *harpax*, a catapult-launched grapnel. With the establishment of the Mediterranean as a Roman lake, the need for naval developments ceased and a reversion to smaller, more cost-effective vessels (*liburnians*) occurred. These developments are traced in subsequent chapters.

The Kyklos (defensive circle)

A defensive tactic adopted by outnumbered or slower fleets was to form a circle, with rams pointing outward. This was used by the Greeks against the Persians at Artemisium. The diagram shows the *kyklos* used by Peloponnesian ships against Athenians off Rhium in 429 BC.

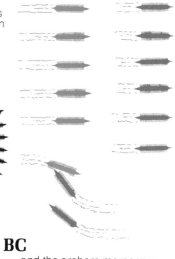

Greek Trireme c500 BC

Length: 125-135ft (38-41m)
Beam: (hull) 10-13ft (3-4m)
(outrigger) 18ft (5·5m)
Oar length: 14-15ft (4·25-4·5m)
Draught: 3-4ft (·9-1·2m)
Crew: 200 -- made up of 170 rowers
62 upper (*thranite*)
54 middle (*zygite*)
54 lower (*thalamite*)
Marines: 10 hoplites
4 archers
(Athens)
Others had up to 40 marines
Deck-hands: 15 plus the captain (*trierarch*) and a flautist to keep time
The rowers were not slaves but highly trained professionals drawn from the lower classes. The hoplites were middle class and the archers mercenary Scythians.

The reconstruction below is based on a variety of sources, including coins (for the general appearance), excavations of the ship sheds that housed these vessels (for the dimensions) and surviving naval records (for number of oars, and colour scheme—large quantities of red ochre paint were used). Literary sources tell us that at this stage there was only one oarsman per oar, and that Phoenician vessels were higher than Greek ones, and carried more marines. This implies that Greek vessels did not have the raised deck of their Phoenician counterparts though some reconstructions show this feature.

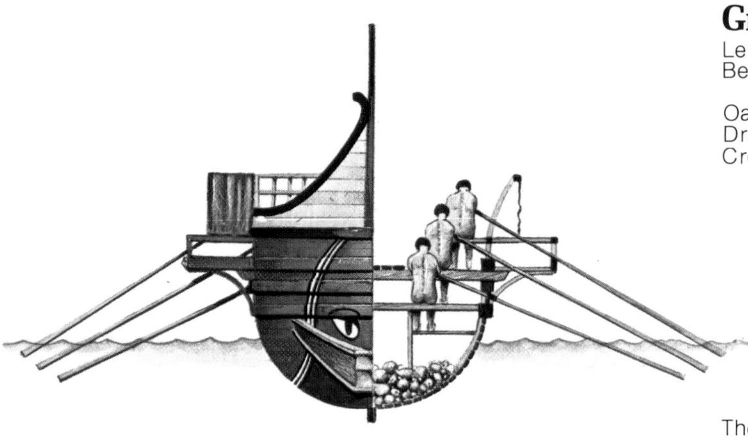

Greek Trireme

492
Persian fleet is severely damaged by storms off Mt. Athos

490
Persian fleet under Datis and Artaphernes crosses the Aegean via Naxos

Eretria (in Euboea) is destroyed

Persians land in Attica but are repulsed by an Athenian army under Miltiades at Marathon

Hippias, son of Pisistratos accompanies the Persian force

a 50-oared galley with oars in a single bank. There were also triaconters, of 30 oars. Homeric ships had as few as 20.

Ancient ships, whether warships or transports, normally made use of single, square-rigged sails, and efficient performance required a following wind. Transports sometimes mounted two or, more rarely, three masts with a single yard and sail on each. Warships lowered their mast and sail before going into action. Steering was by means of two large paddles, one on either quarter. Battle tactics depended to a great extent on ramming the enemy, but boarding operations by heavily-armed troops were also carried out and in this way prizes could be taken. Missiles were also used, although this method of fighting recommended itself more to the Persians than to the Greeks.

Persian Naval Strategy

It is interesting that Xerxes reverted to his father's original plan and decided to invade Greece from the north. He must have considered that his channel through the Athos peninsula eliminated the main hazard of this route. Clearly, he could deploy a much larger army in Greece if his land forces could make their own way along the coast. At the same time, the fleet keeping pace on the army's flank contained transports which considerably eased his supply problem. The land forces carried a good deal of their own baggage and equipment with the help of camels and other beasts of burden. These did not include horses. It was not customary in the ancient world to use

The Periplus (left)
In its simplest form the *periplus* involves the fleet with the larger numbers outflanking its opponents. In the diagram (left) a slightly more elaborate version is shown. The red fleet backs water slowly in front of its blue opponents, keeping its rams facing the enemy, until its flanking ships can execute the *periplus*. This enables the attackers to ram their opponents' sides. At the same time the remainder cease backing water and advance to the attack. This tactic was employed quite frequently, notably at the Battle of Salamis (480 BC) where the Greeks used it against the Persians, with the flanking force hidden behind a headland. The simple version was also successfully used by Demetrius Poliorcetes against Ptolemy at the battle of Salamis-in-Cyprus (306 BC) where he defeated a force of 200 ships.

The Diekplus (right)
The red fleet, speedier and more agile than its opponents, wishes to break the blue fleet's line and bring about a general action in which it will have the advantage. (1) Led by its flagship, it approaches the enemy in line ahead. (2) The red flagship, by quickly backing water on one side turns into an opponent and aided by the blue ship's own momentum, shears off its oars, leaving it helpless. (3) The red flagship picks up speed again and selects its next victim. The crippled blue ship is finished off by the next red ship. Any blue ship turning to aid its sister will expose its own vulnerable side to succeeding red ships. A counter tactic is to deploy two lines, thus making a *diekplus* suicidal. The disadvantage, of course, is that this shortens the battle line, leaving a fleet vulnerable to a *periplus!*

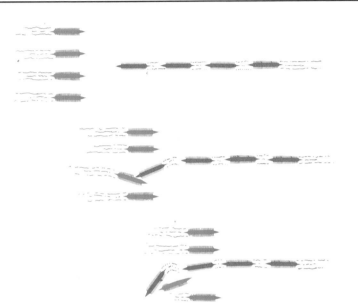

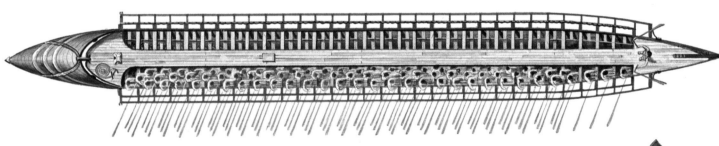

The construction of the vessel itself resembled a modern rowing eight i.e., the shell, of carvel-built planks was constructed first as a rigid monocoque structure and the ribs inserted later. These boats were so light and unstable (due to their narrow beam) that the rowers were expected to throw javelins and sling stones from a sitting position, and later we are told of an admiral who got over a harbour boom by moving his marines aft, thus raising the bows out of the water! The *parablemata* (leather screens) are for the protection of the rowers against javelins and other missiles.
Because of the size of their crews, triremes had to put in to shore at night for water and supplies. This meant that they needed a base to operate from (usually a shelving beach) and this requirement governed tactics to a large extent.

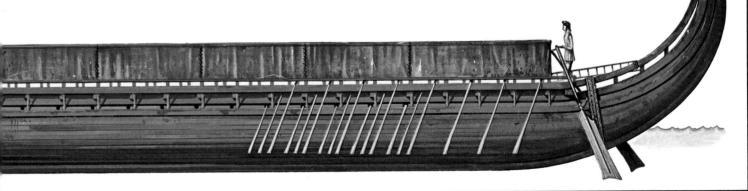

489
Miltiades prosecuted by political opponents at Athens

486
Darius I of Persia dies and is succeeded by his son Xerxes

484
Herodotus, historian, born about this date

BC

31

horses for such purposes and it is noteworthy that Xerxes transported his horses by sea on special ships. Horseshoes were unknown in the ancient centres of civilization, and it is possible that the Persian cavalry might have reached Greece with lame mounts if their horses had been obliged to make the whole journey by land.

Warships were, of course, necessary to protect both the transports and the land forces. Without naval defence, the Persian army would have been exposed to the danger of Greek amphibious attacks on its flank and its rear. Moreover, it was Xerxes' hope that he would crush any Greek naval units immediately, wherever he met them.

He met them first at Artemisium, on the northern promontory of Euboea. Several actions were fought here, with varying outcome. The Greek position was well chosen. In the narrow channel between the Euboean coast and the mainland, the Greeks could not be enveloped by superior numbers. At the same time, they guarded the flank of Leonidas' forces at Thermopylae. If the Persians sailed round Euboea to attack them in the rear, then the Persian land forces would be separated from their seaborne support. What took the Greeks by surprise was the enormous size of Xerxes' force, which despite all reports far exceeded their most pessimistic estimates. It was quite possible for Xerxes to send one section of his fleet round the south of Euboea while he engaged the Greeks at Artemisium with the remainder. Such a manoeuvre entailed no loss

of numerical superiority on either front. But summer storms gathered over Thessaly and aided the Greeks. The very size of Xerxes' fleet meant that there were not sufficient safe harbours to accommodate all the ships; a considerable part of it had to lie well out to sea in rough weather. In this way many ships were wrecked. When a squadron was dispatched to round Euboea and sail up the Euripus strait, which divides the long island from the mainland, this contingent also fell victim to storms and treacherous currents. The task assigned to it was never carried out.

Quite apart from the figures given by Herodotus, events themselves testify to the enormous size of the Persian armada. Despite the heavy losses suffered at Artemisium, Xerxes' fleet still enjoyed the advantage of dauntingly superior numbers when, late in the same season, the battle of Salamis was fought. Even after Salamis, the number of surviving ships and crews was such that the Greek fleet at Mycale hesitated long before attacking them.

Greek Naval Units and Tactics

It is not easy to generalize about Greek naval tactics and techniques of shipbuilding, since these differed from state to state. The Peloponnesians, for instance, relied much more on boarding operations than did other Greeks. The Athenians, the greatest sea power, excelled particularly in use of the ram. In a Greek

Above: *This coin shows a Phoenician warship of about 400 BC apparently drawn up stern first on the beach.*

galley, the ram was formed by the forward tip of the keel, heavily armoured and built up to a point just above the water level. The bows of the vessel were constructed on the basis of the keel, just behind the ram. Apart from this, protruding from the prow, on a level with the rowing decks, were three armoured prongs. If the ram penetrated deep into an enemy ship below the water line, these came into contact with the upper part of the enemy's hull, doing further damage. They also protected the prow of the attacker, and it is easy to see that they could be used with devastating effect on the enemy's oars or steering paddles. It may be said that a war galley so constructed was less a ship with a ram mounted than a ship mounted on a ram.

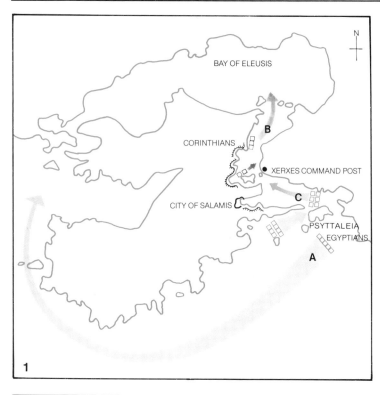

BAY OF ELEUSIS	
	B
CORINTHIANS	
	XERXES COMMAND POST
CITY OF SALAMIS	C
	PSYTTALEIA EGYPTIANS
1	A

Battle of Salamis 480 BC

Greeks	Persians
Fleets	
Athens 150	Phoenicia 100-120
Aegina 30	Egypt 75-90
Megara 20	Ionian Greeks 100
Corinth 40	Cyprus 50
Peloponnese 50	Lycia 20
Others 20	Caria 25
	Cilicia 30
	Others 50

1 The Greek High Command sends a false message to Xerxes that the Greek fleet intends to flee to the Isthmus of Corinth and join the army. Believing this, Xerxes sends his Egyptian squadron to block the Megarian channel (A) and puts his fleet on either side of Psyttaleia to await the attempted Greek escape. The fleet waits all night in vain.

To further the ruse, the Greek fleet puts to sea at dawn and heads north (B). The Corinthian squadron, with some others, leads off under sail (which would be carried in flight but not normally in battle), with the object of defending the Megarian channel and the Greek rear from Egyptian attack. Xerxes orders his fleet to advance up channel (C).

2 The Aeginetans and Megarians advance from their ambush in Ambelaki bay (A) and engage the Ionians. Meanwhile the rest of the fleet back water, luring the Persians on until, crowded and disordered by the narrowing channel, they come up between the Pharmakoussae islands. The Greeks attack (B).

The Phoenician admiral is an early casualty. Leaderless, the Phoenician squadron attempts to back off into more open water, causing confusion as more Persian ships advance. It is morning and the confusion is worsened by a freshening southerly wind. The taller top-heavy Phoenician galleys begin to fall foul of one another (they carried a raised fighting bridge and more marines than Greek vessels). The Phoenicians break and flee, and following the enemy ships down channel, the Athenians attack the Ionians from behind in a classic pincer movement. The Persian fleet is driven back past Psyttaleia and the garrison on the island is destroyed by marines from the Greek fleet. Meanwhile the Corinthians have held off the Egyptians.

The Persians have lost 200 triremes; the Greeks 40.

483
The Athenians, on Themistocles' advice, exploit the Laurium silver-mines to build a fleet

481
Xerxes prepares for invasion of Greece

The Greek city states form a defensive alliance

Xerxes by diplomacy conciliates northern and central Greece

Sicilian Greeks dominated by Gelon of Syracuse do not collaborate

Attack on an enemy's oars and steering gear was sometimes a preliminary to ramming. In the manoeuvre known as *diekplus*, the attacking vessel swung sharply round the stern of its opponent, breaking oars and steering paddle on the way. It then circled back and rammed the crippled and helpless victim as it lay broadside on.

In order to ram, it was necessary to attack the enemy on his broadside, and this could also be achieved by the opportunism of weatherwise commanders. An enemy who was floundering, drifting or not in perfect command of his craft was an obvious target. In order to take advantage of a wind squall or choppy sea, the attacker himself needed to be well in control and unaffected by the elements. In other words, he needed superior seamanship and a ship that stood the sea better than the enemy's. The Athenians, in particular, usually possessed both these advantages.

Tactics such as we have described are exemplified in the battle of Salamis, though there can have been little room for the practice of *diekplus* — which in any case could be frustrated by the adoption of close formations. The Phoenician vessels of the Persian fleet were built with higher sterns and decks than those of the Greeks, and the archers and javelin-throwers who manned them were ready to take full advantage of their superior position. On the other hand, the higher ships were less stable and less manageable in gusty weather. On the advice of Themistocles, the Greeks waited for an expected wind to rise

before launching their attack. The battle was opened by a Greek ship which rammed a Phoenician, smashing its lofty poop. Congestion added to the difficulties of the invaders, and the narrow sleeve of water was soon strewn with their wrecked ships, broken oars, corpses and the debris of battle.

The Battle of Plataea

Let us now pass from consideration of the battle of Salamis to that other decisive victory of the war, the land action fought at Plataea in the following year, 479 BC. Unlike Salamis, the battle of Plataea was won more by luck than judgment. Pausanias, the Spartan general in command of the Greek forces, was admittedly an astute strategist and tactician, who well appreciated the main strengths and weaknesses both of his own and of the enemy forces. But the same may be said of the Persian commander-in-chief, Mardonius. One may guess that Xerxes' departure was an advantage to the Persians. Great organizer though the king was, he was no soldier.

At Plataea, each of the opposing commanders strove to draw the enemy into attacking his own well-chosen and strongly defended positions. Each saw the danger of initiating an attack upon such positions. But while each waited for the enemy to act first, neither could afford to wait indefinitely. The vast Persian army, deprived now of seaborne supplies, must sooner or later find difficulty in feeding itself on enemy terri-

tory. For Pausanias, the problem was tactical and immediate. He had chosen a position in the foothills of Mount Cithaeron; the Persian cavalry, when they issued from Mardonius' stockaded camp across the Asopus river opposite, were driven off with heavy loss, including that of their commander. But Mardonius was too wise to commit his main force, and although his cavalry could not succeed on the mountainous ground which the Greeks now occupied, it was able to interfere with their watering places and supplies.

Pausanias now took up another position. He led his army down into the plain, where a small cluster of hills protected him from a frontal cavalry charge. Mardonius still did not attack. The Greeks' water and supply problem became ever more acute. Pausanias waited ten days, but could wait no longer. However, he kept his head admirably. He did not attempt to force a battle by attacking the Persian camp. Such a course would have been fatal, but even so, the alternative was not free from danger. He decided to withdraw by night to a position nearer his old one, where water would be available and supply lines less exposed. In the difficulty and confusion of the night march, which seemed to some of his officers like a demoralizing retreat, the units of the Greek force became separated from each other and lost contact.

On the following day, Mardonius saw the disorganization of the Greeks, but mistook it for something much more serious than it was. He had been encouraged to think that, given time, the Greek states and their military contingents would quarrel and abandon each other. He had, in fact, devoted much well-judged diplomacy and intrigue towards hastening this end. But in the present instance, Greek difficulties were tactical rather than political. When the Persians surged forward to what they thought would be easy victory, they met determined resistance. The Spartan main body, although separated from the rest of the Greek army, was able to meet an infantry attack with the advantage of superior ground which impeded the use of the Persian cavalry. This was the occasion for which Pausanias had long waited and risked much. In savage fighting the Spartans overcame the enemy before them, killing Mardonius. Although they had no aptitude for attacking fortifications, they then assaulted the Persian camp. Here, they were fortunately rejoined by other Greek units, some of whom had just defeated the invaders' Boeotian collaborators. The camp was at length taken and no

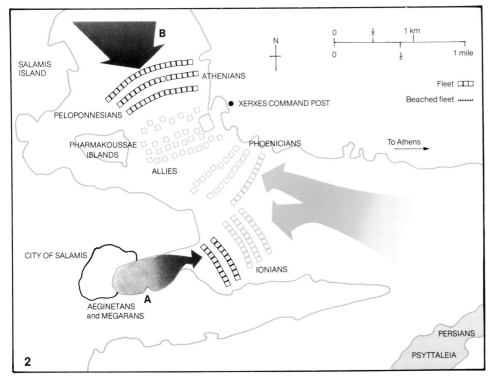

480

Xerxes leads grand army and naval armada into Greece

Greeks fight delaying naval action at Artemisium (north Euboea)

Spartans with other Greeks under Leonidas are annihilated in heroic defence of Thermopylae

Persians pass southwards and seize Athens

Athenians evacuate their population and defeat Persians in naval battle of Salamis

In Sicily, Greeks under Gelon defeat Carthaginian invasion at Himera

BC

33

quarter was given to the defenders, only a few of whom escaped. Another, larger Persian force, whose commander had at the last moment been loath to follow Mardonius' lead, was already on its way back to the Hellespont. The city of Thebes, which had led Boeotia in collaboration with the Persians, was captured after a short siege and its political leaders put to death. A vast amount of treasure, with part of which the Persians had hoped to buy provisions for themselves and their animals without the need of foraging, fell into Greek hands as a result of this victory.

Greek Arms and Armour

In the early historic period (8th and 7th centuries BC), the shields used by Greek warriors were of various shapes and sizes. The evidence of lines written by the Spartan poet Tyrtaeus suggests that his compatriots and contemporaries in the 7th century still used a long broad shield which protected thighs, shins, chest and shoulders, though some modern scholars think that we have here a fanciful allusion to earlier usage. Support for such long shields had been given by a strap which passed round the neck and over the shoulder. In addition to which there was a single grip for the left hand.

Well before the Persian Wars a Greek warrior's equipment and method of fighting had gone through a process of gradual but fundamental change. The role of the heavy infantryman or hoplite (Greek: *hoplites*) was now cardinal in warfare, and the hoplite owed much to his defensive armour. The round concave shield, which had now superseded other types, was about 3 feet (c 1 metre) in diameter. It was made of wood, reinforced or faced with bronze, and very often bore some emblazoned device comparable to the armorial bearings of the Middle Ages. On its inner concave surface, the hoplite's shield usually had two brackets, through one of which the forearm passed, while the other was gripped by the hand.

Above the flat broad rim of his shield, a hoplite's head was well protected by a bronze helmet. The type known as the "Corinthian" helmet could be pulled forward in battle so that it vizored the face, while allowing for eye slits and breathing spaces for nose and mouth. Out of battle it could be pushed to the back of the head, leaving the face uncovered. This is the position in which it most frequently appears in sculpture, vase paintings and coins. There were, however, more complicated types of

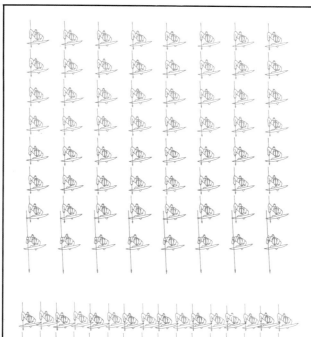

The Phalanx (left)
After the introduction of the *hoplon* shield in the seventh century BC, a new unit of combat evolved. It was usually called the phalanx (although this term had been in use since Homer's time). In this formation the hoplites lined up in files, often, though by no means always, eight deep. These files stood side by side in ranks, each file occupying a 6 to 8 feet (2-2·5m) frontage. This was called open formation (above left) and was the normal formation for manoeuvring. It also left room for skirmishers to pass through to the rear. Just before contact with the enemy, the rear ranks closed up so that each man occupied 3 feet (1m) of frontage and the left side of his shield covered his neighbour. Over this wall of shields the hoplite could thrust his spear. The rear ranks took a man's place as he fell, or pushed behind him as required (left). Because of each man's tendency to edge behind his neighbour's shield, the phalanx had a habit of drifting right which affected the outcome of many battles. The officers, including the king or general (*strategos*), were expected to fight in the front rank alongside the other well-equipped hoplites, and to expose themselves to the same risks as the rest of their troops.

The Hoplite Panoply (left)
Such a panoply was very expensive, being roughly comparable to the cost of a modern car. The figure (far left) wears a costly panoply consisting of an engraved and decorated "Chalcidian" helmet, a similar bronze muscled corslet, and greaves. He carries an alternative to the normal hoplite sword—the *kopis*, a heavy slashing sword. The other figure wears the simplest form of hoplite equipment: an un-reinforced corslet, a simple bell helmet and plain greaves. The possession of hoplite equipment was a mark of the middle classes.

Below: The phalanx tactic is well illustrated on Greek vases and sculpture such as the fourth century BC Nereid monument from Xanthus shown here.

BC 479
Mardonius is defeated at Plataea by Greek army under Spartan regent Pausanias

Persian survivors retreat overland

Greeks destroy Persian fleet at Mycale in east Aegean

478
Despite Spartan opposition, Themistocles secures restoration of Athenian city walls

Pausanias liberates Cyprus and Byzantium from Persians

34

Greek Hoplite (c480 BC)

The colour illustration shows a typical hoplite of the Persian Wars. His slightly old-fashioned helmet is decorated with a natural horsehair crest. Others were black, white, or multi-coloured. He wears a cuirass, reinforced with metal scales for protection. His shield is the *hoplon*. The designs painted on the bronze face at this time were individual ones, animals and mythological creatures, such as the Gorgon's head shown, being particularly popular.

On his legs he wears a pair of bronze greaves shaped to imitate the muscles of the leg, both for decoration and for strengthening. His main weapon is his long spear, which varied in length between 6ft 6in and 10ft (2-3m). The iron head is balanced by a bronze butt-spike, which could be used offensively in the event of the head snapping off. The spear was normally wielded overarm, and its grip is bound with leather thonging. His secondary weapon is a short sword suspended from his shoulder by a baldric. Equipped in this way and partly covered by his neighbour's shield, the warrior is protected from head to foot and has a formidable reach with his long spear. Hoplites such as this defended Thermopylae, fought as marines at Salamis, and won Plataea.

The Hoplite's Sword

Such a sword was made of iron with bronze fittings and had a blade about 2 ft (60cm) long. It was suitable for cutting and thrusting and was carried in a wooden scabbard covered with leather.

Hoplite Defensive Equipment

The shield (*hoplon*) which gave the hoplite his name, and dictated his method of fighting, was of heavy construction and quite large (see above). It was built on a wooden core which was faced with bronze and backed by leather. It was held by an armband (usually bronze) around the forearm and a handgrip. The part of the shield which lay against the arm often had an additional layer of bronze protection. The large size meant that it was quite heavy — approx. 18lb (8kg). Sometimes a leather curtain was hung from the base of the shield as protection for the hoplite's legs against missiles.

The body was protected by a cuirass. The most expensive type was the muscled cuirass made of bronze, but the most common type of protection was a cuirass made up of numerous layers of linen or canvas glued together to form a stiff shirt (*linothorax*). These were often reinforced with metal plates or scales. This type of cuirass replaced the earlier bronze bell type. The cuirass itself consisted of a body piece with armholes cut out and the bottom cut into two layers of "feathers" (*pteruges*). This wrapped around the body and was laced together on the left-hand side, where the join was protected by the shield. A yoke which bent down over the shoulders and tied to the chest completed the cuirass. Several different patterns were used, some with detachable *pteruges* and differing styles of yokes.

The head was protected by a bronze helmet which often, but not always, had a horsehair crest. The type illustrated — called "Corinthian" — appears to have been the most common but many different types were in use (see page 44).

The lower legs were protected by a pair of bronze greaves which were sprung onto the leg and did not have straps. In earlier times, thigh guards, arm guards and foot guards had also been used, but by the Persian Wars these had largely gone out of use as they hampered movement and made the equipment too heavy. Despite this, the hoplite was still well protected.

Accused of treason, Pausanias is recalled to Sparta and commits suicide

Athenians forming Aegean naval confederacy continue war against Persia

c467
Cimon, Athenian commander, defeats Persian forces on Eurymedon river in south Asia Minor

465
After earthquake at Sparta, Messenians revolt (3rd Messenian War)

Xerxes dies and is succeeded by his son Artaxerxes I

BC

35

Battle of Plataea 479 BC

Greeks
Hoplites

Lacedaemon (Sparta and Allies)
10000

Tegea 1500	Hermione 300
Corinth 5000	Eretria 600
Potidaea 300	Chalcis 400
Orchomenos 600	Ambracia 500
Sicyon 3000	Leucas 800
Epidaurus 800	Pale 200
Troezen 1000	Aegina 500
Lepreum 200	Megara 3000
Tiryns and Mycenae 400	
Phlius 1000	Plataea 600
Thespiae 1800	Athens 8000

Light troops

Sparta 35000   Others 35000

Persians   Medizing Greeks
Foot soldiers

Immortals 10000	Thebes 6000
Persia 2000	Thessaly 3000
Media 2000	Locris 500
Bactria 2000	Malis 500
Sakae 2000	Macedonia 2000
India 2000	Phocis 1000
Others 5000	

Cavalry

Guard 1000	Thebes ⎫
Persia 1000	Thessaly ⎬ 5000
Media 1000	Macedonia ⎭
Bactria 1000	
Sakae 1000	

1 The Greek armies, under Pausanias, advance into Boeotia. Mardonius selects a battlefield south of Thebes which would favour his cavalry. The Greeks prudently will not advance beyond the foothills. Mardonius' cavalry tries to lure them on but in the skirmishing its general is killed and it withdraws, having inflicted heavy casualties on the Megarians and Athenians.

2 Pausanias skirts Plataea and takes up a new position astride the Asopus ridge where plentiful water supplies are available. Both sides wait. Mardonius has a supply problem aggravated by Greek guerrilla action. His cavalry captures a supply convoy of 500 wagons at night (A) and so blocks the Greek supply line. For the next 3 days the Persian cavalry skirmishes with the Greeks and poisons their water supply (B). Pausanias must now act. He wishes to get close to the mountains and feigns a retreat, sending his less experienced troops back in the night (C). They lose their way and camp under the walls of Plataea until dawn. At first light the Greek left and right wings withdraw (D) covered by a rearguard.

3 Mardonius orders an all-out assault. His cavalry forces the Athenians to turn. The allied Greeks rush to the Athenians' aid but are handled roughly by the Boeotians (A). Mardonius and his guard cavalry bring the Spartans to bay (B); the Corinthians and other Peloponnesians come to assist them (C). The Persians discharge flights of arrows at the hoplites crouched behind shields. Finally, the Tegeans charge, followed by the Spartans. The Greek heavy infantry soon prevails against brave resistance and Mardonius is slain. The Persian centre under Artabazus breasts the Asopus ridge (D) in time to see the Persian collapse. Artabazus retreats, pursued by Spartans; the Boeotians break off also. Casualties: only 3000 of Mardonius' command survive. 1000 Medizing Greeks are killed. 1500-3000 Greeks are lost.

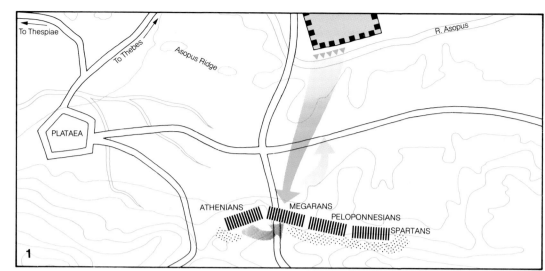

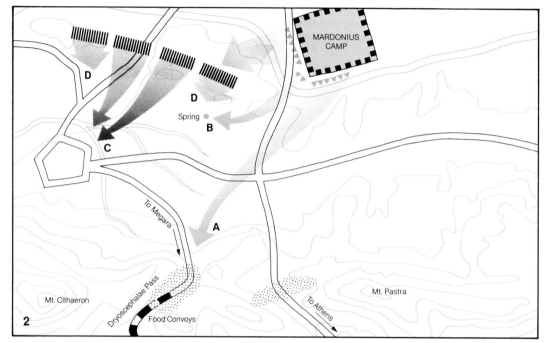

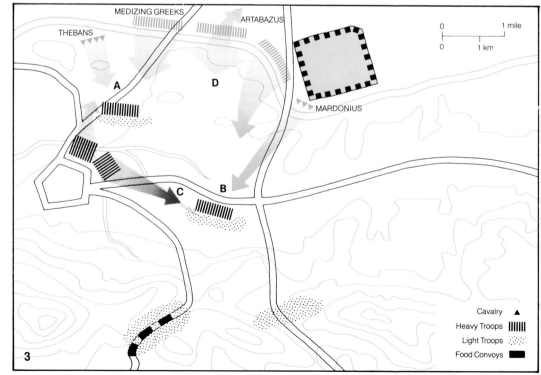

Cavalry ▲
Heavy Troops ▥
Light Troops ⠿
Food Convoys ▰

BC | **462**
Themistocles, accused of implication in Pausanias' intrigues, dies in exile

461
Athenians ally with Argos against Sparta

Cimon, pro-Spartan in sympathy, is exiled from Athens

Pericles, anti-Spartan, dominates Athenian politics

459-4
In Egypt, Athenians support revolt of Libyan prince Inaros against Persian domination

helmet, by no means uncommon, with moveable vizors and cheekpieces. Helmets were frequently surmounted by crescent horsehair plumes, usually in the "fore-and-aft" plane.

Since the round shield used by the hoplite did not cover him below the knee, he also required leg protection, and this was provided by greaves (shin-

Below: Horsebowmen were an important element in the army which Xerxes led into Greece, and were used effectively in the fighting at Plataea.

Bottom: A wine-cup (cylix) painting of a Greek military trumpeter. Such signals were vital in Greek warfare.

guards). Thus the Greek heavy infantry-man remained effectively armoured from head to foot.

The chief offensive weapon of the Greek hoplite was his long lance, up to 9ft (about 3m) in length. Unlike the Homeric spears, these lances were used only for thrusting, not for throwing, and they were tipped with iron. The hoplite also carried a short cut-and-thrust sword for fighting at close quarters.

By contrast with the hoplite, Greek cavalrymen, who were few in number, wore no armour and carried no shield. Their weapons were spears or javelins, of which they sometimes carried two or more. They were recruited from the ranks of the wealthy, for only rich men could afford horses*. Often they wore broad-brimmed hats, as a protection against the elements rather than against the enemy. The Greeks ordinarily rode bareback or used only a saddle cloth. They had no stirrups and no horseshoes.

In addition to heavy infantry and their meagre cavalry, Greek armies also contained lightly-armed troops. These were called 'peltasts' (*peltastai*) from the *pelte* or light shield which they carried. They were armed with a bundle of javelins, and they were used mainly for scouting, reconnaissance or raiding: anything that might involve hit-and-run tactics. They were not expected to be able to sustain a heavy attack.

The Greeks also used archers with their light troops, and at a later date bowmen were sometimes mounted. A standing force of archers at Athens was used for police duties, but these were Scythian slaves bought at public expense from northern Greece. The most celebrated Greek archers were the Cretans. The Cretans, however, did not participate in the Persian Wars.

Hoplite Tactics

Greek hoplite tactics may be regarded either as the outcome or the determinant of hoplite arms and armour. The word *phalanx,* which was used by Homer (almost always in the plural) to denote the rank and file of the army, in classical times was applied especially to the dense formation adopted by the hoplites. There was a steady tendency for the formation to increase in depth, but in Xenophon's time it was four ranks deep; this may be taken as normal in the fifth century. In this formation, the long

*Aristocratic horsemen, it would seem, sometimes rode to war fully armed, but fought dismounted as hoplites. This is reminiscent of Homeric chariot tactics.

lances of the rear rank could project beyond the shields of the front rank to confront the enemy. As the number of ranks in the phalanx increased, so did the length of the lances.

It has often been suggested that the role of the rear ranks was mainly to add weight and that an ancient Greek battle was very much like a modern rugger scrum, with both sides pushing until one gave way. Long lances can hardly have been used with this sort of struggle in mind. To the rear ranks in particular, they would have been merely an impediment. Nevertheless, it is quite likely that battles often developed into this kind of contest. The lance-heads of classical times, unlike the weapons of some ancient peoples, were of mild steel rather than soft iron; by modern standards they were far from being well-tempered and it is probable that they were frequently unable to penetrate the wall of defensive bronze armour opposed to them. In such cases, the "scrum" situation naturally arose. Where it was impossible to cut or force away through the enemy's line, one hoped simply to push it over.

In close order, every shield protected not only its user's left side but also the right side and lance arm of his neighbour. Once formation was broken, this advantage was lost; the army which broke an enemy formation while preserving its own had won a battle. Once its own formation had been broken, an army usually took to flight. The hoplite who wished to escape by running was obliged to throw away his ponderous shield, and the word *ripsaspis,* literally "one who throws away his shield", still means a deserter, even in Modern Greek. Horace, writing in the first century BC, confesses to having thrown away his shield when he fought for Brutus and Cassius at the battle of Philippi. His frankness was presumably encouraged by the examples of early Greek poets who, in several surviving instances, plead guilty to the same offence.

In many ancient battles, there was a disproportion between the gruesome casualties of the defeated army and the trifling losses sustained by the victors. This is because the main carnage occurred not in the battle itself but in the massacre of fugitives which followed. Spartans were not expected to run away. They were exhorted to return either with their shields or upon them—for Tyrtaeus' Spartan shields could be used conveniently as biers. The heavily-armed hoplite was, of course, unable to overtake a fleeing enemy who had discarded his cumbersome shield; this was another role for cavalry and light troops.

457
Athenian Long Walls rebuilt

Athenians are defeated by a Spartan force at Tanagra in Boeotia

Athens dominates Boeotia after victory at Oenophyta

About this date Thucydides, historian, born

Cimon recalled from exile

BC

37

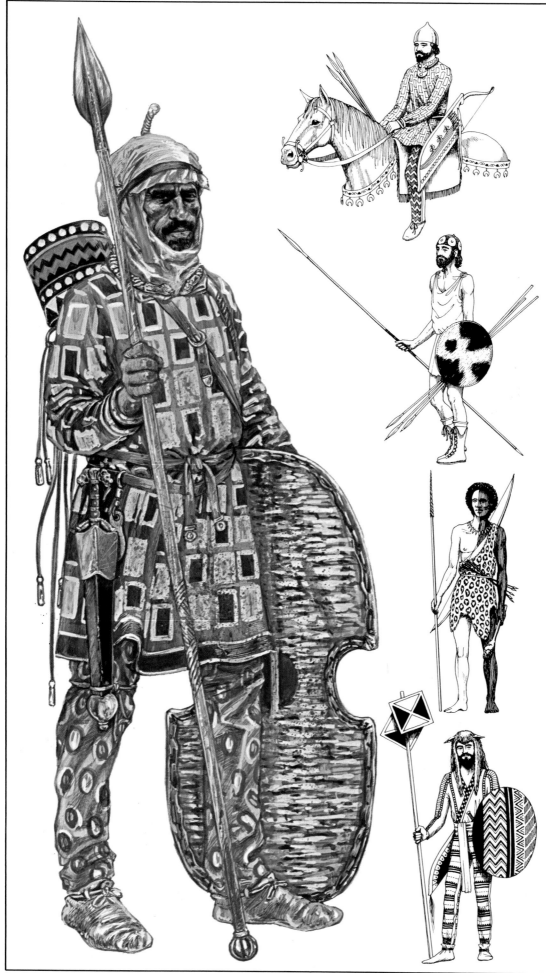

Persian Troops

The main drawing illustrates a Persian "Immortal", so-called because whenever the contingent suffered casualties, its numbers were brought up to a full establishment strength of 10,000.

He was invariably of Mede or Persian race and was a professional soldier, providing the king's guard in peace and the cream of the army in war. He is shown equipped as he would appear on the battlefield, very different from the palace dress shown on the Persepolis reliefs and commonly illustrated. His weapons are a bow, which proved largely ineffectual against the heavily armoured Greek hoplite, and a short iron-headed spear with a silver counterweight (gold for officers). His secondary weapon is a large dagger or short sword decorated with lions' heads at the top of the hilt. For defence he wears a corslet of metal scales under his tunic, and carries a hide-covered wicker shield of traditional shape (the *gerron*). While offering adequate protection against arrows and the like, it would not stop a determined spear thrust—(unlike the Greek *hoplon*). On his head he wears the *tiara,* a soft cloth covering which could be drawn across the face to keep out dust. His loose tunic is highly embroidered and could be crimson, blue, yellow or even white.

Though courageous he suffered in battle against the Greek hoplite because of his inferior shield, lack of helmet or leg protection, and his one advantage, his bow, was largely negated by heavy hoplite armour. Despite this he fought well and only gave way at Plataea after Mardonius had been killed.

Other Troop Types

The top line drawing shows another Persian soldier, in this instance a Mede cavalryman. He wears an embroidered tunic and trousers over a metal scale corslet. On his head he wears a bronze helmet. His weapons are a bow and several javelins. Like most Persians he is richly dressed with gold or silver torque and bracelets. Below him is a Paphlagonian or Phrygian spearman from Asia Minor. He carries a small round shield, javelins and a spear. On his head is a wicker helmet, reinforced with metal plates. Beneath him is an Ethiopian, one of the more bizarre types levied from all over the Persian empire. His weapons are a palm-wood bow, stone-tipped cane arrows, a club and a spear tipped with antelope horn. In battle he daubed himself with war-paint, chalked one side and vermilion on the other. Below is a Scythian standard bearer in a tight, embroidered tunic. He carries a hide-covered, wicker shield, a bow and a dagger. On his head is an animal skin headress. The Scythians provided both cavalry and infantry for the Persians. The Persian army also contained Bactrians, Indians, Arabians, Egyptians, and many other subject races.

BC

454 Revolt in Egypt collapses   Athenian expedition sustains disastrous losses

451 Five-year truce between Athens and Sparta

450 Cimon leads Greek fleet against remaining Persian bases in Cyprus, but dies on active service

Exceptions there will always be. Spartans *sometimes* ran away and shields were sometimes jettisoned by the pursuers as well as the pursued. In this way, Aristomenes, the Messenian leader, once lost his shield in a moment of triumph over his Spartan enemies. He recovered the lost property later, with some difficulty and in curious circumstances. The reader is referred to Pausanias' *Description of Greece* (4.16.6).

Persian Arms and Equipment

Herodotus describes the arms and equipment of Xerxes' army in some detail. The Persians themselves wore floppy felt hats, tunics and armour exhibiting a surface of fishlike iron scales, and trousers. They carried wicker shields. Their weapons were large bows, short spears, and daggers which were suspended from their belts on the right-hand side. Thus equipped, they might or might not be mounted. Persian armies generally relied upon the large numbers of their horsemen and bowmen.

Apart from the Persians themselves, Herodotus gives particulars of the other national contingents which the Persian kings were able to mobilize, although the statistics on which he based his information may have referred to the potential fighting strength of the entire Persian empire rather than to Xerxes' actual expeditionary force, gigantic though this force unquestionably was. We hear of Assyrians and others with bronze helmets; but in general, the Asiatics were protected only by various kinds of soft headgear and they seem to have worn no substantial body armour. Apart from daggers, bows and arrows, their weapons included iron-spiked clubs, axes and lassoos.

Cavalrymen—especially cavalry officers—may have worn more protective armour. Masistius, the Persian cavalry commander who was killed in the early stages of the Plataea campaign, wore gold scale armour under his scarlet surcoat. When his horse was hit by an arrow, he defended himself vigorously on foot and could not be brought down by body blows. At last, the Athenians who surrounded him guessed the secret and struck at his face.

Persian archers, both mounted and unmounted, carried their arrows in a quiver slung on the hip. This practice differed from that of the Greek archers whose quivers were slung on their backs. It is easy to imagine that the hip position was more expeditious when there was a requirement for rapid fire.

Above: *A 5th century Persian bronze helmet from Olympia. Many of Xerxes' soldiers, however, were protected only by cloth or felt headgear.*

Herodotus refers to the war chariots of the Indian contingent, but there is no mention of these chariots being used in the fighting. Persian kings normally went to war in chariots, which were also employed by the Persians for hunting. The Greeks of the classical period used chariots only for sporting events. Generally speaking, by the time of the Persian Wars the war chariot had been replaced by the man on horseback. The change had no doubt been brought about by the improved efficiency of horses' bits, which made it easier for the rider to control his steed.

Causes of Greek Victory

Herodotus pays a tribute to the heroism and physical strength of the Persian infantry. He makes it quite plain that in their hand-to-hand struggle with the hoplite forces of the Greeks at Plataea they were defeated as a result of their inferior arms and equipment. In its final stages, the battle of Plataea amounted almost to a fight between armed and unarmed men. This, however, does not detract from the merit of the Greeks, who needed to be skilled in the use of their weapons and well practised in military manoeuvres. The Persians, as Herodotus remarks, possessed no such skill and fought in disorder.

It must also be stressed that, throughout both Persian invasions, the Greeks were fortunate in their generals, who managed brilliantly to turn the decisive battles into infantry engagements, in which the effect of Persian numbers, cavalry and archers was neutralized.

Apart from the question of weapon-training, the Greeks owed much to robust physical fitness, the product of their athletic habits. The life of Spartan citizens was dedicated to military training; the Spartan state was a war machine and nothing else. But for sheer stamina the performance of the Athenian hoplites at Marathon is commemorated every time we speak of a "Marathon race". This indefatigable force advanced nearly a mile to the attack, at the quick step, each man in armour weighing about 70lbs (32kg). After hard fighting, in which they routed the Persian infantry and assaulted the Persian ships, they hurried back more than 20 miles (33km) to Athens and prepared to resist another landing. Before the battle, the Athenian runner Pheidippides had covered the 152 miles (245 km) between Athens and Sparta in two days in a vain attempt to summon timely help. It is also pertinent to remember that the Olympic Games included a hoplite event which was run in armour, or at any rate with a heavy hoplite shield on the arm.

One must not overlook the psychological aspect of the struggle. Greek resistance was inspired; yet one may wonder if the inspiration was really drawn from patriotism. The Thessalians in the north, who had no hope of active support from other Greek states, understandably collaborated with Xerxes. The Boeotians, led by Thebes, can perhaps be excused for doing the same, since the Peloponnesians, dominated by Sparta, wished to defend themselves by building a wall across the Isthmus of Corinth and abandoning northern Greece to its fate. This they would certainly have done, had it not been for the threat of Athens to withdraw her fleet. The Athenians, as Herodotus admiringly proclaims, provided the true rallying point for Greek patriotism.

Yet the Athenians themselves were a prey to 'fifth column' activities. Hippias the son of Pisistratus, once a benevolent despot at Athens and later an exile at the Persian court, accompanied Darius' fleet in the hope of reinstatement, and there is reason to believe that, just about this time, the powerful aristocratic clan of the Alcmaeonidae, which had connived at Hippias' exile but was now disgusted at democratic developments in Athens, was preparing to collaborate with the Persian invading army.

The true inspiration of Greek resistance was, perhaps, liberty rather than patriotism. But liberty is an equivocal ideal. Too often it means the liberty to impose one's own will upon others. And this is what it came to mean among the Greeks, as the following chapters show.

c450
Aristophanes, Athenian comic poet born

At Rome, the laws are codified

449
Peace between Athens and Persia (The Peace of Callias)

BC

The Peloponnesian War

Two major powers had emerged in Greece: Sparta, a land power, militaristic and authoritarian; Athens, a sea power, comparatively democratic. Political rivalry resulted in wars that tarnished Athens' image and culminated in her defeat.

Ancient Authorities

Thucydides, the Athenian historian on whom we chiefly rely for our knowledge of the long fifth-century war between Athens and Sparta, was particularly well qualified to write on this theme. He was fully contemporary with the events which he described and commanded both troops and ships in the course of the war. It should have been no disgrace to him that he was unable, in 424 BC, to prevent the Thracian city of Amphipolis from falling into Spartan hands; Brasidas, the Spartan general who opposed him, was a commander of rare military genius. However, Thucydides was blamed at Athens for his failure and spent the remainder of the war in exile. During this time, one assumes, he had abundant leisure to collect material for his history, but there are reasons for thinking that he did not actually write it until after his recall to Athens on amnesty terms at the end of the war. Remarks made in the course of his narrative prove that he was aware of the Athenian surrender in 404 BC. Yet his history ends with the events of 411 BC. He apparently died before he could finish.

It should also be noted that Thucydides was politically well qualified as the historian of his own times. He was a relative of the pro-Spartan statesman Cimon and a warm admirer of the anti-Spartan Pericles. His political impartiality is thus not attributable to indifference, but to a two-sided commitment. He must have been a prey to divided loyalties.

Thucydides' history was continued from the point where it left off by Xenophon in his *Hellenica*. Xenophon was himself a military commander of outstanding ability. Whether he really completed the story of the Peloponnesian War is perhaps a question of opinion, for he regarded the war as ending with the destruction of the Athenian fleet at Aegospotami in 405 BC. Certainly, this event deprived Athens of essential supplies and led to the surrender of the city in the following year. Other historians, however, of whose works only fragments survive, took a different view, and regarded the war as ending with the revival of Athens ten years later.

To Plutarch, who flourished in the late first and early second century AD, we are also indebted. His biographies of Cimon and Pericles are obviously relevant to the period which immediately preceded the Peloponnesian War and to its early phases. Indeed, we have only a very imperfect account from Thucydides of the 50 or more years which elapsed between the defeat of the Persian invaders and the beginning of war between Athens and Sparta, so the evidence that a later writer has passed on to us must not be despised.

Xenophon apart, we are unable to compare Thucydides with those who followed him as historians. Of Theopompus, Ephorus and Cratippus we possess only scattered fragments and testimonies. A most impressive excerpt of Greek history, which seems to be a continuation of Thucydides, has been recovered from an Egyptian papyrus manuscript, but this fragment is only 900 lines long. Our loss is all the greater because the balance of advantage does not always and in every way lie with the contemporary historian. History calls for the study of events in relation to their causes and effects. This presupposes that a historian has lived long enough or late enough to be aware of those effects. Yet, when all has been said, we must congratulate ourselves on having inherited the history of an ancient war from the hand of one who took part in it.

Political Background

The conflict between Cimon and Pericles, to which we have alluded, was perhaps to some extent a clash of personalities. It can easily be interpreted as the struggle between a warm-hearted military extrovert and an intellectual—not to say high-

Above right: The historian Thucydides is our main source for the events of this period. Unfortunately he died before completing his work.

Right: Pericles, the renowned Athenian statesman who fostered his city's political and cultural predominance in the years that followed the Persian Wars.

BC

446
Athenian attempts to expand westward are halted by defeat by Coronea in Boeotia

441
Samos revolts against Athenian domination, but is besieged and reduced by Athenian forces

c437
Pericles founds Athenian colony at Amphipolis in Thrace

Pericles' diplomatic and colonising activities in the Black Sea secure the Athenian corn supply

40

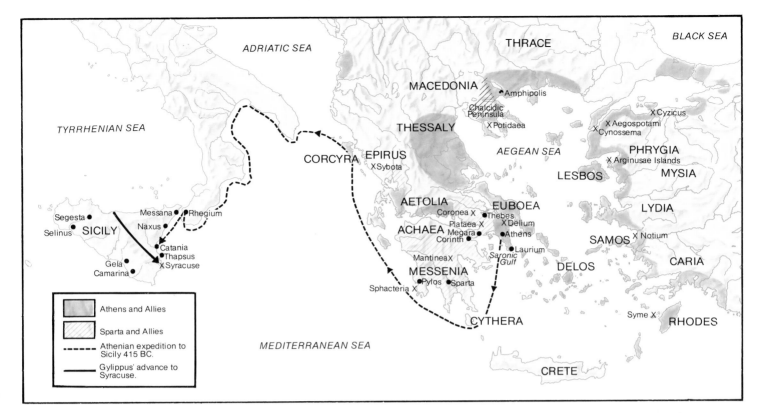

Athenian expedition to Sicily 415 BC.

Gylippus' advance to Syracuse.

brow—orator. But this conflict reflected wide differences of attitude which were evident not only in Athenian politics but in political activity throughout Greece. Were the Greeks to remain united under traditional Spartan leadership, or was it to be accepted that, as a result of the Persian Wars, Athens offered an alternative—if divisive—hegemony?

The question was not purely strategic. Pericles himself, in the early years of the Peloponnesian War, eloquently drew attention to Athenian cultural supremacy. Indeed, Athenian supremacy in this field stood in no need of advertisement. But the polarity of attitudes which expressed itself in the Peloponnesian War was also characterized by acute ideological differences: the differences which existed between democratic and oligarchic structures of power.

In our own day, democracy is a word which means different things to different persons. But the Greek meaning of the word corresponds to no modern usage. Athenian democracy meant the political supremacy of an Assembly open to all citizens. Citizenship was an exclusive privilege. It excluded women, it excluded slaves, and it excluded a numerous section of the community, drawn from other Greek states, which could not lay claim to citizen ancestry. There was no question of representative democracy. Magistrates were elected or appointed by lot, but the Assembly members met, deliberated and voted together, in the open air, simply by virtue of their status as citizens of Athens.

At Sparta, by contrast, power was nominally in the hands of two hereditary kings but rested in reality with five *ephors* (supervisors). They were elected annually by a narrowly-defined citizen assembly. There was also a *gerousia* (senate) of twenty-eight* men over 60 years old, elected by the same assembly from among the most notable families of Sparta. The citizen assembly could approve or reject, by acclamation, the proposals made by the kings, ephors and senate. Otherwise, its members had not the right to speak; they only qualified for attendance on reaching the age of 30.

Compared with Sparta, Athens seems to merit the description of "democracy". In the last resort, all government means control by a minority—for only a minority can produce that unity of directive which the word "government" implies. However, the governing minority may be comparatively large or comparatively small. At Athens it was large; at Sparta it was small. In this sense only is there any correspondence between the ancient and modern uses of the word democracy.

Nevertheless, there is one matter in which Sparta appears to have been more democratic than Athens. This concerns the status of women. At neither city did women possess the right to vote or take part in any political activity. At Athens they enjoyed very few civil and legal rights, although there was an important

*The two kings, by their attendance, raised the membership to 30.

Above: *This map shows the main actions fought during the Peloponnesian war when the sea power of Athens gradually succumbed to the predominantly land-based Spartans.*

distinction between those who were the daughters of citizens and those who were not. Only the former could contract a legal marriage and produce children who were citizens. At Sparta, however, a woman of citizen family possessed one right which was not accorded to any woman in Athens: she might own property. The social consequences—and, in the long run, the political consequences —of this legal right were important. Writing of the Spartan constitution in the fourth century BC, Aristotle accused the Spartans of what we should describe as petticoat rule.

However that may be, the Spartans themselves certainly regarded the ideological aspect of the Peloponnesian War as cardinal. As soon as they had occupied Athens and made themselves masters of Greece, they established oligarchies in all the main cities and provided armed garrisons to ensure the continuance of oligarchic power. Admittedly, the situation did not last; in many instances—above all at Athens—democratic feeling was too strong to be overawed by the presence of a handful of troops. Sparta, in fact, with a declining citizen population, lacked the manpower to garrison Greece, and her reputation as a liberator suffered disastrously from the attempt to do so.

435
Corinth defeated by Corcyra in naval battle arising out of colonial dispute

433
Corcyra saved from Corinthian retaliation by Athenian naval intervention at the battle of Sybota

432
Athenians besiege Potidaea (Corinthian colony)

Corinth wins Spartan support against Athens

BC

41

Archers and Slingers

The colour drawing below shows a typical Scythian archer. Such men were recruited by the Athenian tyrant Pisistratus in the mid-6th century BC and served as mercenaries alongside the Athenian hoplites and also as a police force within the city. It is significant that they appear extensively on Attic vase paintings of this period, often shooting from a kneeling position. They were not with the Athenian army at the battle of Marathon and indeed a contingent of Asiatic Scythians, or "Sakae", fought

with the Persian invasion force. During the 5th century BC the Persians also employed Sakae to teach archery to their troops. This figure is wearing the characteristic long pointed hat mentioned by Herodotus and loose-fitting tunic and trousers. He carries a composite bow and is about to fire a small three-fletched arrow. His bow-case, or "gorytos", is ornamented with painted patterns and contains a second bow and supply of arrows. There is no evidence that Scythians used thumb rings, but rather they employed the normal Mediterranean loose that is used by Western archers today. In this they contrasted with the normal Greek practice which was to pinch the arrow between thumb and forefinger: a weak grip which meant that Greeks were unable to draw the powerful bows of the Scythians. This may in part explain why the full value of bowmen was only gradually appreciated in Greece towards the end of the Peloponnesian War

Above left: A pottery painting of a musician in Scythian costume. His long pipe is strapped to his mouth—a common practice.

The Composite Bow

The drawings (left) show the bow unstrung, in cross-section, and strung. It consists of a wooden core on to which is bound sinew (front side) and horn (back). The elasticity of the sinew means that when the bow is drawn it stretches and is put under tension. By contrast the strips of horn are compressed. Both substances therefore react to propel the arrow. The bow is fitted with horn endpieces into which the nocks for the string are carved. Two types of bronze arrow head are also illustrated. In both cases the shaft of the arrow fitted into the head.

The Slinger

A slinger, typical of the men who fought the Spartans at Sphacteria (see page 53), and his lead projectile are shown here. The bullet was cast and weighed between 25 and 30 grams. It was frequently inscribed

with some suitably belligerent phrase, in this instance "Dexa" ("Take that!"). It would not be seen in flight and was capable of penetrating unprotected flesh to a range of about 100 metres. The figure wears a round hat to protect him from the sun's glare and carries his slingstones in a bag on his hip. He is equipped with a small shield with a single handgrip and wears a loose wool or linen tunic. One end of his sling is looped around his wrist while the other is released when the stone is launched. Rhodian slingers like this amply proved their value during Xenophon's retreat in 401 BC.

Spartan ultimatum to Athens
Spartan king Archidamus invades Attica
Rural population confined within Athenian city walls
Plague at Athens
Potidaea taken by the Athenians

Athenian Sea Power

Spartan weakness at sea, as contrasted with Athenian strength, had been underlined by the events of the Persian Wars. The instrument by which the anti-Persian policy of Cimon was now translated into the anti-Spartan policy of Pericles was the alliance of Aegean maritime states known to modern historians as the Delian League. After the disgrace and recall of Pausanias, the Spartans and other Peloponnesian states at last recognized the reality of Athenian leadership at sea and were content to shed their own naval responsibilities. The League, over which Athenian stewards presided, had its headquarters and treasury at Delos. Member states which could not so conveniently provide ships contributed money. The organization served its original purpose well, but even before peace was reached with Persia some members had vainly attempted secession and had been coerced. The Euboean city of Carystus was even forced to join.

In 447 BC, Athenian ambitions of expansion westward at last met with disaster on Boeotian battlefields. Athens had been involved in war against Corinth, Thebes and Sparta. It was obvious that the Delian League, invoked against Persia, would be used by Athens against other Greek states. At the same time, it must have been clear not only to Pericles but to any intelligent Athenian that the city's independence was conditional on its domination of the Aegean. The situation has many parallels in history. The autonomy of one power can be secured only through the subjugation of others. Already, in 454 BC, the League treasury at Delos had been transferred to the custody of the city of Athens.

For many of the Greek city states at this period, the protection afforded by Athenian sea power had become simply a protection racket. Yet the Athenians could hardly have maintained their position of dominance had they been unable to rely on a nucleus of goodwill among the islands and coastal cities of the Aegean Sea. We have already drawn attention to the way in which ideological considerations often contributed to the creation and preservation of such goodwill. To these, there may also be added colonial and racial ties.

Apart from their sense of Greek nationality and—more importantly—local state citizenship, the Greeks were conscious of racial allegiances. Athenian support for the Ionian Greeks, and subsequent ability to rally their loyalty, owed something to the fact that the Athenians were themselves of Ionian stock. Like the Aeolians of the north-east Aegean, the Ionian Greeks had interbred in prehistoric times with the pre-Hellenic peoples of the Aegean lands. The Dorians, who emerged in Greece at a later date, were examples of comparatively pure Nordic stock. The temperamental differences which resulted are comparable with those which today distinguish Nordic from Mediterranean peoples. Both Sparta and Athens were, on different occasions, able to take advantage of racial sentiment, and the Greeks of the central Aegean were predominantly Ionian.

To these circumstances it may be added that Athens exerted power and influence through her many colonies in the Aegean and Black Sea regions. From as early as the eighth century, colonization had been a well-recognized procedure in Greece in relieving population pressures in a country that was by no

Above: *A marble representation of an Athenian trireme (the Lenormant relief). Three banks of oars are clearly visible but only the top rank of rowers. Such war galleys relied wholly on their oars for speed in battle.*

means fertile. Fleets carrying settlers were sent overseas. The number of these settlers ranged from mere hundreds to a matter of thousands. It was important that they should find suitable territory where no organized political power yet existed. Colonies usually preserved traditional ties with their mother city and could themselves become the mothers of colonies. Ordinarily, colonial foundations of this kind were autonomous, but there was also a type of settlement known as a "cleruchy", where the settlers preserved citizen rights in the founding city. It was common Athenian practice to found cleruchies in conquered territory.

Athenian Diplomacy and Naval Strategy

Athenian wealth, arising from the silver mines at Laurium in south-east Attica, would have been dissipated in communal handouts if Themistocles had not diverted it, during the period between the two Persian invasions, into naval armament. To win support for this measure, he found it more effective to incite jealousy against Athens' seafaring neighbour, the island of Aegina, than to reawaken fears of Persia. But there can be no doubt that his policy saved Greece from Persian domination.

When the tide of invasion receded, Sparta, suspicious of growing Athenian power, attempted to dissuade the Athenians from rebuilding their ruined

429
Athenian fleet wins victories over Peloponnesian naval units near Naupactus

Death of Pericles

Plataea, Boeotian city supporting Athens, is besieged by Thebans and Spartans

428
Lesbos revolts against Athenian domination

Mytilene is besieged by Athenians

BC

43

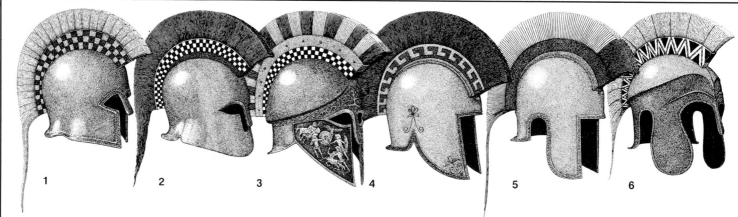

1   2   3   4   5   6

Greek Hoplite Helmets

The evolution of the hoplite and his equipment engendered two main types of bronze helmet, known today as the "Corinthian" and "Illyrian". Such helmets were prized possessions and often passed from father to son. The Corinthian was produced by beating metal over a stake and tailor-made so as to be very close fitting. On pottery and sculpture these helmets usually appear with crests, but a close study reveals that in practice a large number lacked them. Crests were usually made of horsehair set in wood, rather like a broom. As horsehair is difficult to dye, the bristles were normally left unstained; black, white and chestnut were common natural colours. Little is known about helmet linings but it is believed that felt may have been glued inside. What is certain is that skull-caps of felt or wool were worn, to keep hair in position and perhaps as padding. The illustration shows several helmets in use around the 5th century BC. Number **1** is a fairly simply decorated variant of a Corinthian helmet. It offers excellent all-round protection but suffers by severely limiting vision and hearing, as well as being hot and stuffy to wear for long periods. **2** is a south Italian variation from which developed the Etrusco-Corinthian type (see page 109). **3** is the classic Corinthian helmet. It has elongated cheek-pieces to better protect the wearer's mouth and throat. The bowl is strengthened by a cranial ridge which also increases ventilation by making the dome less close

city walls. As a pretext, it was urged that the cities of northern Greece should dismantle their fortifications in order to deprive any future invader of a Greek base—such as Thebes had been for Mardonius. Themistocles ingeniously protracted negotiations on the matter while the Athenians hastily rebuilt their city walls, and Sparta was soon faced with a *fait accompli*. Such, at least, is the story told by Thucydides. Plutarch quotes Theopompus' view that Themistocles bribed the Spartan ephors into acquiescence. Indeed, there is room for both stories: artful diplomacy may have been combined with bribery.

Themistocles was also responsible for the fortification of Piraeus, the main port of Athens. This represented a reversal of traditional Athenian policy, which had been concentrated on agricultural self-sufficiency. Later, Long Walls were built connecting the city with Piraeus and with the minor port of Phaleron. The double walls to Piraeus were about four miles (6·4 km) long and provided a corridor about 200 yards (183m) wide by which sea-borne supplies could reach the city in defiance of besieging armies.

It needed only one more step to complete the grand strategy which Themistocles had initiated; the establishment of a network of naval bases in the Aegean. Such a network was provided by the so-called Delian League. Its importance can be understood by reference to the structure of ancient ships. These were light and comparatively frail and were not made to endure rough weather for long. They hugged the coast and made for shelter at the first sign of a storm. It was not necessary to find an anchorage; a beach was good enough, for the same light construction that endangered these vessels in storms permitted them easily to be drawn up on shore. But beaches were inconveniently few on the rocky and inhospitable coastline of the eastern Mediterranean. Most good anchorages served as ports to city states, whose position they had perhaps originally determined. It was essential, both for war and for trade, to make use of such bases, and this end could best be guaranteed by political domination of the states concerned. The Athenian people well understood their needs, and they identified their needs with their rights.

The funds which accrued from the contributions to the League were no less vital to the maintenance of a powerful navy. Apart from the expense of building, maintaining and repairing ships, rowers had to be paid, and in a trireme these were numerous—upwards of 150 in a single vessel*. Rowers were recruited from the lower citizen classes at Athens and were paid a daily wage. Those who pulled at the longer, upper-bank oars sometimes earned more money than those rowing in the lower banks. The armed marines on each vessel were hoplites, drawn from the wealthier, arms-bearing classes. Even for hoplites, the state latterly provided a spear and shield, while requiring the individual to furnish the rest of his panoply.

*4th century Athenian triremes each had 170 rowers.

The Outbreak of the Peloponnesian War

Athenian westward ambitions, rather than possession of Aegean bases, provoked the Peloponnesian War. Such ambitions were bound to be entertained mainly at the expense of Corinth, a maritime city with an enviable position on the Isthmus, facilitating that westward economic expansion to which the Athenians so eagerly aspired. In 459 BC, the Athenians had intervened on behalf of the smaller and nearer Isthmus city of Megara against Corinth. In 435 BC, intervention was still the political weapon and Corinth still the enemy. The Corinthians were at this time involved in a quarrel with their own colony of Corcyra (Corfu). After a naval battle near Sybota, off the coast of Epirus, they would have overwhelmed the colonists if Athenian ships had not intervened to save Corcyra.

The next clash, at Potidaea, was also an involvement with Corinth. The Potidaeans were unwilling members of the Delian League and, encouraged by the Macedonian king, would have seceded from it. Potidaea, on the western coast of the Chalcidic peninsula, was a colony of Corinth and, faced with Athenian

Right: *Painted pottery showing an armourer at work on a helmet. The "Corinthian" style of helmet in particular called for fine craftsmanship, being produced from a single sheet of bronze.*

BC | 427
Surrender of Mytilene | Plataea falls to Thebans and Spartans | At Corcyra, triumphant democrats, supported by Athens, massacre their political opponents | 426 The Athenian general Demosthenes campaigns in Aetolia | 425 Demosthenes occupies Pylos on west coast of Peloponnese

44

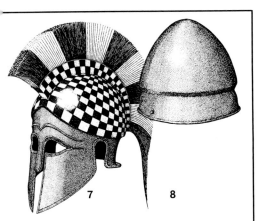

fitting. This particular helmet is richly decoated with relief sculpture. **7** is a late Corinthian with cut-outs to improve hearing, while **6** is a more open development known as the "Chalcidian" type. **4** and **5** show similar developments in Illyrian helmets. **8** shows a cheaper, mass produced piece popular in the Peloponnese and known as the "Pylos" type. It was simply attached by a leather strap.

coercion, appealed to the mother city for help. Despite this, the Athenians besieged and eventually captured the city in 430 BC. Pericles' attempt at this time to gain control of Megara by an economic blockade may be regarded as a retaliatory threat for what happened at Potidaea. No doubt, he would gladly have applied the same treatment to Corinth herself. But the larger city, unlike Megara, lay on

the west of the Isthmus, with outlets to the Gulf of Corinth. The port of Megara was situated on the Saronic Gulf.

Other states saw themselves threatened by Athenian policy and actions, especially Thebes and the Boeotians, who would be encircled by a traditionally hostile power if Athens held the bases at which she aimed on the Gulf of Corinth. In the face of the general Athenian threat, Sparta, with its Peloponnesian satellites, was with some difficulty persuaded to support the struggle against Athens. Throughout the war, she remained the least bitter of Athens' enemies and at the end of it was the most clement of the victors ranged against her.

The war had begun as a naval conflict with Corinth and continued in this way throughout its earlier phases. Corinthian ships were now supplemented by those of Peloponnesian allies, but Athens still controlled the seas. In 429 BC, the Athenian admiral Phormio, by brilliant ramming tactics, twice defeated the Corinthian and Peloponnesian fleets at the mouth of the Gulf of Corinth.

However, as the war went on the Corinthians learned their lessons and designed war galleys of a new type. A high prow had given their boarding parties and missile throwers an advantage, but in ramming tactics the upper part of the prow never came into collision with the enemy. The lower war galley of the Athenian fleet made an impact both with water-line ram and

pronged prow. Taught by disasters, the Corinthians introduced lower, reinforced prows. This facilitated naval tactics of a new kind: head-on ramming. The Athenian galleys, lightly structured for manoeuvre and broadside ramming, were in their turn at a disadvantage.

Spartan Strategy

Spartan strategy in the early phases of the war seems to have been singularly ineffectual. The Spartans did not attempt to besiege Athens but contented themselves with a yearly invasion of Attica, ravaging as much Athenian farmland as they had time for and hoping thereby to provoke the Athenians into a pitched battle. This was the situation which had been foreseen by both Themistocles and Pericles. The Athenian rural population drove its flocks and herds to Euboea for safety and itself withdrew behind the city's walls. The Long Walls to the coast safeguarded the access to seaborne supplies, and the Athenian navy, merchant fleet and chain of Aegean bases guaranteed the transport of corn from the other side of the Aegean, particularly the Black Sea area. Admittedly, as a result of unhealthy crowding within the walls, plague exterminated a large proportion of the population. But that was hardly due to strategic calculation on anybody's part.

The Peloponnesian war afforded very few instances of classic hoplite engagements. Just as the Spartans knew better than to attempt a siege, so the Athenians were wise enough not to challenge Sparta to a pitched battle. There was one spectacular exception. In 418 BC, after a period of uneasy truce, an Athenian detachment, at the instance of Alcibiades, the city's brilliant younger statesman and general, was sent out in support of Sparta's rebellious satellite allies and a pitched battle resulted at Mantinea in the northern Peloponnese.

The Spartans proved that their flair for hoplite fighting had not suffered from lack of practice. On going into action, a hoplite battle-line often developed a dangerous left-to-right drift, as a result of which the left wing could easily become enveloped by the enemy's right. This was because the man on the extreme right instinctively edged outwards for fear of exposing his unshielded right flank; the remainder closed up on him, as each man sought the protection of his neighbour's shield arm. At Mantinea (418 BC), both armies tended to outflank the opposing left wings because of this.

Fearing to be encircled, the Spartan king, Agis, attempted at the last moment

Fighting develops round Pylos and adjacent island of Sphacteria

Spartan garrison on Sphacteria surrenders to Cleon and Demosthenes

424
Athenians defeated by the Thebans in Delium

The Spartan general Brasidas captures Amphipolis in Thrace

In Persia, Darius II succeeds his father Artaxerxes I

BC

45

to extend his left wing and to reinforce the attenuated line of battle with troops from the right. Two officers who were responsible for the reinforcing movement did not obey. In the resulting confusion, the line developed a gap through which the enemy poured. However, the troops on the right so quickly rolled up the forces opposed to them that they were able to turn round and overwhelm the enemy centre—until that moment victorious. The superiority of the Spartan hoplite, even when hindered by bungling generalship, was once more demonstrated in this action.

The Spartan Army

Concerning the battle of Mantinea, Thucydides points out that a Spartan king in the field could rely upon an established chain of command through which his orders quickly reached all units. Subordinate to the king were the "polemarchs", who transmitted his commands to the troops through the officers in charge of units. At Mantinea, the largest Spartan unit was the *lochos*: rather less in numerical strength than a modern battalion. It was divided into 4 *pentecostyes,* each consisting of 4 *enomotiai*: companies and platoons respectively. The Spartan army on this occasion contained 7 battalions.

The whole battle front measured 448 men from one wing to the other; behind these were supporting ranks, for the most part eight deep. The members of the king's bodyguard were referred to as *hippeis* (knights), though by the time of the Peloponnesian War they served mostly on foot. At Mantinea, mounted troops were in fact deployed on either wing of the Spartan army to protect the flanks. But to judge from King Agis' anxieties, either their quality or their quantity inspired little confidence.

Thucydides seems to approve the efficiency of the Spartan chain of command, remarking in effect that the Spartan army was really an officer corps in which every man felt responsible for seeing that orders were carried out. However, one is familiar with the situation in which there are "too many chiefs and too few Indians". Organization of this kind does not always produce the best discipline. At the battle of Plataea, the refusal of a Spartan junior commander to obey Pausanias' order to retreat created widespread and dangerous confusion. At Mantinea, the polemarchs on the right, disregarding the king's word of command, proceeded to win the battle in their own way. They were subsequently put on trial in Sparta

Spartan Army Organisation
There are two fairly detailed but differing accounts of the organisation of the Spartan army. According to Thucydides, writing near 400 BC, the organisation was based on an average file of 8 men, 4 files making up an *enomotia,* or platoon, commanded by an *enomotarch;* four *enomotiai* comprising a *pentekostys* or company, and commanded by a *pentekonter;* and four *pentekostyes* making up a *lochos,* or battalion, and led by a *lochagos.* 7 *lochoi* comprised an army. Xenophon, who like Thucydides was an officer in the field and is therefore an equal authority, gives only two *enomotiai* as comprising a *pentekostys,* two *pentekostyes* making up a *lochos* and four *lochoi* a *mora,* or regiment, commanded by a *polemarch.* The army comprised six *morae.* Population decline later affected total strength, but that of the *mora* (variously reported as 500, 600 or 900) depended on the age groups called up. The *enomotiai* marched one behind the other in column. When deploying for battle, rear units formed up on the left of the leader so making a phalanx of four columns, sixteen abreast and eight deep, with two metres between columns. On the command to form close-order the rear half of each *enomotia* would move up to fill the gap on each file's left.

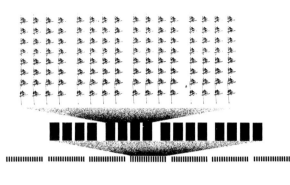

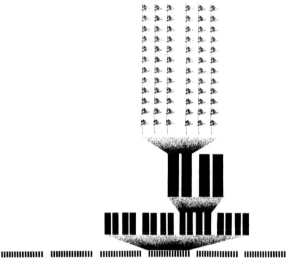

Other Troop Types
The foot soldier shown was mostly of *helot,* or serf, stock and accompanied his master into battle. Armed with a javelin or alternatively a sling, he would also support his master with refreshment, carried in a goatskin bag. The trooper seen here carries a bunch of javelins, each one of which has a loop attached. The loop was twisted round the shaft and then around the first two fingers of the thrower, enabling him to impart greater leverage and spin to the weapon, thus increasing accuracy and range. The cavalryman, a Thessalian, wears unusual headgear, probably made from cowskin, and carries no shield. Like all ancient horsemen he lacks stirrups and sits well back to maintain control of his horse.

BC	423		422	421	
	One year truce between Athens and Sparta	At Amphipolis, Cleon, the Athenian commander, and Brasidas, the Spartan commander, are killed	Hostilities renewed	Athens and Sparta agree to peace (The Peace of Nicias)	Boeotia and Corinth refuse to accept the peace treaty

The Spartan Hoplite

The Spartan hoplite is seen here in full battle array. His Corinthian helmet is of brass and decorated with a transverse crest; his shield, with Spartan blazon, is brass-faced, as are the full-length "muscled" greaves. The white linen corslet, worn over a red tunic, replaced the heavy "bell" cuirass and was made from several layers of material glued together. The lower part was cut into strips to facilitate bending down. The corslet found favour because of its lightness but was often reinforced with plates. The red cloak seen in the illustration was the characteristic Spartan uniform. It was discarded in battle. Before the time of Alexander, beards were usually worn in Greece and long hair characterised Spartan adult men. Herodotus describes how the Spartans; awaiting the Persian onslaught at Thermopylae, passed their time in taking exercise and combing their hair. This hoplite is binding a leather handgrip around the shaft of his spear to enable him to obtain a firm purchase when thrusting it overarm over the wall of phalanx shields. Unlike other hoplites, the Spartan trained all his life as a soldier, and was thus a "professional". His drill and weapons-skill were thus superior to, and more fearsome than, that of other hoplites.

and sentenced to banishment, for cowardice, so Thucydides says; one might have expected the charge to be disobedience.

Commands were, in any case, difficult to give to a hoplite army in action. Helmets—especially of the Corinthian type—must have seriously impaired their wearers' hearing. But trumpets were used for signalling and the Spartan army marched to the sound of the flute— which apparently had a steadying effect. Hand signals were also given. It has been suggested that the supposedly ill-judged order at Amphipolis which exposed the Athenian column to an enemy sally on its unshielded side was an instance of signals being misunderstood. The use of signals was also sometimes employed in a tactical ruse. In an early battle with the Argives at Sepeia (494 BC), the Spartans sounded a signal which meant "fall out for dinner" and thus threw the enemy off guard before mounting an unexpected attack. Comparable tactics were used by the Spartan admiral Lysander against the Athenians at the crucial battle of Aegospotami. In this case, the signal for the surprise attack was a bronze shield flashed in the sunlight.

The Athenian Army

At Athens, ten generals (strategoi) were elected yearly by a show of hands in the Assembly. Unlike other officials, they could be re-elected and in this way, like Pericles who was re-elected repeatedly, they might exercise great personal influence and ensure an all-important continuity of policy. Their responsibilities were those of defence and security which, as we know from modern politics, are often of cardinal importance. Fortifications and munitions, both military and naval armaments, recruitment of soldiers and seamen and the imposition of war taxes all fell within the scope of their administration.

As in Sparta, there was a military hierarchy to administer the armed forces. The infantry was commanded by ten taxiarchoi, with junior officers (lochagoi) in charge of companies. The cavalry were under the command of two senior officers (hipparchoi); subordinate to them were ten phylarchoi—literally "tribal leaders". For recruitment, both of cavalry and infantry, was based on "tribes", the ten local groupings of the civil population. We may compare our own county regiments.

Apart from administration, all the above-mentioned officers, including the elected generals, might be commanders in the field, taking responsibility for

420

418

BC

Athens temporarily allied with Spartans against Boeotians, Corinthians and Megarians

Boeotian alliance with Sparta resumed

Athens forms alliance with Argos (previously neutral) against Sparta

Argives and Athenians defeated by Spartans in battle of Mantinea

47

Siegecraft at Plataea 429-427 BC
1 The Peloponnesian besiegers construct a mound using layers of criss-crossed logs as a basic structure and in-filling with earth. As the mound nears the wall, the

Plataeans counter by erecting a scaffold covered with hides to protect the men, and by raising the walls behind this screen.
2 Once the mound reaches the wall, the Plataeans tunnel through wall and try to undermine it. The Peloponnesians counter by using solid wattle and clay to provide a tough facing to the ramp. They then deploy rams against the raised wall but the Plataeans

and try to undermine it. The Peloponnesians counter by using solid wattle and clay to provide a tough facing to the ramp. They then deploy rams against the raised wall but the Plataeans

respond by dropping heavy beams on chains to snap off the rams' heads and by trying to lasso them with nooses.
3 Although the mound is undermined, parts of the wall

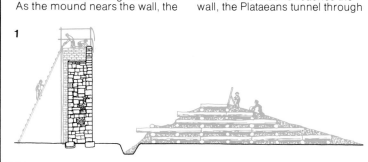
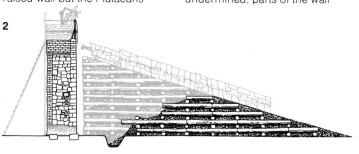

strategic and—up to a point—tactical decisions. But once a hoplite battle had been joined, the din and density of the fray was such as to leave little room for command or manoeuvre, while the light-armed troops, both at Sparta and at Athens, seem to have been subject to very little organization of any kind.

The advantage which the Spartan hoplite corps enjoyed over all other such forces in Greece lay in the fact that it was a professional army, devoting its whole time to military training and activities. This was the result of political and economic circumstances; the Spartan citizens regarded themselves as a small garrison dominating a population of potentially hostile serfs. They could also

Above: *Vases do show helmeted horsemen, but helmets were not worn by early Greek cavalry when in battle.*

rely on this population, together with the community of free farmers who did not enjoy the franchise, to nourish and maintain them. The full citizen thus had the wherewithal to pay the necessary military mess fees.

The Athenian citizen, although his case was different, did not lack military training and experience. At the age of 18, Athenians of the well-to-do hoplite

classes were called up for a two-year course of military training. This included instruction in the use of arms, tactics and fortifications. After that, they remained on the register as liable to military service until the age of 60, although those under the age of 20 or over 50 could be called on only for garrison duties, ie, service in Attica. Speaking in 431 BC, Pericles claimed that Athens possessed 13,000 hoplites, with 16,000 more on garrison duty. This latter number included not only the older and younger citizens, but also those of the resident aliens who could afford heavy armour.

The Athenians used cavalry in the Peloponnesian War, but did not always put it to the best possible use. As at Sparta, membership of the order of cavalry carried with it important social implications. But some of the wealthier citizens continued to serve as "knights" on the battlefield. During the earlier period of the war, when the Spartans were invading Attica yearly, Pericles sent out cavalry detachments to chase off enemy raiding parties. About this time, there was a cavalry skirmish between the Athenians and their Thessalian allies, on the one hand, and the Boeotian cavalry on the other. The Athenians held their own until hoplites came to the aid of the Boeotians. At Mantinea, the Athenian cavalry was able to extricate many of the Athenian fugitives from the battle, and at Delium in 424 BC, where good use of cavalry made the Thebans victorious, the Athenians at least had sufficient cavalry on their own side to protect some of their infantry in the retreat. Alcibiades, then a young officer, was himself mounted and was able to come to the aid of the philosopher Socrates, who was serving on foot.

The Athenians also underestimated the value of light-armed troops until quite late in the war. In this respect, they learned their lesson as a result of painful experience. They had themselves, in 429 BC, suffered disastrously at the hands of

the Chalcidian cavalry and light troops, when the cities of that area revolted against the Athenian League. The Athenian hoplite campaigns in western Greece, among the peasant communities of Aetolia, had also run into serious trouble in 426 BC, when beset by light-armed guerrilla fighters. Javelins, slings and sometimes bows were the main weapons of the light-armed fighter, who avoided coming to grips with the hoplite. He carried a sword only for emergencies. Apart from guerrilla tactics, missiles were of obvious importance in a siege.

Sieges of the War

By the beginning of the Peloponnesian War, Greek siegecraft had, in contrast to earlier times and despite Spartan tardiness in this direction, become highly sophisticated. In the first years of the war, the Boeotian town of Plataea near the Attic frontier became an object of contention and was besieged by a combination of Boeotian and Peloponnesian forces. There remained in the town only a military garrison, the non-combatant population having taken refuge in Athens.

The besiegers built an earthen ramp reinforced with timber against the town wall, but the Plataeans raised the height of their own wall and sapped the ramp from beneath. The Peloponnesians plugged the gap made by the sappers with clay and wattle; to which the Plataeans replied by building new fortifications within the threatened sector of their walls. When battering-rams approached, their heads were lassoed or broken off by heavy beams dropped from above. An attempt was made to fire the town, but this was foiled by a drenching thunderstorm. A double crenellated and turreted circumvallation was then built with a view to starving the defenders. The outer wall was a precaution against any surprise by an

416
The Athenians, capturing the neutral island of Melos, massacre and enslave the inhabitants

Athenians intervene in Sicily in favour of Segesta against Syracuse

415
Athenian expeditionary campaigns against Syracusans

Alcibiades recalled from Sicily to face prosecution at Athens, escapes to Sparta

414
Athenians besiege Syracuse

collapse under the battering. The besieged then construct an interior wall so that the enemy will break through into another walled enclosure. In reply the besiegers fill this enclosure with wood and pitch and fire it. A chance rainstorm, however, douses the blaze. As described below, the garrison only succumbed to starvation after prolonged resistance.

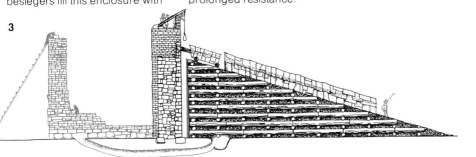

3

Athenian relief force, but the Athenians feared to be involved in a pitched battle with Spartan hoplites and no relief was sent. At last, the Plataeans, having equipped themselves with scaling ladders, captured a section of the double wall and held it, while 200 of their number escaped to Athens, having first deliberately taken the wrong road to mislead their pursuers. In the following summer, a Spartan assault on the walls had some success, but the besiegers allowed starvation to do its work. The remaining 200 men of the garrison surrendered and after some specious legal proceedings were put to death.

At Plataea, a sledgehammer had been taken to crack a nut; other sieges were of greater military significance. In 425 BC, an Athenian fleet put a landing party ashore at Pylos in the western Peloponnese and, after some discussion, built a fort there. In this area, it might serve as a garrison to the Messenian population, already disaffected subjects of Sparta. The Spartans blockaded Pylos and occupied the island of Sphacteria, which stretched across the mouth of the adjacent bay. However, an Athenian fleet arrived and the Spartans in Sphacteria were themselves besieged. An Athenian hoplite force surprised and annihilated a Spartan outpost at the southern extremity of the island. Bowmen and slingers were then landed in overwhelming numbers. Woodland on the island had been destroyed by a chance fire and the Spartan force, originally 420 strong, deprived of all cover and unable to come to grips with the enemy, was forced to surrender (see plan on page 53).

The most significant and the most sensational of all sieges during the war was that of Syracuse on the east coast of Sicily, which ended catastrophically for the Athenian besiegers and finally put an end to Athens' dreams of westward expansion. On landing, the Athenians soon established a base. They built a double wall across the plateau to the west of the city, to sever land communications with the rest of Sicily, while their fleet controlled the seas. As the besiegers extended their walls southwards, the Syracusans, starting from their own city walls, built counter-fortifications at right-angles across the intended course of the Athenian ramparts. The Athenians, however, overcame these obstacles.

In the north, the besiegers' walls had been left incomplete, and through this gap 3,000 Sicilians led by the Spartan general Gylippus brought relief to the city. Northward extension of the Athenian walls was soon blocked by a counter-wall, which this time the Athenians were unable to surmount. The northern gap remained open and the defenders were able to pass through it. Under the leadership of Gylippus, the Syracusans soon

The Siege of Syracuse 416 BC

1 The Athenians approach Syracuse through Euryalus, and, after a brief battle, capture the Epipolae plateau. They build two forts, one at Labdalum on the northern front and a round fort (the Circle) to guard the south-western front. From the Circle they build twin walls of circumvallation.
2 The Syracusans build a counter wall, but this is captured and dismantled.
3 The Syracusans now construct a ditch and palisade across the marshes, but this is also captured in a two-pronged attack by the fleet and the army (who cross the marshes on planks).
4 The Athenians complete their walls on the southern front, widening at the shore to protect the fleet, but Nicias, the Athenian commander, leaves the northern wall incomplete – a great blunder.
5 The Syracusans appeal to Sparta, who refuse to send an army, but send a general, Gylippus, who collects 3000 irregular troops and enters Syracuse without meeting resistance. Gylippus assumes command in Syracuse, captures Labdalum, and builds a wall between the city and the fort. This is the turning point in the siege.
6 Nicias asks Athens to call off the siege, but instead the city sends reinforcements. Nicias establishes three forts at

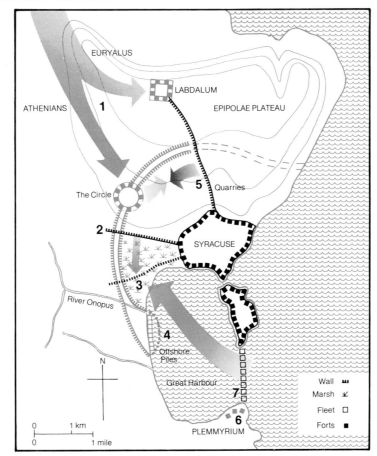

Plemmyrium at the southern end of the great harbour and transfers the fleet there.
7 Both sides now receive reinforcements. Gylippus attacks by land and sea and, after a series of naval battles, captures Plemmyrium and bottles up the Athenian fleet in its stockade, blocking the harbour mouth with a chained row of ships. Meanwhile, the Athenian army is trapped in the marshes, and is ravaged by disease. The Syracusan navy retires and modifies its ships after the Corinthian style, altering the old hollow bow and rendering it more resistant to impact (as shown on the trireme p30–31, and similar to the bow of the vessel pp98-99). This, with the strengthened outriggers, allows head-on ramming as a deliberate tactic. Head-on ramming and the use of small boats moving under the oars and attacking the rowers totally demoralise the Athenian fleet. The fleet fails to break out of the great harbour, and it is decided to abandon the ships and escape overland. The Syracusan cavalry and light troops constantly harass the Athenians. Weakened by disease and tormented by thirst, the survivors surrender.
This is Athens' greatest defeat. Together with her Greek, Etruscan and Italian allies, she has lost 150–200 ships and 40,000–50,000 men.

Wall
Marsh
Fleet
Forts

EURYALUS
ATHENIANS
LABDALUM
EPIPOLAE PLATEAU
1
The Circle
5
Quarries
2
SYRACUSE
3
River Onopus
4
Offshore Piles
N
Great Harbour
7
6
PLEMMYRIUM
0 1 km
0 1 mile

Spartan commander Gylippus brings reinforcements to Syracuse

Spartans, on Alcibiades' advice, occupy Decelea in Attica

Demosthenes brings reinforcements from Athens to Nicias' army at Syracuse

Total destruction of Athenian forces in Sicily

Nicias and Demosthenes captured and put to death by victorious Syracusans

In India at this time, the Nanda dynasty is established in the Ganges kingdom of Magadha

assumed the offensive and the Athenians were besieged within their own double walls. At last, even their base was taken and they were hemmed in on the harbour beach. All escape by sea was eventually cut off by the victory of the Syracusan fleet in the harbour itself. New ships on the reinforced Corinthian model had been built and the tactics of head-on ramming were employed. The whole Athenian expeditionary force, together with the large reinforcements which had reached them, was utterly destroyed.

Victories of the besiegers over the besieged during the period which we are considering were often achieved by starvation. This had produced the final surrender of Plataea and Potidaea. The Athenians themselves, deprived of their fleet, were eventually overcome by hunger; before beginning his blockade of the city, the Spartan admiral Lysander had sent all Athenian captives taken elsewhere into Athens to swell the numbers of the starving.

The New Spartan Strategy

Peculiar circumstances had led the Spartans to send Gylippus with his small force of Peloponnesians to rally Sicilian resistance against Athens. Alcibiades had been recalled from the Syracusan expedition and threatened with prosecution by his jealous political enemies at Athens. He had saved himself by deserting to Sparta, offering advice in return for asylum; the Spartans had acted on his advice.

Apart from intervention in Sicilian affairs, Alcibiades had made other useful suggestions, recommending that as an alternative to their annual ineffective invasions of Attica the Spartan army should occupy a permanent base on Attic soil, which would constitute a continuous menace to the Athenians—not merely a seasonal inconvenience. On their next visit to Attica, in 413 BC, the Spartans accordingly occupied Decelea, a small township situated some 14 miles (23 km) north of Athens.

The Thracian Peltast

After the experience of the Persian Wars, the Greeks realised the value of lightly-armed missile troops such as archers, slingers and peltasts. Originally peltasts were Thracian tribesmen fighting in their native dress, but later the term came to denote a particular type of foot soldier. His name derived from his shield, the *pelta* which was frequently crescent-shaped but which might also be circular or oval. It was made of wicker and covered with goat or sheep skin. The use of the *pelta* and the peltast's lack of armour enabled him to evade the charge of heavily equipped troops and yet hold an advantage over lighter troops, such as archers, in hand-to-hand fighting. Another advantageous factor was that peltasts were far cheaper to equip and maintain than hoplites. Their weapons were a bundle of javelins. Although they are conventionally illustrated with only two, it is clear from accounts of battles in various ancient texts that more were carried, the number depending on their length which varied between 3·5ft (1·1m) and 5ft (1·6m). The colour drawing shows a typical Thracian peltast wearing the characteristic foxskin cap and high boots. His cloak (*zeira*) bears the characteristic pattern evident in all extant references. His cloak and tunic are girded up to allow greater freedom of movement and to ease the throwing action. During the Corinthian War peltasts acquired such a deadly dexterity that hoplite units could not withstand them in combat. The battle of Lechaeum (see p 57) illustrates their potential admirably. Of course on the occasions when hoplites did manage to engage them, they suffered severely.

The Throwing Sequence
The series of drawings above shows how the peltast delivered his javelin. The missile is gripped lightly with the third and fourth fingers while the second and third are inserted into the loop of the thong that is bound round the shaft. The thong adds greater leverage to

BC   412

Spartans recognise Persian control of Ionian cities in return for naval and financial aid

Alcibiades, unpopular at Sparta, becomes adviser to Persian satrap Tissaphernes

411

Oligarchs temporarily gain power at Athens

Athenian fleet wins victory over Spartans at Cynossema in the Hellespont

50

The position was well chosen; it was, in fact, Alcibiades' own choice. The raids made by the Peloponnesians were now unremitting. In earlier days, the Athenian farmers had been able to occupy and enjoy their property outside the campaigning season but the situation had changed radically. Decelea also proved to be a point of refuge for runaway slaves, many of whom possessed valuable skills. The Athenians lost an estimated 20,000 slaves in this way. Their flocks and pack animals were also subject to depredation and the Athenian cavalry, much taxed in driving off enemy raids over rocky ground, found itself increasingly immobilized by lame horses. It

should be remembered in this context that horseshoes were unknown to the ancient Greeks. In addition to these difficulties, supplies which had previously arrived overland from Euboea now had to be brought at great expense by the circuitous sea route. The city walls required to be guarded, both summer and winter, by Athenian troops, in daytime on a roster basis and at night by the whole garrison.

The Spartans retained their grip on Decelea throughout the years that followed and in 406 BC, King Agis, who was in command there, actually launched a night attack in the hope of rushing the city walls of Athens. He caught the outposts off their guard but

the defenders on the walls were alerted just in time. Agis' force on this occasion consisted of 14,000 hoplites and the same number of light-armed troops, with 1,200 cavalry. This marks a great departure from the earlier Spartan reliance on predominantly hoplite armies.

Although the Athenians were shaken by the event, the challenge of the Spartan attack was answered resolutely by the Athenian garrison army, which issued from the gates to give battle. However, it took up a position immediately beneath the walls, where it could be covered by missiles from above. Agis wisely judged that it would be inadvisable to fight under such conditions. He retired and the Athenians showed no inclination to follow him.

Spartan Naval Weakness and its Remedies

Sparta had never been an important naval power, but the Athenian disaster in Sicily presented her with the opportunity of becoming one. This opportunity was taken, thanks largely to the vigour and enterprise of the Spartan admiral Lysander. The Athenians were striving to repair their devastating naval losses at Syracuse, but in the meantime they had lost their grip on the eastern Aegean. The Persian satraps of Asia Minor, Tissaphernes in the south and Pharnabazus in the north, encouraged the Greek cities of the League to revolt against their old "protector". This made the Persians the natural allies of Sparta—although their long-term objectives were, of course, different. A formal agreement was reached, the Persians promising to supply ships and pay rowers, the Spartans recognizing the Persian claims over the Greek Ionian cities. However, the agreement did not take effect as smoothly as the Spartans had hoped. Alcibiades, who had left Sparta hastily when the Spartan queen Timaea became pregnant by him, had now taken refuge in Asia Minor with Tissaphernes. Once more, he offered advice in return for hospitality. His advice to Tissaphernes was that the Persians should delay their help to Sparta and, by so doing, preserve a balance of power between the contending Greek states.

A balance of power in the eastern Aegean certainly resulted, as was illustrated by a series of naval engagements which took place between 411 and 405 BC. At Cynossema, a headland in the Hellespont, the Athenians were

the delivery, significantly improving the mechanical efficiency of the throw. The twist imparted also greatly aids the accuracy of the missile.

Tactics versus Hoplites
Peltasts in open order (right) run forward in groups and throw javelins. They then retire on their fellows. Unencumbered by armour, they never need come to grips with their heavier enemy.

Other Troop Types
The black and white drawing (right) shows a Dii tribesman who was armed with a large slashing sword (*machaira*) unlike most Thracians at this time. His shield is a variant of the *pelta*. The grips were either similar to those fitted to the *hoplon* (ie using a central armband and handgrip fixed near to the rim) or simple handgrips fixed centrally on the back of the shield. He wears the earflaps of his foxskin cap tied back, revealing a metal skullcap beneath. The figure (far right) illustrates a later type of peltast. This is the sort of man that marched with Xenophon and figures so prominently in his epic retreat from Persia. He is a mercenary and carries his *pelta* slung over his shoulders to aid movement. The bag on his right hip contains provisions and, possibly, plunder! His javelins are bundled together for ease of carriage. The tactical importance of light-armed troops is more fully explored on page 57 in Chapter 4.

410
With Alcibiades' help, Athenians defeat Spartans at naval battle of Cyzicus

408
Cyrus, son of Darius II, assumes supreme political control of Persian provinces in Asia Minor

408/7
Lysander commands Spartan navy

407
Return of Alcibiades to Athens

BC

51

able to turn what initially looked like a defeat into a last-minute victory over the Spartan admiral Mindarus. In the following year, 410 BC, they gained a complete victory over the Spartan-led fleet, killing Mindarus and destroying his ships at Cyzicus, while the crews with difficulty escaped overland. Alcibiades, who had collaborated with the Athenian naval force in the Hellespont and had contributed largely to the result of Cyzicus, was welcomed back to Athens and soon given a command against Lysander. However, in 406 BC, while Alcibiades was temporarily absent on liaison duties, his deputy, acting against orders, provoked an unnecessary naval engagement at Notium, opposite Samos, and was defeated with heavy loss. As a consequence, Alcibiades fell from popularity and retired again to private life in a castle refuge near the Hellespont, put at his disposal by Pharnabazus.

In the same year, a victory was won by the Athenian navy at the Arginusae Islands near Lesbos. The Athenians were no longer confident of superiority in naval tactics and sailed defensively in double line, to guard themselves against that manoeuvre of *diekplus* of which they themselves had once been the most able exponents. In the event, they sank 75 of the enemy ships. The Spartan commander Callicratidas, who had succeeded Lysander, was lost overboard. But faced with the choice between rescuing their own wrecked survivors and exploiting their victory, the Athenians attempted both and achieved neither. Their loss of life was great and the commanders of the fleet were put to death for negligence when they returned to Athens.

The decisive action of Aegospotami which destroyed the Athenian fleet in 405 BC cannot be described as a naval battle. Lysander, who had now resumed command of the Spartan naval forces, launched a surprise attack from the opposite shore of the Hellespont and captured the Athenian ships and their crews on the beach. Only the Athenian admiral, Conon, escaped with a handful of ships.

The history of these closing years of the war is complicated by the fact that a virtual state of civil war existed between the Athenian fleet based on Samos and the arms-bearing oligarchy which had been established by a *coup d'état* in Athens in 411 BC. True, a compromise government soon followed, but political animosities remained intense. The social division in the Athenian forces was not between officers and other ranks, but between

hoplites and rowers. Both the Spartans and the Persians should have been able to take advantage of the situation, but they themselves were divided by internal jealousies. The Spartan home government was, not without reason, suspicious of Lysander's autocratic attitude and the Persian satraps were jealous of each other; ultimately, the ambitious young prince Cyrus was empowered by his royal father to supersede them both.

Alcibiades, in these final years of conflict, continued to act like a city state in his own right. Soon after the Athenian surrender, he was killed in a mysterious raid on his home in Phrygia. Lysander and Pharnabazus were possibly responsible. There were many persons both in and out of politics who must have been glad to get rid of Alcibiades, including his enemies in Athens. One story had it that he was killed by the brothers of a local lady whom he had seduced.

Atrocities and the Conventions of War

The Peloponnesian War was bitterly contested and marked by atrocities throughout. After subduing Mytilene, the people's Assembly at Athens voted that all the adult male Mytileneans should be put to death and the women and children enslaved. The sentence was revoked by another vote on the following day and the order of reprieve reached Mytilene just in time. But later, when a similar sentence was passed on the islanders of Melos, no reprieve followed.

At the beginning of the war, the Plataeans summarily executed a party of armed Thebans who had infiltrated their town with a view to seizing control. This was done after the Theban supporting force had been induced to retire by a promise of clemency to the captured party. Later, when the Plataean garrison surrendered, the Thebans insisted, despite Spartan reluctance, that all of them should be put to death. The Spartan admiral Alcidas stupidly and cruelly slaughtered captured rowers who had been forced into Athenian service from the Aegean maritime cities. Nevertheless, of all the Greek states involved, the Spartans were on the whole the most restrained. It is true that at Plataea, and afterwards at Aegospotami, they yielded to the will of their allies, authorizing the massacre of prisoners, with some show of judicial procedure. But after the surrender of

Below: *Bronze figurine of a Spartan warrior. His helmet is drawn forward to provide a vizor. The enveloping cloak could also serve as a blanket, but it was not worn in battle.*

Athens, the Spartan government disregarded the wishes of Corinth and Thebes and refused to impose a sentence of massacre and slavery upon their conquered enemy.

Leaving aside the atrocities produced by civil strife at Corcyra, the Athenians generally behaved with greater brutality than other Greek states. They had been the heroes of the Persian Wars, but they were the villains of the Peloponnesian War. Particularly in the final stages, when they feared the growth of Spartan naval power, they reacted with ruthless savagery. The Assembly ordered that mercenary rowers captured in enemy service should have their right hands cut off. The Athenian

Alcibiades commands for Athens in the eastern Aegean

Alcibiades' officer is defeated in a naval engagement at Notium by Spartans

Athenian naval victory over Spartans at Arginusae

Athenian commanders executed at Athens for failing to pick up survivors at Arginusae

Euripides and Sophocles, Athenian tragic poets, die

Assault on Sphacteria 425 BC

Athenians	Spartans
Hoplites	
Athens 800	Sparta 440
Messenia 200-300	
Light troops	
Archers 800	Helots c560
Peltasts 800	
Rowers	
5000-7000 from 70 triremes	None

General Situation The Spartans on Sphacteria are part of a force blockading Athenians on Pylos. An Athenian naval victory, however, turns the tables, but attempts to starve out the Spartans are foiled by swimmers who manage to evade the blockade. Fire destroys the trees on the island leaving the Spartans without cover. Demosthenes plans to attack. Cleon arrives from Athens with archers and peltasts boasting of victory within 20 days.

1 Athenian hoplites land before dawn, overrun the outposts and advance up the island. The main Spartan force advances.

2 The Spartans cannot close with the Athenian hoplites for fear that enemy peltasts will fall on their flanks and rear. The peltasts, unencumbered by armour or heavy shields, can easily avoid the formidable Spartan charge over rough ground. The Spartans are constantly harried by sling bullets, arrows and javelins, all launched from a range of 50 yards or so. Their commander, Epitadas, is killed and his second-in-command wounded. They withdraw to their hilltop outpost in a ruined fort.

3 The Spartans hold out until a Messenian officer leads his light troops along the clifftop and surprises the Spartan rear. Surrounded and exhausted, they surrender. 292 hoplites are taken prisoner, including 120 "Spartiates" (the officer class). Athenian casualties number only 50 or so.

The battle amply demonstrates the value of light troops as the Spartans are defeated without the hoplite forces coming to blows. All Greece is amazed at the fact that they choose to yield rather than die at their positions.

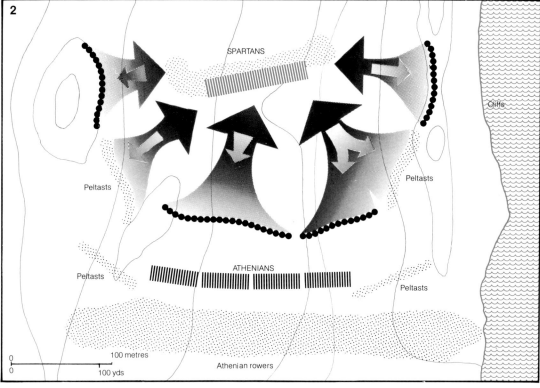

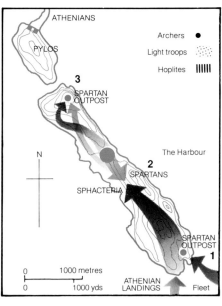

Archers ●
Light troops (dotted)
Hoplites ||||||

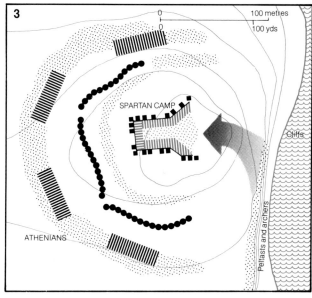

commander Philocles, himself executed with the rest after Aegospotami, had directed that the crews of two captured triremes should be thrown over a cliff.

The massacre of prisoners was certainly not without precedent in Greece. The ever-pressing problem of food shortage would alone have made it impossible to guarantee quarter for all who surrendered. But it was common to ransom or exchange prisoners, or to negotiate their return as part of a peace settlement, as was done with the Athenian prisoners after the battle of Coronea in 446 BC.

Questions of humanity apart, Greek warfare in the classical period exhibited a singularly conventional appearance. Hoplite conflicts seemed almost "staged"; more like a medieval ordeal by battle than like battle itself. Fighting tended to recur in the same places, as if in traditional arenas. But this was the effect of Greek geography. In a mountainous country, difficult to negotiate even on foot, the armies of succeeding epochs inevitably tended to clash in the same plains and mountain passes: Thermopylae, Mantinea, Coronea, Chaeronea.

Once a battle had been won, the victors set up a trophy, a monument assembled from the captured arms and armour of the vanquished. The defeated army asked for a truce in which to recover its dead. These were the formal ways of claiming victory and acknowledging defeat.

Truces, with safe conduct for pilgrims, were in force at all temples. Athletic contests were closely associated with religious cults — the Olympian games were in honour of Zeus and the Pythian games in honour of Apollo — and local truces permitted the celebration of the games even in wartime, although religious truces were sometimes broken and recriminations full of casuistry resulted. Heralds and ambassadors were sacrosanct and inviolable, although incidents could occur in which their inviolability was not respected as it should have been according to the established conventions.

The Decline of Sparta and Ascendancy of Thebes

In the 4th century BC the "March of the Ten Thousand" illustrated the increasing importance of cavalry and light troops, which was seen to the full in the defeat of the Spartan hoplites at Leuctra and in the armies of Philip of Macedon.

Ancient Authorities

Xenophon is our most valuable authority for the greater part of this period. After continuing Thucydides' history of the Peloponnesian War as far as the surrender of Athens and the events of the year 403 BC, Xenophon left an interval of two years—later to be filled in—before proceeding with his account of Greek history more or less uninterruptedly down to the year 362 BC. Other contemporary historians are known to us through later writers such as Plutarch, Diodorus Siculus and Cornelius Nepos. Nepos unfortunately mentions more sources than he uses. But it is questionable whether the elegant fourth-century testimony of Ephorus or Theopompus, even if it had survived in connected form, would be as valuable as that of Xenophon, who himself played an important military and political role in his own times and could consequently rely on his own experience of warfare among Greeks

and non-Greeks, not to mention his close acquaintance with leading personalities of the epoch.

Apart from Greek history, Xenophon also set down in his *Anabasis* the record of a great military venture, the expedition of a Greek mercenary army into the heart of the Persian empire. The expedition was not successful and Xenophon inherited command of the Greek troops after their leaders had been treacherously killed. The qualities of leadership and military resource which he then displayed extricated the men for whom he had accepted responsibility and saved the whole adventure from ending in complete disaster. The story is told from the standpoint of a professional soldier.

Xenophon wrote two other works of professional military interest. One is the *Hipparchus*: a description of the duties and functions of a cavalry commander. The other is a more general work on horsemanship, together with its military applications. Composed in an epoch when the importance of

cavalry in Greek warfare was being increasingly realized, these works are often illuminating, though curiously enough Xenophon seems to underestimate rather than exaggerate the importance of the cavalry arm. In this, he differs from most writers, who tend to insist on the importance of their own subject, if only as a form of self-advertisement. One would guess that Xenophon, for all his experience, was a conservatively minded officer, writing in the latter part of his life and still thinking in terms of warfare as it had been carried on in an earlier generation than his own.

The battle of Mantinea, with which Xenophon's history closes, marks the end of the brief Theban hegemony which had superseded that of Sparta. In modern jargon, it may be said that the result was a "power vacuum" in Greece: a situation of which the ambitious king of semi-Hellenized Macedon in the north was well able to take advantage. For this period of history, we have excellent testimony in

BC

404
After Athenian surrender, Sparta supports an oligarchy (The Thirty Tyrants) at Athens

The Thirty Tyrants are overthrown by Athenian exiles under Thrasybulus

Democratic government re-established with Spartan acquiescence

401
In Persia, Cyrus revolts against Artaxerxes II using a Greek mercenary army (Xenophon's expedition)

After the death of Cyrus at Cunaxa, the Greeks march home via the Black Sea coast the surviving speeches of Athenian orators, most notably Demosthenes. He was violently opposed to the aspirations of Philip II of Macedon; it is fortunate that we also possess the writings of Isocrates, who regarded Philip with favour and saw in him a leader capable of uniting Greece. Isocrates was hardly an orator. His political writings were produced for distribution rather than declamation and he has been fairly described as a political pamphleteer. In any case, he offers the best antidote to Demosthenes' unquestionably sincere but heavily one-sided view of the Greek political scene in the middle of the fourth century.

The Political Situation

Throughout the classical period the Greek peoples were beset by a dilemma which sometimes convulsed and sometimes paralysed their political activities. This was the result of a deep emotional conflict. They had never decided whether loyalty to their respective cities or to their common nationality had the prior claim. The Persian Wars had seen the unification of Greece against the invader. Those cities which had sided with the Persians had done so very much under stress of *force majeure*. However, the liberty which the Greek states had won by their victory over the Persians was the liberty to fight each other and, during the following century, they took full advantage of this liberty. Only at the

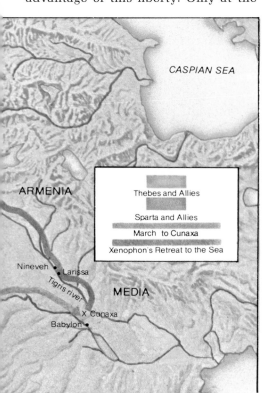

end of the Peloponnesian War, when the Persian satraps bought back from Sparta their control of the Ionian cities, did the Greeks become once more conscious of Persia as a political force. Persia, by that time, was no longer the vigorous power that it had been and Greek strategists, looking eastward, saw in the empire of the Great King either an economic ally against their enemies in Greece or a tempting target for plunder and acts of aggression.

Persian policy towards Greece still based itself consistently on the principle of "divide and rule". But Greek leaders were learning that the same policy could be applied to the Persians themselves. More than 10,000 Greek mercenary troops supported the claims of Prince Cyrus to the Persian throne on the death of his father, Darius II. When Cyrus was killed in battle at Cunaxa near Babylon in 401 BC, his elder brother Artaxerxes II was left as undisputed ruler and the two satraps of the Aegean coast, free from Cyrus' discipline, were left once more to plot against each other. The way was open for any Greek commander in the eastern Aegean to take full advantage of Persian dissension.

Left: *The extent of the March of the Ten Thousand into Persia can be seen in the right hand portion of this map, while the campaigns of Thebes dominate the Greek mainland.*

Above: *A Persian dignitary seated on his camel. The Persian army included camels during this period, but careful handling was required as they tended to unsettle the cavalry.*

Meanwhile, Sparta had become unpopular among the other Greek states. After the surrender of Athens in 404 BC, the Spartans, under Lysander's guidance, had installed garrisons, established oligarchies and exacted tribute to pay mercenaries, nominally in aid of the common defence. In so doing, they were repeating the Athenian error of the preceding century. The difference was that their puppet régimes were oligarchic, not democratic. However, a change in Spartan policy occurred when Lysander, the victor of Aegospotami, fell from power and King Agesilaus, whom he had originally hoped to use as a political instrument, superseded him in authority. The lesson of Cyrus' expedition was not lost upon Agesilaus. At Cunaxa, under the young Persian prince, an Asiatic force with the support of the Greek mercenary body already mentioned had defeated a Persian army reputedly some four times its own size, and would thereby have determined the Persian royal succession had it not been for the death of the pretender himself. After this, the Greeks, under improvised leadership, had been able to withdraw and return

CASPIAN SEA

ARMENIA

Thebes and Allies

Sparta and Allies

March to Cunaxa

Xenophon's Retreat to the Sea

Nineveh • Larissa

Tigris river

MEDIA

X Cunaxa

Babylon •

| 400 | | 399 | | 397 | | BC |

400
The Spartans invade Persian territory

399
Judicial murder of the philosopher Socrates by an Athenian democratic court

397
In Sicily, Dionysius I of Syracuse captures Motya from the Carthaginians

55

to Greece again, despite the difficulties of a thousand-mile march and in defiance of every attempt to bar their way. The fundamental military weakness of the Persians was exposed and successive Spartan commanders in the east Aegean took full advantage. No longer awed by the satraps or the Great King, they liberated from the Persians those Ionian Greek cities which Lysander had sold for financial support against Athens. Nor did the Spartans rest content with this patriotic achievement, but carried war far into the Asiatic mainland, where they reaped a rich reward in terms of booty. In such enterprises no one was more thoroughgoing and successful than Agesilaus himself.

The Persian reaction was once more economic and diplomatic rather than military. Harassed by Agesilaus' offensive, the Persian satrap who had succeeded Tissaphernes transferred his financial subsidy from Sparta to Sparta's enemies in north Greece. The result was the Corinthian War of 395-387 BC, fought in and around the Isthmus, as Thebes, Corinth, Athens and Argos struggled, in alliance, to overthrow Spartan supremacy. The Persian policy was eminently successful: even too successful to please the Persians, as it turned out. Agesilaus at once marched back to Greece by the route that Xerxes had taken more than a century earlier; with a highly mobile force, quite unlike the vast and cumbersome Persian array, he completed his march in only 30 days. He then defeated the opposing Greek forces at Coronea in 394 BC and the Spartan power on land was once more established. But the Corinthian War permitted the Athenians to recover their sea-power, together with some of their overseas allies and possessions. Conon, the Athenian admiral who had escaped from Aegospotami, defeated the Spartans in a naval battle at Cnidus, almost on the eve of Coronea, and in the following year he assisted in rebuilding Athens' Long Walls between the city and Piraeus.

The Persians were much alarmed by this revival of Athenian power and again switched their support. A compromise peace was negotiated with the satrap at Sardis by the Spartan commander Antalcidas. Broadly speaking, the terms were that Persia should keep the Ionian islands and that Sparta should continue to dominate Greece, having proper regard to the independence of other Greek states and to Athens' claim over her lately-recovered Aegean possessions. The peace in

practice was more of what a modern politician would call a "cold war" than a genuine peace. It was characterized by treacherous interventions and *coups de main* carried out by the Spartans. From these acts of aggression, Thebes suffered more than any other Greek state—as indeed she had done by the terms of Antalcidas' treaty. The Theban reaction was violent; Spartan hegemony in Greece eventually received its death blow from Thebes at the battle of Leuctra in 371 BC. Nor were the Spartans able to re-establish themselves when, after a decade of meteoric ascendancy, Theban power was suddenly extinguished.

Mercenary Troops and Xenophon's Ten Thousand

Agesilaus, in his incursions into the Persian mainland, had re-employed many of the famous "Ten Thousand" who had served under Cyrus and followed Xenophon back to Greece. Xenophon himself, in fact, was serving with Agesilaus' army at Coronea, although as an Athenian he should have been on the other side. These facts remind us of the ever-increasing importance of mercenary troops in fourth-century Greek warfare. Throughout the eastern Mediterranean and adjacent lands, Greeks had from very early times served as mercenaries. Even westwards, as far as Spain, as archaeological evidence shows, Greek arms and armour were appreciated. Even more appreciated were the men

Left: *A tombstone dating from the 4th century BC. Even after the Peloponnesian War cavalry was still used chiefly as a light-armed skirmishing force, and was not inclined to face heavy infantry at close quarters.*

who knew best how to use them. So much is suggested by ancient Egyptian and Asiatic inscriptions. The Greeks themselves were making use of Thracian and Scythian mercenaries before the Persian Wars, and they were still making use of them during the Peloponnesian War. At Amphipolis in Thrace, in the action of 422 BC which saw the death of the Spartan general Brasidas and the Athenian Cleon, troops hired locally were employed on both sides. On the whole, the Greeks tended to export hoplites and import light-armed troops and cavalry. But the commerce was not carried on exclusively between Greeks and others. Greeks also hired Greeks. At Syracuse, the Arcadian mercenaries from Mantinea, now in the service of the Athenians, were in no way daunted or discouraged by the fact that other Arcadians were fighting on the opposite side from them.

The Spartans could indeed draw on forces from Arcadian cities like Mantinea and Tegea, in virtue of treaties which they had imposed upon these cities, but they also found it worthwhile to levy mercenary bodies from the same area, thus raising forces greater than those to which their treaty rights entitled them. Brasidas, for instance, used Peloponnesian—almost certainly Arcadian—as well as local mercenaries, at Amphipolis. The Arcadians were a robust, pastoral people deprived by their inland position of trading outlets; in war they served mainly as hoplites. Another well-known source of Greek mercenary troops was Crete. The characteristic contribution of the Cretans was archers. Similarly, the Rhodian mercenaries specialized as slingers.

The expedition of Cyrus, in which Xenophon took part, marked a new era, mainly on account of its unprecedentedly large mercenary element. But apart from the question of professionalism, the tactical lessons which it taught pointed curiously in opposite directions. The battle of Cunaxa was conspicuous for the success of the Greek hoplites. It proved once again that the lightly-armed troops of the Persian empire were no match for the Greek heavy infantrymen. At Cunaxa, Cyrus was killed in the moment of victory and his Asiatic supporters

396/5
Agesilaus II of Sparta campaigns victoriously against the Persians in Asia Minor

395
In Greece, an alliance of city states against Sparta is supported by Persian funds

In Boeotia, Lysander is killed fighting against the Thebans

394
Spartan victory over allied Greek states at Nemea

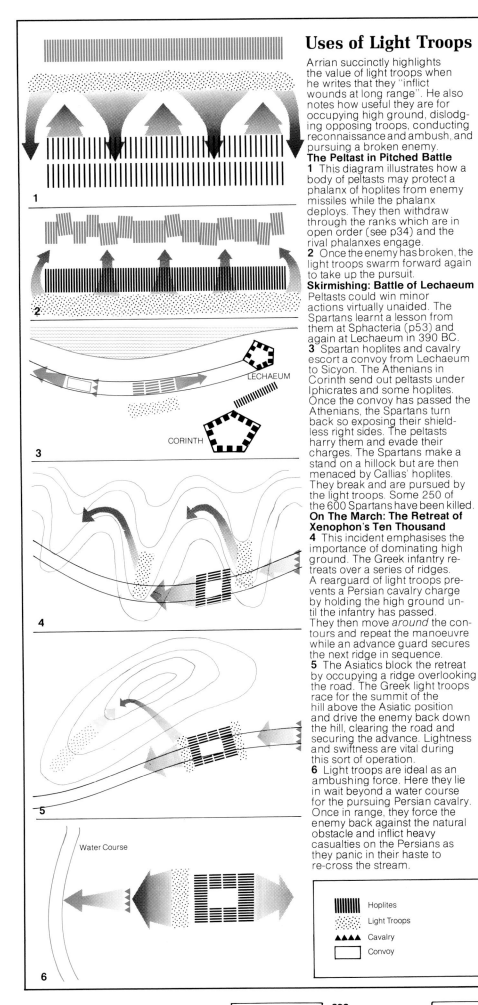

Uses of Light Troops

Arrian succinctly highlights the value of light troops when he writes that they "inflict wounds at long range". He also notes how useful they are for occupying high ground, dislodging opposing troops, conducting reconnaissance and ambush, and pursuing a broken enemy.

The Peltast in Pitched Battle

1 This diagram illustrates how a body of peltasts may protect a phalanx of hoplites from enemy missiles while the phalanx deploys. They then withdraw through the ranks which are in open order (see p34) and the rival phalanxes engage.

2 Once the enemy has broken, the light troops swarm forward again to take up the pursuit.

Skirmishing: Battle of Lechaeum

Peltasts could win minor actions virtually unaided. The Spartans learnt a lesson from them at Sphacteria (p53) and again at Lechaeum in 390 BC.

3 Spartan hoplites and cavalry escort a convoy from Lechaeum to Sicyon. The Athenians in Corinth send out peltasts under Iphicrates and some hoplites. Once the convoy has passed the Athenians, the Spartans turn back so exposing their shield-less right sides. The peltasts harry them and evade their charges. The Spartans make a stand on a hillock but are then menaced by Callias' hoplites. They break and are pursued by the light troops. Some 250 of the 600 Spartans have been killed.

On The March: The Retreat of Xenophon's Ten Thousand

4 This incident emphasises the importance of dominating high ground. The Greek infantry retreats over a series of ridges. A rearguard of light troops prevents a Persian cavalry charge by holding the high ground until the infantry has passed. They then move *around* the contours and repeat the manoeuvre while an advance guard secures the next ridge in sequence.

5 The Asiatics block the retreat by occupying a ridge overlooking the road. The Greek light troops race for the summit of the hill above the Asiatic position and drive the enemy back down the hill, clearing the road and securing the advance. Lightness and swiftness are vital during this sort of operation.

6 Light troops are ideal as an ambushing force. Here they lie in wait beyond a water course for the pursuing Persian cavalry. Once in range, they force the enemy back against the natural obstacle and inflict heavy casualties on the Persians as they panic in their haste to re-cross the stream.

▚▚▚	Hoplites
∴∴∴	Light Troops
▲▲▲▲	Cavalry
☐	Convoy

immediately fled. The Greeks were thus deprived of employment and leadership, but this does not alter the military significance of their exploits both up to and after the action at Cunaxa in 401 BC.

As they made their way northward to the Black Sea coast, at first pursued by the regular Persian troops of Tissaphernes, then harassed by guerrilla mountaineers and finally in conflict with the forces of the northern satrap Pharnabazus, the Greeks learned not only the uses but also the limitations of a hoplite body. The lessons of the later phases of the Peloponnesian War were, in fact, reinforced. Xenophon came to understand increasingly the importance of the cavalry role; although he still perhaps underestimated it. Even more important was the potential effect of light missile troops, armed with bows, slings and javelins. In the circumstances, to men cut off from their base by many hundred miles of enemy territory, the supply of arrows and sling bolts presented a major problem. But the Cretan archers gathered the enemy's spent arrows and used them with their own bows. Some of the villages through which they passed also provided bowstrings and lead for sling bolts. Frequently, the Greeks were obliged to improvise or fight under unaccustomed conditions. For the javelin-throwers it was important to win the advantage of high ground; when attacked by guerrillas from the rocks above, the Greeks' own light troops, at a hopeless disadvantage, were hemmed in amid their hoplites,

393
Conon rebuilds the Long Walls at Athens

390 (or 387)
In Italy, invading Gauls defeat the Romans at the Allia and temporarily occupy Rome

BC

Agesilaus, returning to Greece overland, defeats the allies at Coronea

Conon, Athenian admiral, wins naval battle against Spartans at Cnidus

57

whose shields they needed for shelter. The army was only able to make its way down the deep mountain defiles when its light missile troops had occupied the highest points, thus making the lower crags untenable to enemy guerrillas.

Various incidents in the march of the Ten Thousand testify to a fusion of traditional and changing attitudes. The soldiers formed a professional not a citizen army and they thought in professional terms. Xenophon's appeal to the Rhodians to come forward and exercise their native skill as slingers was accompanied by an offer of improved pay and conditions; the Rhodians had not joined up as slingers and slinging was no part of their original bargain. On a later occasion one member of the Rhodian unit was ready with an ingenious suggestion for crossing a river by means of inflated skins; he expected to be paid well for his plan. Elsewhere, Xenophon, exhorting the troops to resolute action, conceded frankly that they had no ambition to be considered as heroes— merely to get safe home.

On the other hand, religious duties were scrupulously observed. Omens were consulted and Xenophon was conscientious in sacrificing to the gods before any impending trouble, even when there seemed to be very little time for the practice of strict piety. Such attitudes in themselves bear witness to a kind of patriotism which was perhaps more valuable than the old, narrow allegiances fostered by independent city states. The gods were the gods of all the Greeks and the observance of Greek religious rites sprang from that sense of Greek solidarity which did so much to hold the Ten Thousand together.

Another Greek tradition, religious in origin, which the army upheld was the singing of the "paean" as they went into battle. The paean was a hymn which was sung on various solemn occasions. It was no doubt calculated to strike terror into the hearts of the enemy and certainly seems to have had this effect on Asiatic forces. The singing of the battle paean was not, in fact, a universal Greek practice; the Spartans replaced it with flute music, the object of which was to steady their own rather than shake the enemy's nerves. But the paean was adopted by the Ten Thousand, although their leadership was largely Spartan. Xenophon recounts one amusing incident when the women whom the soldiers took along with them as mistresses joined in the battle cry after the paean had been sung.

Right: *A mounted warrior as depicted on a Thracian 4th century BC silver helmet which was discovered in Romania. Greek and Macedonian warriors were often involved in Thracian wars.*

The ululating battle cry was distinct from the paean. The paean was sung when the enemy were still at some distance. The battle cry was raised at the moment of entry into battle. A slogan for identification purposes was also used and was circulated before an engagement in the manner of a password. The Greek battle cry at Cunaxa was "Zeus the Deliverer and Victory."

The Military Career of King Agesilaus

Xenophon was the friend and admirer of the Spartan king Agesilaus; Agesilaus, for his part, was anxious to emulate Xenophon's exploits in Asia. He too believed in the use of mercenaries and was glad when reluctant conscripts from subject Greek cities bought themselves out. The money thus raised could be used to pay for keen professional soldiers and good horses. Unlike the Spartan commanders of an earlier generation, Agesilaus believed in cavalry. Xenophon, at the outset of his homeward march from Cunaxa, had converted captured horses, used as baggage animals, to form a small cavalry unit 50-strong, but this force was apparently not sufficient to protect the Greek foraging parties who were set upon by Pharnabazus' cavalry east of the Hellespont as the long journey was nearing its end. On this occasion the Greeks lost 500 men; when Pharnabazus' horsemen were finally routed, their defeat was precipitated by a hoplite charge, thus confirming an axiom of Greek military wisdom that it was folly for cavalry to engage with heavy infantry.

Agesilaus, however, placed much more reliance on cavalry than did Xenophon. Indeed, he had more at his disposal. He scored one notable victory during his march through Thessaly to confront the rebellious Greek states who challenged him at Coronea in 394 BC. The cavalry which he had assembled in Asia easily overcame the Thessalian cavalry ranged against it. The Thessalian cavalry was the best in Greece, but Thessalian horses were no match for Asiatic breeds.

Agesilaus was eminently flexible both as a strategist and as a tactician. When operating against Tissaphernes

in Asia Minor, he deceived the enemy by an ingenious double-bluff. His intention of attacking Lydia was proclaimed with such an obvious eye to publicity that the enemy took it for a feint and concentrated in Caria to the south. The offensive, however, was made against Lydia, as Agesilaus had from the first intended, and in the absence of any planned defence was easily pressed home.

This very unconventional Spartan king was equally ready to buy off his enemies or to fight them, employing either method freely as circumstances dictated. His swift return from Asia to Greece was expedited by opportunism of this kind.

The tactics which Agesilaus adopted at Coronea exhibited a mixture of traditional usage and innovation. The battle was begun as a conventional hoplite engagement, with the almost predictable result that Spartan and Theban forces on the right wing each routed their enemies' allies on the opposing left wings. The Thebans relaxed their pursuit, only to find that Agesilaus' army stood between them and the safe mountain country whither their fleeing Argive allies had already retreated. When they attempted to rejoin the Argives by a southward march to Mount Helicon, Agesilaus, wheeling round, made a frontal attack on them. But he was unable in this way to break their line. He therefore withdrew and reformed his army in open order, allowing the Thebans to pass through the gaps in the hope of attacking them on the flank. The flank attacks, however, were not very successful and the Thebans reached the mountains in good order. Agesilaus

BC 389
Plato, visiting Sicily, interests Dion in his concept of a "philosopher king"

386
The "King's Peace" introduces a period of "cold war" in Greece

Dionysius I consolidates conquests in south Italy

384
The autocrat, Jason of Pherae, dominates Thessaly

58

Persian Troops

The fully armed horseman seen here is a member of Cyrus the Younger's bodyguard, his dress revealing a number of Greek influences. The bronze helmet is decorated with a horsehair plume; the corslet is of linen, reinforced with bronze scales and having *pteruges* on the lower half. In addition to his two iron-headed javelins he would be carrying a normal Greek short sword. Note that his left, bridle arm is protected with a leather binding. Unlike the Greeks, the Persian extra-heavy cavalry wore bronze-scale leg protectors, similar to cowboys' chaps. Leather moccasins are the only foot protection. His horse, bred from the Median plains, is comparatively large. He is also protected by a bronze scale apron which is sewn to a leather and cloth backing. The bridle is made of bronze discs, and the chamfron is decorated with a winged motif. The figure is the first appearance of a cavalry type that later evolved into cataphracts.

Other Troop Types

The light cavalryman seen below wears a typically Persian head-dress, or *tiara*, and a bright red quilted cuirass over a brown and white tunic. He carries two heavy throwing javelins, as Persian cavalry operated as missile troops rather than shock cavalry. His Greek-style sword is intended for self defence. Some cavalrymen carried a single-handed battle-axe rather than a sword, and it was reputedly a blow from one of these that split Alexander's helmet at the Battle of the Granicus. The horse's bridle is made of brass, the harness leather, while his forelock and tail are tied up with red ribbon. The foot soldier's kit shows the influence that Greek equipment had on the Persian army. He carries a hoplite-type shield and sword, but not the expensive body armour which only the cavalry could afford. Some troops may, however, have worn scale corslets beneath their tunics for protection. His short thrusting spear is counterweighted on the butt.

remained in possession of the field, but he had not destroyed the enemy.

The method of allowing an impetuous enemy to pass through one's ranks, spending his force and exposing himself to flank attack, was one that had been used by the Ten Thousand against scythed chariots in Asia; it was to be used by the Romans against Carthaginian elephants at a later date. Xenophon criticizes Agesilaus for attempting a frontal attack on the Thebans in the first place. If he had been content to wait, he could have attacked their flank as they made their way southward, at a moment of his own choosing and to his advantage.

Later, in the days of Theban supremacy when enemy forces had occupied Spartan territory, Agesilaus, with courage and resource, successfully organized the defence of Sparta itself, though the city had no permanent walls or impregnable citadel such as most Greek cities possessed. Indeed, the Spartans had always relied on fighting

their wars on enemy territory. But on this occasion they fortunately had at their head a man well qualified to deal with unprecedented situations.

After the collapse of Thebes, King Agesilaus, at the age of 80, again led mercenary forces abroad, first into Asia then to the Nile Delta in support of Egyptian rebels against Persia. The rebels in Egypt quarrelled between themselves and Agesilaus was left in no very dignified position, hiring himself to one side against the other in a petty war. Even here, however, he demonstrated his flair for military stratagem. Being besieged by a vastly superior number of inexperienced troops, he allowed them to construct a wall and trench around his own encircled forces. When the circumvallation was complete but for a short gap, he suddenly led a sally through the opening. The enemy, for all their superior numbers, were hindered by their own ramparts from attacking him in the flank or rear. The Greek force

with its Egyptian allies was not only extricated but inflicted heavy losses on the besiegers, who were hemmed in between their own trenches.

Agesilaus died at the age of 84 on the way home from Egypt. There seems to have been something unhappily circular in the defence economy over which he presided: mercenary expeditions raised money by which the Spartan state was enabled to hire more mercenaries. However, it may be pleaded that Agesilaus was in fact trading military expertise for manpower.

The Challenge to the Spartan Hoplite

Agesilaus' death marks the end of an epoch in Greek history. His skilful operations had to some extent concealed the serious decline in the fighting potential of the Spartan citizen army. The development of new forms of warfare had been in itself an admission

Battle of Leuctra 371 BC

Spartans and Allies	Thebans
Hoplites	
Sparta 2000	6500
Phocis 1500	
Acarnania 1000	
Corinth 2000	
Arcadia 2000	
Achaea, Eleia and Sicyon 1500	
Cavalry	
1000	1500
Peltasts	
Sparta 300	1000
Thrace 500	
Phocis 300	

1 The Spartans and their allies under King Cleombrotus invade Boeotia, and camp at Leuctra, near Thebes. The Thebans (who include their *corps d'elite* the Sacred Band, under Pelopidas) sally out commanded by Epaminondas. They are badly outnumbered but Epaminondas persuades them to fight. The Spartans form up on the plain in a shallow crescent. The Thebans weight their left wing and refuse their right.
2 On the Theban left wing the cavalry drive back the Spartan cavalry and Pelopidas and the Sacred Band reinforce this attack. While the Theban cavalry prevents outflanking, the Theban phalanx crashes into the Spartan.
3 A furious battle develops around Cleombrotus, and the weight of Theban numbers drives back the Spartans.
4 Cleombrotus and many officers are killed and the Allies retreat to their camp, harried by Theban cavalry. The Spartan left wing has seen no action. 500 Spartans are killed in battle, 400-500 in retreat. 300 Thebans are killed.
The generalship of Epaminondas has given the outnumbered Thebans a great victory over the best army in Greece.

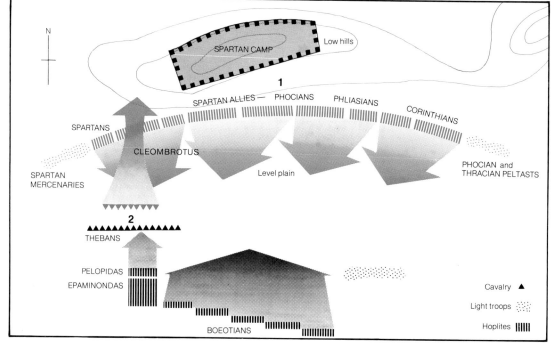

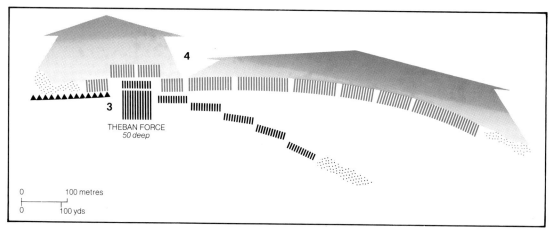

BC 376
Chabrias, Athenian commander, wins naval victory against Spartans off Naxos

372
In China (politically divided at this epoch) the sage Mencius (Meng K'o) was born

371
Pact of non-aggression and independence is proposed at inter-state conference at Sparta

Epaminondas' claim to represent all Boeotia is rejected by Agesilaus

60

that the supremacy of the Spartan hoplite phalanx was at an end. Since the Peloponnesian War, the Spartan army had been substantially remodelled; this in itself reflected a decline in numbers of the fully-enfranchised citizens who formed the backbone of the heavy infantry. The decline could in some degree be paralleled by population decline in other Greek states, but apart from all general tendencies Spartan military strength had also been seriously affected by the losses suffered in a devastating earthquake which occurred as far back as 465 BC—before the Peloponnesian War had even begun.

The Spartan army in the fourth century consisted of six battalions (*morai*). Each of these was under the command of a *polemarch* and, according to contemporary historians, consisted of 400 or perhaps 600 men. Both citizens and non-citizens served in it. Within the *mora*, there was subdivision into smaller units, as previously with the *lochos*. During the Corinthian War, a Spartan *mora*, after escorting a contingent of allied troops back to the Peloponnese, was intercepted in the Isthmus and routed with crippling losses by the Athenian commander Iphicrates. In numerical terms, casualties of 250 out of a total strength of 600 men, which on this occasion the unit contained, were extremely serious. The strategy and tactics of Iphicrates were even more significant; his victory was gained against hoplites by the use of light-armed troops. The Spartan débâcle, which occurred outside Corinth, can be paralleled by others in Greek military history, where (as at Amphipolis in the Peloponnesian War) incautious troops marching close under enemy walls exposed themselves to a sally from the city gates.

The action, however, was still more reminiscent of Sphacteria. The Spartans were overwhelmed by missiles and never allowed to come to grips. At Sphacteria, Spartan lack of foresight, combined with some bad luck, had produced the fatal situation, but Iphicrates was the deliberate architect of his own victory, which vindicated to the full his new strategic and tactical concepts of light-armed warfare. Indeed, there is a third reason for regarding Iphicrates' success on this occasion as historically significant: the troops he commanded were mercenaries and their victory was gained against a predominantly citizen force.

Another great professional commander of the fourth century was

Chabrias the Athenian. He was distinguished for the resistance which he offered to Agesilaus in Boeotia during the Corinthian War. Expecting to be charged by the enemy, he ordered his men to kneel down and present their spears, with shields resting on their knees. Agesilaus was deterred from making the attack. Perhaps well-chosen ground, as much as the kneeling posture, deterred him. But Chabrias, honoured with a statue, was at his own request portrayed by the sculptor in a kneeling position such as he and his men had adopted on the battlefield. In fact, kneeling statues derived from this precedent soon became fashionable even among victorious athletes.

Chabrias, in the course of his long military and naval career, had a fine record of patriotic service, but this in no way prejudiced his thoroughly professional outlook. He served with Agesilaus in Egypt, where he was put in charge of the Egyptian navy while the Spartan king commanded the land forces. Agesilaus was disappointed, for he had expected to command both by land and sea. However, there is no suggestion that either of the two men, while campaigning as comrades-in-arms under the same Egyptian monarch, was in the least troubled by the thought that they had previously encountered each other as enemies on Greek battlefields in their own land.

Light-armed Troops

The efficient organization and equipment of light-armed troops was an important fourth-century development. When one speaks of light-armed troops in the context of Greek military history, the term includes javelin-throwers, archers and slingers. Of these, javelin-throwers had the longest tradition of service in historic times. They came to be called *peltastai* from the type of shield which they carried: the *pelta*, an importation from Thrace. Pisistratus, autocratic ruler of Athens in the sixth century BC, had enlisted a mercenary corps from the Thracian hinterland after a period of exile in those regions; Athenian familiarity with the *pelta* seems to have dated from that time. The *pelta* was a small buckler made of animal skins stretched over a wicker framework. It had no metal fittings or trimmings and was light enough to be held in the left hand, without forearm support. Characteristically, it was formed in the shape of a broad crescent moon, but the word also applied to

Above: *Scythian archers featured on a gold dress ornament of Graeco-Scythian origin dating from the 5th or 4th centuries BC and found near the Black Sea. The bow persisted as the Scythians' characteristic weapon.*

other shapes made of the same light material. The javelins which the peltasts carried were fitted with leather loops about halfway down the shaft. The first and second fingers engaged the loop, while the shaft of the javelin, supported on the hand, was gripped by the thumb and remaining fingers. This enabled the thrower to exert greater leverage and added to the force with which the missile was launched. Peltasts, like other combatants, also carried a sword (originally short) or dagger in case of emergency, although they did not normally count on coming to sword strokes with the enemy ranged against them.

Both the construction and use of bows and arrows varied considerably in Greece. In Crete, the practice of archery had been maintained since the earliest times, but in the rest of Greece it had generally been neglected. By the fourth century, the use of Cretan mercenary archers had become common. Before the Persian Wars, the Athenians had employed Scythians in the same capacity; but the Athenians, according to Herodotus, had no archers at the battle of Marathon. The Athenian police force, nevertheless, continued to rely on Scythian mercenaries and a policeman was ordinarily referred to as an "archer".

The most common type of bow in ancient Greece was a composite fabrication, but bows consisting of a single flexible wooden staff, like the English longbow, were in use outside Crete. Homer describes a bow made from a pair of wild goat's horns. Horns, united by a core of pliant wood, might certainly have provided an effective bow. But other evidence suggests a

The Spartan king Cleombrotus is defeated and killed by the Thebans at Leuctra

370
Jason of Pherae is assassinated

Epaminondas invades the Peloponnese and threatens Sparta

366
At Syracuse, Dionysius II succeeds his father Dionysius I

BC

61

less simple process of manufacture, involving strips of horn, wood and dry gut—apart from the bowstring, which was normally made of gut or sinew. Among the Scythians, not only the fabrication but also the use of the bow was complicated. The Scythian, although holding the bow in his left hand, normally contrived to rest his arrow on the left side of the bow when taking aim. Moreover, the archer usually held the arrow on the bowstring between the first and second fingers of his right hand using his first three fingers to draw the string—the conventional Mediterranean loose. Scythian arrows were short with small bronze tips, unlike the heavy arrowheads of the Cretans, but in his capacious quiver the Scythian carried both his bow and a great many diminutive arrows.

Different usages prevailed among archers in different parts of the Persian empire. In some of the hill tribes that Xenophon encountered, archers gained extra leverage by bending the bow against the foot. The arrows of some tribal archers were so long that they could be gathered and used as javelins by the Greeks. Persian arrows were shot from longbows. These missiles could be re-used by Xenophon's Cretan archers, who practised high-trajectory shooting for greater range. It was perhaps possible, even with the short Cretan bows, to draw the long Persian arrows to the ear, if not to the right shoulder. Greek archers normally drew the bowstring only to the chest.

Unlike the Cretan archers, the Greek slingers from Rhodes, when properly equipped, had the advantage of their opposite numbers in Asia. A leaden Greek sling bolt had twice the range of the heavy stones used by the Persians in their slings. Sling bolts of this kind have been discovered by modern excavators. They are sometimes inscribed with the name of the commander for whose service they were destined. Sometimes, also, they were ironically addressed to the recipient, with some such inscription as "Take that!"

Hoplite Tactics and the Theban Phalanx

Despite the new developments in light-armed and cavalry warfare, Spartan supremacy in Greece was finally brought to an end by developments in hoplite warfare itself. At Leuctra in 371 BC, under the inspired leadership of Epaminondas and Pelopidas, the Thebans massed a phalanx of 50 ranks in depth on their left wing, against a Spartan phalanx only 12 deep. As it attacked, the Theban line was deliberately slanted forward towards the left, so that the Spartan right wing (the traditionally strong wing of a Greek phalanx) was overwhelmed before the less reliable contingents of Thebes' allies had time to engage. When Cleombrotus, the Spartan king in command, saw what was intended, he tried at the last moment to reinforce the threatened wing and to envelop the attacking Thebans, but the prompt and vigorous charge of the ·Theban *corps d'élite*

Engines of War

Siege techniques were not greatly developed by the Greeks until c450 BC, but during the Peloponnesian War Plataea, Athens' Boeotian ally, was besieged by the Spartans who brought all their craft to bear in capturing the city (see pages 48-9). The defenders were as resourceful as the attackers and it took two years —429-427 BC—before the Spartans were successful. There is little doubt that the experience inspired Greek engineers to develop their war machine and the ensuing years saw some ingenious inventions.

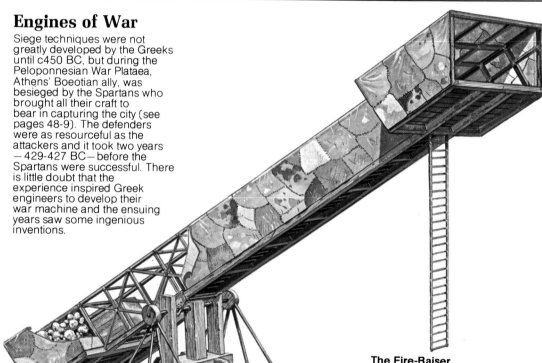

The Sambuca

The Fire-Raiser
Fire-raisers were used at the siege of Delium, in 424 BC, by the Thebans against the Athenian stockade. The iron cauldron, filled with lighted coals, sulphur and pitch, was kept aflame by a soldier blowing through the main beam by means of bellows. The wooden beam was split in half, hollowed out and rejoined with an iron tube running down the centre. That part of the beam nearest the cauldron was covered with iron plating to prevent it catching fire.
Transport was effected by the simple method of strapping

The Sambuca
Designed by Damis of Colophon, the *sambuca,* or siege ladder, was a great advance on the conventional ladder as there was no need to estimate the height of a wall accurately, the defenders had no chance to push it away before the attackers were upon them, and it could be used further away than the traditional type, for example across a surrounding ditch or moat. The method of attack was for an assault party of ten men to mount by a short ladder the compartment situated furthest from the carriage. Some 2½ tons of counterweights were then loaded into boxes in the rear and the device wheeled to the wall, being covered by supporting fire from siege towers. Two men then worked the vertical capstan and, aided by the counterweight, the ladder rose to the battlements. The ladder was enclosed by reinforced sides and roof to protect the men from missiles.

the device to two wooden carts, enabling the machine to be pushed against the palisade while covering fire was given to the soldiers manipulating the engine and to the man responsible for keeping the bellows working and the fire alight in what was an exposed position.

BC   **365** Dionysius II, unsuited for role of philosopher king, rejects Plato and Dion   **364** Pelopidas killed in victorious battle of Cynoscephalae against Alexander of Pherae   **362** Epaminondas defeats Spartans, Athenians and other allies at Mantinea, but is killed in the action

62

(known as the "Sacred Band") gave the Spartans no time to complete the necessary manoeuvre. The Spartans were caught in disarray and Cleombrotus himself was killed at an early stage in the battle.

Consideration of what happened at Leuctra prompts some general observations on the evolution of hoplite fighting. When Xenophon, on the outward march to Cunaxa, mounted a military display to entertain a vivacious Asiatic queen, his hoplite formation was drawn up four deep. This he refers to as being normal practice. At first sight, it would seem surprising that descriptions of ancient hoplite battles in which the depth of formation is mentioned nearly all specify eight or more ranks. But such formations may well have earned mention precisely because they were not normal at the time of writing; although perhaps, as the fourth century advanced, they tended to become normal.

At Coronea, Agesilaus' allies on the left wing, who included veterans of Cyrus' expedition, routed the enemy ranged against them when, as Xenophon tells us, they came "to spearpoint" with them. However, when the Spartans clashed with the Thebans in the second stage of the battle, shield was set against shield. It was a question of pushing rather than thrusting. The Thebans knew as well as the Spartans how to use the shield as an offensive weapon and they gained added weight from the depth of their formation. These tactics, although still in process of development, were certainly not new to the Thebans. They had defeated the Athenians at Delium with a phalanx 25 deep—against which the Athenians had ineffectively mustered a mere eight ranks.

A phalanx was not necessarily drawn up in uniform depth throughout. At Mantinea in 418 BC, the depth of the Spartan line was left to the decision of the junior commanders who were in charge of different sectors. The depth of formation here must have depended, at any given point, on whether a thrust-ing spear-fight or a pushing shield-fight was intended. The junior commander knew the individual soldiers of his unit and could judge for which type of combat they were better qualified. On the other hand, the lack of uniformity could have a disorganizing effect. This was particularly evident at Nemea, during the Corinthian War, when Athenian, Argive, Boeotian, Corinthian and Euboean allied contingents apparently wished to adopt the formation to which each was accustomed, without regard for the coordination of allied tactics as a whole.

Citizen Morale and the Sacred Band

The dramatic defeat of Sparta at the battle of Leuctra lent new impetus to the revival of citizen morale throughout Greece in general and in Thebes in particular. But realization that the Spartan hoplite phalanx was not invincible dated, as we have seen, from the Corinthian War. Sparta owed it to the ability of Agesilaus both as general and statesman, rather than to her traditional methods of warfare, that she had obtained peace with honour at the end of that war. Even so, the peace had been dictated by a Persian arbitrator, not a Spartan victor. In military terms, despite the growing use of mercenary troops, the revival of citizen confidence meant revived confidence in the effectiveness of citizen armies.

Lysander had been killed invading Boeotia early in the Corinthian War and there was no Spartan admiral of comparable ability to replace him. This fact enabled the Athenians, after the rebuilding of the Long Walls, to re-establish their old imperial system based on the combination of sea power with the encouragement of ideologically sympathetic governments in the Aegean states. When the Spartans, by an unprovoked *coup de main* in 382 BC, installed a puppet government at Thebes, they were attempting to imitate Athenian methods. But their action was too clumsy and too blatant and in the long run it turned out to be counter-productive, making them the objects of bitter resentment at Thebes and of hostile suspicion in the rest of Greece. Thebes was also humiliated by the Persian king's peace which, to satisfy Sparta, deprived her of her traditional control of the smaller Boeotian cities.

Once the Spartan puppet government had been violently liquidated and the Spartan garrison expelled from Thebes,

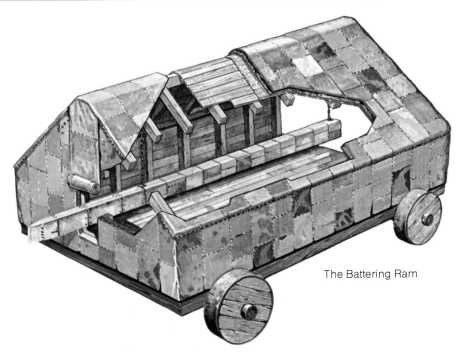

The Battering Ram

The Battering Ram
The battering ram was used to shake down a section of wall, create a breach or undermine the wall so that troops could force an entry. The model shown here is after the style of the "tortoise" ram, much used by the fourth century BC. The actual ram is metal-plated at the forward end and the serrated tip was often of bronze. Propelled over rollers, the ram would be given considerable impetus. It was pulled back by a rope-and-pulley system. It was fire-proofed by compressing layers of seaweed between ox-hide as an overall protective cover.

The Fire-Raiser

360
Agesilaus dies after revenue-raising campaign in service of King Tachos in Egypt

359
At the death of Perdiccas III of Macedon, his brother Philip becomes king

358
Philip gains victories over Paeonians and Illyrians

BC

63

Theban patriotism expressed itself in the military organization of the citizen body, relying much more heavily on civic loyalty than on mercenary or allied support. The most striking feature of the Theban military revival was the *corps d'élite* known as the "Sacred Band". The Greek words might perhaps be explained as meaning the "Dedicated Band"; but ancient historians have given other explanations. "Sacred" was an epithet that was commonly applied to the citadels of Greek cities; it was said that the Sacred Band at Thebes had originally been instituted as a guard for the citadel. At the time of the battle of Leuctra, the Sacred Band had been organized and trained by Pelopidas, although it was reputedly created by another Theban leader, Gorgidas, earlier in the same decade.

According to tradition, the 300-strong Sacred Band was formed by pairs of lovers—for the Greeks did not regard homosexuality as perverse. The idea of a lovers' squad was, in fact, older than Pelopidas' Sacred Band. In Homer's *Iliad*, it is suggested that a unit composed of close kinsmen would be good for military morale; Plato records the view, not necessarily his own, that a regiment composed of lovers would fulfil the same purpose more effectively. Each partner of a loving couple would find in the other's presence an inspiration which would spur his efforts and forbid him to disgrace himself on the battlefield. Xenophon, however, who hated homosexuality, would have none of this and protested that a friendship based on anything more than admiration of mind and character could only corrupt, not raise, a fighting man's morale.

At Chaeronea, the battle which in 338 BC finally put an end to the independence of the Greek city states, the Sacred Band suffered severely, each man falling in the place where he had fought. The victor, Philip II of Macedon, is said to have shed tears over them, exclaiming: "Perish any man who suspects that these men either did or suffered anything that was base!" Philip evidently professed Xenophon's views as to the nature of friendship.

Epaminondas in the Peloponnese

After Leuctra, Epaminondas, serving as commander-in-chief of the Theban armed forces, repeatedly invaded the Peloponnese and would have captured Sparta itself if Agesilaus had not been present to improvise its defence. The military and political strategies of Epaminondas were linked to each other in a way which disciples of Clausewitz must approve. He encouraged those areas in the central and western Peloponnese which had long been dominated by Sparta to assert their liberty; this end was secured by the construction of fortified cities in what had previously been wild and rural areas. It was a case of the punishment fitting the crime, for the war had been provoked by Sparta's refusal to recognize Theban supremacy over the Boeotian townships.

The cities of Mantinea, Megalopolis and Messene, which Epaminondas established or restored, stood like a chain of fortresses barring Sparta's northwestward communications. Mantinea had been a flourishing Arcadian centre before Agesilaus besieged it in 385 BC. The Spartans at that time diverted the river which ran through the city, so that its waters lapped against the outside walls and eroded them. When the Mantineans surrendered, they were forced to abandon their homes and accept dispersal in villages. Epaminondas restored the scattered people to their city and saw to it that they were well protected by fortifications. These, indeed, were much needed, for Mantinea lay in the middle of an open, featureless plain.

Messene was originally the name of a territory, not a city, but on Epaminondas' initiative a city of that name was raised near the old Messenian stronghold of Mount Ithomé. As for Megalopolis (as the Romans called it), it was a new city. The Greek form of the name was *He Megale Polis,* meaning simply the Big City. It was situated in a plain through which the Alpheus river flowed northwestward towards Olympia and the Eurotas river southeastward to Sparta and the Laconian Gulf. Rivers and river beds were used by the ancient Greeks as substitutes for roads—which they conspicuously lacked. Megalopolis thus enjoyed good communications while obstructing those of Sparta. Its population was drawn from the inhabitants of 40 Arcadian villages. Unfortunately, the villagers did not take any more kindly to city life than the citizens of Mantinea, dispersed by Agesilaus, had done to village life.

The ruins of the three cities just mentioned are all visible today. Those at Messene are particularly impressive. It is disappointing that the archaeology of fortifications in Greece cannot always be so neatly related to history. The walls of Aegosthena in Attica resemble those of Messene in style, but their date and purpose remains mysterious. During the fourth century, fortifications became increasingly sophisticated, as is demonstrated by surviving technical treatises on the subject, like that of Aeneas Tacticus (about 357 BC) or of Philon of Byzantium in the following century.

During the Peloponnesian War and earlier, fortifications had been intended mainly for the protection of cities and citadels. In the fourth century they were often built to enclose large areas of territory adjacent to the city centres. The fortifications themselves exhibited many of the features which we associate with medieval castles, being

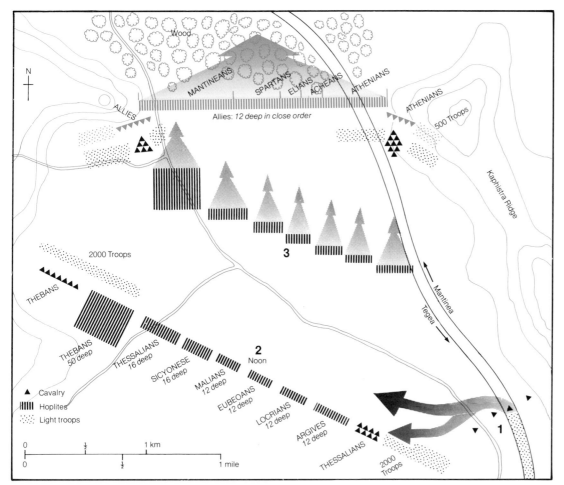

Battle of Mantinea 362 BC

Allies	Thebans
Hoplites	
Mantinea 7000	Thebes 10000
Sparta 3000	Thessaly 2000
Elis 2000	Euboea 1500
Achaea 2000	Malis 1500
Athens 6000	Locris 3000
	Sicyon 3000
	Argos 5000
Cavalry	
Athens 1000	Thebes 1500
Others 1000	Thessaly 1500
Light troops	
Mercenaries 1000	Mercenaries and Thessaly 4000

1 Epaminondas' Boeotians advance on Mantinea. The Mantineans and Allies block the road between two steep ridges.
2 The Thebans march across their front and ground arms. The Allies stand down not expecting the Thebans to attack.
3 Epaminondas suddenly advances in oblique formation against the enemy right while his cavalry and light troops pin down the left flank. The Theban cavalry drives off the Allies and attacks the exposed right while the massive Theban phalanx crashes in frontally. The Mantineans flee but Epaminondas is killed. Mortified by his death, the Thebans give up pursuit and some of their marauding troops are killed.

The battle shows Epaminondas at his best. He uses his cavalry and light troops to pin down the left and expose the right flank on which he launches an assault.

---

provided with turrets, battlements, moats, posterns and sallyports. Sallies were made from the right-hand side of a projecting bastion, so that issuing troops had their shield arms towards the enemy. Walls were characteristically of brick superimposed upon masonry. Apart from city defences and the larger territorial enclosures, the ruins of many smaller fortresses are to be found in Greece, dating from the fourth or fifth centuries. These were sometimes watchtowers or signal towers and, where they occur on the coast, may well have been built as a defence against pirates.

The Mantinea Campaign and its Consequences

Both the strategy and tactics of Epaminondas sometimes appeared indecisive, but this appearance was deceptive. He aimed always at surprising the enemy and was often unwilling to strike where he could not achieve surprise. In 363 BC, a dispute broke out in the northern Peloponnese arising from the misuse of temple funds at Olympia. As a result, the Arcadian cities were divided, Mantinea and Tegea appearing respectively at the heads of rival coalitions. Tegea supported Thebes; Mantinea was pro-

Left: *Air view of the ruined walls of Mantinea which stood in a plain unlike most fortified Greek cities. The Theban Epaminondas fought his last battle here.*

Spartan: this produced a corresponding ideological conflict of democratic and oligarchic sympathies.

The Athenians, who eight years earlier had received the news of Leuctra with less enthusiasm than had many Greek states, were now in open alliance with Sparta. Epaminondas hoped to intercept the Athenian contingent in the Isthmus as it marched to help Sparta, but in this he was disappointed, for the Athenians decided to make the journey by sea. With an army drawn from Boeotia and other northern Greek territories, he now established his headquarters and base at Tegea, in a walled and well-supplied city, where he was advantageously placed between the Spartans and their allies at Mantinea. When Agesilaus, at the head of a Spartan force, marched northwards via Pellene in Laconia, Epaminondas made no attempt to confront him but, avoiding the enemy, led his army straight on Sparta itself, expecting to find it stripped of defenders. Unfortunately for the Thebans, information of the move had reached Agesilaus through a deserter and the king hurried back to Sparta — just in time.

The element of surprise had been lost and Epaminondas did not press his

Philip occupies Pydna and Potidaea, formerly subject to Athens

The Phocians penalised by the Amphictionic Council (Trustee states for Delphic temple)

Phocians involved in Sacred War (355) against Thessalian and Boeotian communities

attack on the city but, returning by an abrupt night march, renewed his threat to Mantinea. Here again, the advantage of surprise eluded him. An Athenian cavalry unit had just arrived in support of the Mantineans and it clashed with Epaminondas' advance guard of Theban and Thessalian horsemen, forcing them back. Sparta, aided by her allies, now had time to assemble an army before Mantinea, blocking the way northward at a point where the plain was constricted on either side by mountain slopes one mile apart. In the ensuing battle, Epaminondas at last achieved the surprise which he had been seeking. After marshalling his army for battle, he suddenly swerved westwards and, taking up a position on the adjacent foothills, commanded his troops to ground arms. It appeared that he had abandoned the intention of fighting that day and the enemy was thrown off guard. Then, unexpectedly, Epaminondas attacked, as at Leuctra, with a heavily-loaded left wing, trailing his right. The unforeseen move brought him victory, but he was mortally wounded in the battle and died urging his countrymen to make peace. Ironically, the ruse which succeeded against the Spartans at Mantinea was very similar to that which they themselves had long ago used against the Argives at Sepeia, and not so long ago against the Athenians at Aegospotami in 405 BC.

Epaminondas' death may almost be said to have turned his victory into a defeat. The enemy was not pursued. As if from that moment, Theban military power, naval ambitions and political influence went into a swift decline. Unified leadership meant so much to a Greek city state. Always harassed by the jealousy of fellow-citizens, only a man of outstanding qualities could retain a commanding position long enough to implement a consistent policy. One may make comparisons with Pericles at Athens, with Lysander and Agesilaus at Sparta. Epaminondas'

policy had stemmed from his realization that for the Thebans attack was the best method of defence.

Thebes now fell back on its old strategies, content if it could dominate the smaller cities of Boeotia; its vitality was soon sapped by petty and exhausting warfare with the neighbouring peoples of northern Greece.

Autocrats and their Armies

The character of Epaminondas was much admired both by his contemporaries and in later antiquity—perhaps because he was a dedicated constitutionalist. The ancients, even under the Roman Empire, never ceased to cherish a sentimental regard for constitutional government, which—very much as we do—they equated with the ideal of political liberty. From a military point of view, however, constitutional governments often find themselves at a disadvantage when confronted with despotic régimes. The despot is not embarrassed by consultative procedures and is often better placed to take prompt decisions. His decisions, of course, are not necessarily right. But in time of war, it may happen that even a wrong decision is better than indecision and vacillation.

The political evolution of the Greek cities in Sicily and the western Mediterranean contrasted sharply with that of mainland Greece. Under despots the Sicilian Greeks had repelled threats from Carthage and Etruria, and despite interludes of moderate democratic government, constitutionalism was alien to their way of life. Autocrats who could not rely on the loyalty of local citizen armies naturally tended to recruit mercenaries, and with mercenary armies they developed the use of cavalry, light-armed troops, sophisticated fortifications, siegecraft and artillery devices—as well as shipbuilding and naval tactics. We have already seen that in this respect the

Syracusans proved themselves more than a match for the Athenians. Hoplite forces, of course, were also in use, and these often consisted of citizen troops interspersed with mercenaries. The concentration on hoplite armies in mainland Greece was the outcome of constitutional conservatism. It meant that warfare (and therefore, to a large extent, foreign policy) was in the hands of a well-to-do citizen class, which could afford to pay for arms and armour. When the citizens of Syracuse rebelled, they sought aid from the Greek mainland. Dion, the friend of Plato, mustered a small officer corps in Greece, with which he sailed to Sicily and led the democratic revolt against Dionysius II. At a later date, the Syracusans appealed for help to their mother city, Corinth; Corinth sent them the brilliant general Timoleon, who successfully championed the Sicilian Greeks both against their own despots and the Carthaginians. But the mainland and central states were on the whole

Left: *The plain of Chaeronea as it is today. In 338 BC Philip, King of Macedon, won a resounding victory here against the combined forces of Thebes and Athens, thereby ensuring Macedonian domination of the Greek states and laying a foundation for further conquests in Asia.*

more inclined to export leadership and ideology than they were to import technical development.

The military advantages enjoyed by despots became increasingly evident during the fourth century. In the east, the decline of Persian power especially facilitated the rise of local autocrats. In Cyprus, Evagoras, once a tributary of Persia, emerged as an independent prince and contributed significantly to the Athenian victory at Cnidus (394 BC) and the demise of Spartan naval power. More important still was Mausolus of

Halicarnassus. Although once ranking as one of the Great King's satraps, he came to rule his own empire, seduced several of the Aegean naval states from their Athenian allegiance and involved Athens in wars with her former allies.

An even greater threat to the Greek city states was posed by the despotisms of the northern Greek peninsula itself. The massive military preparations of Jason of Pherae in Thessaly were beginning to alarm the whole of Greece when his career was cut short by assassination in 370 BC. The inevitable

Iphicrates' Reforms

The Athenian general Iphicrates was a great innovator who saw the potential of peltasts and used them with considerable success against Spartan hoplites (as at the battle of Lechaeum — see p. 57). In the light of this experience, he also introduced modifications to the traditional hoplite equipment, making it lighter, and thus increasing the hoplite's chances against peltasts The colour drawing shows these changes. The large, heavy, metal-faced *hoplon* has been replaced by a smaller, lighter, leather-faced shield. His metal greaves are discarded — replaced by boots called *Iphicratids* after the general. His cuirass is of quilted linen rather than stiff layers, and his helmet is of the latest "Thracian" type. This style of cuirass is fairly typical of the 4th century BC — Plutarch describes a similar corslet worn by Alexander at the battle of Gaugamela. Of course, our figure now has less protection than the traditional hoplite, so, to compensate, his spear is lengthened to 12ft (3·6m) to enable him to outreach his heavier opponent. This equipment did not supplant the traditional panoply, which remained as popular as ever.

The Later Peltast

During this period peltast kit tended to become heavier. The peltast has a larger wicker shield, now oval in shape (this could also be hide-covered). As a mercenary, he is able to afford a reasonable helmet. His weapons are the usual javelins, sword and now a short spear to enable him to defend himself fighting hand-to-hand. By the time of Alexander's successors he had acquired body armour and his oval shield could be made of hide-covered wood.

blow to Greek constitutional liberty was finally struck by Philip II of Macedon. It might well have come earlier from Jason, but Philip was able to proceed further with his plans before being assassinated.

Philip of Macedon

Philip of Macedon was a man of many-sided genius. His conquests were founded in the first place upon solid political and economic organization. He created an army on a new model and used it in war with brilliant strategic and tactical ability. The political unification of Macedonia itself—by no means a cultural or ethnic unity—was a great achievement. Philip's first expansionary moves placed at his disposal the trading wealth of the Chalcidic peninsula and the precious metal deposits of Thrace.

His fighting force, remarkable for its sheer numerical strength, among other things, was based on a combination of the phalanx with cavalry and light troops which protected it from flank attack and which could themselves easily develop an outflanking movement against the enemy. The word phalanx, as used by modern historians, is often applied to the Macedonian phalanx in particular. This differed significantly from earlier Greek fighting formations. When moving in open order it could be more mobile. It made use of extremely long pikes*, which the phalangists grasped with both hands. This type of pike—called a *sarissa*—must have given the formation greater thrusting power, with a denser array of spearheads projecting beyond the shields of the first rank. The depth of the Macedonian phalanx developed in time from eight to sixteen ranks; it is noteworthy that in this respect Philip did not find it necessary to imitate the very deep Theban phalanx. It would seem that the Macedonian formation was equally prepared to thrust with its pikes or push with its shields. Since both hands were used to grip the heavy pike, one assumes that a phalangist's shield was slung round his neck and perhaps manoeuvred with his elbow or forearm as required.

Another Macedonian speciality was the corps of *hypaspistai*. A hypaspist was originally a shield-bearer or squire to a heavily-armed fighting man. In Philip's army, the hypaspists were foot-guardsmen, perhaps armed more lightly

*It is not possible to give a precise measurement as estimates vary.

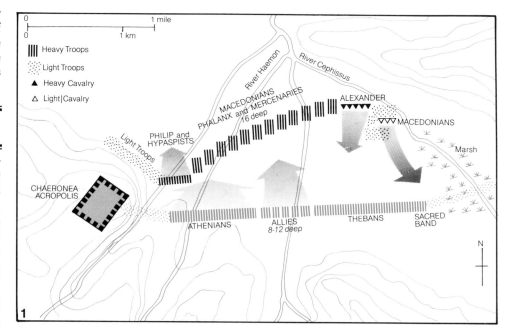

Key:
- ||| Heavy Troops
- ∷ Light Troops
- ▲ Heavy Cavalry
- △ Light/Cavalry

River Haemon • River Cephissus • MACEDONIANS PHALANX and MERCENARIES 16 deep • ALEXANDER • MACEDONIANS • Marsh • Light Troops • PHILIP and HYPASPISTS • CHAERONEA ACROPOLIS • ATHENIANS • ALLIES 8-12 deep • THEBANS • SACRED BAND • N

BC   **347** The death of Plato   **346** Philip forces the Phocians to capitulate   Philip receives their forfeited voting rights in the Amphictionic Council   In Sicily, Dionysius recovers Syracuse

68

Battle of Chaeronea 338 BC

Greek Allies	Macedonians
	Infantry
Athens)	Hypaspists 3000
Euboea) 10000	Phalanx 24000
Corinth)	Mercenaries 5000
Megara)	(includes
Leucas) 8000	Thracian peltasts
Corcyra)	slingers and
Thebes 12000	javelinmen)
Mercenaries 5000	
(mostly peltasts)	
	Cavalry
None	Heavy cavalry 1800
	Light cavalry 400

In 339 BC Philip of Macedon invades central Greece. This prompts the enemy cities of Athens and Thebes to form an alliance to oppose him. First they block the passes and prevent Philip's advance with the aid of numerous mercenaries but at Amphissa Philip destroys the guarding force. The allies hastily muster at Chaeronea.
1 The allies hold a strong position between the Acropolis and the river. Philip leads his Macedonian hypaspists on the right while Alexander commands the cavalry on the left. Philip makes an oblique advance—reminiscent of the tactics of his master, Epaminondas. When engaged he retreats (this movement is presumably a feint) and the Athenians surge forward, creating a gap in their centre.

2 Alexander drives through the gap in the wedge formation and turns on the Theban rear. As Philip's central phalanx advances, he checks his retreat and attacks the Athenians. They break in disorder. Meanwhile, the Macedonian light cavalry strikes at the flank of the Sacred Band. The Thebans are surrounded by the twin cavalry movements and cut down where they stand. Of the 300 men in the Sacred Band, 254 are killed and the remainder all wounded. One thousand Athenians are lost and 2000 taken prisoner. Theban losses are similar.
This battle marks the ascendancy of the professional pikeman over the citizen hoplite; Greece lies at Philip's mercy.

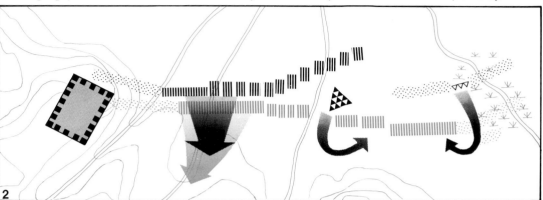

Above: *Coins of Philip II of Macedon commonly feature a mounted figure and the name "Philippos"—the Greek name meaning "lover of horses".*

Left: *The grave of the Thebans who fell at the battle of Chaeronea was marked by this massive stone lion. In the intervening years the memorial has been much restored.*

than the phalangists but more heavily than the peltasts. They played a prominent part in the tactics of Chaeronea where, by a feigned withdrawal, they lured the inexperienced Athenian left wing forward, thus creating a fatal gap in the opposing Greek line, which allowed the Thebans on the right to be surrounded and annihilated.

Philip II of Macedon came to power in 359 BC in difficult circumstances. However, he rid himself of his dynastic rivals, bought off the Paeonian tribal invaders, and repelled the Illyrians. As a boy of fifteen, he had been a hostage at Thebes and had there acquired an admiration for the Greek way of life and a knowledge of Theban military tactics —particularly the use of massed infantry as developed by Epaminondas.

By his seizure of Amphipolis in 357 BC, Philip controlled the approach to the gold mines of Mount Pangaeus, thus securing Macedon's economic and political future. He secretly offered Amphipolis to the Athenians in exchange for Pydna, a valuable port, and when they acquiesced, occupied both Pydna and Potidaea (356 BC), but did not surrender Amphipolis. He presented Potidaea to Olynthus, the leading city of the Chalcidic Confederacy, but in 349 BC, when the time was ripe, he besieged and ruthlessly destroyed Olynthus, subjugating the other cities of the Confederacy.

Seizing another opportunity, Philip intervened in 353 BC on behalf of Thebes and her satellites against the adjacent state of Phocis. The original quarrel was religious in character, relating to temple property at Delphi. Philip was at first unsuccessful in his war with the Phocians, but in 346 BC he crushed them completely and usurped their place on the Amphictyonic Council of states which was responsible for administering the Delphic temple and its property.

In 340 BC, Philip was diverted by war on his north-eastern front, when Athens, as well as Persia, alarmed and resentful at his policies, encouraged Perinthus and Byzantium to defy him. Though he was unable to capture either of these cities, he conducted successful wars against the Scythians and other Balkan tribes, and in 339 BC his opportunism again enabled him to intervene in Delphic disputes. Thebes was directly threatened by Macedonian armed strength, and sensing their own danger, the Athenians, urged by Demosthenes, made common cause with their traditional Theban enemies. Philip, however, overwhelmed the Greek armies combined against him at Chaeronea in 338 BC.

Philip was now master of northern Greece. After a congress at Corinth, he presided over a Pan-Hellenic confederacy which he used as a pretext for garrisoning the strategic points of Thermopylae, Chalcis, Thebes and Corinth. He was assassinated in 337 BC as a result of a domestic intrigue. Olympias, his queen, repudiated in favour of a rival, was later accused by political enemies of complicity in Philip's murder, but the Macedonian people continued to revere Olympias, despite her admittedly vindictive nature. She was later murdered herself.

Philip was not affected by the reckless impulses which repeatedly involved Greek states in war against each other. He was well able to cloak his intentions and sentiments until the moment for action arrived. But though in this respect an accomplished hypocrite, he was free from self-deceit. His admiration for Greek culture was genuine, and he probably believed in all sincerity that Greece needed him as a leader. Indeed, there were eminent Greeks who shared this view, and such sympathisers contributed in an important degree to his success. His son, Alexander the Great, continued his policy and carried out conquests such as he had planned—though perhaps to an extent which Philip had not dreamed.

Alexander the Great

Few military commanders approach the status of Alexander III of Macedon who, in his brief lifetime, established an empire extending from Greece to India. Had he lived, his dream of the consolidation of the known world under his rule might have been realised.

Ancient Authorities

Alexander the Great, third king of Macedon of that name, the son of Philip II, had many biographers and the story of his conquests was recorded by many ancient historians. Among extant works, that of Arrian (Flavius Arrianus) is the most comprehensive and the most reliable. Arrian lived in the second century AD. He was both a philosopher and a man of action. He was governor of Cappadocia under the Roman Emperor Hadrian and in this capacity resisted and repelled an invasion of imperial territory by the Alans, a nomadic people of south Russia. As a soldier, as a native of eastern Asia Minor and as one whose military experience had been gained in that part of the world, he was admirably qualified to chronicle the wars of Alexander in Asia. He uses judgment in selecting his sources and authorities and he relies mainly on the

Below: *A mosaic found at Pompeii in 1831 showing Alexander and Darius at Issus. The mosaic is based on the work of a Greek artist contemporary with Alexander the Great.*

earlier but no longer extant history of Alexander's general Ptolemy, the founder of the Egyptian dynasty which ended in 30 BC with the death of Cleopatra a year after Actium.

In addition to Ptolemy, Arrian also uses the account of Aristobulus, another of Alexander's trusted officers who was a technician and served the Macedonian army in a technical capacity. Arrian's work is called the *Anabasis of Alexander. Anabasis* is the Greek word which Xenophon used in the title of his work recording Cyrus' expedition; in the context it means "a journey to the interior". Arrian also retails the account of Nearchus, who was commander of Alexander's fleet. This work is called the *Indica*. It begins with an account of India and its customs, but its main theme is the voyage completed by Alexander's ships, under the command of Nearchus, in support of the Macedonian army as it returned from India to Persia—from the mouth of the Indus to the Tigris.

Arrian also tentatively includes in his account evidence from the works of such other writers as he considers to have some historical value. His discriminating remarks on the subject suggest, however, that a great deal of

what was written about Alexander had very little historical value. To some writers, Alexander was simply a legend into whose life story it was possible to interpolate all sorts of romantic or sensational material. His adventures with the Amazons and their queen, to which Arrian alludes with little conviction, fall under this head. Other biographies of Alexander reflect the Greek liberal tradition which regarded Alexander and his father as the assassins of Greek liberty. Such works are unscrupulously slanderous. Ptolemy and Aristobulus, as loyal officers of Alexander, were naturally biased in his favour, but this bias cannot be corrected by reference to other writers who acknowledged no sort of commitment to truth.

Plutarch in his life of Alexander seems to have based himself on very diverse sources and his work consequently suffers in point of consistency. Quintus Curtius Rufus, another biographer, writing in the first century AD, presents a garbled account, from which some useful information may nevertheless be derived, as it may also from Diodorus Siculus. But both Curtius and Diodorus relied heavily on Clitarchus, who wrote, it would seem,

BC

341
In Sicily, Timoleon defeats the Carthaginians at the Crimisus

341/40
Perinthus and Byzantium aided by Athens and Persia successfully defy Philip

338
Taking advantage of Amphictionic disputes, Philip re-enters Greece

70

in the third century BC. Clitarchus' reputation as a historian stood very low in the ancient world and it is difficult for a modern historian to know how much truth he mingled with his fiction.

The Political Situation at Philip's death

Let us examine the situation which Alexander inherited from his father. After the battle of Chaeronea in 338 BC, Philip was in a position to dictate terms, but he was obviously concerned that the peace which followed should appear to be the outcome of negotiation. After a conference at Corinth, he formed a league of Greek states with himself at the head. Most of the important Greek cities belonged to this federal league, the only conspicuous exception being Sparta. Philip then declared war in the name of Greece against Persia, in alleged retaliation for the Persian invasion of Greece at the beginning of the previous century. It was customary for Greek declarations of war to be based ostensibly on some ancient quarrel or injury. Such revivals of past wrongs lent dignity to a cause and imparted to it the air of a crusade. The Peloponnesian War had begun with recriminations of this kind. But quite apart from Philip's expansionist ambitions, anyone who wished to unite Greece could not fail to identify Persia as an enemy. The Persians still retained control of many Ionian cities and were quite blatantly dedicated to keeping the free Greek states divided against each other by means of bribery and diplomacy.

At the news of Philip's death, the cities of the Greek League immediately repudiated the federal agreement; but Macedonian garrisons still occupied strategic points in Greece, including the citadels of Thebes and Corinth, and when Alexander, with characteristic speed, hastened southwards at the head of an army, resistance collapsed. Alexander was on this occasion not in the least vindictive; the Corinth federal agreement was quietly and firmly re-established.

More serious was the military threat from Macedon's northern tribal neighbours in Thrace and Illyricum. In dealing with them, both the Macedonian war machine and Alexander's ability to handle it were thoroughly tested, but both emerged from the test with enhanced reputation.

Apart from the menace of external enemies, Alexander had found himself confronted by a more intimate challenge in the heart of Macedon itself. Questions had arisen over succession to the throne during Philip's lifetime, for the king had set aside Alexander's mother, Olympias, to marry a new queen, Cleopatra. The mere existence of the resulting uncertainty must have encouraged the ambitions of other royal scions. But despite the resentment which Alexander had felt against his father, he promptly punished Philip's assassin with death and followed this up by executing three possible pretenders to the throne, who might or might not have been accessories to the murder. Olympias, without Alexander's approval, completed his task by procuring the death of Cleopatra and her infant daughter. Despite the Macedonian patronage of Greek constitutional ideals, politics in Macedon itself were frankly dynastic and disputes were settled by normal dynastic methods.

Meanwhile, preparations for the invasion of the Persian empire had proceeded apace. Philip had already dispatched a force of more than 10,000 men, supported by a fleet, across the Hellespont; the Greek cities of Asia Minor welcomed him as a liberator. The force in question was, indeed, a mere vanguard and at the time of Philip's death had been awaiting his arrival with the main body. The time was certainly opportune, for the Persian court itself had recently been convulsed by palace intrigue and regicide. Here also was a matter which called for Alexander's prompt attention.

Alexander's Character

Alexander was only 20 years old at the time of his father's death. Experience usually comes with age, but it had come to Alexander while he was still extremely young, qualifying him as a soldier, an administrator and a diplomat. At the age of 16, he had acted as regent while his father was absent on an expedition against Byzantium and on his own initiative had led a force against rebellious Thracian tribes, expelled them from their chief city and repeopled it, under the name of Alexandropolis, with various immigrants. At the battle of Chaeronea, he had led Philip's élite cavalry regiment in its charge against the Theban Sacred Band, winning a reputation for dauntless courage. He had also been sent with other envoys to Athens after the conclusion of peace, conveying to that city the ashes of the Athenian dead.

As a military commander, Alexander showed great resource and a flair for ingenious improvisation. These qualities were demonstrated in the campaign in Thrace which followed his father's death. On one occasion, the enemy tried to overwhelm his troops by launching a fleet of unharnessed chariots down a steep slope on to their heads. Alexander ordered the Macedonian phalangists to open their ranks and allow the chariots to hurtle through;

Left: *A typical tract of land in Cappadocia through which Alexander campaigned. After his conquest of the Persian Empire, Cappadocia became independent and it later separated from Pontus in the north.*

those who could not evade the danger in this way were to lie down, link shields for protection and let the wheels pass over them. These orders were obeyed and there were no Macedonian casualties.

On his campaigns, Alexander made light of physical obstacles. When the Thessalians barred his march into Greece at Tempe, his pioneer corps cut a military road through the rocky cliffs of Mount Ossa, so that he swiftly outflanked the waiting enemy. He showed similar resourcefulness in his campaign against northern tribesmen, when he made a surprise crossing of the Danube by requisitioning local fishing boats for transport.

Alexander, like Philip and earlier Macedonian kings, was very anxious to appear Greek. The Macedonians were a semi-Greek people and their language was a Greek *patois* which had absorbed many barbarous elements, so that it could no longer be understood by Greeks. Noble Macedonians, however, spoke both Greek and Macedonian, worshipped the Olympian gods, and were accepted by the Greek athletic authorities as competitors in the Olympic games. Alexander's tutor had been the philosopher Aristotle and the young prince's enthusiasm for Homer and Greek culture in general was well known. He was, in fact, not even content with being Greek, but wished to proclaim himself a Greek god, the son of Zeus, who had approached his mother, it was rumoured, in the form of a serpent.

In view of such Philhellenic commitments, it seems astonishing that Alexander should have given offence, after his conquest of Persia, by adopting Persian dress and customs and obliging his Macedonian officers to do the same. His Philhellenism was perhaps a natural enthusiasm, while his orientalism was a matter of policy, aimed at conciliating a conquered empire. Indeed, Alexander's character was full of contradictions. His indifference to danger and hardship was combined with heavy drinking and outbursts of passionate anger which led him into crimes and atrocities. In a moment of drunken fury, he murdered his old friend and veteran officer, Clitus; for a mere whim, he burnt down the captured city of Persepolis, although such an act went quite contrary to his general policy of conciliation. Having made prisoners the women of Darius' family, he behaved towards them with a courtesy and chivalry that would have done credit to a knight of medieval legend, but he had been quite

Macedonian Infantry

The Syntagma* (right)
The basic infantry unit in the phalanx was the 256 man *syntagma* made up of 16 files (*lochoi*) of 16 men; the whole battalion being commanded by the *syntagmatarch* on the right. The unit was capable of performing complex doubling manoeuvres and to this end a number of subordinate officers existed. Each file was led by a *lochagos*, while his second-in-command, *ouragos*, took the rear. The *hemilochites* was the half-file commander and the *enomotarch* the quarter-file commander. Across the front of the unit the chain of command was as follows: 2 files were led by a *dilochites*, 4 by a *tetrarch*, 8 by a *taxiarch* and 16 by the *syntagmatarch*. Five others followed the unit: a herald, signaller, trumpeter, *extra-ouragos* (to bring up stragglers) and an aide.

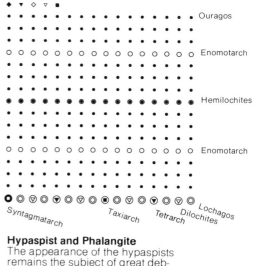

(Theoretical drill book formation according to Asclepiodotus 1st century BC)

Hypaspist and Phalangite
The appearance of the hypaspists remains the subject of great debate. We know that they formed a contingent distinct from the phalanx but opinions differ as to their equipment. Our figure (left)

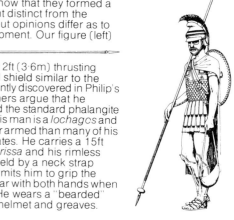

carries a 12ft (3·6m) thrusting spear and shield similar to the arms recently discovered in Philip's tomb. Others argue that he resembled the standard phalangite (right). This man is a *lochagos* and so is better armed than many of his subordinates. He carries a 15ft (4·5m) *sarissa* and his rimless shield is held by a neck strap which permits him to grip the heavy spear with both hands when in battle. He wears a "bearded" Thracian helmet and greaves.

merciless to the survivors of Tyre and Gaza—not to mention Thebes. At the distance of over two millennia, we can only notice these inconsistencies, not explain them. As Alexander died at the age of 32, it may be argued that his character scarcely had time to form.

Alexander's Army

It would have been impossible for Alexander to make his far-reaching conquests if he had not been able to foster high morale among the men whom he led. Such morale was very largely the product of his own courage and ability as a leader. Apart from this, the Macedonian army was organized with a view to encouraging *esprit de corps*. The old citizen hoplite army of the fifth century had gained in this respect from the fact that it represented an exclusive social élite. The mercenary armies of the earlier fourth century had been held together—to the extent that they were held together—by a sense of professional allegiance. Well-trained mercenaries had confidence in each other and valued the opportunity of

Below: *This head of Alexander the Great was found at Pergamon in Asia Minor and dates from the 2nd century BC. Portraits of Alexander always show him youthful and beardless.*

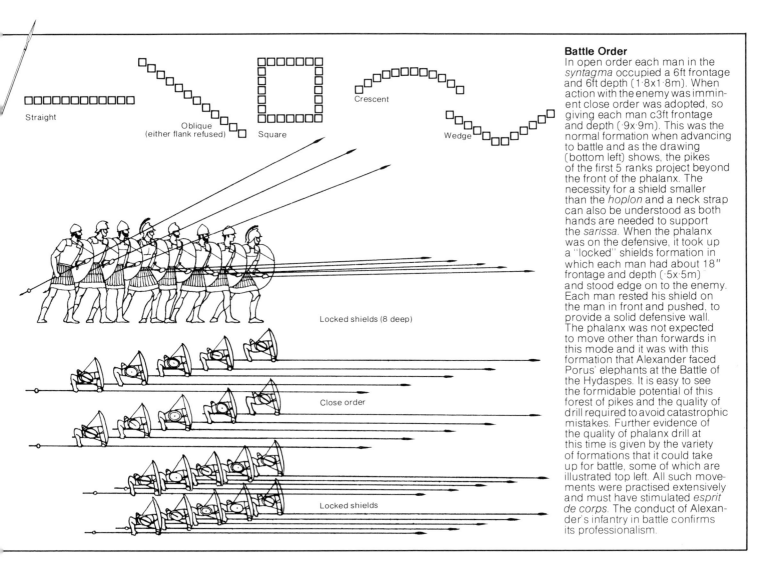

Straight

Oblique
(either flank refused)

Square

Crescent

Wedge

Locked shields (8 deep)

Close order

Locked shields

Battle Order

In open order each man in the *syntagma* occupied a 6ft frontage and 6ft depth (1·8x1·8m). When action with the enemy was imminent close order was adopted, so giving each man c3ft frontage and depth (·9x·9m). This was the normal formation when advancing to battle and as the drawing (bottom left) shows, the pikes of the first 5 ranks project beyond the front of the phalanx. The necessity for a shield smaller than the *hoplon* and a neck strap can also be understood as both hands are needed to support the *sarissa*. When the phalanx was on the defensive, it took up a "locked" shields formation in which each man had about 18″ frontage and depth (·5x·5m) and stood edge on to the enemy. Each man rested his shield on the man in front and pushed, to provide a solid defensive wall. The phalanx was not expected to move other than forwards in this mode and it was with this formation that Alexander faced Porus' elephants at the Battle of the Hydaspes. It is easy to see the formidable potential of this forest of pikes and the quality of drill required to avoid catastrophic mistakes. Further evidence of the quality of phalanx drill at this time is given by the variety of formations that it could take up for battle, some of which are illustrated top left. All such movements were practised extensively and must have stimulated *esprit de corps*. The conduct of Alexander's infantry in battle confirms its professionalism.

---

serving under a gifted commander. Alexander certainly employed mercenaries in his invasion of Asia Minor, and he relied more upon them in his operations farther east. At the same time, for reasons which we have noticed, it was not in the interests of an autocratic ruler to maintain a hoplite corps drawn from the wealthier citizen classes of his own territory. For these reasons if no other, the monarchs of Macedon had to find a new basis for "team spirit".

We hear of Foot-companions and Hypaspists—a word which originally meant simply "squires" or "armour-bearers". The King's own mounted Guard led the Companion squadrons; and late writers refer to an infantry detachment of "Silver-shields". Such terminology is suggestive of elite units, and generally speaking elitism was an important principle in Alexander's army. Elite bodies characterised Macedonian armies from early to late times. In battle, they constituted spearheads, and a spearhead unit was known as an *agema*. The word *agema* in Greece had meant "that which is led" (for this use see Xenophon *Lacedaemonian Constitution* 11.9), and might denote an entire field army. Among

the Macedonians, the significance was rather "that which leads". The Macedonian *agema* could be the spearhead of an infantry or cavalry corps. There was an *agema* of Hypaspists and the Royal Squadron of cavalry (*ile*) was the *agema* of the Companions—themselves an elite. In Alexander's eastern campaigns, after the reorganisation of the cavalry into hipparchies (*hipparchiai*), the *agema* still persisted as a cavalry spearhead.

The army was also technically diversified and highly sophisticated from a practical point of view. It represented the culmination of the fourth-century tendency to arm light troops more heavily and heavy troops more lightly; yet differences between different fighting arms were sharply preserved, as between instruments appropriate for different tasks. The Companions were armoured heavy cavalry. By contrast, the Thracians and Macedonian scouts (*prodromoi*) represented lighter cavalry units. Alexander also used archers, slingers and peltasts, and the fighting-men were followed by a large body of technicians and engineers, whose ability was amply demonstrated in the ambitious sieges undertaken.

In some ways, Alexander's tactical handling of his army may seem stereotyped and to that extent unlikely to secure the advantage of surprise. The main instrument of attack was the Companion heavy cavalry; the attack was made on the flank, while the phalanx barred the enemy's advance in the centre and the lighter cavalry on the left wing guarded the phalanx itself from being outflanked. However, this general pattern left room for flexibility. The timing of the attack, which could easily convert a defensive into an offensive action, was all-important, and in this respect Alexander's judgment proved unerring. Furthermore, the phalanx was itself a highly flexible unit, capable of assuming various formations; it could form a square, extend itself into rectangular shape with broadside presented to the enemy, or it could become a solid column, capable of being directed either head-on or inclined at an angle against the enemy battle-line. In addition, it could adopt a wedge or arrow-head formation. Even if the full-length sarissa was 17 feet (5·2m) long, some of the phalangists seem to have been equipped more lightly than others. The positioning and employment of variously equipped troops would have been another factor making for flexibility. Certainly, the *sarissa* of Alexander's phalangists was shorter than that of later armies. (Ancient measurements are given in cubits and standard cubits differed locally. This variance may account for much of the modern controversy over measurements in the ancient world).

The Rebellion of the Greek States

Before penetrating into Asia, it was necessary for Alexander to secure his bases in mainland Greece and the Balkan peninsula and his lines of communication in the Aegean. His campaigns in Thrace and Illyricum had subdued the peoples in those regions and he had, no doubt, hoped for suffi-

cient political sympathy among the Greek states to ensure support for the Macedonian garrisons which Philip had placed in Thebes and other cities after Chaeronea. In this, he must have been disappointed. While he was fighting against Illyrian tribes, a rumour circulated that he had been killed. At Athens, the anti-Macedonian orator Demosthenes produced an eye-witness to Alexander's death and procured money from Persia to promote Theban revolt. At Thebes, two Macedonian officers were murdered and the Macedonian garrison besieged. It says much for Alexander's personal prestige, even at this early stage, that the mere rumour of his death was enough to inspire rebellion. As it was, he was provided with a pretext for more stringent action than he had previously taken. He marched swiftly into Greece. Thebes was captured by assault and, on the ostensible authority of the Greek League which Philip had originally

formed, the city's walls and buildings were razed and its surviving citizens sold into slavery. In the massacre which accompanied the capture of the city, the Phocian and Boeotian enemies of Thebes, who had been glad to take sides with Alexander, showed themselves more merciless than the Macedonians. Alexander dealt mildly with Athens, and at Thebes insisted, with marked respect for Greek religion and culture, that the city's temples and the descendants of the renowned poet Pindar should be spared. Other exemptions were families with Macedonian sympathies and connections. If it was in Alexander's character to be both magnanimous and ruthless as occasion demanded, this was no less than the functions of a military commander required. Such alternative attitudes are perhaps necessary at any time. Vindictiveness may stiffen resistance, but persistent attempts at conciliation are easily taken for weakness.

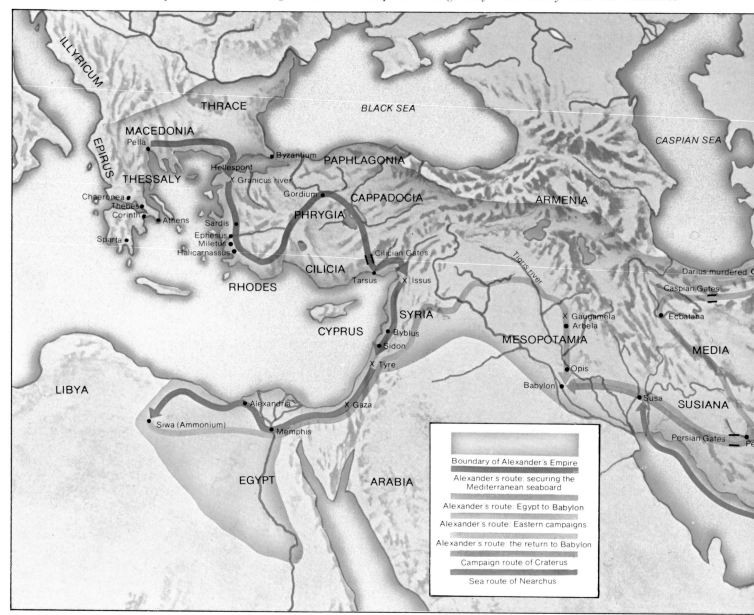

Alexander crosses into Asia

Alexander defeats the Persian satraps of Asia Minor at the Granicus river

Memnon escapes and rallies resistance at Miletus and Halicarnassus

Alexander marches southward, leaving Parmenio with a garrison at Ephesus

About this date in Sicily, Timoleon dies

In 334 BC, Alexander crossed the Hellespont with 40,000 men and joined the Macedonian force which had already been posted by his father as a bridgehead in Asia. Mainland Greece was secure. The Peloponnesians had taken no part in the revolt. Thebes no longer existed, and Athens, apart from the fact that it contained many Macedonian sympathizers, was cowed by the example of Thebes. To the Greek cities of Asia Minor, the arrival of Alexander promised liberty, as they understood it, and they awaited him as ready-made allies. His plan was to dispense with elaborate lines of communication and to supply his army from ever-increasing conquered territory. Nevertheless, he could not march

Below: *This map illustrates the sequence of events in Alexander's great campaign of conquest. The diversity of the terrain in which he operated is remarkable.*

eastward leaving substantial enemy forces in his rear; and such forces existed, both in the form of the Persian army which three satraps had assembled on the banks of the Granicus river near the Hellespont and in the Phoenician naval potential, against which he could muster comparatively few ships. His fleet, although it contained a Macedonian element, was contributed for the most part by the states of the Greek League and numbered about 200 vessels in all. Alexander's strategy, however, was to destroy the enemy's navy on land by capturing its bases. This expedient was one which often recommended itself in ancient warfare and it was an obvious stratagem in view of the modest size and simple structure of ancient ships. Fleets would not long remain at a distance from a hospitable coast. They could, moreover, easily be replaced when lost. The Persians had ample money to pay for new ships and

crews if they wished to do so, and it was therefore more important to occupy ports and shipyards than to destroy the ships themselves.

The Battle of the Granicus

After marching into Asia, Alexander could not advance southwards until he had disposed of the Persian army which menaced his eastern flank. He therefore led his forces towards the enemy by a route roughly parallel with the southern shore of the Hellespont, sending scouts in front of him. The use of scouts and look-outs had in the past been much neglected by Greek commanders—it could, for example, have spared the Athenians their overwhelming defeat at Aegospotami—but Alexander had been well trained in his father's army and the Macedonian war machine operated scientifically.

The Persians were numerically almost equal to the invaders, though slightly inferior in infantry strength. A part of their force was made up of Greek mercenaries, who presented a formidable hoplite opposition. These numbered somewhat under 20,000 men. The figure has been suspected of overestimate, but Arrian, who records it, is our most reliable source. The Persian position was well chosen, on the farther bank of a deep river. Parmenio, Alexander's second-in-command, who had, under Philip's orders, led the vanguard into Asia, counselled a waiting policy, but Alexander was of a different opinion and decided to attack at once.

Despite the difficulties of the terrain and the obstacle presented by the Granicus river, the tactics of the ensuing battle conformed to type. The phalanx engaged the enemy, while the cavalry launched an attack from the right wing. The resulting fight, which took place in the river and on its banks, assumed the hand-to-hand, body-to-body aspect of an infantry battle. In this fighting, the Macedonian cavalry, armed with long lances, had an advantage over the Persian horsemen with their short javelins. At the same time, the Persians were able to make use of their scimitars at close quarters—to which weapons Alexander himself almost fell a victim.

Arrian's account of the action reads at one point like an epic narrative, with its emphasis on single combat, centred in the duels between leaders on either side. It was evidently the Persian plan to strike down Alexander himself. His

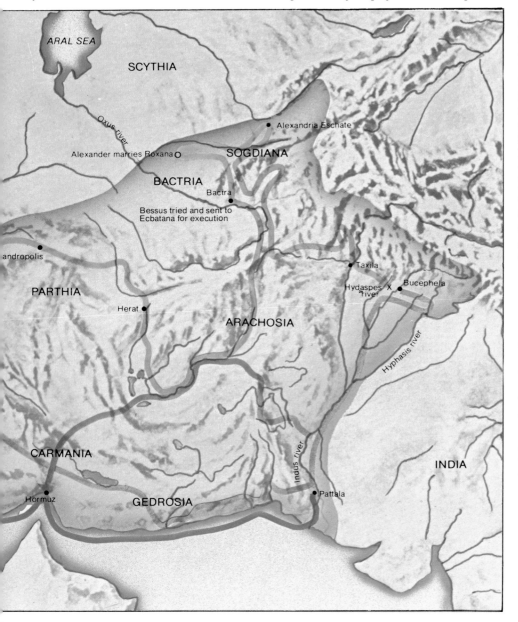

333
Memnon dies Alexander rejoins Parmenio at Gordium   Alexander reaches Tarsus by way of a pass over Taurus mountains (Cilician Gates)   Alexander defeats Darius III of Persia at the battle of Issus: he refuses Darius' peace terms   BC

75

splendid insignia and entourage made him easy to recognize—and it was perhaps remembered how the death of Cyrus at Cunaxa had transformed even a victory into a defeat. Cyrus himself had on that occasion singled out King Artaxerxes for personal attack; selection of the enemy leader as a special target may well have been regular Persian practice.

Alexander's scouts were the first to approach and enter the river and they must have signalled the best points for crossing. The Granicus, although capable of being forded, was running comparatively deep, as one would expect in springtime. In the deep water, horsemen enjoyed some advan-tage. The Persians rained missiles from the high banks opposite, but the Macedonian cavalry must have been well-protected by their armour. Alex-ander led his forces obliquely down-stream. It must thus have been possible for the head of the column to establish itself at a point where the bank was lower; those following would have been able to face round towards the enemy, in the manner of a slanting battle-line, once the bridgehead was secured.

The Macedonian advance party which first crossed the river suffered severe casualties. But Alexander, with the Companion cavalry, followed hard on their heels. Unlike the Persian kings, he was not surrounded by his body-guard, but led it. This may be inter-preted as a mark of his courage or an instance of his rashness.

As the Macedonian cavalry emerged from the riverbed in ever increasing numbers, they bore down the enemy horsemen opposed to them and the two wings of the Persian army eventually broke and fled. The Greek hoplite mercenaries, who held the centre, remained in position; not, as Arrian ungenerously remarks, through any rational plan of action, but paralysed by the magnitude of the disaster. They were soon clasped against the thorny breast of the phalanx by Alexander's encircling cavalry on either wing and relentlessly mown down. Hardly any

Battle of the Granicus 334 BC

Alexander	Persians
Cavalry	
Companions 1700	Bactria 2000
Prodromoi 800	Hyrcania 1/2000
Thessaly 1700	Paphlagonia 1000
Greece 600	Cappadocia 1/2000
Paeonia 200	Others 8/10000
Heavy Infantry	
Phalanx 12000	Greek mercenary
Allied Greek	hoplites 5/8000
hoplites 7000	
Hypaspists 3000	
Peltasts	
Thrace 6000	Greek mercenary
Greek	peltasts 1/2000
mercenary peltasts 5000	
Light Troops	
Illyricum 1000	Local troop
Agriania 500	levy 5/8000
(javelinmen)	(archers
Crete 500	and
(archers)	spearmen)

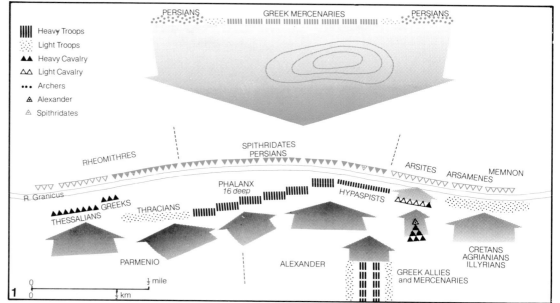

1 The Persian Satraps decide to bring Alexander to battle and advance towards the Granicus. Alexander learns of this and races for the river. The Persian cavalry gets there first and means to hold the bank until the infantry arrives. Alexander deploys his army as it comes up ex-tending to the left. Wanting to pre-empt the Persian infantry, he orders an immediate attack. His light cavalry and one squad-ron of Companions storm across and gain a foothold. Alexander and Companions hurl themselves across aiming obliquely at the Persian centre. General advance by Alexander's army.
2 A furious *mêlée* develops around Alexander and Spithri-dates who is killed. His Hyrcan-ians assailed by Hypaspists and Companions, break, upon which a general rout ensues. The Persian infantry follows suit although the Greek mercenaries prepare a more orderly withdrawal.
3 A further charge by Alexander pins half the Greek infantry on a low hill until they are surr-ounded by the Macedonian infan-try. Deciding to make an ex-ample of these "traitors", Alex-ander refuses to accept their surrender. When many have been killed, Alexander takes the rest prisoner and sends them in chains to the Macedonian mines as an example.

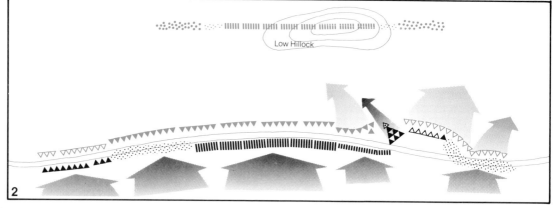

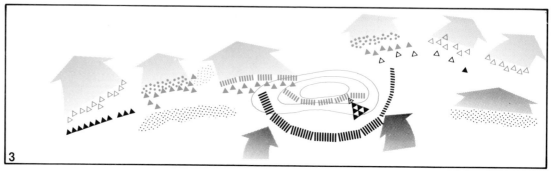

BC	332				
	Alexander besieges and captures Tyre: most Palestinian cities submit to him	Gaza is besieged and captured	Alexander leads his army into Egypt, but meets no resistance	Alexander plans the foundation of Alexandria	Alexander visits the oracle of Zeus Ammon (at Siwa) in winter 332/1

76

escaped; 2,000 were taken alive and were sent back in chains to Macedon to serve a sentence of hard labour, as traitors to the Greek cause. For Alexander regarded the Macedonians who composed nearly half his army as Greeks; the cities of the Greek League, with some Greek mercenaries recruited by Alexander himself, supplied certainly over one quarter, the rest being recruited from Thracians, Paeonians and other northern peoples. However, a leader of the defeated Greek mercenary force, Memnon of Rhodes, eluded both death and capture and lived to fight another day. He had in any case advised against fighting at the Granicus and had hereby incurred some odium among the Persians.

After the Granicus

The result of the Granicus battle must have reaffirmed the faith placed by the Persian king, Darius III, in Memnon. The Greek mercenary commander's strategy had been sound. He had wished to avoid a pitched battle, conduct a scorched-earth policy in Asia, fortify maritime and naval bases on the coast and cut Alexander off from the sea. While Memnon himself survived, there were still considerable prospects of putting this plan into effect. However, many coastal cities, as well as the important road junction of Sardis, soon fell to Alexander with little or no resistance. Miletus held out in the hope of relief from a Persian force inland. It also received encouragement from Phoenician and Cyprian ships based on Mycale. But Alexander forestalled both naval and military relief and captured the city. Memnon fell back on Halicarnassus and fortified it strongly. Driven from there, he tried to establish naval bases on the major Aegean islands, not only threatening Alexander's flank from the sea but providing a springboard for a counteroffensive against Greece and Macedon. Unfortunately for the Persians, Memnon suddenly fell ill and died. Those who inherited his command persisted for some time in the same strategy, but were eventually deterred by quite a small show of naval strength by Antipater, the Macedonian governor whom Alexander had left in charge of mainland Greece.

Alexander had left Parmenio with the main body of the army at Sardis. With his own striking force, he marched round the south-west extremity of Asia Minor and along the southern coast, digressing northward to join Parmenio again at Gordium in the interior. Strategically, the move seems superfluous, but Alexander's expeditions sometimes wore the aspect of exploration, pilgrimage or even tourism. In any case, he lost no opportunity of acquainting himself with the features of an empire which he already regarded as his own.

Having joined forces with Parmenio, Alexander marched southward again into the Cilician plain and threatened Syria. A Persian force, inadequate to defend the vital mountain pass, fled at his approach, but the main Persian army, under command of Darius himself, was waiting farther south in Syria. At this point, Alexander was suddenly incapacitated by a bout of fever and his advance was checked.

Emboldened by the delay, Darius made a circuitous march and descended, by a northern mountain pass, on the town of Issus, where he brutally put to death the Macedonian sick who had been left there. This manoeuvre placed him at Alexander's rear. Alexander was surprised but not dismayed at the move, for it had carried the Persian army (600,000 strong) to a point where the plain was pinched between the mountains and the sea. Here, their superiority in men and missiles could not be deployed to advantage. However, the position in some ways resembled that which the satraps had chosen at the Granicus. Darius' army was drawn up with a riverbed in front of it. The channel was now dry, since it was late autumn (334 BC). The king's mercenary hoplites were placed in the centre. His cavalry held the wings, his right wing being more heavily loaded, since the mountains left little room for deployment on the left. He also hoped to break through on the right wing and cut Alexander off from the sea. It must be remembered that after Darius' encircling march the two armies had exchanged positions.

Much of Alexander's success seems in general to have been due to good reconnaissance work. Darius had relied on preventing an outflanking move from the Companion cavalry by posting a substantial force on the mountain slopes above. Having ascertained this plan, Alexander provided a light detachment of his own to meet and ward off the threat. He also sent the Thessalian cavalry, under Parmenio, to reinforce his left wing. It was possible for Alexander to make all such changes shortly before battle was joined; his advance was leisurely, and the Persians kept their positions, leaving him the initiative.

The battle conformed to the pattern of many ancient battles. The right wing of the Macedonian army, in encircling the enemy, placed the central phalanx under strain. As the phalangists on the right strove to maintain contact with the cavalry on the wing, they parted company with the phalangists on their left and a dangerous gap appeared, which Darius' Greek mercenaries were quick to exploit. It then became a question of whether Alexander with his Companions could encircle the mercenaries before the mercenaries could break through the centre and encircle him. Alexander won, ploughing devastatingly into the mercenary flank and rear. In danger of capture, Darius fled precipitately in his war-chariot, and even the Persian forces of the right, who had held back Parmenio's cavalry, soon

Early Catapults

The earliest known artillery piece, an obvious advance on man-powered missile launchers, was invented in Syracuse c 400 BC and subsequently developed into sophisticated artillery. The illustrations show early developments.

The Gastraphetes: (Belly-bow) This was originally an extremely powerful bow with a mechanical draw-device added. It consisted of a bow, a stock with ratchets attached and a slider with trigger mechanism. To operate it, the slider was drawn forward and a claw engaged the bow-string (see illustration). The bow was placed against a solid object such as a wall or the ground and the operator then leaned on the stock, grasped the handles and used his weight to compress the slider one ratchet at a time, until the string was drawn. A bolt was then placed in the groove on the slider, the weapon aimed, and fired by pulling back the bar of the trigger. This allowed the claw to pivot upwards releasing the string. The use of a mechanical device allowed a more powerful bow to be used (some 150-200lb [68-90kg] as opposed to a hand-bow's 40-60lb [18-27kg] draw-weight). Because of their weight and slow rate of fire the use of such devices was largely confined to sieges.

The Oxybeles: (Bolt-shooter) The next obvious development, c 375 BC, was a larger and more powerful machine too big to carry, thus requiring a stand. The even more powerful bow was drawn back by a winch and levers. These improvements meant an increase in range and accuracy.

The Oxybeles (Torsion powered) Having reached the limit of power of the composite bow, catapult designers turned to a new source of power: torsion. The earliest type consisted simply of two bundles of sinew rope looped over a rectangular frame. More power again was obtained by twisting these slightly and this led to the sinew "springs" being placed within the frame. The ropes were stretched on a special frame before being inserted, and final tightening and tuning was done by turning the "keys" at top and bottom (see illustration). Such machines were known by the general name *katapeltes*, literally, shield-piercer, because they were capable of penetrating a man's shield and armour at ranges in excess of ¼ mile (400 metres). As they increased in size they were adapted to throw stones.

The Lithobolos: (Stone-thrower) These machines threw stones of 10lb (4·5kg) to 180lb (82kg) in weight. They all looked alike and differed only in size: the dimensions being calculated by a complex mathematical formula based on the spring diameter. The illustration shows a 60 pounder (27kg). Such machines were normally brought to point-blank range (150-200 yds [157m-185m]) where they were capable of stripping battlements from fortified walls.

Ammunition

Darts and bolts varied in size, as did the machines. Both finned and finless projectiles were used. The most popular size was around 27" (68cm). Heads also varied. The stones used were carefully shaped into spheres. Several "ammunition dumps" of such stones have been found. As a quick expedient, rough stones were sometimes given a coating of clay to render them spherical so ensuring an efficient ballistic shape. The disadvantage of this of course was that such projectiles did not cause as much damage as solid shot. Stone-throwers were occasionally adapted to sling large darts by simply replacing the slider and the bow-string.

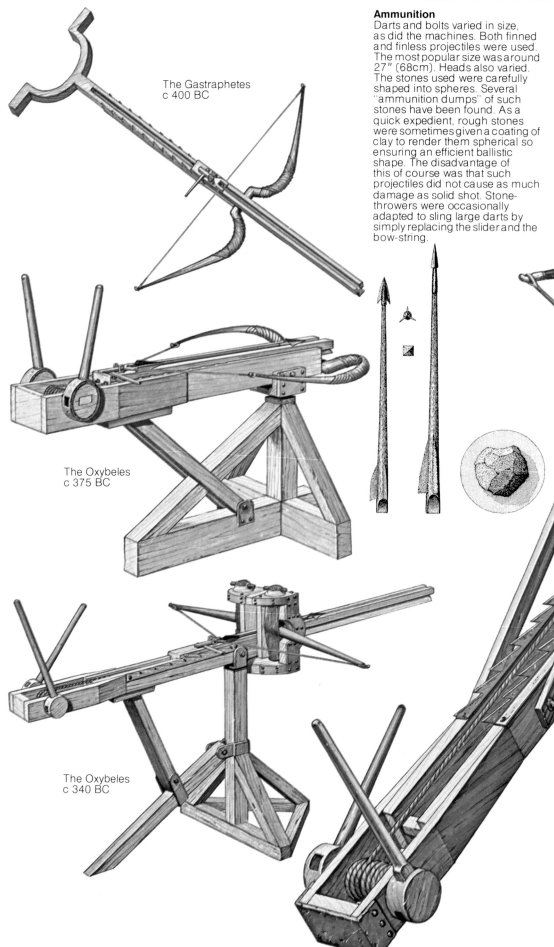

The Gastraphetes
c 400 BC

The Oxybeles
c 375 BC

The Oxybeles
c 340 BC

Alexander captures Persepolis | Alexander pursues Darius eastwards | Darius, now a fugitive in the power of the usurper Bessus, is murdered | Philotas, son of Parmenio, Alexander's officer, is accused of conspiracy and executed | Parmenio, commanding the garrison at Ecbatana is murdered on Alexander's orders

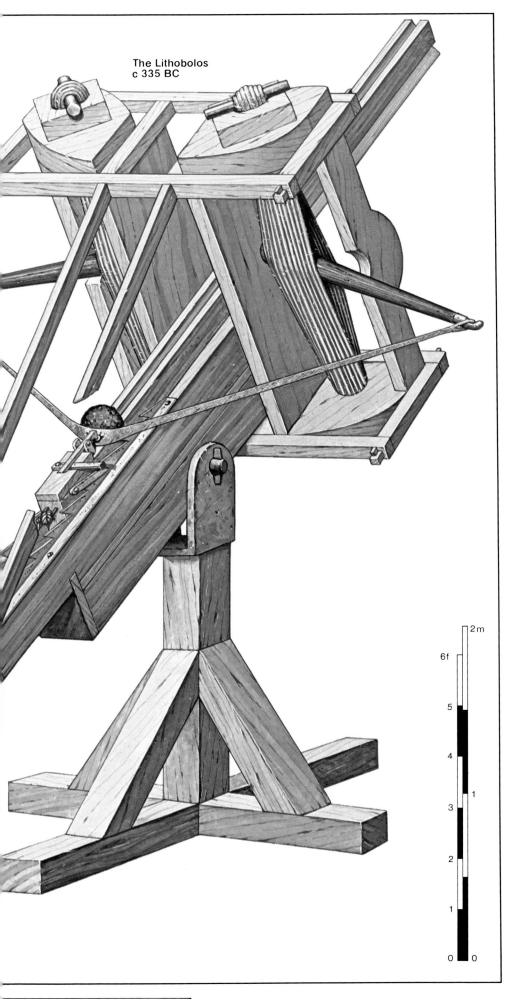

The Lithobolos
c 335 BC

followed their king's example. Darius'
mother, wife and children, who had
accompanied the army, were left
prisoners in Alexander's hands.

The Siege of Tyre

Such was the battle of Issus. It would
have been understandable if Alexander,
possessed of his royal hostages, had
determined there and then to march
eastward into the heart of the Persian
empire, before Darius had time to
mobilize fresh forces. However, he
adhered to his original plan of securing
the Levant coast. The prudence of this
strategy is beyond question. While
Persian and Cyprian fleets were
amenable to Persian control, they
remained, despite the death of Memnon,
capable of launching a counter-
offensive against mainland Greece and
Macedonia itself. The bizarre logic of
such a move might be that the armed
forces on either side would end by
occupying each other's countries.

Alexander continued his march
southwards down the Syrian coast.
Awed by the result at Issus, Sidon and
Byblus surrendered to him without
opposition. Tyre, however, while
offering to accept his suzerainty,
refused him entry into the city
precincts. Undaunted by the fact that
Tyre was built on an offshore island in
a seemingly impregnable position,
Alexander at once resolved upon a
siege. His small naval force could not
hope to match the number of Tyrian
ships in the open sea, so he began to
construct a causeway from the land. As
the causeway was extended into
deeper water the task became more
difficult; the builders were soon within
range of missiles from the city walls
and the Tyrian ships. Alexander
replied by constructing two towers on
the causeway, from which he was able
to use siege artillery (sling and
crossbow-types) to ward off the
attack, at the same time screening his
builders. The towers themselves were
protected by hides from the sharp,
flaming darts of the enemy. However,
the Tyrians managed to burn down the
towers eventually by launching fireships
against them.

Alexander widened his causeway
and brought up more siege-engines. He
was also now able to muster a large
fleet; Sidon and Cyprus, overawed by
his victorious progress, contributed
ships and sailors. The Tyrians were
surprised by the size of the naval
armament brought against them and
refused to fight in the open sea; but

Alexander campaigns in
the eastern Persian
empire

Arachosia is subdued

Alexander marches
through the Afghanistan
mountains

In Italy, Rome is
victorious over the
Volsci and founds more
Latin colonies

they used their own ships to block the island's northern and southern harbours which faced towards Sidon and Egypt respectively.

The causeway was at last completed and Alexander's siege engines were turned against the walls of the city. But the Tyrians countered his towers with wooden towers of their own, superimposed upon the city battlements—which were already 150 feet (46m)

high. Approach to the walls was in any case made difficult by rocks which had been dumped in the sea at the base of the walls. Alexander ordered these rocks to be hauled away, but the ships detailed for this work were thwarted by armoured Tyrian ships which cut their mooring cables. Alexander set armoured vessels of his own to protect the workers; when Tyrian divers were used to cut the cables, the Macedonians

anchored their ships with chains. In the end, they lassoed the rocks and used their catapults to hurl them into deep water where they would present no obstacle to them.

The Tyrian ships now mounted a surprise sally against the Cyprian naval force which guarded the north harbour. Alexander, however, was on the alert and took timely measures. Other ships were sent to seal the

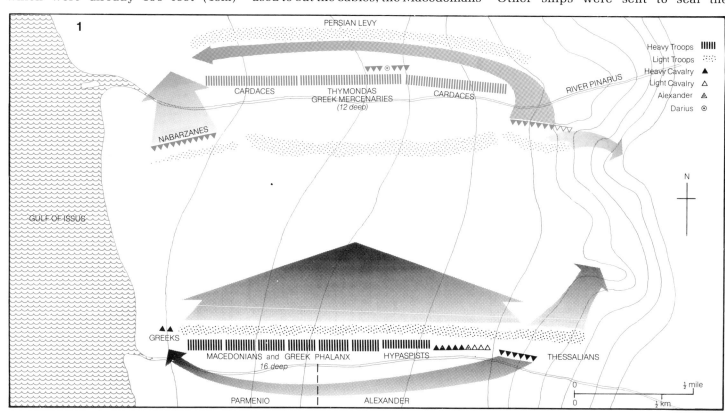

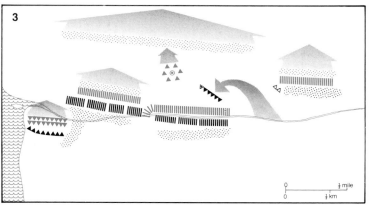

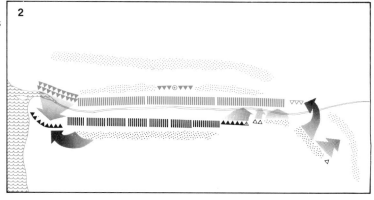

Battle of Issus 333 BC

Alexander	Darius
Infantry	
Hypaspists 3000	Greek
Phalanx 12000	mercenary
Greek allied	hoplites 8/10000
infantry 7000	Cardaces 20000
Light Troops	
Thrace 6000	12/15000
Illyricum 1000	General levy of
Crete 1000	tribesmen 50000
Mercenaries 5000	
Cavalry	
Companions 2100	Nobles 3000
Thessaly 2100	Others (extra-
Greek allied 750	heavy, heavy
Prodromoi 600	and light)
Paeonia 300	8/10000

1 By clever strategy Darius has cut Alexander off from home, so Alexander must turn to face him. Darius deploys his vast army behind a screen of cavalry and light troops between the hills and the sea. As Alexander advances, Darius' screen retires to the flanks revealing a line of Cardaces (Asiatics armed with *hoplon* shields and weapons) while the mercenary Greek hoplites hold the centre. As the foot hills are unsuitable for horsemen Darius switches the bulk of his cavalry to the right wing; Alexander moves his Thessalians

to the left as a counter and plugs the resulting gap with Companions and peltasts. He also sends light troops to oppose the Persians on the hills.
2 Alexander's light troops push back the Persians on the hills while Alexander edges right to protect the wing. Parmenio presses forward and a gap develops in the Macedonian line. Alexander outflanks the Persian left and routs it. A desperate struggle rages in the centre as the phalanx tries to cross the River Pinarus. Meanwhile the Persian cavalry comes to grips with the Thessalians who are supported by skirmishing light troops; the line holds.
3 Alexander swings left after Darius and a bitter struggle ensues around his chariot. Alexander is wounded in the thigh. Darius sensing that the Macedonians are gaining the upper hand, flies the field. His Greek mercenaries are giving the phalanx a hard time but the Companions wheel into them. The Persian right, seeing Darius run, also breaks and panic spreads. Darius evades Alexander's pursuit. The mercenaries manage to extricate themselves but suffer badly and many of them are killed. Darius' wife and family are taken.

Alexander's army meets with hard fighting in Bactria and Sogdiana (Russian Turkestan)

Bessus is captured and executed as a regicide

In Italy, Roman colonisation of Fregellae leads to Second Samnite War

harbour entrance once more, and he himself with some hastily-manned vessels sailed round the island to intercept such Tyrian triremes as had broken through. Most of these he managed to disable, although the crews saved themselves by swimming.

The besiegers now brought up engines on ships to the north wall of the city, but the masonry resisted their efforts. A similar attack from the south, however, was more successful and a breach was made. The first attempt to penetrate by means of gangways failed, but eventually the breach was enlarged and the city was entered. Alexander gained possession of the walls, but the Tyrians made a last desperate stand within the city. This was overcome by Alexander and his hypaspists and the defenders were massacred. A few pilgrims and visitors from Carthage were spared, but women and children were enslaved.

The Battle of Gaugamela (331 BC)

While Alexander was still besieging Tyre, Darius sent him envoys offering all territory west of the Euphrates, with the sum of 10,000 talents and the hand

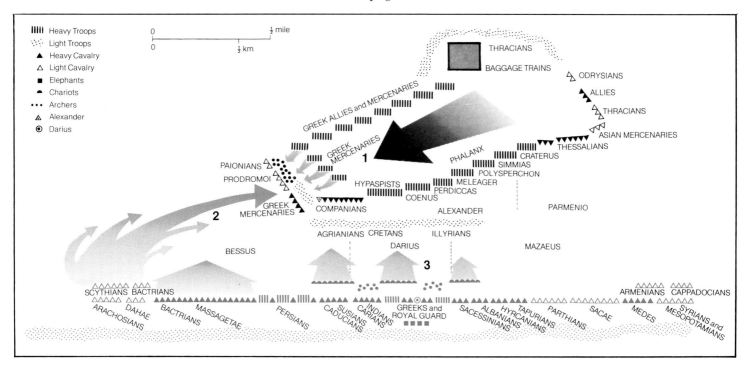

Battle of Gaugamela 331 BC

Alexander	Darius
Infantry	
Phalanx 12000	Royal Guard 2000
Hypaspists 3000	Greek mercen-
Greek mercen-	aries 2000
Greek allies 7000	
Greek mercenaries 8/9000	
Light Troops	
Thrace 6000	Mardi 2000
Illyricum 1000	General levy
Agriania 1000	of peasants
Crete 1000	c50000
Cavalry	
Companions 2100	Persis 1000
Thessaly 2100	Royal Guard 1000
Greek allies 750	India 1000
Prodromoi 600	Caria 1000
Paeonia 300	Susiana 1000
Thrace 500	Cadusii 1000
Asia 300	Sacessinia 1000
(mercenary archers)	Media 2000
Greek mercen-	Albania 1000
aries 400	Hyrcania 1000
	Tapuritae 1000
	Dahae 1000
	Arachosia 2000
	Massagetae 2000
	Bactria (heavy) 6000
	Bactria (light) 1000
	Cappadocia 1000
	Armenia 2000
	Syria 1000
	Parthia 2000
	Mesopotamia 1000
	Scythia 4000
	Scythed chariots 200
	Elephants 15

1 Darius clears a battlefield for his cavalry. Alexander takes up oblique formation (left refused)

and edges diagonally right off cleared area. Bessus tries to outflank this movement.
2 Skirmishing: Macedonian right is pushed back by heavy cavalry, Ariston's men shore up the line.
3 Chariot charge is disrupted by light troops. Some pass through phalanx but are destroyed by the army grooms behind the line.

4 Companions charge weak spot created by Bessus stretching his line leftwards; the phalanx charges frontally and the centre crumbles. Bessus makes no headway.
5 Mazaeus launches all his cavalry against Parmenio.
6 Two units of the phalanx become detached and some Persians ride through gap to

attack the baggage trains. In turn they are attacked by Macedonian reserves.
7 To help Parmenio Alexander wheels left to roll up Mazaeus' flank. Fierce fighting against Parthians and Hyrcanians; 60 Companions killed; many wounded. Aided by Thessalians Alexander triumphs.

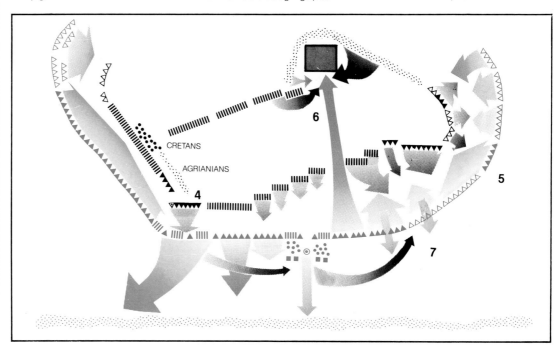

Alexander, in a drunken dispute, kills his trusted officer Clitus

Alexander marries Roxana, a Sogdian noblewoman

Alexander begins the invasion of India

Companion Cavalryman

This illustration depicts a member of Alexander's Companion cavalry as he might have appeared in battle. It was under the generalship of Philip and Alexander that the horseman really assumed a significant place in combat, rather than being used as a skirmisher or mounted archer as he had been in the 5th century BC. Alexander himself led one squadron (*ile*) of the Companion cavalry (*hetairoi*)

Cavalry Formations

and a study of his tactics at once highlights the importance of Macedonian cavalry as shock assault troops. They seem to have been fairly heavily armed and to have been used to drive home a concentrated punch; their disciplined manoeuvring at speed adding to their formidable power. In addition, Alexander also used contingents of light cavalry, known as *prodromoi*, who may have been armed with longer spears.

The main figure is shown in a Boeotian helmet, a very popular cavalry type as it afforded excellent all-round vision. He wears a bronze corslet with *pteruges*, strap-on greaves (which were optional), open-toed sandals and carries a straight sword, although the curved *kopis* was also popular. The black and white drawing illustrates a Companion in march order. He is laden with kit, lacks greaves and wears a Thracian helmet. As is evident, neither stirrups nor saddles were used at this time.

Cavalry Formations

The diagrams above show the types of formation the cavalry used. The Greeks favoured a square, 16 wide and 8 deep. (Frontage c4ft, 1·2m per man; depth c11ft, 3·35m per man). Light cavalry adopted more open order. Scythians favoured a wedge which was taken up by the Thracians and Macedonians. The Thessalian rhomboid cavalry formation lent itself to sudden changes of direction. In Alexander's army, *ilai* of 200 men were at one time organised so that 4 *ilai* constituted a *hipparchia*.

Alexander crosses the Indus

Alexander defeats and captures the Indian king Porus on the Hydaspes river (Jhelum)

Alexander's men refuse to march eastward beyond the Hyphasis river

Alexander has boats built and transports his army down the Indus

of his daughter in marriage, in exchange for the restoration of his family and the conclusion of a treaty of friendship and alliance. Alexander rejected the offer on the grounds that the possessions offered were already within his grasp and that he would marry Darius' daughter, if he chose, with or without Darius' consent.

Like Tyre, the Phoenician city of Gaza resisted Alexander. It was built on a lofty eminence which seemed to defy siege, but to Alexander obstacles were merely opportunities for demonstrating his invincibility. He was wounded at Gaza, but captured the city, leaving no male adult survivors and enslaving the women and children.

After such a demonstration, the Persian satrap in Egypt thought it prudent not to resist. The Egyptian population, which had only recently been re-subdued by Persia, regarded Alexander as a liberator. He was acknowledged as Pharaoh, founded a city on the Greek pattern at Alexandria and marched his army across the inhospitable desert to Siwa, where the oracle of Ammon (Zeus to the Greeks) was interpreted as declaring him to be the god's own son.

In 331 BC, Alexander led his forces back eastward. The coastline had now been secured and his programme of eastern conquest began in all seriousness. He marched up through Syria, crossed both the Euphrates and the Tigris and confronted Darius on the other side of Mesopotamia, in the plain of Gaugamela, near the town of Arbela. This was the scene of his final and decisive battle against Darius.

The Persian king had assembled a host which for its size and picturesque variety was reminiscent of that which Xerxes had led into Greece a century and a half earlier. It contained scythed chariots, elephants, camels and contingents of many nationalities, including Indians, Scythians and Bactrians, with the traditional Persian regiments of "apple-bearers", so called from the globular gold and silver pommels on their spear butts. Darius' now depleted ranks of Greek mercenaries, however, required reinforcement by Asiatic infantry and tribal levies.

As usual, Alexander prepared for the battle with painstaking intelligence and reconnaissance work. From the interrogation of prisoners, he ascertained Darius' entire order of battle. He also led in person a cavalry reconnaissance of the ground on which he meant to fight. It was necessary to make sure that there were no cavalry-traps in the form of pits or spikes. Darius had, in fact, caused the ground to be levelled in preparation for the use of his scythed chariots.

As at Issus, Darius would willingly have left the initiative to Alexander, but in the circumstances this became inexpedient. Alexander led his right-wing cavalry still farther to the right and the more numerous and extensive Persian line moved correspondingly in the same direction, so that it might continue to outreach him on the flank. Had this drift persisted, both armies would have slid away from the ground which had been levelled for the chariots. Darius therefore ordered his left-wing cavalry to attack. The fighting at this point was at first indecisive, but eventually Alexander prevailed. As for the scythed chariots, they proved a fiasco, as they had done nearly 70 years previously at Cunaxa. The Macedonians opened their ranks and allowed them to pass through, while the light troops bombarded them with missiles, grasped the reins of the horses and dragged down the drivers.

Meanwhile, as Alexander drove the routed Persian left wing before him, the central phalanx found itself unable to follow, especially as the left wing under Parmenio was recoiling before the Persian right. Alexander had foreseen this situation and had posted flanking guards to the phalanx, but as gaps appeared between the main divisions of the army, Persian and Indian troops broke through and attacked the Macedonian baggage train, rescuing Persian prisoners and mowing down the guards. Eventually, the rear formation of the phalanx, which had been placed in reserve, saved the situation and drove the enemy from the baggage.

At this stage, Alexander, summoned by an appeal for help from Parmenio, abandoned his pursuit of the enemy and rode with his Companions across the battlefield to save the left wing of his army. The course of events was complicated when he collided with enemy cavalry in flight from the centre; this delayed the help which he was able to bring to Parmenio. However, Parmenio's Thessalian cavalry had managed to hold out and the Persians were already beginning to retreat in this sector of the field. Alexander was thus enabled to renew his pursuit of Darius, who had fled when the Persian left wing crumbled. As at Issus, the Great King's example was followed by his entire army. If a more resolute leader had been in command of the Persian forces, either at Issus or Gaugamela, the results might have been very different.

Above: *This coin was probably struck to commemorate Alexander's victory over Porus at the Battle of the Hydaspes. Such objects help us to build up a picture of troop types.*

Farther East

Alexander now took possession of the great capitals of the Persian Empire—Babylon, Susa, Persepolis and Ecbatana—with all their accumulated treasure. Darius became a refugee in the wilder northern provinces, where he was eventually murdered by one of his officers. Alexander was then free to assume the title of King of Persia and, when he captured Darius' murderer, handed him over to Persian justice for barbarous execution.

The subjugation of the central territories of the Persian Empire was not difficult, but conquest of the eastern provinces involved three years of arduous mountain warfare in the areas now comprised by Khorasan, Russian Turkestan and Afghanistan. But Alexander's experience qualified him for all types of warfare, and his marriage to Roxana, daughter of a Bactrian tribal chief, perhaps did something to conciliate what was otherwise a hostile population.

During the years which followed Gaugamela, Alexander's problems became increasingly political rather than military. With the assumption of despotic power, his character revealed itself as despotic and tyrannical. He killed Clitus—the officer who had saved his life at Granicus—in a drunken rage. Philotas, the son of Parmenio, once Alexander's trusted commander of the Companions, was accused of treason and executed. Fear of reprisal then led Alexander to procure the murder of Parmenio.

Alexander realized that he could not hold the Persian empire without con-

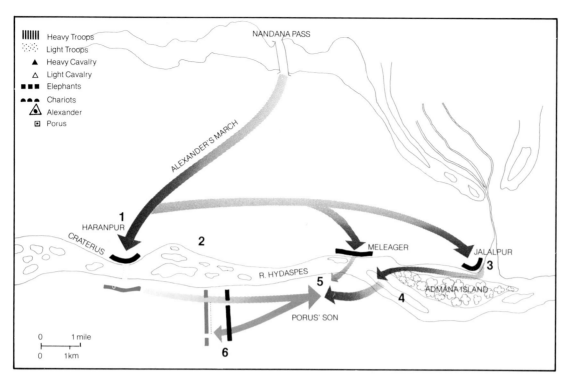

Heavy Troops
Light Troops
▲ **Heavy Cavalry**
△ **Light Cavalry**
■■■ **Elephants**
▲▲▲ **Chariots**
⬭ **Alexander**
⬜ **Porus**

NANDANA PASS

ALEXANDER'S MARCH

1
HARANPUR
CRATERUS
2
R. HYDASPES
MELEAGER
JALALPUR
3
5
ADMANA ISLAND
4
PORUS' SON
6

0   1 mile
0   1km

Battle of the Hydaspes 326 BC

Alexander	Porus
Infantry	
Phalanx 14000	30000
Hypaspists 3000	
Greek mercenaries 8/10000	
Light troops 6/7000	
Cavalry	
Companions 2100	Horse 4000
Bactria 500	Chariots 300
Sogdiana 500	Elephants 80/100
Scythia 500	
Dahae horse archers 1000	
Mercenaries 1000	
Arachosia 500	
Parapanisadae 500	
Indian allies 700	

1 Alexander reaches the Hydaspes river to find Porus blocking the ford. After many feints (**2**) he decides to cross behind Admana island (**3**). He moves by night during a storm leaving Craterus and a force (2000 cavalry, 9000 infantry) at the ford and dropping off Meleager with 1000 cavalry and 16000 infantry *en route*. He embarks with the remainder, accidentally lands on an island (**4**) and finally struggles ashore across the swollen river while boats bring up the phalanx. The

ciliating its inhabitants; he progressively adopted Persian manners and dress and required his officers to do the same. But by these conciliatory gestures to the Asiatics, he alienated the Macedonians and the Greeks, who grew indignant and rebellious. However, the prestige of a triumphant war-leader will carry any political ruler a long way. It carried Alexander on another march eastward into India. Perhaps he felt that a career of continued military conquest was essential to his political power. On the banks of the Hydaspes (Jhelum river), he defeated the Indian king Porus.

Elephants figure conspicuously in the accounts of Alexander's Indian warfare; in the battle of the Hydaspes, where they seriously disrupted the Macedonian phalanx, they presented Alexander's men with a new challenge. Although Darius had assembled elephants at Gaugamela, they had not played any conspicuous part in the fighting there. Apart from their novelty, the Indian elephants did not constitute a very serious menace. The animals' drivers were vulnerable to missiles and, deprived of their drivers, frightened and uncontrolled, elephants were as dangerous to their own side as to the enemy, trampling underfoot whatever stood in their way. At the same time, their fighting value cannot have been negligible, since they were widely adopted by both Greek and Macedonian armies during the succeeding century. After the battle of the Hydaspes, Alexander captured a

Indian Enemies

These drawings show the troops that Alexander defeated at the Hydaspes. The war elephant is ridden by a mahout and rajah armed with bamboo javelins. The elephant's tusks are reinforced with brass. The 6ft (1·8m) bamboo longbow was the primary Indian weapon; it fired a long (3ft, 1m) arrow. The long broadsword (44", 112cm) had an extremely wide blade and could be used one-or two-handed. The shield was made of hide.

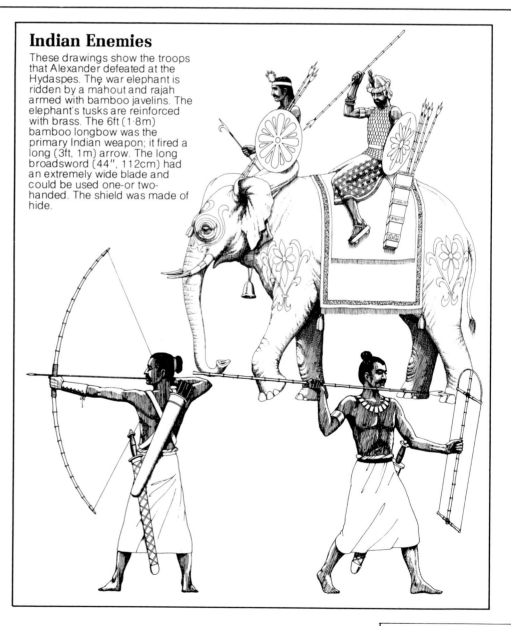

Alexander and his army reach Susa

Officials guilty of corruption during his absence, are punished

Macedonians, offended by Alexander's orientalising policies, mutiny at Opis

Alexander receives ambassadors from Carthage, Spain, Gaul and Italy

In Greece, Demosthenes is forced into exile

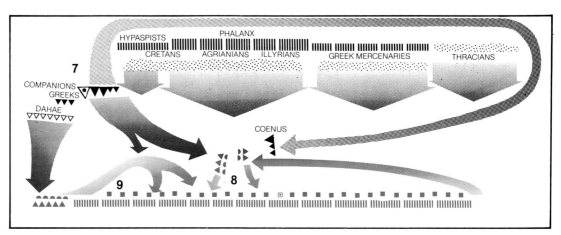

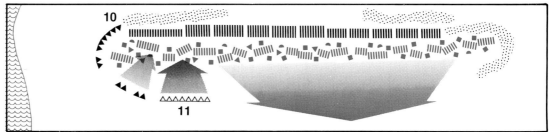

cavalry, with a screen of mounted archers, moves off (**5**) while Porus sends his son to intercept them. Alexander realises that Porus is not following and his cavalry overwhelms the Indians whose chariots are stuck in the mud. Porus' son is killed here. Porus moves his army to confront Alexander whose cavalry manoeuvres in front of his infantry (**6**) giving them time to form up. Porus' infantry is screened by elephants. Alexander's cavalry moves to the right (**7**) while Coenus makes a circling move to the left. When the Macedonian horse hits the Indian left, Porus switches his right wing horse in support. Coenus chases them; Alexander charges and they take refuge among the elephants (**8**). Greek light troops harry them (**9**) and the remaining Indian cavalry is pushed back by Alexander when trying to wheel on the light troops (**10**). Reunited, Alexander's cavalry attacks the infantry as the phalanx moves in. The elephants run amok, the cavalry is crushed and surrounded by Craterus' force (**11**). Porus is defeated (his losses are catastrophic).

Alexander's Return

Having traversed the Punjab, Alexander wished to march across the desert to the Ganges. But here his army rebelled; even the magnetism of his personality could not persuade them to follow him further. He had intended to reach the Ocean which, according to Greek geographical theory, embraced the circumference of the world's land mass. This, he hoped, would enable him to open a sea route to India; with a sea voyage in view, he had brought Greek shipwrights with him on his long march. He now consoled himself with the prospect of a return journey by sea. Building a fleet, he sailed for hundreds of miles down the Indus to its mouth. Long before this was reached, his officer Craterus with the main body of the army, which had marched alongside the ships on the river, was sent back towards Persia by an inland route. Nearchus, Alexander's admiral, commanded the fleet on its hazardous voyage along the coasts of the Indian Ocean and the Persian Gulf. Alexander himself marched meanwhile with his army on land across the Gedrosian desert, with the intention of creating bases and assembling provisions for the fleet. In this march, the army suffered horribly from every kind of

privation and hardship and many died in the wilderness. Alexander rejoined his fleet on the Carmanian coast (near Hormuz), but gave orders to Nearchus to continue the voyage as far as the mouth of the Tigris, at the head of the Persian Gulf.

On his return to Persia, Alexander dealt severely with cases of corruption and conspiracy that had occurred during his absence. Subsequently, he gave time to public works and the suppression of brigandage. He then began preparing a new voyage of discovery, planning to bring a fleet down the Euphrates and sail round Arabia as a preliminary to conquest of that territory. His attempts to fuse his Macedonian followers with the Persian population continued apace. Already, before setting out for the eastward frontiers of empire, he had done much to secure military fusion, training Persians in Macedonian methods of fighting. There were now units of Persian Companions and Persian "Silver-shields". This policy remained a source of grievance with the Macedonians; at Opis, near the mouth of the Tigris, Alexander's veterans, fearing to be made redundant, came near to mutiny. However, he succeeded in reassuring them and emotional scenes of reconciliation followed.

Apart from his Arabian designs, Alexander had apparently not forgotten his plan to navigate the Ocean. By this route, he hoped that he might sail round the inhabited world, as it was then conceived, conquer the territories

dominated by Carthage and curb the growing power of Rome. It is not beyond possibility that if he had lived he would, in pursuit of this aim, have taken a fleet round Africa. As it was, the western nations felt that he was a political and military force which they could no longer afford to ignore. Near Babylon in 324 BC Alexander was approached by conciliatory envoys from Libya, Carthage, Spain and Gaul: representatives of remote peoples, whose very names were in some instances unknown to the Macedonians.

Alexander's death, after a short, sudden illness, at Babylon, his chosen capital, in 323 BC, took the whole world by surprise. In addition to Roxana, he had married Statira, Darius' daughter; and Barsinè, Memnon's widow, had been his cherished mistress. Arrian, on the authority of Aristobulus, mentions also another Persian wife*. The Macedonians, unlike the Greeks, do not seem always to have observed a monogamous tradition. Roxana bore Alexander a posthumous son, but the prospects of infants and children in such circumstances were negligible. Alexander had never nominated, let alone prepared, anyone to inherit his authority. Had he lived, however, he would predictably have been an absentee emperor and his regents would no doubt have fought each other as his successors did.

---

*There is some confusion in ancient accounts as to the number of Alexander's wives and mistresses.

Alexander's Successors and the Later Greek World

After Alexander's death, his empire was riven by wars of succession, while the city-states of Greece once more struggled for independence. The machinery of war now included heavier and faster warships—like the galleys on which the rising power of Carthage depended.

Ancient Authorities

In addition to his account of Alexander's exploits, Arrian also wrote a book about events after Alexander's death. Unfortunately, this work has survived only in fragments; thus our chief ancient authority for the period remains Diodorus Siculus, who flourished in the second half of the first century BC. He wrote what he called a "Library" (*Bibliothekè*) of history, which aimed at being a complete World History down to the wars of Julius Caesar. Diodorus makes use of various sources, some of which enjoyed a good reputation in antiquity. Others did not. For the epoch of Alexander's immediate successors, he relied extensively on the Athenian historian Diyllus, who had continued the record of events as far as the year 297 BC. Diodorus also owes much to Hieronymus of Cardia, whose military and official career well qualified him as the historian of the half century which followed Alexander's death. By contrast, Duris of Samos was

a sensational writer with no very firm commitment to truth. Regrettably, Diodorus is not at pains to distinguish the value of his respective sources. This task is left to his readers.

Diodorus, himself remembered as a Sicilian, is at his best on the subject of Sicilian history. In this area, his authority is often Timaeus (352-256 BC), another Sicilian Greek, who was contemporary with many of the events which he described. A contemporary writer is naturally well placed to observe his material, but to the extent that he is personally involved in it, he is bound to have formed prejudices; Timaeus, although his testimony in general commanded respect among the ancients, was not always unbiased.

Fortunately, we are also helped by Plutarch's *Lives*. Plutarch himself, at the beginning of his *Life* of Alexander, takes trouble to stress that he is a biographer rather than an historian and that he does not undertake to supply the comprehensive information expected of an historian. Many of Plutarch's *Lives* are those of influential

Greek soldiers and statesmen who flourished during or close to the period with which we are now concerned; they contribute in an important way to our knowledge of an epoch which is not on the whole well documented. Moreover, the Greek world had moved into an historical phase in which events centred more than ever on the activities of dominant individuals. The connection between history and biography is to that extent closer.

To the foregoing sources we may add such knowledge as can be gained from Justin (Marcus Junianus Justinus) who wrote probably in the third century AD. In a Latin "epitome", Justin summarized the universal history of Pompeius Trogus, whose Latin work, composed at the beginning of the Christian era, relied on Greek sources that had been composed at an earlier date.

Below: *During the 22 years between the death of Alexander and the Battle of Ipsus, the empires of the successors changed vastly. This map shows one of the distributions of territory.*

BC

323/2
Philip Arrhidaeus is nominal successor to Alexander's Empire

Alexander's posthumous son by Roxana shares Philip's title

Perdiccas, Alexander's officer, is regent of the Asiatic empire

Antipater and Craterus are joint regents of Western territories

For the present work, concerned as it is with military action and methods of warfare, we must be grateful that various ancient text books on military science and technology have survived. These include the work of Aeneas Tacticus (late fourth century BC) and Philon of Byzantium, who probably wrote at the end of the third century BC. Also important is the engineer Athenaeus, whose tract on mechanical devices may be assigned to the first century BC and, without attempting a bibliography, Biton's booklet on siege engines should be noticed. It was written perhaps in the third century BC (an exact date is not known).

The Political Situation after Alexander's Death

After Alexander's death, the disputed succession led to a long series of wars in which his senior officers were the contenders. Of these, Perdiccas, Craterus and Eumenes were soon killed. Antipater and his successors remained in possession of Macedonia and Greece, Lysimachus of Thrace, Antigonus of Phrygia and much of Asia Minor, Ptolemy of Egypt and Seleucus of the eastern territories as far as India. In 319 BC, Antipater died and left power in the hands of one of his officers, disregarding the claims of his son Cassander. Before long, Cassander asserted himself. But Macedon, weakened by internal division, now played a less important role and Antigonus, with his geographically

central position in the empire, was the only ruler who dared aspire to the whole of it. His ambition soon led to combinations against him and he and his son Demetrius were finally defeated at Ipsus in 301 BC, Antigonus himself being killed in the battle. Ipsus was the only battle among many in that period which can in any way be considered as decisive, for it established that there could never be any single successor to Alexander's power and that political partition was the destiny of the vast territory which he had conquered. This did not, of course, put an end to warfare among the rulers of the separated areas. On the contrary, their relationship was depressingly reminiscent of that which had existed among the Greek states during the preceding century and a half. No single power was capable of dominating the others; and yet, without a dominant central authority, nothing could be expected but a pattern of eternally shifting hostilities and alliances, with their inevitable concomitant of bloodshed, destruction and wasted resources.

To some extent, the flagging cause of Greek freedom benefited while Alexander's successors fought each other in remote eastern theatres of war, although the freedom of the Greek states amounted, as always, mainly to a freedom to quarrel among themselves. As soon as the news of Alexander's death had reached Greece, Athens revolted and in alliance with the Thessalians and Aetolians succeeded in blockading Antipater in the Thessalian town of Lamia. However, he held out until, facilitated by Athenian reverses at sea, Macedonian reinforcements reached him, and then defeated his Greek enemies at Crannon. Demosthenes, as ever the inspiration of anti-Macedonian sentiment at Athens, was forced to flee to the island of Calauria (now Poros). He was sentenced to

death at the instance of his Athenian enemies and Antipater's men provided the execution squad. They pursued him to Calauria, but Demosthenes killed himself by taking poison before the sentence could be carried out.

Sparta was one of the few cities in mainland Greece which had not fallen directly under the domination of Philip or Alexander, but Alexander had detached from the Spartans the support of their traditional Peloponnesian allies and reduced them to impotence. When Sparta, subsidized by Persian funds, had attempted to assert its power, Antipater had completely crushed the Spartan army at Megalopolis in 331 BC.

Warfare among the Greeks was now carried on not so much by cities as by leagues. Epaminondas, in the early part of the fourth century, had attempted to unite the Arcadian cities at Sparta's expense, on the model of the ancient Boeotian League. Philip, Alexander and Antipater had exercised authority as leaders of the Greek League which had been formed at Corinth after Chaeronea. The most powerful league

Below: *A portrait bust thought to represent Lysimachus who ruled Thrace after Alexander's death. He fought with other "successors" and died in battle against Seleucus in 281 BC.*

Battle of Ipsus 301 BC

Commanders:
Antigonus (Monophthalmos)
Seleucus Nicator supported by separatist rulers, Ptolemy, Cassander and Lysimachus.
Numbers:
Antigonus: 70000 foot, 10000 horse, 75 elephants.
Seleucus: 64000 foot, 10500 horse, 400 elephants, 120 chariots.

1. Demetrius, Antigonus' son, commanding cavalry routs and pursues Antiochus, Seleucus' son.
2. Seleucus' elephants prevent return of Demetrius.
3. Antigonus without cavalry support is threatened.
4. Seleucus delays his attack by feints and manoeuvres.
5. Seleucus' psychological warfare is successful. He attracts deserters from Antigonus.
6. Other Antagonid troops are demoralized and disperse.
7. Seleucus launches attack on Antigonus' main position.
8. Antigonus dies fighting.
9. Demetrius with 5000 foot and 4000 horse escapes via Ephesus to Greece (according to Plutarch).

Greeks, in revolt, besiege Antipater in Lamia | Antipater defeats Greeks at Crannon | About this time, Chandragupta Maurya dominates northern India | The death of Aristotle | BC

87

to emerge during the third century was the Achaean League, which soon included other than Achaean states and inevitably came into collision with the military power of Sparta.

In 244 BC, Agis IV came to the throne in Sparta. Seeking a remedy for Sparta's decline, he tried to restore the traditional system of government and discipline and to incorporate many non-citizens into the exclusive and dwindling citizen body. Agis was seized and put to death by order of the ephors. A few years later, Cleomenes III abolished the ephorate and made himself absolute ruler, but he was defeated in battle and driven out by a combination of the Achaean League and the Macedonian power. Another absolute ruler of Sparta, more ruthless than Cleomenes, arose in the person of the usurper Nabis. Like Cleomenes, he was opposed by the Achaean League, which now invoked Rome as an ally, in place of Macedon. Nabis was finally defeated in 193 BC and assassinated in the following year.

The Naval Power of Rhodes

One Greek constitutional state which continued to prosper and grow strong in a world of warlords was Rhodes. Like the political leagues of the Greek mainland, the Rhodian federal government enjoyed an advantage over more narrowly conceived city states. The Dorian Greek settlers of the island had originally founded three main cities: Ialysus, Lindus and Camirus. Despite its Dorian population, the island had, throughout most of the Peloponnesian War, been a member of the Athenian League. Only in 411 BC, when Athenian power was in decline and Lysander had, with Persian financial support, made Sparta a naval force in the eastern Mediterranean, did Rhodes renounce her Athenian allegiance. About this time, the cities of the island formed a federation, with a newly-founded capital city and a central government. Each member city, however, preserved a large measure of local autonomy.

Rhodes had grown rich by carrying corn and other cargoes in its ships; Alexander's destruction of Phoenician Tyre rid the island state of a dangerous trade competitor. At the same time, the Macedonian mastery of the entire Persian empire and the consequent abolition of political frontiers in the eastern Mediterranean threw open new coasts and harbours to Rhodian vessels. In the time of Alexander's Successors, Rhodes managed to hold a balance of power and ingeniously preserved its independence. The Rhodians flattered and conciliated the contending dynasts around them, refusing to enter into any alliance with one against another. This in itself would not have been enough to secure the island's liberty if Rhodes had not possessed a strong navy of its own. Such a navy, however, the Rhodians were wise and bold enough to maintain. In their moderate form of democracy, the rowing crews of the ships were recruited from the poorer classes, while the officers were drawn from wealthier families. They did not need to rely upon mercenaries, either to serve in or command their navy.

Rhodes was, in fact, the successor of Athens as the leading Greek naval power. As at Athens, such power was dependent largely upon civic patriotism. But as a comparatively small island, Rhodes enjoyed some advantages which the Athenians had not possessed. The Rhodians could rely entirely upon their navy for defence. Immune to land invasion, they were not obliged to organize an army or build Long Walls to secure communications with their docks and shipyards. Indeed, the famous Rhodian slingers served for the most part as mercenaries in foreign armies and may best be considered as a source of "invisible earnings". Moreover, the island's rocky coast lent itself admirably to fortification against sea-borne attack, as the Crusaders of a later age were not slow to realize.

Rhodes' naval supremacy in the eastern Mediterranean was also a bulwark against piracy. Unfortunately, any power strong enough to subdue pirates in the ancient world usually felt at liberty to behave with piratical lawlessness itself; such protection as it offered became a "protection racket". Rhodes, however, was an exception in this respect and, deeply committed to constitutional principles, evolved a code of maritime law which the Romans later imitated and embodied in their own laws. Indeed, modern law, based upon the Roman, may indirectly owe something to Rhodes.

The Rhodian foreign policy, bent on preserving a balance of power, could not at all times be sustained. Forced at last to take sides either with Ptolemy or Antigonus, the Rhodians considered that their best prospects lay in alliance with the former. Rhodes was accordingly blockaded and stormed by Antigonus' celebrated son, Demetrius the Besieger (*Poliorcetes*). This ordeal, however, the island triumphantly survived, re-emerging with enhanced power and prestige.

Siegecraft

Any further allusion to the siege of Rhodes is perhaps best prefaced by some general remarks on the evolution of Greek and Macedonian siegecraft in general. Even before the Peloponnesian War, Pericles had used battering rams against the island of Samos, when it revolted from the Athenian League in 441 BC, and we have already referred to the siege of Plataea (429-427 BC), in which the Spartans and their allies used rams in conjunction with an earthen ramp, flaming arrows, fire faggots and elaborate walls of circumvallation. In the fifth century, the advantage lay with the besieged and the prospect of taking a town by assault presented enormous difficulties. The Athenian Long Walls were never stormed and the Athenians themselves

Right: *In the 4th century BC there was a general tendency to lighten the armour of heavy infantry and to render them more mobile. Greaves, however, persisted; those shown in this illustration derive from Dherveni near Salonika.*

Perdiccas killed by mutinous troops

Seleucus (Nicator) becomes satrap of Babylonia

Demosthenes threatened with arrest by Antipater's men, commits suicide

In Italy, a Roman army, trapped in a mountain pass (the 'Caudine Forks') surrenders to Samnites

Craterus killed in battle against Eumenes, former chief of Alexander's Secretariat

Later Greek Helmets

Throughout the 5th and 4th centuries BC the Greek helmet continued to evolve, still with a view to improving ventilation, hearing and vision without sacrificing protection. The "Chalcidian" helmet (**6**) continued to be very popular in its original form but improved versions (**3**) with a cranial ridge for better protection and hinged cheek-pieces for better ventilation appeared. The nasal piece also became smaller and disappeared entirely from some helmets, giving rise to the "Attic" style of helmet in which the only vestige of the nasal piece was an inverted V over the brow. This type was extremely popular in Italy, where it survived until the 2nd century AD or later. The example shown (**7**) is Italian and combines a Greek-style crest with typical Italian cheek-pieces. Others bore the "Chalcidian" style cheek-pieces. From the 4th century onwards these became more elaborate and **4** shows a highly decorated Attic helmet in the form of a lion's head. This helmet is borne by Alexander the Great on the so-called Alexander Sarcophagus. Others, such as that of Alexander's cousin, Pyrrhus of Epirus, had cheek-pieces in the form of rams' heads. Such helmets show the armourer's decorative talent at its height. One of the most popular forms between the 5th century and Macedonian times was the "Thracian" type. Its name does not signify that it derived from Thrace but rather that it resembled the Thracian bonnet (as worn by the peltast on p51). It is characterised by its backward sweeping bowl, usually swept forward again at the peak, and its very long cheek-pieces resembling the lappets of the bonnet. Numbers **2**, **5** and **8** are all examples of this style, **8** being the earliest form. The long cheek-pieces offer excellent protection for the neck and throat. The cranial ridge also added strength, while the peak protected the forehead and shaded the wearer's eyes. **2** is similar but shows the new style of falling crest which began to replace the classic upright crest in the late 5th century BC, possibly under Italian influence. **5** shows a typical Thracian helmet but with highly decorated cheek-pieces in the form of a beard. Naturally the various helmet styles influenced one another, and **1** illustrates a "Thraco-Attic" type which has features of both genres. The practice of painting helmets flourished and, judging by surviving paintings, may even have gained in popularity. **7**, for example, has a black bottom half and red top while others were decorated with red, black and white hoops (as evidenced by Macedonian tomb paintings). More expensive helmets were ornamented with black enamel inlay called niello. This was an amalgam of sulphur and (for instance) copper with which the engraved lines were filled.

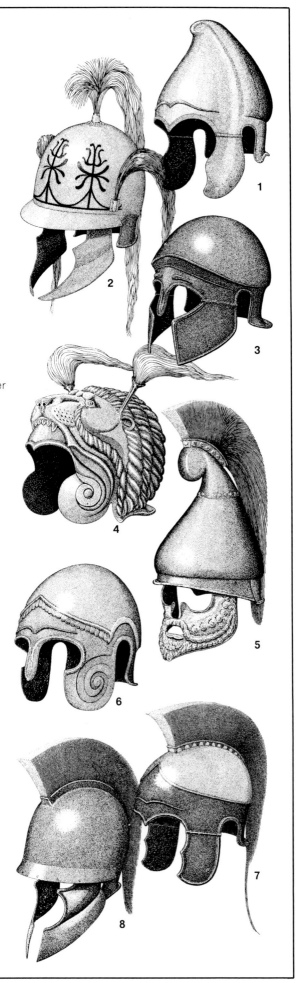

succeeded in taking Potidaea only after a long blockade. These circumstances are explained largely by the Greek weakness in archers and slingers and their general neglect of missile warfare. In default of covering fire, all siege operations were exposed to counter-attack from the besieged walls, as happened at Plataea, where the heads of the battering rams were broken off by heavy beams dropped from the fortified walls above.

With the introduction of missile warfare, the situation was crucially altered. The greater use of hand missiles was soon followed by the employment of artillery engines, depending for their projectile power on cables of twisted sinew. The introduction of the arrow-firing catapult was attributed to Dionysius I of Syracuse. This machine was a giant crossbow mounted on a heavy wooden frame, launching a correspondingly heavy-headed dart. Philip II of Macedon used such machines when he besieged Perinthus in 340 BC. But the first use of catapults to hurl rocks probably came rather later. Alexander certainly had such catapults at the siege of Tyre.

Artillery of this kind could, of course, be employed by the besieged as well as the besiegers. In fact, its use operated to the advantage of those within the walls, since their fortifications were of a more solid and permanent nature and could be built with narrow ports, embrasures and battlements, behind which the artillerymen could operate under cover. Besieging armies countered this advantage by constructing elaborate towers and penthouses, with ports for artillery which matched those of the defenders. Such structures also sheltered battering rams. The obvious way of operating a battering ram was to suspend it from an overhead beam and swing its head against the target. It could also be mounted on wheels and thrust violently against the wall under attack by a large and muscular crew. More sophisticated types were developed, in which the shaft of the ram slid in a wooden channel; it was then repeatedly winched back, as if in a catapult, and projected against the wall.

Penthouses, often on wheels, could also be used to screen the operations of miners and sappers or those who wished to fill in the fosse before an enemy rampart. Covered by artillery and missile support, assault with scaling ladders became increasingly effective. Ladders were not always of wood; a kind of leather and cord network ladder was also in use.

The defenders, for their part, sometimes hung on their battlements wooden placards which could be shifted in such a way as to dislodge any scaling ladders placed against them. These protective placards must, of course, in turn have been exposed to the assailants' fire darts. As is the way of military technology, the series of devices and counter-devices was capable of endless prolongation, inevitably involving both attackers and defenders in enormous expense. A simpler and cheaper method of capturing a city was by means of treachery, and by treachery cities were often captured. This method, with all the precautions and counter-measures which we class under the heading of "security", was allotted scientific consideration in the treatise of Aeneas Tacticus (late fourth century BC).

The Siege of Rhodes

Demetrius brought to the siege of Rhodes a vast armament of men and ships. Apart from his own fighting fleet of 200 vessels and his auxiliary fleet of more than 150, he had enlisted the aid of pirate squadrons. One thousand private trading craft also followed him, attracted by the wealth of Rhodes and the prospect of spoil. The whole operation was, in fact, a gigantic piratical enterprise. But Demetrius seems to have felt that it was "a glorious thing to be a pirate king".

The Helepolis at Rhodes

Height: 130-140ft (40-43m)
Base: 72ft (22m) square
Armament: Lowest floor: 2x180 lber (82kg) catapults; 1x60 lber (27kg) catapult
1st floor:
3x60 lber (27kg) catapults
Next five floors:
2x30 lber (14kg) catapults
Top two floors: 2x dart-throwers.
Construction: main beams are fir or pine, wheels and horizontals are oak. All major joints are reinforced with iron plates. To protect the machine from fire-missiles, its exterior is clad with iron plates on 3 sides.
Propulsion: the machine is mounted on eight wheels each 15ft (4·6m) in diameter. It is propelled by a capstan and belt drive, with a suitable mechanical advantage, (manned by roughly 200 men). Additional thrust could be provided from the rear.
Weight: Probably around 150 tons.
Siege towers had existed since Assyrian times. That illustrated is the famous *helepolis* built by Epimachus of Athens for Demetrius "Poliorcetes" (the Besieger) in 304 BC. This was the largest siege-tower of ancient times and descriptions of it survive in the accounts of Vitruvius, Diodorus, Plutarch and the so-called Athenaeus Mechanicus. Most siege towers were smaller than this gigantic structure and were hide and wool or hide and seaweed covered. Many had drawbridges, but this one apparently did not. In action it was brought up within missile range of the walls, supplying suppressing fire against the defenders. The large stone-thrower could even destroy ramparts and curtain-walls. Once this had been accomplished attackers could bring up battering rams and drills, or undermine the walls. Alternatively an assault could be mounted with ladders, drawbridges *sambuca* etc.

The main harbour at Rhodes, as well as the city, was fortified with towers and walls. Here the Rhodian fleet could safely rest; nor was Demetrius able to prevent ships with supplies from running his blockade. His first concern, therefore, was to capture the harbour. He at once proceeded to build his own harbour alongside, constructing a mole and protecting his seaborne siege operations from counter-attack by means of a floating spiked boom. At the same time, his army ravaged the island and built a huge camp on land adjacent to the city but out of missile range.

In the course of the siege, both sides employed the technical devices we have just described. Mining operations by the besiegers were met by the counter-mines of the besieged. At a fairly early stage, Demetrius' men secured a footing on the mole of the main harbour, but the Rhodians prevented him from exploiting this bridgehead and he never captured the harbour. Later, as the result of a land attack, he actually penetrated the walls of the city, but the attack was contained by the Rhodians and those who had entered were mostly killed.

The most sensational feature of the siege was Demetrius' mammoth tower, which was nicknamed the *helepolis*, "city-taker", although in the event it failed to take the city. The *helepolis*

tower was based on a huge square grille of timberwork, covering an area of 5,200 square feet (484 sq m). The tower was about 140 feet (90 cubits, 43m) high and the uppermost of its nine storeys was 900 square feet (84 sq m) in area. As a protection against fire, the tower was armoured with iron plates on its three exposed sides; it was mounted on gigantic castors, the wheels of which were themselves plated with iron. The artillery ports of the *helepolis* were made to open and close by mechanical means and were padded with leather and wool as a protection against the shock of missile attack. Communication with the upper storeys was by means of two staircases, for ascent and descent respectively.

The machine was moved, presumably in relays, by 3,400 specially selected strong men. Some pushed from inside the structure, others behind. Diodorus assures us that the whole monstrous contraption could be rolled in any direction very smoothly. The *helepolis* was in effect a mammoth tank, far larger than any that have ever been driven by petrol engines. Despite every precaution, however, the Rhodians managed to dislodge some of the tower's iron plates; when there was a real danger of it being set on fire, Demetrius ordered it to be withdrawn from action.

The entire Greek and Macedonian world, constitutionalists and dynasts alike, sympathized with the Rhodians during the siege. The conflict was, after all, one between law and piracy. Influenced perhaps by the unpopularity of his operations and convinced at last that he could not win, Demetrius came to terms with the Rhodians and went away to look for a war somewhere else. The Rhodians, overjoyed, rewarded the sacrifice of citizens, slaves and resident aliens as they had promised.

Demetrius had left his engines strewn around the city and the scrap metal which they yielded provided material for the huge statue which the Rhodians erected at their harbour entrance: the Colossus of Rhodes, one of the Seven Wonders of the World. A prodigy itself, the Colossus was a fitting memorial to a prodigious siege.

Fortifications

Fortifications during the generations which followed Alexander the Great were required to meet the challenge of increasingly sophisticated siegecraft and of armies equipped with larger, more abundant and more powerful machinery. Great importance was attached to counter-attack and to the creation of vantage points from which the besieger could be threatened on his flank by missiles. With this in view, ramparts were sometimes built on a saw-tooth pattern. Either the wall itself followed a saw-tooth contour or a straight wall was given a saw-tooth facing on its outer surface. The advantage of this device was that one saw-tooth projection gave covering fire to the next. Fortifications at Samikon, in the western Peloponnese, exemplify the asymmetrical, slanted pattern of saw-tooth fortification and may be contrasted with the equilateral zig-zag which was adopted, for instance, at Miletus on the coast of Caria.

As a defence against the approach of siege towers, deep moats were often dug in front of the walls of a fortified position. Such moats had been dug in front of the Athenian city walls after the battle of Chaeronea and they were improved during the course of the succeeding century. On archaeological evidence, these moats appear to have reached a depth of 13 feet (4m) and a

Left: *The walls of Side on the coast of Pamphylia (southern Turkey). Its robust fortifications bear witness to an epoch that saw rapid developments in the art of siegecraft.*

Right: *Tomb painting of a soldier of the 3rd or 2nd century BC from western Asia Minor. Alexander's successors commanded troops so armed.*

width of 33 feet (10m). In some instances, moats were filled with water; when they surrounded cities, further protection was often given by a wall or palisade on the inner edge.

The construction of towers on the ramparts had long been a feature of Greek cities. These frequently projected in the manner of bastions and permitted a flanking attack on the besiegers. At the same time, the missile men who garrisoned them had the advantage of superior height and were in a position to oppose any siege towers. Such defensive towers tended to become increasingly numerous. They were also increasingly independent of the curtain walls which linked them. At Myndos, near Halicarnassus, Alexander's besieging force managed to destroy one defence tower, but its collapse did not affect the solidity of the wall. Conversely, during the siege of Rhodes, Demetrius' forces were able to destroy the curtain wall on each side of a tower without destroying the tower itself. Towers were square, polygonal, semi-circular or horse-shoe in plan. The number of artillery loopholes and embrasures introduced by the builders tended to increase. Curtains between towers must have been built higher to the extent that the towers themselves were. Archaeological evidence suggests that walls of about 29·5ft (9m) in height were normal during the fourth century; if attacks by a *helepolis* were expected, they were probably built higher. The height of a city's walls was sometimes increased by the defenders during the course of a siege. The summit of a wall normally provided a communicating alley between towers and also a fighting platform fronted by a crenellated parapet. Such parapets, like the towers, might support tiled roofs; in which case they featured windows.

Both at Tyre and Rhodes, the besieged walls were difficult to attack on account of the rocks which lay in front of them. Considerable use was made of sites fortified by nature, even where the most defensible points did not closely correspond with the area needing to be defended. For this reason, city walls frequently embraced an area considerably greater than the city itself. It followed that some of the most imposing fortifications were constructed in areas where nature gave little help, and much effort was needed to strengthen the position.

Mercenary Armies, Pay and Booty

The siege of Rhodes, if one disregards its political futility, offers an interesting case study, since it presents a mercenary army at war with a citizen garrison. A citizen army was at its best fighting in its own homeland, in defence of its own womenfolk, children and property. A mercenary army, on the other hand, had the greatest inducement when it was an invading army, free to plunder and live off enemy country. This situation is illustrated by a late third-century Cretan inscription which, in recording the terms of a treaty, specifies that a soldier's daily ration shall be one *choinix** of corn, except when he is quartered in enemy territory from which corn can be obtained. In the fifth century, citizen armies and navies serving away from home, whether provided with their rations in kind or in cash, expected no more than a subsistence allowance. Persian subsidies raised the daily ration allowance for trireme rowers from a half to a whole drachma, but there was difficulty in obtaining what had been promised.

---

*This measure varied locally. Its range was between approximately 1·5 pints (850 cc) and about a quart (rather more than a litre).

The drachma may be taken as containing 66·5 grains (4·3 gm) of silver; readers who are accustomed to inflation accounting may calculate what this means in terms of today's commodity values.

The main reward for mercenary service during the fourth and third centuries was booty, not pay. Ready coin was often inadequate to provide payment. Cleomenes III of Sparta was hurried into a disastrous engagement at Sellasia in 222 BC because he lacked cash for the retention of his mercenaries. It should be noticed that Cleomenes was conducting a defensive campaign on his own territory. In an offensive war such as he had waged earlier in Arcadia, booty had been available and mercenary remuneration could be based on results.

Prisoners might often change hands for cash ransoms. Before the siege of Rhodes, the Rhodians came to an agreement with Demetrius, according to which a freeman captured by either side should be exchanged for 1,000 drachmas and a slave for 500 drachmas. But most booty was in kind and captives were commonly sold as slaves. An invading army, as at Rhodes, was followed by a horde of expectant traders. Among these, slave-dealers constituted a numerous community; after a victory, captives could be sold on the spot.

Apart from the inevitable fickleness of a mercenary army, its appetite for booty significantly conditioned the course of such wars as it was employed to fight. Even with citizen armies, it was hard for any commander to retain control over his men once they had fallen to plundering; for this reason a battle won in one sector of the field was often lost in another. It was an outstanding tribute to Alexander's discipline at Gaugamela that he was able to withdraw his victorious Companions at the moment when the enemy was in flight and a rich spoil invited them, in order to help his hard-pressed left wing at that phase of the battle.

Except for a small nucleus of Macedonians who perhaps felt themselves to be united with their leaders by a tie of common nationality, the armies of Alexander's Successors depended mainly on mercenaries; this fact goes far to explaining why the wars which they fought were usually so inconclusive. A mercenary force possessed of the baggage train of a defeated army—let alone a town or territory which had sheltered the enemy—in its preoccupation with plunder would have little incentive to

Polysperchon's son, Alexander, defies Antigonus' and Cassander's troops in the Peloponnese

After Alexander's death in action, his widow, Ctesipolis, suppresses revolt in Sicyon

The Rhodians ally themselves with Antigonus

follow up a victory or pursue fugitives. Indeed, it was hardly in the mercenary's interest to eliminate the opposing forces completely. By so doing, he would have deprived himself of employment and so a living.

War Elephants

The kings and generals who commanded armies in the Graeco-Macedonian world seem to have had a taste for massive equipment; their wide use of war elephants was perhaps consistent with this taste. We have already noticed that elephants could be defeated easily enough by flexible tactics, but at the same time they must have had some substantial advantages to justify their continued use. The elephant could inflict casualties by trampling enemies underfoot or seizing them with its trunk. And—not least important—it offered a higher platform from which missiles could be launched. The turret mounted on an elephant's back might accommodate a crew of four. A consideration of siege, mountain and naval tactics should remind us that the ancients attached great importance to a point of vantage based on superior height. The archer who threatened his enemy from above gained a wider view and a greater range.

As compared with cavalry, elephants were less manoeuvrable, although at the same time they might easily frighten horses and make them unmanageable. On the whole, the elephant was best employed against a stationary enemy; in this connection we should remark that the Macedonian phalanx, against which elephants were used, had itself become less mobile. This may be another example of the general military tendency to make everything bigger and heavier. Demetrius' armourer produced for him a cuirass which completely withstood a catapult dart at 26 paces and was considered light, at a weight of 40 lbs (18·1 kg). A similar cuirass was supplied to one of Demetrius' lieutenants, although this officer had been accustomed to a panoply weighing two talents. A more normal weight was one talent. The talent in Attic weight has been estimated at 57lbs (25·86 kg), by the Aeginetan standard at 83lbs (37·80 kg). In any case, such armour must be regarded as heavy. It would be no wonder if ponderously equipped phalangists found it difficult to perform the essential evasive manoeuvre of opening ranks with all the alacrity that an elephant charge demanded.

Special anti-elephant devices were adopted. The most effective seems to have been that of planting the ground with spikes. The poor beasts, maddened by pain, soon became incapable of control. But perhaps the best answer to the elephant threat was an opposing force of elephants. In this case, the larger elephants could have been expected to enjoy an advantage, not only on account of their weight but because of the superior position occupied by the archers on their backs. The Seleucid rulers, with their ready access to India, at first had the monopoly of elephants and of the Indian mahouts who could control them. The Ptolemies soon equalized by training African elephants captured in Ethiopia. The African elephant which they enlisted was not a larger species than the Indian; on the contrary, ancient authorities who describe it as

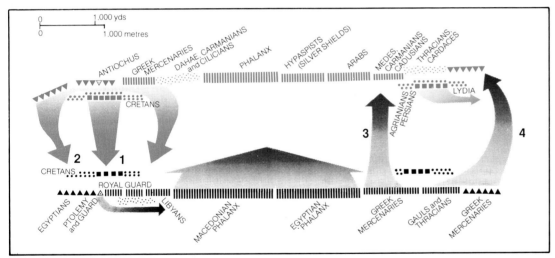

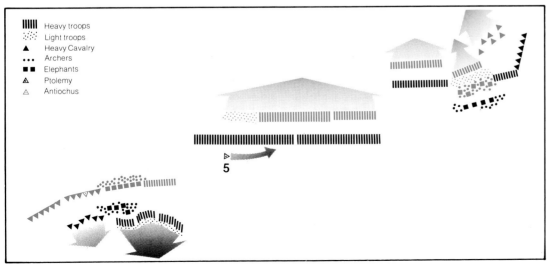

	Heavy troops
	Light troops
▲	Heavy Cavalry
•••	Archers
■ ■	Elephants
△	Ptolemy
△	Antiochus

Battle of Raphia 217 BC

Ptolemy	Antiochus
Cavalry	
Guard 700	Horse 6000
Egypt 2000	
Greek Mercenaries 2000	
Elephants 73	Elephants 102
Infantry	
Royal Guard 3000	Phalanx 20000
Phalanx 25000	Hypaspists 10000
Greek	Greek Mercenaries
Mercenaries 8000	5000
Crete 3000	Crete 2500
Thrace) 6000	Persia) 2000
Gaul)	Agriania)
Egypt 20000	Arabia 10000
Libya 3000	Media)
	Cadusia) 5000
	Carmania)
	Lydia 1000
	Cardaces 1000
Peltasts	
2000	7000

1 Antiochus' Indian elephants charge and force back the opposing African elephants, which disrupt Ptolemy's Guard cavalry and infantry. **2** Antiochus attacks opposing cavalry; his peltasts defeat Ptolemy's peltasts and Libyans. Antiochus pursues them. **3** Ptolemy's elephants refuse to charge on the right but his mercenaries attack the Arabs while (**4**) his cavalry evades the elephants and sweeps away its opponents. **5** Ptolemy takes cover behind his phalanx. Stripped of their wings the two phalanxes close. Urged on by Ptolemy, the larger Egyptian force triumphs. Antiochus returns too late. He loses 10000 infantry, 300 horse 5 elephants; Ptolemy's casualties amount to 1500 infantry, 700 horse, 16 elephants.

312

Demetrius, son of Antigonus, defeated by Ptolemy at Gaza

Seleucus recovers Babylon with Ptolemy's help

At Rome, Appius Claudius Caecus becomes censor

During Appius' censorship, the Appian Way is constructed between Rome and Capua

Plebeians are admitted to the Senate

BC

93

smaller were familiar with a North African sub-species, found in the regions of the Red Sea and of the Atlas Mountains—where it was used by the Carthaginians. When Ptolemaic African elephants clashed with Seleucid Indian elephants at the battle of Raphia, near Gaza, in 217 BC, the Seleucids had the better of it. But in any case, numbers on this occasion told in their favour.

Elephants could also be used to force the entrance to a city. However, when the Macedonian commander attempted this at Megalopolis in 318 BC, the defenders laid large gates studded with spikes on the ground over which the elephant attack was expected and the operation ended in disaster.

Quinqueremes and Heavier War Galleys

The word trireme (Greek *trieres*) is usually taken to mean a war galley with three banks of oars, superimposed one above another. Representations of galleys with two and three banks of oars have survived; in the fifth century, Athenian rowers were divided into *thranitai, zygitai,* and *thalamitai,* according to the tier in which they rowed. The *thranitai,* who pulled at the longest oars, sometimes received extra pay, as happened at the outset of the Athenian expedition against Syracuse in 415 BC. However, the word *trieres* contains no allusion to banks of oars; its original meaning may simply have been "triply-furnished". After the end of the Peloponnesian War, quadriremes and quinqueremes came into general use. Both are mentioned by Arrian in his description of Alexander's operations at Tyre. In later history, we hear of "ten-furnished", "twenty-furnished" and even "forty-furnished" galleys. Unless one contemplates a floating skyscraper, it is impossible to suppose that these numbers denoted superimposed banks of oars.

The allusions to "forty-furnished" ships are particularly unconvincing; we may perhaps discount them altogether, but a problem still remains. In a trireme, the rowing benches furnished for any one triplet of rowers were probably staggered in the fore-and-aft dimension as well as in cross-section, so that opposite numbers in the upper tiers did not sit directly over the heads of those below. However, even granted such an arrangement, we cannot attribute five banks of oars to a quinquereme without arriving at a top-heavy hull. The deployment of the oars themselves would in any case have

been complicated and would have presented other problems. Modern scholars, therefore, usually draw the conclusion that a quinquereme was a galley which seated five rowers at one oar, or which shared two or three oars among five rowers. Perhaps the larger denominations take into account rowers on each side of the ship or rowers seated facing each other over a single oar. Those who make conjectures rely on the analogy of Venetian galleys in medieval and Renaissance times, where practice is known to have varied considerably. One thing seems clear: the ancient classification of war galleys cannot have been consistently by reference to banks of oars.

There is a further implication. If Greek galleys were classified by reference to rowers and not to oars, a single-banked galley furnished with benches for three rowers at each oar should still have qualified for description as a trireme, or triple-furnished ship. The slant of the oars would have meant that the rowers still sat in tiers; those on the inside would still have had the heaviest work, so that the tiers might still have been differentiated as *thranitai, zygitai* and *thalamitai.* There is no evidence that this was or was not so. It simply follows logically from what seem necessary assumptions. On the other hand, it is possible that the ancients were not consistent in their use of terms. By the word for a trireme, they may always have meant a galley with three oar banks, even though a quinquereme was not a galley with five oar banks (see page 98).

Whatever we decide about the quadriremes and quinqueremes that figured so prominently in the navies of Alexander's Successors, they were bigger and heavier boats, rowed by more men and larger oars. The trireme had been used in battle for ramming or attacking enemy oars and steering gear. It had also served as a platform from which missiles or boarding parties could be launched. The vessels of the late fourth century could in addition carry heavy siege engines on their fore-decks and were capable of towing horse-transport craft.

Demetrius' navy even featured "fifteen-furnished" and "sixteen-furnished" galleys. They were highly spectacular and no doubt had great propaganda value, but do not seem to have been in general use. For many purposes, Demetrius, like any other admiral, was obliged to rely on light, undecked ships, including a "one-and-a-half" type of vessel (more literally translated, "a three-halver"). Whether

Above: *A 2nd century BC relief of a Greek galley carved on the rocks of the Acropolis at Lindos in Rhodes. The stern is shown and the large steering paddles are easily seen.*

this was supplied with one and a half banks of oars or one and half tiers of rowers remains open to conjecture.

Sicilian Warfare

One cannot adequately discuss the war resources of Alexander's Successors without referring to warfare as it was waged in the western Mediterranean, both contemporaneously and during the earlier part of the fourth century. Sooner or later, the dynasts of the Greek mainland and eastern Greek world were bound to become involved with the west, and to a considerable extent, the Macedonian war machine as developed by Philip and Alexander was the result of western inspiration. The siege of the Carthaginians at Motya on the west coast of Sicily by the Greeks under Dionysius I of Syracuse, in 398 BC, strikingly anticipates the great eastern siege operations such as those mounted against Tyre and the island of Rhodes.

Motya was valuable to the Carthaginians both as a mercantile and naval base. The city itself was built on an island about 1·5 miles (2·4 km) in diameter, in an encircling bay approximately 2 miles (3·2 km) wide, and it was linked to the mainland by a causeway. As the Greek army and its supporting fleet approached the island, the defenders destroyed the causeway. But Dionysius soon began to build a new causeway, by means of which the city was eventually attacked and

Successor War Elephant

Alexander was so impressed by Porus' elephants that he incorporated them into his own army, and under his successors the pike phalanx and elephant dominated warfare. It brought into use the fighting tower which usually housed a pikeman and an archer or javelinman. The driver, normally an Indian, was also armed with javelins. The elephant's main advantages in battle were its size and the sheer terror it inspired. It was especially useful against cavalry as horses unused to it would panic at the sight and sound of such an animal. Thus a chain of elephants at 20-50m intervals could effectively block a cavalry advance. It had one major disadvantage, however. Though difficult to kill, many pin-prick wounds or the loss of its driver could cause it to panic and become as great a danger to its own side as to the enemy. Elephants were therefore accompanied by a protective escort of light infantry. Later Successor elephants acquired a permanent detachment of light troops, a larger four-man tower and hoops of leather or metal armour to prevent hamstringing. Smaller African forest elephants were also used by the Ptolemies in Egypt and by Carthage. It is uncertain if Carthage employed fighting towers although Egypt certainly did so. The elephant shown is typical of the period 280-200 BC. The tower consists of a padded saddle on top of which is a rawhide-covered frame.

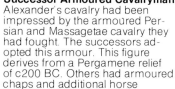

Successor Armoured Cavalryman
Alexander's cavalry had been impressed by the armoured Persian and Massagetae cavalry they had fought. The successors adopted this armour. This figure derives from a Pergamene relief of c200 BC. Others had armoured chaps and additional horse armour and were known as *cataphracts* (literally: covered-in).

taken. The besiegers' rams, catapults and six-storey siege towers triumphed at last, despite some enemy sucess in firing the wooden towers. Another technical feat of the siege appears in Dionysius' use of rollers to drag his ships across the encircling arm of the bay. This permitted his more numerous fleet to be deployed to advantage, not compressed within the narrow harbour entrance, where the Carthaginian admiral had hoped to challenge it. As a result the relief fleet from Carthage was obliged to sail away, leaving Motya to its fate.

Later in the fourth century, Timoleon, the widely esteemed champion of the Sicilian Greeks, again liberated them from the threat of Carthage. He had originally been invited from Corinth to assist the Syracusans in a struggle against their own tyrant, Dionysius II, and other designing despots. In 341 BC, Timoleon emerged as a leader against the Carthaginians and defeated them at the Crimisus river, though his Greek enemies frustrated him by siding with the Carthaginians. The example of Timoleon as a constitutionally-invoked liberator and national champion can hardly have been lost on his contemporary, Philip of Macedon, whose policy and strategy were founded on pious intervention.

In the time of Demetrius the Besieger, another formidable Greek war leader arose in Sicily. This was Agathocles, who had served with military distinction in Timoleon's epoch. Subsequently, he had espoused popular politics and after some vicissitudes made himself absolute master of Syracuse. This brought him into conflict with other Greek cities and with the Carthaginians, who in some cases united with Sicilian Greek communities to oppose him. He suffered a defeat at the hands of the Carthaginians and being hard-pressed decided to retaliate with a counter-offensive in Africa. He watched for his opportunity and, eluding the Carthaginian fleet, conducted his own flotilla to the African coast. Here he persuaded his men to burn their boats (literally), in order that they might be committed to the occupation of Carthaginian territory; with help from the North African Greek city of Cyrene, he launched a successful military campaign, almost capturing Carthage itself. Meanwhile, the Carthaginians in Sicily had failed to take Syracuse and Agathocles was able to return to the city. A later African expedition did not succeed, but Agathocles' domination of Sicily remained secure.

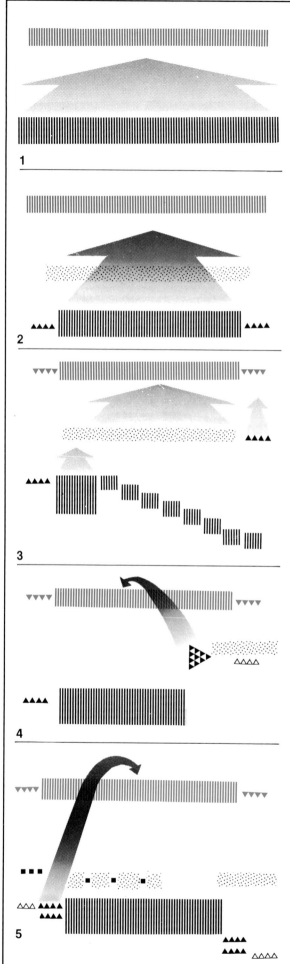

Tactics in Greek Warfare

The Greek Phalanx
1 This diagram shows how the Greek phalanx fought at Marathon in 490 BC. The phalanx attacks en masse in a solid line. It is composed of men in close order (3-4ft frontage per man) and may be four or more ranks deep.

Introduction of Cavalry and Light Troops
2 The addition of horsemen and light troops to an attacking force granted an army a measure of tactical flexibility. The cavalry are available to protect the vulnerable flanks of the phalanx while the peltasts employ their small shields to screen the hoplites from enemy arrows, stones and javelins. Such tactics can be observed at the battles of Solygia, Delium and Coronea in the late 5th and 4th centuries BC. (See page 57 for further information).

Theban Tactics
3 The battles of Leuctra (371 BC) and Mantinea (362 BC) exemplify the tactical advances of the Theban fighting formation under the leadership of Epaminondas. In an oblique attack, one wing of the phalanx is "weighted" and used to deliver the main punch while the other wing is refused and the enemy line pinned down by light troops and cavalry.

Macedonian Variations
4 Examination of the major battles of Philip and Alexander reveals further developments. The phalanx has been deepened (16-20 ranks) but not as spectacularly as the Theban model. The killer blow is, however, delivered by a furious cavalry charge which swings on to the enemy's rear while the phalanx engages frontally. The phalanx may advance in line (as at Issus) or obliquely (Chaeronea, Gaugamela).

Developments of the Successors
5 The various conflicts of the Diadochian Wars illustrate further tactical elaboration. All the previous elements are employed: the echeloned attack, heavy cavalry delivering the main blow, light cavalry protecting the heavy, and light troops screening and skirmishing. A new factor, however, is introduced in the form of elephants. They are used to discourage enemy cavalry and to disrupt the enemy line. The phalanx is deployed mainly as a pinning force. Whereas it was the vital element at Marathon, by the time of Ipsus and Raphia it is but one of many interdependent components.

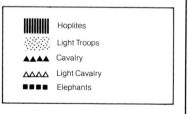

‖‖‖‖	Hoplites
░░░	Light Troops
▲▲▲▲	Cavalry
△△△△	Light Cavalry
■■■■	Elephants

BC 309
In Sicily, Acragas (Agrigentum) leads a combination of Greek cities against Syracuse

308
Ophellas, Ptolemy's officer allies himself with Agathocles against Carthage

Agathocles murders Ophellas and assumes command of his army, but cannot take Carthage

307
Agathocles finally returns from Africa to Syracuse

In Epirus, Pyrrhus reigns as a minor

96

Agathocles' strategy of counter-offensive suggests that which Memnon of Rhodes, but for his untimely death, might have employed against Alexander. It also demonstrated what Alexander's own campaigns had done much to make apparent, that an army did not need a base as long as it was in a position to threaten enemy bases. One guesses that the later fourth-century war leaders of both the eastern and western Mediterranean studied and learned from each other's strategic methods.

As for Agathocles, his incorrigible delight in warfare led him to exploits in Italy and Corcyra, and before he died he came into contact—and conflict—with the Successors of Alexander. But his own succession was in dispute and to spite his family he renounced all dynastic pretensions in favour of the people—although this did little to render Syracusan politics any more stable. He might have been regarded as a benevolent despot in some quarters, but Timaeus the historian was one of his political victims and so Agathocles' posthumous reputation suffered.

Carthage and its Sea Power

For the western Greeks, and for the Greek Sicilian cities in particular, Carthage had long been the most formidable national enemy, playing in this respect much the same role as Persia had done in the east. In other ways, however, Carthage offered a very sharp contrast to Persia, and its power was based on very different resources. Persia was a territory; Carthage was a city. Persia became a great land empire, for the most part employing other nations to carry on its sea warfare. Carthage was a great commercial and naval power and for preference hired foreign mercenaries to fight its land wars.

The city of Carthage had been founded by Phoenician settlers from Tyre on the north African coast, in what is now Tunisia, during the ninth or eighth century BC. The Carthaginians were a Semitic-speaking people, racially distinct from the Greeks. The Persians, by contrast, were racially akin to the peoples who had entered the Greek and Italian peninsulas and they spoke an Indo-European tongue which belonged to the same linguistic group as both Greek and Latin. The social and economic institutions of Carthage, however, resembled those of the Greeks far more closely than did the Persian. Carthage was never a des-

potism. Aristotle, in his treatise the *Politics,* praised the Carthaginian constitution and compared it to the Spartan. The Carthaginian pattern of colonization also resembled the Greek. Itself an offshoot of Tyre, Carthage founded colonial trading cities throughout the western Mediterranean, including southern Sardinia and Spain. The object, however, was to establish trading contacts rather than relieve population pressures, and the consequent tie between colonial settlement and mother city was on the whole closer than that which existed in the Greek world. Certainly, the Carthaginian cities of Sicily were strenuously supported from north Africa in their wars against the Greeks.

To protect their merchant fleet, the Carthaginians maintained a substantial navy of war galleys. At Carthage, there were two harbours, an inner and an outer, both landlocked, artificially-excavated basins. The galleys were normally manned by citizen rowers, but the number of crews available, as well as the size of the harbours and the competing claims of a large merchant fleet, may have been a factor which limited the size of the navy.

The Carthaginians and Phoenicians in general were the boldest seafarers of the ancient world. Yet their success in naval warfare against the Greeks—and subsequently against the Romans—was surprisingly slight. Like the Phoenicians of the eastern Mediterranean, the Carthaginians seem often to have enjoyed a numerical advantage in ships, but vessel for vessel in a sea-fight, they do not seem to have been by any means superior—rather the contrary. Certainly, they carried smaller complements of armed men, and this

Below: *In 306 BC Demetrius Poliorcetes (the Besieger) won a naval victory against Ptolemy of Egypt off Salamis in Cyprus. This coin shows victory mounted on a ship's prow.*

placed them at a disadvantage, not only in boarding tactics but in missile warfare at sea. In the fifth century, on Xerxes' Phoenician vessels, the military force of marines had been supplied by the Persians themselves. The Carthaginians remained deficient in this respect. Agathocles' invasion flotilla, nearing the African coast, was all but overtaken by a superior Carthaginian naval force. The Greeks, however, were able to hold off the pursuers when they were within missile range, for Agathocles had a larger complement of archers and slingers on his galleys.

As seamen, supporting the war of their compatriots in Sicily, the Carthaginians faced a challenge which the invasion forces of Xerxes had been able to avoid. Their army had to be transported across a wide expanse of open sea and could not hug the coast. Admittedly, this meant that the ships were in less danger of being driven on to a lee-shore, but it was rather a question of "Hobson's choice". For the large Carthaginian invasion fleet which set out for Sicily in 311 BC met with a storm in which it lost 60 out of 130 triremes, as well as 200 transport vessels.

It should be noticed that the galleys in this ill-fated expedition were all triremes. The Carthaginians also developed the use of the quinquereme. In fact, it is thought that the invention of the quinquereme, ascribed to Dionysius I of Syracuse, was originally a Phoenician innovation. The quinquereme was certainly found to have some advantages in naval warfare—even if it did not possess every advantage over lighter vessels. One cannot exclude the possibility that it was originally introduced with mainly navigational considerations in view: a heavier and more substantial ship to resist heavier seas. Among the Carthaginians, as with the Greeks, the tendency was always towards heavier craft. The Carthaginian ships which had been engaged against the Phocaean Greeks off Alalia in Corsica in 535 BC were probably pentekonters like those of their enemies.

A feature of Carthaginian war galleys which Greeks and Romans seem sometimes to have imitated was a small auxiliary sail which could be hoisted on the prow of the vessel — (it was known as the *akation* in Greek) — perhaps from a yard on a large bowsprit. This may have assisted the ship in sailing at an angle to the wind. It could also be useful in a combat emergency. The mainmast in a galley could not be mounted at short notice, but Diodorus relates how a Carthaginian warship, in danger of being overtaken by Agathocles' rowers, raised its auxiliary foresail to take advantage of a favourable breeze and so escaped.

The Carthaginian Land Forces

Although the Carthaginians depended for their land forces mainly upon mercenary troops, it should be noticed their citizen army was not to be despised. It was, admittedly, small: in the Carthaginian armada against Agathocles, citizens numbered only 2,000 as compared with 10,000 Libyan troops. But Carthage possessed a picked citizen corps d'élite which the

Greeks described as a "Sacred Band", and when the Carthaginians were called upon to fight against a combination of their own mercenaries and the rebellious population of their subject cities in north Africa, at a time when Carthage was already threatened by Rome, they ultimately triumphed — after a war marked by many atrocities.

Carthaginian troops had fought in Sicily against Timoleon. Plutarch in this connection speaks of 10,000 foot-soldiers armed with white shields, whom the Greeks guessed to be all Carthaginians on account of their splendid arms and the slow pace and good order of their advance. Of course, one has to distinguish between the citizens of Carthage itself and the

Carthaginian citizens of the overseas settlements. But in any case, it would be wrong to describe the Carthaginians as an unmilitary nation.

They used elephants with considerable effect, both in their first wars against Rome and against their mercenary rebels. The Carthaginian use of elephants differed from that which the Macedonian dynasts had learned from India. There was no turret-like howdah, manned by archers, on the animal's back. The Carthaginian war elephant was controlled by a single driver with a goad, and it was relied upon mainly to trample the enemy underfoot.

Elephants seem to have superseded chariots in the Carthaginian armies, but the Carthaginians also employed

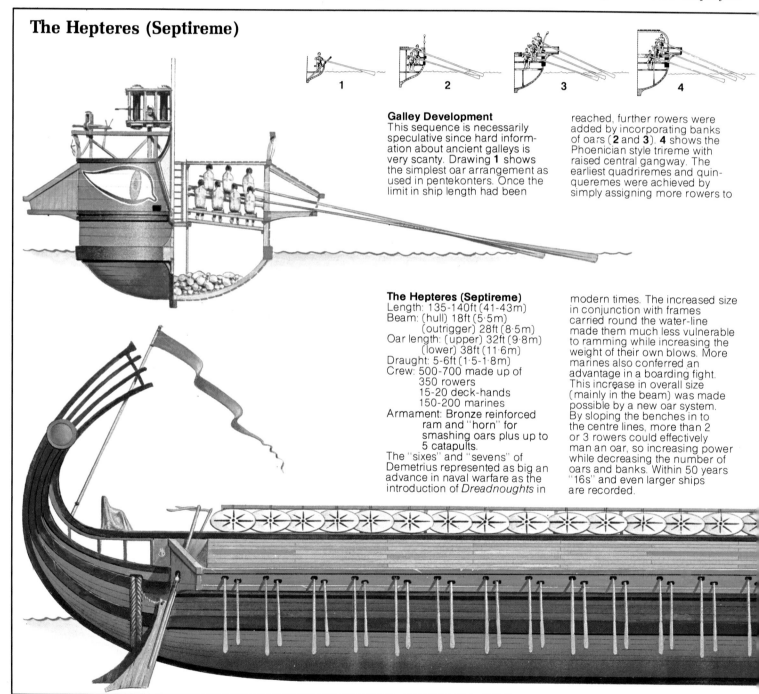

The Hepteres (Septireme)

Galley Development
This sequence is necessarily speculative since hard information about ancient galleys is very scanty. Drawing **1** shows the simplest oar arrangement as used in pentekonters. Once the limit in ship length had been reached, further rowers were added by incorporating banks of oars (**2** and **3**). **4** shows the Phoenician style trireme with raised central gangway. The earliest quadriremes and quinqueremes were achieved by simply assigning more rowers to

The Hepteres (Septireme)
Length: 135-140ft (41-43m)
Beam: (hull) 18ft (5·5m)
     (outrigger) 28ft (8·5m)
Oar length: (upper) 32ft (9·8m)
     (lower) 38ft (11·6m)
Draught: 5-6ft (1·5-1·8m)
Crew: 500-700 made up of
     350 rowers
     15-20 deck-hands
     150-200 marines
Armament: Bronze reinforced ram and "horn" for smashing oars plus up to 5 catapults.
The "sixes" and "sevens" of Demetrius represented as big an advance in naval warfare as the introduction of *Dreadnoughts* in modern times. The increased size in conjunction with frames carried round the water-line made them much less vulnerable to ramming while increasing the weight of their own blows. More marines also conferred an advantage in a boarding fight. This increase in overall size (mainly in the beam) was made possible by a new oar system. By sloping the benches in to the centre lines, more than 2 or 3 rowers could effectively man an oar, so increasing power while decreasing the number of oars and banks. Within 50 years "16s" and even larger ships are recorded.

chariots in historic times, including four-horse chariots, such as the Greeks used only for racing. For chariot fighting suitable terrain was essential. The Persians made considerable use of chariots in their Asian armies, but the latest instance of chariot warfare in Greece occurred in the Lelantine plain of Euboea, in the seventh-century struggle between the cities of Chalcis and Eretria. Four-horse chariots were mobilized against Timoleon in Sicily and exercised a disruptive effect on the Greek cavalry at the battle of the Crimisus. On that occasion, a thunderstorm and torrential downpour supervened to the Greek advantage; the Carthaginian foot-soldiers, with their heavy iron mail, were seriously handicapped and the mud must have done much to immobilize the chariots. Plutarch's comments on this battle are interesting. Although the armour of the Carthaginians made them impervious to Greek spears, they could not compete with the Greeks in sword fighting, which called for special skill. Tactics had changed since the epoch of the Persian Wars. Plutarch also remarks that an unprecedented number of Carthaginian citizen troops perished in the battle. Usually, a greater number of Africans, Spaniards and Numidians—whose loss was lightly felt—were engaged in the Carthaginian armies.

Carthaginian mercenary forces were drawn both from north Africa and from the many countries with which the Carthaginians had established trading relations. Different mercenary and allied national contingents seem often to have specialized in different arms. The Numidians, a nomadic people who lived to the west and south of Carthage, bred horses and contributed cavalry. They were renowned as horsemen and are referred to as riding without bridles. The Libyans were charioteers; Agathocles, campaigning in Libya against Carthage, was able to enlist Libyan chariots in his own army. The Balearic islanders provided the Carthaginians (and later the Romans) with slingers. This speciality of the Balearic troops is comparable with that of the Rhodians in the eastern Mediterranean, as has been noted in earlier chapters.

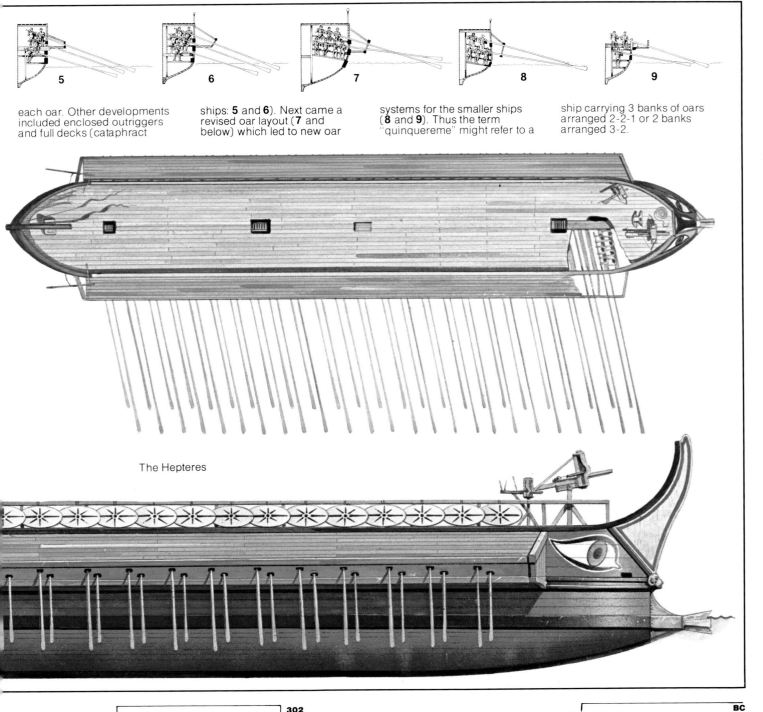

5

6

7

8

9

each oar. Other developments included enclosed outriggers and full decks (cataphract

ships: **5** and **6**). Next came a revised oar layout (**7** and below) which led to new oar

systems for the smaller ships (**8** and **9**). Thus the term "quinquereme" might refer to a

ship carrying 3 banks of oars arranged 2-2-1 or 2 banks arranged 3-2.

The Hepteres

In Italy, Cleonymus II of Sparta campaigns with mercenary army in aid of Tarentum

Pyrrhus is driven from Epirus by Cassander

Pyrrhus is received and championed by Ptolemy

Cassander allies himself with Lysimachus and Ptolemy against Antigonus

Pyrrhus of Epirus and the Roman Republic

**Rome's progress towards domination of southern Italy
was opposed, in the early 3rd century BC, by Pyrrhus of Epirus, whose hard-won victories
added a new term to the military vocabulary.**

Ancient Authorities

The career of Pyrrhus of Epirus is obviously in the essence of our theme. For the life of Pyrrhus, Plutarch is our main extant source; Plutarch relies on the valuable contemporary evidence offered by Hieronymus of Cardia. Hieronymus' *Histories of the Successors* provided important material for the relevant period in Diodorus' *Bibliothekè*, as well as for Arrian's history of post-Alexandrian events; it was also a source for Plutarch in other *Lives*: those of Eumenes and Demetrius. Hieronymus had fought in the army of Eumenes who, like himself, was a native of Cardia in the Thracian Chersonese (Gallipoli peninsula). When Eumenes was captured and put to death by Antigonus, Hieronymus, with a facility characteristic of the times, transferred his allegiance to the latter. He witnessed the battle of Ipsus in 301 BC and was later made governor of Boeotia by Demetrius, Antigonus' son. The *Histories of the Successors* included events at least until the death of Pyrrhus and perhaps until even later.

Nearly all our knowledge of early Roman history is derived from later writers. Before the fourth century BC, some records were kept at Rome. Presumably, they will have suffered at the sack of Rome by the Gauls in 390 BC. From the early fourth century, at any rate, the compilation and display of yearly calendar events, under the names of magistrates for the year, was the responsibility of the Roman chief priest (Pontifex·Maximus).

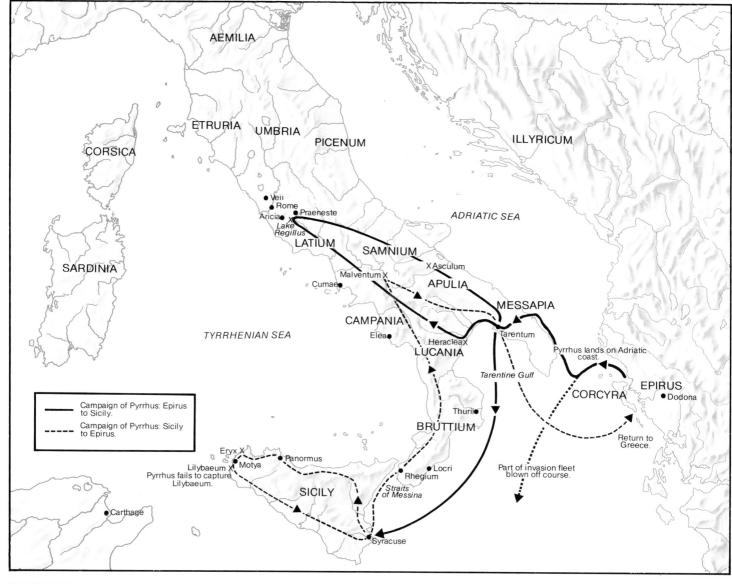

Campaign of Pyrrhus: Epirus to Sicily.
Campaign of Pyrrhus: Sicily to Epirus.

301
Death of Antigonus I (Monophthalmos) at Ipsus in battle against other Successor kings

300
Agathocles, Syracusan autocrat, after intervention in Italy captures Corcyra

Seleucus Nicator founds Antioch

About this time Euclid, the mathematician, flourished at Alexandria

The first Roman historians were themselves public men: often senators who had held important offices. Their purpose was largely patriotic and they wished to present Roman history in a favourable light to the Greek world, in which the writing of history was a cultured and honourable preoccupation. The early Roman writers, like Quintus Fabius Pictor, who took part in the second war against Carthage, wrote in Greek. But Marcus Porcius Cato (Cato the Censor) compiled his work in Latin, and from his time (234-149 BC) the use of Latin in historical writing became general. Such writing made use of the early pontifical annual records; its exponents are known as annalists. The culmination of their vogue was the publication in the late second century BC of 80 books of annals by the pontifex Publius Mucius Scaevola. These records, regarded as authoritative, were little questioned or disputed by the annalistic historians of the following century.

The work of the early annalists was used not only by the Roman historians of the first century BC and after, but by Greek historians who dealt with Roman history, including both Diodorus and Dionysius of Halicarnassus, a contemporary of Livy. However, the contents of the annalistic accounts relating to early centuries of Rome's history are best known to us through Livy's work. His prose epic, spanning the period between Rome's foundation (traditionally 753 BC) and his own times (59 BC-17 AD), is permeated by a sense of national destiny. Of its original 142 books, Books 1-10 and Books 21-45 have survived. Apart from excerpts and fragments of the remainder, summaries of Livy's complete work, made by later writers, are still extant. Unfortunately for our subject, Livy had no experience of warfare, but the annalistic records from which he notably derived his method and much of his material had in many cases been assembled by men who played a leading part in the wars and politics of their nation. Conversely, Livy's literary genius ensured that the testimony of these writers would not be lost; hardly any Roman historical records prior to the first century BC have been preserved independently.

Archaeology has done much to distinguish fact from legend in the early

history of Rome. It has tended very often to confirm the ancient literary traditions; for example, by providing evidence as to the prosperity and decline of towns at certain epochs. Ancient coins and inscriptions supply their own form of documentation. Of course, the credibility of the old stories which inspired the Roman poets remains largely controversial, but the main outlines of early Roman history are generally accepted. For example, without crediting every legend that relates to the Roman kingdom, no one would wish to deny that Rome was originally governed by kings who normally reigned for life after accession, but that in the sixth century BC some fundamental change transferred sovereignty into the hands of two annually elected magistrates, who were afterwards known as consuls.

Historical Background

In the middle of the fourth century BC, the Dorian Greek colonists of Tarentum in southern Italy had appealed to Sparta, their mother city, for help against the indigenous population which threatened them. At a time when northern Greece was crucially involved against Philip of Macedon, Sparta had sent a force under King Archidamus III, who had subsequently been killed fighting in Italy. Later, when Alexander the Great was in the east, his mother's brother, also named Alexander, who

Left: *This sculptured head of Pyrrhus is to be found in Naples. The relationship between Pyrrhus and the Romans was one of chivalrous hostility. His costly victories merely enhanced Roman prestige.*

had made himself ruler of the tribes and cities of Epirus, gladly accepted another Tarentine invitation to intervene in southern Italy. He too was killed fighting there. A third episode of this kind occurred in 303 BC, when Cleonymus, a Spartan mercenary general, with 5,000 men, championed the Tarentines against Italian neighbours. Cleonymus used Italy as a base against Corcyra (Corfu) and eventually quarreled with the city which had engaged him. For Tarentum, the most natural sources of Greek aid in these recurrent situations were Sparta, their mother city, and Epirus, conveniently situated opposite the heel of Italy across comparatively narrow seas. In 281 BC, at last in open conflict with Rome, the Tarentines issued an invitation to King Pyrrhus of Epirus.

Among the tribal peoples of Epirus, the comparatively Hellenized group of the Molossi were a dominant force. Their kings traced descent from Achilles, and the sanctuary of Zeus at Dodona, celebrated throughout Greece for its oracle, lay in their vicinity. The contact of Epirus with Greek civilization was facilitated by many Corinthian and Elean settlements on the eastern shores of the Adriatic. Alexander had done much to enrich the country before embarking on his Italian adventure and Pyrrhus' father, the Molossian king, had married a lady of the Thessalian nobility. In general, Epirus may be classified, like Macedonia, as a semi-Greek territory.

Pyrrhus inherited his title to the throne as a child and as a consequence his position long remained precarious. However, he at last enlisted the help of Ptolemy and, after establishing himself powerfully in Epirus, ruled at first jointly and then as sole monarch. In this capacity, he allied himself with the Thracian dynast Lysimachus to drive out Demetrius, who had claimed the throne of Macedon on the death of Cassander in 297 BC. Demetrius' claim was based on his marriage to Antipater's daughter Phila and he derived support from some of the Greek states, to whom he had at one time presented himself as a champion of constitutional liberty. Pyrrhus and Lysimachus, in combination, succeeded in defeating Demetrius, but when the victors competed for domination of the Macedonian kingdom,

298
In India, death of powerful northern ruler, Chandragupta Maurya

Independent kingdom of Bithynia established under Thracian dynasty

297
Pyrrhus rules Epirus jointly with Neoptolemus

Death of Cassander, ruler of Macedonia

About this time, independent kingdom of Pontus established under Mithridatic dynasty

BC

101

Right: *Italic spearheads. It will be observed that the spear-shaft fitted into the socket in the bronze head, not the head into the wood as in a Roman pilum at a later date.*

Pyrrhus was forced to withdraw. Thus frustrated, he was ready to direct his ambitions westwards.

The Tarentines, who gave Pyrrhus his opportunity, had an old treaty with Rome, perhaps describable as obsolete, according to which the Romans were not to send warships into the Tarentine Gulf. In 282 BC the Romans installed supporting garrisons in the Greek cities of Thurii, Locri and Rhegium. These measures were directed against the Italian people of Lucania, to the north. Thurii, however, lay at the western corner of the Tarentine Gulf and, probably as a demonstration of strength, the Romans sent warships there.

The matter could have been overlooked by the Tarentines, but they were already anxious at the expansion of Roman power and decided on war. They accordingly attacked and sank several Roman warships, drove the Roman garrison from Thurii and sacked the city. The violence of their reaction may be explained ideologically by the hatred of Tarentine democrats for Thurian oligarchs. Committed now to war against Rome, the Tarentines made their invitation to Pyrrhus not only in their own name but on behalf of other Greek cities in Italy. As a contribution to the common war effort, they offered both their own armed forces and substantial levies of indigenous Italian troops, comprising Lucanians, Messapians and Samnites: in all, according to Plutarch, 20,000

Below: *This Samnite breastplate with its trefoil design was a widely distributed type. It was common in southern Italy in the 4th century BC and was adopted by the Carthaginians.*

cavalry and 350,000 infantry. Whatever the accuracy of the figures, they were high enough to attract Pyrrhus and to arouse popular enthusiasm for the war in Epirus.

Pyrrhus' Invasion Force

Pyrrhus immediately sent Cineas, his Thessalian staff officer and diplomat on whose education and intelligence he placed great reliance, to Tarentum with an advance party of 3,000 men, while he himself assembled the main body of the invasion forces. Vessels for the convoy and an accompanying escort of war galleys were provided by Tarentum itself. In the past, Cleonymus had been similarly supplied. In a fleet which included horse-transports and a variety of flat-bottomed boats, Pyrrhus embarked 20 elephants, 3,000 cavalry, 20,000 infantry, 2,000 archers and 500 slingers. According to Plutarch, a rough crossing awaited them and an unseasonal north wind began to blow when they were halfway across. The result was that many ships were

carried southwards past Sicily and towards Libya. It became impossible to round the heel of Italy and enter the Tarentine Gulf; those vessels which had not been blown hopelessly off course evidently looked for a haven on the Adriatic shore. Plutarch says that the on-shore wind that first battered many of them on the harbourless coast veered suddenly and prevented Pyrrhus' own flagship from reaching the shore. Perhaps it is not necessary to assume a diametric change of wind. Ships closely following the irregular contours of the coastline must themselves often have altered course. There was in any case a danger that it would be impossible to beach the royal galley at all, and rather than be blown out to sea again Pyrrhus transferred to a small boat* while it was still dark and reached shore, exhausted, in the light of dawn. The wind dropped and some other elements of the scattered fleet came up with him. They were well received by the local Messapian inhabitants, who were Tarentine allies and did their best to help. At last, having collected 2,000 infantry, very few cavalry and two elephants, Pyrrhus pushed on overland to Tarentum to join his advance party.

Plutarch's account of the storm is rather garbled and seems to be affected by the confusion of the event itself, but the episode is worthy of note to anyone who is interested in ancient navigation. It appears that Pyrrhus' flagship alone of all those which had hugged the inhospitable Italian coast had been able to hold its course in the heavy sea. Perhaps this galley is to be identified with the septireme which Pyrrhus later used in Sicily and which, according to Polybius†, ultimately fell into the hands of the Carthaginians. In any case, we have here additional testimony as to the enhanced seaworthiness of the larger and heavier vessels. Plutarch says explicitly that Pyrrhus' ship was preserved by its great size and strength.

As the king approached Tarentum, Cineas came out to meet him with such forces as were already stationed in the city. Whatever the precise terms of Pyrrhus' agreement with the Tarentines, he was very careful not to do anything which might offend them until his own widely dispersed fleet had at last made its way into harbour at Tarentum. He

---

*Plutarch. *Life of Pyrrhus*. 392. The Greek could mean that he plunged into the sea and swam, but this seems unlikely.

†Polybius I.23

BC	296	295	294
	Seleucus extends his kingdom to the Mediterranean through Syria and Cilicia	Rome defeats Gauls, Samnites and other Italic peoples at battle of Sentinum	Demetrius Poliorcetes acclaimed as king of Macedonia

102

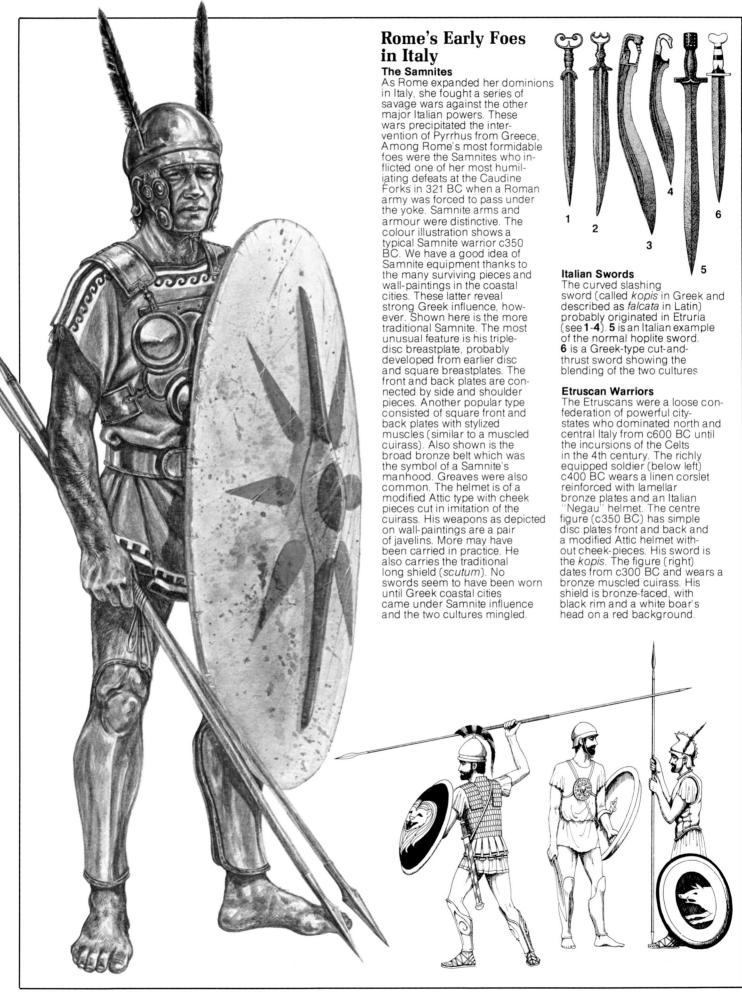

Rome's Early Foes in Italy

The Samnites

As Rome expanded her dominions in Italy, she fought a series of savage wars against the other major Italian powers. These wars precipitated the intervention of Pyrrhus from Greece, Among Rome's most formidable foes were the Samnites who inflicted one of her most humiliating defeats at the Caudine Forks in 321 BC when a Roman army was forced to pass under the yoke. Samnite arms and armour were distinctive. The colour illustration shows a typical Samnite warrior c350 BC. We have a good idea of Samnite equipment thanks to the many surviving pieces and wall-paintings in the coastal cities. These latter reveal strong Greek influence, however. Shown here is the more traditional Samnite. The most unusual feature is his triple-disc breastplate, probably developed from earlier disc and square breastplates. The front and back plates are connected by side and shoulder pieces. Another popular type consisted of square front and back plates with stylized muscles (similar to a muscled cuirass). Also shown is the broad bronze belt which was the symbol of a Samnite's manhood. Greaves were also common. The helmet is of a modified Attic type with cheek pieces cut in imitation of the cuirass. His weapons as depicted on wall-paintings are a pair of javelins. More may have been carried in practice. He also carries the traditional long shield (*scutum*). No swords seem to have been worn until Greek coastal cities came under Samnite influence and the two cultures mingled.

Italian Swords

The curved slashing sword (called *kopis* in Greek and described as *falcata* in Latin) probably originated in Etruria (see **1-4**). **5** is an Italian example of the normal hoplite sword. **6** is a Greek-type cut-and-thrust sword showing the blending of the two cultures

Etruscan Warriors

The Etruscans were a loose confederation of powerful city-states who dominated north and central Italy from c600 BC until the incursions of the Celts in the 4th century. The richly equipped soldier (below left) c400 BC wears a linen corslet reinforced with lamellar bronze plates and an Italian "Negau" helmet. The centre figure (c350 BC) has simple disc plates front and back and a modified Attic helmet without cheek-pieces. His sword is the *kopis*. The figure (right) dates from c300 BC and wears a bronze muscled cuirass. His shield is bronze-faced, with black rim and a white boar's head on a red background.

293
Demetrius controls Greek states

About this time, the Athenian comic dramatist, Menander died

292
Seleucus shares his throne with Antiochus his son

290
Rome subdues the Samnites

BC

103

then took charge of the situation, placed the whole city on a war footing, closed all places of entertainment and sport, suspended all festivities and social events and conscripted the population for military service. Some of the citizens, who objected very strongly to this treatment, left the town.

Pyrrhus soon learned that a formidable Roman army was approaching, plundering the Lucanian hinterland on its way. The large force of allies which had been promised him by the Tarentines had not yet arrived, and Pyrrhus would gladly have waited until he had the support of greater numbers. To delay longer, however, leaving all initiative to the enemy, would clearly have been strategically inadvisable and bad for morale. He therefore led out his men to confront the Romans. Perhaps for the sake of further procrastination, he sent forward a herald to enquire whether the enemy would accept him as an arbitrator of their differences with Tarentum. The reply was, as at this stage he might

Below: *Young elephants campaigned with their parents. Florus describes how a cow-elephant, anxious for her offspring's safety, spread havoc among Pyrrhus' troops in Italy.*

have expected, that the Romans neither wanted him as an arbitrator nor feared him as an enemy.

Pyrrhus watched from his camp near Heraclea as the Romans crossed the river Siris and was impressed by their good order and military discipline, which, as he remarked to one of his officers, seemed surprising in "barbarians". More than ever, he was disposed to wait for his reinforcements, but this was precisely what the Romans were determined to prevent him from doing. Pyrrhus deployed his men along the river bank in defensive positions, but the Romans were beforehand. Their infantry crossed the river at fordable points in some strength, and Pyrrhus' men, threatened with encirclement, had to withdraw.

The Battles of Heraclea and Asculum

In the circumstances which we have just outlined, the battle of Heraclea began. Pyrrhus realized that he must seize the initiative without further delay and, adopting the time-honoured tactics of the great Alexander, left his phalanx to hold the enemy in front, while he himself led a cavalry charge at

the head of 3,000 horse. But unlike Alexander, he had timed the move badly. His attack came too late. The Romans themselves were usually weak in cavalry, but on this occasion they seem to have been well supported by the horsemen of their Italian allies, and Pyrrhus' Thessalian cavalry were driven back. The king then ordered his phalangists to attack, though an offensive role was not normal or suitable for them and they might well have found themselves encircled by the opposing cavalry if the enemy's horses had not taken fright at the elephants and become uncontrollable. In these circumstances, the Thessalian cavalry was able to resume the offensive and soon carried all before it.

The victory, though not decisive, was something better than what we usually describe as "Pyrrhic". Roman casualties were, according to Dionysius, 15,000; according to Hieronymus, 7,000. Pyrrhus' casualties were, by Dionysius' account, 13,000; by Hieronymus', 4,000. Perhaps we should not sneer at such widely divergent statistics. Casualty reports from modern theatres of war often show similar discrepancies. In any case, Pyrrhus possessed himself of the abandoned Roman camp, and his prestige was very much enhanced, so that many of the hesitant Lucanians, Samnites and other allies, whom he had awaited in vain before the battle, now joined him.

Pyrrhus did not expect to take Rome itself, but he advanced northwards, to within 37 miles (60 km) of the city walls, hoping to negotiate out of strength. However, his presence by no means intimidated the Romans. No fear that he would detach their allies from them, ravage their lands or lay siege to the city itself induced them to make peace on terms that would safeguard the Tarentines. Their friendship remained conditional on the unconditional departure of Pyrrhus and his army from Italy.

Meanwhile, two Roman consular armies had been brought up to strength and remained at large in Italy. Pyrrhus could not afford to ignore them. They might threaten his rear; they might threaten his communications; they might threaten his allies. Above all, prestige and morale were at stake. He must not appear reluctant to engage the enemy. He broke off negotiations with the Roman government and went campaigning again. Confronting the Romans at Asculum in Apulia, he fought them on rough and wooded ground which gave little opportunity to his elephants or cavalry and turned the

BC | 289 Death of Agathocles of Syracuse | 288 Pyrrhus and Lysimachus, king of Thrace, combine to invade Macedonia | Demetrius expelled from Macedonia | In Sicily, the Mamertines (community of Italian mercenaries) occupy Messana

104

fight into an infantry engagement. The ground seems also to have hampered the phalanx; the Romans prolonged the battle all day and night fell without a decision having been reached.

On the following day, Pyrrhus contrived to fight on open ground which was less to the enemy's advantage, giving them no occasion for the tactics of flexible response, such as they had adopted in the wilder country. Even so, the Romans, with their short swords, striving desperately to reach a decision before the elephants could be brought into action, seem to have been a match for the long pikes of the Greek phalanx. In the end, the elephants once more gave Pyrrhus his victory—which this time was more "Pyrrhic" in character. The Romans merely retreated into their camp. Pyrrhus himself was wounded in the arm. Hieronymus' figures are of 6,000 Roman casualties, as compared with 3,550 on Pyrrhus' side. But many of Pyrrhus' ablest officers were among the dead and he was not in a position to recruit new troops, as the Romans were.

Pyrrhus was a brave and inspiring if rather flamboyant commander, who was well capable of keeping his head even in the middle of a most desperate fight. Yet he does not seem to have excelled either as a strategist or a tactician. At Heraclea, by waiting for reinforcements, he conceded a valuable initiative to the Romans, without receiving the reinforcements for which he had waited. The timing of the cavalry charge with which he had opened the battle was also tardy. At Asculum, he could not make the right choice of ground until a day of indecisive fighting had taught him costly lessons.

Pyrrhus in Sicily

Two new warlike prospects now invited Pyrrhus. Both offered him the opportunity—which he always coveted—of championing Greek civilization. One opportunity lay in Greece itself, where an irruption of Celtic hordes from the north had produced turmoil; the other lay in Sicily, where the Greek cities, lacking a military successor to Agathocles, were again menaced by the Carthaginians. Pyrrhus chose the Sicilian venture. Certainly, it looked less like a retreat from his present unsatisfactory situation. To the disgust of the Tarentines, after unsuccessful peace overtures to Rome, he suspended operations in Italy, placed a garrison in

Above: *Mamertine coin. The Mamertines were Italic mercenaries originally employed by Agathocles of Syracuse. They later set up an independent state at Messana (Messina).*

Tarentum, and sailed for Sicily with 30,000 infantry and 25,000 cavalry. His consequent success was quite unequivocal; he swept the Carthaginians before him, soon reaching Eryx, their strongly fortified city at the western extremity of the island.

Eryx was taken by storm. A trumpet blast gave the signal for a missile barrage which dispersed the defenders on the walls. Scaling ladders were swiftly brought up and Pyrrhus was himself the first man to mount the battlements, dealing death to left and right of him and emerging at last unscathed. This was a victory after his own heart and he celebrated it, as he had vowed to do, with athletic events and displays in honour of Heracles.

The Carthaginians having been thus subdued and already inclined to negotiate terms, Pyrrhus found himself in the role of a keeper of the peace. A community of Italian brigands, originally hired from Campania as mercenary troops by Agathocles, had been in the habit of extorting payments from Sicilian cities. These lawless and violent men, who styled themselves *Mamertini* ("The War God's Men" in their dialect), were to play a crucial part in later history; but for the time being Pyrrhus managed to suppress them, defeating them in pitched battle and capturing many of their strongholds. Even here, however, his achievement was incomplete. The Mamertines survived to embarrass the Mediterranean world at a later date.

As for the Carthaginians, Pyrrhus refused them the peace they asked and required that they should totally evacuate Sicily. But by this time he had himself begun to quarrel with the Greek Sicilian cities, some of whom were ready to support the Carthaginians, while others rallied surviving Mamertines to their aid. News that the people of Tarentum and other Greeks of the Italian mainland were hard pressed by the Romans in his absence now gave him the opportunity of extricating himself from yet another deadlock, and he took it.

In Sicily, Pyrrhus' reputation, both as a triumphant war-leader and as a liberal ruler, had ultimately suffered. He had failed to capture the remaining stronghold of Lilybaeum, which the Carthaginians had established on the westernmost point of Sicily after the destruction of Motya at the beginning of the previous century. Planning the invasion of Africa, in imitation of Agathocles, he had made himself unpopular by what amounted to press-gang recruitment of rowing crews. But at the same time it must be admitted that the Greeks were never an easy population to deal with. Every successful champion of their liberties was sooner or later bound to be suspected as a potential tyrant.

It is related that Pyrrhus left Sicily conscious that it would become a battlefield for hostilities between Rome and Carthage. Perhaps the remark attributed to him on this occasion was the invention of historians who enjoyed the advantage of hindsight. But Sicily had always been a cockpit and it was easy to see here an area in which any widely expanding power must be challenged.

287
Pyrrhus occupies Macedonian territory

Antigonus II (Gonatas), son of Demetrius, inherits control of Greek states

At Syracuse, about this date, Archimedes is born

At Rome, the Hortensian law gives legal force to resolutions of the plebeian assembly

BC

105

Rome and Carthage as Allies

At the time of Pyrrhus' operations in Italy and Sicily (281-275 BC), Rome and Carthage were in fact associated by a series of treaties which dated from very early times. The precise number of these treaties is a subject on which neither ancient historians nor modern scholars agree. Polybius, the Greek historian of Rome's wars against Carthage, paraphrases these treaties, the earliest of which was preserved at Rome in an archaic form of Latin. According to Polybius, the treaty forbade the Romans to sail south of the "Fair Cape" (just north of Carthage) unless driven there by weather or warfare. A Roman finding himself accidentally in this area was not allowed to carry anything away with him save what was necessary for repairs to his ship or sacrifice to the gods, and he was obliged to leave the country within five days. Any business contracts in the scheduled zones were to be concluded in the presence of a herald or notary. Such contracts could be enforced by law in Libya and Sardinia. In Sicily, a Roman was to enjoy equal rights with others. Carthage, for her part, was bound to maintain friendly relations with Rome's Latin satellites, and this applied even to other Latin cities, though rather equivocally: if the Carthaginians captured such a city, they were obliged to hand it over to Rome without sacking it. The Carthaginians, moreover, were forbidden to build any fort in Latin territory, and if Carthaginians by chance entered the territory under arms, they were not to pass the night there.

At a later date, says Polybius, another treaty was made. Areas in which the Romans might neither trade nor practise piracy were more specifically defined. If the Carthaginians captured any Latin city, they could retain valuables and captives but must surrender the city itself to the Romans. There are detailed provisions relating to the taking of slaves, and again a reference to Sardinia and Libya as sensitive Carthaginian zones. The Romans were not to trade or found settlements in either of these territories.

The last of the three treaties mentioned by Polybius was occasioned by Pyrrhus' invasion and may confidently

Right: *Samnite horsemen as depicted in a 4th century tomb at Paestum. The Samnites were implacable enemies of Rome in this period.*

be assigned to 279 BC. It provided that, should either the Romans or Carthaginians subsequently reach terms with Pyrrhus, these should be subject to a reservation: namely, that if either of the two parties became a victim of the king's aggression, they might both collaborate within the resulting theatre of war. In any such case, the Carthaginians would provide ships for transport and hostilities, but each government would pay its own troops. The Carthaginians would assist in war at sea but could not be obliged to land any forces. The representatives of the contracting parties swore solemnly to this agreement, each by his own gods, and the terms of the treaty, inscribed on bronze tablets at Rome, were preserved at the temple of Jupiter. Polybius expressly denies the assertion of the pro-Carthaginian Greek historian, Philinus, that another treaty existed according to which the Romans and Carthaginians were respectively forbidden to enter Sicily and Italy.

It is not always easy to distinguish between the commercial and strategic activities of the ancient world. A major sector of commerce was the slave trade and the capture of slaves was

Right: *A Lucanian warrior as shown on a 4th century tomb painting at Paestum in southern Italy. Paestum had been a Greek colony, but in 390 BC it was captured by the Lucanians.*

necessarily accompanied by violence and warlike action. Nor was piracy regarded as an infringement of any international code, although one might be obliged to refrain from it locally under treaty pledges. However, the first two of the above-mentioned treaties seem to have been mainly commercial in scope; the third, military and naval. The underlying principle seems to have been that Carthage should offer naval aid in return for Roman military support.

It is indeed on record that, hoping to hinder Pyrrhus' intervention in Sicily, a Carthaginian admiral arrived with 120 ships to dissuade Rome from making peace with the king. The Romans were not at first willing to commit themselves. The Carthaginians then sailed off to negotiate with Pyrrhus. These negotiations also led to nothing, but when the Carthaginian mission returned again to Rome, the Romans were more amenable. The Carthaginian negotiators

Lysimachus occupies Macedonia and Thessaly

Antigonus Gonatas loses Thessalian territory to Pyrrhus

Driven from Macedonia, Demetrius is captured by Seleucus in Asia

Rome at war with Celts in north Italy

even transported 500 Roman soldiers to Rhegium, on the straits of Messina, in order to reinforce the garrison.

The End of Pyrrhus

The Carthaginian diplomatic initiative against Pyrrhus certainly seems to have borne fruit. Moreover, the Carthaginian navy attacked the king's forces as they returned from Sicily and destroyed a substantial number of his ships. About 1,000 Mamertines had also crossed into Italy to afflict Pyrrhus with guerrilla warfare. Their crossing had no doubt been much facilitated by the Carthaginian fleet.

In Italy, the Samnites, disgusted by Pyrrhus' neglect of their cause, were no longer willing to rally round him in great strength. Two Roman armies, respectively under the two consuls of the year, were now campaigning separately. Pyrrhus detached half his force to deal with the enemy in Lucania, while he himself marched northward to confront the Romans near Malventum (later renamed, more propitiously, Beneventum). Here, he attempted a night attack. Night attacks, in ancient warfare, were notoriously prone to miscarry. It will be remembered that Alexander had refused to be tempted into night operations at Gaugamela. Pyrrhus' attempt was no exception to the general rule. His advancing forces lost their way in wooded country during the hours of darkness and at dawn found themselves deployed in positions for which they had never bargained. The Romans, at first alarmed by the unexpected presence of the enemy, soon realized that it was possible to attack the isolated vanguard and rout it. Thus encouraged, the cautious consul gave battle to Pyrrhus' main body in the open plain. On this occasion, the Romans seem to have discovered a method of dealing with elephants; though the animals at first moved onward with their usual irresistible momentum, they were eventually frightened and induced to turn against their own troops. As a consequence, Pyrrhus was obliged to retreat.

He was now left in command of 8,000 infantry and 500 cavalry and, as Plutarch convincingly assures us, for lack of money to pay them, he was obliged to look for a new war. This he found in Macedonia, which Antigonus Gonatas, Demetrius' son and successor, proceeding from his rather precarious foothold in Greece, now occupied. Gauls, whose presence in southern

Battle of Beneventum 275 BC

Commanders:
   Pyrrhus v Consul Manius Curius.
Numbers:
   Pyrrhus' force: 20000 foot, 3000 horse, (2 elephants have been recently killed in action against the Mamertines).
   Roman force: 1 consular army, approximately 17000 foot, 1200 allied cavalry.
1   Pyrrhus detaches force to divert other consular army.
2   In night march against Curius' camp Pyrrhus' troops get lost in wooded country—delays.
3   They fail to achieve complete surprise at dawn.
4   Roman sally repels Pyrrhus' advance guard.
5   Romans forced to retreat as elephants enter the action.
6   Roman reserves from their camp counter-attack and capture some elephants.
7   Pyrrhus' army is forced to make a retreat.
Result:
   Pyrrhus returns to Epirus with only 8000 foot, 500 horse. Enhanced Roman prestige in Italy.

Europe was at this period a menace to Mediterranean civilization, were, like Illyrians, nevertheless found useful by Greek warlords; both Pyrrhus and Antigonus employed them. Pyrrhus was successful against Antigonus' elephants and won over the opposing Macedonian infantry by an appeal made to them on the battlefield. Antigonus fled, but the Macedonian population was soon alienated from Pyrrhus; the Gauls, whose military advantage was that they required little cash payment, remunerated themselves by the plunder of friend and foe alike. On this occasion, they ransacked some royal tombs for treasure, scattering the bones of the occupants. Pyrrhus' Greek sentiments were outraged, but he could do nothing about it.

As ever, turning from a task which, left uncompleted, would have been better unattempted, Pyrrhus answered an invitation to meddle in Spartan politics, hoping thereby to make himself master of the Peloponnese. He was killed in Argos during a street fight, having been felled by an accurately aimed tile from a woman's hand.

Meanwhile, in Italy, the garrison which Pyrrhus had left at Tarentum defied the Romans until 272 BC. It then surrendered, but was allowed to withdraw on honourable terms, while the Tarentines gave hostages to Rome and accepted a Roman garrison. The Romans dealt sternly but not vindictively with the Italian populations which had supported Pyrrhus. Important sectors of their territory were confiscated in order to provide for Latin

had made their point. The 120 ships could be thrown into either scale; Rome continued its war against Pyrrhus' allies in Italy. In fact, the Carthaginian commander, on his way back to Sicily,

BC

colonial settlements, linked to Rome by ties of citizenship. At Rhegium, the garrison installed by the Romans had been composed largely of Campanian mercenaries; Campania, like Arcadia in Greece, was a traditional source of mercenaries. These had mutinied and attempted to pursue an independent line in the manner of the Mamertines (who were also of Campanian extraction). When the Romans reoccupied Rhegium, they showed no mercy to the mutineers and 300 of them were executed in Rome.

The Political and Military Emergence of Rome

Rome now dominated southern and central Italy, including Etruria and the Greek cities. Northern Italy, of course, remained largely occupied by the Gauls, and the Gauls remained a menace. The process by which Rome had developed from a small military outpost on a river-crossing to become the dominant power of the Italian

Left: *An Etruscan bronze statuette of the 5th century BC. The cheek-pieces of the helmet, as often in such Etruscan figures, are turned up. Compare hinged Greek types.*

peninsula had been by no means swift or continuous. It had taken the greater part of five centuries, and during that time Rome itself had twice been occupied by a foreign power.

According to traditional stories, the last of Rome's kings, Tarquinius Superbus, an Etruscan, had been expelled late in the sixth century BC after his son had villainously raped the wife of a noble kinsman. Etruscan armies under Lars Porsenna had attempted to restore Tarquinius but had been thwarted by the heroism of Horatius who, with two comrades, defended the Tiber crossing against them until the demolition of the bridge was completed. The Latin cities to the south had then combined to replace the exiled monarch on his throne, but had been defeated by the Romans at the battle of Lake Regillus (where the Romans were assisted by the gods according to the legend!).

Illustrated Etruscan tomb inscriptions, taken in conjunction with the existing legends, suggest that the underlying historical facts were very different. It is clear that Porsenna was not the friend but the mortal enemy of Tarquinius, his fellow Etruscan. He probably conspired with aristocratic, partly Etruscan elements in Rome to precipitate Tarquinius' downfall, and then himself occupied Rome. He certainly advanced south of Rome, to fight the Latins and their Greek allies of Cumae — where according to one story Tarquinius ultimately took refuge. When the Etruscans were defeated by the Latin League at Aricia (as described by Livy), their fugitives were received and protected in Rome. Moreover, Livy stresses the friendship of Porsenna towards the Romans and his chivalrous respect for their way of life. One would guess that Rome had accepted the position of subject ally to Etruria. The Roman population, despite its Etruscan overlordship, was of course Latin; their Etruscan allegiances brought them into conflict with the other Latin cities, who were allied to the Greek maritime states — Etruria's commercial rivals.

At Rome, Latin patriotic sentiment may have accepted Etruscan kings and welcomed their leadership against Etruria itself, just as English patriotic feeling in the Middle Ages accepted French-speaking Plantagenet kings as leaders against the French. The early Roman historians, however, did not

like to contemplate their city as a mere catspaw in Etruscan dynastic politics, let alone a puppet state to be employed against their Latin brothers. Consequently these chroniclers substituted history of their own invention, assigning fictional roles to historic characters.

As the strength of Etruria diminished, Rome asserted its authority over both the Etruscans and the Latins, but at the beginning of the fourth century the city was overwhelmed, after the disastrous battle of the Allia, by a vast horde of Gallic raiders. The Romans retreated into their citadel on the Capitoline Mount; they eventually bought off the Gauls, whose immediate interest was in moveables and not in land. Roman history records that the great Camillus, Rome's exiled war leader, was recalled to speed the parting Gauls with military action, but this thinly veils the fact that the Gauls departed of their own accord, having obtained what they wanted. Livy blames Roman decadence and impiety for the disaster, but the Romans must in any case have been vanquished by sheer weight of numbers. Apart from that, they were never at their best when dealing with a strange foe whose weapons and methods of warfare were new to them.

Roman military history is chequered by catastrophes. Few great empires can have sustained more major disasters during the period of their growth. Nobody would deny that the Romans were a formidable military nation; yet the genius which enabled them eventually to dominate the ancient world was as much political as military. Their great political instrument was their concept of citizenship. Citizenship was not simply a status which one did or did not possess. It was an aggregate of rights, duties and honours, which could be acquired separately and conferred by instalments. Such were the rights of making legal contracts and marriages. From both of these the right to a political vote was again separable; nor did the right to vote necessarily imply the right to hold office. Conquered enemies were thus often reconciled by a grant of partial citizenship, with the possibility of more to come if behaviour justified it. Some cities enjoyed Roman citizenship without the vote, being autonomous except in matters of foreign policy. Even the citizens of such communities, however, might qualify for full Roman citizenship if they migrated to Rome; where this right was not available, citizenship could be obtained by those who achieved public distinction in their own communities.

282
Roman protective garrison in Thurii, Locri and Rhegium

Tarentines attack Roman naval flotilla

281
Seleucus defeats and kills Lysimachus at Corupedium

Tarentum invites Pyrrhus to intervene against Rome

Seleucus murdered

The Roman Army in Early Times

Citizenship, of course, implied a military as well as a political status. For the duties which it imposed were, above all, military. The Latin and other Italian allies, who enjoyed some intermediate degree of citizenship, were in principle required to supply an aggregate of fighting men equal to that levied by the Romans themselves. In practice, the Romans relied on their Italian allies particularly for cavalry; an arm in which they themselves were notoriously weak. The Greek cities did not normally contribute military contingents, but supplied ships and rowers. They were known as "naval allies" (*socii navales*) because of this function.

Any army whose technical resources are comprised by hand-arms, armour and horses, will, at all events in the early years of its development, reflect an underlying social order. Combatants who can afford horses and armour will naturally be drawn from the aristocracy.

Others will have little armour and less sophisticated, if not fewer, weapons. This was true of Greek armies and also of medieval armies. It was certainly true of the Romans. At Rome, indeed, the military class differentiation was defined with unusual care and with great attention to detail. The resulting classification is associated with the military and administrative reorganization of Servius Tullius, traditionally sixth and penultimate King of Rome. His name suggests a sixth-century date for the reforms in question, though some scholars think that the so-called Servian organization was introduced later than this.

The "Servian" infantry was divided into five property classes, the wealthiest of which was armed with swords and spears and protected by helmets, round shields, greaves and breastplates. All protective armour was of bronze. In the second class, no breastplate was worn, but a long shield was substituted for the round buckler. The third class was as the second, but wore no greaves. The fourth class was equipped only with spears and javelins; the fifth was composed of slingers. There is no reference to archers. The poorest citizens were not expected to serve except in times of emergency, when they were equipped by the state. However, they normally supplied artisans to maintain siege engines and perform similar duties.

The army was also divided into centuries (ie, "hundreds"), as the citizens were for voting purposes. However, a century soon came to contain 60, not 100 men. The first property class comprised 80 centuries; the second, third and fourth class had 20 centuries apiece; the fifth class had 30. A distinction was made between junior and senior centuries, the former containing young men for front-line action, the latter older men, more suitable for garrison duty. A single property class was equally divided between the two age groups.

The cavalry was recruited from the wealthiest families to form 18 centuries. A cavalry century received a grant for the purchase of its horses and one-fifth

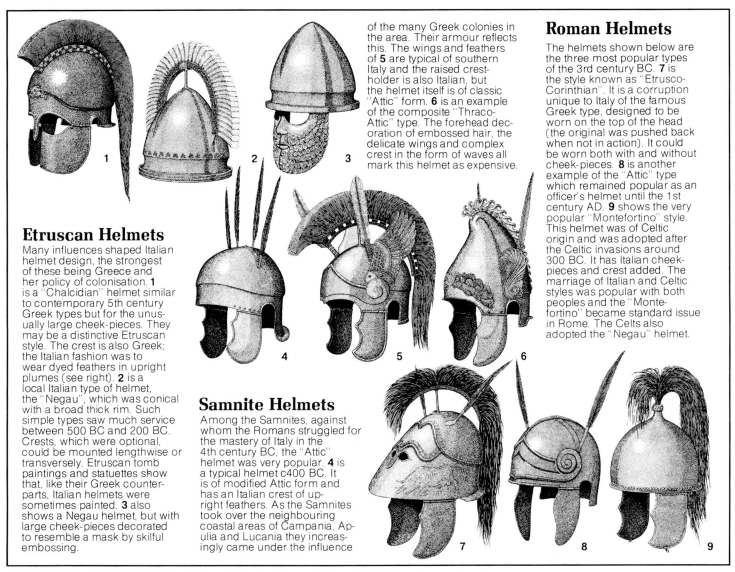

Etruscan Helmets

Many influences shaped Italian helmet design, the strongest of these being Greece and her policy of colonisation. **1** is a "Chalcidian" helmet similar to contemporary 5th century Greek types but for the unusually large cheek-pieces. They may be a distinctive Etruscan style. The crest is also Greek; the Italian fashion was to wear dyed feathers in upright plumes (see right). **2** is a local Italian type of helmet, the "Negau", which was conical with a broad thick rim. Such simple types saw much service between 500 BC and 200 BC. Crests, which were optional, could be mounted lengthwise or transversely. Etruscan tomb paintings and statuettes show that, like their Greek counterparts, Italian helmets were sometimes painted. **3** also shows a Negau helmet, but with large cheek-pieces decorated to resemble a mask by skilful embossing.

Samnite Helmets

Among the Samnites, against whom the Romans struggled for the mastery of Italy in the 4th century BC, the "Attic" helmet was very popular. **4** is a typical helmet c400 BC. It is of modified Attic form and has an Italian crest of upright feathers. As the Samnites took over the neighbouring coastal areas of Campania, Apulia and Lucania they increasingly came under the influence of the many Greek colonies in the area. Their armour reflects this. The wings and feathers of **5** are typical of southern Italy and the raised crest-holder is also Italian, but the helmet itself is of classic "Attic" form. **6** is an example of the composite "Thraco-Attic" type. The forehead decoration of embossed hair, the delicate wings and complex crest in the form of waves all mark this helmet as expensive.

Roman Helmets

The helmets shown below are the three most popular types of the 3rd century BC. **7** is the style known as "Etrusco-Corinthian". It is a corruption unique to Italy of the famous Greek type, designed to be worn on the top of the head (the original was pushed back when not in action). It could be worn both with and without cheek-pieces. **8** is another example of the "Attic" type which remained popular as an officer's helmet until the 1st century AD. **9** shows the very popular "Montefortino" style. This helmet was of Celtic origin and was adopted after the Celtic invasions around 300 BC. It has Italian cheek-pieces and crest added. The marriage of Italian and Celtic styles was popular with both peoples and the "Montefortino" became standard issue in Rome. The Celts also adopted the "Negau" helmet.

The Roman Army (3rd century BC)

These figures illustrate the soldiers (*milites*) of this period Those eligible for service through owning property at a set level were assembled and selected for service. A citizen was liable for service from the age of 17 to 46, but in an emergency this could be extended to 50 or more. Men were then graded into 4 types which formed the various lines of battle. The *velites* (below) were the youngest and poorest. They were armed with 4ft (1·2m) javelins, sword and a 3ft (1m) diameter shield made of wicker and covered with hide. Their only other defence was a helmet. Polybius mentions that many of them wore wolf or bear skins over their helmets. The figure (far right) shows a *hastatus* or *princeps*. They formed the first two lines of heavy infantry respectively. The *hastati* were the young men full grown. They were armed with a heavy, long *scutum*, 2 *pila* (heavy and light) and a short, straight cut-and-thrust sword (*gladius*) Armour was provided by each individual and thus varied. The soldier shown here wears a small, square back and breast plate, a greave on the left leg only and a Montefortino helmet. The *principes* were the family men "in their prime" as Polybius says. They were armed as the *hastati*. The figure (right) shows a *triarius*, one of the older veterans, who carried a long thrusting spear (*hasta*). This one is able to afford a mail coat and he wears an Etrusco-Corinthian helmet and two greaves. The shield designs are uncertain but are based on contemporary Italian and known later Roman designs.

BC

279
Battle of Asculum — another costly victory for Pyrrhus

Celtic irruption into Macedonia and Thrace

278
Celts invading Greece are routed near Delphi

Antigonus Gonatas destroys Celtic host at Lysimachia in Thrace

110

The Roman Battle System

1 The legion forms up, *hastati* and *principes* in open order, *triarii* in close order. The gap between lines might vary between 0 and 250ft (0-76m). The *velites* skirmish and distract the enemy. When all is ready the *velites* are recalled and pass through the open ranks to the rear.

2 The *prior* centuries of *hastati* move right and the *posterior* centuries advance to form a solid line. At about 150yds (137m) both sides charge. The front ranks of *hastati* throw their light *pila* at about 35yds (32m) from the enemy, quickly followed by their heavy *pila*. They draw swords and close up on the run and hit the enemy with as much impact as possible. Succeeding ranks throw *pila* over the front ranks. The battle is a succession of furious combats with both sides drawing apart to recover. This might go on for several hours.

3 During one of these pauses the *hastati* are given the recall. The *posterior* centuries back away and the *prior* centuries slide across in front of them. Then the maniples of *hastati* withdraw in close order, to reform behind the *triarii*. Meanwhile the *principes* move up in open order and pass through the *hastati*. The enemy is unable to take advantage as a continuous front is presented.

4 The *posterior* centuries deploy to the left of their *prior* centuries, the *principes* manoeuvre to within charging distance, and the tired enemy is faced with a fresh foe and another fierce charge.

5 If the enemy is not broken before the *principes* too are exhausted, then their place is taken by a thin (3 deep) line of *triarii* spearmen.

6 The army can now withdraw or prepare to start again. The phrase "*Inde rem ad triarios redisse*" ("The last resource is in the triarii") passed into the language as a description of a desperate situation. Naturally not all battles went "by the book" and for variations see the battles of Zama (p121) and Cynoscephalae (p124).

Against a pike phalanx the second and third lines were used to give weight to the front ranks in an attempt to resist the push of the 16 deep phalanx. The beauty of the system was that its flexibility allowed the lines to adapt to differing situations.

Symbol	Label
	Velites
	Triarii
	Principes
	Hastati
	Posterior century
	Prior century

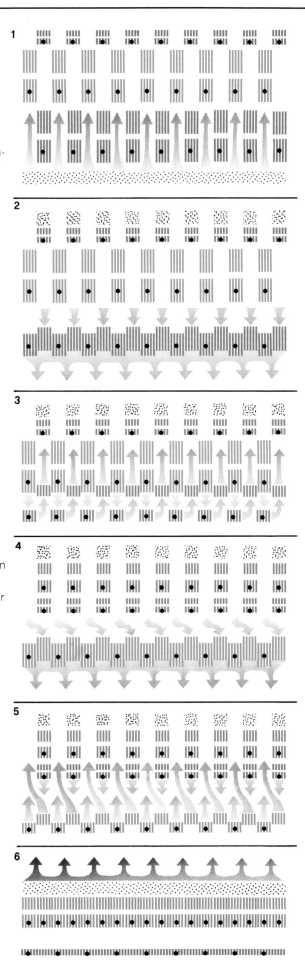

of this amount yearly for their upkeep. The yearly grant was apparently provided by a levy on spinsters! In general, the financial burden of warfare was shifted from the poor on to the rich. For this imposition, the rich were compensated by what amounted to a monopoly of the political suffrage. Inevitably, it was felt in time that they were over-compensated, but that is a matter which must not detain us here.

During the early epochs of Roman history, as archaeological evidence indicates, Greek hoplite armour was widely imitated throughout the Mediterranean area. Italy was no exception to this rule and, as Livy's description suggests, Rome was no exception in Italy. Greek weapons called for Greek skill in their use, and this in turn assumed Greek tactical methods. The Romans were in contact with Greek practice, both through their Etruscan northern neighbours, who as a maritime people were more susceptible to overseas influences, and through direct contact with Greek cities in Italy, notably Cumae. The Roman army, as recruited on the Servian basis, must have fought as a hoplite phalanx, in a compact mass, several ranks deep, using their weight behind their shields as well as their long thrusting spears. The light troops afforded by the fourth and fifth infantry classes will have provided a skirmishing arm, and the cavalry held the wings on either side of the phalanx. There were also two centuries of artificers (*fabri*) attached to the centuries of the first class, and two of musicians (made up of horn-blowers and trumpeters).

The Military Reforms of Camillus

The next great landmark in Roman military organization is associated with the achievements of Camillus. Camillus, credited with having saved Rome from the Gauls and remembered as a "second founder" of Rome, was a revered national hero. His name became a legend, and legends accumulated round it. At the same time, he was unquestionably a historical character. We need not believe that his timely return to Rome during the Gallic occupation deprived the Gauls of their indemnity money, which was at that very moment being weighed out in gold. But his capture of the Etruscan city of Veii is historical, and he may here have made use of mining operations such as Livy describes. Similarly, the military changes attri-

277
Pyrrhus in Sicily
Antigonus establishes his authority in Macedonia

275
Pyrrhus returns to Italy
Pyrrhus fights the Romans at Beneventum without success
Pyrrhus returns to Epirus

BC

111

The Post-Camillan Roman Army

The basic fighting unit of the Roman army was the maniple which consisted of 120-160 men organised into two centuries. Each maniple elected a centurion who then nominated another to command the other century. The first century commander was styled "*prior*" and the second "*posterior*". The most senior centurion was the commander of the first century of *triarii* and was known as "*primipilus*". The drawing (top right) shows a century of *hastati* in open order. Every alternate rank is displaced laterally from the one in front to allow room for throwing the two *pila*. Once the front two ranks have hurled their *pila*, the second rank closes up with the front rank and swords are drawn. The third and fourth ranks then throw *pila*, close up and draw swords. This continues until the entire century is in close order (see drawing right). A late writer says that in close order each man occupied a 3ft (·9m) frontage and depth (other writers give varying dimensions). The centurion's second-in-command was known as an *optio* and was assisted by a *tesserarius* (orderly-sergeant). Signals were passed by the *cornicen* (trumpeter) so drawing attention to the *sig—nifer* (standard bearer). His movement of the *signum* indicated the expected direction of movement. Unlike the *hastati* and *principes* a maniple of *triarii* consisted of only 60 men; they constituted the last line of defence.

As noted on p111 Roman troops in battle order were drawn up in three lines. The *hastati*

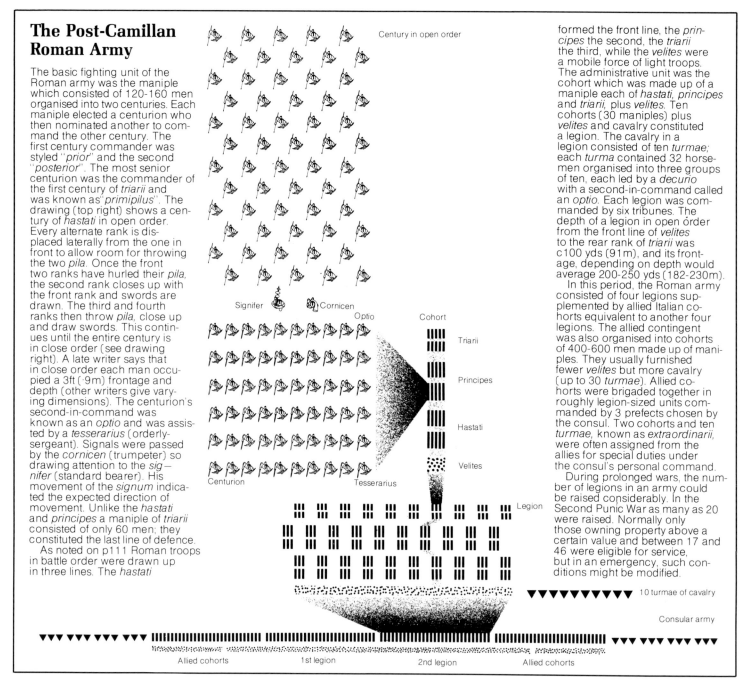

Century in open order

Signifer   Cornicen

Optio   Cohort

Triarii

Principes

Hastati

Velites

Centurion   Tesserarius

Legion

10 turmae of cavalry

Consular army

Allied cohorts   1st legion   2nd legion   Allied cohorts

formed the front line, the *principes* the second, the *triarii* the third, while the *velites* were a mobile force of light troops. The administrative unit was the cohort which was made up of a maniple each of *hastati, principes* and *triarii*, plus *velites*. Ten cohorts (30 maniples) plus *velites* and cavalry constituted a legion. The cavalry in a legion consisted of ten *turmae*; each *turma* contained 32 horsemen organised into three groups of ten, each led by a *decurio* with a second-in-command called an *optio*. Each legion was commanded by six tribunes. The depth of a legion in open order from the front line of *velites* to the rear rank of *triarii* was c100 yds (91m), and its frontage, depending on depth would average 200-250 yds (182-230m).

In this period, the Roman army consisted of four legions supplemented by allied Italian cohorts equivalent to another four legions. The allied contingent was also organised into cohorts of 400-600 men made up of maniples. They usually furnished fewer *velites* but more cavalry (up to 30 *turmae*). Allied cohorts were brigaded together in roughly legion-sized units commanded by 3 prefects chosen by the consul. Two cohorts and two *turmae*, known as *extraordinarii*, were often assigned from the allies for special duties under the consul's personal command.

During prolonged wars, the number of legions in an army could be raised considerably. In the Second Punic War as many as 20 were raised. Normally only those owning property above a certain value and between 17 and 46 were eligible for service, but in an emergency, such conditions might be modified.

buted to him may in part, if not entirety, be due to his initiative.

Soon after the withdrawal of the Gauls from Rome, the tactical formation adopted by the Roman army underwent a radical change. In the Servian army, the smallest unit had been the century. It was an administrative rather than a tactical unit, based on political and economic rather than military considerations. The largest unit was the legion of about 4,000 infantrymen. There were 60 centuries in a legion and, from the time of Camillus, these centuries were combined in couples, each couple being known as a maniple (*manipulus*). The maniple was a tactical unit. Under the new system, the Roman army was drawn up for battle in three lines, one behind the other. The maniples of each

line were stationed at intervals. If the front line was forced to retreat, or if its maniples were threatened with encirclement, they could fall back into the intervals in the line immediately to their rear. In the same way, the rear lines could easily advance, when necessary, to support those in front. The positions of the middle-line maniples corresponded to intervals in the front and rear lines, thus producing a series of quincunx formations. The two constituent centuries of a maniple were each commanded by a centurion, known respectively as the forward (*prior*) and rear (*posterior*) centurion. These titles may have been dictated by later tactical developments, or they may simply have marked a difference of rank between the two officers.

The three battle lines of Camillus' army were termed, in order from front to rear, *hastati, principes* and *triarii*. *Hastati* meant "spearmen"; *principes*, "leaders"; and *triarii*, the only term which was consistent with known practice, meant simply "third-liners". In historical accounts, the *hastati* were not armed with spears and the *principes* were not the leading rank, since the *hastati* were in front of them. The names obviously reflect the usage of an earlier date. In the fourth century, the two front ranks carried heavy javelins, which they discharged at the enemy on joining battle. After this, fighting was carried on with swords. The *triarii* alone retained the old thrusting spear (*hasta*). The heavy javelin of the *hastati* and *principes* was

BC

274
In India, Asoka extends the empire of Chandragupta Maurya far southwards

272
Pyrrhus, campaigning in the Peloponnese, is killed in street fighting at Argos

Surrender of Tarentum to Rome

112

Above: *Italic bronze breast-plate with buckle-like attachments. The design of early Italic arms and armour often shows the influence of Greek originals.*

the *pilum*. It comprised a wooden shaft, about 4·5 feet (1·4m) long, and a lance-like, iron head of about the same length as the shaft; which fitted into the wood so far as to give an overall length of something less than 7 feet (2·1m). The Romans may have copied the *pilum* from their Etruscan or Samnite enemies; or they may have developed it from a more primitive weapon of their own. The sword used was the *gladius*, a short cut-and-thrust type, probably forged on Spanish models. A large oval shield (*scutum*), about 4 feet (1·2m) long, was in general use in the maniple formation. It was made of hide on a wooden base, with iron rim and boss.

It has been suggested that the new tactical formation was closely connected with the introduction of the new weapons. The fact that the front rank was called *hastati* seems to indicate that the *hasta*, or thrusting spear, was not abandoned until after the new formation had been adopted. Indeed, cause and effect may have stood in circular relationship. The open formation could have favoured new weapons which, once widely adopted, forbade the use of any other formation. At all events, there must have been more elbow room for aiming a javelin.

Apart from these considerations, open-order fighting was characteristic of Greek fourth-century warfare. Xenophon's men had opened ranks to let the enemy's scythe-wheel chariots pass harmlessly through. Agesilaus used similar tactics at Coronea. Camillus was aware of the Greek world —and the Greek world was aware of him. He dedicated a golden bowl to Apollo at Delphi and Greek fourth-century writers refer to him. It is at least possible that the new Roman tactical formation was based on Greek precedents, as the old one had been.

Officers and Other Ranks

The epoch of Camillus also saw the first regular payments for military service. The amount of pay, at the time of its introduction, is not recorded. To judge from the enthusiasm to which it gave rise and to the difficulty experienced in levying taxes to provide for it, the sum was substantial. It was a first step towards removing the differences among property classes and standardizing the equipment of the legionary soldier. For tactical purposes, of course, some differences were bound to exist: for instance, in the lighter equipment of the *velites*. But the removal of the property classes produced an essential change in the Roman army, such as the Greek citizen army had never known. The Athenian hoplites had always remained a social class, and hoplite warfare was their distinctive function. The Spartan hoplites had been an élite of peers, every one of them, as Thucydides remarks, in effect an officer.

At Rome, however, the centuries of which the legions were composed were conspicuously and efficiently led by centurions, men who commanded as a result of their proven merit. The Roman army, in fact, developed a system of leadership such as is familiar today — a system of officers and other ranks. Centurions were comparable to warrant officers, promoted for their performance on the field and in the camp. The military tribunes, like their commanding officers, the consuls and praetors, were at any rate originally appointed to carry out the policies of the Roman state, and they were usually drawn from the upper, politically influential classes.

Six military tribunes were chosen for each legion, and the choice was at first always made by a consul or praetor, who in normal times would have commanded two out of the four legions levied; as colleagues, the consuls shared the army between them. Later, the appointment of 24 military tribunes for the levy of four legions was made not by the consuls but by an assembly of the people. If, however, additional legions were levied, then the tribunes appointed to them were consular nominations. Tribunes appointed by the people held office for one year. Those nominated by a military commander retained their appointment for as long as he did.

Military tribunes were at first senior officers and were required to have several years of military experience prior to appointment. In practice, however, they were often young men, whose very age precluded them from having had such experience. They were appointed because they came from rich and influential families and they thus had much in common with the subalterns of fashionable regiments in latter-day armies. Originally, an important part of the military tribune's duties had been in connection with the levy of troops. In normal times, a levy was held once a year. Recruits were required to assemble by tribes (a local as distinct from a class division). The distribution of recruits among the four legions was based on the selection made by the tribunes.

"Praetor" was the title originally conferred on each of the two magistrates who shared supreme authority after the period of the kings. The military functions of the praetor are well attested, and the headquarters in a Roman camp continued to be termed the "praetorium". In comparatively early times, the title of "consul" replaced that of "praetor", but partly as a result of political manoeuvre, the office of praetor was later revived to supplement consular power. The authority of a praetor was not equal to that of a consul, but he might still command an army in the field.

The command was not always happily shared between two consuls. In times of emergency—and Rome's early history consisted largely of emergencies—a single dictator with supreme power was appointed for a maximum term of six months, the length of a campaigning season. The dictator chose his own deputy, who was then known as the Master of the Horse (*magister equitum*).*

The allies, who were called upon to aid Rome in case of war, were commanded by prefects (*praefecti*), who were Roman officers. The 300 cavalry attached to each legion were, in the third century at any rate, divided into ten squadrons (*turmae*), and subdivided into *decuriae*, each of which was commanded by a *decurio*, whose authority corresponded to that of a centurion in the infantry.

---

*The late revival of the dictatorship against Hannibal was in many ways exceptional.

┐ **271**
The Romans recapture
Rhegium

┐ **266**
Athens allied with the
Peloponnesians and
Ptolemy II in war against
Macedonia (Chremonidean
War)

BC

The Punic Wars and Roman Expansion

In spite of the military genius of Hannibal, Carthage was destroyed as the result of three wars between 265 and 146 BC. Macedon and Syria were quelled, but the war against Jugurtha of Numidia revealed weakness at the heart of Roman power.

Ancient Authorities

We have now once more reached a period of history for which there is important first-hand evidence. This is provided by the work of Polybius, who was born about 200 BC and died some time after 118 BC. He wrote the history of Rome's conquest and domination of the ancient world during the third and second centuries and the scope of his work was extended to include a more or less favourable assessment of the resulting Roman supremacy. His original *Histories* contained 40 books, but of these only the first five, together with excerpts and fragments from later books, remain extant.

Polybius was a citizen of Megalopolis, the city originally founded by Epaminondas as a bulwark against Sparta. About 170 BC he was serving as a cavalry commander in the Achaean League, but after the collapse of Macedon and the consequent control of Greece by the Romans, Polybius was deported with other political suspects to Rome and was indefinitely detained in Italy, on no explicit charge. This detention, however, seems to have been regarded by him as an opportunity; he became intimate with influential political and literary circles in Rome, being personally acquainted with some of the characters who figure eminently in his history. Afterwards, he had the opportunity of travelling widely. He wrote a book on tactics and a history of the war which the Romans waged round Numantia in Spain, but these works are unfortunately lost. As it is, we have in Polybius' surviving books the testimony of one who was in close contact, at the highest level, with the military and political life of his day.

For Hannibal's war against Rome and the period which immediately followed it, Livy is of course our most extensive authority. Perhaps it is not possible for a historian to be completely objective, but one must remember that Livy was inspired by patriotic motives, as were many of the writers on whose

Above: *The head seen on this Carthaginian coin is believed to be that of Hannibal, Rome's greatest enemy.*

evidence he depended. In addition to this, family pride and flattery often played an important part in shaping the accounts given by Roman historians; it is easy to feel that if the successes of some Roman commanders in Italy had been as great as Livy suggests, Hannibal would have been defeated much sooner than, in fact, he was. Apart from the early history of Rome down to 294 BC, Livy's surviving books narrate events from the beginning of the Hannibalic War down to the conquest of Macedonia and defeat of the Seleucid power in the second century BC. Were the entire 142 books extant, we should possess the history of Rome in the full form which he gave it, down to the year 9 BC. As it is, nearly all the contents of Livy's lost books have been transmitted to us by later writers in summarized form. Historians of the imperial epoch in many instances either used Livy as a source or had access to the sources which he had used. These included the important Greek historians Appian and Dio Cassius, who were both born during the second century AD.

By contrast, Sallust (Gaius Sallustius Crispus, about 86-35 BC), the historian

Above: *A Carthaginian coin minted in Spain. The head may be that of Hasdrubal Barca, Hannibal's brother.*

of the war against Jugurtha, lived close to the events which he described, having both the oral and written testimony of men who took part in them. But although Sallust served in Julius Caesar's African campaign of 46 BC, his interests were of a political rather than a military nature.

Historical Outline

Punicus is the Latin for "Carthaginian". The first Punic War was provoked by those perennial troublemakers the Mamertines who, based on Messana (Messina), appealed to the Carthaginians against Hiero II, the Greek king of Syracuse. Their object achieved, the Mamertines wished to be rid of the Carthaginian garrison which had protected them, and they appealed to Rome. The Carthaginian threat across the narrow straits was too great, the

Right: *This map illustrates the major campaigns of the Second Punic War 218-201 BC. Scipio's intervention in Spain and finally in Africa itself succeeded in turning the tide of Carthaginian domination.*

BC	264	263	260	259
	Rome supports the Mamertines against Hiero of Syracuse and his Carthaginian allies	Hiero makes peace and alliance with Rome, but war against Carthage continues	Roman naval victory over Carthaginians at Mylae	Roman successes in Corsica and Sardinia

opportunity of removing it too good, and Rome intervened in 264 BC.

To win the war in Sicily, Rome built a fleet with which she defeated the Carthaginians. Imitating the strategy of Agathocles, the Roman general Regulus crossed into Africa and launched an offensive, but the Carthaginians employed a brilliant Spartan mercenary leader, Xanthippus, and Regulus was defeated and captured. The Romans' newly achieved command of the sea, however, enabled them to win the war, despite the fact that their fleets were repeatedly destroyed in storms. Isolated in east Sicily, Hamilcar Barca, the great Carthaginian commander, was at last obliged to come to terms with the Romans and surrender his command of the island in 241 BC.

Before the next outbreak of hostilities with Carthage, Rome was involved against the Gauls in North Italy. The Romans also found it necessary to subdue an Illyrian queen who, encouraged by Macedon, had extended her power southward in support of the piracy which was the mainstay of her nation's economy. Carthage, meanwhile, was threatened with a gruesome revolt of her own mercenaries, abetted by subject populations in North Africa. From this so-called "Truceless War", the city was barely saved by the military ability of Hamilcar Barca. Of

Rome and Carthage in this period, it might be said that either nation would have been quicker to take advantage of the other's difficulties, but for its own. As it was, the mercenary war had forced Carthage temporarily to withdraw from Sardinia, and the Romans, opportunists as previously, intervened in this sensitive Carthaginian area.

Hamilcar now concentrated on Spain, both as a military base and as a zone for further economic expansion. After his death in action, his son Hannibal pursued the same policy. War followed the siege and capture of Saguntum, a city friendly to Rome. Hannibal then invaded Italy via the Pyrenees, the Rhone and the Alps. His invasion may be compared with that of Pyrrhus. The defeats which he inflicted on the Romans were overwhelming and unambiguous in a way that Pyrrhus' dubious victories certainly were not, but, like Pyrrhus, he was unable to detach Rome's Italian allies from her, let alone capture or come to terms with Rome in the course of his campaigns.

On the initiative of Publius Cornelius Scipio, later honoured with the surname of Africanus, the Romans again applied the remedy of an African counter-offensive. Hannibal, recalled by the Carthaginians and defeated at Zama in 202 BC, was driven into exile.

At Zama, invaluable cavalry support

had been provided by Masinissa the Numidian king, who had abandoned his alliance with Carthage. In the peace which followed, Masinissa took full and shameless advantage of the protected position which he enjoyed as a Roman ally, and Rome did little to discourage him. Thus provoked by the Numidian, Carthage in retaliation infringed the Zama peace treaty. Using this as a pretext, the Romans disingenuously induced the Carthaginians to make what amounted to an uncondi-

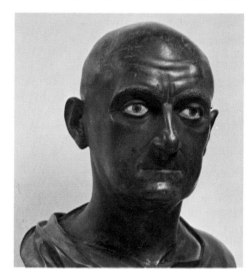

Above: *A portrait bust of Scipio Africanus who defeated Hannibal in the battle of Zama in 202 BC.*

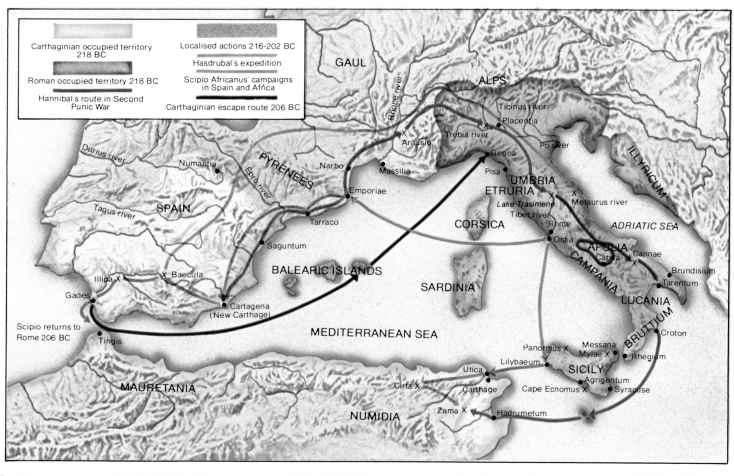

256
The Roman commander Regulus invades Africa, after Roman naval victory at Ecnomus

255
Defeat of Regulus by Carthaginians under the Greek commander Xanthippus

254
The Romans capture Panormus in Sicily

250
Romans repulse Carthaginian counter-offensive on Panormus

BC

115

tional surrender; when, however, the Romans next required them to vacate their city and their coast and resettle as homeless wanderers in the interior, they resisted. After a long siege by land and blockade by sea, the Romans captured, sacked and utterly destroyed Carthage in 146 BC.

Since the Second Punic War, Rome had found itself surrounded by nations which, whether they had been the allies or enemies of Carthage, were now in a position to inherit that city's much dreaded power. In pursuit of stable frontiers, the Romans were obliged to fight in Spain and North Africa. Here, frontiers were offered by the Ocean and the Sahara Desert respectively. In other directions, the situation did not lend itself so readily to conclusive results. In the East were three great dynasties, the Macedonian, the Seleucid and the Ptolemaic, controlling Alexander's European, Asian and North African legacies respectively. In the north of Italy, the Gauls were still not completely subdued, and those beyond the Alps posed problems for the future. The second and first centuries therefore found Rome involved in far-flung theatres of war, driven by fear of encircling enemies into a policy of continual expansion.

The Roman Naval Effort

A remarkable feature of the Punic Wars was that Rome, with virtually no naval tradition, contrived to dominate the seas almost throughout, while Carthage, which was by comparison an unmilitary power relying on mercenary armies, produced two supremely brilliant generals in the persons of Hamilcar and Hannibal.

The first Roman naval success came at Mylae in 260 BC, in support of the struggle for Sicily. The victory had been preceded by an effort of shipbuilding and naval training which must be regarded as prodigious, even if we do not believe all that ancient historians wrote on the subject. For instance, we are told that a wrecked Carthaginian ship which fell into Roman hands was used as a model for building the new fleet. In fact, the Romans had previously possessed a small fleet. Consisting of 20 ships, it had operated under the orders of two officers known as *duoviri navales*; one such officer had commanded the squadron which came under Tarentine attack in 282 BC. The diminutive Roman fleet was, admittedly, composed of triremes, and heavier vessels were

now required to match those of the Carthaginians, but one would have thought that sea-going Greek allies were capable of supplying Rome with quinqueremes for imitation, and that Hiero II of Syracuse, who, after the early days of the war, had resumed his alliance with the Romans, could have offered instruction in shipbuilding.

The ancient world affords other examples of navies successfully built in haste, and it must be remembered that even the heavier galleys of Roman times were small compared with the sailing ships of later European history. In the First Punic War, it is estimated that Rome had a fleet of approximately 160 vessels, whereas the Carthaginians

had about 130. Both sides were limited in their building programmes by the number of available rowers. The useful Roman superiority was probably again derived through Greek assistance.

Roman naval victory, however, was mainly the product of tactical and technical innovation. From the first, the Romans renounced the traditional ramming manoeuvres and concentrated on boarding tactics, which would permit them to fight what were virtually land battles at sea. To this end, they effectively developed an iron-beaked grappling device, known as a "raven". Polybius described the structure and operation of this mechanism in great detail, although a diagram would have made his meaning clearer. In Greek, the "raven" was a *corax* (Latin: *corvus*), and a hooked instrument called a *corax* had previously

been used in siege warfare for grappling fortified walls.

The "raven", as used by the Roman navy, was a swivelling, derrick-operated gangway, mounted in the prow of a warship. Its pivoting base allowed it to be effective in at least three directions, and its iron beak, when lowered to a horizontal position, spiked and gripped the enemy's deck. A boarding party then poured across the gangway. To this device the Punic fleet proved extremely vulnerable.

According to Polybius, the derrick section of the gangway was 24 feet (7·3m) long and the horizontal, turntable section on which it hinged (like a flail) measured 12 feet (3·6m). Some scholars

Above: *Ancient ruins at Carthage. In 146 BC the Romans captured Carthage and razed it to the ground. Later they colonised the site.*

think that an apparatus so large would have caused the ship on which it was mounted to capsize; others believe that it did indeed cause accidents and was therefore discontinued. It could, in any case, have been dismounted when not in use. It may be remembered that Demetrius the Besieger erected siege towers on his war galleys at Rhodes. We also have ancient representations (1st century BC) of Roman warships with turrets mounted on the deck. These turrets are apparently iron-plated, like Demetrius' *helepolis,* and in any case must have been heavy. Some suggest that they were painted to resemble stone or even built of stone

BC
249
A Roman fleet defeated at Drepana
247
The birth of Hannibal
Arsaces overthrows the Seleucid satrap and becomes first king of Parthia
244
Hamilcar Barca maintains Carthagian base on Mt Eryx in Sicily

116

Battle of Lake Trasimene 217 BC

Romans	Hannibal
	Infantry
2 legions 10000	Africa 10/12000
	(4000 light)
Italian allies 10000	
Crete 1000	Spain 7/8000
(archers)	(4000 light)
Peltasts 1000	Celts 10/15000
	Cavalry
Rome 600	Numidia 4000
Allies 2/3000	Celtic heavy 4000
	Spanish heavy 2000
	Elephants 1

The Roman consul Flaminius is following Hannibal in the hope of "pincering" him between his own and his fellow consul's army. He makes his camp late. During the night Hannibal posts his troops on the wooded heights above the lake; he plans a massive ambush. At first light Flaminius continues his "pursuit". A mist fills the valley. The front ranks* make contact with Hannibal's light troops and deploy, as do the right wing Allied cohorts behind them. The Roman rearguard is still in the bottleneck between the hills and the lake and the ferocity of the Celtic charge drives them into the lake. The bulk of the Romans around Flaminius are caught in marching order and cannot form their triple line. Flaminius is killed by Celtic cavalry. The Carthaginian light troops cannot hold the deployed Romans, most of whom fight their way up Mt. Castelluccio and escape.

The battle is over in 3 hours; some 15000 Romans have been killed and 4000 more taken prisoner. The 6000 or so who have escaped are surrounded by Carthaginian cavalry and light troops and forced to surrender. Hannibal's losses number only 1400-2500 dead; his classic ambush has ensured total victory.

*They are presumably the *extraordinarii* who generally led the army column on the march.

CARTHAGINIAN CAMP

HANNIBAL SPANISH and AFRICANS

EXTRAORDINARII

ALLIES

SPANISH

CELTS

NUMIDIANS

CELTS

CELTS

CELTS

ALLIES

Baggage train

Ancient shoreline

I LEGION

II LEGION

ROMAN CAMP

▥	Heavy troops	
⠂	Light troops	
▲	Heavy cavalry	
△	Light cavalry	
▲	Hannibal	
⊙	Flaminius	

blocks. Polybius' account of the "raven" should not be hastily rejected. According to one reading of Diodorus, Demetrius at Rhodes had built twin towers on two galleys yoked, for stability, alongside each other. In action, the "raven" would have been similarly balanced by the enemy ship.

Hannibal's Long March

The unprecedented Roman naval achievement was paralleled on the Carthaginian side by Hannibal's unprecedented overland advance from Spain to Italy. In Spain, treaty agreements defining the Carthaginian sphere of activity as south of the Ebro were equivocal; for Saguntum, south of the Ebro, was a Roman all . Hannibal was in no flagrant breach of treaty when he

beseiged and captured the city, but he intended war—and war ensued.

Before crossing the Pyrenees, Hannibal saw to it that Spain and North Africa were well garrisoned, but he did not intend to preserve his own communications with either of these areas. He could hope to create a new base in North Italy. His route, via the Rhone and the Alps, had been well prepared by diplomacy and reconnaissance and he expected to live off the land during his long march. This being so, the attitude of the Gauls and Alpine tribes who lay along his route varied from place to place. Either they might speed him on his way as soon as possible, or they might resist.

The tribe whose territory straddled the Rhone crossing-point was in two minds. The inhabitants on the west bank gave Hannibal maximum assistance and cooperated in building boats of all shapes and sizes, but those on the farther bank opposed his crossing. However, a small Carthaginian force under an officer called Bomilcar, guided by friendly Gauls, crossed the river at a point one day's march upstream, where the current was split by an island. Rafts were used and cavalry ferried across, while the Spanish infantry swam with their shields beneath them. The whole move, initiated by a night march, was made in secret. When Hannibal's main body crossed, the enemy suddenly found himself encircled by Bomilcar's force and dispersed in panic. Some ingenuity was required to transport the elephants, but three days later a Roman army newly-landed at Massilia (Marseille) in the hope of intercepting Hannibal found only his empty camp. The Roman general Scipio (father of Africanus) did not attempt any further pursuit but turned his attention towards Spain, to ensure that no reinforcements should be available from that quarter.

The march over the Alps makes epic reading; even in Livy's hostile narrative, Hannibal emerges as its hero— rather like Satan in Milton's *Paradise Lost*. There is no precise agreement about the points at which either the Rhone or Alps were crossed. Indeed, the latter was much debated even by ancient historians. Certainly, Hannibal did not approach the Alps by the shortest route, but marched four days northward up the Rhone valley, to avoid any further Roman interference with his plans. In this area, he won the goodwill and assistance of a Gallic tribe by successfully arbitrating in a disputed succession to the chieftainship. His ascent on the north side of the Alps, however, met with opposition and treachery from the mountain peoples. Hannibal sustained frequent losses of men, animals and stores, but by his indefatigable courage and resource repeatedly extricated the army from traps which man and nature placed in its way. The descent into Italy was begun when fresh autumn snow was already falling. Icy conditions, landslides and precipices impeded the famished troops but, when all else failed, timber was hewn, vast fires lit and the men's sour-wine ration poured on the hot rocks blocking the path in order to crack them. A snaky track was thus chiselled down the sheer mountainside. Hannibal is recorded as having reached Italy in the fifth month after leaving his Spanish base; the crossing of the Alps took him fifteen days.

Ancient reports vary considerably as to the number of men he led into Italy. Polybius' account, derived from an inscription left by Hannibal in southern Italy, puts the figure at 20,000 infantry and 6,000 cavalry. Livy bases himself on the account of the historian Lucius Cincius Alimentus, who had at one time been Hannibal's prisoner. But he regards Alimentus' estimate of 80,000 cavalry and 10,000 infantry as inflated. It would seem, in any case, that Hannibal may have lost upward of one-quarter of his entire force during the march. Perhaps even this cannot be described as a crippling loss. But the fact remains that during the ensuing 15 year campaign in Italy, despite brilliant victories on the field of battle, Hannibal was continually faced with acute problems of recruiting, winning allies and receiving reinforcements. To none of these problems did he find an entirely satisfactory answer.

Hannibal's Victories

Publius Cornelius Scipio, consul in 218 BC, having despatched his own army into Spain under command of his brother Gnaeus, returned with exemplary speed to North Italy and took command of the legions there. He met Hannibal's invading army, which had already occupied the area of Turin, in the angle of the Po and the Ticinus, its northern tributary. In the cavalry battle which followed, Scipio was repulsed and wounded, and retired on Placentia. The fight had proved Hannibal's cavalry superiority and the consul hoped to divert future warfare away from the open country which favoured cavalry tactics.

In face of Hannibal's threat, the other consul, Tiberius Sempronius Longus, preparing for an invasion of Africa, was posted northward to join

Early Roman Warships

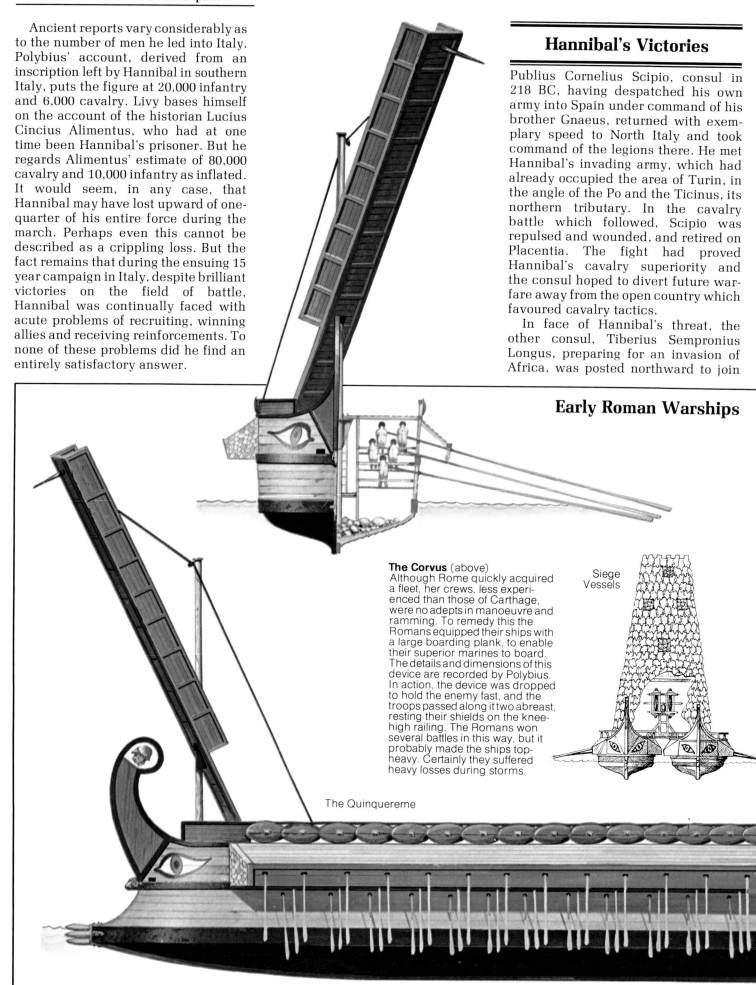

The Corvus (above)
Although Rome quickly acquired a fleet, her crews, less experienced than those of Carthage, were no adepts in manoeuvre and ramming. To remedy this the Romans equipped their ships with a large boarding plank, to enable their superior marines to board. The details and dimensions of this device are recorded by Polybius. In action, the device was dropped to hold the enemy fast, and the troops passed along it two abreast, resting their shields on the knee-high railing. The Romans won several battles in this way, but it probably made the ships top-heavy. Certainly they suffered heavy losses during storms.

Siege Vessels

The Quinquereme

c232
In India, death of the great Buddhist Emperor, Asoka

229
Hamilcar Barca killed on active service in Spain

Hamilcar's work is carried on by his son-in-law Hasdrubal

225
In Italy, Gauls defeated by the Romans at Telamon

forces with Scipio. With Scipio severely wounded, Sempronius virtually took charge of the situation and, encouraged by a successful cavalry skirmish, fought a battle on the Trebia, a southern tributary of the Po, in bitter winter conditions. Hannibal, after a personal reconnaissance, had cleverly used wild country to mask a cavalry ambush. The Romans lost about two thirds of their army. But even so, 10,000 Roman legionaries, although encircled, forced their way through the enemy centre and found safety in Placentia. The Roman horses, though not the Roman soldiers, were still terrified by elephants. But Roman light-armed troops (*velites*) managed to turn back the big animals and, by spearing their rumps (the tender skin under their tails), almost succeeded in stampeding the poor creatures.

Icy conditions prevented Hannibal from following up his victory, and as he picked his way southward in the following spring, his own army suffered badly in areas flooded by melting snow. Afflicted by an opthalmic complaint which eventually cost him the sight of one eye, Hannibal himself rode on the one remaining elephant, barely high and dry. The rest of the elephants had succumbed either to war or weather.

Publius Scipio was sent into Spain with a new command. In Italy, the succeeding consul, Gaius Flaminius, who guarded the western side of the Appenines, was bent on a decision, and now followed the Carthaginian army. On the north shore of Lake Trasimene in Etruria, Hannibal lured the Romans through a bottleneck between the hills and the water on to a pocket of level ground. The ambush which he had posted on the high ground overlooking the lake was hidden by mist. As the Romans advanced to meet his frontal challenge, the troops from the mountain slopes swept suddenly down and, catching the legions still in column of march, drove them into the lake amid frightful butchery and confusion. Two legions were annihilated and Flaminius killed. This victory was followed up by an ambush against the forces of the other consul, when the Romans lost some 4,000 cavalry.

Feeling the need of unified command as an emergency measure, the Romans now appointed a dictator, Quintus Fabius Maximus, and a Master of the Horse, to replace the surviving consul.

Hannibal, meanwhile, needed allies. The Gauls of North Italy, although he had recruited many of them, had proved disappointing. The previous summer, their renewed warfare at the prospect of Carthaginian invasion had diverted Scipio and crucially delayed his arrival on the Rhone. But now the tribes were hesitant and lukewarm. Hannibal accordingly hoped to find

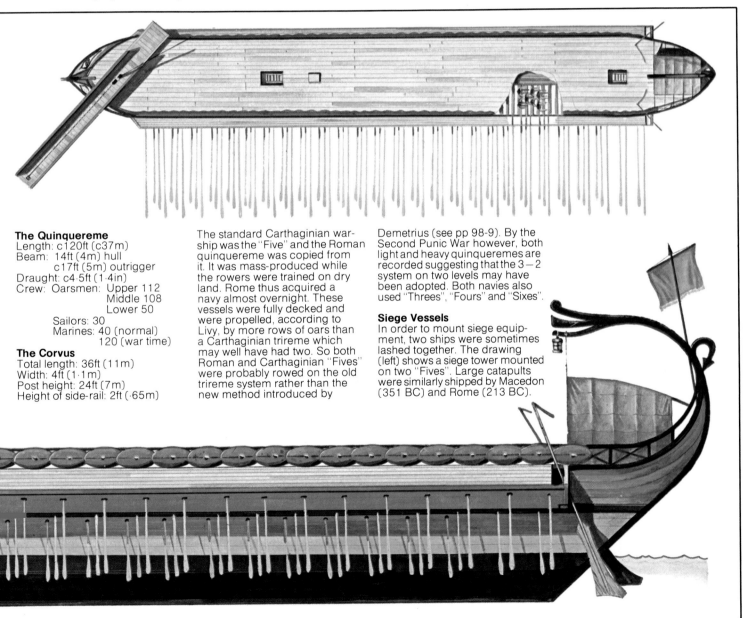

The Quinquereme
Length: c120ft (c37m)
Beam: 14ft (4m) hull
c17ft (5m) outrigger
Draught: c4·5ft (1·4in)
Crew: Oarsmen: Upper 112
Middle 108
Lower 50
Sailors: 30
Marines: 40 (normal)
120 (war time)

The Corvus
Total length: 36ft (11m)
Width: 4ft (1·1m)
Post height: 24ft (7m)
Height of side-rail: 2ft (·65m)

The standard Carthaginian warship was the "Five" and the Roman quinquereme was copied from it. It was mass-produced while the rowers were trained on dry land. Rome thus acquired a navy almost overnight. These vessels were fully decked and were propelled, according to Livy, by more rows of oars than a Carthaginian trireme which may well have had two. So both Roman and Carthaginian "Fives" were probably rowed on the old trireme system rather than the new method introduced by

Demetrius (see pp 98-9). By the Second Punic War however, both light and heavy quinqueremes are recorded suggesting that the 3—2 system on two levels may have been adopted. Both navies also used "Threes", "Fours" and "Sixes".

Siege Vessels
In order to mount siege equipment, two ships were sometimes lashed together. The drawing (left) shows a siege tower mounted on two "Fives". Large catapults were similarly shipped by Macedon (351 BC) and Rome (213 BC).

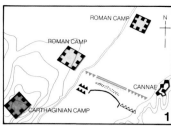

Battle of Cannae 216 BC

Romans	Hannibal
Infantry	
8 legions 40000	Africa 10/12000
Allied	(4000 light)
cohorts 40000	Spain 7/8000
	(4000 light)
	Celts 20/25000
	(some light)
Cavalry	
Legionary 2400	Numidia 4000
Allied	Spain 2000
cohorts 3500/4000	Celts 4/5000

1 Rome masses all its strength and sends both consuls (Varro and Paullus) to join armies of previous year's consuls (Servillius and Atilius). Atilius' command taken over by Minucius. Hannibal camps north of the Aufidius river; Rome sends ⅔ of her force to camp opposite him—the rest stay on the other side of river to limit Carthaginian foraging. The Romans take up battle lines; Hannibal follows suit. The Romans form up extra deep because of the narrowness of the plain; they aim to crush Hannibal's centre. Hannibal pins his hopes on his cavalry, placing his heavy cavalry on the left and Numidians on the right. He bows his centre forward, also making it deeper than the flanks in order to delay the legions' advance. The African infantry is kept in reserve behind each flank of the crescent. Both sides leave troops to guard the camps—the Romans aim to capture Hannibal's camp.

2 The battle opens with skirmishing. Hannibal's left cavalry are launched and hit the Roman right which gives way under weight of numbers.

3 The heavy infantry clash and the Spaniards and Celts are forced back. The Numidians skirmish with the Allied cavalry, while Hasdrubal swings his heavy cavalry across the back of the Roman infantry towards the Allies. Thus threatened they break and run taking Varro with them. Meanwhile the crescent is holding and the Africans advance in columns on the flanks and then turn inwards.

4 Hasdrubal turns into the Roman rear while the Carthaginian light troops move around into the rear as well as supporting the centre. Paullus strives to keep the Romans fighting, even ordering his escort to dismount but to no avail. 45500 infantry and 2700 cavalry are killed; 3/500 infantry and 1/2000 cavalry are captured. Paullus, Servilius and Minucius are dead. 7000 escape to the smaller camp, 2000 to Cannae but they are surrounded and captured. Hannibal takes both camps and more prisoners. He has only lost 6/8000 infantry.

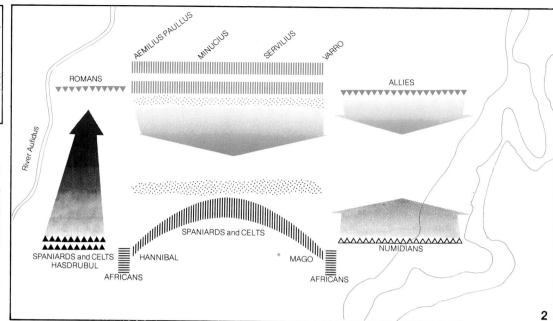

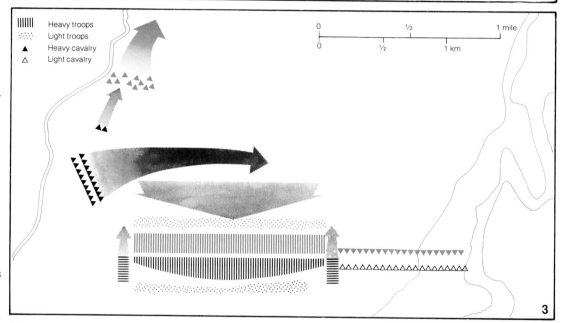

Heavy troops
Light troops
Heavy cavalry
Light cavalry

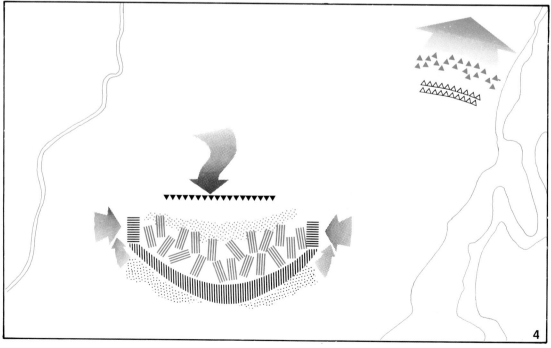

BC	217		216		215
	Romans heavily defeated at Lake Trasimene	In Palestine, victory of Ptolemaic forces over Antiochus III (Seleucid dynast)	Overwhelming defeat of Romans by Hannibal at Cannae	Hannibal in Capua	Hannibal's treaty with Philip V of Macedon

120

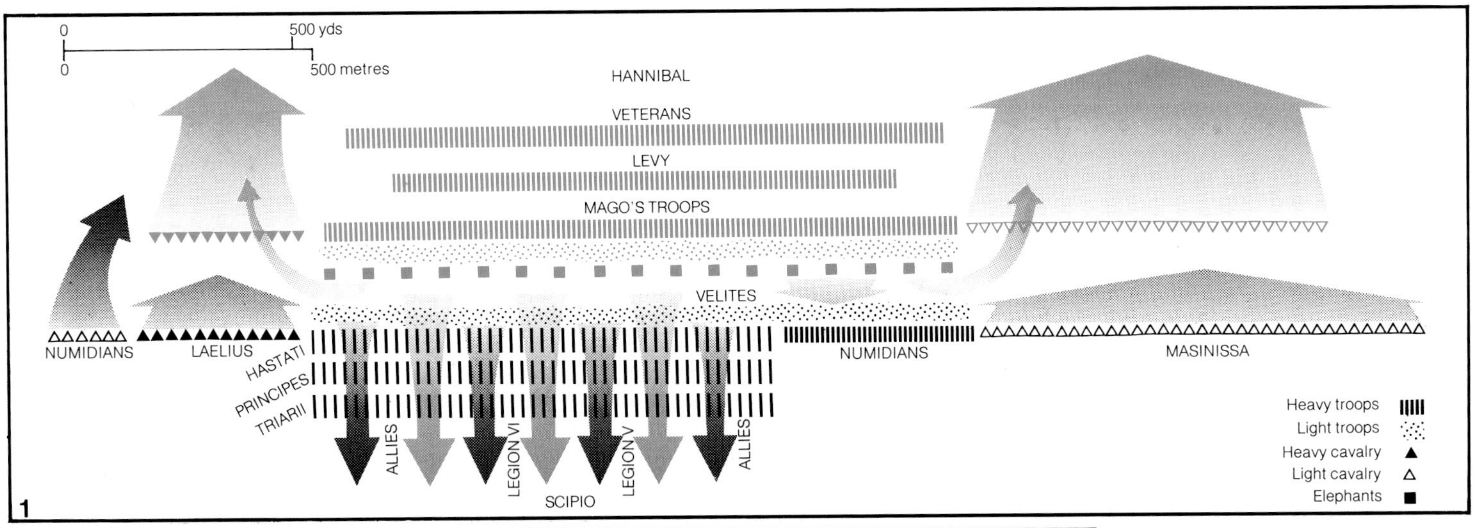
0
500 yds
0
500 metres
HANNIBAL
VETERANS
LEVY
MAGO'S TROOPS
VELITES
NUMIDIANS
LAELIUS
HASTATI
PRINCIPES
TRIARII
NUMIDIANS
MASINISSA
ALLIES
LEGION VI
LEGION V
ALLIES
SCIPIO
Heavy troops
Light troops
Heavy cavalry
Light cavalry
Elephants
1

Battle of Zama 202 BC

Scipio	Hannibal
Infantry	
Legions V and VI 10/11000	Veteran Italian army 12/15000
Allies 12/13000	Mago's Italian army 5/6000
Numidia 5/6000 (under Masinissa)	Carthage) Africa) 10/12000
	Numidia) Moors) (light) 3/4000
Cavalry	
Numidia 4600 (light)	Numidia) Moors) (light) 2/3000
Rome) Italy) (heavy) 2000	Carthage) Africa) (heavy) 2000
	Elephants 80

Scipio invades Africa; Carthage recalls Hannibal and his dead brother Mago's army from Italy. Hannibal raises a levy of local troops and confronts Scipio some 105 miles (70km) south-west of Carthage. He forms up his army in 3 lines: Mago's army and light troops in front, the African levy in the middle, the veteran army from Italy in the rear. His cavalry are on the wings; elephants ranged in front of the infantry. His veterans are held in reserve to prevent encirclement and hold off superior Roman cavalry. Scipio positions his maniples of *principes* behind the *hastati* to leave "elephant lanes" which the *velites* temporarily occupy to conceal the stratagem.

1 Light cavalry skirmish. The elephant charge is disrupted by Roman yells and they confuse Hannibal's cavalry. The Roman cavalry sees this and drives its opponents from the field. Other elephants are goaded into and herded down the "channels" by *velites*.

2 The infantry closes; Hannibal's first line is forced back on to the second which will not admit it. The infuriated Celts and Ligurians stream around the flanks and force the centre.

3 The Carthaginian second line cracks; the veterans will not let them pass. Scipio sounds the recall. Both sides re-form: the remains of Hannibal's front lines on the flanks; Scipio brings his *principes* and *triarii* on to the wings to counter this move. The Romans advance implacably. The struggle is evenly matched until the Roman cavalry returns and charges enemy rear. Slaughter ensues; Hannibal escapes. He has lost 20/25000 men; 8/10000 are taken prisoner. Rome has lost c 2000 while 2/3000 of Masinissa's Numidians are dead.

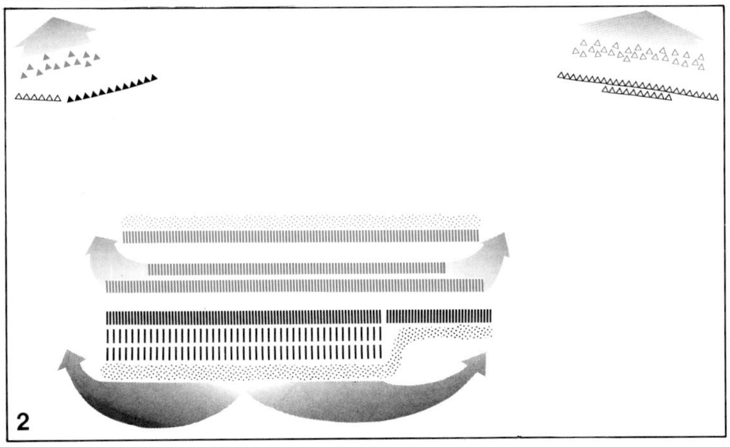
2

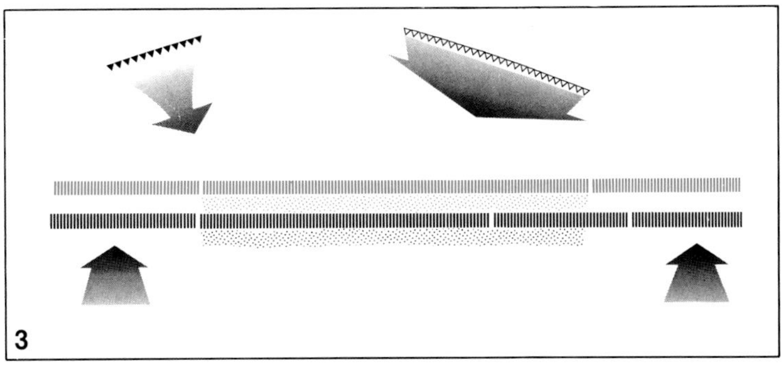
3

Italian allies in the south, but here he was even less successful. He also tried to bring the Roman dictator to battle, but Fabius, with a strategy which became proverbial, could not be tempted into combat.

Hannibal ravaged Apulia and Campania and provoked discontent with Fabius' strategy. Consuls were once more appointed, and their joint armies were overwhelmingly defeated at Cannae in Apulia, in 216 BC. In this battle, Hannibal's central infantry, mainly Spaniards and Gauls, advanced in a wedge-like formation, with Hannibal himself commanding in this sector. The Romans drove back the wedge and turned it into a dent, so that the Carthaginian battle-line changed in form from convex to concave. This event, however, was not unforeseen by Hannibal. The central retreat was controlled and, at a well-chosen moment, the already enveloping wings of the Carthaginian army closed around and encircled the Romans.

Hannibal was a great exponent of ambush. The Trebia battle had been won largely through a cavalry ambush. Trasimene had been based on an ambush. At Cannae, where the terrain did not lend itself to ambush, a ruse served his purpose. A party of about 500 Numidians pretended to desert to the Romans, throwing down their weapons. But they had other weapons concealed under their clothes and these they soon used to devastating effect in the rear of the Roman troops.

Hannibal was also extremely weather-wise and quick to take advantage of climatic conditions. At the Trebia, in freezing weather, he had seen to it that his men were well fed and rubbed down with oil to preserve the suppleness of their muscles, while the Romans went into battle numb with cold and without breakfast. At Trasimene, his ambush had made full use of the morning mist which rose from the lake. At Cannae, he had so placed himself that the wind blew from behind his army, driving dust at the Romans.

The Romans' political dedication to the separation of powers was often their military undoing. At the Trebia and at Cannae, one consul called for caution while the other counselled action. A similar disagreement arose between Flaminius and his officers before Trasimene. Minucius, Fabius' Master of the Horse, who had been appointed by the people and not, in the traditional

213
Hannibal occupies Tarentum

About this time, Chinese victories over the Huns

The Great Wall of China built

211
The Romans recover Capua

The brothers Gnaeus and Publius Scipio killed in operations against the Carthaginians in Spain

BC

Hannibal's Army

Like most Carthaginian armies, Hannibal's was mainly composed of mercenaries. After crossing the Alps he had, according to Polybius, 12000 African and 8000 Spanish infantry, and 6000 cavalry (Spanish and Numidian). He also added Celts and Italians.

Spanish Infantry
These consisted of Balearic slingers; *caetrati,* light infantry armed with small round bucklers; and *scutarii,* heavy infantry with a flat *scutum* (shown right). His weapons are a short sword, spear, and a heavy javelin— either a *pilum* or a *saunion,* a thin weapon made entirely of iron. Polybius' detailed description of these troops refers to purple-edged white tunics. This was not "true" purple, but a mixture of indigo and madder. He wears typical Spanish headgear —a sinew cap—and his boots are home-made. He wears captured Roman armour, and might also have had a helmet.

Africans and Numidians
The small illustration below shows a Numidian light cavalryman. These superb horsemen rode without a bridle, and were armed with a small shield and quite large javelins. Hannibal's Spanish cavalry looked similar to the *scutarii* and *caetrati.* The Numidians played an important part in Hannibal's victories, and their defection to Rome led indirectly to Hannibal's defeat at Zama. The African infantry (below right) were of mixed Libyan and Phoenician descent. Originally armed in Hellenistic fashion, after Hannibal's early victories they were equipped with the choicest captured Roman arms. He is thus shown wearing mail, like the best equipped Roman troops. However, he probably retained his Greek-style shield, in order to avoid being mistaken for the enemy.

BC	207		206		203
	Hasdrubal, brother of Hannibal, crosses the Alps with a relief force	Hasdrubal is defeated and killed on the Metaurus	The Numidian king Masinissa, former ally of Carthage, joins the Romans	In China, the beginning of the Han dynasty	Recall of Hannibal to Africa

Above: *A view of the site of the battle of Cannae showing the Aufidius river, close to which Hannibal won his great victory over the combined armies of two Roman consuls.*

way, by the dictator, regarded himself as Fabius' equal and frequently frustrated his strategy and defied orders given by him.

Perhaps these differences of opinion have been too much stressed. Rome hesitated between strategies of action and caution; and Livy, as much a dramatist as a historian, repeatedly personified such strategies. One must also allow for the prejudices of the earlier Senatorial historians on whom Livy based himself. They were ever inclined to exonerate men of their own class and consequently throw blame on popular leaders.

Rome's Survival and Triumph

After Cannae, Capua and many southern Italian localities defected to Hannibal. The Romans besieged Capua and, to divert their troops from this quarter, Hannibal feinted with a march up to the walls of Rome itself. The Roman reaction, however, was not what he hoped; unable to relieve Capua, he led his army off into Apulia.

The two elder Scipios had campaigned successfully against three Carthaginian generals in Spain, but in 211 BC they were both at last, through lack of resources, defeated and killed. In the following year, the younger Scipio (Africanus) landed in Spain and soon captured New Carthage (Cartagena). He could not, however, prevent Hasdrubal Barca, Hannibal's brother, from slipping across the western Pyrenees with reinforcements for the Carthaginian army in Italy. Hasdrubal, wintering unmolested in Transalpine Gaul (Southern France), crossed the Alps in a more clement season and more propitious circumstances than his brother had done, and the Alpine tribes, by now convinced that the Carthaginian objectives lay farther south, were not hostile.

However, in trying to join forces with his brother, Hasdrubal was defeated by two Roman consular armies and killed, in a battle on the river Metaurus in Umbria (207 BC). Hannibal, remembering the difficulties of his own pioneer Alpine crossing, had been surprised at his brother's early arrival and was slow to move northward. A message to him from Hasdrubal was intercepted by the Romans, and the two consuls, Marcus Livius Salinator and Gaius Claudius Nero, were able to combine their armies in secret. For Nero, despite his morose temperament,

showed rare initiative and—for a Roman general—an even rarer ability to collaborate with a consular colleague. Hasdrubal, suddenly surprised to find that he faced two Roman armies in place of the one which he had supposed to be encamped before him, attempted to withdraw, but he was overtaken by the superior Roman forces and obliged to fight at a disadvantage. His defeat was the product of brilliantly conceived and efficiently executed strategic manoeuvre, and in the long term it produced decisive strategic results. From then on, Hannibal could not hope for reinforcement.

Scipio, after his successful war in Spain, returned to Italy. Politically and strategically, he found himself in opposition to the war policies of Fabius, but the time for vigorous counter-offensive had now arrived and Scipio was allowed to cross with an army into Africa. His campaign here began inauspiciously when he failed to take Utica, on the coast northwest of Carthage, but after wintering on a coastal promontory he defeated the Carthaginians and their ally King Syphax in the battle of the "Great Plains", in the North African interior. Carthaginian difficulties were such that Hannibal was eventually recalled from Italy; although peace negotiations were afoot, his presence resulted in the continuation of the war.

202
At Battle of Zama,
P. Scipio (Africanus)
defeats Hannibal

201
Carthage makes peace
with Rome
Masinissa established as
king of Numidia in
alliance with Rome

200
Rome at war with Philip V
of Macedon

BC

123

Hannibal's last great battle and first serious defeat is generally referred to as having occurred at Zama (202 BC), although there were several places of this name and various alternative names and sites have been suggested. Some of the 80 Carthaginian war-elephants which opened the battle with a frontal charge were turned back in panic by the pandemonium of shouts and trumpet blasts which the Romans raised; the rest were allowed to pass through gaps in the Roman ranks. For this purpose, the Roman maniples were ranged directly behind and in front of each other, not in their usual quincunx formation, covering intervals. The way was now clear for a cavalry battle. While in Spain, Scipio had captured the young Numidian prince Masinissa and had won him over to the Roman cause. Masinissa was now a Roman ally and as a result Scipio possessed a strong Numidian cavalry contingent which, with the Roman cavalry, routed Hannibal's horsemen, already thrown into confusion by the rioting elephants. The two front lines of the Carthaginian army were scattered and forced out on to the wings by those behind, who refused to let them retreat any farther. Scipio took advantage of the chaotic situation to give his men a breathing space rather than press his attack. He reformed his army in a single line with *principes* and *triarii* on the wings and *hastati* in the centre, presumably because he feared to be outflanked in an infantry battle. At the same time, he hoped anxiously for the return of his cavalry, which had been drawn away too far in pursuit. The critical moment came as the Romans faced the remaining Carthaginian line, veterans of the Italian wars whom Hannibal had till now held in reserve. But, fortunately for Scipio, his Roman and Numidian cavalry returned to the battlefield just in time to decide the issue in his favour. Outflanked on either side, the Carthaginians were cut to pieces. Hannibal, with a few horsemen, escaped first to Hadrumetum on the coast and thence to Carthage, where he advised the government to make peace.

The Legions against the Phalanx

Rome had clashed with Philip V of Macedon when he cautiously allied himself with Carthage. Roman military commitments had then led to a compromise peace, but war was renewed two years after Zama. The Romans did not wish for a bad

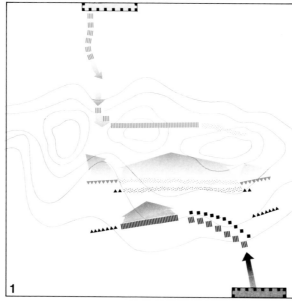

1

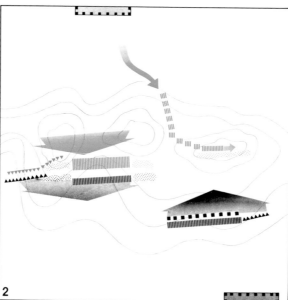

2

Battle of Cynoscephalae 197 BC

Romans	Macedonians
Infantry	
2 legions 8400	Phalanx 16000
Allies 10000	Mercenaries 1500
(2 legions)	Peltasts 4000
Phalanx* 4000	(2000 Thracians)
Peltasts* 2000	Illyricum 2000
*=Aetolian league	(light)
Cavalry	
Rome 400	Macedonia 1000
Allies 1800	Thessaly 1000
Aetolian league 400	
Elephants c20	

Skirmishing forces from either side meet in the mist of Cynoscephalae ridge. Macedonians have the upper hand until Roman reinforcements push Philip's men back. Philip's cavalry and mercenaries arrive and the Romans make an orderly retreat.
1 Both armies are led out. Philip marches half the phalanx and Thracians up the pass and deploys leftwards on the summit. Flaminius orders his right to hold its ground and leads the left (1 legion + Allies) to relieve his light troops, forcing back the Macedonian light troops who retire through the line as do the Roman light infantry. Both sides reorganise. Philip orders phalanx and peltasts to double depth, thus halving front and leaving room for his left wing hastening up in column.
2 Philip charges downhill and forces back the Romans. His left wing is still deploying across the ridge. Flaminius orders his right plus elephants to attack.
3 The echeloned Macedonian left is easily pushed back, but the Roman left is still in trouble. Seeing this, a tribune peels off 20 maniples and hits Philip's phalanx in the rear slaughtering the exposed phalangites. The Macedonians, in retreat, raise their pikes in surrender but the uncomprehending Romans cut them down. They lose 7/8000 killed, 4/5000 prisoners; Rome: c 1000 dead.

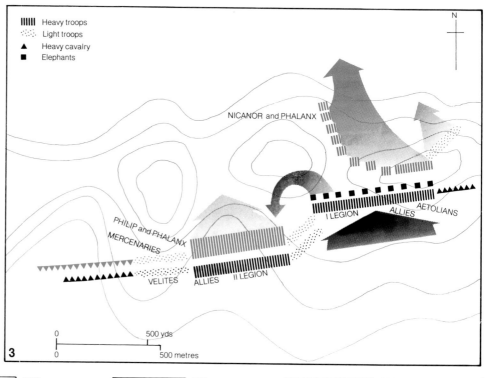

‖‖‖‖‖	Heavy troops
⋰⋰⋱	Light troops
▲	Heavy cavalry
■	Elephants

NICANOR and PHALANX

PHILIP and PHALANX

MERCENARIES

VELITES   ALLIES   II LEGION

I LEGION   ALLIES   AETOLIANS

N

3

0 _____ 500 yds
0 _____ 500 metres

neighbour on the other side of the Adriatic, let alone one who often emerged as the ally and patron of pirates. Pretexts for intervention in Greek and Macedonian affairs were not far to seek. Since 273 BC, Rome had been on friendly terms with the Ptolemaic dynasty of Egypt. Ptolemaic succession difficulties had now arisen, and with avid opportunism Philip had allied himself to Antiochus III, who ruled Syria—the rump of the Seleucid empire—in an attempt to seize the Ptolemies' overseas possessions. As usual, in a struggle between the successor powers, would-be neutrals were reluctantly involved, and Rhodes and Pergamum, a Greek Asiatic kingdom of culture and dignity which had recently stemmed Celtic inroads and defied the Seleucids, appealed to Rome.

The Roman commander who eventually took charge in Greece was Titus Quinctius Flaminius, an ardent phil-hellene. He finally defeated Philip at the battle of Cynoscephalae in Thessaly (197 BC). Cynoscephalae in Greek means "dog's heads", the shape of local hillocks suggesting the name. The uneven ground seriously hindered the Macedonian phalanx, but heavy mist early in the day also hampered Roman mobile tactics. On both sides, the right wing was victorious, but the scales were tipped in Rome's favour by a tribune whom history has not named. On his own initiative, he diverted 20 maniples from a point where victory was already assured, to surprise the enemy phalanx in the rear. Flaminius, thus victorious, was welcomed as liberator of Greece. Subsequently, however, in 183 BC, he appeared in a less generous light, attempting to extradite the aged Hannibal, who as a harmless exile now lived in the Asiatic kingdom of Bithynia. Hannibal took poison. Even Roman senators, on receipt of the news, did not approve Flaminius' action, condemning it as officious and harsh.

Rome's terms with Philip were not unduly severe, but war already loomed with Antiochus, his eastern ally. The logic of Roman military expansion is clear enough. For the sake of security and trade, Rome wanted peace in the eastern Mediterranean, but since she could not countenance any power strong enough to act as peacemaker, she had to exert her own strength in this capacity. Antiochus neglected rather than suspected Roman power and he had, perhaps tactlessly, employed the exiled Hannibal in a military capacity. In the war which followed, Antiochus' fleets were unable

Above: *T. Quinctius Flaminius is seen on this coin. After defeating the Macedonians, he was proclaimed liberator of Greece. In effect, Roman power soon replaced Macedonian.*

to resist the Roman grappling and boarding tactics which had destroyed Carthaginian naval supremacy. On land, he was defeated first at Thermopylae (191 BC), then at Magnesia near Sipylus (190 BC), in Lydia. This last battle proved decisive. The Roman legions, as at Zama, had the advantage of good allied cavalry support, provided here by Eumenes, king of Pergamum. In their desire to tempt Antiochus from his defensive position, the Romans exposed their right wing, but Eumenes' attack anticipated and threw into confusion the outflanking movements by Antiochus' heavily armoured cavalry. The Roman left wing was thrown back by a charge of oriental horsemen under Antiochus' personal leadership, but the victors in this section of the field continued their pursuit too long and left the central phalanx unsupported. The phalanx, stationed in dense formations, at intervals, with elephants filling the gaps, was broken when the Romans successfully stampeded the elephants and breached the line.

The peace terms which followed Magnesia reduced Antiochus to impotence as far as the Mediterranean was concerned. But Rome fought a third Macedonian war with Perseus, son of Philip V. The decisive battle which finally established Rome as arbiter of the eastern Mediterranean world came at Pydna in Macedonia (168 BC). The pikemen of the Macedonian phalanx were again at a disadvantage on broken ground and the Roman legionary swordsmen were able to exploit gaps in their ranks. Roman tactical flexibility was, on this occasion, well turned to

account by the generalship of Lucius Aemilius Paullus, son of the consul who had been killed at Cannae.

Rome's victories in these eastern wars cannot be understood unless it is realized that the ponderous Macedonian phalanx of the second century differed completely from the original flexible and mobile phalanx of Philip II and Alexander the Great. With the growing tendency towards heavier weapons and armour, it in effect reverted in character to the rigid Greek phalanx of the fifth century. At Cynoscephalae, the phalanx, attacked by Flaminius' tribune in the rear, had been unable to wheel about even to protect itself. This helplessness compares significantly with the alacrity of Alexander's phalangists at Gaugamela, who faced sharply about to rescue their baggage train from a Persian breakthrough.

Ever since the days of Camillus, when the maniple formation had been introduced, the Romans, unlike the Macedonians, had developed consistently in the direction of flexibility. To this development, the genius of Scipio Africanus had given great impetus, and the commanders who fought Rome's eastern wars in the second century BC had thoroughly absorbed his tactical principles.

Weapons and Tactics

The confrontation between the legion and the phalanx raises questions as to the comparative effectiveness of sword and pike. The pike, of course, had the longer reach, but the sword was a more manageable and less cumbersome weapon, giving greater opportunity for skill in its use.

At Pydna, the Italian allies serving under Aemilius Paullus hurled themselves with reckless heroism at the enemy pikes, trying to beat them down or hew off their points. But they sacrificed themselves in vain; the pike points pierced their shields and armour, causing terrible carnage. The phalanx was eventually shattered as the result of cool tactical judgment. Paullus divided his force into small units with orders to look for gaps in the pike line and then exploit them. The gaps appeared as a result of the rough ground which prevented the phalangists from moving with uniformity and keeping abreast. Forced at last by the infiltrating legionaries to abandon their pikes and fight at close quarters, the Macedonians found that their small swords and shields were no match for the corresponding Roman arms.

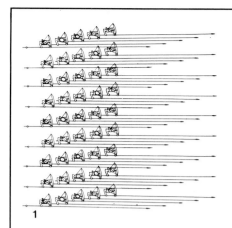

Pike versus Pilum

1 The phalanx advances 16 deep, pikes levelled, in close order. The Roman maniples, in open order, may be 12 deep or more (this would vary according to the opponent). At c35 yards (32m) light *pila* are thrown in a volley. These could penetrate armour or weigh down a shield as the neck of a *pilum* would bend under the impact.
2 As the lines close heavy *pila* are also thrown, the *hastati* draw swords and adopt close order. The *pila* will have taken their toll and the oncoming phalanx will be hindered by dead bodies and shields weighed down by pila.

The Macedonian dynasts who relied upon the phalanx were perfectly aware of the dangers to which it was exposed, and their awareness explains the hesitation to join battle which marked their encounters with the Romans. The phalanx was considered secure while it remained stationary. The Romans consequently tried to tempt it into action but, even so, had to beware lest in provoking an attack they rendered themselves too vulnerable.

Gaps, of course, might be opened in the enemy lines by the *pilum*. Something could be expected from the volley of weighted javelins with which the legions normally commenced a battle. But against this, the phalangists were heavily armoured: Perseus' phalanx at Pydna drew its title of "Bronze Shields" from the round bucklers which his men wore slung round their necks and drew in front of them as fighting started. But wooded or uneven country was the legionary's best chance against armies of the Macedonian type. The Romans had learnt their lesson as early as the battle of Asculum against Pyrrhus, where they had been able to withdraw nimbly before the intact line of the phalanx, only to rush in where ground obstacles created ready-made breaches in the pike formation.

A similar confrontation of sword and spear is to be found in Italy in 225 BC, when, in the period between the First and Second Punic Wars, Rome fought with invading Gauls at Telamon in Etruria. On this occasion the Romans were the spearmen and the Gauls the swordsmen. The Roman general, in fact, placed some of his *triarii* in the front line in order that their spears might blunt the Gallic swords: the Gauls, like the Italian soldiery at Pydna, tried to parry or hack away the spear heads. Gallic swords were sometimes made of very soft iron. In fact, Polybius tells us that the Gallic sword was so soft that after striking a blow the swordsman was obliged to straighten the bent iron against his foot*.

Incidentally, Plutarch tells the same story of poorly-tempered Gallic swords

---

*Polybius' account perhaps reflects an epoch when Roman pike tactics were regarded as an answer to the Gallic long sword. At a later date, skilled swordsmanship in the use of the *gladius* was recognised as the right answer. As for Celtic iron, it is praised in some ancient texts. Its quality would naturally be determined by geographic rather than ethnographic considerations.

Right: *Masada. Roman camps dating from the Jewish revolt of AD 66 reveal siege methods like those employed at Numantia in the 2nd century BC by Scipio and other Roman generals, who invested the Spanish town for eight months in 133 BC.*

BC	150	c147	146	
	Rome provokes new war with Carthage (Third Punic War)	In Spain, Viriathus rallies Lusitanian resistance to Rome	Corinth, in revolt against Roman control of Greece, is sacked by Mummius	Romans capture and destroy Carthage

126

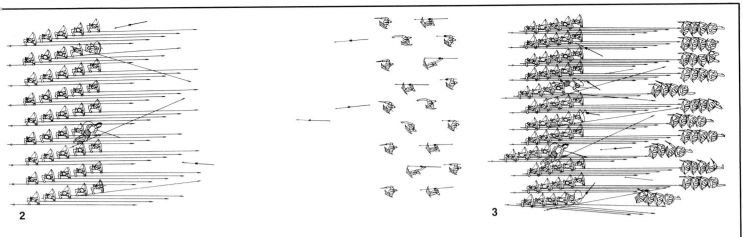

2

3

3 If the phalanx continues to advance, the two sides rush together and the legionaries take the impact of the pikes on their *scuta*. A pushing match develops which normally favours the deeper formation. However, wherever a casualty or a natural obstacle creates a gap in the phalanx's line, the Roman opposite number will try to close with his enemy. Another tactic is to out-flank the ponderous phalanx. In either case, once the expert Roman swordsman gets to grips with the phalangite he will generally get the better of him, as the phalangite is not a trained swordsman and carries a smaller shield than his Roman foe.

in his *Life of Camillus*. The Gauls seem to have relied on carrying all before them at the first onset; this is understandable if their swords were rendered so quickly unserviceable. Perhaps the defect was localized in certain tribes where ironworking had not advanced beyond a primitive stage or where facilities for obtaining good weapons did not exist. At Cannae, although the Spaniards in Hannibal's army fought with their short thrusting swords, the Gauls preferred their normal, unpointed, slashing weapons. However, there is no mention here of soft iron and the Gauls, so far from despairing when immediate victory eluded them, doggedly retreated in the face of Roman pressure, until Hannibal's tactical plans matured. In any case, one feels that Hannibal's astute generalship would not have permitted the use of soft iron weapons among his troops.*

Polybius gives a graphic account of the Gallic invaders of 225 BC. Although the rear ranks wore cloaks and trousers, the huge men of the front line, with traditional bravado, fought stark naked save for their gold collars and armlets. The sight was formidable, but the prospect of acquiring the gold stimulated Roman efforts to kill the wearer. The shields of these reckless fighters were not large enough to protect them; the bigger the warrior, the more exposed he was to the Roman *pilum*. The Roman legionary regularly carried two *pila*, one more slender than the other, perhaps for convenient reservation in the shield hand. The

long, barbed, iron head was riveted so securely to the shaft that it would break rather than become detached from the wood. However, this very solidity was later felt to be a mixed blessing, for a spent missile, intact, could be recovered and used by the enemy. Technical measures were taken to neutralize the danger.

Sackers of Cities

Advantages cease to be advantages when one becomes too dependent on them. Rome's dependence upon overseas power and wealth led to neglect of the old self-sufficient Italian economy. Roman overseas wars assumed the aspect of predatory exploits rather than peace-keeping missions; the struggles of the later second century characteristically terminated in the pitiless sack of cities rather than decisive battles followed by peace terms. When the Achaean League and its ally Corinth revolted against the Roman settlement of Greece, the Corinthians treated Roman senatorial ambassadors with disrespectful violence. After the short war which followed, the Roman consul Lucius Mummius razed Corinth and enslaved its inhabitants. Mummius was hardly a philhellene. For Greek art treasures, he displayed the enthusiasm of a collector rather than a connoisseur.

The same year (146 BC) had seen the destruction of Carthage, bringing the Third and last Punic War to its bitter end. The Carthaginians had recalled from exile an able general—another Hasdrubal—who organized their very solid defences. Against the 45-foot (13·7m) city walls, the Romans made

slow progress. The Roman besieging army itself, at one time in grave danger, was saved only by the energy and resource of Scipio Aemilianus, son of Aemilius Paullus, victor of Pydna, and grandson by adoption of the Scipio Africanus who had defeated Hannibal. When the Carthaginians were successful in running the Roman blockade by sea, Scipio built a mole across the gulf into which their harbour issued, thus cutting them off. The Carthaginians dug a canal from their inner (naval) harbour basin to the coast and put to sea with a full fleet, but the Romans defeated them in a naval engagement. The walls of Carthage were finally breached. Hasdrubal surrendered and was reserved for the day when Scipio triumphed as a victorious general in Rome, but his wife and children preferred to perish in the flames which enveloped the Carthaginian citadel and temples.

Another appalling siege was that of Numantia in 133 BC. For Rome, the capture of Numantia marked the successful culmination of a savage and often shameful war in which, after the elimination of Carthage, the Romans aimed to impose their rule on the native peoples of the Spanish peninsula. The siege operations at Numantia were, like those at Carthage, conducted by Scipio Aemilianus.

Scipio was something of an expert in sieges. Appian says that he was the first general to enclose with a wall an enemy who was prepared to give battle in the open field. It might have been expected that such an enemy would prove impossible to contain. But Scipio's measures were very thorough.

Numantia was beset with seven forts and surrounded by a ditch and

---

*Hannibal had, in fact, issued many captured Roman weapons to his army, but these were unsuitable for use by slashing Gallic swordsmen.

palisade. The perimeter of the circum-vallations was twice as long as that of the city. At the first sign of a sally by the defenders, the threatened Roman sector had orders to hoist a red flag by day or raise a fire signal by night, so that reinforcements could immediately be rushed to the danger spot. Another ditch was built behind the first, also with palisades, after which a wall 8 feet (2·4m) high and 10 feet (3m) wide (not including parapets) was constructed. Towers were sited at 100-foot (30·5m) intervals along the wall, and where the wall could not be carried round the adjacent marshland its place was taken by an earthwork of the same height, thicker than the wall.

The river Durius (Douro), on which Numantia stood, enabled the defenders to be supplied by means of small boats, swimmers and divers. Scipio therefore placed a tower on either side of the river, to which he moored a boom of floating timbers. These timbers bristled with inset knives and spearheads and were kept in constant motion by the strength of the current. They acted as a barrage, effectively isolating the city from any help which might reach it along the river.

Catapults and all kinds of siege engines were now mounted on Scipio's towers and missiles were accumulated along the parapets, the forts being occupied by archers and slingers. Messengers were stationed at frequent intervals along the entire wall in order that headquarters might be informed immediately of any enemy action, whether by day or night. Each tower was furnished with emergency signals and each was ready to send immediate help to another in case of need.

Thus invested for eight months, the Numantines starved. They took to cannibalism, and at last 4,000 surviving citizens, now mere filthy and ragged skeletons, surrendered unconditionally.

Roman Camps

Excavations at Numantia have brought to light 13 Roman camps in the vicinity. Seven of these have been identified as Scipio's. Others were those of his less successful predecessors in Spain. The Numantine excavations of Schulten testify in general to the accuracy of Polybius' description of Roman camps, though some notable differences in internal arrangements and dimensions must be recognised.

A camp containing two legions with an equivalent strength of Italian allied contingents, commanded by a consular

Above: *This coin celebrates Rome's victory over Macedon. In 168 BC Aemilius Paullus, by his victory at Pydna, ended the Macedonian dynasty.*

general, was normally built in the form of a square. A main road (*via principalis*), 100 feet (30·5m) wide, separated the headquarters of the general, with those of his paymaster (*quaestor*)*, staff of officers and headquarter troops, from those of the legionaries and attached cavalry. The *via principalis* issued on either side through gates in the camp wall. The headquarter section of the camp covered one-third of its total area. The remaining two-thirds was itself bisected by another road (*via quintana*), 50 feet (15·2m) wide, parallel to the main road. The word *quintana* indicated that it was adjacent to the tents of the fifth maniple and its attached cavalry. Both these roads were bisected at right angles by a third road, which ran to the general's headquarters from a gate in the farthest wall. The headquarters (*praetorium*) was connected by a short road, on the other side, to a gate in the nearer wall.

Between the camp ramparts and the tents inside, a margin (*intervallum*) of 200 feet (61m) was left vacant. This placed the tents out of reach of enemy missiles—especially fire darts. In exceptional cases also, the camp could accommodate extra troops, and there was room to stow booty. Before the battle of the Metaurus, Claudius Nero had managed to smuggle his own legions into the camp of his colleague Livius without the enemy being aware of it. Hasdrubal only knew that he faced two consular armies instead of one when he heard the same trumpet call sounded twice in the same camp.

*The quaestor's *duties included responsibility for pay and rations, disposal of booty and sale of captives to slave dealers.*

Above: *Trajan's Column—Roman soldiers build a turf-and-log camp. Despite its later date, the relief could suitably be used to illustrate descriptions of camp building such as we find in Republican authors.*

A Roman army never halted for a night without digging itself a camp. The perimeter was formed by a ditch, normally about 3 feet (·91m) deep and 4 feet (1·22m) wide. The excavated earth was flung inside to form a rampart, which was surmounted by a breastwork of sharpened stakes. For the purpose of constructing such a camp, each soldier on the march carried a spade, other tools and sharp stakes to set in the rampart.

In wartime, a Roman army encamped at a chosen spot for the winter. In this case, the camp comprised a more solid structure. The tents made of skin were replaced by huts thatched with straw. Each tent or hut held eight men, who messed together. Polybius' account suggests that the huts or tents were

BC | 133 | | | 124 | | 121

In Spain, Romans capture Numantia

Political violence at Rome leads to the death of Tiberius Gracchus

Gaius Gracchus, brother of Tiberius, is tribune

Gaius Gracchus dies amid mob violence

128

the narrow military caste which governed Rome was no longer competent. The war in Africa underlined the fact that it was also corrupt. Gaius Marius, who at length assumed command against Jugurtha, was a "new man" and came from outside the hereditary ruling class. He had new military ideas and was in many ways a living repudiation of aristocratic claims to superiority and privilege. However, his success in North Africa was only partial and the war was at last brought to an end by his *quaestor*, Lucius Cornelius Sulla. A *quaestor*, although exercising the functions of paymaster and purser, could be called upon to act in a military capacity, deputising for the general under whom he served. In such circumstances, Sulla secured the capture of Jugurtha. His success was made possible by the treachery of Bocchus, king of Mauretania, who had been an ally of Jugurtha. In his negotiations with Bocchus, Sulla himself was exposed to possible treachery, but it so happened that, presented with the interesting choice, Bocchus chose to betray Jugurtha to Sulla rather than Sulla to Jugurtha.

Jugurtha later perished in prison at Rome, after being led in triumph by Marius (104 BC), but the enterprising *quaestor* did not hesitate to claim credit for having ended the war. Unlike Marius, Sulla came from an old aristocratic, though not very prominent, family; it was perhaps foreseeable that the antagonism which had begun as professional jealousy would issue in political conflict, although few could have guessed the extent to which it was destined to convulse and create divisions in the Roman state.

Admirers of Roman institutions and ethics may deplore the fact that Jugurtha was betrayed into Roman hands, not vanquished by them. Similarly, the heroic Lusitanian chief, Viriathus, had defied Roman armies in Spain until the Romans had suborned his trusted associates to cut his throat as he lay sleeping. In the preceding century, Roman standards of honour had won the respect of Pyrrhus, who was a chivalrous character if nothing else. By the end of the second century, however, Rome had been obliged to deal frequently with barbarous foes who not only found it inconvenient to honour solemn undertakings—as civilized politicians often find it—but freely entered into undertakings which they had no intention of honouring. In a wider and more wicked world, the Romans fought their enemies cynically with their own treacherous weapons.

laid out in long lines with streets between them, but the evidence of Numantia excavations points to the grouping of maniples round a square.

The War against Jugurtha

As in Spain, so in Africa, Rome's succession to Carthaginian power and influence did not ultimately go unchallenged. After Zama, Masinissa, Scipio's Numidian friend, captured King Syphax, an ally of Carthage, and his beautiful Carthaginian queen, Sophonisba. With the latter, Masinissa immediately fell in love. But Scipio, fearing her influence, insisted that Sophonisba should join the other captives destined for Rome. Unable to renounce his friendship with Scipio, Masinissa regretfully offered her, as an alternative to Roman captivity, a cup of poison—which she drank without demur.

However, even while Rome used Masinissa as a catspaw to apply her vindictive policies against a crippled Carthage, she was alarmed at his growing power and, at his death, arranged for the distribution of his kingdom among his three legitimate sons, thus averting the potential threat of a united Numidia. But unfortunately, Jugurtha, Masinissa's grandson, united Numidia once more under his own rule. When a Roman army was sent against Jugurtha, it would seem that he either bribed its commander or used the influence of Roman friends to secure easy terms. Jugurtha was given a safe-conduct to Rome in order that he might account for his actions. On this occasion, he contemptuously bribed his way through all difficulties. Another Roman army was sent against him, but he defeated it. Later Roman generals had more success but could not bring the war to an end.

It is a sad reflection that Rome's great reign of peace was made sound at the circumference only to crumble at the centre—in Italy and in the city itself. The war in Spain had shown that

113	112	107	104	BC
Romans defeated by Germanic tribes (Cimbri and Teutones) at Noreia (near Ljubljana)	Rome at war with Jugurtha (Masinissa's grandson)	First consulate of Gaius Marius	Jugurtha led in triumph by Marius	

129

Marius and Sulla

Rome dominated the eastern Mediterranean, and her armies, strengthened by the military reforms of Marius, repulsed the barbarians. However, civil strife troubled the Roman world from within. The immense political power of a successful general was demonstrated in the struggle of Marius and Sulla.

Ancient Authorities

Sulla wrote his memoirs (*Commentarii*) and these, despite their personal bias, as a first-hand account by a protagonist in the main conflict of the epoch, would have been an invaluable source of knowledge if they had survived. As it is, Sulla's testimony reaches us at second-hand in the writing of Sallust and Plutarch. In Sallust's *Jugurthine War*, the effect produced is one of inconsistency; Sallust's hero was Gaius Marius, and Sallust's political orientation placed him on the side of the Popular party. Plutarch's account of Sulla's contemporaries and, of course, his biography of Sulla himself owe much to the memoirs.

Unfortunately, Sallust's only other extant work is his monograph on the conspiracy of Catiline which shook Rome in 63 BC and led to full-scale military operations. Sallust also wrote *Histories* relating to the period 78-67 BC, but his work has been lost except for a few fragments, some of them important, preserved by later writers.

Other valuable contemporary evidence for the earlier and middle decades of the first century BC is to be found in Cicero's speeches. Here, we have the words of a participant in the violent political struggles of the day. Cicero rose to prominence after the death of Sulla, but his early career was passed in the period with which we are here concerned, and both his forensic and political orations contain allusions to it. One does not, of course, expect from Cicero the impartial detachment of a historian, but his references to contemporary and near-contemporary events merit such regard as is due to the pronouncements of a moderate man.

Our knowledge of the period is also derived from later writers. Many of these preserve the substance of Livy's lost books. They include Velleius Paterculus, who was an officer in the Imperial army early in the first century AD. He wrote a summary history of Rome down to the year AD 30. His contemporary Valerius Maximus composed a text book for students of rhetoric, based on a collection of memorable historic utterances and actions. Early in the second century AD, in the time of the Emperor Hadrian, Lucius Annaeus Florus wrote a summarized history of all Roman wars down to Imperial times. Other compilers of historical summaries are Eutropius, in the fourth century AD, and Orosius, a Christian writer of the fifth century. These chroniclers all wrote in Latin and, while availing themselves of various sources, to an important extent transmit the material of Livy's lost books in their works.

Appian, who was a Greek of Alexandria, flourished in the early second century AD. He moved to Rome, and held high official posts there. His work dealing with the history of the Roman world was arranged mainly on a geographical and ethnographical plan. The *Civil Wars*, however, form a distinct section of five books. Of these, the latter part of the first book is mainly relevant here. Appian has access to many sources; it should be noted that he drew upon Sallust and is indebted to Sulla's memoirs.

Some earlier books of Dio Cassius (Cassius Dio Cocceianus) and later books of Diodorus Siculus were also relevant to the epoch which here concerns us, but unfortunately these have survived only in fragments.

Below: *This map illustrates the migratory routes taken by the Germanic tribes who left their homes in Jutland and confronted the Roman army in a series of fierce battles.*

JUTLAND

GERMANIA

BELGICA

Rhine river

NORICUM

Danube river

Noreia

PANNONIA

ALPS

GAUL

Rhone river

X Vercellae

Po river

X Arausio

Massilia X Aquae Sextiae

ITALY

SPAIN

CORSICA

Rome · Arpinum

SARDINIA

TYRRHENIAN SEA

MEDITERRANEAN SEA

SICILY

Migratory route of the Cimbri, Teutones and Ambrones

Possible route of dispersal of the Teutones and Ambrones

Possible route of dispersal of the Cimbri

BC | 105 | 104

105
Cimbri and Teutones destroy Roman armies at Arausio

Marius' first consulate

104
Marius' second consulate (elected in his absence)

Marius assumes command in Gaul and trains his army

130

Political and Social Background

The Roman civil wars of the first century BC were in some sense 200 years overdue. In semi-legendary times, the class struggle between the privileged patricians and the unprivileged plebeian majority had centred on the right demanded by the plebeians to hold high offices of state. In eventually winning these rights, the plebeians secured for themselves other rights into the bargain, which theoretically made them the dominant partners in the Republic. For the plebs possessed their own officers (tribunes*) and the power to pass resolutions in their own assemblies which had the force of law, binding on the whole community. A tribune had also the right to veto any action of a Roman magistrate. Indeed, significantly, as it later turned out, he possessed the right of veto against his fellow tribunes.

The Senate, by contrast, had always been a consultative body and its resolutions did not amount to laws. But it advised the consuls and other magistrates, who were normally elected for yearly terms. Its own membership, in the early days of the Republic, was based on the selection of the consuls and continued to include men who had served as consuls. Its wisdom and experience provided a thread of continuity which was otherwise lacking and its consuls were indispensable. The annual elections were a precaution against tyranny, but such precautions could have led only to chaos in foreign policy and defeat in war, if the Roman people had not been willing to accept senatorial guidance, together with the supremacy of those noble families which provided the nucleus of the Senate.

The fact that the Romans were willing, although by no means legally obliged, to accept such guidance meant that the Republic, in the early centuries of its development, closely approached the ideal of aristocratic government — just as fifth-century Athens had been able to present itself as the model of democracy. But with the meteoric rise to Mediterranean dominion, the Roman ruling caste was faced with problems and temptations which proved too great for it, and

*Tribuni plebis, not to be confused with military tribunes (tribuni militum). By the middle fifth century BC, they were ten in number.

Above: *This portrait bust of Plutarch is set up in his home town of Chaeronea. His description of Sulla's victory here owes something to knowledge of local traditions.*

public confidence in its wisdom and integrity consequently declined.

The constitutional weapons for the class struggle which had been forged in the fifth, fourth and early third centuries were at last put to use at the end of the second century by Tiberius Gracchus, a high-minded aristocratic reformer. But the weapons proved two-edged. As we have observed a tribune could veto a fellow tribune, as well as a magistrate, and it was not difficult for the ruling oligarchy (nobiles) to find a tribune who would defend their interests. Passions were aroused and Tiberius Gracchus was assassinated amid scenes of civil disturbance.

The main cause which Tiberius had championed was that of the unemployed farmers who were forced out of business by Rome's newly-found access to cheap overseas grain. The struggle was carried on by Tiberius' brother Gaius. Since tribunician power had proved inadequate, Gaius invented new weapons with which to attack the nobles. He encouraged the wealthy but unprivileged class of equites to attack the exclusive noble clique who enjoyed senatorial dignity. The equites were the old Servian cavalry class whose military recruitment had been based on property qualifications. But in war, the cavalry was now supplied by allied contingents; the last known instance of the Roman equites having served as

cavalrymen is in the fighting at Numantia. Equestrian rank therefore remained merely an economic and social classification. Thanks to Gaius Gracchus' legislation, the juries of the law courts were now recruited from the equites. Provincial governors, normally of senatorial rank, on quitting office were frequently sued by those whom they had governed, on grounds of extortionate practice; but the fact that such trials had taken place before senatorial juries guaranteed the acquittal of the accused. Tried by the equites, they were now, regardless of justice, certain to be convicted—unless the jury was bribed. But the senatorial party was able to outbid Gracchus in demagogy. Roman domestic politics became increasingly violent. Gaius Gracchus, circumvented and discredited, was eventually found dead by a hostile mob which had pursued him; it appeared that he had ordered a faithful servant to kill him.

The Military Achievement of Marius

In the days when Marius had first served in North Africa, the nobiles were once more in precarious control of Roman politics. They were at least sufficiently in control to mismanage foreign wars. When Marius, a member of the equestrian class, declared his intention of standing for the consulate, his aristocratic commanding officer insulted him. However, Marius possessed ability, energy, wealth, influential family connections and a flair for intrigue. He became consul in 107 BC and superseded the general who had slighted him. However, no amount of intrigue could have raised Marius to the eminence for which he was destined if events had not conspired to demonstrate his very real military ability, both in the Jugurthine War and the campaigns against the barbarians.

A land-hungry Germanic tribe, the Cimbri, had left their homes in Jutland and together with other tribes, including the Teutones, whose name is remembered above all in this connection, had migrated southwards, carrying with them their entire families and moveable possessions. The Romans were alarmed and a consular army met the migrants in Noricum, a Celto-Illyrian area northeast of the Alps. In the ensuing battle the Romans were badly defeated. The Cimbri and their allies must have found that the Alps presented a more formidable barrier than the Rhone and they fortunately avoided Italy, moving

Saturninus, turbulent tribune at Rome, becomes Marius' political agent
Marius' victory over the Teutones at Aquae Sextiae

Above: *Battle scene from a Roman sarcophagus. The German tribesmen in conflict with the legionaries may well resemble the warriors of the Teutones and Cimbri, Marius' foes.*

westwards into Gaul (Southern France), an area which was by now under Roman control. Several Roman armies attempted to eliminate the barbarian menace, but they met with a series of humiliating defeats culminating in a major disaster at Arausio (Orange) in 105 BC, which much disturbed Rome.

The campaigns against the migrants could be regarded as offensive wars. The German tribes were fighting in defence of the families they had with them, and the Romans had rigidly, though not unwisely, refused to negotiate or concede any right of settlement to the barbarians. After Arausio, however, the way to Italy lay open to the Germanic invaders and Rome was unquestionably on the defensive. A full state of emergency existed and in these circumstances Marius, who had recently emerged as conqueror of Jugurtha, was elected consul for the second and successive year (105 BC). Legally, ten years should have elapsed before his second election. Constitutional precedent required that the consul should be sponsored by the Senate. But the Popular Assembly, as the legislative body of the Republic, was free to do as it chose. In any case, the Romans rarely insisted on constitutional niceties where they conflicted with military expediency.

Marius gloriously justified his appointment. Fortunately, the Germans had not immediately attempted the invasion of Italy but moved westwards towards Spain. This gave Marius time to train his troops for the coming conflict. Much of his success may indeed be attributed to good military discipline and administration. He was appointed consul for the third time before he came to grips with the enemy. He even had leisure to improve his supply lines by setting his men to dig a new channel at the mouth of the Rhone river.

The Teutones and the Ambrones (another allied German tribe) parted company from the Cimbri and the Tigurini (a Celtic people who had joined them). While the former confronted Marius on the Rhone, the latter made for Italy by a circuitous march over the Alps. Marius restrained his men in their camp to allow them to become accustomed to the sight of the barbarians who surrounded them, calculating that familiarity would breed contempt. When the Teutones marched on towards Italy, bypassing his camp, he led his own men out and overtook the enemy near Aquae Sextiae (Aix-en-Provence). Here, he fought a battle on favourable ground and, making use of a cavalry ambush posted in the hills, completely annihilated the Teutones. Their allies the Ambrones had already been slaughtered in great numbers in a fight at a watering place two days earlier.

Marius's consular colleague in North Italy fared by no means so happily and was forced to withdraw before the invading Cimbri into the Po valley, leaving them to occupy a large part of the country. In 101 BC Marius's legions were brought to reinforce the North Italian army, Marius being now in his fifth consulate. A battle was fought at Vercellae (perhaps near Rovigo). The barbarians' tactics were not utterly devoid of sophistication and had some success. Nor were the Germans ill-armed. Their cavalry wore lofty plumes on helmets grotesquely shaped like animal heads. Their breastplates were of iron and they carried flashing white shields, two javelins each and heavy swords for hand-to-hand fighting. The summer heat may have been in favour of the Romans, who were accustomed to the Mediterranean climate. Fighting was confused on account of a heavy dust storm. The Roman victory may be ascribed to superior training and discipline. Sulla, on whose account Plutarch relies, suggested that Marius' tactics were mainly designed to secure glory for himself at the expense of his consular colleague. Sulla himself fought in the battle, but one would not expect his evidence to be unbiased. In any case, the entire Germanic horde was destroyed and Rome was spared a catastrophe that might have proved conclusive to its political existence. For unlike the victors of the Allia, three centuries earlier, the Cimbri were in search of land, not gold. The greatest threat presented by the northern barbarians lay in their numbers, estimated at a total of 300,000; some ancient historians thought that this

BC | 101 | | | 100
Marius' fifth consulate | Marius' victory over the Cimbri at Vercellae | Glaucia as tribune collaborates with Saturninus | Marius' sixth consulate | Exile of Metellus Numidicus, Marius' former commander

132

was an underestimate. The Romans at Vercellae were a little more than 50,000 strong. At the same time, the barbarians' great trek southward from Jutland, let alone their subsequent victories over Roman armies, cannot have been achieved without leadership. It is surprising that the names of the Germanic leaders are not at least as celebrated as that of Brennus.*

Recruitment

The wars against the Cimbri and the Teutones are poorly documented. Marius emerges as both strategist and tactician, a leader possessing formidable discipline and great physical courage. Yet the secret of his success may well have lain in his ability as a military administrator and the intelligence of his military reforms.

One has only to consider his methods of recruitment. Constitutionally, these were outrageous and exposed him to the ever-increasing hostility of the Senate. But from a social and strategic point of view, they were precisely what Rome needed. Since the time of the Servian reforms, the poorest section of the population (*proletarii*) had not qualified for enrolment in the legions, except in times of grave national emergency. The name *proletarii* in fact signifies those who contributed only their children (*proles*) to the community —not their taxes or their military service. Plutarch suggests that only the propertied classes were required in the army, since their possessions were some sort of a security for their good behaviour. In any case, it must have been felt that they had a greater stake in the society which they defended.

At the time when Marius had been appointed by 'the People' to his first term as consul, Roman citizens were undergoing a process of proletarianisation. The land, from which the farmer was being forced by low overseas corn prices, was bought up by wealthy absentee landlords, who were able to run their estates with the help of cheap labour, supplied by a multitude of enslaved war captives. Meanwhile, the small farmer moved into the city, where he could at least take advantage of the cheap and subsidized corn which often proved to be the price of his political support.

The Senate had ruled that extra

*Boeorix, king of the Cimbri, negotiated with Marius before the battle of Vercellae, but does not appear as a conspicuous character.

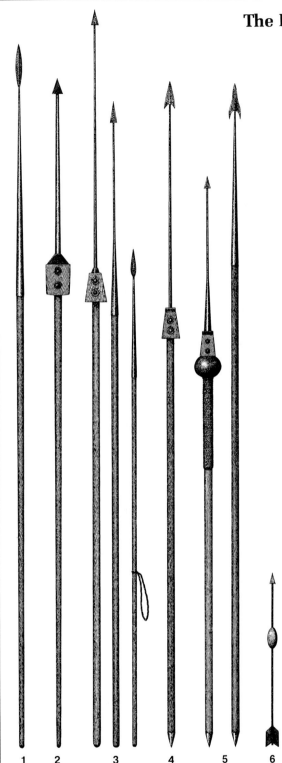

The Evolution of the Pilum

The *pilum* was a heavy type of javelin. It was possibly invented by the Etruscans, since the earliest examples come from 5th century BC Etruscan graves (**1**). The weapon consists of a long pointed iron shank fitted to a wooden shaft either by means of a socket in the iron or a penetrating riveted tang (**2**, a 4th century BC example). The *pilum* came into prominence during the Celtic invasions. Its weight gave excellent penetration, and the long metal shaft prevented its being cut away. Caesar speaks of *pila* pinning together Celtic shields— which implies penetrating ½-1″ (13-25mm) thickness of oak and hide. Handicapped by a *pilum* the shield became useless. Caesar recounts Celts throwing away such encumbered shields, preferring to fight without them. Additionally, the thin metal shaft bent or buckled on impact preventing the weapon being thrown back. **3** shows *pila* as used by the Romans in the 3rd century BC. They relied on them increasingly, equipping first the *hastati*, then *principes* and, by Marius' day, the whole legion with them. Each legionary carried 2 *pila*, one more slender and lighter than the other. The *velites* carried a smaller javelin —called *verutum*, usually with a throwing thong (*amentum*) attached. The heavy *pilum* is over 7ft (2·1m) long, the *verutum* some 4ft (1·2m). As time went by the heavy *pilum* got smaller and the light larger, until by the 1st century AD they were identical (**4**). By 100 AD the *pilum* had shrunk further, and a bronze weight was added to maintain armour piercing capability (**5**). Also shown is a Celtic version called a *gaesum* used by Roman auxiliaries of Celtic origin. Remains of these have been found near Hadrian's Wall. The Celts, of course quickly adopted *pila*. By the end of the 3rd century AD the Romans' main enemies were chiefly horsemen, and the *pilum* was replaced by a spear more suitable for fending off cavalry. Vegetius also refers to a *plumbata*, apparently a lead-weighted throwing dart capable of outranging all other hand missiles (**6**).

1   2   3   4   5   6

levies should be raised for the Jugurthine War. Marius, finding the measure inadequate, and always ready to provoke the Senate, recruited not only volunteers and time-expired veterans—which it was open to him to do—but also offered enlistment to members of the proletariat who wished to go soldiering. Whereas previously the field for recruitment had been progressively narrowing as property requirements became harder to satisfy,

Marius, by his initiative, raised a strong army and at the same time produced one remedy for the problem of unemployment.

As long as he enjoyed the support of the People's Assembly and its tribunes, the Senate could not check Marius' recruiting activities. His methods, however, had an ominous aspect. Roman soldiers, though now members of a fully professional army, owed personal loyalty to the general who enrolled and employed them. This loyalty was enhanced by traditional Roman concepts of the semi-sacred relationship which existed between a protector (*patronus*) and his protégé (*cliens*): a relationship which in some contexts acquired legal definition. Marius, at any rate, became a patron to his veteran soldiers, securing for them, through his political associates, a grant of farmland on retirement. The day of private armies, when soldiers owed prime allegiance to their generals rather than to the state, was not far off.

Army Reorganization

At the battle of Aquae Sextiae, Marius gave the order to his men, through the usual chain of command, that they should hurl their javelins as soon as the enemy came within range, then use their swords and shields to thrust the attackers backwards, down the treacherous slope. The instructions to discharge javelins and then join battle with swords and shields is such as we might expect to be given to an army which had adopted the *pilum* and the *gladius*, but the offensive use of shields and the application of pushing tactics sounds like a reversion to the old fifth and fourth century phalanx as it had been used both in Greece and Italy. The probability is that the traditional manipular formation with its three-line quincunx deployment had generally been superseded. In the course of the preceding century, Rome had come into conflict with a wide assortment of enemies, variously equipped and accustomed, and the Romans were nothing if not adaptable. They were ready to improvise and to adopt such tactics as suited the terrain and were most likely to prove effective against the type of enemy with whom they had to deal in any particular battle. There were no longer any routine tactics. The maniple which had been the unit of the old three-line battle front was in the first place a tactical unit (see page 112). Once it had ceased to be tactically effective, there was no reason for its retention. Marius recognized this fact and reorganized his army accordingly.

For purposes of administration a larger unit than the maniple was convenient; and in this, subdivisions were necessary. The legion was consequently divided into ten cohorts, and every cohort contained six centuries, each commanded by a centurion, whose titles, ranging from that of the exalted *primus pilus* to *hastatus posterior,* reflected differences of

Marius' Legionary

Marius' reforms simply formalised a growing trend for the Roman army to become necessarily more professional as Rome's empire expanded. All legionaries were equipped much as the soldier (left). The helmets shown on p. 109 — particularly the "Montefortino" type — were all popular. Mail shirts though expensive, became universal. Greaves disappeared, except on centurions. The *pilum, scutum* and *gladius* continued in use, plus a dagger (*pugio*). Another of Marius' reforms was to reduce the size of the baggage train (*impedimenta*). The troops thus had to carry much of their gear, hence the wry description: "Marius' mules". The soldier is depicted in marching order. In addition to the equipment shown right, he has a bedroll and cloak, 3 or more days' ration of grain and hard-tack, and an entrenching tool virtually identical to modern ones. The whole, including arms and armour, weighed an estimated 80-100lb (35-44kg). Each squad (*contubernium*) of 8 men was also allowed one mule, which carried heavier items such as the squad's leather tent and mill-stones.

The Scutum (below)
Polybius describes the shield as being curved, 24" (·66m) wide, 44" (1·1m) long or more, and as "thick as a palm." Archaeology bears this out, but additionally shows that the thickness of individual shields might vary between ·5-·75" (12·5-19mm). He continues, "... of a double thickness (sometimes more) of planks glued together ... a binding of iron which protects it from cutting strokes ... (and) an iron boss, which deflects the more destructive blows ..." Its construction thus resembled modern plywood. It also had a leather cover.

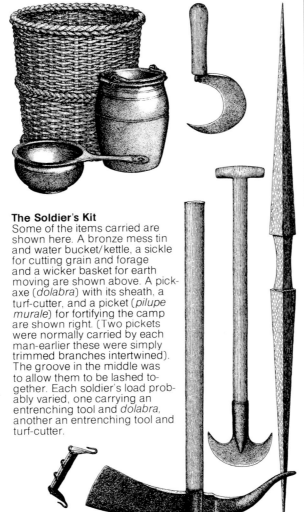

The Soldier's Kit
Some of the items carried are shown here. A bronze mess tin and water bucket/kettle, a sickle for cutting grain and forage and a wicker basket for earth moving are shown above. A pickaxe (*dolabra*) with its sheath, a turf-cutter, and a picket (*pilupe murale*) for fortifying the camp are shown right. (Two pickets were normally carried by each man-earlier these were simply trimmed branches intertwined). The groove in the middle was to allow them to be lashed together. Each soldier's load probably varied, one carrying an entrenching tool and *dolabra*, another an entrenching tool and turf-cutter.

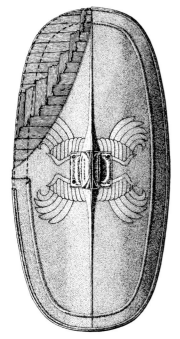

The Caliga (right)
This heavy sandal was very tough and long-wearing. The sole consisted of several layers of leather and was c ·75" (20mm) thick and studded with hob-nails. The upper was cut in one piece and sewn up at the heel. The front was laced up. In winter they could be stuffed with cloth or fur for warmth. The Emperor Gaius derived his nickname "Little boot" (Caligula) from having worn specially-made *caligae* as a child.

The Mail-Cuirass (right)
This was the standard armour of the legionary, and most likely was of Celtic origin. It was made of iron rings of two sorts: solid rings and open, linking rings which were butted or riveted shut. This provided an excellent defence against cuts and a good one against thrusts, while also being very flexible. The illustration has been opened out to clearly show the structure.

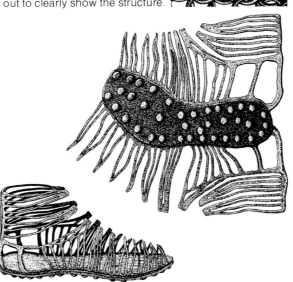

position on the battlefield, rank and seniority. Before Marius' time the cohort, notably as used by Scipio in Spain (134 BC), was often a purely tactical formation, employed to cope with special circumstances. On the other hand, it had originated as an administrative infantry unit among the Italian allies. Cohorts had been mobilized originally as 500 and 1,000 strong respectively. Each had been under the command of a *praefectus*. As a legionary unit, the cohort was 500-600 strong. Its division into six centuries meant that these were each somewhat under 100 strong, larger than the old manipular centuries, which in practice had sometimes contained as few as 60 men.

Marius abolished the *velites*, the skirmishers of the ancient Camillan army; and with them, their characteristic arms of light spear and small buckler (*parma*) disappeared. The *pilum* was now used by all legionaries, and Marius introduced a change in its manufacture. In place of one of the iron rivets which had secured the head to the shaft, he had a wooden peg inserted. When the javelin impaled an enemy shield, the peg broke on impact and the shaft sagged and trailed on the ground, though still attached to the head by the remaining iron rivet. Not only was the javelin thus rendered unserviceable to enemy hands, but it encumbered the warrior whose shield it had transfixed. According to Plutarch, this novelty was introduced in preparation for the battle with the Cimbri at the battle of Vercellae. At a later date, in Julius Caesar's army, as a further refinement, the long shank of the *pilum* was made of soft iron, so that it bent even while it penetrated.

Marius was at pains to ensure that every soldier in his army should be fit and self-reliant. He accustomed his men to long route marches and to frequent moves at the double. In addition to their arms and trenching tools, he insisted on them carrying their own cooking utensils and required that every man should be able to prepare his own meals. Flavius Josephus, the Jewish historian who wrote in the first century AD, describes the legionary as carrying a saw, a basket, a bucket, a hatchet, a leather strap, a sickle, a chain and rations for three days, as well as other equipment. If this was a legacy of Marius' reforms, it is easy to understand why the men who patiently supported such burdens were nicknamed 'Marius' mules'. Of course, campaigning in enemy country or where there was a danger of sudden

Legionary Helmets

1 shows a type of bronze helmet made in Gaul to meet the Roman army's demands. It is known as "Coolus" type and is distinguished from the "Montefortino" by its larger, flatter neck-guard and Gallic cheek-pieces. These entered service around 50 BC and continued in use until around 100 AD. They are fastened like the earlier types by a strap passing from the rear under the ears, through the cheek-pieces and tied under the chin. The horsehair crest and feathers were worn only on parade or in battle. **2** shows an early type of iron helmet known as "Imperial-Gallic" which appeared around 15 BC. It is closely related to the "Agen" helmet worn by Gallic chiefs (see p.143). The peak of this and the "Coolus" helmets gave added protection against downward cuts. The prominent "eyebrows" also added strength and were a common Gallic feature. **3** shows a more developed form of this style of iron helmet, dating

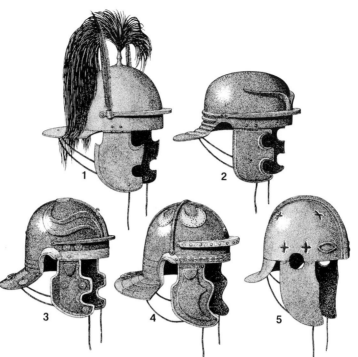

from the second half of the 1st century AD. The neck-guard is now deeper and extended ear-protectors have been added, together with a band around the brow-edge, both of bronze. The cheek-pieces are turned outward at the rear to deflect blows. The eyebrows have grown more ornate, and wider. This example is fitted with a crest-holder and Gallic-style enamelled bronze bosses. Crests were now no long worn in battle. Altogether this helmet has a more finished look than earlier types and represents the legionary helmet at its peak of design. **4** is similar and dates from around 100 AD. It is an Italian-made copy of the Gallic types, but of inferior quality. The peak is of down-turned "L" section and it has a cruciform reinforce over the bowl. **5** shows a cheap early 4th century AD helmet. The huge increase in the size of the army necessitated simplifying equipment. This helmet is made in two halves, joined by a ridge with separate neck and cheek-pieces.

attack, the Romans marched lightly equipped and ready for action at short notice, while the soldiers' packs (*sarcinae*) were carried with the baggage train. Marius is also said to have introduced a quick-release system for the pack.

Military Standards and Banners

Another of Marius' innovations was the introduction of a single silver eagle (*aquila*), mounted on a staff, as a legionary standard. It is difficult to know just what significance should be attached to this change, because we have no clear information about the military standards which were previously in use. The eagle was a bird sacred to Jupiter. According to one source, there had previously been five legionary standards. Apart from the eagle, these exhibited the forms of wolves, bears, minotaurs and horses, and they were carried severally before the several ranks of the army in battle. But from Marius' time, they were relegated to subordinate and ceremonial usages.

The legionary eagles were later made of gold and they were embellished with wreaths and other ornaments. In peacetime, they were kept in the state treasury (*aerarium*) at Rome, the old temple of Saturn. In wartime, they were carried with the legion and had a little sanctuary allotted to them in the camp. They were objects of quasi-religious veneration.

This quasi-religious function of the standards was in conflict with their practical purpose. In so far as the standard was a sacred object symbolizing the corporate existence of a military unit, it qualified for the care and protection of the soldiers whom it represented and could not properly be exposed to danger of capture by the enemy in battle. Its loss was, in fact, regarded as a great disgrace. The standard therefore had to be placed behind the front line and surrounded by troops who would defend it.

Schoolboys are — or used to be — familiar with Caesar's anecdote of the standard-bearer who leapt down from his ship as it beached on the Kentish coast, with an exhortation to the hesitant legionaries to follow him if they did not intend the betrayal of their eagle into enemy hands. An earlier example of the same attitude occurs in Plutarch's account of the battle of Pydna. On this occasion, a captain of one of the Italian contingents seized his unit's ensign and flung it into the enemy phalanx. Thus blackmailed by the threat of dishonour, his men redoubled their efforts to break the phalanx. For, as Plutarch observes, the Italians in particular regarded it as ignominious to desert their standards.

If, however, the standard was a sacred object which required protection, it could not discharge its practical function — which was to serve as a rallying point. As such, its place was in the forefront of the battle. The legionaries could not be expected to

look over their shoulders to discover where they should take their stand. The very name of the standards in Latin, *signa*, suggests that they were in fact signals, and as tactics became increasingly mobile and less uniform, the need for them increased. Incidentally, the Greeks of the fifth century BC had made no corresponding use of military standards in their compact phalanx battles.

A study of ancient references to the position of the standards on the battlefield suggests that they may have been located immediately behind the front line. They were thus protected, and yet at the same time sufficiently far advanced to serve as marking signals for the greater part of the army. On the other hand, the whole point of Marius' innovation may have been to confer a single standard on the legion which would serve its emotional needs, at the same time leaving the standards of the smaller units free to be used, without sentimental inhibitions, for practical purposes. By contrast with legionary standards, the old signalling staves of the maniples had embodied no sacred animals. They had exhibited the open palm of a hand on a raised spear, but were later decorated with garlands and other emblems. When maniples were absorbed into cohorts, the cohort took the leading maniple's standard.

Similarly, the cavalry standards (*vexilla*), consisting of flags suspended from a kind of yard-arm and identifying units, would lose their more emotional significance with the adoption of the

BC | 91
Legislation by M. Livius Drusus hostile to the *equites* | Drusus murdered | Outbreak of Social War (Rome against Italian allies) | | 90
Spread of Social War | Marius commands on northern front

136

Auxiliary Infantry Helmets

The auxiliaries were not as well paid as the legions, nor was their status as high, and their equipment reflected this. **6** is the sort of helmet worn by auxiliaries from the middle of the 1st century AD. It is a bronze copy of contemporary legionary types, but very much simplified. **7** is also a simplified legionary design, this time from around 100 AD. Similar helmets are shown in use on Trajan's column. **8** shows another helmet of around 100 AD worn by Eastern archer units. It is of typical Eastern design, being conical and made of segments of iron, bronze, or horn held in a metal frame. Roman features are the decorated browband, ear-guards and cheek-pieces. As it was relatively simple to make, this type was widespread. **9** shows a 4th century helmet from Egypt, the number of segments has been reduced for simplicity and a nose guard added. This is the origin of the "Spangenhelm" of the Dark Ages.

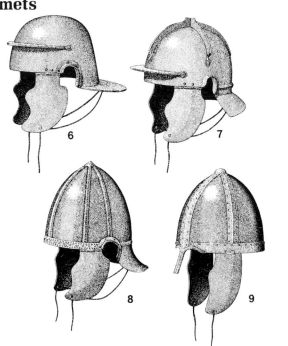

Above: *After the military reforms of Marius' time, Roman cavalry was recruited from outside Italy. Arms and equipment, however, were still in the Roman style, as this relief shows.*

uniform legionary emblem. By Marius' time, the Italian cavalry had largely been superseded by overseas cavalry forces (*auxilia*), who perhaps did not share the Italian veneration for standards and banners. The eagle remained a permanent symbol throughout later centuries of military development. But other forms of standard were also imitated from the usage of outlying peoples on Rome's frontiers. An interesting example is the *draco*, which was a windsock of coloured silk, with the silver head and gaping jaws of a dragon.

The Italian captain distinguished by his gesture at Pydna had been a Pelignian. Marius came from Arpinum, a town which had enjoyed full Roman citizen rights since the beginning of the second century. Arpinum was not far from the territory of the Peligni, and Marius was perhaps acutely conscious of the importance of military standards and banners in terms of local sentiment. As an eminently practical commander, he must also have been aware of the difficulties which such sentiments created. It is possible to regard the silver eagle as his solution

The Social War and its Consequences

Marius apparently had a parade-ground voice and manner, which were extremely effective in the army, but as they were accompanied by no inkling of statesmanship, they made him a ludicrous figure in politics. After his defeat of the barbarian hordes, he was hailed as a third founder of Rome, a worthy successor to Romulus and Camillus, but during his sixth consulate, in which he was called upon to exercise the faculties of a civil administrator rather than a general, his popularity rapidly declined. The violent demagogues who had secured his previous extensions of office also fell foul of the mob and themselves perished as victims of violence. Unable to obtain a seventh appointment as consul, Marius left on a private tour of Asia Minor, which was already threatened by the growing power of

Mithridates, king of Pontus. Marius was perhaps looking for a new war in which he would again have a chance of demonstrating his exclusively military talent. In the course of his travels, he was hospitably entertained by Mithridates, but contrived nevertheless to offend him. After that, the ex-general returned to Rome, where he was no longer a very important person.

Civil violence on the old party lines was now temporarily suspended. But a new kind of threat arose. An austere and dignified reformer, Marcus Livius Drusus, had proposed that full Roman citizenship should be conferred on the Italian allies. In earlier times Rome had readily and generously granted such extensions of her citizenship, but latterly, able to recruit cavalry and auxiliary support from overseas, the Senate had felt itself in no need of conciliating the Italians. Drusus was eventually assassinated, and the Italians whom he had championed soon realised that the Popular party was as exclusive in its attitudes towards the franchise as were the nobles. Although the Latins, who possessed almost full citizen rights, remained loyal, the other Italian peoples, notably the Marsi, broke out in angry armed revolt. Their object was no longer to obtain the citizenship, but to establish an independent Italian state.

In the ensuing so-called 'Social War' (ie, war with the *socii*, or allies), Marius found himself once more serving the Republic in a military capacity, in company with senatorial commanders who would have been his enemies if the emergency had left time for party politics. As it was, he was disappointed by the modest powers entrusted to him on the northern front, while Sulla, operating south of Rome, gained distinguished victories. Perhaps there was no justification for jealousy. Sulla was about 20 years younger than Marius—who was by now 67 years old.

After a second year of struggle, the Romans gained the upper hand over the Italians and wisely decided to negotiate out of strength. Without undue loss of face, they were able to confer full citizenship on all Italy, and with this concession the extremist movement for an independent Italian state collapsed. The conciliatory Roman attitude may be praised as a return to exemplary political wisdom and moderation, but if it had manifested itself earlier, two years of bloody fighting would have been avoided.

Roman military organization had always been closely linked to the constitutional and social establishment.

Legislation conceding citizenship to the Italians   Nicomedes of Bithynia restored by Romans   End of Social War   Mithridates involved against Bithynia   Mithridates clashes with Rome (First Mithridatic War)   **BC**

The constitutional changes that followed the Social War had foreseeable military consequences. The Italian populations, being now enfranchised, qualified for enlistment in the legions. There was no longer any question of separate Italian allied contingents. Indeed, these had already been made redundant by the use of overseas auxiliaries: a circumstance which must be counted among Italian grievances before the Social War. The new prospects of enlistment, especially in view of the proletarian opportunities provided by Marius' reforms, let alone the prospect of land grants to retired veterans, must have gone far to conciliating the aggrieved Italians. All that was now required was a new war to provide employment and new conquests to provide more land for the veterans. With Mithridates menacing the countries of the eastern Mediterranean, the pretext was not far to seek. In any case, Rome had never welcomed a large consolidated power on the frontiers of her territory.

Sulla's March on Rome

Sulla's prestige after the Social War was considerable. He was made consul in 88 BC, and the Senate placed him in command of operations against Mithridates. For the inevitable eastern war had by now broken out. But once the Italian allies had been placated, party politics in Rome reasserted themselves, and the same unscrupulous and violent methods were employed. In the People's Assembly, at the instance of another tribunicial demagogue, the Senate's appointment of Sulla was overruled, and command in the Mithridatic War was transferred to Marius, who was, even at his advanced age, ambitious to restore his waning reputation by some new military achievement.

At the time when the new legislation was due to take effect, Sulla hastened to rejoin his army in Campania, where it was preparing for the eastern campaign. He tested the consensus among his legionaries and found them ardently loyal to himself. Officers who came from Rome to arrange for the transfer of Sulla's troops to Marius were roughly handled by the men and driven away with contumely. With six legions at his back, abandoning all pretence to constitutional procedure, Sulla marched on Rome. After a few hours of street-fighting, he was in control of the city. Marius was outlawed and fled, and the tribune who

had legislated so blatantly in his favour was killed. However, although this action was made possible by the wholehearted support of Sulla's men, his officers, with one exception, were appalled at the unprecedented violence of the action and firmly dissociated themselves from it.

Having purged the city ruthlessly of his political opponents, Sulla established his own partisans in power and left Rome once more in preparation for his Mithridatic expedition, which he rightly felt himself well qualified to undertake. For he had already, in the period between the Cimbrian and Social Wars, successfully championed the cause of a Roman protégé ruler in Asia Minor.

Roman Standards

Throughout the history of the Roman army standards played an important part. They represented the spirit of each unit, and were held in religious awe, being decorated with precious oils and garlands on special occasions. In battle, the standards had a key function, since orders were relayed through them. Each maniple had a standard which was normally stationed between the centuries, hence the terms *ante-signani* (before the standards) and *postsignani* (behind the standards). The senior maniple of a cohort carried the cohort standard, and the senior cohort carried the legion standard — originally an eagle, a wolf, a Minotaur, a horse or a boar. These may have been of tribal origin. Marius made the eagle the symbol of the legion, but other symbols were carried: astrological ones such as a bull, capricorn or ram, relating to the unit's foundation day, and in Imperial times a small portrait statue of the emperor (*imago*). Flags called *vexilla* were also carried by detachments from units.

Standard-Bearers
The colour illustration shows a Praetorian standard-bearer (*signifer*) in parade dress with a crimson tunic over his armour. He carries a manipular standard, symbolised by the hand at the top. Portraits of the emperor and empress, various awards for bravery, and the traditional symbolic tuft, (originally grass or leaves) complete the standard. Next to him is a *vexillarius* wearing his "medals" (*phalerae*) and torques awarded for bravery. *Vexillarii* and eagle bearers (*aquiliferi*) were traditionally bareheaded, while the Praetorians wore lionskin capes, the legions bearskin and the auxiliaries bearskin with the face cut away. The small figures show

(left to right) an auxiliary standard-bearer, a legionary cohort *signifer* and an auxiliary cohort *signifer* with a leather tunic over his armour. These are all in battle array. All the figures are 1st-2nd centuries AD. Above are shown an eagle and a maniple standard from the late 2nd century AD and a *draco*, a type of windsock, which became the most common standard in the 4th century AD.

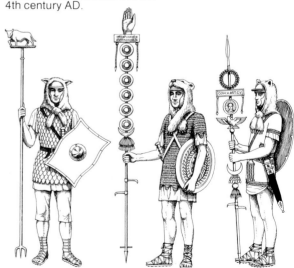

BC | 88

Sulla is consul | Sulla marches on Rome: Marius flees to Africa | In the East, massacre of 80,000 Romans on Mithridates' orders | Sulla lands with 5 legions in Epirus, besieges Mithridates' allies in Athens | 87 — L. Cornelius Cinna, Marius' collaborator is consul

138

Left: A scene from Trajan's Column showing the army on the march. Both legionary and Praetorian standards are prominently displayed. Though of Imperial date, it shows the form taken by signa after Marius' reforms.

Sulla's undisguised appeal to armed force as a political weapon in Roman internal politics certainly marked a new departure. But in a sense, this was merely the logical development of methods and policies which Marius had already initiated. The provision of land grants for retired veterans had the forseeable—and no doubt foreseen—effect of securing the allegiance of the troops to their general rather than to the State. Troops who had confidence in the ability of their leader to manipulate legislation to their material advantage in this way were ready to give him enthusiastic support. It was only required in addition that he should offer the prospect of continuous warfare in which new land for distribution could be conquered and new spoils won. Sulla, as a gifted leader, certainly met both these requirements.

The relationship between political and military power became increasingly clear. It was a circular relationship in which political power was the reward of military achievement and military support was guaranteed by the use of political power. In these circumstances, although the Romans—sentiment apart—had an interest in the survival of the Roman State and its ascendancy over barbarous regimes, the allegiance of the armed forces was to their generals rather than to their republican institutions—or indeed to the State itself. It is noteworthy that Julius Caesar's standard-bearer, a generation after Sulla's march on Rome, as he leapt down into the sea on the steeply-shelving Kentish beach, shouted aloud that he himself at least would do his duty to the Republic and to his general. To a constitutionalist, the order in which he proclaimed his allegiances must seem that of right priority. Such a priority, however, was not by any means universally reflected in military attitudes during the first century BC, as the enduring conflict between Marius and Sulla reveals.

Sulla's War in Greece

The kingdom of Pontus, south of the Black Sea, over which Mithridates reigned, had once been a satrapy of the Persian Empire, but after the time of Alexander the Great its rulers had established themselves as an independent dynasty. The population may have contained Thracian, Scythian and Celtic elements such as had entered from the north, but it was dominated by Iranian feudal and priestly castes, and its kings adopted, or at any rate

Attempt to repeal Sulla's legislation leads to violence and massacre of Marius' enemies

Marius dies and is replaced by Valerius Flaccus

Sulla, though outlawed at Rome, captures Athens

Sulla defeats Mithridates' general Archelaus at Chaeronea and Orcho-menos

Valerius Flaccus leads army through Greece to Asia, as Rome's legiti-mate commander

affected, Greek culture. Mithridates VI, with whom we are here concerned, had presented himself as a champion of Greek civilization, and in this role he had given military protection to the Greek cities on the northern shores of the Black Sea, firmly imposing his authority on this area. As a result he had access to fertile grain-growing lands and to the resources of wealthy Greek maritime states, including a substantial navy.

However, when Mithridates turned his attention southwards into Asia Minor he came into conflict with rulers who were friends and allies of the Roman People: that is to say, Roman buffer states and protectorates. In this connection, he had already exercised Sulla's considerable diplomatic ability in 96 BC, when the Roman had been appointed governor of Cilicia. Mithridates was not unwary, but Rome's preoccupation with Jugurthine, Cimbric and Social Wars, let alone its own internal dissensions, offered him opportunities which he could not resist. In 88 BC, when a Roman commander, less adroit that Sulla had attempted to use puppet forces against him—much as Masinissa had been used against Carthage—Mithridates reacted strongly and inflicted humiliating defeats not only on the puppets but on the Roman armed forces themselves. He then quickly extended his power throughout Asia Minor and the Aegean, where many Greek cities, tired of Roman extortions, at first welcomed him. In these cities, Mithridates got rid of the Roman business population by massacring men, women and children, to the reported number of 80,000. He then sent his armies under Greek generals into Greece. Athens was already dominated by a disreputable popular tyrant, who was willing to serve as a Pontic puppet. The Roman governor of Macedonia and the officer whom he delegated acted with vigour and resolution and held the Pontic armies at bay in North Greece, but the arrival of Sulla and his five legions in Epirus (87 BC) was timely.

Sulla laid siege to Athens, starved the city for some time and finally took it by assault. The operation was expensive, but Sulla cut down sacred groves to provide timber for his siege works and appropriated the wealth of Greek temple treasuries to defray costs. He had a superstitious belief in his own good fortune, from which he and his men derived much confidence, but evidently did not worry unduly about the feelings of the gods. The siege of Athens was marked by elaborate

Above: *Mithridates VI of Pontus, Rome's inveterate enemy, is seen here. He lived to an old age but the youthful portraiture is reminiscent of Alexander the Great.*

mining operations. When the Roman earthworks subsided, the besiegers quickly divined the cause and dug a counter-mine. The sappers of the two sides met underground and fought a desperate battle with their spears amid subterranean gloom.

Sulla permitted the partial sack of Athens, then called a halt to it out of respect for the city's historic past. Mithridates' commander Archelaus still controlled the seas, and the rocky terrain of Attica did not provide food for the Roman army. Sulla moved off into the corn-growing Boeotian plain, already the destination of Pontic reinforcements. Here he fought two victorious battles at Chaeronea and Orchomenos.

Mithridates' armies were a characteristic compound of Greek and Oriental elements. With a Macedonian-type phalanx, the king had put into the field a large contingent of scythe-wheel chariots. There was also a unit which bore the traditional name of 'Brazen Shields'. Superior numbers, perhaps, as well as the imposing display of flashing gold and silver arms and armour, at first daunted the Romans. At Chaeronea, therefore, Sulla took up a defensive position and set his men to digging protective entrenchments on their flanks. As he had intended, they soon grew tired of the digging and showed willingness to fight. In the battle which followed, the Pontic phalangists appear to have been poorly trained, and the scythe-wheel chariots were a complete fiasco, provoking the Roman soldiers to open laughter and ironical applause. Casualty figures are

derived from Sulla's own record and seem very unconvincing. He reported 100,000 enemy dead, whereas Roman losses were confined to 14 missing, of whom two were found next day. But in any case, the result was a resounding success for Roman arms.

The flexible generalship of Archelaus cannot be blamed. He made the best of his multitudinous but unseasoned troops—some of whom were freed slaves recruited for the occasion. The phalanx broke under the impact of the Roman javelins and catapult missiles. The Pontic cavalry and light-armed troops continually menaced the Romans with encirclement. But Sulla and his officers averted danger thanks to their own vigilance and the mobility of the men under their command.

Archelaus, who escaped the battle, spent the following winter in the island of Euboea, where he was protected by his navy from Roman attack. Sulla and his army wintered in Athens. In the following spring (85 BC), the two armies met once more in Boeotia, in idyllic country near Orchomenos. Sulla again precipitated an engagement by digging entrenchments. But this time it was the enemy who were provoked, for they were in danger of being confined by Sulla's earthworks to the marshland around Lake Copais. The Pontic cavalry had some initial success, but Sulla by his personal example saved the situation. Renewed assaults on the Roman entrenchments only exposed the Pontic army to counter-attacks, and Archelaus' archers, finding themselves all too soon at grips with the legionaries, were reduced to using their arrows as swords. Sulla's men continued their digging and on the following day, when the whole of the enemy force was committed to interrupting them, the Romans attacked suddenly, captured Archelaus' camp and slaughtered his scattered troops amid the marshes. Archelaus himself again escaped.

War within a War

After Sulla's dramatic march on Rome in 88 BC, Marius had tried to escape by sea, but found himself stranded on the west coast of Italy, where the local people, anxious only to back the winning side, did not know

Right: *Mithridates' campaigns in 88 BC prompted swift Roman reaction. Sulla's intervention in Greece and his successes at Chaeronea and Orchomenos forced Mithridates to make peace.*

| Cinna consul | Valerius Flaccus killed in mutiny incited by his officer C. Flavius Fimbria | Fimbria assumes command: success of Fimbria against Mithridates | Lucullus, Sulla's officer, refuses to collaborate with Fimbria | Fimbria's troops desert to Sulla: suicide of Fimbria | Peace of Dardanus between Sulla and Mithridates |

whether to protect or betray him. As a way out of the difficulty—according to Plutarch—a volunteer Gaul was secretly sent in to murder him. But Marius bellowed at the man in his parade-ground voice and the would-be assassin fled in confusion. The story may not be true, but it is in character.

Finally, Marius reached North Africa. Here, he was *persona grata* among the settlements of his own retired veteran soldiers. In the following year, Sulla being now occupied with Mithridates, party strife again broke out in Rome, and Marius, seeing his opportunity, landed in Etruria, where more of his old soldiers were settled. With the help of forces raised by his political associates, he sacked Ostia, captured Rome, and launched a reign of terror in which his political opponents were ruthlessly butchered. But the consciousness of Sulla's power, still poised against him in the East, preyed on his mind. He took to heavy drinking and died during his seventh consulate.

The Popular party, however, remained in power and had sent into Greece legions which purported to be the true army of the Republic. Sulla, now outlawed, was denounced, and an appeal was made to his men to desert him and accept the authority of the legitimate Roman commander. However, when the new legions in Greece,

Above: *Bocchus, King of Mauretania, is delivering Jugurtha, his son-in-law, into the hands of Sulla. Marius triumphed over Jugurtha in 106 BC but Sulla claimed the credit.*

respectful of Sulla's military record, showed every inclination to leave their legitimate commander and join the outlaw, they were tactfully led away through Macedonia and Thrace to concentrate their efforts against Mithridates across the Hellespont. Gaius Flavius Fimbria, a highly efficient, if treacherous, officer had now taken command of them, having

secured, in the course of a mutiny, the murder of the commanding officer originally appointed.

Sulla's friends in Rome had been massacred, his houses burnt, and his wife and children had barely escaped into Greece to join him. In order to return to Rome, to square accounts there, he was now ready to negotiate with Mithridates, and to this end he negotiated with Archelaus at a convenient temple precinct on the Boeotian coast. It was suggested to Sulla that he should accept Mithridates as an ally against his own Roman enemies. Sulla responded with a suggestion that Archelaus should betray Mithridates. Archelaus appeared shocked: upon which, Sulla, who excelled in such negotiations, professed himself equally shocked at Archelaus' treacherous offer. In the end, it was agreed that Mithridates should retain his kingdom, but give up his conquests, with much of his fleet, and pay an indemnity.

Sulla's legions were offended by such a compromise peace. They felt patriotism for their nation, even if they cared nothing for its present government, and the Romans who had perished in Mithridates' massacres were not forgotten. Sulla placated them with the rather specious argument that he would have been unable to fight against both Fimbria and Mithridates

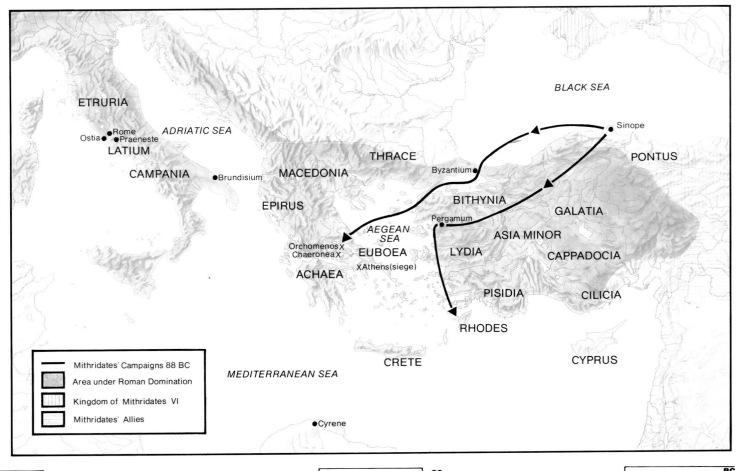

84
Fourth consulate of Cinna

Julius Caesar marries Cornelia, Cinna's daughter

Cinna murdered by mutinous troops

83
Renewal of war against Mithridates by Sulla's officer Murena

Archelaus deserts to the Romans (Second Mithridatic War)

BC

141

together. To be fair to Fimbria, he would have succeeded in capturing the Pontic king, if Lucius Licinius Lucullus, Sulla's trusted officer, who had by now assembled a fleet, had not deliberately permitted Mithridates to escape.

With the Pontic menace temporarily removed, Sulla moved his army close to Fimbria's camp in Lydia and settled down to entrenching operations—his characteristic military gambit. Fimbria's men, dressed for fatigue duties, soon came over and helped with the digging; Fimbria, accurately assessing the situation, committed suicide. Sulla at once took charge of the deceased general's troops. He punished the Greek cities who had acquiesced in Mithridates' massacres with enormous financial impositions, which they were unable to support without more help from Roman money-lenders. Leaving Fimbria's legions to garrison the East, Sulla then returned with his own army, like an avenging angel, to Italy.

Sulla's army, when it landed at Brundisium (Brindisi), was vastly outnumbered by the armed forces of the Popular Party, but his men were dedicated to him, while those of his enemies were lukewarm. Officers in command of substantial units also joined him, particularly the sons of Marius' victims and opponents, including Gnaeus Pompeius, who, as a result of the nickname which Sulla later bestowed on him, became known to history as Pompey the Great. Nevertheless, Sulla reached Rome too late to prevent the massacre of his supporters. He was also unpopular with the Samnite Italians, against whom he had fought in the Social War. These allied themselves with the Popular faction and constituted the most serious threat with which Sulla had to deal, but he was at last victorious over them in a fierce battle in Rome's Colline Gate. Soon after, Marius' son, besieged in Praeneste in Latium, committed suicide.

Sulla slaughtered his captives in large numbers. Completely in control of Rome and Italy, he drew up a series of lists outlawing his political opponents —who were accordingly massacred. He had himself made dictator in due constitutional form, and remained dictator in the modern sense, even when he had relinquished the formality, until his death from disease in 78 BC.

Lucullus and his Navy

Despite what has been said above, the achievements of Lucullus, while serving under Sulla against Mithridates,

Above: *Mountainous country in Cappadocia. In the 1st century BC, interference in this area by Mithridates of Pontus was thwarted by Rome.*

deserve honourable mention. Lucullus was connected with Sulla by marriage; dedication to the mighty warlord seems to have been the dominant motive in his life. Lucullus served with distinction during the Social War, and during the march on Rome in 88 BC he was apparently the only officer in Sulla's force to applaud the coup. He was a man of rare literary and scholarly gifts. Sulla dedicated his memoirs to him, and he became Sulla's literary executor. His negotiations with Fimbria, on the occasion to which we have already alluded, most clearly demonstrate his attitude. If Mithridates were prevented from escaping by sea—so it was urged —then Lucullus and Fimbria would share the glory of his capture, to the exclusion of Sulla. Neither self-interest nor loyalty to the Republic can have led Lucullus to reject Fimbria's proposal. He must have been governed simply by his fidelity to Sulla.

While Sulla was laying siege to Athens—though himself cut off from supplies by the enemy's navy—Lucullus had been detailed to raise a fleet from such maritime states in the eastern Mediterranean as had resisted Mithridates. He sailed from Greece for Alexandria in midwinter, over seas infested by Pontic and pirate squadrons, in a small sailing craft, with three other light ships and three Rhodian galleys as an escort. He won political support for the Romans in Crete and was accepted by the citizens of Cyrene as an impartial arbitrator in their own internal disputes. Changing ships several times to baffle enemy intelligence, he at last reached Alexandria, after narrow escapes from pirates in

which he lost more than one vessel. But the young Ptolemy of Egypt did not wish to be committed, and his support went no further than a royal welcome, generous hospitality and gifts.

Around Cyprus, enemy war galleys lay in wait, and Lucullus was forced to slip away inconspicuously, hoisting sail only at night and relying on oars by day. But, fortunately, Rhodes had taken a firm stand against the Pontic menace and, with a nucleus of ships which the Rhodians placed at his disposal, Lucullus won over or conquered other Greek islands and steadily enlarged his fleet. In these operations, he was careful not to associate himself with cities which had become pirate havens. Apart from his innate respect for law and order, any such association would have offended his Rhodian allies.

Lucullus later fought two victorious battles with Mithridates' navy in the north-east Aegean. At Tenedos, he led his fleet into action aboard a Rhodian quinquereme. The enemy admiral, however, came full tilt at the Rhodian with the intention of head-on ramming. On this occasion, the master of Lucullus' flagship executed an unusual manoeuvre. Afraid to encounter the attacker head-on, he swung round, presented his poop and, backing water, met the enemy stern first. The configuration of the Rhodian ship's hull was apparently such that in this posture it sustained no damage.

BC 82

Sulla's return to Italy: battle of the Colline Gate against Marians and Samnite allies

Sulla becomes dictator, massacres his political enemies; narrow escape of Julius Caesar

In the East, Murena defeated by Mithridates; operations halted by Sulla

81

In the Aegean, Mitylene revolts against Roman taxation

Julius Caesar recruits ships from Nicomedes for the operations against Mitylene

Caesar's relationship with Nicomedes becomes notorious

142

The Gauls

These fierce warriors were among Rome's most implacable foes. They conquered and colonised northern Italy, destroying the Etruscans in the process. Rome subdued them in three stages: in north Italy, south France and finally by Caesar's conquest of northern France. During this time the Celts and Italians freely exchanged ideas and weapons. The Celts, supreme iron workers of their day, pioneered iron helmets, and probably invented chain-mail around 300BC. The Italians contributed the *scutum* and helmet cheek-pieces. The colour illustration shows a chieftain or noble from southern France (1st century BC). Celtic cavalry used a type of horned saddle (and snaffle bit), which the Romans adopted. His iron pot helmet is of the type known as "Agen". He is rich enough to afford the latest style of mail armour and wears a gold torque and bracelets. His weapons are the long Celtic sword and an 8ft (2·4m) spear with characteristic large Celtic head and concave edges, as are described by Diodorus. His horse ornaments around the harness depict human heads. They were of ritual significance: the Celts were fierce head-hunters. He wears short breeches (*braccae*) and leather shoes. Longer trousers were worn in northern France (see black and white figure). Cavalry led by chiefs such as this fought both against and for the Romans. The bulk of the cavalry had little or no armour and some carried circular shields rather than the long flat type shown here.

Celtic Infantryman (below)
The illustration shows a typical tribesman wearing the check or tartan trousers of northern France. He carries the usual weapons—long shield and sword. Like the Romans, the Celts wear their swords on the right of their bodies. His hair is coated with clay and lime (see p165).

80
Sulla is consul   Pompey (Cn. Pompeius   Capture of Mitylene
                    Magnus) suppresses
                    Marians in Sicily and
                    Africa

79
Sulla returns to private
life

78
Death of Sulla

BC

143

Pompey and his Epoch

Gnaeus Pompey's victories preserved Roman dominion in the East and broke the Mediterranean pirates, while in Italy Crassus crushed the slave rebellion and Catiline's conspiracy was put down. The death of Crassus at Carrhae left Pompey supreme—save for Julius Caesar.

Ancient Authorities

In the generation which followed Sulla's death, Roman Republican politics were at first dominated by Gnaeus Pompey, then brought within sight of their end by Julius Caesar. This period is well represented by Plutarch's *Lives*. Although Plutarch insisted that he was a biographer and not a historian, the combined effect of the biographies of Pompey, Lucullus, Sertorius, Crassus, Cato, Cicero and Caesar is to convey a general picture of political and military events as they unfolded themselves in the last years of the Republic. Even Plutarch's anecdotes, though often apocryphal, in many cases aptly illustrate personality, and Roman history in this period was largely one of personalities and personality conflicts.

Cicero was born in the same year as Pompey (106 BC). Although without military experience, and anything but a soldier, the great orator rather astonishingly managed to become consul in 63 BC. As a consul he was in some ways the diametric opposite and counterpart of Marius, who had been a military man in need of political agents to manage his civil commitments. Cicero, in a world of ever-increasing political violence, needed military support. For this, he relied on no man more than Pompey, and his extant orations throw considerable light on the military realities of his day. His speech in favour of Manilius' legislation* shows him eloquently committed to the support of Pompey, faithfully reflecting the moderate opinion of his times. The extent of his personal reliance on the illustrious general, amid the lawless conditions then prevailing in Rome, is apparent in his defence of Milo on a murder charge, which followed the bloody recurrence of political gang warfare in the city and its vicinity. The defence of Murena contains allusions to the Catiline conspiracy which Cicero, if anybody, could take credit for exposing and suppressing, although the relevant military operations were

*The Manilian law gave Pompey command in the war against Mithridates.

Above: *Pompey the Great ("Magnus"). He wished to be the constitutional servant of a state that depended helplessly on his military power.*

placed in the hands of others. Historically significant, also, is the prosecution of Verres after his term as governor of Sicily, which offers startling evidence of the helplessness of Roman naval forces in the face of an often quite highly organized pirate menace: the menace which Pompey was ultimately called upon to combat. Drawing on Cicero, one can easily multiply examples to demonstrate the interdependence of Roman military and political power in the 1st century BC.

To the subject of Catiline's war, Sallust devotes a whole monograph. He, too, was writing of events which had occurred during his lifetime. But his account is sometimes hard to reconcile with Cicero and with Plutarch, and if Sallust was relying on his memory, his version may not be the most accurate. For instance, Plutarch, citing Cato's demand for the death sentence on Catiline's accomplices, tells us that the whole of Cato's speech was recorded in shorthand (then an innovation) by Cicero's clerks, and that as a result it was the only one of Cato's speeches to remain extant. Sallust's version of the speech is very different from Plutarch's and, whether

or not his memory played him false, may well be an invention of his own.

Other authorities for the period are those noted in the foregoing chapter. Appian is particularly instructive on the renewed Mithridatic War and on Roman operations in the East.

Military Command and Political Power

Sulla had tried to impose constitutional government by armed force. This attempt in itself was doomed to failure, for constitutional regimes depend upon a substantial element of consent and consensus among the population. In Sulla's day, such an element was lacking, and the legislation by which he tried to make good the deficiency was in many ways anachronistic. He was perhaps justified in depriving the *equites* of rights and honours which Gaius Gracchus had conferred on them, but his laws reduced the People's Assembly to a position which it had occupied in the years of struggle between Patricians and Plebs. He wished to guard the state against another Marius by reinforcing the old rules that had applied to consular elections. It was now required that magistracies should be filled by any one individual in strict order of ascent. A man could become consul only after first serving as *quaestor*, then as *praetor*; age qualifications secured that there would be a time interval between one appointment and the next. Re-election to the same office was *a fortiori* hampered by time regulations.

However, the new threat to the constitution came not from consuls and praetors, as Sulla had anticipated, but from proconsuls and propraetors. The exigencies of overseas wars had rendered the delegation of executive and administrative power inevitable. Distance, if nothing else, made it impossible to interrupt a war for the

Right: *This map illustrates the way in which the Roman provinces were partitioned between Pompey, Caesar and Crassus in 55 BC following the initial division of 59 BC.*

sake of an election, and the need for continuity of command was too obvious to be overlooked. Apart from that, the consuls were two in number, and the wide areas over which Rome now ruled could not be administered by a couple of magistrates, even allowing for their assistance by praetors. By contrast, constitutional precedent did not limit the number of pro-magistrates who could be appointed.

The first proconsul had held his office as an extension of his consular power in 326 BC. It had been an *ad hoc* measure to meet a military situation. Sulla had wished to limit the term for which pro-magistracies could be held to a single year, but the tasks which the pro-magistrates were called upon to perform often required a longer tenure of office. Pompey set a new precedent by having power conferred on him for a term of three years. Obstacles placed in the way of the consulate did not operate in the instance of special overseas commands. It was even possible for one who was not a magistrate at all to hold command in a province as a "private person" (*privatus*), and such commands were normally both military and civil in their scope. Admittedly, a proconsul's power was limited to a certain area. But this area, as in the instance of Pompey's command against the pirates in 67 BC, could be very large.

Sulla had provided that a consul should officiate for one year at home before being sent abroad with proconsular power. But in practice, it was possible for a consul in Rome to control foreign provinces through his senior officers (*legati*). Pompey, both on active service and while administering from a distance, made extensive use of

Above: *Pompey's Pillar stands on the highest point in Alexandria. Though it is dedicated to Diocletian, it reminds us that Pompey died in Egypt and was thought to mark the site of his tomb.*

legati. Originally, such officers, appointed to a general's staff by the Senate, had been three or four in number. But Pompey in his campaign against the pirates made use of 24 *legati.* Both with proconsular responsibility for Spain from 55 BC and as consul in 52 BC he governed the province by proxy through the use of *legati.* But by this time, Sulla's constitution had been completely eroded.

The delegation of authority, in one way or another, though expedient and formally constitutional, was a practice which hastened the downfall of the Republic. Nobody availed himself of this practice more than Pompey, and in many ways he was in the same paradoxical position as Sulla. He was, of course, a more amiable character and merely upheld, rather than imposed, a constitution by force.

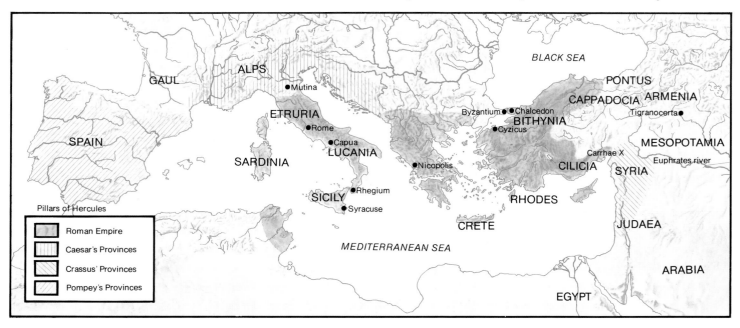

Pompey appointed to assist Metellus Pius in Spain against Sertorius

Pompey takes up appointment in Spain

In Palestine, Alexander Jannaeus, expansionist ruler of the Jews, dies

Alexandra Salome, Alexander Jannaeus' widow, succeeds him and conciliates the Pharisees

The Early Career of Pompey

In 82 BC Pompey had himself been appointed as Sulla's *legatus* first to Sicily then to North Africa, where leaders of the Popular party—who now had very little to lose—tried to rally resistance against the dictator and his establishment. In both theatres of war, Pompey had been wholly successful, and Sulla, whose concessions, no less than his ruthlessness, sometimes took men by surprise, permitted the junior general to celebrate a triumph.

The triumphal procession of a victorious general to the temple of Jupiter Capitolinus, with his army, spoils and captives, attended by senators, magistrates and officials, sacrificial beasts, banners and admiring crowds, was granted under certain conditions. The commander of the Roman Popular forces in North Africa had allied himself with an African king, so that Pompey's victory could be claimed to have taken place over a foreign power. But triumphs were the prerogative of consuls, praetors and dictators, and Pompey was not a

magistrate of any kind. Nevertheless, Sulla, though an ardent constitutionalist, did not always justify his decisions on constitutional grounds. Nor were the celebrations in any way subdued. Pompey had, in fact, intended to have his triumphal chariot drawn by African elephants, but they were too big for the city gates and horses had to serve his turn.

After Sulla's death another attempt was made to rally the Popular faction in Italy by men whom Pompey had himself raised to power. However, he showed himself at once a champion of the *status quo*, besieged the dissidents with their forces in Mutina (Modena), received their surrender and then executed them. Lepidus, the ringleader of the movement, fled to Sardinia and died there. Pompey's military power and prestige now alarmed the Senate, and they were glad to post him to Spain, where Sertorius, another one-time supporter of the Popular party, had set up what amounted to an independent state.

Since the death of Gaius Marius, Quintus Sertorius was probably the only good general that the Popular party had possessed. When his

partisans in Italy were menaced by Sulla, he seems to have realized that the single hope of resistance lay in adoption of an overseas base. He already knew Spain, having served there as *quaestor,* and in conflict with Celtiberian tribes had shown himself able to match the tribesmen in the employment of ruses and guerrilla tactics. In the years that followed Sulla's return to power, Sertorius had repeatedly worsted Roman senatorial forces. He identified himself with local aspirations and came to figure rather as the leader of a Spanish nationalist cause than of any Roman political faction. Pompey had considerable difficulty in dealing with his Romano-Spanish guerrilla tactics and strategy, and might never have emerged victorious if treachery had not played its part. For Sertorius was murdered as the result of a conspiracy formed by his lieutenant Perpenna. Perpenna, however, was not such an adroit guerrilla fighter as Sertorius, and Pompey, laying a trap, soon captured him and put him to death.

In this early stage of his career, at least, Pompey resembled Sulla in his good luck. During his five years'

75-74	74		
Rome acquires Bithynia by bequest of Nicomedes IV: occasion of Third Mithridatic War	Lucullus is consul	Lucullus secures command in Cilicia and Asia	Propontic Greek city of Cyzicus resists Mithridates

absence in Spain, Italy had been terrorized by a massive slave revolt. The slaves had defeated several Roman armies, but had at last been crushed by Marcus Licinius Crassus, one of Sulla's old officers, now an ambitious politician and general. Even so, 5,000 survivors of Crassus' victory managed to escape and retreat northward into Etruria, where Pompey, returning from Spain with his legions, met and destroyed them. He did not hesitate to claim major credit for this successful operation, a claim which hardly improved his relations with the influential Crassus. Pompey had no unconstitutional ambitions, but he attached great importance to his own public reputation and this sometimes made him tactless.

The Revolt of Spartacus

In the ancient world, the fate of war captives, if it was convenient to spare their lives, was normally to become slaves. Victorious Roman wars had consequently, before the beginning of the first century BC, filled Italy and Sicily with a slave population whose size had become an obvious danger. There had been violent slave revolts in Sicily in 139 and 104 BC, both of which had dragged on for several years, but the most serious of all such insurrections was that to which we have referred above (73 BC). It was led by Spartacus, a Thracian gladiator, a man of noble character and no mean intelligence, who was endowed with some Greek culture. Together with a band of comrades, he broke out of a gladiatorial barracks managed by private enterprise at Capua. The runaways equipped themselves with knives and spits from a local cookshop, afterwards supplementing these with a store of gladiatorial weapons. A military force from Capua was sent against them, but they routed the soldiers and took possession of their arms—a valuable acquistion for the slaves.

Now 3,000 troops from Rome, under a praetor, were sent against the insurgents. Spartacus and his followers were temporarily besieged on a precipitate summit, but they twisted the branches of wild vines to make ladders and escaped down a sheer rock face. Spartacus' army was joined by runaway slaves of all nationalities, from all parts

Left: *Gladiators in combat with wild animals. Gladiators were a commonplace of Roman life; it was thought good for morale that the public should be accustomed to the sight of death.*

Above: *These gladiators date from the 3rd century AD but their use is recorded as early as the 3rd century BC.*

of Italy, and seems to have reached a strength of 90,000—a figure which would account for its continued success against the Roman armies that confronted it. The consuls in Italy still normally shared four legions between them, while much bigger armies were posted abroad under pro-magistrates. However, the very size of the slave force, with its lack of men able to take command and the multitude of nationalities that went to its making, did not contribute to good order and discipline within its ranks. Spartacus led his men northward in the hope that they might pass the Alps and disperse to their homes, but many of them preferred a life of brigandage in Italy, and he was persuaded to turn south again.

Crassus, when appointed to deal with the rebels, was by no means immediately successful. One of his officers, commanding two legions, engaged the enemy in contravention of orders and was defeated with heavy casualties, while many legionaries, fleeing from the battlefield, left their weapons to increase the enemy's already growing store. Crassus issued new arms on payment of deposit and apparently punished the cohort chiefly responsible for the rout by decimation, a traditional Roman military punishment: selected by lot, one man out of every ten was beaten to death.

Spartacus' purpose in returning southwards, apart from that of satisfying his followers, had been to cross into Sicily and fan the embers of slave revolt which had continued to smoulder in the island since the earlier insurrections. Many slaves in this area were of Greek language and origin, and perhaps he hoped for some sense of national coherence such as would give him more control over his forces. He negotiated with a band of pirates—many of whom now ranged freely in the western Mediterranean far from their Cilician strongholds—but they failed to provide him with the transport which they had promised and kept the deposit which he had paid for it.

Crassus at last managed to blockade Spartacus in a small peninsula at Rhegium, by means of an elaborate four-mile earthwork and fosse across the isthmus. But on a wild, wintry night, Spartacus contrived to fill in the ditch and sallied out with a large part of his forces. It looked as though the slaves might march on Rome, but in Lucania some of them mutinied and formed a separate camp. These were engaged by Crassus, after some preliminary manoeuvring, and slaughtered to the number of 12,000. Spartacus, however, with the main body of the army, still remained at large. Crassus' quaestor, who had pursued him into mountain country, was heavily defeated and was himself lucky to be carried away wounded. But discipline in the slave army remained poor, and Spartacus could not resist the demands of his followers for further confrontation with the Romans. This was precisely what Crassus wanted, being already afraid that Pompey and Lucullus, by their arrival from the West and East respectively, would steal credit for the victory which he had promised himself. In a decisive battle, Spartacus died fighting. Those of the slaves who survived the slaughter were captured by Crassus or Pompey and crucified.

Crassus' trenching operations near Rhegium are worth noticing. The recourse to trench warfare, not necessarily associated with the blockade of a city or the fortification of a camp, was a Roman as distinct from Greek development. It was perhaps what one would expect from a nation of engineers who excelled in building roads, aqueducts and drainage systems. Perhaps it was a natural extension of camp construction, or perhaps we may see it as a logical step from Scipio Aemilianus' fortifications at Numantia, where, as Appian observes, he was the first general to enclose within a wall an enemy who would have been willing to fight in the open field. If Scipio was the first, subsequent Roman commanders certainly showed themselves willing to learn from example, and it will be remembered how trenching operations had earlier played an important part in Sulla's eastern campaigns.

The Pirates

Spartacus' negotiation with the pirates is just one among many instances testifying to their ubiquity in the Mediterranean world in the early first century BC. The Romans were not prepared to maintain a fleet in peacetime for mere police operations. In the emergencies of the Punic Wars, they had hastily constructed a navy. Against Mithridates, neither Sulla nor Fimbria had been given a fleet of warships. It had remained for Lucullus to buy or borrow one. In the eastern Mediterranean, Rhodes had been a great bulwark against piracy, but the Romans, dissatisfied with the Rhodian attitude in the last of the Macedonian Wars, spitefully damaged the island's trading position by conferring on Delos the status of a free port. With Delos as a highly competitive trading centre, Rhodian sea-power had declined. Not only were the Rhodians unable to suppress piracy on the high seas or on the Aegean shores, but Delos, unlike Rhodes, provided the pirates with a market in which their booty could fetch its price and their captives be sold as slaves. The legality of such dealings went unchallenged.

In this connection, it is pertinent to recall some famous incidents in Julius Caesar's early career. Caesar's Julian pedigree marked him as the scion of an ancient patrician clan, but his aunt had been wedded to Marius, and while still a mere youth Caesar was on Sulla's "wanted" list. Flitting between one rural hiding place and another, he was at last arrested by Sulla's manhunters, but after bribing the officer in charge, escaped overseas to Bithynia, where King Nicomedes received him hospitably. While in the East, the young Caesar fell into the hands of Cilician pirates, who released him for a ransom. Manning some ships at Miletus, he then pursued, arrested and crucified the pirates, as he had often pleasantly threatened to do during his captivity. Caesar, however, was lucky in being able to afford a ransom, let alone organize a punitive expedition. Plutarch describes how Roman citizens, after being treated with ironic deference by their pirate captors, were at length assured that they were free to go and flung overboard in mid-sea.

Roman punitive forces were not always so successful against the pirates as Caesar's expedition was. The Cilician pirates were not to be despised as a fighting force. They roved the sea not merely in ships but in fleets. They negotiated with civil powers often on equal terms; it was as if they had achieved some kind of citizen status in a cosmopolitan pirate community. Mithridates was anxious

    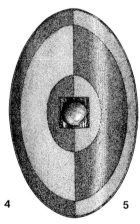

1   2   3   4   5

The Legionary Shield

These drawings trace the development of the legionary shield (*scutum*). Its basic dimensions and construction are shown on p135. **1** shows the traditional curved *scutum* in use in Italy from the 7th century BC onward. This is the shield described by Polybius. It had acquired bronze or iron edging some time before the Punic Wars, and a metal reinforcing plate over the boss (*umbo*) which enabled it to be "punched" and thus used offensively. It gradually faded from use in Augustus' day, but lingered on as a ceremonial shield in the Praetorian Guard until after AD 150. The design shown is one which appears on the Arch of Orange (Arausio) and is probably the badge of *Legio II Augusta*. **2** shows the first modification made to this type c 10 BC. The top and bottom are shorn off to reduce weight. This type survived in service until after AD 175. The design is taken from a shield c AD 75 on a relief at Mainz. **3** shows the next development. The old wooden spindle-shaped boss is eliminated — again to save weight — and the handgrip hole covered only by a circular bronze or iron *umbo*. This appeared c AD 20. The design shown is the famous "thunderbolt" emblem. Different legions carried variations of this motif. It appeared during Augustus' reign and by AD 100 was almost universal. **4** illustrates the next change — a straightening of the sides and the addition of "L" shaped reinforces in the corners. This type came into service c AD 40-50 and was used until after AD 200. The design is from Trajan's Column. **5** reveals a return (c AD 150) to the oval shape, which survived until the end of the Empire. The design in maroon and yellow is that of the *Thebaea legio palatina*

Lucullus defeats Mithridates in Pontus   Successes of Spartacus in Italy   Pompey captures and executes Perpenna in Spain

to enlist their help, as indeed Sertorius had been. When a pirate ship fell into the hands of Verres, governor of Sicily in 73-71 BC, members of the crew were re-employed by him for the various skills which they possessed and the pirate captain was allowed to ransom himself. Here indeed was a contrast to Caesar's ruthless action, but Caesar after all had had a private score to settle with his captors.

Later, when Verres was still in office, a whole pirate squadron descended on the Sicilian coast. According to Cicero, the Greek commander in charge of the governor's fleet was drunk at the time, and was the first to escape in his quadrireme as soon as the pirates had been sighted. The provincial navy was undermanned, its crews unpaid and half-starved although they might have put up a fight if it had not been for their commander's example. But the quadrireme, which by reason of its bulk should have been more than adequate to deal with the light pirate craft, outstripped the other vessels in headlong flight to a neighbouring port, where the panic-stricken commander and crew precipitately disembarked to seek refuge inland. The pirates overtook the hindmost ships of the governmental flotilla and in the evening burnt them, together with the quadrireme and other abandoned vessels, on the shore.

Next day, they sailed unopposed into the harbour of Syracuse, taking the opportunity of a sightseeing expedition—as Cicero ironically suggests—while Verres was still governor.

The Sicilian *débâcle* resulted largely from the fact that money levied for the payment of rowers and marines had been diverted into the governor's privy purse. Though a flagrant example, this was far from being the only case of its kind. Moreover, it in some way reflected at a provincial level the policy of the Republican government as a whole. The maintenance of navies merely for police operations seemed not worth the financial outlay. However, in Verres' time, pressures were already mounting which were destined to change public attitudes.

Pompey against the Pirates

The Illyrian and Macedonian Wars had for a time forced the pirates of the Ionian Sea northwards into the Adriatic. At the beginning of the first century BC, the main piratical menace came from Cilicia, where the wild coastline and hinterland provided the pirates with remote bases and obscure hiding places. Rome had created a Cilician province, which was in effect a base for anti-piratical operations. The official

thinking was characteristically military rather than naval, and the main strategy relied upon the time-honoured expedient of winning a naval war on land by depriving the enemy of his harbours. In other parts of the Mediterranean, however, especially Crete, the problem was more intractable.

In 67 BC a corn shortage in Italy, linked to supply problems over seas which were increasingly unsafe, brought the question of piracy to a head. Pompey, as a result of a popular proposal by a minor politician, was given far-reaching powers to deal with the menace. By this time, thanks in part to encouragement from Mithridates, piratical enterprise had reached a high degree of cohesion and organization. The rovers had become to some extent a land power as well as a sea power. They exacted tribute from maritime cities, built beacons and watch-towers on the coasts where their arsenals and harbours were situated, employed skilful pilots, and were led by men who in earlier days had been used to administrative business and executive command. Their conduct, so far from being furtive, was marked by con-

Below: *The boarding party of marines is clearly illustrated on this Roman warship. Pompey's campaign against the pirates revealed his skill in the use of such naval resources.*

Lucullus completes expulsion of Mithridates from Pontus

Mithridates becomes a fugitive with Armenian king Tigranes, his son-in-law

In Italy, Crassus defeats Spartacus

Pompey captures and executes fugitives from Spartacus' army

Above: *This coin was issued by Q. Nasidius, Sextus Pompeius' moneyer, in 44-3 BC. It bears Pompey the Great's portrait on the obverse and a typical galley of the period on the reverse.*

spicuous bravado. Plutarch refers to silver-plated oars, gilded spars and purple-woven sails, not to mention leisure hours of music, dancing and feasting on the coasts which they controlled. Many of them were devotees of the popular eastern religion of Mithras, but this did not prevent them from plundering the temples of the more traditional gods and goddesses. Nor was the coast of Italy free from their attentions. On one occasion, they seized two Roman praetors, complete with their official staff and entourage; in another raid they kidnapped and held to ransom the daughter of a distinguished Roman general. Plutarch says that at the time of Pompey's appointment they possessed 1,000 ships and dominated 400 cities.

The terms of Pompey's command gave him authority over all seas within the Pillars of Hercules (ie, east of Gibraltar) and over the whole coastline to a distance of 50 miles (80km) inland. He was authorized to appoint 24 senior officers to serve directly under his orders, each one of whom would rank as praetor. He had power to raise up to 125,000 men and 500 warships, and the vast resources of money voted for the enterprise were wholly adequate to support such a force. In the event, Pompey did not use all the money placed at his disposal, and so far from occupying the three years to which special legislation entitled him, he was able to report the successful completion of his task in a matter of months.

His work was carried out very methodically. The western Mediterranean was first combed of pirates, each of 13 naval squadrons having been assigned its separate operational zone. Pompey then proceeded eastward with

60 of his best ships to attack the main enemy strongholds. The western sea had been cleared in a mere 40 days. Within three months, the pirate bases of the east had also been stormed and occupied. The bulk of the enemy fleet had been destroyed in a major naval engagement, and those pirates who had sought refuge in inland fortresses with their families were besieged amid the mountains and captured. Prisoners numbered 20,000. Among many vessels captured were 90 warships complete with their equipment.

If Pompey ever deserved the title of Magnus ("the Great") it was now. So far from simply crucifying all his captives—which would have been the normal reaction to the situation—he realized that the pirate menace had been the product of a social situation, not merely a military and naval challenge. The pirates had been desperate men with nothing to lose, whom ruthless wars and bloodstained politics had rendered homeless and destitute. In the circumstances, death in battle was preferable to starvation, and crucifixion well worth risking. Showing clemency to his prisoners, Pompey offered an amnesty to those who were still at large and as a result received massive surrenders. The ex-corsairs and their families were successfully settled in agricultural colonies at well-chosen points throughout the eastern Mediterranean lands.

Pompey's great victory was unfortunately marred by an administrative clash. It must have been obvious from the start that in warfare against an elusive and highly mobile enemy, his authority over littoral zones was likely to conflict with that of previously appointed Roman governors, responsible for the interior. Metellus, the governor of Crete, was bent on merciless extermination of the pirates, many of whom hoped to take advantage of Pompey's amnesty. One of Pompey's officers, sent with a contingent to Crete, finished by fighting in league with the pirates against Metellus. Pompey was made to look foolish and Metellus got his way in the end.

Lucullus against Mithridates

Pompey's suppression of the pirates was the finest achievement of his career, and one which he owed almost entirely to his own ability. The news of his victories swiftly arrived in Rome, and before he could himself return to Italy, new and sweeping powers of

command were assigned to him. He was to take charge of the war against Mithridates. Here, however, as on other occasions in his life, he owed much to the work of a predecessor.

Taking full advantage of Roman preoccupations in Italy and Spain, allying himself with the pirates and accepting a military mission from Sertorius, Mithridates had gone far to re-establishing the military potential of which Sulla had temporarily deprived him. Sulla's deputy in the province of Asia (ie, west Asia Minor), suspicious of the king's designs, had renewed military operations against Pontus without authorization from Rome. When he was worsted in battle, Roman prestige suffered as a direct consequence.

Above: *Roman ruins in Cilicia. After putting an end to pirate activity in this area, Pompey was appointed to succeed Lucullus in the war against Mithridates further north.*

Full-scale war had again broken out when Mithridates invaded Bithynia, a province which Rome had acquired by the bequest of its late monarch in 75 BC. Nobody was better qualified than Lucullus to undertake operations in this theatre, but in order to secure command of Cilicia and Asia during his consulate (74 BC), he had found it necessary to intrigue deviously with the mistress of a political adversary. He was immediately obliged to rescue his colleague in Bithynia who, anxious to take sole credit for a quick victory, had been defeated by Pontic forces both on land and in sea battles.

Mithridates, learning perhaps equally from his own past experience and from Sertorius' military mission, had remodelled his army and navy. It is true that his large Oriental host still included such lumber as scythe-wheel chariots, which were usually ineffective because they needed an excessively long run in order to gather impetus. He had, nevertheless, equipped his infantry with short swords and long shields on the Roman pattern, and had adopted Roman tactical formations. In general, his forces were now equipped more obviously for war than for ceremonial occasions as they previously had been.

Mithridates besieged the Romans in Chalcedon (opposite Byzantium) and pressed farther westward along the south shores of the Propontis (Sea of Marmara) to attack Cyzicus. Lucullus, however, after successful actions by land and sea, relieved both these cities and, dispersing Mithridates' invading armies, launched a counter-offensive into Pontus, where he soon penetrated the chain of fortress towns that defended the western territories of the kingdom. Mithridates, once more defeated in a pitched battle, fled eastward to take refuge with his son-in-law Tigranes, king of Armenia. Lucullus sent an embassy to demand the fugitive's extradition and, while waiting for an answer, did much to restore the economy of the Asiatic cities, still crippled by Sulla's impost. When the Armenian king refused to surrender Mithridates, Lucullus marched his legions into Armenia and, in a battle which showed him an astute tactician, defeated Tigranes' multitudinous host. He then captured the newly-built capital of Tigranocerta and inflicted a further defeat on Tigranes and Mithridates farther east. But the war threatened to extend itself interminably eastward, and it now seemed likely that Lucullus would involve himself against the Parthians, south of the Caspian sea. His troops mutinied and it was impossible for him to carry his conquests any farther.

Indeed, not only was a halt called to Lucullus' victorious advance, but the Roman army in Armenia was paralysed by indiscipline, and the prolongation of Lucullus' command was already in question. In these circumstances, Mithridates, who was nothing if not resilient, mustered new forces and reoccupied Pontus. At the same time, Tigranes resumed the offensive and entered Cappadocia in eastern Asia Minor. Shocked by news of Roman defeats in Pontus, the mutinous troops at last followed their general back westward to rescue the legions which had been left to garrison that territory. But such was their mood that it was not possible to restore the situation, and this unhappy state of affairs still persisted when Pompey arrived to assume command of the war.

Lucullus was a man of very independent mind, always determined to rely on his own ability and integrity in a world where sycophancy and demagogy were prerequisites of success. Consequently, he lost the support not only of the legionaries under his command but of his own staff, at the same time giving opportunities to his political enemies in Rome. He was a firm disciplinarian, but that was not enough. Perhaps the greatest grievance of his soldiers was that he prevented them from plundering the cities of friendly and subject peoples—in a way that Sulla would certainly have allowed.

In 63 BC, Lucullus managed at last to celebrate a well-deserved triumph, after which he retired from war and politics to live a life of refined luxury. Unfortunately, he became insane in his old age. His supersession by Pompey must have been extremely galling to him. The two men had been rivals ever since the days when they both served under Sulla. But Sulla, always unaccountable, had consistently favoured Pompey, though he had more confidence in Lucullus.

The End of Mithridates

By their dogged resistance to Lucullus, Mithridates and Tigranes had ultimately exhausted not only the Roman forces but their own. The mutiny among Lucullus' troops had found its counterpart in palace intrigues and family dissensions in the despotic establish-

Below: *A triumph for Roman arms (the Glanum monument in France). The power that Pompey gained by his victories in the east led Julius Caesar to imitate him in Gaul.*

ments of Pontus and Armenia. One of Mithridates' sons had already set up a separatist government in South Russia and had been recognized by Lucullus. Tigranes' son was soon to adopt a similarly independent line. The mere prospect of Pompey's vast resources thrown into the scale against the Asiatic kingdoms was enough to increase already existing strains to breaking point.

Lucullus had overcome enemy armies many times larger than his own. Plutarch, quoting Livy, says that in the great battle which preceded the capture of Tigranocerta the Romans were outnumbered by more than twenty to one, and Livy must be presumed more accurate on history near to his own times than on semilegendary antiquity or even the Hannibalic wars. The situation, however, was now very much altered. Pompey possessed huge financial resources still untapped, increased by plunder taken from the pirates, not to mention the ships which he had captured. The Asiatic despots had lost heavily in men and Pompey had added the army of Lucullus to the massive forces which he had deployed against the pirates. Making full use of his naval strength, Pompey set his ships to guard the Asiatic coast from Syria to the Bosphorus, a precaution against any attack by the Pontic navy in his rear. He then left his Cilician base to confront Mithridates in the north. His striking force

was not unduly large. Certainly, it was not unwieldy, and it was as much as he needed, for he had already by adroit diplomacy managed to involve Tigranes against the Parthians, and the king of Pontus was conveniently isolated.

Mithridates and his staff seem not always to have been alert to their opportunities. The Pontic army encamped at first in a strong mountain fastness, but retreated to worse positions as a result of water shortage. Pompey occupied the stronghold thus vacated, deduced from the vegetation that water existed at no great depth, and successfully dug wells. Subsequently, however, despite Pompey's trenching operations, designed to cut him off, Mithridates slipped away eastward with a still substantial army. Pompey followed him as far as the Euphrates and a great battle* was fought there by moonlight. The low moon, behind the Romans' backs, threw long shadows ahead of them and confused the enemy marksmen. Mithridates' army was routed, but he himself broke through the Roman ranks with a body of 800 cavalry. He at last escaped with only a few faithful followers, including a hardy young concubine who was dressed and armed like a Persian horseman. Pompey had been dubious about the wisdom of

---

*Pompey later founded Nicopolis (Victory City) near the site of the battle.

68
Lucullus campaigns in Armenia.

Lucullus' troops (incited by P. Clodius) mutiny

Mithridates recovers much lost territory

In Palestine, sons of Alexandra, Hyrcanus and Aristobulus, quarrel

night operations, but had yielded to pressure from his officers—as he did with less fortunate results 18 years later against Caesar at Pharsalus.

Tigranes would no longer grant asylum to his father-in-law, and Mithridates made his way via the headwaters of the Euphrates into the Black Sea region. He still hoped to repair his fortunes and even contemplated the invasion of Italy by an overland route, but the rebellion of another son, who probably represented public opinion, made all such schemes futile. For the first time in his life, Mithridates, now 68 years old, gave way to despair. Suspicious of assassination attempts, he is said to have rendered himself immune to poison by the continuous administration of small doses. Now that he had

decided to end his own life, his immunity proved a disadvantage, but in obedience to his orders one of his bodyguards despatched him.

Pompey had meanwhile made peace on sufficiently generous terms with Tigranes. He did not attempt to follow Mithridates northwards, but found himself involved in gruelling warfare with the Caucasian tribes. Later, operations southward, in Syria, Judaea and Arabia, claimed his attention and exposed him to criticism as neglecting the Pontic threat. He was in this area when news of Mithridates' death reached him by letters. Apparently, the camp contained no platform of turfs such as a Roman general on campaign usually mounted when addressing his men, but Pompey climbed up on a pile

of pack-saddles, and his announcement was the signal for sacrifices and feasting, as if in victory celebration.

Catiline's Conspiracy

While Pompey was in the East, Italy was shaken by the conspiracy and armed insurrection of Catiline (Lucius Sergius Catilina). The relevant facts have reached us almost entirely through Sallust and Cicero. Sallust was anything but politically unbiased, and Cicero, as the man whom Catiline conspired to murder, and who ordered the execution of Catiline's accomplices, was obviously not impartial. The events, as we know them, may be summarized as follows.

The Roman Army after Marius

The Roman army kept evolving throughout its history, but Marius' reforms provide a convenient point at which to examine it. Rome's expansion after the Punic Wars required her to fight battles further afield over a period of more than one "season". This was very unpopular with the property owning classes liable for military service, who had their own affairs to run. Furthermore, numbers of men liable for service diminished as wealth began to concentrate. Recruits were scarce. Marius resolved this dilemma by opening the army to all citizens regardless of property qualification. Naturally many could not afford arms and armour and the state had to supply them. This led to standardisation and the old cavalry, *velites, triarii* etc disappeared. All the maniples of a cohort were armed alike with *pila, gladius* and *scutum*. The larger centuries which appeared towards the end of the 2nd Punic War now became standard. The legion thus came to consist of 10 cohorts each of 3 maniples of two centuries of around 80 men, giving a total of c4,800. Standardisation also did away with the cohort organised into three lines. Instead, each of the lines (*acies*) consisted of a series of cohorts. The front line consisted of 4 cohorts, arranged 10 wide by 8 deep (c240 yds, 220m front) the remaining 2 lines of 3 cohorts

each were arranged 12 wide by 6 deep, giving a similar frontage.

Caesar formed his legions in 1, 2, 3 or 4 lines as circumstances demanded though 3 lines (*triplex acies*) was usual. The depth of each line would also vary as could the space between lines. The legion was thus extremely flexible. The system of marching one line through another was now used less often, but the centuries still initially formed up behind one another to leave intervals for light troops and/or cavalry to pass. The outcome of the Social War also led to the disappearance of the Allied cohorts, since most of these were now eligible to join the legions. This and the redundancy of the *velites* meant that light troops and cavalry had to be provided by auxiliaries. They were recruited from the non-citizen provinces or Allies. A good example of an army of this period is that of Caesar when he became a provincial governor (below). It consisted of 4 legions, numbers VII, VIII, IX, and X plus 2-3000 Balearic slingers and Cretan archers organised into cohorts. In addition there were 2000 Spanish and Gallic cavalry, organised into 4 *alae*. This army would normally occupy some 1500 yds (1370m) frontage. As Caesar's campaigns in Gaul extended, so the army grew to 10 legions. It is interesting to

compare "paper" strengths with actual numbers. Caesar's legions averaged 3-4000 in battle because of sickness, detachments, casualties etc. After particularly hard campaigns the average could fall as low as 2800-3000 (see eg Pharsalus p171).

Maniple

Legion

Cohort

Cavalry   Legio X   Legio IX   Legio VIII   Legio VII   Cavalry

Light infantry, slingers and archers

Corn shortage at Rome   Pompey, given command against the pirates, gaining a naval victory at Coracesium   Q. Metellus asserts his authority against Pompey in Crete   Caesar marries Pompeia

Catiline had been involved in an earlier plot to overthrow the constitution and seize power in 65 BC. He was influential and well connected and on this occasion there had been no question of bringing any charge against him. His second plot, again the product of political disappointment and, we are encouraged to believe, sheer viciousness, was matured in 63 BC. The original plan was to co-ordinate widespread disturbances throughout Italy, with the main uprising concentrated in Etruria, where old soldiers who had become bankrupt farmers might be relied upon for support. When Cicero, as consul, obtained information of this plot, the conspirators held an emergency meeting at Rome in the Street of the Sickle-makers and adopted a more desperate programme. They resolved to murder Cicero next day, set Rome on fire, and incite the slave population to rebellion and looting. Meanwhile, their sympathizers in other parts of Italy were to take up arms without further delay and the insurgents of Etruria were to march on the terrorized city. Cicero, who was consistently well informed, received prompt warning of his danger and denounced Catiline to his face in the Senate—of which the accused was a member. After this, Catiline fled from Rome to join his army in Etruria.

Other conspirators, however, remained in Rome. Hoping to gain further supporters among the Gauls, they made contact with some envoys of a Gallic tribe then in the city. Cicero's informants again served him well. Through the agency of the Gauls, he obtained signatures on incriminating documents and arrested five of the leading conspirators. Their fate was debated before the Senate. Caesar pleaded for life imprisonment. But Cicero was supported by Cato, the much respected great-grandson of Cato the Censor, and ordered the execution of the conspirators without trial. His justification was the state of emergency which then existed, but not everyone considered him justified. Once the conspiracy at Rome had failed, Catiline's mainly ill-armed forces in Etruria had little hope of success. Regular troops were sent against him. His line of retreat northward was cut off, and he was overwhelmed and killed in a battle at Pistoria.

Catiline's blundering plot hardly amounted to a war, yet it had considerable military significance. Italy was the strategic centre of the Mediterranean world, but it was at the same time the most vulnerable area in

The Parthians

The "Parni" were a people of Scythian origin—one of the three tribes of Dahae, who fought both for and against Alexander. Between 250 BC and 130 BC they conquered an empire stretching from Armenia to Afghanistan. Over the next three centuries they were to clash repeatedly with their western neighbour, Rome, as the Roman leaders sought new lands to conquer farther east.

Parthian Cataphracts (left)
Three main influences combined to persuade the Parthian nobility to develop armoured cavalry more than other peoples: the neighbouring Massagetae invented such cavalry; their foes in the successor kingdoms had improved the equipment; and the new empire provided the necessary resources. The drawing (left) shows a noble around 50 BC. He and his horse are covered in bronze or iron scales. Others wore mail. The armour on his limbs is leather—metal appeared much later. His weapons are a long *kontos*, a sword or axe, and frequently a bow as well. The horse armour is shown opened for ventilation.

BC | 66

Pompey given command against Mithridates: he supersedes Lucullus   Mithridates is defeated but escapes   Tigranes' son deserts to the Romans   Surrender of Tigranes   Aretas, Nabataean (Arab) king, invoked by Hyrcanus against Aristobulus, besieges Jerusalem

154

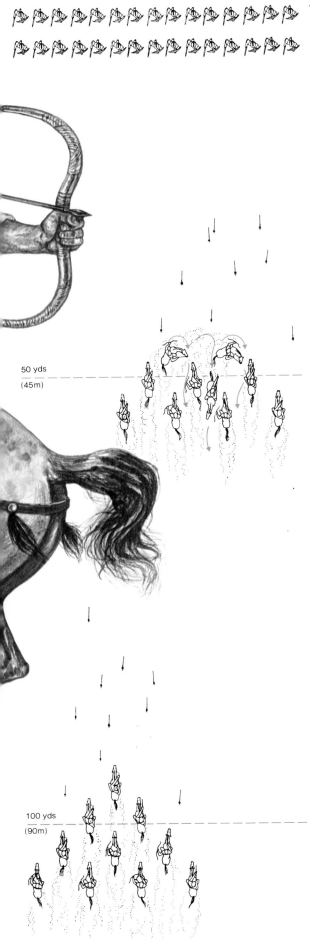

The Parthian Army

The Parthians were orignally nomadic horse-archers, but as they expanded, they employed mercenaries, (mainly infantry), like other successor states. A mercenary revolt in 128 BC altered matters and subsequently they only raised militia from subject cities, and relied mainly on their own cavalry. Indeed on some occasions, notably at Carrhae (see p156), their forces were entirely mounted.

The Parthian Horse-Archer (left)

The bulk of the Parthian cavalry was provided by the nobles' retainers and slaves who served as light horse archers. One of these is shown left executing the "Parthian shot"—a phrase which has become proverbial. The highly embroidered clothing and style of headdress reveal his Scythian origin, as does the traditional *gorytus* (bow-case). To protect his embroidered trousers he wears very baggy leggings which are held up only at the back, giving the front of each legging distinctive folds. Strapped to each thigh, like a cowboy's pistols, are two long daggers or short swords. By AD 100 the cap was less common, and a simple headband was worn instead; a longer knee-length tunic was fashionable, and a cylindrical quiver replaced the *gorytus*. The archer is shown using a thumb-ring to loose the string of his composite bow. The thumb-ring, of metal or bone, originated in the Steppes before 200 BC and was in use in Syria by AD 100 having spread via Persia. Its use necessitated placing the arrow on the right of the bow, rather than the left as in a conventional release. Its main advantage was said to be that it gave a slightly easier loose.

The Tactics of Horse-Archers

Light cavalry form up in loose order, generally with about 6ft (2m) frontage as shown in the diagram left. The Scythians are said to have invented the wedge formation illustrated, and others, such as Thracians and Macedonians to have copied it from them. When the horse-archer attacks, he places one arrow on his bowstring and holds more in his bowhand. He then advances at a canter. At about 100 yds (90m) he breaks into a gallop and fires 2-4 arrows. At about 50 yds (45m) he wheels, generally to the right (since a horse-archer can only fire to his left) and gallops along the front still firing. Alternately, he reins in and skid-turns as shown left and fires behind him as he retreats. This manoeuvre became known as the "Parthian shot", though all Asiatic nomads practised it. Such charges and volleys of arrows, as swarms of riders darted in and out of the dust clouds, were calculated to demoralize the enemy. The Parthian terrain, with its numerous hills and dunes, favoured such hit-and-run tactics and the Romans were greatly shocked by them, as they differed from anything previously encountered.

50 yds
(45m)

100 yds
(90m)

that world. Ever fearful of military despotism, the Senate preferred to see Rome's legions deployed in distant and overseas provinces, while Italy, comparatively denuded of troops, remained an attractive prey for any armed adventurer who could rally sufficient malcontents to his support. Catiline's insurrection had its precedent in that of Lepidus in 77 BC. Lepidus' attempt had been crushed with Pompey's valuable aid. Catiline had timed his uprising to take place when Pompey was no longer at hand. That Pompey might return from the East, bringing retribution, as Sulla had done, was a possibility which the conspirators had been forced to take into account, and they had accordingly planned to seize Pompey's children as hostages. Apart from that, any military regime which could control Italy possessed the advantage of interior communications, the importance of which remained to be demonstrated in later Roman history. It is hard to see how Catiline could have hoped ultimately to make himself despot of Rome. We do not know precisely what his plans and intentions were. But he certainly could have created great havoc before being subdued, if it had not been for Cicero's highly efficient "secret service".

The Parthians

In the course of their eastern wars, the Romans had several times come into contact with the Parthians. Sulla, reaching the Euphrates, had negotiated with them on friendly terms. Lucullus, distrusting them as allies, had prepared to attack them. Pompey, invoking their aid, had promised them Armenian frontier territory, but failed to keep his promise after Tigranes' humble submission. Like other Asiatic kingdoms, Parthia was a succession state of the Seleucid empire, the Parthian leader Arsaces having founded an independent dynasty in the middle of the third century BC. With this Arsacid dynasty the Romans had to deal.

The culture of the Parthians was in many ways a characteristic legacy of Alexander's eastern conquests: a discrepant and sometimes grotesque blend of Greek and barbaric traditions. But their way of warfare owed little to Macedonian precedents. There was no clumsy imitation of the phalanx, such as Mithridates had used. The Parthian army was a cavalry army, and its cavalry was of two kinds. The nobility, not unlike medieval knights, were lancers, protected by coats of chain mail and mounted on strong horses that were also mail-clad. These heavy cavalrymen are referred to by Greek writers as *cataphractoi*. The word literally means "covered over". But the more typical Parthian warrior was a mounted bowman who wore no armour and, relying on his mobility, rode swiftly within arrowshot of the enemy to let fly a deadly shaft as he wheeled his horse and made off. The modern expression "a Parthian shot" is a reminder of this highly skilful man-oeuvre. Given an Asiatic terrain of undulating hills or dunes and skylines that could conceal without impeding such horsemen, Parthian tactics were a formidable threat to a less mobile enemy. In addition, it should be noted, their bows were strong and their arrows penetrating, being capable of nailing a shield to the arm that supported it or a foot to the ground.

Before conflicting with the Parthians, the Romans had some experience of cataphracts. Tigranes' army had included 17,000 heavily mailed horsemen. Lucullus, observing that these had no offensive weapons save their lances and were hampered by the weight and stiffness of their armour, had ordered his Thracian and Galatian cavalry to beat down the lances with their swords and attack at arm's length. Similarly, he had instructed the legionaries not to waste time hurling their javelins, but to close with the

Above: *This coin shows King Orodes I of Parthia (80-76/5 BC), one of the Arsacid dynasty which the Romans never succeeded in finally conquering.*

enemy at swordpoint, attacking the legs of the armoured riders and hamstringing their horses; for their mail did not cover them below the waist. The purpose of coming to grips quickly was also to prevent the enemy from using his archers. In the mountainous country of Armenia, the tactics of the Parthian horse-bowman would in any case have been impossible.

The Parthians were masters of ruse, adepts in feigned retreats and ambushes. Their country was remote and, to the Romans at any rate, little known, and they were in a position to plant

spies and false information on an invader who necessarily made use of local guides. They rallied their troops not with military trumpets but with an ominous and disconcerting roll of drums—perhaps like the beating of tom-toms. They would also wheel their galloping steeds close to the ranks of the enemy, raising dust clouds which had the effect of a smoke-screen. Their methods of warfare were utterly different from those which the Romans had encountered in Pontus and Armenia, and the discovery of this fact came as a great shock to the Romans.

The Disaster of Carrhae

The Romans were never able to subdue or dominate the Parthians, and their first campaign against this untried enemy, led by Marcus Crassus in 53 BC, ended in a major disaster near Carrhae in Mesopotamia. In his youth, Crassus had, like Pompey and Lucullus, seen military service under Sulla. He had grown rich at the expense of Sulla's outlawed victims. The Social War and the operations against Spartacus had proved that he possessed real military ability, but, throughout his long political career, money had been his chief weapon. Only the spectacle of Pompey's success and, latterly, Caesar's victorious campaigns in Gaul, had revived his ambition for

Battle of Carrhae 53 BC

Crassus	The Surena
Infantry	
7 legions 25/28000	None
Light troops 4000	
Cavalry	
Gaul 1000	Cataphracts 1000
Syria)	Light horse
Cappadocia)3000	archers 6/8000
Arabia)	*Camels 1000
(plus unknown	*Waggons 200
number of non-	(*for baggage)
combatants)	

General situation Eager to establish a military reputation, Crassus plans to invade Parthia. On his march towards Seleucia he encounters Parthian cavalry and forms a defensive square, taking up position near a stream. Many of the Romans want to rest here, but, urged on by his son Publius, Crassus decides to march on. He soon runs into the main Parthian force whose horse archers surround and harass the defensive square using the tactics shown on p 155.
Day 1 Crassus tries to subdue the archers with light troops, but they are forced back to the legionaries' line. The Parthians are resupplied with arrows from the baggage train. Publius then attempts a major sally with 8 cohorts, 500 archers and 1300

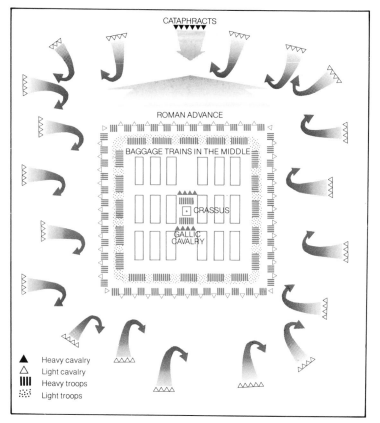

CATAPHRACTS

ROMAN ADVANCE

BAGGAGE TRAINS IN THE MIDDLE

CRASSUS

GALLIC CAVALRY

▲	Heavy cavalry
△	Light cavalry
IIII	Heavy troops
:::::	Light troops

cavalry including the Gauls. The Parthians yield and Publius gives chase, but the Parthians then turn on Publius and their archers and cataphracts surround his force. Despite the bravery of the Gallic cavalry, Publius' men are overwhelmed, only 500 being taken alive. He kills himself and his head is taken on a pike to taunt Crassus. Night falls; the Parthians withdraw; the Romans decide to retire leaving behind the wounded despite pleas for mercy.
Day 2 Most of the Romans reach Carrhae. The Parthians slaughter stragglers and the wounded (c4000) and 4 cohorts lost on the march (c1500). Besieged in Carrhae, Crassus decides to fall back by night on the mountains as provisions are scarce. Again many are separated in the confusion of the march.
Day 3 Cassius and 500 horse are back in Carrhae, whence they flee to Syria. 5000 Romans hold a strong position in the hills. They turn back, however, to help Crassus and his men lagging behind. Realising that the Romans may escape, the Surena lures Crassus to a parley where he and his officers are killed. Some of the Romans surrender; other flee and are hunted down by the Arabs. Total Roman losses are 20000 killed; 10000 captured.

Pompey intervenes in Palestine: he captures Aristobulus and establishes Hyrcanus

Catiline's second conspiracy

Mithridates' suicide: his son Pharnaces makes peace with Pompey

Lucullus granted triumph at Rome

Catiline's accomplices executed on Cicero's orders

darkness, but gave chase again during the day, when the straggling Roman columns, as a result of their night march, had lost contact with each other. Crassus' officer Gaius Cassius, better known to history for his action on the Ides of March nine years later, led 10,000 men back to safety. Without more detailed information, we cannot confidently praise him for saving his men or blame him for deserting his general. Other officers, under pressure from the demoralized army, accompanied Crassus to a parley which Surena had proposed with obviously treacherous intent. In a contrived scuffle, the Roman negotiators were cut down; Crassus' head was carried in triumph to the Parthian king, then concluding peace with the Armenians. In the whole campaign, the Romans are reported to have lost 20,000 killed and 10,000 prisoners. These last were settled by the Parthians as serfs in provinces farther east.

Despite the crushing defeat of Crassus, the Parthians made no attempt to follow up their victory. Unlike the Gauls or the Germans, they were under no pressure to migrate at the expense of other nations. Perhaps they also realized that the country into which Crassus had imprudently ventured was among their greatest military assets, and their way of fighting could not be equally successful on any other terrain. For many years, the Romans felt the disaster of Carrhae as a deep disgrace; apart from all else, their standards had fallen into enemy hands. But no sense of emergency was entailed. The Parthians did not even present a threat comparable with that which had been posed by Mithridates or the Cilician pirates.

Treachery apart, the Parthians were also indebted for their victory to the generalship of Surena—though what we hear of his character does not suggest the hardihood of a great military leader. When he travelled privately, Surena was accompanied by an enormous retinue, which included 200 waggons for his concubines. This made him look hypocritical when he expressed disgust at the pornography discovered in the baggage of the defeated Roman army. However, his personal ability is not in question. Indeed, his success excited the jealousy of the king whom he served, and soon after Carrhae he was put to death.

military honour. As a result of a tripartite political agreement, in which Pompey and Caesar were his partners, he obtained Syria and Egypt as his province, seeing the opportunity for a prestigious war against Parthia.

Crassus launched hostilities without any authority from Rome and without any provocation from the Parthians, although a hostile atmosphere had been created by Pompey's broken promises and the support given to a Parthian royal pretender by Pompey's deputy in Syria. When Crassus occupied frontier cities in Mesopotamia, he was met by a challenging embassy from the Parthian king. Defiant language was used on both sides, and a state of war immediately existed.

Having based himself on Carrhae (Biblical *Haran*; modern Harran), Crassus with his army began to march on Seleucia, the old Babylonian capital of Alexander's successor. The Roman legions very soon became a constant target for the enemy's missiles, nor were their light-armed skirmishers numerous enough to ward off the

attacks. Surena*, the Parthian general, made sure that his bowmen were continuously supplied with ammunition, using an efficient camel corps to transport load upon load of arrows.

Crassus sent forward his son Publius with 8 cohorts, 500 archers and some 1,300 cavalry. The Gauls, like Publius, had served with distinction under Caesar, and they had some success against the Parthian cataphracts, nimbly grasping the enemy's long lances and stabbing the horses in their unprotected bellies from underneath. But in the end, Publius' force, separated from the Roman main body, was annihilated, and the triumphant Parthians were able to taunt Crassus with the sight of his son's head on a pike.

The Romans were now obliged to retreat by night, but they were by this time exhausted, and 4,000 wounded were abandoned to be butchered by the enemy. The Parthians were content to remain inactive during the hours of

*Surena was head of the Suren clan and was therefore entitled "the Suren".

Catiline defeated and killed at Pistoria	Sacrilegious scandal involving P. Clodius leads to divorce of Pompeia	Cicero gives evidence against Clodius	Pompey's triumphant return to Rome	Pompey divorces Mucia on grounds of adultery with Caesar

Julius Caesar

In a series of brilliant campaigns, Caesar subdued Gaul and the Germanic tribes and made incursions into Britain. Military achievement and political ambition were interwoven in Caesar's character, and in 49 BC he led his legions across the Rubicon to drive Pompey from Rome.

Ancient Authorities

We have now reached a chapter in which biography and autobiography may readily be identified with history. Caesar's record of his *Gallic Wars* is the best known of his writings and is of particular interest to British readers, as it describes the first Roman military expeditions to Britain. The narrative of the *Gallic Wars* spans the period of 58 to 52 BC inclusive, and each of its seven books corresponds with a year in this period. To Caesar's seven books, his officer Aulus Hirtius added an eighth, which brought the historical record up to 50 BC. Caesar's account of the war (49 BC) which, after his return from Gaul, he fought against Pompey is given in the three books of his *Commentaries on the Civil War*. The story of his military career is then carried further by an anonymous history of his eastern campaigns, ending with the battle of Zela against Mithridates' son in 47 BC. This work may also have been written by Hirtius. Another anonymous account describes Caesar's victorious war in North Africa (47-46 BC), where Cato had joined other surviving Pompeians. A third narrative from an unknown hand relates to the last of Caesar's wars, fought against the sons of Pompey in Spain and leading to the final victory at Munda in 45 BC. Unfortunately, the *Spanish War* is not intelligently or clearly written, although the writer, perhaps a junior officer, seems to have been an eyewitness of operations which he describes.

Apart from Plutarch's *Life*, we have a biography of Caesar by Suetonius (Gaius Suetonius Tranquillus), who was probably born in AD 69 and survived well into the second century, holding secretarial positions under the Emperor Hadrian, posts to which he was perhaps helped by another distinguished writer, the younger Pliny (Gaius Plinius Caecilius Secundus). Almost the only extant work of Suetonius is his *Lives of the Caesars*. It contains 12 biographies, beginning with that of Julius Caesar and continuing with the line of Roman emperors who followed him in absolute power, as far as Domitian.

As to Julius Caesar's political career before his appointment to command in Gaul, much is to be learnt from Cicero and Sallust, but despite the biographies of Plutarch and Suetonius, our knowledge of him as a young man is fragmentary and imprecise. While Sulla's energies were concentrated on meting out retribution to the Marian party in Italy, Mithridates, temporarily subdued, had once more become active, and Caesar, then in the East, enthusiastically participated in military action against him. While raising a fleet in Bithynia, he was suspected of a homosexual relationship with the Bithynian king, but Suetonius, who records this circumstance, was notably addicted to scandal. While still a young man, Caesar achieved military distinction in the eastern wars and after an action at Mitylene was awarded a civic

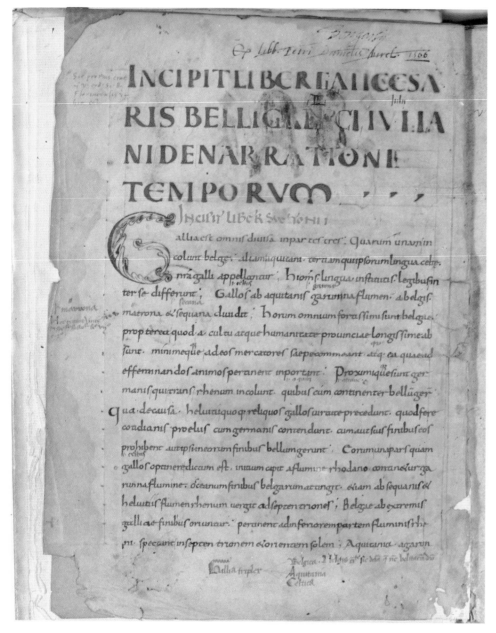

Left: *"All Gaul is divided into three parts..." The first page of Caesar's* De Bello Gallico *from a 9th century manuscript preserved in Amsterdam.*

oak-leaf crown for saving the life of a fellow-soldier. Like Crassus, he seems to have abandoned the military life for politics and then to have realized later that, in the world in which he found himself, military command and victory were prerequisites of political success.

Apart from war and politics, Caesar was deeply committed to the cultivation of literature. He had interrupted his earlier career in order to pursue literary studies at Rhodes, and he wrote books on literary criticism, now lost. In these works, he is known to have advised the avoidance of unusual or recondite words, and his own war commentaries are models of lucidity, because he practised what he preached.

Below: *Caesar's campaigns against the enemies of Rome and against Pompey and his successors took him from one end of the Empire to the other in the space of only 13 years.*

Political Background

The clan of the Julii claimed to be older than Rome itself. On the other hand, Caesar was connected by marriage with leaders of the Popular party. As a result, he could command the support of the mob, while he talked to aristocrats on equal terms: against which it must be admitted that he was distrusted by both parties. His early career was certainly not calculated to inspire confidence. He was a manipulator of political violence, an apologist for disreputable causes, an unscrupulous demagogue of the kind which Rome already knew only too well—except that his Latin was impeccable. His dress was fastidious and effeminate, and anyone could be pardoned for believing stories about the king of Bithynia. Notwithstanding, Suetonius

cites an impressive list of distinguished Roman ladies whom he is said to have seduced, including the wives of Pompey and Crassus.

To promote his political plans, as well as his personal living standards, Caesar borrowed heavily from Crassus—who ran a kind of political finance business. This, of course, placed Caesar's demagogic art at Crassus' disposal, and was liable to involve the demagogue in cases against which his natural sagacity would otherwise have warned him. Catiline's conspiracy may have been an instance of such involvement. At the same time, Caesar possessed an insight into realities which enabled him to see, as Cicero was unable or unwilling to see, that the real rulers of Rome were Pompey and the army which he could at any time summon to his support. All the constitutionalism which had survived as outworn tradition or had been violently

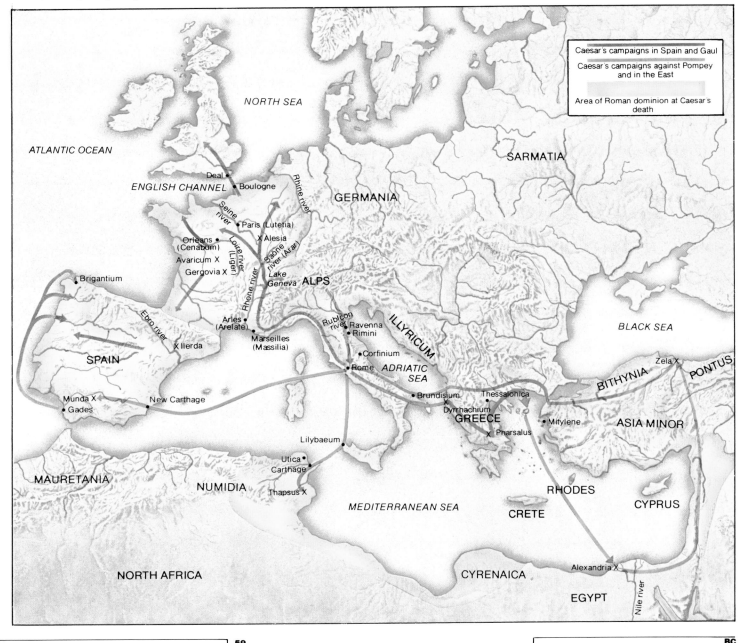

Caesar's campaigns in Spain and Gaul

Caesar's campaigns against Pompey and in the East

Area of Roman dominion at Caesar's death

Caesar's first consulate

Caesar granted proconsular power in Italian Gaul, Illyricum and Transalpine Gaul

Caesar marries Calpurnia; his daughter Julia marries Pompey

BC

imposed by Sulla was a mere facade. If the constitutional illusion persisted, this was due only to Pompey's reluctance in his political role. That great man's ambition was purely professional. He wished at heart merely to be Rome's leading general, not its autocrat.

With financial help from Crassus, Caesar obtained a military command in Spain in 61 BC. Here, the pacified Roman province still needed to be protected against the hill tribes of the northwest, and there was abundant scope for military action, Caesar proved to himself what he must have suspected: the military ability which he had shown in the East as a young man had not deserted him on the threshold of middle age. Spoil and slaves were the ordinary perquisites of successful war. One has furthermore to take into account the normal extortionate practices of a Roman governor. Caesar returned to Rome, once more a rich man, free from the burden of his debts to Crassus. He must now also have realized that he had it in him to be a general at least as great as Pompey.

In 60 BC Caesar, as consul, quietly and confidently disregarded the Republican constitution and left only a few opponents helplessly remonstrating. Power was now in the hands of Pompey, Caesar and Crassus, and the sources of their power, exerted in person or through agents, were military force, mob rule and money. By refusal to make reasonable concessions to any of them, the Senate drove its three potential enemies into alliance. Yet it must be admitted that any concessions could easily have proved the thin ends of unconstitutional wedges. At least, the triple alliance, while it lasted, meant peace. If the constitutionalists had chosen to exploit jealousy among the opponents of their authority, they might have preserved some measure of independence, while making Italy once more the theatre of war between armed contenders. From the point of view of Republicans like Cicero or Cato, the situation had to be seen as one which admitted no happy issue.

The Helvetii and Ariovistus

It may be asked whether Caesar's conquest of Gaul was in fact a great achievement in the Roman national interest or whether it was simply a means to personal prestige and political power at home. The same question may be asked of many Roman military exploits in the first century BC. In the instance of Crassus' disastrous Parthian expedition, the motives were obviously personal, while of all commanders at this time, Pompey was probably the most ready to await rather than create his opportunities. Caesar's operations in Gaul were more demonstrably directed towards the security of Rome than Crassus' eastern campaign would have proved, even if it had not been such a disaster.

Caesar's command as proconsul in 59 BC was at first limited to Italian Gaul* and Illyricum. It was then extended to Gaul beyond the Alps. There was good reason for posting Roman forces in this area. German and Gallic tribes were once more on the move and Roman memories of the Cimbric war were only half-a-century old. The Helvetian Gauls had, at the time of Caesar's proconsulate, already been forced southwards into north Switzerland by pressure from the Germanic Suebi. When the Suebi, intervening in Gallic tribal disputes, infiltrated west of the Rhine, the Helvetii, now in danger of being isolated from the rest of Gaul, decided to migrate westwards, and asked in 58 BC permission to move peacefully through the Roman Province (southern France). Caesar, as he explains, unable to see where such a movement might

---

*The Romans called the Gallic regions of north Italy Cisalpine Gaul (*Gallia Cisalpina*), ie near-side Gaul. North of the Alps lay Transalpine Gaul (*Gallia Transalpina*).

---

end and remembering that the Helvetii, in alliance with the Cimbri, had once inflicted humiliating defeat on a Roman army, refused his permission and built an elaborate 19-mile* (28 km) earthwork, complete with forts and command posts, between Lake Geneva and the Jura mountains, to block the migrants' southward exodus. The extent of this fortification and the speed with which it was constructed are further testimony to the growing part played by military engineering in Roman strategy during this period of their history.

Caesar had already gained time by a rather disingenuous protraction of negotiations with the Gauls, and he was able to collect five legions in north Italy before the Helvetii, frustrated by his Geneva line of fortifications, had made their way with difficulty across the Jura mountains and the valley of the Saône. He attacked the Helvetii and inflicted a defeat on the clan that formed their rearguard as it waited to follow the main body across the Arar river (Saône). Very swiftly bridging the river, Caesar followed in their tracks for some two weeks until, encouraged by difficulties which he had with his corn supply, they unwisely took the offensive. After a battle which lasted into the night, the Helvetii were defeated. As a result, other tribes, fearing reprisals from Caesar, refused to supply them with corn. Starvation forced them to surrender, and Caesar resettled them in their Swiss homeland. If his ambition had been less far-

---

*Roman miles.

sighted, it would have been simple and lucrative to sell them all as slaves. But the Helvetii, apart from their inconvenience elsewhere, were required in their original location—as a buffer state against the Germans.

This move, of course, made no sense unless the German infiltration into Gaul were at the same time halted. After an uncompromising diplomatic exchange with Ariovistus, king of the Suebi, Caesar found himself committed to a new war—which indeed he must have expected. The generation of Roman soldiers which Caesar commanded—if one discounts experience gained against Spartacus' German followers—had not previously encountered German warriors, and the new enemy's towering physique and warlike reputation dismayed them. At one point something like a panic occurred. But Caesar's charismatic leadership and the fearlessness which he communicated especially to the Tenth Legion, his *corps d'élite*, soon rallied officers and men alike. His truculent oratory, capable of kindling mobs, could also inspire an army. The Romans defeated Ariovistus in a major battle in the plain of Alsace and drove him back across the Rhine—which he never recrossed. In this action, Publius Crassus, who was to meet so untimely a death at Carrhae six years later, was in charge of Caesar's cavalry, and at a difficult moment his initiative swung the

Roman reserve line into action on the hard-pressed left wing, turning a doubtful issue into a certain victory.

Caesar and the Belgic Gauls

After the victory over Ariovistus, Caesar travelled south to perform his judicial functions as governor in Italian Gaul. Meanwhile, he left his army, under command of a deputy, encamped for the winter west of the Jura mountains. But the Belgic Gauls to the north, who were of mixed Celtic and Germanic extraction, were preparing for war.

In the following summer, after arranging for some diversionary operations by the Aedui, a friendly Gallic tribe, Caesar met a combined force of Belgic tribes, some 40,000 strong, in a battle on the Axona river (Aisne). Caesar's camp had been fortified on a low hill, with the bend of the river embracing it. The corn supply was again in question and the position was chosen not only for tactical defence but to prevent an enemy encircling movement which might cut the Romans off from friendly country in their rear—the source of their provisions. Anticipating battle on level ground in front of the camp and being heavily outnumbered, Caesar protected his flanks on either side by digging trenches; these extended from the Roman camp at one end to terminal forts in which artillery engines were installed. A battlefield was thus prepared, as in a kind of arena.

However, despite skirmishing in which Caesar's cavalry had the advantage, neither army would risk attacking across the intervening marsh. The Belgians then found fords on the

river, and attempted to cross in order to cut Roman communications in the rear. This plan was defeated by Caesar's prompt use of cavalry and light-armed troops which, attacking the enemy in the water, inflicted heavy losses. The Belgians had already, in the course of their march, failed to capture a Gallic town to which, as an ally, Caesar had sent timely aid; now, finding themselves short of provisions, they became disheartened. It was decided that the tribes should disperse, each to its own territory, on the understanding that all should reassemble for the defence of any one that was attacked. Their retreat, however, was so disorderly and unplanned that the Romans were able to fall upon the various contingents separately and massacre them amid scenes of confusion.

Most of the Belgic tribes were now glad to make peace with Caesar, but the strongest of them, the Nervii, still defied him. Having gained intelligence of the normal Roman order of march, they decided on a surprise attack. Mainly an infantry force, they issued from a wooded hilltop, driving Caesar's cavalry vanguard before them, then swept across the Sabis river (Sambre) and uphill, to attack the Romans as they made ready to entrench their camp. Six Roman legions had marched in front of the baggage, which was guarded by two rear legions. This differed from the arrangement which the Nervii had been led to expect, for when there was no immediate likelihood of fighting, each legion was separated by its baggage from the next.

Above: *Gold torques of ancient British Celts. Ornaments of this kind were in themselves a form of wealth, and conquering Romans regarded them as honourable trophies during their wars with the Gauls of Italy.*

Left: *A torque is worn by the dying Gaul in this well-known statue. Celtic invaders of Asia Minor were defeated by Attalus I of Pergamon in the 3rd century BC and were accordingly depicted in Pergamese art.*

<table>
<tr><th colspan="2">Caesar v Ariovistus 58 BC</th></tr>
<tr><td colspan="2">Numbers:</td></tr>
<tr><td></td><td>Caesar: c 21000 legionaries plus Gallic horse (c4000) and other auxiliaries.
Ariovistus: German tribal levy en masse (from community of 120000); includes 6000 horsemen with 6000 footmen and 16000 light infantry.</td></tr>
<tr><td>1</td><td>Ariovistus pitches camp 2 miles (3km) from Caesar, cutting his supply lines.</td></tr>
<tr><td>2</td><td>Caesar offers battle. Ariovistus declines. Cavalry skirmishes ensue.</td></tr>
<tr><td>3</td><td>Caesar marches past Germans. He pitches a second camp so restoring the supply route.</td></tr>
<tr><td>4</td><td>2 legions in new camp, 4 in old.</td></tr>
<tr><td>5</td><td>Next day: Germans attack new camp. Battle noon to sunset.</td></tr>
<tr><td>6</td><td>Next day: Caesar leads triple line from old camp.</td></tr>
<tr><td>7</td><td>Germans give battle. Hand-to-hand struggle, no javelins used.</td></tr>
<tr><td>8</td><td>Germans defeated on the left.</td></tr>
<tr><td>9</td><td>Publius Crassus switches third line to support hard-pressed Roman left.</td></tr>
<tr><td>10</td><td>Rout and slaughter of Germans.</td></tr>
</table>

Even then, the surprise was so effective that the Romans scarcely found time to put on their helmets and remove the covers from their shields. Snatching a shield from one of his rear men, Caesar made his way to the front line, rallying his troops in person in the thick of the fight. The Romans suffered serious casualties, but were saved from disaster largely by their training and by the fact that officers and men knew what to do without being told. The Nervii, who had relied on surprise and superior numbers, found themselves fighting at a disadvantage when the Roman rear legions arrived. Many of them fell in battle, resisting with desperate courage, but the Romans now had control of the situation; on that day the Nervii were utterly destroyed as a fighting force.

Caesar completed his conquest of Belgic Gaul in a brief campaign against the Aduatuci, a Germanic tribe which had been associated with the Cimbri. They had set out to help the Nervii but, too late for the battle, found themselves isolated. Caesar demanded the surrender of their weapons, but some were secretly retained, and the Aduatuci attempted an armed sally from their town by night. For this kind of action Caesar was prepared with signal fires. He inflicted heavy losses in the fighting which followed, and sold the whole of the surviving population as slaves—350,000 persons in all.

Tidal Seas

Publius Crassus, in the same campaigning season, had been sent to force the submission of the Gallic states on the Atlantic seaboard. This submission was soon received, and it should be noted that Caesar now regarded as suspect any tribe which did not approach him with offers of peace. In the following year, however, the Veneti (of the south Brittany region) led neighbouring tribes in a resistance movement and seized Roman officers who had been sent on forage missions among them, the object being to force the release of hostages whom they themselves had previously given. Indignant at this act of treachery, Caesar prepared for war against the maritime Gauls. This demanded the use of a navy. At the mouth of the Liger river (Loire) he built ships, recruited rowers from the Province (south of France) and engaged sailors and pilots.

The south Brittany coast is indented by a series of estuaries which, even today, impedes motor traffic. The Veneti and their neighbours built their strongholds on coastal eminences, which were islands when the tide flowed and peninsulas when it ebbed. Any land attacks on these citadels would be frustrated by the incoming tide, whereas a naval force would be left on the rocks when the water receded. The Romans, with great effort, built moles and raised siegeworks to provide themselves with a base of operations. But when the defenders were seriously threatened, their navy always arrived and evacuated them, together with their possessions, and the Romans were obliged to repeat the same engineering feat elsewhere.

The destruction of the enemy's fleet thus offered the only solution. But here again the Romans were at a disadvantage. The Gallic ships were built of oak, with massive transoms fixed by iron nails of a thumb's thickness, and they relied on stout leather sails. These ships were intended to resist the Atlantic wind and waves, and they also resisted the rams of the Roman war galleys. At the same time, their greater height made them difficult to grapple and thus invulnerable to boarding parties. The Gauls again were at an advantage when missiles were exchanged at sea, launching their weapons from a higher platform. Even when the Romans mounted turrets on their decks, it did not raise them above the enemy's lofty poops. Moreover, the Gallic ships were constructed with flatter bottoms and were in less danger of being stranded in the shoals, while their navigators had intimate knowledge of the coast and the tides.

However, with perseverence, ingenuity and good luck, the Romans, under command of Decimus Brutus (who was destined later to be one of Caesar's assassins), were at last victorious in a decisive sea battle. With sickle-like hooks fitted on long poles, they attacked the enemy's rigging and tore away his halyards. With the consequent collapse of their yards and sails, the Gauls were powerless, for their ships did not make use of oars. It was thus possible for two or three Roman galleys to attack a single Gaul and destroy the enemy fleet in detail. It also happened that the wind dropped, and fleeing Gallic ships were becalmed and overtaken. Once the fleet of the maritime Gauls had been thus eliminated, Caesar had no difficulty in subduing the states of the Atlantic coast, which had depended completely on their ships. He was quite merciless, for he considered that the arrest of his officers, after a negotiated submission, was a breach of international law. All the leading men of the Veneti were executed and the rest sold as slaves.

Right: *Detail of a relief over the triumphal arch at Orange (Arausio) which was erected c30 BC and to which Tiberius added his inscription in AD 25, half a century after Julius Caesar's time. Trophies of arms include conspicuous shields.*

BC   56

Caesar's campaign against the Veneti and Decimus Brutus' naval victory   P. Crassus' campaign in Aquitania   At Luca, Caesar, Pompey and M. Crassus renew their coalition

162

Operations in Germany and Britain

Caesar's campaigns in Gaul had begun as a defensive operation designed to keep the Germans out of Gaul. If the Romans did not intervene in Gallic tribal disputes, taking full advantage of Gallic political instability, then the Germans were certainly willing and able to do so and, after the experience of the Cimbri and the Teutones, western Europe dominated by land-hungry German invaders was a prospect which no Roman could regard with equanimity. The continued success of Caesar and his officers in various parts of Gaul was consequently greeted by periods of recurrent public thanksgiving in the city.

In the north and west of Gaul, however, Roman action was no longer purely defensive. It becomes clear from the tone of Caesar's commentaries that he regarded himself and his army as the agents of a civilizing mission. He also intended that the Gallic habit of tribal warfare should give way to widespread Roman law and order, and that the whole country as far as the Rhine to the east and the Channel to the north should be accessible to Roman trade, enterprise and public works. His desire to ensure that these frontiers should remain inviolate led, in 55 BC, to campaigns (both northward and eastward) against the peoples who inhabited the lands beyond them.

In this year, German tribes, already threatening the Meuse region, crossed the Rhine under pressure from the Suebi. Caesar negotiated with the migrants, but realized that they were only playing for time. He eventually took them by surprise and defeated them with great slaughter. He then, in ten days, built a wooden bridge over the Rhine and marched his legions across, for a reconnaissance in force which lasted 18 days. He did not attempt a battle with the Suebi but retired again into Gaul, destroying his bridge, having frightened his enemies and put heart into his allies.

It was already late summer in the same year when Caesar set on foot an expedition to Britain. British help to his Gallic enemies provided a military pretext, but his motives, personal ambition apart, were partly those of an explorer. He sent his trusted officer Gaius Volusenus to carry out coastal reconnaissance, and he dispatched Commius, a friendly Gallic chief, to negotiate on amicable terms, if possible, with the natives. Some British tribes had already sent conciliatory embassies to Caesar in Gaul.

When preparations were completed, Caesar sailed with two legions in 80 transport vessels, escorted by warships, across the Channel (probably from a point near Boulogne). The British were assembled on the cliffs when he arrived, but the cliffs alone made landing impossible until he found an open beach seven miles farther up-

Channel (probably between Walmer and Deal). Here the Roman legionaries landed under great difficulties, wading through water with full packs while British cavalry, chariots and infantry attacked them. Fortunately, it was discovered that the Britons had never seen oared galleys and were frightened by the Roman warships. The movement of the oars possibly suggested the legs of a sea monster. Caesar also used the warships' dinghies, together with light reconnaissance craft, to aid his men as they struggled in the surf. Landing was eventually effected and the Britons were driven back. But the Roman cavalry, embarked in a separate transport fleet, had been forced by foul weather to return to the continent, and without them Caesar's characteristically swift pursuit of a conquered enemy was made impossible.

The Romans at once fortified a camp. Caesar received a chastened embassy from the conquered Britons, and Commius, who had been held in chains, was now released. But the spring tide unexpectedly filled the beached Roman galleys with water and heavy storm damage rendered the whole fleet unseaworthy. In these circumstances, the Britons immediately took heart and renewed hostilities. However, with foresight Caesar had laid in corn supplies, and he now repaired his less seriously damaged ships with wood and bronze material which he salvaged from the 12 total wrecks. He again imposed himself on the Britons

Roman Cavalry Shields

It is uncertain just when cavalry began to use shields. Some of the Indian cavalry opposed by Alexander probably carried small shields, but the earliest examples we know of are depicted on Tarentine coins from southern Italy c400 BC. These are small bucklers and are probably those described by Polybius as made of ox-hide, and shaped like a bossed cake, when he writes of early Roman cavalry shields. It is likely that the well known Lacus Curtius relief depicts this type. Cavalry shields came into widespread use around 250 BC and it seems that large wooden *hoplon*-type shields were adopted from the Greeks by Italian cavalry. Again coins and Polybius' works are our sources. Traditionally, Rome's allies provided the bulk of her cavalry. They were mainly Italian, but Celtic and Spanish cavalry were also recruited. 1 shows the flat spined shield which dates from c200 BC and may be of Italian origin, though commonly associated with Celtic cavalry. The winged horse motif was a

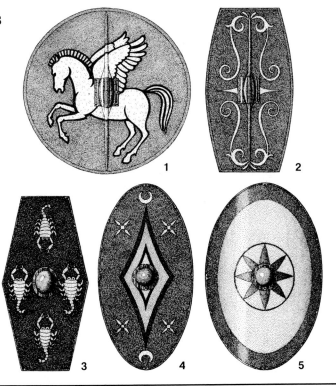

popular one and, together with the eagle, wolf, boar, and Minotaur was an emblem of Rome at this time. It is around 40" (100 cm) in diameter. 2 illustrates a shield used by the Celts and Germans who provided the bulk of Caesar's cavalry in the 1st century BC. It is simply a flat, oval Celtic shield with top and bottom cut off, a practice also adopted by the legionaries around this time. The design shown is a typical Celtic motif. 3 is a hexagonal type, commonly associated with Germany in the latter half of the 1st century AD. The scorpion design is one shown on a Trajanic monument and may be that of the *equites singulares*, a German unit of guard cavalry. 4 shows the normal 1st and 2nd century AD oval cavalry shield. It is some 48" x 27" (122cm x 68cm), and flat. Like legionary shields it is made of ply covered with leather, with a metal rim and boss. The design is from Trajan's Column. 5 is a typical design c AD 300. By this time the shield has become slightly dished and rounder (41" x 36") (104cm x 91cm). The design is of an unknown cavalry unit taken from the *Notitia Dignitatum*.

55

Caesar's campaigns against the Germans   Caesar crosses the Rhine   Caesar's first expedition to Britain   Pompey and Crassus are consuls

BC

163

and was promised that hostages would be sent to him in Gaul. He then recrossed the Channel before the autumn equinox. Only two tribes complied by sending hostages.

In the following year, despite turbulence among the Gauls, Caesar made an expedition with five legions, 2,000 horse and a correspondingly larger fleet, to his previous point of landing in Britain. On this occasion he penetrated inland, forded the Thames, and subdued the British king Cassivellaunus, who ruled over the Hertford area. Caesar again returned to the continent before winter, having once more been obliged to repair a fleet damaged by storms.

The two expeditions to Britain amounted to extended raids rather than invasions. It is surprising that no British ships attempted to interfere with the Roman landing on either occasion. No doubt they would have been heavily outnumbered. Perhaps the Britons had lost ships helping the Veneti, or perhaps they were warned by the example of that unhappy people.

Another point of interest is the British use of chariots. These were not employed in warfare by the Gauls of Caesar's time. In Britain, by contrast, Caesar writes respectfully of their military value. The charioteers could manoeuvre with great skill and drive down steep slopes without losing control. In the early stages of a battle, the chariots were driven among the enemy cavalry to create confusion. Missiles were thrown from them, the chariot crews being able to balance themselves, if necessary, in a kind of tight-rope act, on the poles that supported the horses' yokes. The noise of the wheels was daunting, though there is no mention of scythe attachments. At a later stage in the battle, chariot-borne warriors dismounted and fought on foot, while drivers waited at a distance, ready to pick them up and drive them from the battlefield at speed if circumstances

The Enemies of Caesar

Early German Tribesmen
The drawings (below) show German warriors of c100 BC-AD 100. They are, (left to right):

Chauci Noble
He is equipped with a large flat shield, a long 12ft (3·6m) spear as described by Tacitus, and a locally made imitation of a Roman *gladius*. He wears a tight tunic and trousers, and his hair is tied in a "Suebian knot".

Young Chatti Warrior
This man is a commoner, his sole garments are a short fur cloak and loin-cloth. His hair and beard remain uncut until he fulfils his vow to kill an enemy. His weapons are the national *framea*, a short assegai-like weapon suitable for thrusting or throwing, and a number of javelins with hardened wooden points.

Aestii Tribesman
This warrior carries a hexagonal shield and club. Men such as this fought for the Romans and are shown on Trajan's Column. The first two figures are reconstructed from weapons and clothing found in Germany and Denmark. The Germans were mainly infantry and fought in large wedge formations. Cavalry units included infantry troops.

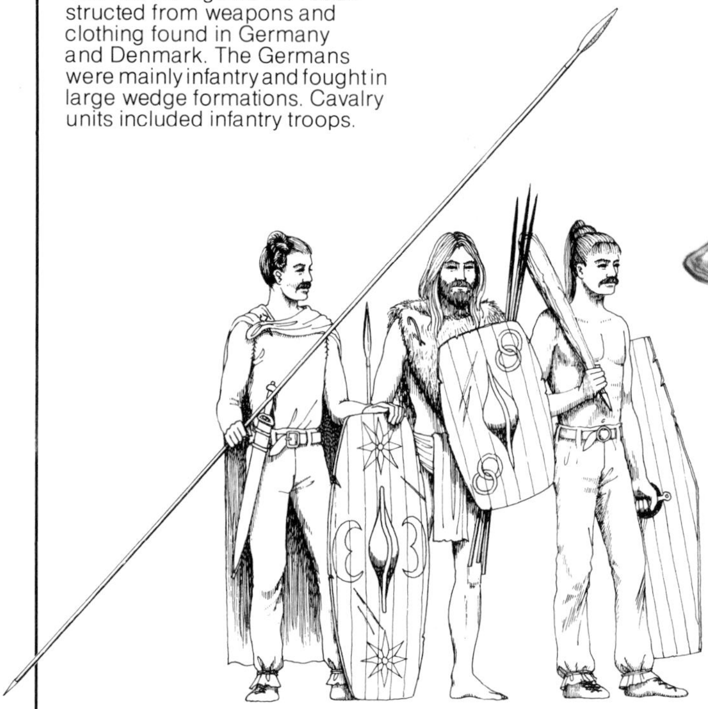

The Celtic Chariot
The reconstruction above is based on various coins, a funeral *stele* from Padua in Italy, and the descriptions of Diodorus, Strabo and Caesar, as well as archaeological findings. In all cultures chariots tended to disappear once large cavalry horses became available. The last recorded use of them in battle in continental Europe is at Telamon in 225 BC, though Strabo records some Gauls using them as late as Caesar's day. The Britons certainly had them and they are recorded in use by Picts as late as the 3rd century AD. These chariots are small with wheels of 3ft (90cm) diameter and are very light and manoeuvrable. Caesar records their ability to gallop and turn on steep hills, and seems impressed by them. They were drawn by 2 ponies via a yoke-pole and traces which probably fastened to the axle.

BC   54

Caesar's second expedition to Britain: he defeats British king Cassivellaunus   Belgic tribes revolt: Cotta and Sabinus, Caesar's officers, defeated and killed   Q. Cicero survives attack   Labienus defeats Indutiomarus   Death of Caesar's daughter Julia (Pompey's wife)

164

thus dictated. One is reminded of Homeric accounts of chariot warfare.

Caesar against Vercingetorix

Caesar's initial conquest of Gaul had been deceptively simple. The Gauls did not remain docile, and Gallic uprisings alternating with Roman reprisals soon assumed the aspect of a vicious circle. Not long after Caesar's British campaign, the Belgic tribes revolted. Two of Caesar's senior officers were lured out of their camp and killed with almost their entire force, while another Roman camp was relieved by Caesar's arrival in the nick of time. The Germans once more intervened and a new retaliatory expedition across the Rhine became necessary. Caesar built a bridge even more quickly than he had done on the previous occasion. But when he had subdued the Gauls in the north-east, he had one of their leaders flogged to death. The resentment and apprehension which this execution caused was a stimulus to further revolt.

During the period of the Gallic Wars, Caesar spent every winter in north Italy where, apart from all other considerations, he was able to keep in touch with Roman politics. Returning to Transalpine Gaul in 52 BC, he found the whole country in a state bordering on general rebellion. At Cenabum (Orleans), a massacre of the Roman trading community had taken place. The situation was so dangerous that when Caesar reached the Roman Province in south France, he dared not summon his legions to him from their stations farther north, lest they should be attacked while he was not present to command them in person. Nor dared he travel through Gallic territory unattended by his army.

However, he gathered some troops in the Province, marched up into the Cevennes amid winter snows, and then

Celtic Warriors
The crew shown with the chariot are typical Celtic warriors. They fight stripped to the waist and sometimes naked. To emphasise their fearsome looks, they often coated their hair with clay and lime and combed it into stiff spikes. The Britons also occasionally tattooed or painted themselves with woad, a blue-green dye. The Picts (painted ones) derived their name from this practice. Depictions show that the driver normally sat rather than stood, with the warrior behind him. Both moved around freely—Caesar records charioteers running out along the yoke-pole. The warrior also dismounted to fight, as shown here, while the chariot remained nearby, should a quick retreat prove to be necessary. Celtic shields appear to have been copied from the similarly sized Italian *scutum*, but they were flat not rounded. They were made of oak or linden planks varying in thickness from ·5″ (13mm) in the middle to ·25″ (6mm) at the edges and covered with hide.

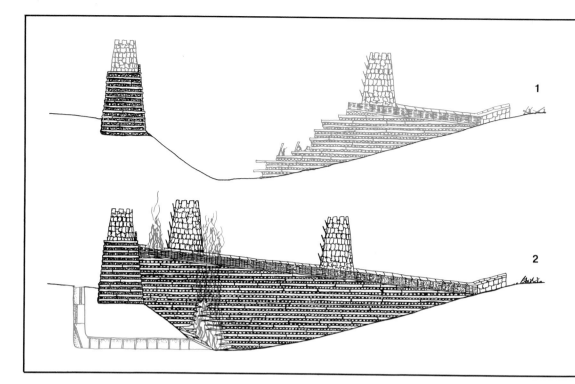

The Assault on Avaricum

Caesar: 8 legions (c30000) plus cavalry and auxiliaries (c8000) Garrison: 10000 picked Gauls. Total population 40000.

This Gallic city was situated on a hillock surrounded by marshes which made a conventional siege impossible. The only approach was along the spur of a ridge. An assault was also necessary since rams were ineffectual against reinforced Gallic walls. Caesar therefore raises an *agger* (earthwork) some 80ft (24m) high, 330ft (100m) wide and 250ft (75m) long. This consists of earth and rubble with timber supports laid criss-cross. Probably only the 2 lateral "banks" were built on timber to make the structure cohere and support the weight of the siege towers mounted on either side. As these are pushed towards the walls the Gauls hastily erect hide-covered towers of their own to counter them (**1**). The crews who propel the siege towers are protected from missile fire by side screens, and the workers by

left his force to occupy the enemy's attention, while he himself travelled so swiftly north-eastwards, through once friendly areas, that his old Gallic allies had no time to organize treachery, even if they would have wished it. Thus rejoining his legions, Caesar captured several rebel strongholds and avenged the massacre at Cenabum, but he now faced an enemy leader of great courage and skill in the person of Vercingetorix, chief of the Arverni tribe in central Gaul. At the siege of Avaricum (Bourges), both Romans and Gauls suffered intense hardship, for Vercingetorix' scorched-earth strategy inflicted terrible privations on enemies and friends alike. Meanwhile, the Gauls had learnt to counter Roman siege techniques. The defenders set fire to Caesar's assault towers and undermined the ramp which he had raised against their walls; many Gauls were by occupation iron-miners. But the Romans took Avaricum at last. Caesar says that only 800 out of 40,000 persons escaped to join Vercingetorix in his impregnable camp amid the

Right: *The head of Vercingetorix. This Gallic chief was able to unite the bickering Celtic tribes under his leadership and defy Julius Caesar's forces in 52 BC.*

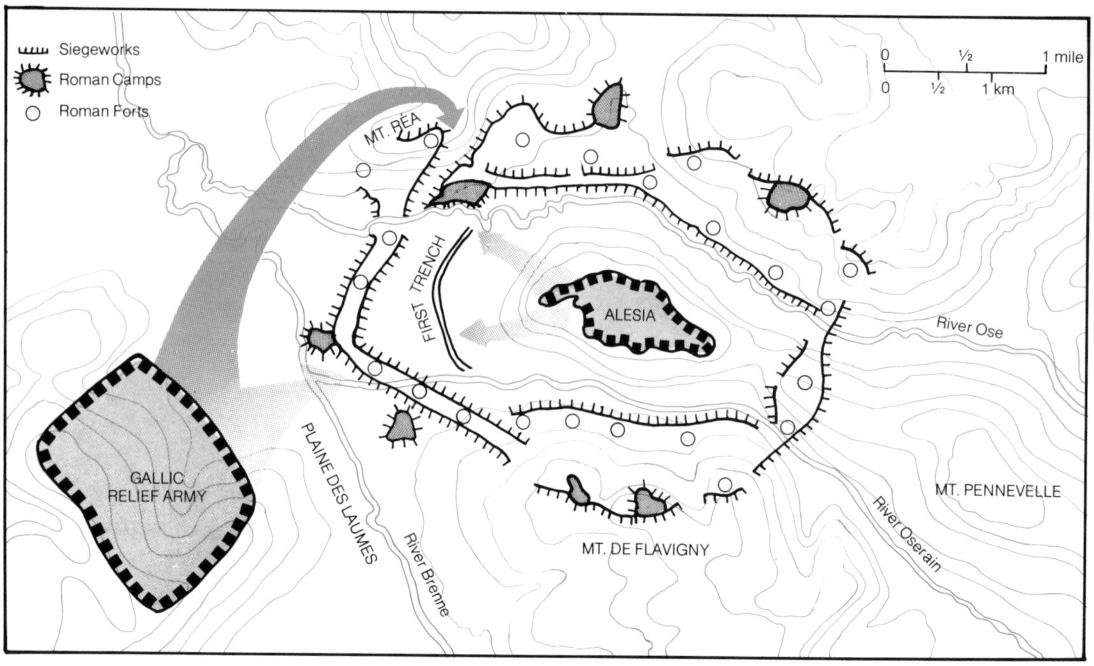

The Siege of Alesia 52 BC

Caesar	Vercingetorix
Troops	
10 legions 40000	Infantry 80000
Cavalry and auxiliaries 10000	Cavalry 15000
	Relief army:
	Infantry 250000
	Cavalry escaped
	from Alesia 8000

Caesar follows Vercingetorix' army of tribesmen to Alesia and begins the massive task of blockading the plateau. While the works are under construction the Gauls' cavalry attempts to break out. It is repulsed with heavy loss, but eventually escapes by night, before the works are finished, to raise a relief army. The first attacks by this army are repulsed. Finally, 60000 picked men launch an attack on Caesar from around Mt Réa, where they can overlook the defences. Even though this combines with a simultaneous attack from Alesia, it too fails. The relieving army then disperses and Vercingetorix surrenders.

Map labels: Siegeworks · Roman Camps · Roman Forts · MT. RÉA · FIRST TRENCH · ALESIA · River Ose · GALLIC RELIEF ARMY · PLAINE DES LAUMES · River Brenne · MT. DE FLAVIGNY · River Oserain · MT. PENNEVELLE

Vercingetorix is leader of combined Gallic states   Caesar takes Avaricum   After repulse, Caesar abandons siege of Gergovia   Surrender of Vercingetorix at Alesia   Near Rome, P. Clodius is murdered by rival gangster Milo

rows of sheds (*vineae*). The *agger* is completed in 25 days. To counter it the Gauls, who include iron-miners in their number, dig several tunnels, fill them with pitch and timber and fire them and the props, hoping to collapse the *agger*. Rising smoke alerts Caesar around midnight and the siege towers are withdrawn. A Gallic sally is repulsed, and by dawn the fires are under control (**2**). Caesar repairs the damage, and moves 1 siege tower forward again. Lulled by success the Gauls slacken guard. Under cover of a swirling rain storm, the Romans filter into the *vineae*. Emerging suddenly, they quickly scale the walls with ladders and the sentries are overwhelmed. The city is lost, only 800 escaping. The plan view (**3**) shows the *agger*, the 2 siege towers and the rows of *vineae*. Behind are the catapults, *ballistae* and *scorpiones* protected by mantlets. The structure by which the siege tower is propelled is also visible on the right, while the crew is shown in action (left).

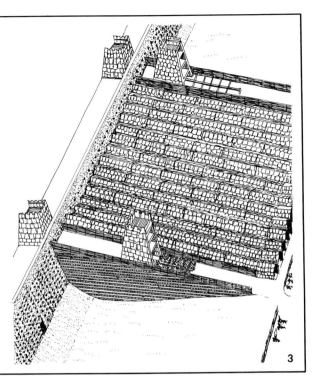

Caesar reproved the survivors, although he would no doubt have commended their initiative had they been successful. For the sake of prestige and morale, he now waited until his cavalry had gained some minor victories before evacuating his positions at Gergovia.

Operations at Alesia

The action at Gergovia amounted to the most serious reverse that Caesar faced in the whole of the Gallic Wars. He had for some time been contemplating withdrawal, to deal with threats elsewhere in Gaul. But the mere fact of his withdrawal encouraged revolt and led to the defection of the Aedui, whose old allegiance to him had been wavering as a result of Vercingetorix' continued success. In the north, several tribes did not join the general rebellion, and Belgians who revolted were overcome by Caesar's deputy, Labienus, on the Seine near Lutetia (Paris). Vercingetorix had now collected a vast force of cavalry and launched an offensive against the Gallic peoples on the frontiers of the Roman Province. Caesar, however, had enlisted the help of German cavalry from Rhine tribes with whom he had previously come to terms. Vercingetorix was seriously repulsed and retired to Alesia in a territory subject to the Aedui (almost certainly at Alise-Sainte-Reine).

The Gallic leader hoped to repeat the experience of Gergovia, but he now saw that Caesar was bent on a massive blockade. Before the Roman circumvallations could close round him, he sent out his cavalry contingents each to

marshes. Vercingetorix now retreated to another impregnable position, this time deploying the tribes under his command on a mountainous plateau before the town of Gergovia in Arverni territory. Caesar managed to occupy a hilly eminence opposite the town and established here a small garrison, which he connected with the main camp by means of a double ditch and rampart. The result was to impede the enemy's supplies of food and water, but the move was not decisive, and while Caesar faced Vercingetorix at Gergovia he was not available for operations elsewhere. Once, when his departure was temporarily necessary

to deal with a threatened revolt among the Aedui, the enemy launched a sortie against the force which he had left behind him and the Roman camp was defended only with difficulty.

In these operations, Vercingetorix used archers and other missile-troops in great numbers and with devastating effect. The Romans retaliated vigorously with catapult artillery. Finally, a Roman assault on the fortified plateau miscarried, although it had been carefully planned by Caesar. Legionaries who broke through the defending wall and tried to push their attack into the town itself were repulsed with heavy loss. They had exceeded their orders and

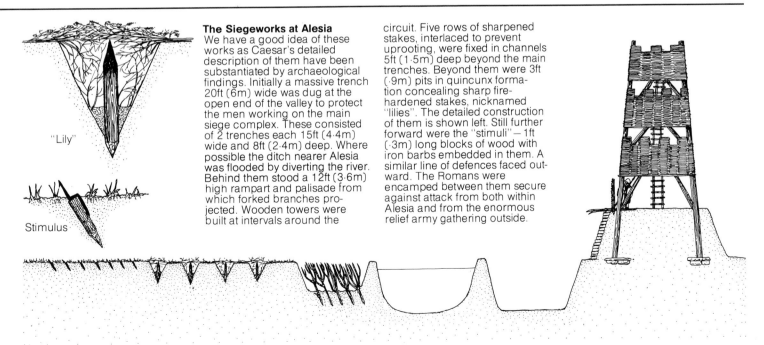

The Siegeworks at Alesia
We have a good idea of these works as Caesar's detailed description of them have been substantiated by archaeological findings. Initially a massive trench 20ft (6m) wide was dug at the open end of the valley to protect the men working on the main siege complex. These consisted of 2 trenches each 15ft (4·4m) wide and 8ft (2·4m) deep. Where possible the ditch nearer Alesia was flooded by diverting the river. Behind them stood a 12ft (3·6m) high rampart and palisade from which forked branches projected. Wooden towers were built at intervals around the

circuit. Five rows of sharpened stakes, interlaced to prevent uprooting, were fixed in channels 5ft (1·5m) deep beyond the main trenches. Beyond them were 3ft (·9m) pits in quincunx formation concealing sharp firehardened stakes, nicknamed "lilies". The detailed construction of them is shown left. Still further forward were the "stimuli" — 1ft (·3m) long blocks of wood with iron barbs embedded in them. A similar line of defences faced outward. The Romans were encamped between them secure against attack from both within Alesia and from the enormous relief army gathering outside.

"Lily"

Stimulus

Cavalry Helmets

The Roman cavalry of Republican times, drawn from the wealthier classes, had worn mainly "Attic" style helmets rather than the mass-produced "Montefortino" style (p 109). The auxiliaries of Caesar's day wore their native helmets. Under the Empire, the regular cavalry *alae* wore elaborate helmets based on "Attic" types. **1** shows one of these c AD 40. It is made of iron, sheathed in bronze embossed to imitate hair. Unlike infantry helmets, cavalry helmets cover the ears, but still have flanged ear-guards attached. **2** shows a crested helmet c AD 75, probably an officer's. It is of iron with bronze re-inforcement and decoration. Arrian describes helmet plumes as yellow. **3** shows a bronze helmet c AD 120. It has a peak and cruciform reinforcement. Similar iron helmets also exist. **4** is an elaborate iron and bronze helmet c AD 200. The knob is drilled to take a falling plume. **5** (c AD 250) could be iron or bronze, and has a single mask held on by a strap instead of hinged cheek-pieces. **6** is an iron helmet c AD 350 with a separate neck-guard. It is made in halves, joined by the central ridge, and reveals strong Persian influence.

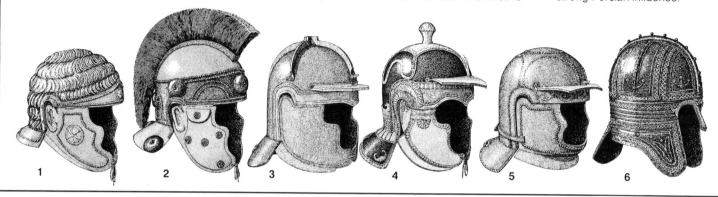

its own tribe, to organize relief forces from every direction. Caesar had soon to deal with these relief forces. But his double circumvallation was so effective that he was able to hold off all attacks from outside and from within, until Vercingetorix and his force were starved into surrender. Vercingetorix was held captive for six years, for exhibition in Caesar's triumph in Rome. He was then executed, according to the usual custom, when the celebrations were over. Pompey would have behaved more chivalrously.

In Caesar's commentaries, engineering operations around Alesia are described in great detail. The Roman entrenchments linked an encircling chain of camps and forts. The inner ditch was 20 feet (6m) wide, with sheer sides (ie, not tapering at the bottom), and the main circumvallation was constructed 400 paces* behind this ditch. Here, there were two trenches each 15 feet (4·4m) wide and 8 feet (2·4m) deep; the river was diverted to carry water into the inner trench wherever possible. Behind the trenches was a 12-foot (3·6m) earthwork and palisade, with antlered prongs projecting from it. Breastworks and battlements were overlooked by turrets at intervals of 80 feet (23·6m). Caesar also sowed the ground beyond his fortifications with prongs and pitfalls of various patterns, illustratively or humorously termed "lilies" and "stingers" (*stimuli*). A parallel line of fortifications was then provided as an outer circumvallation

*1 pace (*passus*) = 5 Roman feet
1 Roman foot = 11·65 inches (296mm)
400 paces = 1,942 English feet (592m)
The above measurements are in Roman feet, as given by Caesar.

Above: *This coin celebrates the victory of Caesar over Vercingetorix, who is here shown as a captive under a trophy of Gallic armour. Vercingetorix was put to death in Rome after appearing in Caesar's triumph.*

against the inevitable relief force. The inner perimeter was 11 Roman miles (10·1 miles/16·3 km) long; the outer 14 Roman miles (12·9 miles/20·7 km).

Caesar writes that the Gallic relief force, when it came, amounted to 250,000 infantry and 8,000 cavalry. Belgic troops were rallied by Commius, Caesar's old friend, who now preferred liberty to civilization and had at last taken sides with Vercingetorix. Meanwhile, the non-combatant population of Alesia had been driven out by the Gallic garrison—perhaps a preferable alternative to the slaughter and cannibalism that had been proposed. The wretched outcasts begged to be accepted as Roman slaves and fed as such. But Caesar, who had laid in military provisions only for 30 days, forbade them to be fed.

When the Romans were attacked simultaneously by the huge relief force and the desperate men from Alesia, the issue remained for some time uncertain, but Caesar had apparently held his German cavalry in reserve and his use of it late in the day routed the enemy cavalry and exposed to massacre the archers and light-armed troops who had accompanied them.

The besieged garrison now made a night attack on the Roman positions. The Gauls had become more sophisticated in their methods of siege warfare, and were armed with ladders and grappling hooks. Many missiles were exchanged in the darkness, and Caesar seems to imply that casualties were caused on both sides accidentally by what had been intended as "covering fire". Meanwhile, the Roman legionaries had taken up their stations on pre-arranged plans and the Gallic sortie was contained and repulsed.

The final assault on the Roman circumvallation, which was made simultaneously from within and without, was again decided by cavalry action. Caesar had unostentatiously sent out a cavalry force, which took the outer enemy in the rear, just at the moment when they were heavily engaged on the ramparts. At this moment, in particular, the situation at Alesia must have been that of a nest of boxes. In the centre was the town. Vercingetorix had fortified the surrounding plateau with a six-foot (1·8m) wall, to protect his camps in the enclosure. Outside this was the Roman double circumvallation, now attacked by the Gallic relief forces from beyond. But these finally had been surprised by the appearance of Caesar's cavalry behind their backs.

50
Caesar returns to Italy   Disputes between Caesar's
political friends and foes
at Rome

After this action, which forced the surrender of Alesia, many Gallic leaders fell into Caesar's hands. But Commius, after further adventures, escaped to Britain, where he ruled over a migrant branch of his own Belgic tribe in what is now Hampshire.

Tactical Considerations

The organization and equipment of Caesar's army in Gaul was virtually that which had been introduced by Marius. There was no question of manipular quincunx formation. The army ordinarily fought in three unbroken lines. In any one legion, four cohorts in front and three apiece in the rear ranks was normal distribution. Sometimes the legions themselves appear as tactical units, as for instance in the battle against the Nervii, where Caesar ordered his tribunes to close up the gap between the isolated Seventh Legion and the rest of the battle line, thus obviating the danger of encirclement. On occasion, a two-line battle formation might be adopted, as it was by Publius Crassus while fighting against the Gauls of Aquitania.

In his earlier Gallic campaigns particularly, Caesar seems to have made full use of hillside positions. This, however, was not an advantage if the enemy possessed a strong archer force which outranged the Roman heavy javelin. Publius Crassus, leading the ill-fated advance guard of his father's army at Carrhae, discovered this to his cost. For on a sandy hill, the rear ranks were raised above the front ranks only to offer better targets to the Parthian bowmen.

The Roman javelin (*pilum*), as used by Caesar's armies against the Gauls, embodied the Marian principle of buckling on impact. This effect was achieved not by a breakable wooden peg but by soft iron in the shank of the javelin, which bent and was hard to remove. In many instances, Gallic shields, which had evidently overlapped each other when their owners adopted a close formation, were pinned together by a single *pilum*. In such circumstances, the Gauls had abandoned their shields and fought unprotected. In the later battle against the Nervii, however, we hear of *pila* being intercepted and launched on a

Right: The triumphal arch at Arausio where Roman armies were defeated by German tribes in 105 BC. The Helvetii, Caesar's enemies in 58 BC, were then allied to the Germans.

return journey. Perhaps these were javelins which fell flat to the ground, without head-on impact. Perhaps, also, the bending of the iron was produced not so much by the impact as the attempted withdrawal. In any case, the "interception" of javelins can hardly have involved catching them as they hurtled through the air!

The adoption of a three-line or two-line formation must have been determined largely by topographical considerations. In Caesar's battle against the Belgic confederacy, the plain on which he planned to fight yielded a battle front co-extensive with the adjacent wall of his camp. However, in warfare against consistently superior forces, there was an ever-present danger of encirclement, and apart from the normal use of cavalry on the wings, Caesar made tactical use of fortifica-

tions. In the battle against the Belgic confederates, he protected his flanks with an earthwork on either side. Tactical fortifications were indeed a conspicuous feature of Roman warfare in the first century BC. Caesar was able to develop their use on account of the astounding speed and efficiency with which his technical arm did its work. We may compare his building of bridges and fleets.

Caesar relied on a skilled corps of artificers for specialist work. But the legionaries were still responsible for digging trenches and raising the earthworks round camps. However, though *dolabrae* were carried, the Roman soldiers, operating usually in enemy country, often travelled light, leaving their equipment to be transported by large mule trains located at intervals between the marching legions. The

Above: *Battle scene at Arausio, recalling bloody wars of conquest rather than the subsequent Pax Romana.*

legionaries were thus ready to resist a sudden attack, and to provide against such a contingency, they sometimes marched in four parallel columns (*quadratum agmen*), which could abruptly turn and face toward either side in the form of a battle line. When surrounded, the Romans might also adopt the formation of a ring (*orbis*)—an ancient counterpart of the 19th century British square.

When Caesar assumed command in Transalpine Gaul, there had been only one legion stationed there. Caesar finished the Gallic Wars with ten legions under his command, but these were not up to the strength of those which Marius had levied (5,000 men). A legion of Caesar's army was not usually more than 3,500 strong. It will be realized from this how enormously the Romans were outnumbered in the course of the Gallic Wars. Caesar himself says that the siege of Alesia could not have been undertaken without recourse to his elaborate fortifications. Without the aid of ramparts and ditches, towers and pits, he had not sufficient troops to surround the Gallic positions.

The Roman was traditionally a foot-soldier. However, cavalry was essential to Caesar, not only for flank protection, but for swift pursuit of a defeated enemy. Such speed in pursuit was, in fact, characteristic of his generalship and goes far to accounting for the decisiveness of his victories. Since Marius' time, the Romans had regularly used foreign (non-Italian) cavalry. Caesar's horsemen were mainly drawn from Spanish and Gallic allies. Similarly,

he used Cretan and Numidian archers and Balearic slingers. But against Vercingetorix he also made great use of Germans from the tribes which he had conciliated beyond the Rhine. It was not simply that Gauls in this campaign were less available or less trustworthy. German horsemen were hardy riders, who despised the use of saddlecloths. Their horses were physically inferior to Gallic mounts but were very highly trained. German cavalry fought in conjunction with infantry, operating in couples, each composed of a horseman and a footman, associated in a kind of knight-and-squire relationship. If necessary, the footmen could support themselves in fast moves over long distances by hanging on to the horses' manes*. Caesar himself noticed the advantage of combining infantry with cavalry; one of the assets of the British war chariot was that it combined the mobility of horsemen with the stability of foot soldiers. Again, typically Roman in his respect for military traditions, Caesar did not attempt to impose foreign methods of fighting on his own men, but employed foreign troops which operated according to their own traditional methods, while making good Roman deficiencies.

In this context, it should also be noted that Caesar recruited a legion of Gallic infantry, who later received Roman citizenship. Their purpose was to replace two Roman legions which, on orders from the Senate, he had sent back to Pompey in 51 BC—for use in a Parthian campaign which never materialised. The Gallic legion was

---

*A mixed unit of cavalry and infantry (*cohors equitata*), modelled on German practice, later formed a regular part of the Roman auxiliary forces.

known as the *Alaudae* ("Skylarks"). The reference was perhaps to their helmet crests, and the nickname may have been one which the Gallic legionaries conferred on themselves, for *alauda* (cf, French *alouette*) is a word of Gallic, not Latin, extraction.

Caesar against Pompey

The fall of Alesia did not automatically bring Gallic resistance to an end, but it deprived the Gauls of unifying and co-ordinating leadership. During the following year (51 BC) Roman armies were able to deal with their opponents piecemeal as they had done before the emergence of Vercingetorix, and as Caesar's term of office and command approached its end, he could justly claim to have conquered and subdued the rebellious warriors of Gaul.

In a political situation delicately balanced amid a variety of competing interests, Caesar's enemies at Rome, who possessed what amounted to a casting vote, managed to face him with a clearcut option which admitted of no compromise. Either he must disband his army and return to Rome as a private person, without so much as a bodyguard, or else he must descend upon Rome at the head of an invading army, as the enemy of the Republic. The former alternative meant suicide in a political, and perhaps even a more literal, sense. In 49 BC Caesar, with his army, crossed the Rubicon river (between Ravenna and Rimini) which divided Italian Gaul from Roman Italy. Pompey had with some hesitation placed his loyalty to the constitution before his old alliance with Caesar. He, also, could now have exclaimed "The die is cast!". For both men had been called upon to make difficult decisions. Lucius Domitius Ahenobarbus, appointed as Caesar's provincial successor, refused to be advised by Pompey and tried to resist Caesar at Corfinium (near Corfinio). Caesar captured him, released him and took command of his troops. No Sullan or Marian massacre ensued at Rome, but Caesar tried unsuccessfully to prevent Pompey from embarking his army at Brundisium, whence it was skilfully piloted, from among the Caesarian entrenchments and moles, across the Adriatic, to form the nucleus of a new base in Greece. The rulers and governors of the East owed their positions to Pompey's goodwill, and he could rely on them for financial and military support.

Caesar lacked a fleet and could not therefore immediately follow Pompey. Instead, he turned his attention to Spain, the provincial territory which Pompey had governed from Rome through his *legati*. Marching through the south of France, Caesar found the Massilians hesitant and, while he negotiated with them, Domitius Ahenobarbus—abusing the clemency shown him at Corfinium—arrived with a few merchant ships and rallied local support for Pompey. Caesar built 12 ships at Arelate (Arles), in the Rhône delta, and left them with Decimus Brutus—victor over the Veneti—for the purpose of blockading Massilia (Marseille). From the cutting of the timber to the launching of the ships, the work took only 30 days. The wood was, of course, unseasoned, but Roman fleets were often built quickly and *ad hoc*, and they were not required to last. Other forces were also left to besiege the Massilians by land.

Fighting in Spain centred on Ilerda (Lérida) on the Sicoris (Segre) river, a tributary of the Ebro. The Pompeians, accustomed to guerrilla tactics like those used in Spain by Sertorius, fought in a flexible and loosely organized way, which at first disconcerted Caesar's troops. The corn supply was once more of crucial importance, as always where, in consequence of latitude or altitude, crops ripened late in the season. Lucullus had had the same trouble in the Armenian mountains. Caesar's supplies were cut off when the river, abnormally swollen by melting spring snows, swept away his bridges. At a later stage, he crossed the river in boats of hide stretched on light wooden frames, which were conveyed to the water on trailer-linked wagons. Caesar says that his British experience had taught him so to construct boats.

At last, Pompey's *legati*, Afranius and Petreius, were themselves cut off from supplies and forced to capitulate. After much fighting, Massilia (Marseille) also surrendered. Caesar returned to Italy, ready for an offensive against Pompey himself. Despite the Pompeian fleet, which had been detailed to prevent his crossing into Greece, Caesar managed to transport his troops unexpectedly in winter across the Adriatic. A further contingent, left behind with Marcus Antonius (Mark Antony) for lack of ships, crossed the Adriatic without further difficulties later in the winter.

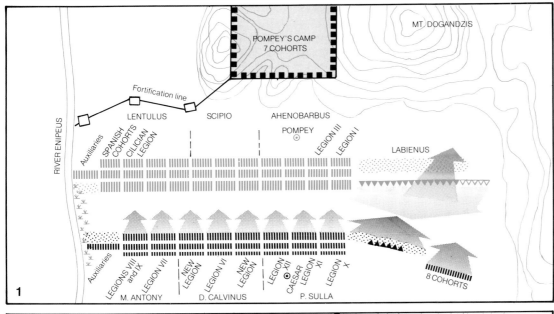

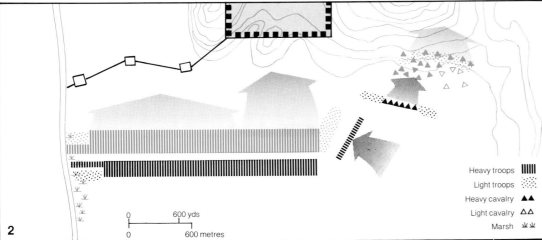

Battle of Pharsalus 48 BC

Caesar	Pompey*
Infantry	
Elements of 9 legions 23000 (82 cohorts, many under-strength) Allies and auxiliaries 5/10000	Elements of 12 legions + 7 Spanish cohorts = 50000 (some cohorts under strength) Allies and auxiliaries 4200
Cavalry	
Gaul) Germany) 1000 (+ 400 light infantry)	Allies 7000 (*Perhaps subtract campaign losses of 3/7000)

Caesar camps north of Enipeus river in Thessaly; Pompey camps 3 miles north-west of him. After much jockeying for the better position, battle lines are drawn. Pompey means to outflank Caesar's right with his superior cavalry; Caesar in anticipation stiffens his cavalry with light infantry and stations 8 cohorts as further cavalry support.
1 The armies close to c150 yds (137m). Pompey does not order a charge—he hopes by this tactical innovation that Caesar's men will exhaust themselves by charging double distance. However they foresee this trap and spontaneously halt halfway to redress. The lines then close. Pompey's cavalry pushes back Caesar's, whose 8 cohorts then charge and scatter Pompey's horse. Light-troops and cavalry pursue.
2 The 8 cohorts wheel into Pompey's flank and Caesar orders his third line into battle. Pompey, potentially encircled, flees and seeing this his army breaks under all-round pressure. In two hours Pompey has lost 6/10000 killed, Caesar some 1200 dead.

Heavy troops ▐▐▐▐▐
Light troops ⋮
Heavy cavalry ▲▲
Light cavalry △△
Marsh ⚶⚶

0 — 600 yds
0 — 600 metres

The armies of Caesar and Pompey confronted each other at Dyrrhachium (Durazzo). Caesar's force was the smaller, perhaps three-quarters the size of Pompey's, but it was the better army. Pompey realized this and wisely avoided a pitched battle, choosing instead to fortify an enclave on the Adriatic coast, 15 Roman miles (13·8 miles, 22·2 km) in perimeter. Caesar characteristically enclosed this enclave with his own outer circumvallation.

The Supreme Victor

Military history in general tends to familiarize us with battles which are decided on a fateful day and battlefields which are reminiscent of playing fields. By contrast, Caesar's mode of fighting, with its reliance on earthworks and ditches, anticipates protracted twentieth-century struggles amid extensively prepared positions. At Dyrrhachium, Pompey's determination not to be drawn into a pitched battle was in every way wise. He had access to seaborne supplies and reinforcements, while Caesar, without a navy, was cut off from Italy. The besiegers grew hungrier than the besieged, but lacking corn they resorted to digging up a local root which could be mixed with milk and made edible.

Eventually, Pompey, who had been growing ever stronger, broke through Caesar's lines at a weak point near the sea. Caesar's counter-attack on one of Pompey's camps proved a very costly and almost disastrous failure. The

---

Battle of Dyrrhachium 48 BC

Commanders:
Caesar v Pompey
Numbers:
Caesar: c25000 legionaries; a few cavalry and auxiliaries.
Pompey: c36000 legionaries; a strong cavalry force.

1. Pompey mobilises in the East (500 war galleys plus unspecified number of other craft).
2. After subduing Pompey's legions in Spain Caesar crosses Adriatic in winter with 7 legions.
3. Caesar surrounds Pompey's larger force at Dyrrhachium with a circumvallation.
4. Pompey continuously reinforced and supplied by sea.
5. Early Spring: Mark Antony crossing the Adriatic reinforces Caesar with 4 legions.
6. Pompey succeeds in breaking through Caesar's lines.
7. Caesar's counter-attack is repulsed with heavy loss.
8. Pompey fails to take advantage.
9. Caesar raises siege and marches eastward to Thessaly.
10. Pompey imprudently follows him to Pharsalus.

Above: *Metellus Scipio. After Pompey's death he commanded Pompeian partisans in North Africa. Caesar defeated him at Thapsus and he subsequently committed suicide.*

Caesarian cohorts, approaching the camp — which had been much ramified and extended — lost their way around the ramparts and mistook an entrenchment which connected the camp with the neighbouring river for part of the camp itself. Demolishing the rampart in order to make their way through, they were taken at a disadvantage by a Pompeian force, with resulting confusion and panic in which nearly 1,000 were killed. If Pompey had exploited his opportunity as they fled, he might have finished the war on that day.

Caesar's strategy at Dyrrhachium thus ended in fiasco, and he marched away into Thessaly, perhaps threatening Thessalonica or perhaps mainly in search of corn. If he hoped at the same time that Pompey would be encouraged to take the offensive, then his optimism was eventually justified. Pompey was persuaded by his influential and aristocratic officers to offer battle. He did so reluctantly, but should not be accused of weak-mindedness. His advisers were highly placed men who could easily have swayed the sympathies of the legions under his command. At Pharsalus, Caesar reserved 8 cohorts for attack on the enemy's larger but inexperienced cavalry force. These cohorts advanced irresistibly, thrusting with their javelins at the faces of the young horsemen. Once the cavalry had been routed, the Pompeian legions were unable to withstand the impact of Caesar's third line, now thrown fresh into the battle. Pompey escaped and made his way to Egypt, where he was murdered on arrival by orders of the ruling Ptolemy, who dared not offer hospitality to a loser.

On arrival in Alexandria, Caesar obliged Ptolemy to accept Cleopatra (his sister and wife, according to Ptolemaic precedent) as joint ruler of Egypt. However, hostilities soon followed, as a result of which Ptolemy XIII was drowned in the Nile and his brother Ptolemy XIV placed on the throne as a mate for Cleopatra, only to be murdered by her orders. Caesar himself had already obtained Cleopatra as a mistress; she had a son "Caesarion" (Little Caesar) after the conqueror's departure from Egypt.

Meanwhile, Pharnaces, the son of Mithridates, had taken advantage of Roman civil strife to attempt the reconstruction of his father's empire. Caesar, avenging an unsuccessful deputy, defeated the ambitious ruler at Zela in Pontus, and immortalized the event with his laconism "*Veni, vidi, vici*" (I came, saw and conquered).

After brief political activity in Italy, Caesar crossed into North Africa to deal with surviving Pompeians, some of whom had, more than two years earlier, with Numidian help, defeated his officer Curio. The battle of Thapsus (46 BC) was here decisive. After Caesar's victory, Cato, left with the hopeless task of defending Utica, philosophically committed suicide. Petreius and the Numidian king Juba made a suicide pact, involving an after-dinner duel to the death. Metellus Scipio, who had commanded at Thapsus, successfully stabbed himself. Afranius was captured; Caesar, whose clemency did not usually extend to second-offenders, had him executed. Domitius Ahenobarbus had already been killed at Pharsalus.

In the west, however, Caesar's enemies rallied. His old second-in-command in Gaul, Titus Labienus, had defected to Pompey. A survivor of the Greek and African campaigns, Labienus now aided the sons of Pompey in a desperate battle at Munda in southern Spain. Nobody had a better insight into Caesar's mind and methods than Labienus. But it was a case in which enemies understood each other better than allies. A tactical move by Labienus was misinterpreted as flight. Flight resulted, and Labienus was killed. Of the two Pompey brothers, Gnaeus was overtaken and killed, but Sextus lived to fight another day. Caesar, before his assassination in 44 BC, was planning new eastern conquests, but he could hardly have undertaken them before settling the outstanding account in Spain. With Sextus Pompeius at large, the victory at Munda remained incomplete.

	46			
Caesar's third consulate	Pompeians in Africa defeated at Thapsus	Suicide of Cato	Caesar appointed dictator for 10 years	Caesar adjusts and reforms the calendar: the year 46 BC (708 AUC) contained 445 days

The Centurion

Following the reforms of Marius, centurions ceased to be elected and instead became professional officers. Their importance grew and by Caesar's day they were the men who actually commanded the troops, while the still amateur and youthful tribunes, nominally superior to them, held mainly staff appointments. In imperial times the legion had 59 centurions, comprising five in the 1st cohort and 54 in the remainder. Those of cohorts 2-10 were equal in rank and differed only in seniority. Above these ranked the senior centurions (*primi ordines*) who each commanded a double size century of the first cohort. This arrangement of the 1st cohort (see p 187) probably dates from Caesar's day, since

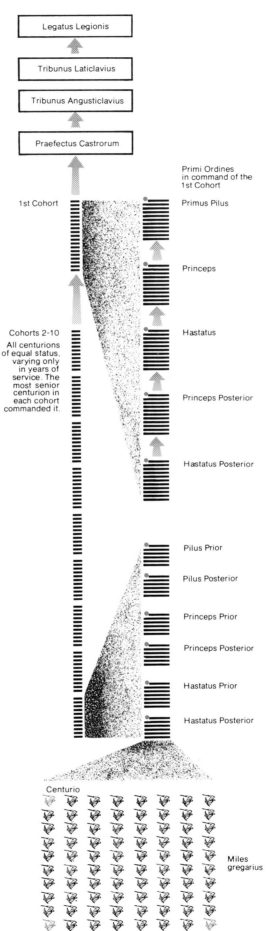

Legatus Legionis

Tribunus Laticlavius

Tribunus Angusticlavius

Praefectus Castrorum

Primi Ordines in command of the 1st Cohort

1st Cohort

Primus Pilus

Princeps

Hastatus

Princeps Posterior

Hastatus Posterior

Cohorts 2-10
All centurions of equal status, varying only in years of service. The most senior centurion in each cohort commanded it.

Pilus Prior

Pilus Posterior

Princeps Prior

Princeps Posterior

Hastatus Prior

Hastatus Posterior

Centurio

Miles gregarius

Tesserarius

Optio
Second-in-command

he mentions a senior centurion leading a double sized century, and often writes of the *primi ordines*. Caesar's respect for his centurions is revealed by his many tales of their courage and leadership. The figure (left) is a centurion of the 1st century AD. With an earlier style of helmet, he would also be typical of Caesar's day. His rank is denoted by his transverse crest which might be of horsehair or feathers as here. His rank is also signified by his vine "swagger stick", which was sometimes used to administer corporal punishment. His armour is of mail or scales, and, unlike the legionaries' was richly decorated and was sometimes silvered. The centurion carried his *gladius* on the opposite side to the legionaries, and in battle carried shield and *pila* like his men.

The Legion's Command Structure
On joining his century as a recruit, having signed on for 20 years (16 in Caesar's time), the *miles gregarius* (common soldier) found himself commanded by a *tesserarius* (guard sergeant), an *optio* (the second-in-command) and his centurion. There were 54 such centurions in cohorts 2-10. The senior centurion in each cohort commanded it since each centurion was of the same rank. As the diagram shows, the designations of each centurion reflected the battle lines of the early Republican legion. Above them ranked the senior centurions of the 1st cohort (*primi ordines*) from *hastatus posterior* up to *primus pilus*. The ordinary soldier might hope to reach the exalted rank of *primus pilus* but it was a rare achievement. The career of Petronius Fortunatus provides a typical example. He joined *Legio I Italica* and was promoted to centurion after 4 years. For the next 42 years he served in 12 different legions but was never promoted to the *primi ordines*. The 3rd-in-command of the whole legion was the camp prefect (*praefectus castrorum*). Above him ranked the tribunes, 5 of whom were tribunes of the equestrian order (*tribuni angusticlavii*) who in earlier times had commanded two cohorts each, but who now held staff appointments, leaving the centurions to lead the men in battle. The other tribune was of the senatorial order (*tribunus laticlavius*) and was a young man who would later command a legion and was serving his "apprenticeship". He acted as second-in-command of the legion. Above him was the legate (*legatus legionis*), a mature senator, usually in his thirties. The legion headquarters also contained an adjutant (*cornicularius*), clerks (*librarii*) and orderlies (*beneficiarii*). Since the legion was self-sufficient, it also included many tradesmen (*immunes*) in its ranks. They are far too numerous to list here, but included surveyors, engineers, armourers, medics, catapult-operators, farriers, architects, smiths, musicians and the like. They were exempt from fatigues and other duties.

The Wars of the Triumvirate

In 44 BC Caesar fell to the daggers of conspirators anxious to preserve the Republic. However, in the power struggle that ensued, culminating in Antony's defeat at Actium, the Republican era ended and Octavian—the future Emperor Augustus—emerged victorious.

Ancient Authorities

The period with which we are now about to deal comprises the years between Julius Caesar's assassination and the battle of Actium in 31 BC. This battle may conveniently be regarded as marking the end of the Roman Republic. Contemporary evidence, such as was available to later ancient historians, derived in an important degree from one of the main military and political protagonists of the epoch. This was the man who had in 63 BC begun life as Gaius Octavius and received (according to normal usage) the name of Gaius Julius Caesar Octavianus (Octavian) when he became the adoptive son of his great-uncle Julius Caesar. After Actium, recognizing in himself a benevolent despot at the head of the Roman imperial establishment, Octavian assumed the title of Augustus (meaning "revered"), and he is generally referred to by this title when the imperial stage of his career is under consideration. He died in AD 14.

Augustus wrote his memoirs, and on these Livy was able to rely. They thus provide material for Dio Cassius, who made use of Livy's now lost books. The relevant portion of Dio's *Roman History* is fortunately extant in complete form. Augustus' memoirs themselves do not survive, but an important official record of his own career, which he wrote for posterity, has been preserved in inscriptions, the best copy being that discovered in 1555 at Ancyra (Ankara). This invaluable record is generally known as the *Res Gestae*.

Contemporary witnesses of events, let alone participants in them, possess an obvious advantage. But to the extent that their personal interests are affected, they are often more biased than historians of subsequent ages. Augustus, even if he had wished, could not afford to be generous to Antony, his defeated rival. Since he was himself not only a writer but the patron of a gifted literary generation which included Virgil, Horace and Livy, he had every means of ensuring that a view of history favourable to himself would be transmitted to posterity.

Above: *Cicero, seen here in civilian dress, was one of the minority of Roman statesmen whose career was not based on military achievement. He was proscribed and eventually put to death at Antony's instigation.*

Fortunately, history was also written by Gaius Asinius Pollio, who had been one of Julius Caesar's officers. In the fighting that followed Caesar's death at the hands of Brutus and Cassius and their fellow conspirators, Pollio had served under Antony. After the victory of Antony and Octavian at Philippi (42 BC), Pollio's intercession on behalf of his fellow poet had prevented Virgil's property from being allocated to one of the veteran soldiers who had defeated the armies of Brutus and Cassius. Even when the victors of Philippi had clashed and Antony's suicide had followed the defeat at Actium, Pollio never wholly acquiesced in the supremacy of Augustus. His view of history tended to correct a more one-sided version which might otherwise have gained exclusive currency. Unfortunately, Pollio's own writings, apart from some letters to Cicero, do not survive. But Appian made considerable use of him, and so did Plutarch in his *Life of Antony*. Plutarch, incidentally, draws on the accounts of some other interesting eye-witnesses, including Quintus Dellius, who served as Antony's officer against the Parthians in 40 BC, and Olympus, who is remembered as Cleopatra's medical adviser.

Other important contemporary evidence is to be derived from Cicero's *Philippics*, a series of fourteen orations in which Antony was bitterly attacked. The title of these speeches invites us to compare them with those directed by Demosthenes against Philip of Macedon. They belong, of course, to the literature of invective and do not pretend to impartiality, but like Cicero's letters written at this time, they shed great light on the politics of the period.

We may also notice among almost contemporary writers the historian Velleius Paterculus, who was born in 19 BC, when Augustus was firmly established in power. Velleius was certainly in no position to be impartial, and he made no attempt to be so.

Further evidence is preserved in Suetonius' *Life of Augustus*. Suetonius had access to many official documents now lost. His pronounced interest in scandal was not associated with any political bias and, writing in the second century, at a comfortable distance from events, he was under no particular pressures. He is not, however, a useful military historian.

Political History

The conspirators by whose swords Caesar died at a meeting of the Senate in 44 BC were old-fashioned constitutionalists. They were extremely stupid men. They could not see that a constitution which needed to be upheld entirely by military force was no constitution. It had been Pompey's weakness that he made too many concessions to constitutional appearances; Caesar was murdered because he made too few. But military power was the only real basis of authority in Rome during the first century BC.

The conspirators were surprised to find that their action was unpopular. Yet Caesar had always been lavish in the pursuit of his political ends—even

Right: *The Triumvirate apportioned Rome's dominions between themselves as shown. The territories granted to Sextus Pompeius in 39 BC were won back from him by force of arms.*

in the days when he had been sustained by loans from Crassus. With the proceeds of world conquest at his disposal, he had been considerably more lavish. Nor did this largesse end with his death, for the terms of his will, apart from other public benefactions, included a cash hand-out to the citizens.

Mark Antony, surviving Caesar's death, made sure that Caesar's will was publicised and assumed the powers of an executor. He was able to do this because Marcus Aemilius Lepidus (whom Caesar in his recently relinquished role of dictator had made Master of the Horse) was available with troops not far from Rome. Antony won the support of Lepidus, and the conspirators, now thoroughly on the defensive, were glad to concede a highly honourable public funeral to Caesar in return for an amnesty.

It is easy, with the advantage of hindsight, to approve the judgment of Cassius, who had urged that Antony as well as Caesar should be killed. But while it could be hoped that the single murder of Caesar would look like tyrannicide, the assassination of both consuls, to a generation which still remembered Sulla, could portend the beginning of new massacres and provoke more opposition than it removed. Brutus was perhaps right about this. Certainly, the skill with which Antony now exploited the situation had not been foreseeable. He had served Caesar well in a military capacity, but his civil administration of Italy during Caesar's absence had done little to make him popular.

At the same time, Caesar's will was a great disappointment to Antony. For it named as principal heir Gaius Octavius, Caesar's great-nephew, now receiving military training in Illyricum* in preparation for Caesar's projected campaign against Parthia. At Caesar's

---

*He had been stationed at Apollonia, the Roman military base, a point of disembarkation on the eastern Adriatic coast, already connected by road (the Via Egnatia) with Thessalonica.

death, the young man, completely without political experience, boldly returned to Italy, and his boldness was rewarded. But even the vast financial resources and the prestigious name of Caesar, conferred on him by the terms of the will, would not have enabled him to survive, let alone predominate, if he had not possessed innate political and military ability. His possession of such ability was something which was unforeseen by Antony, by the conspirators and by Cicero, who, although not one of the assassins, approved their constitutional principles.

The ensuing conflict, which resulted in heavy fighting round Mutina (Modena), wore the aspect of a four-cornered struggle. The non-violent constitutionalists represented by Cicero were already allied with the conspirators, and they enjoyed the temporary support of Octavian, for in 43 BC Antony, who promised to be a more oppressive autocrat than Caesar, grudged Octavian his inheritance and treated him with corresponding cool-

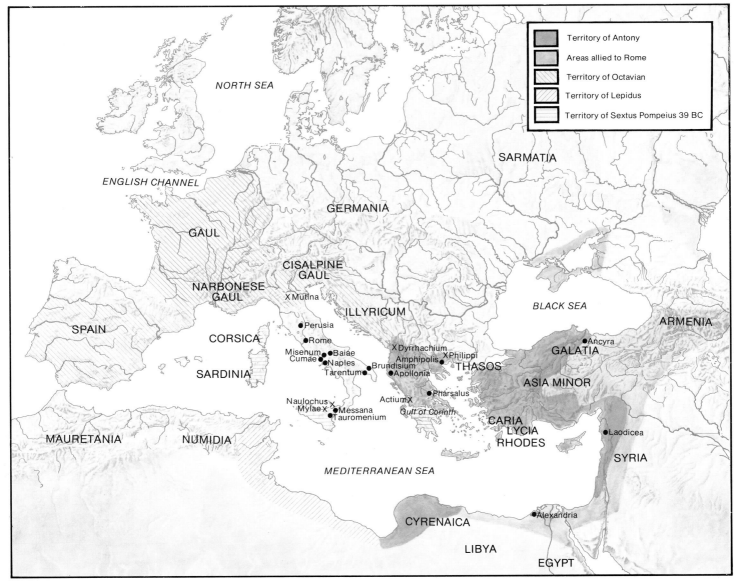

43
Triumvirs established · Quintus Labienus sent by Cassius as ambassador to Parthia · The Mutina campaign · Cassius captures Rhodes

BC

175

Right: *A military portrait statue of Augustus found at Rome. The Emperor wears a metal cuirass. Portrait statues were designated as* loricatae *or* togatae, *depending on whether the subject wore armour or civilian dress.*

ness. However, the future both of Antony and Octavian depended on respect for Caesar's memory, and after the Mutina fighting—in which Antony fared ill and Octavian revealed his powers—the two men were reconciled, to the exclusion of the constitutionalists. Lepidus, now governor of Gaul, wavered but eventually joined them. The triumvirs, as they now became, jointly wielded dictatorial power, and their power was recognized by a formal legal enactment. They were the committee of three, appointed for the establishment of the constitution.

Modern historians sometimes refer to the Triumvirate as the "second triumvirate", regarding the informal agreement of Caesar, Pompey and Crassus as the first. But the authority conferred on Antony, Octavian and Lepidus in 43 BC more closely resembled that enjoyed by Sulla, and they used their authority as Sulla had used his. Their proscriptions (formal outlawry followed by systematic massacre) were singularly cold-blooded. Friends and relatives of each triumvir were ruthlessly sacrificed to the malice, suspicion and self-interest of the others, nor could the goodwill of Octavian protect Cicero from Antony's murderous resentment.

The Mutina Campaign

The strategy and tactics of the Mutina campaign were almost as complicated as its politics. The multi-sided nature of renewed civil strife became evident when Antony had himself appointed to supersede Decimus Brutus, Caesar's old admiral, as governor of Italian Gaul. Decimus had treacherously participated in Caesar's assassination, and he enjoyed the confidence of the Senate. He now refused to hand over his province to Antony. Antony marched against him with those legions whose loyalty he could command and occupied the major towns of the province. Decimus pretended to withdraw southwards towards Rome, but suddenly occupied Mutina and prepared for a siege, killing and salting cattle. His preparations were well advised. Antony blockaded him in Mutina, encircling the city with a rampart and a trench, and maintained this position until Decimus' supplies began to fail.

Meanwhile, the newly-appointed consuls for the year, Hirtius and Pansa, with the Senate's authority marched northward from Rome to raise the siege. Guided by Cicero, the Senate still regarded Caesar's assassins as champions of the constitution. In the circumstances, Cicero was also disposed to accept Octavian as an ally—if only for the reason that he was now in conflict with Antony. Octavian, with loyal Caesarian troops, whom he was able to pay out of his private resources, having received the title of propraetor, accompanied Hirtius. Approaching Mutina, the two commanders found their cavalry involved in skirmishes with Antony's horsemen, who were numerically superior but hindered by a terrain intersected by torrent beds. Pansa, with some veteran legions and raw levies, came to the support of his fellow consul. Octavian's headquarters cohort was sent out to guide and escort him as he approached. However, Pansa's troops, together with their escort, were ambushed by Antony's forces on the road and a fierce battle was fought, for the legions on either side regarded their enemies as traitors. The battle was, in fact, threefold. For the high embankment which carried the road over the marsh made the combatants on one side of it invisible to those on the other, while the headquarters cohorts of Antony and Octavian clashed with each other on the road itself above the opposing forces.

Octavian's cohort was eventually annihilated, and Pansa's veteran legionaries fell back to defend the camp, into which his raw troops, prudently instructed to take no part in the battle, had already retreated. Pansa himself was mortally wounded.

Hirtius now marched eight miles (13 km) from his camp near Mutina with fresh troops and defeated Antony's exhausted men. Night fell, and the dangers presented by the marshes stopped him from pursuing the enemy, while Antony's cavalry extricated many of their lost and wounded comrades. Some of these were placed on the horses' backs, with or without the usual riders. Others hung on to the horses' tails and were led away.

Antony's besieging force still surrounded Mutina. When Hirtius and Octavian seemed about to break through the blockading lines at their weakest point, Antony withdrew two legions from other points on the circumvallation in order to oppose them. But he again had the worst of a battle. Hirtius himself broke through into Antony's field headquarters, where he was killed fighting.

Despite contrary advice from his staff, Antony now raised the siege. He was afraid that with the arrival of enemy forces he might in turn be besieged himself. When he had withdrawn, Decimus Brutus cautiously thanked Octavian from the other side of the river for his action, but Octavian coldly indicated that he had come to oppose Antony, not to help Caesar's murderers. Antony, with great difficulty, made his way northwards to the Alps and found eventually, as he had hoped, an ally in Lepidus, governor in Narbonese Gaul (southern France).

Decimus was confirmed in his command by the Senate, but the troops who had served under him decided otherwise and deserted to Octavian. Decimus' position deteriorated until he was left a mere fugitive. While trying to

escape through wild territory, to join Marcus Brutus in Macedonia, he fell into the hands of a Gallic chief friendly to Antony and was put to death.

Cassius against Rhodes

The Senate showed consistent favour to Caesar's assassins. Having declared Antony a public enemy, it conferred the province of Macedonia, which he had previously regarded as an unacceptable alternative to Italian Gaul, upon Marcus Brutus. Cassius was assigned Syria, with responsibility for making war on Publius Cornelius Dolabella, who had originally secured the consulate left vacant at Caesar's death. Dolabella had, in Rome, favoured the constitutionalists, but in his subsequent provincial appointment he had changed sides and treacherously murdered the governor of Asia, Gaius Trebonius, one of the Ides of March conspirators. Dolabella, soon defeated by Cassius, committed suicide at Laodicea in Syria.

Brutus and Cassius probably did not at first regard war with Antony—let

alone Octavian—as inevitable. But they found it prudent to build up their military and financial position. This involved hostilities against states which would not pay them tribute, and among such states the courageous and highly respectable community of Rhodes was conspicuous. The Rhodians, in fact, resisted Cassius in the same fearless and independent spirit that their ancestors had shown in resisting Demetrius Poliorcetes and Mithridates. Sadly, on this occasion, their heroic resolve was in vain.

Rhodes, like Laodicea, had supported Dolabella, so Cassius had a good prextext for plundering it. The Rhodians hoped to resist his heavy war galleys with lighter ships of their own which employed the old Greek manoeuvres of *diekplus* and broadside ramming. Cassius had been educated at Rhodes and did not underestimate the naval prowess of his enemies. Basing himself on the island of Myndus, off the Carian coast, he carefully prepared his own fleet with its full complement of personnel and trained his crews.

The Rhodians with 33 galleys met Cassius' fleet in the open sea near Myndus. Cassius himself watched the battle from a high point on the shore. At first, the nimble Greek tactics of the Rhodian seamen were effective, but Cassius had the advantage of numbers and was able to surround the Rhodians who, thus confined, soon found it impossible to carry out the manoeuvres on which they had relied. Whether it was a question of ramming or boarding, the heavier Roman ships with their larger complements gained the upper hand. Two Rhodian vessels were captured, together with their crews. Two were rammed and sunk, and the remainder escaped to Rhodes.

Cassius now based himself on the Asiatic mainland. He then embarked troops in transport ships and landed a military force on the island of Rhodes in order that they might attack the city from the land, while he himself sailed against it with 80 ships. The Rhodians again tried to fight at sea, but the numerical odds were too great and, after losing two more ships, their navy was forced into harbour and blockaded. The Roman fleet had carried siege towers, prefabricated in sections; in the event, these proved unnecessary. Cassius, with a picked troop of men, suddenly appeared in the middle of the city, persons unknown having opened the gates to him when it became evident that Rhodes was completely unprepared for a siege.

Cassius put to death 50 of the leading citizens and seized all the gold and silver that he could lay hands on. His naval victory, though it owed much to his prudence and experience, was also the result of superior numbers. The mere fact that the Rhodians had undertaken to fight him with lighter ships meant that heavier galleys were no longer regarded as self-evidently more effective. The use of lighter against heavier vessels was to be vindicated 12 years later at the battle of Actium where Octavian's ships defeated Antony's less manoeuvrable fleet.

Strategy before Philippi

Cassius was ready to proceed against Cleopatra, who had helped Dolabella. She had been established by Caesar with her son in Rome, but returned to Egypt after Caesar's murder. Naturally, she was to be counted among the Caesarians. But before Cassius could launch a punitive expedition against Egypt, he was warned by Brutus, who had, with gentlemanly expressions of regret, been plundering the cities of Lycia (southern Asia Minor), that Antony was preparing an eastward offensive from Brundisium. Brutus and Cassius united their forces and concentrated them on the Gulf of Melas, in the north-east corner of the Aegean, from which point they could best advance through Thrace to meet Antony's expected invasion. The triumvirs

were certainly well advised to seize the initiative. After their savage proscriptions, Brutus and Cassius might have been regarded as deliverers if they had been allowed to land in Italy.

Among the troops now assembled to confront the triumvirs were 19 legions, not all fully up to strength. Most of them had been inherited from official predecessors, though Brutus had taken over one legion from Antony's brother Gaius, whom he had defeated and killed in Macedonia. Accompanying cavalry and auxiliaries included Gauls, Spaniards, Thracians, Illyrians, Parthians, Medes and Arabs; and these were joined by the armies of various allied potentates. Thanks to the methods already described, the two "liberating" generals had ample funds for the maintenance of these forces.

Meanwhile, Cleopatra was contemplating naval aid to Antony. This would

---

The Ballista: (Stone-thrower) This is described in detail by Vitruvius, one of Caesar's experts, who wrote c25 BC. The *ballista* shown is of the most common size—60lb (27kg). In comparison with earlier machines the springs are angled slightly forward within their frame to form a shallow "V". This had the effect of increasing the angle through which the arms could be twisted. This required a more complex frame structure, and was not thought worthwhile

for arrow-firers. The other significant improvement is the use of oval, rather than circular, holes and washers. This allowed more rope to be inserted without necessitating enlargement of the whole machine. The *ballista* is shown at rest. To load it, the slider was pushed forward until the trigger engaged the string and then wound back by the levers, the ratchet preventing the string from flying forward until the desired moment of release.

The Scorpio: (Dart-thrower) This too is described by Vitruvius, and one of the most common size, a three-span machine firing a 27" (67cm) bolt, is shown below left. It incorporates the oval holes and has curved arms to obtain an increased twist (see left). Many bolts from this type of machine survive. They usually have pyramid-shaped heads and 3 wooden or leather flights.

The Cheiroballistra
The next major improvement in catapult design, the introduction of metal frames, came some time before AD 100. They were sturdier than wood and allowed the springs to be wider spread, as well as further increasing the angle of twist. Stone-throwers also came to have metal frames. The springs are encased in bronze cylinders to protect them from the weather. The wider spaced frames also allow easier sighting while the small arch assists aiming. (Modern tests have shown that these machines were impressively accurate.)

Mechanical Efficiency
The diagram (left) shows, top to bottom; a Greek arrow-firer, the *scorpio* and the *cheiroballistra*. It illustrates how improvements brought about an increase in twist, and hence power.

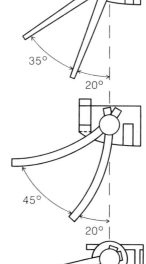

The Ballista c50 BC

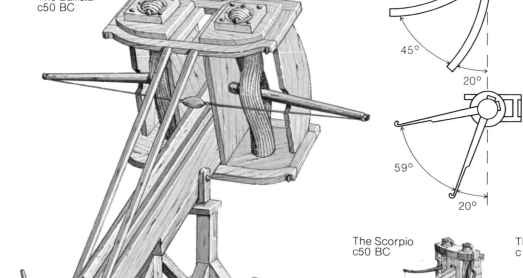

The Scorpio c50 BC

The Cheiroballistra c AD 100

Lucius Antonius surrenders at Perusia

Herod escapes Parthians and takes refuge at Rome

Fulvia, Antony's wife, dies in Greece

Pact of Octavian and Antony at Brundisium: Octavia married to Antony

Lepidus governor in Africa

indeed have been valuable, for the triumvirate was weak at sea. But Cleopatra and her fleet were wrecked on the Libyan coast; she herself returned to Alexandria with great difficulty, feeling very ill. Cassius' commander, who had been lying in wait near the southernmost promontory of the Peloponnese to intercept her, having already employed his time profitably in plundering Greece, now sailed to prevent Antony from crossing the Adriatic. It was not the first time that Antony had faced this particular challenge, having previously ferried reinforcements across the Adriatic, in the teeth of opposition, to support Caesar at Dyrrhachium.

Octavian had been absorbed by naval operations against Sextus Pompeius who, after making a living by piracy during the years that followed Munda, had on Caesar's assassination

been recognized by the Senate as the commander of a Republican fleet. Clashing with Octavian's officer in Sicilian waters, he had the better of some naval fighting. The fleets of the triumvirs, however, were now combined at Brundisium, and they eventually managed to slip across the Adriatic with a strong following wind which enabled the troop transports, under sail, to outstrip the streamlined war-galleys of escorts and enemies alike. They even eluded interception on the return journey and made a second crossing with more troops. Antony and Octavian thus transported 28 legions, out of the total of 43 legions at the disposal of the triumvirate, into Macedonia. Lepidus guarded Italy with the remainder.

At Dyrrhachium, Octavian fell ill. Antony pushed on eastward to face Brutus and Cassius. Food supplies

were his major problem. The wreck of Cleopatra's fleet had left his enemies indisputably in command of the sea, and to make matters worse there had been a failure of crops in Egypt, with resultant famine. It was therefore necessary for Antony to seize what grain-growing areas he could and to force a military decision as soon as possible. He sent an advance guard to hold the mountain passes of Thrace against Brutus and Cassius, thus assuring himself of control over the cornlands farther west.

The purpose of this strategy was not lost on Brutus and Cassius. They sent a naval force along the Thracian coast, outflanking Antony's advance guard and compelling the officer in command of it to abandon his forward positions. They then led their armies through the pass. When a second defile was defended by Antony's force, a friendly

Later Catapults

Constant refinements and technical improvements in Hellenistic times led to significant increases in the range and power of catapults. Agesistratus records that the best of them now had a range in excess of 880 yds (800m). The inventive Greeks also produced a chain-operated "Gatling Gun" catapult but this was not a success, lacking the power of the normal machines.

that were then in operation. Other experiments involved metal springs but these too were failures. The principal catapults used in Roman times are shown here. The major difference between these and the earlier machines (see pp 78-79) is the ratchet-and-pawl system that replaced the straight ratchet formerly used. This can best be seen on the *onager*. All the drawings are to the same scale, to give an idea of the relative size of the machines.

The Onager: (Wild Ass)
This one-armed catapult is mentioned as early as 200 BC by Philon, and again by Apollodorus c AD 100 but was not common until the 4th century AD when it is described by Vegetius and Ammianus. Its principle of operation is similar to a household mouse-trap. The inset drawing shows it fully wound up and at the point of release. The larger illustration shows a 180-lber (80kg). Large machines such as

this were wound up by 8 men. The trigger mechanism can be clearly seen and the bar was normally struck by a hammer to ensure clean release. The machine had to be mounted firmly on an earth or brick platform; it could not be wall-mounted, because of the vibration from its heavy recoil. Compared to 2-armed throwers it is simple to construct, and does not require "tuning", but on the other hand, it cannot be elevated, or trained as easily.

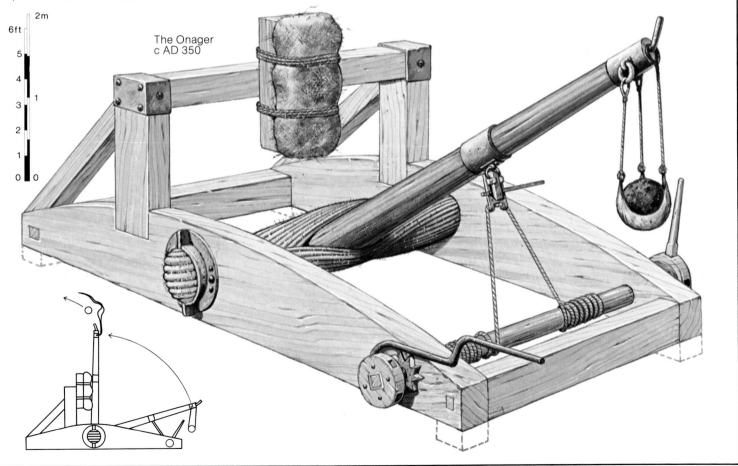

The Onager
c AD 350

39
Antony's Lieutenant
Ventidius repels Labienus
and Pacorus

Death of Labienus

Treaty with Sextus
Pompeius at Misenum

BC

179

Thracian prince showed them a difficult and hazardous way round it. But the prince's brother, who supported the other side, gave warning of the move, and Antony's officer was able to fall back on Amphipolis in Macedonia before he was encircled. The armies of the "liberators" then linked up with their naval squadron and fortified a position not far from the sea at Philippi, within the Macedonian frontier.

Fortifications at Philippi

Antony pushed on in haste to Amphipolis and was extremely glad to find it already occupied by his own advance guard. As September, 42 BC, drew to its close, the supplies of Macedonian and Thessalian corn were limited. Other difficulties apart, Sextus Pompeius with his active fleet would ensure that no grain reached the triumvirs from Spain or Africa. The need for a decisive battle became ever more imperative.

The camps of Brutus and Cassius were about one Roman mile apart, straddling the road to Asia. A trench, rampart and palisade of the usual military type connected the two camps, cutting the road and featuring a central gate through which troops from either camp could issue against the enemy and be deployed in the plain beyond. This plain was flanked by mountains and rocky gorges inland and by marshes southward towards the sea. The pathless mountain area prevented Brutus' camp from being outflanked in the north, and there remained only a short stretch of open terrain between Cassius' camp and the marsh. When Antony approached more quickly than expected and fortified a position only one mile in front of Brutus' and Cassius' camps, Cassius promptly closed the vulnerable gap on his left, so that there was a continuous rampart from marsh to mountains.

Antony's apparent eagerness for battle at a point which was not of his own choosing surprised Brutus and Cassius. But battle was his only hope, even though, at Philippi, tactical as well as strategic factors militated against him. As long as the enemy did not move, he would face the necessity of attacking uphill against extremely strong positions. Nor had the enemy any reason to move. They had secured a well-stocked base on the island of Thasos, not many miles offshore in their rear. Opposite the island, a gulf in the mainland coast offered a convenient

Above: *Octavia, sister of Octavian. She was widely respected and brought up Antony's surviving children by Cleopatra as well as her own family. She died in 11 BC.*

anchorage for their galleys, and a river ran alongside their fortifications, providing an easily accessible water supply. Antony was obliged to find water by digging wells.

When it became clear that Brutus and Cassius, apart from cavalry skirmishing, did not intend to take the initiative, Antony acted with energy and ingenuity. Under cover of the tall swamp reeds, while distracting attention with a show of frontal activity, he built a causeway through the marsh without Cassius' knowledge. Hurrying men along the causeway, he then occupied strong commanding points in Cassius' rear. The latter, however, responded vigorously, building another causeway, fortified by a palisade, through the marsh, more or less at right-angles to Antony's, severing all communications with the strong-points which had been occupied.

In the course of these operations, however, Cassius' forces were necessarily dispersed. Antony suddenly launched a violent attack on the rampart between the camp and the marsh, brought up ladders, filled in ditches, demolished the palisade and overran the position. He then turned on the almost unguarded camp and captured it. Meanwhile, the forces of Brutus, encamped on the northern hill, were presented with an excellent opportunity, for as Antony attacked Cassius, his flank was completely exposed. Without waiting for orders, they charged down from the higher ground, created havoc in Antony's rear, found themselves suddenly face to face with Octavian's legions but routed them also, and went on to seize the camp which had been jointly occupied by the triumvirs' armies.

In the course of these operations, enormous clouds of dust had been raised and the situation was confused. Cassius seems to have thought that Brutus' camp, like his own, had fallen into enemy hands. Certainly, he did not realize that Brutus' men had occupied the enemy camp. Indeed, it is not certain that Brutus himself knew. He never ordered the attack. The suicide of Cassius, which followed, and the exact nature of his misapprehension have been variously explained. One theory current among ancient historians was that he had been murdered by his slave, who contrived to make the act look like suicide.

Both sides now withdrew from the enemy positions which they had occupied, both realizing that their own bases were in danger. Even so, as Appian says, they looked more like porters than soldiers, being intent on carrying off whatever plunder they could. In the swirling dust clouds, friends were indistinguishable from enemies, and Brutus' troops, who had begun the battle without any authorization, may have felt at liberty to terminate it as and when they chose. But when the dust cleared, Antony and Octavian, who, though still in poor health, had arrived in time for the fighting and accompanied his men to the battlefield, were back in their camp. At the same time, Brutus had reoccupied Cassius' lost positions.

The Days of Decision at Philippi

On the day that Cassius met his death at Philippi, his officer commanding the Adriatic naval contingent enjoyed a major success. In an attempt to ferry reinforcements, the triumvirs' commanders at Brundisium tried the experiment of running across under sail once too often. The wind dropped and they were caught. The small escort of warships that had sped them on their way was no match for the enemy's 130 galleys. The troops in the transports, when they saw there was no way of escape, lashed their ships together to provide a fighting platform and prevent single vessels from being isolated. However, the enemy plied them with fire darts and thus obliged them to separate, lest flames should spread from one ship to another. Many eventually surrendered; others drifted in derelict hulks, dying of hunger, thirst and burns.

The news, when it reached Philippi, was obviously a blow to the triumvirs

Octavian blames Sextus for breach of treaty	Sextus gains naval victories over Octavian at Cumae and Messana	Phraates IV becomes king of Parthia after murdering his father Orodes II	Agrippa as governor of Gaul subdues Aquitanian revolt	Defeat and death of Pacorus

and put heart into Brutus, who was now titular commander of Cassius' army as well as his own. He would willingly have continued his static strategy, but his officers, as well as his men, were otherwise inclined. They had already gained one victory without his permission and felt themselves quite capable of repeating the achievement. The triumvirs' men did everything they could to provoke an engagement, approaching close to Brutus' lines and challenging the soldiers with jeers and insults: a naive procedure which was nevertheless often adopted in ancient wars. Apart from this, political warfare was waged and messages were flung across the ramparts, promising rewards to deserters. Brutus retaliated by sporadic night attacks, and on one occasion diverted the river into the enemy camp. But a general engagement was still no part of his plan.

The triumvirs had sent a legion southward into the Peloponnese to forage in Achaea, but their corn supply remained a crucial problem. In their attempts to break the stalemate, they had some minor success. There was a hill close to the camp which Cassius had commanded. But as the hill was within bowshot of the camp, and therefore difficult for an enemy to hold, Brutus now evacuated it. Seeing an opportunity, Octavian promptly occu-

Below: *Trajan's Column shows legionaries receiving medical attention at an advanced dressing station. Once patched up, the wounded would be transferred to a proper field hospital.*

pied the position with four legions, who protected themselves against arrows with screens of wicker and hide. With this strongpoint as a base, it was possible to establish a series of outposts southwards towards the sea, leading perhaps to another outflanking attempt through the marsh. However, against all such possible springboards, Brutus built and garrisoned bastions.

Morale and discipline, meanwhile, especially in the defeated army which Brutus had inherited from Cassius, continued to be bad and tended to worsen as the result of inaction. Under pressure from his staff, Brutus at last consented to fight a pitched battle. He did so with great reluctance, comparing himself to Pompey in a similar situation at Pharsalus. The engagement which followed was not preceded by the usual exchange of javelins, nor was any attempt made at tactical manoeuvre. Fighting closely resembled that of the classical Greek phalanx, except in so far as swords took the place of spears. Appian says that Octavian's legionaries gradually rolled the enemy back as if they were revolving some kind of heavy mechanism. Brutus' infantry at first retreated in good order, step by step; but under relentless pressure, this order was eventually lost. Gaps appeared in the ranks. The front line became intermingled with the rear. Congestion, confusion and full-scale flight resulted. Octavian's men, following instructions, though exposed to missile attack from the ramparts, captured the central gateway in the enemy's fortifications and prevented

any withdrawal by this route. Antony's soldiers hunted down fugitives both in the direction of the sea and the mountains, while Octavian kept watch on the enemy camp, which had not yet fallen into the triumvirs' hands. Brutus himself, having been cut off, retreated northward into the mountains and spent the night there, with less than four legions, hoping to return to his camp under cover of darkness. But his return was blocked by Antony, and his officers and men were too demoralized to attempt a breakthrough. Perceiving that he survived only as the champion of a lost cause, he persuaded a loyal member of his staff to kill him.

After Philippi

Philippi was followed by a redistribution of authority among the triumvirs. Octavian was left in charge of Italy and most of the western provinces, while Antony, though retaining Gaul, undertook to re-establish Roman authority in the East. Lepidus, who had been suspected of collusion with Sextus Pompeius, despite his much diminished role, was eventually permitted to control Africa. With power, Octavian inherited many problems. The claims of veteran soldiers to the land promised them as a reward for service could only be satisfied by the flagrant injustice of evicting present occupants. Moreover, Octavian was naturally concerned to satisfy his own veterans in preference to those of the absent Antony. In these circumstances, Lucius Antonius,

brother of the triumvir, tried to assert his constitutional position as consul and champion the injured parties. Since Lucius was a titular head of state, one can hardly say that he "raised a revolt", but in terms of political and military realities that was what it amounted to. A minor war resulted. Octavian besieged Lucius in Perusia (Perugia) and starved him into surrender. Perusia, reserved by the victor for plunder, was burned down as the result of a fire started by one of its desperate inhabitants. At least, the city qualified more plausibly for enemy status than did those other unoffending Italian territories which had been allocated to victorious troops. But Octavian was still trying to avoid

conflict with Antony. Lucius was consequently pardoned and sent as governor to Spain.

A more serious problem was presented by Sextus Pompeius. The pirate son of a man who had done more than any Roman to suppress piracy, Sextus now occupied and controlled Sicily, where he had been joined by fugitives from Philippi, as well as the Adriatic fleet commanded by Cassius' officers. He was thus in a position to deprive Italy of its overseas corn supply. After the Perusia episode, Mark Antony had himself arrived in Italy, and war between the two triumvirs had narrowly been averted by a treaty made at Brundisium in 40 BC. This was followed in the next year by another

treaty made at Misenum, near Naples, with Sextus Pompeius. According to its terms, Sextus was appointed governor of Sicily, Sardinia, Corsica and Achaea. That was the price of corn for Italy. But the treaty broke down and naval warfare resulted. Octavian was twice defeated in sea battles off Cumae and Messana, though Sextus never assumed an offensive role or made any bid for supreme power.

One secret of Octavian's success was his ability to delegate authority, and he had an outstandingly efficient officer in the person of Marcus Vipsanius Agrippa, who had been his comrade as a young man, while training in Illyricum. Agrippa, who had rendered distinguished service in Gaul

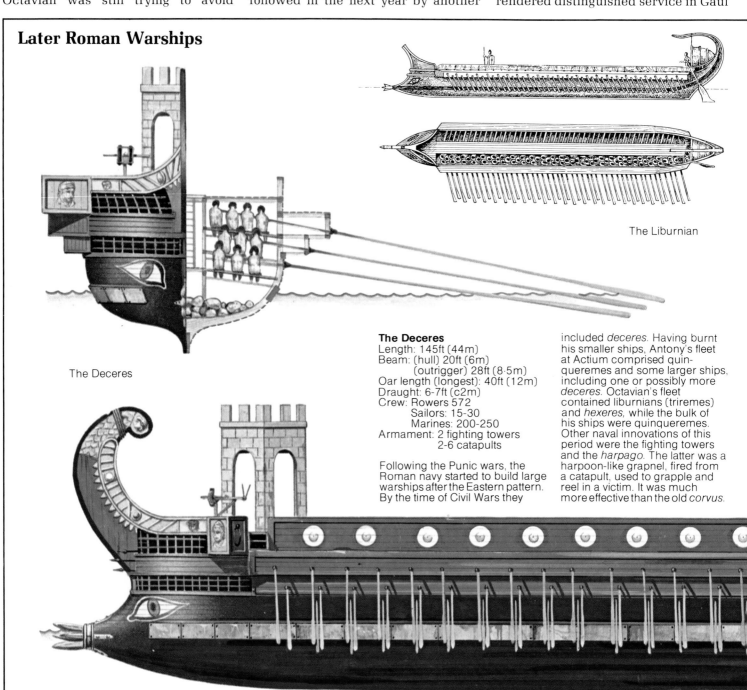

Later Roman Warships

The Liburnian

The Deceres

The Deceres
Length: 145ft (44m)
Beam: (hull) 20ft (6m)
(outrigger) 28ft (8·5m)
Oar length (longest): 40ft (12m)
Draught: 6-7ft (c2m)
Crew: Rowers 572
Sailors: 15-30
Marines: 200-250
Armament: 2 fighting towers
2-6 catapults

Following the Punic wars, the Roman navy started to build large warships after the Eastern pattern. By the time of Civil Wars they

included *deceres*. Having burnt his smaller ships, Antony's fleet at Actium comprised quinqueremes and some larger ships, including one or possibly more *deceres*. Octavian's fleet contained liburnians (triremes) and *hexeres*, while the bulk of his ships were quinqueremes. Other naval innovations of this period were the fighting towers and the *harpago*. The latter was a harpoon-like grapnel, fired from a catapult, used to grapple and reel in a victim. It was much more effective than the old *corvus*.

BC | 36

Antony defeated in Parthia   Sextus Pompeius defeated in naval battles of Mylae and Naulochus   Cleopatra's third child by Antony born (Ptolemy Philadelphus)   Lepidus deposed from triumvirate

182

and contributed to the defeat of Lucius Antonius at Perusia, now proved himself as able on sea as on land. Though Octavian suffered another naval defeat near Tauromenium (Taormina), Agrippa overcame Sextus' fleet at Mylae. This was followed by another victory at Naulochus, which proved decisive. Octavian, by land operations, with the help of Lepidus, had already deprived the enemy of supply centres in Sicily. Sextus fled to Asia, where he was eventually captured and executed at Antony's orders.

Agrippa was noticeably alert to the possibilities of technical innovation. In order to create a suitable naval base for war on Sextus Pompeius, he had cut a canal through the narrow strand which carried the Herculean Way between Baiae and Puteoli, thus linking the inland Lucrine lagoon(*lacus Lucrinus*) with the Bay of Naples. A second canal connected the Lucrine waters with those of Lake Avernus beyond. The combined basins provided a training area in which Octavian's fleet could carry out manoeuvres and tactical exercises whenever they desired.

Sextus Pompeius' success had, throughout this war in Sicilian and southern Italian waters, been dependent very largely on his use of war galleys which were lighter and smaller than those manned by his enemies. As in Cassius' attack on Rhodes, we find evidence that the lighter galley was returning to favour and that the tactics of manoeuvre and ramming were being reintroduced against the heavier ships which provided a basis for grappling and boarding. Strategically, the light ship, with its vulnerability to wind and weather was at a disadvantage. But in localized inshore operations, it often proved its tactical value. Where fighting took place in a choppy sea, the light ship could ride the waves and was more flexible in manoeuvre. Sextus had demonstrated this even before Philippi. If by misadventure his vessels were grappled by the enemy, the crews abandoned ship at once by flinging themselves into the water. They were then picked up by friendly lifeboats, which followed the battle collecting anyone who had abandoned ship.

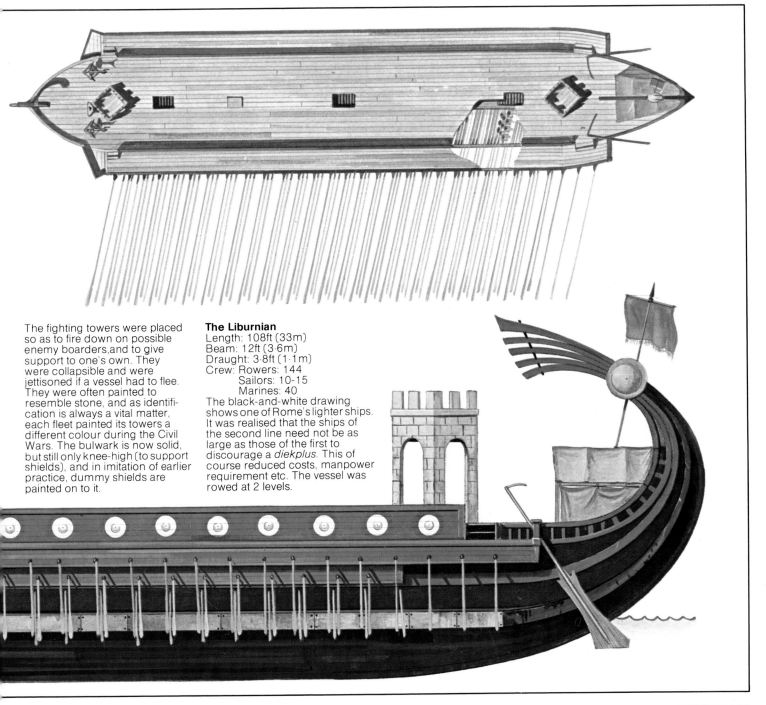

The fighting towers were placed so as to fire down on possible enemy boarders, and to give support to one's own. They were collapsible and were jettisoned if a vessel had to flee. They were often painted to resemble stone, and as identification is always a vital matter, each fleet painted its towers a different colour during the Civil Wars. The bulwark is now solid, but still only knee-high (to support shields), and in imitation of earlier practice, dummy shields are painted on to it.

The Liburnian
Length: 108ft (33m)
Beam: 12ft (3·6m)
Draught: 3·8ft (1·1m)
Crew: Rowers: 144
Sailors: 10-15
Marines: 40
The black-and-white drawing shows one of Rome's lighter ships. It was realised that the ships of the second line need not be as large as those of the first to discourage a *diekplus*. This of course reduced costs, manpower requirement etc. The vessel was rowed at 2 levels.

Admittedly, Agrippa used a new type of harpoon (see pp 182-3) which made it easier to grapple the elusive Pompeians, but it is also apparent that he himself was in part a convert to the tactics of manoeuvre and ramming.

The Parthians Again

In the East, Antony may seem to have had a simpler task than that which awaited Octavian. It was, at least, less invidious to plunder foreign treasuries than to expropriate Italian farmers. But Antony also faced a Roman enemy. Quintus Labienus, the son of Julius Caesar's officer, had taken sides with Brutus and Cassius; before Philippi he had been sent on a mission to the Parthian king to solicit military aid. The events at Philippi had been reported to him while still in Parthia, and he can hardly be blamed for not hastening homeward into a world of which his political enemies had now acquired control. But Quintus Labienus did not remain aloof. He joined the Parthian prince Pacorus in invading Syria, and defeated the Roman provincial governor, who had been one of the officers commanding Antony's advance guard in the Philippi campaign.

The legionaries in Syria showed themselves ready to serve under Labienus' command. With Pacorus, he went on to occupy territories in Asia Minor, but was checked at last by Antony's officer Ventidius and, like Pacorus, met his death in the campaign which followed. These operations are interesting because they show how ineffective the Parthians could be when not fighting on suitable terrain, such as they found in their own country. This is only what one would expect of an army composed almost entirely of cavalry. Labienus, with the troops which had seceded to him, might well have supplied Pacorus with a much needed complement of infantry, but liaison between the Parthians and their Roman allies was bad. In hilly country, the Parthian mounted archers were unable to carry out their characteristic manoeuvres, and even the heavy, mailed lancers were at a disadvantage. Encouraged by memories of success against Crassus, the Parthians charged uphill at Ventidius' legions and were completely routed as a result. Ventidius' victory (39 BC) had come at a time when Antony was still settling his affairs with Octavian and Sextus Pompeius in Italy. But as soon as he returned to the East, feeling a political need for some patriotic military gesture,

Antony planned an offensive war against Parthia, on the pretext of recovering standards and prisoners captured by the enemy during Crassus' ill-starred campaign.

Once more, the Parthians, fighting on their own ground, had the advantage. They employed their traditional tactics, and Antony was forced into a retreat, throughout which the Romans suffered formidable losses, both from sickness and enemy action. Antony himself was much to blame for the costly failure. He had sacrificed too much to the hope of a lightning victory, abandoning, among other valuable siege equipment, an indispensable 80-foot (24m) ram. Admittedly, the lessons of Crassus' ghastly experience were not wholly forgotten. Antony had arranged to take with him a large body of Asiatic cavalry, but the reluctantly allied king of Armenia, who should have provided these troops, deserted him at a critical phase. Antony's Gallic and Spanish

Above: *The head of Quintus Labienus is seen on this coin. Note that he styles himself as "Parthicus".*

horsemen were not competent to deal with the Parthian cavalry. Although the mounted archers were repeatedly driven away, they were seldom overtaken in their flight. Few were captured or killed, and they returned again and again to the attack. Antony's men marched, as Crassus' had done, in square formation, ever ready for action at short notice, and they at last discovered a way of surviving the highly penetrative Parthian arrows. Standing legionaries held their shields in front of others who were kneeling: the overlapping shields gave the necessary protection of double or treble thickness. By feigning dead or wounded, the Romans also sometimes induced their light-armed assailants to fight at close quarters, and this was the only way in which they were able to

inflict appreciable casualties on the enemy. Antony was better prepared for treachery than Crassus had been, and was wise enough to reject the offer of safe conduct across plains which would have provided the horde of Parthian bowmen with ideal conditions. His decision to march by a gruelling mountainous route, which was the only alternative, saved his army.

On the other side, the Parthians themselves had learnt some lessons and, overcoming their ordinary repugnance to a night march, followed up the Romans during the hours of darkness. With feelings of profound relief, Antony and his men at last reached the safe mountainous regions of Armenia. They had recovered no standards or prisoners, but there was reason to be thankful that the enemy had not added to his acquisitions in this respect. The campaign again demonstrated the Parthians' invincibility "at home".

War-Lords and their Womenfolk

The treasure of Egypt had escaped Cassius' "itching palm", for he had been summoned away to meet the triumvirs' armies just when his attentions began to turn towards Alexandria. In 41 BC Antony, aware of this untapped source, reprimanded Cleopatra for her allegedly lukewarm support of the Caesarian cause and summoned her to meet him in Asia Minor. Serving under Julius Caesar, he had known her when a girl. But she had changed since then. Antony spent the winter months with her in Alexandria, indifferent to war, politics or even money.

News of his brother Lucius' ill-judged action in Italy and of the Parthian invasion abetted by Labienus at last caused the triumvir to bestir himself. He set out to confront the Parthians but, on receipt of letters from his wife Fulvia, turned against Italy with 200 ships. Fulvia was a strong-minded woman with a flair for political intrigue. Lucius Antonius had taken up arms in defence of his brother's interests largely at her instigation. By forcing a crisis of this kind, it was said, she hoped also to recall Antony from the embraces of Cleopatra. After Perusia had surrendered amid an elaborate network of circumvallations, Fulvia fled to Greece, where Antony, accepting the current estimates of her motives, met her in no very friendly spirit. She fell ill and died soon after. In the ensuing rapprochement at Brundisium, all concerned were glad to

Agrippa active in Octavian's Illyrian war

Antony annexes Armenia

Antony's donation of all lands formerly ruled by Alexander to Cleopatra and her children

Idumaea (Edom) though encouraged by Cleopatra, fails to gain independence of Herod

Antony	Agrippa/Octavian
	Fleets	
Warships 230	Warships 400
(not all crewed)	
Transports 30/50	
	Marines
Legionaries 20000	
Archers 2000	Legionaries 40000

Antony's supply route from Egypt is cut by Agrippa's naval blockade; Octavian harasses his land supplies. Antony favours a land battle but Octavian will not be provoked. Antony's rowers succumb to disease and starvation and a naval breakout under Sosius fails. Antony pulls all his forces back to the southern promontory and plans for a full scale naval breakout to Egypt where 7 legions are waiting.

1 To take advantage of the prevailing north-westerly winds and clear Leucas Island, Antony must get well out to sea. He embarks with sails stowed, an unusual tactic revealing his intention to run rather than fight to the finish. His 3 squadrons form up in 2 lines with merchant ships, pay chest and Cleopatra following behind. Octavian's ships also form 2 lines and wait, not wishing to be lured inshore.

2 Antony advances at midday, left wing forward hoping to peel back Octavian's line and so open a route south. Octavian backs water to draw him on into open water where superior numbers will tell. The fleets engage and missiles rain down. Agrippa extends his second line north and south, a move which Antony counters by thinning out his centre where his larger ships are holding their own. Antony's flanks are losing but a gap develops in the centre and Cleopatra's squadron bursts through and hoists sail, followed by as many of Antony's ships as can break off (70/80). Antony transfers to a quinquereme and also runs. The rest of his force is surrounded and surrenders, the troops defecting to Octavian.

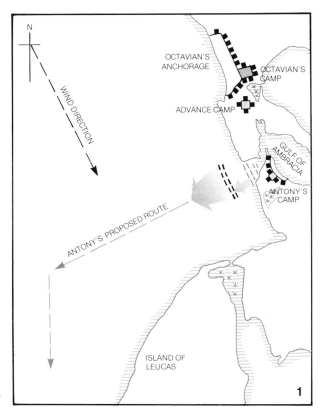

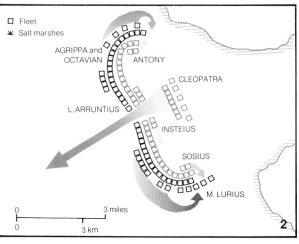

planning yet another eastern offensive to avenge his losses. In addition to her claims as his wife, she brought military equipment, stores and supplies, together with 2,000 magnificently armed legionaries to serve as headquarters troops. To prevent the triumvir from taking this bait, so Plutarch relates, Cleopatra exerted all her charms and wiles. Antony abandoned not only Octavia but his eastern military projects, and returned to Alexandria for another holiday. On the other hand, the contribution which accompanied Octavia may have appeared so inadequate as to explain Antony's disgust and the deferment of his plans.

Octavian was swift to take advantage of the insult offered to his sister. It gave him an honourable pretext for war, though Octavia, on her return to Rome, still maintained her peace-keeping role. But her brother, with his shrewd political insight, now realized that Cleopatra as a foreign enemy was worth more to him than Antony as a Roman friend. By a unilateral decree, he deprived Antony of his position of triumvir. A patriotic war against Cleopatra was the logical outcome.

The Decision at Actium

The inevitable war was destined to be fought at sea, because Cleopatra wished it so. Antony seems to have been, as Octavian proclaimed, a slave to her wishes, and the sea at any rate offered the best prospect of speedy flight in the event of defeat. The armed conflict was preceded by dramatic challenges which emphasize the personal nature of warfare at this epoch. Octavian offered Antony a beachhead in Italy, with space for a camp, in order that a pitched battle might be fought there. Antony replied first with an invitation to single combat, then to a pitched battle at Pharsalus on the site of Julius Caesar's victory. Both these offers were refused by Octavian. He had accepted a similar challenge, defining time and place, from Sextus Pompeius five years earlier and had won the decisive battle which followed. But his fleet now consisted largely of light ships, which he was perhaps reluctant to expose to the hazards of the open sea. In any case, he probably crossed in summer when the weather and the sea conditions were favourable, at a time of his choosing.

It is even possible that Octavian's hesitance to fight in Greece was feigned and that he hoped merely to throw the enemy off his guard. Antony,

blame the dead Fulvia, and a new wife was found for Antony in the person of Octavian's sister, Octavia, a serious and attractive young widow. Naturally, she inherited Cleopatra as a personal and political enemy, and against the Alexandrian liaison Octavia's delicacy availed no more than Fulvia's determination. She bore Antony two daughters, not the great heir to a reign of concord which Virgil in his poem addressed to Pollio had hopefully anticipated. At the same time, Octavia kept peace between her husband and her brother as long as it was possible.

Tension steadily mounted. At Tarentum, in 37 BC, the assembled fleets and armies of the two triumvirs—for Lepidus could now be discounted—confronted each other but, thanks to Octavia, conciliatory negotiations followed and war was once more averted. She arranged that her brother should give Antony two legions for use against the Parthians and receive in return 100 war galleys. As a result of further pleading, she also secured 20 light ships for use by Octavian against Sextus Pompeius, in exchange for another infantry contingent, 1,000 strong, to augment her husband's land forces. Antony then returned to the East, leaving Octavia with her brother to look after his children.

Antony no sooner arrived in Syria than Cleopatra joined him. He flatteringly placed under her dominion a number of Roman protégé territories and officially acknowledged her children by him. After the costly Parthian campaign, Octavia tried once more to meet him in Athens, while he was

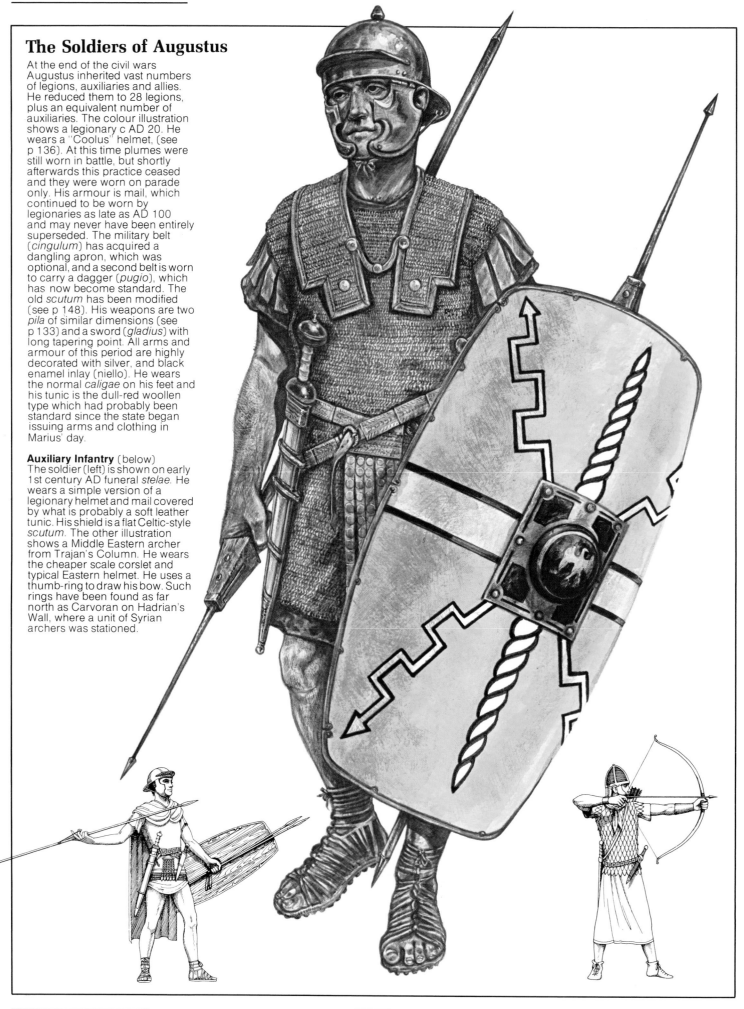

The Soldiers of Augustus

At the end of the civil wars Augustus inherited vast numbers of legions, auxiliaries and allies. He reduced them to 28 legions, plus an equivalent number of auxiliaries. The colour illustration shows a legionary c AD 20. He wears a "Coolus" helmet, (see p 136). At this time plumes were still worn in battle, but shortly afterwards this practice ceased and they were worn on parade only. His armour is mail, which continued to be worn by legionaries as late as AD 100 and may never have been entirely superseded. The military belt (*cingulum*) has acquired a dangling apron, which was optional, and a second belt is worn to carry a dagger (*pugio*), which has now become standard. The old *scutum* has been modified (see p 148). His weapons are two *pila* of similar dimensions (see p 133) and a sword (*gladius*) with long tapering point. All arms and armour of this period are highly decorated with silver, and black enamel inlay (niello). He wears the normal *caligae* on his feet and his tunic is the dull-red woollen type which had probably been standard since the state began issuing arms and clothing in Marius' day.

Auxiliary Infantry (below)
The soldier (left) is shown on early 1st century AD funeral *stelae*. He wears a simple version of a legionary helmet and mail covered by what is probably a soft leather tunic. His shield is a flat Celtic-style *scutum*. The other illustration shows a Middle Eastern archer from Trajan's Column. He wears the cheaper scale corslet and typical Eastern helmet. He uses a thumb-ring to draw his bow. Such rings have been found as far north as Carvoran on Hadrian's Wall, where a unit of Syrian archers was stationed.

poised against Italy, with sea and land forces at Actium on the Ambracian Gulf in North Greece, was certainly taken by surprise when Octavian's armada arrived on the coast of Epirus, not far north of his own position. He was in every sense unprepared. His fleet was not yet manned. As a desperate ruse, he drew his ships up in line of battle and put out the oars, even where there were no rowers to work them. This bluff was effective and Octavian temporarily withdrew.

However, in the strategic manoeuvring and land skirmishing that followed, Antony was unable to shift the enemy from his position, while Octavian's fleet, under Agrippa, gained important vantage points among the Ionian islands and in the Gulf of Corinth, thus cutting off Antony from his sources of supply in the Peloponnese. Morale among his officers and

eastern allies had deteriorated, and among influential deserters to the enemy was Domitius Ahenobarbus, the son of Julius Caesar's officer. But even when the decisive naval battle was imminent, Antony maintained a defensive posture, from which he was drawn only by the threat of encirclement.

Tactics, as well as strategy, reflected a trial of strength between light and heavy ships. Octavian's slender vessels (*liburnae*, as they were called) were able to manoeuvre in groups of three or four around single galleys of Antony's ponderous fleet, exchanging missiles with them; although fear of being grappled and boarded by the swarms of marines which these leviathans carried deterred them from coming too close. In such circumstances, as one might expect, a decision was not quickly reached. But while Antony's flagship on the right was engaged against

Agrippa's squadron, his own centre and left began a mysterious withdrawal. Cleopatra's loss of nerve has been blamed by historians. Her contingent had been anchored in the rear, laden with the treasure on which Antony's war economy largely depended. The Egyptian squadron, taking advantage of a sudden favourable wind, hoisted sail and deserted the scene of the battle. Whatever motives underlay events, Antony certainly followed his mistress in her flight. Most of his fleet, left at the enemy's mercy, in a state of leaderless confusion, was destroyed.

When Octavian invaded Egypt during the following year, Antony and Cleopatra had no prospect of defending themselves. Antony, abandoned by his officers and troops, committed suicide. Cleopatra was captured by Octavian, but contrived to kill herself before she could adorn the conqueror's triumph.

The Early Imperial Legion

The major legionary change since Marius' time was in the size of the first cohort. This now consisted of 5 double-sized centuries, each commanded by a senior centurion. This may have been introduced as early as Caesar's day, since he writes of such a double century at Pharsalus. The legion now consists of 9 cohorts of 480 men and 1 of 800, plus supernumeraries, totalling some 5,200 men. 120 men were drawn from the ranks, and mounted as scouts (*exploratores*) and messengers. Others acted as gunners, since the legion now had 1 *ballista* (stone-thrower) per

cohort and 1 *scorpio* (bolt-thrower) per century, though in practice a total of 50 or so catapults per legion was usual. Earlier armies had siege-trains of catapults but it is not until Caesar's day that they were frequently used in the field. The legion was still recruited from Roman citizens, but by AD 100 most were non-Italians. They were supported by an equal number of auxiliary units (see p 123). The keynote to success was flexibility. Thus a small raid would be contained by the nearest auxiliary cohort. A rebellion such as that of Boudica in AD 60 might be handled by a

legion or two plus their attendant auxiliaries. A punitive campaign such as Corbulo's against the Parthians in AD 59-63 might involve 3-4 legions and a full scale invasion, such as Trajan's attack on Dacia (AD 101) could involve 8-10 legions and 50,000 auxiliaries, cavalry and allies. The total land forces at this time numbered 30 legions plus a similar number of auxiliaries giving 250-300,000 troops. By AD 100 it was unusual for a full legion to take the field. Normally 1 or 2 cohorts were left behind as a fortress garrison. A typical force in order of battle is illustrated.

Cestius Gallus' army against the Jewish Revolt in AD 66:
Legio XII (8 cohorts — c4000)
Legio III (4 cohorts — c2000)
Legio XXII (4 cohorts — c2000)
6 auxiliary cohorts — 4800
4 *Alae quingenariae* (cavalry) — 2000
Allied kings:
Antiochus of Commagene: 2000 horse archers, 3000 bowmen
Agrippa of Judaea: 1,500 horse archers, 3,000 bowmen
Soaemus of Emesa: 1,200 horse archers, 1,500 bowmen and 1,000 javelinmen
This army drawn up as shown would occupy a 2,400yds (2250m) frontage. (Armies of this period were normally drawn up in 2 lines. Sometimes the front line would be auxiliaries, with the legions in a single line of cohorts behind).

Maniple

Double century of 1st cohort

1st cohort

Legion

Cohort

Horse archers Cavalry 3 auxiliary cohorts 8 cohorts of Legio XII 4 cohorts of Legio III 4 cohorts of Legio XXII 3 auxiliary cohorts Cavalry Horse archers

Light infantry, archers and javelinmen

Octavian invades Egypt: suicide of Antony

Octavian's entry into Alexandria: suicide of Cleopatra

Antony's eldest son (by Fulvia) executed on Octavian's orders

Caesarion (Ptolemy Caesar) executed by Octavian

The Military Task of Imperial Rome

Under the rule of Augustus the Empire achieved relative stability, but the weakness of some Imperial successors led to the emergence of pretenders supported by provincial armies. In the early centuries AD, Roman military power both preserved the Empire—and divided it.

Ancient Authorities

For the early part of the long period which we are now considering, many writers already mentioned provide valuable testimony. Indeed, they often have greater value to the extent that they are dealing with subject matter nearer to their own times.

The system of imperial government inaugurated by Augustus (as Octavian called himself from 27 BC onwards) meant that strict impartiality could be a dangerous virtue in a historian of contemporary events. On the other hand, emperors were often happy to be compared with their predecessors to the detriment of the latter. Handsome tribute to the Emperor Nerva thus provided Tacitus with a pretext for unflattering portraits of earlier emperors —an indirect outlet for his Republican sentiments. Such sentiments were common among the literary men of his time. Virgil, Horace and Livy had cherished no illusions.

Cornelius Tacitus was born about AD 56. The exact date of his death is unknown, but he was consul in 97 and proconsul in 112-113. Coming from one who held high administrative posts, his evidence on contemporary events is naturally of historical importance. Tacitus' two major works, which have partly survived on the basis of tenuous manuscript tradition, are known as the *Histories* (probably covering in their complete form the period AD 69-96) and the *Annals,* which must originally have spanned the whole period from the death of Augustus in AD 14 to that of Nero in 68. Of the *Histories,* the first four books and part of a fifth are extant. Of the 16 books of the *Annals* which evidently existed, Books VII-X are lost, while V, VI and XVI are incomplete.

Tacitus also wrote a monograph on Germany and the German peoples, an ethnic study tinged with admiration for primitive virtues. But more important for our theme is his *Agricola.* Gnaeus Julius Agricola enjoyed a distinguished military and administrative career in

Above: *Dacians of the lower Danube surrender to Rome (from Trajan's Column). Under their king Decebalus they posed a threat to the empire until subdued by Trajan.*

Britain, having served as tribune in the army of Suetonius Paulinus, who crushed the revolt of Boadicea (Boudica) in AD 60. It is fortunate for students of history that Tacitus was Agricola's son-in-law.

Contemporary with Tacitus, there lived a remarkable historian with a very different background. Flavius Josephus, born AD 37, was a patriotic Jew who, though opposed in principle to the act of rebellion, himself commanded Jewish resistance forces against the future Emperor Vespasian in AD 67. When captured, he was first spared, then patronized by Vespasian, whose rise to imperial power (in AD 69) he had happily prophesied. Apart from an account of the war in which himself was involved, preceded as it is by a lengthy introduction, Josephus wrote, originally in Aramaic and available to us in its Greek edition, the history of his own country. He began his history with the creation of the world and tried to place Biblical and Graeco-Roman history in context with each other. In this endeavour, he was later followed by Christian writers like Eusebius,

Bishop of Caesarea in 313, whose *Ecclesiastical History* and *Chronicon* contain matter which adds to our knowledge of the Roman Empire in the first three centuries AD.

The historians Zosimus and Aurelius Victor wrote after the adoption of Christianity as an imperial religion, but they are pagan in outlook and sympathy. Although their authority, particularly that of Zosimus, for fourth-century events is more valuable, we owe to them summary accounts of the pre-Christian Empire: notably the resurgence of Roman military strength under Claudius Gothicus and Aurelian.

The autocratic system of government naturally led to the equation of history with imperial biography. Unfortunately, for many periods during the third century, we are obliged to rely heavily on the *Historia Augusta*, a name given by the French scholar Isaac Casaubon

BC ⌐ 27
Octavian assumes title of Augustus

*749 AUC
Death of Herod the Great, shortly after Birth of Christ

*753 AUC
Beginning of Christian era according to accepted chronology

* = From The Foundation of Rome (Anno Urbis Conditae)

9AD
Roman legions under Varus meet disaster in Germany

In China, power of Han emperors temporarily usurped

188

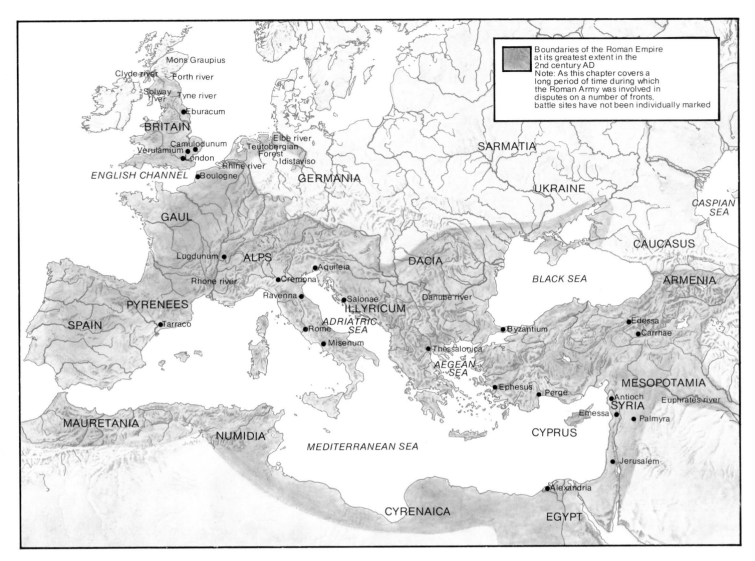

Above: *The Roman Empire at the time of Trajan's death in AD 117—a high-water mark. At no time did Rome simultaneously dominate all the territories that she conquered.*

(1559-1614) to a collection of Roman imperial biographies relating to the years between 117 and 218. The six historians who contribute to this record are uncritical in their approach, and the documents on which they purport to base themselves are often to be considered suspect.

In prefacing a chapter which concerns itself at last with events AD, it is perhaps pertinent here to notice a chronological anomaly. Herod, the Idumaean (Edomite) king, whom Mark Antony, after the Parthian invasion of Syria and Palestine, established as ruler of Judaea, died 749 years after the foundation of Rome. In the sixth century, the Christian abbot Dionysius Exiguus assigned the birth of Christ to the 753rd year after the foundation of Rome; and the years of our era are numbered on the assumption that he was correct. However, the gospels make it plain that Christ was born shortly before the death of Herod, in 4 BC (or slightly earlier) according to the accepted Dionysian reckoning.

Political and Military Considerations

Augustus was able to establish the authoritarian regime on which Roman maintenance of widespread law and order depended, largely because he had assumed power while young and lived to be nearly 77 years old. Longevity is at any time a matter of some luck. In Roman political circles, whether of the Republican or Imperial epoch, it was a matter of great luck. The unity and continuity provided by a single head of state, exercising uninterrupted power for 44 years, was in fact fortunate for the whole Roman world.

Augustus never contemplated abolishing the time-honoured magistracies of the Republic. He simply assumed all the key titles himself: consul, tribune, proconsul and, after the death of his old triumviral colleague Lepidus, *Pontifex Maximus* (Supreme Pontiff). He called himself *Princeps*—a word which in its most general sense meant "leading man". This was in addition to his other constitutional title of *princeps senatus* or "leading senator". He presided over an exhausted world, which had reluctantly realized that law and order can be worth more than liberty, and that authority was destined in the foreseeable future to be based on military power, whatever constitutional forms were adopted. Julius Caesar had shown more respect for constitutional appearances in his last years, as a dictator, than in his early years as a demagogue. It may have been memories of his early career rather than the conduct of his late life that exacerbated Republican sentiment and brought about his murder. Augustus was at all events at great pains to preserve the outward forms of a constitution.

The real source of his power was not merely the army, which now accepted his unrivalled supremacy. From the days which had immediately followed his great-uncle's death, he had realized

14	21	25	37	41	AD
Death of Augustus and accession of Tiberius	Revolt of Sacrovir in Gaul	In China, restoration of the Han dynasty	Death of Tiberius: Gaius (Caligula) becomes emperor	Caligula assassinated: Claudius proclaimed emperor	

189

and were each commanded by a tribune. In practice, their political significance became comparable to that of the Praetorians, though they were not paid so highly.

In addition, there were seven cohorts called *cohortes vigilum,* who served as firemen and night police. Other troops regularly stationed in Italy were the marines at the naval bases of Misenum and Ravenna. These contingents were sometimes used for fatigue and pioneer duties in support of the army or in aid of public works.

The Frontiers of Empire

The Roman navy, at such times as it could be said to exist at all, was always the junior service. However, Augustus was at pains to maintain it, for he needed to preserve lines of communication between Italy and the provinces. Of no small account were the naval forces whose allegiances had been transferred to him after the defeat of Antony and Cleopatra, and he was able to establish fleets in the eastern and western Mediterranean and in the Black Sea. Other naval squadrons operated on the Danube, the Rhine and in the English Channel. Campaigns in Illyricum, under Augustus' destined successor, Tiberius, had safeguarded the route to the east by the *Via Egnatia* and Thessalonica, and the freedom of the Adriatic from pirates was further assured by the construction of the naval base at Ravenna. The Mediterranean in general was well policed under Augustus, and his was the last Roman administration to take effective measures against piracy.

Preoccupation with sea routes was the logical accompaniment of provincial road-building which proceeded under the Empire. Italy in the time of the Republic had acquired a good road system. Apart from that, the *Via Egnatia,* referred to above, and the *Via Domitia,* which led from the Rhône to the Pyrenees, were also Republican achievements. In Augustus' time, new Alpine roads were made and communications facilitated with the Danube. The characteristically straight Roman roads, adhering where possible to high ground, were planned to satisfy military requirements. But at the same time, of course, they opened the way to trade and assisted official contacts.

the political importance of finance. After Philippi, lack of funds had considerably embarrassed him, but with the downfall of Cleopatra, the vast treasury of Egypt, which for different reasons Cassius and Antony had both failed to commandeer, was at his disposal. His "privy purse" (*fiscus*) was administered separately from the Roman state treasury (*aerarium*), but in practice he controlled both funds. Similarly, there was a distinction between imperial and constitutional procedure in provincial administration. The outlying frontier provinces, in which the Roman legions were stationed, were more obviously under command of the emperor; in home territories, where war was not expected, administration was more apparently civil and senatorial.

If we wish to stress the constitutional aspect of Augustus' rule, we may refer to it as the Principate, but the term Empire is that which has best survived in history, the word "emperor" being derived from *imperator,* the title by which a victorious general had normally been acclaimed by the celebrating populace in the later days of the Republic.

Apart from the legions in military provinces at the circumference of the Roman world, it was important to the emperors that they should be able to rely on a nucleus of armed strength at the centre. The Republican general's unit of headquarter troops, the praetorian cohort, developed in Imperial times into the Praetorian Guard, a privileged *corps d'élite.* The Guard, quartered in the vicinity of the city, was originally composed of nine cohorts, each probably 1,000 strong, and included both infantry and cavalry elements. These served as a bodyguard to the emperors.

In 2 BC, two officers (*praefecti*) were appointed to command the praetorian cohorts, and as praetorian prefect, Sejanus (Lucius Aelius Seianus), the adviser of Tiberius, Augustus' successor, attained dangerous power. Later, the Praetorians realized only too well the extent of the emperors' reliance on them. They became makers and breakers of emperors.

Three urban cohorts were also created for police purposes in the city. They served under their own prefect

AD	54	60	68	69	70
	Death of Claudius: accession of Nero	Revolt of Boudica (Boadicea)	Suicide of Nero: Galba becomes emperor	The year of the four emperors: accession of Vespasian	Capture of Jerusalem by Romans under Titus

1st Century AD Legionary

A common soldier of c AD 75-100 is shown here. His helmet is of the type known as "Imperial-Gallic" and his armour is of the segmented style which came into service around AD 30-40. The *scutum* now has straight sides. The design is one of those shown on Trajan's Column, and is probably that of a Praetorian guard cohort. The two *pila* are of the weighted variety introduced before AD 80. The *gladius* has been slightly modified and now has parallel sides and a short point. The conventional woollen tunic and *caligae* are worn, together with a scarf to prevent the neckplates chafing. Scarves quickly became fashionable with the auxiliaries, even though they wore mail armour, not the plated sort. The *cingulum* is still worn, but the belt fittings are now less elaborate. This trend towards simplification was to continue in the second century, with decorated studs disappearing, the *cingulum* growing shorter, and eventually being replaced by *pteruges* and the armour becoming simpler. The legionaries also began to wear breeches beneath their tunics like the auxiliaries. The figure is shown wearing the early type of segmented armour, with elaborate bronze hinges and strap-and-buckle fastenings.

Lorica Segmentata (above)
The drawing shows the simpler "Newstead" type of armour in use from c AD 75-80. The bronze hinges have been replaced by simple rivets, and the belt-and-buckle fastenings by strong hooks. The bottom two girdle plates have been replaced by one wide plate. The individual plates, held together by internal leather straps can be clearly seen. The inset shows the front fastenings in detail. This type of armour was worn until the third century AD or later. It must be emphasised that obsolescence as we know it did not exist in ancient times and earlier styles of armour also remained in service in parallel with this type.

The legions which in the first century AD extended and, later, defended the frontiers of the Empire were distinguished by names and numbers, though some of the numbers were duplicated. The names commemorated the patrons or creators of the legions, as for example the *Legio Augusta,* or else they referred to some event in regimental history, or marked a local connection, as in *Macedonica* or *Gallica.* Augustus' army originally contained 28 legions. But three of these were annihilated in the great Roman military disaster of AD 9, when Augustus' general, Publius Quinctilius Varus, was treacherously ambushed by the German chief Arminius in the Teutoburgian Forest. The numbers of these three ill-starred legions were as a consequence never allotted to Roman legions at a later date.

A Roman governor, in charge of an imperial province, ordinarily ranked as a *legatus* of the emperor. Legions apart, auxiliary troops including cavalry contingents were an important element in the garrison of a province. Under Augustus, auxiliaries, which during the first century BC had been composed of foreign troops, once more began to recruit Roman citizens. This was in part because Roman citizenship itself had by now been conferred on many communities and individuals

Above: *The Emperor Claudius. At first considered weak-minded, he showed great ability as a military administrator and empire builder.*

outside Italy. The social distinction being lost, auxiliaries tended to be integrated with legions. In permanent frontier stations auxiliary cavalry and infantry were posted at first from distant provinces. But as a matter of convenience, auxiliaries came to be recruited locally and the distinction between the legionaries and *auxilia*

was accordingly once more obscured. However, military policy favoured independent cavalry tactics. From the reign of Trajan onwards, tribal non-Romanised units, known as *numeri,* were recruited; their role corresponded in some ways to that of *auxilia* in more ancient times.

The disaster which the Romans suffered in Germany under Varus was the result of an attempt to establish frontiers farther east, on the Elbe. Its effect was that Roman emperors were from that time onward content, as Julius Caesar had been, to rely on punitive and retaliatory action in order to assert a Roman presence on the Rhine. Augustus himself, at the end of his life, made it quite clear that his territorial ambitions were not unlimited. Defence, however, often entails offensive initiative, and he had been at great pains to secure the line of the Danube.

The most suitable location of frontiers was a question which left room for uncertainty, above all in the reign of an emperor of unbalanced mind, such as Gaius (Caligula) proved to be. His inexplicable vacillations could well have been damaging to Roman prestige, and the expansionist policies of the mild-mannered Claudius, who succeeded him, may have been necessary to ensure that enemies

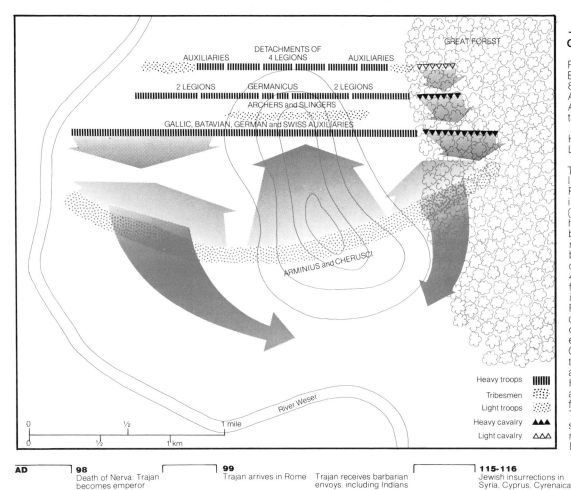

Battle of Idistaviso AD 16

Germanicus	Arminius
Infantry	
Praetorian 1000	German tribes-
Elements of	men 40/50000
8 legions c 28000	(includes some
Auxiliaries 30000	light javelin
Allied German	armed horse)
tribesmen 4/6000	
Cavalry	
Heavy 6000	See above
Light 1/2000 (horse-archers)	

The two armies draw battle lines just north of the Weser River. The German right extends into a forest, the centre (Cherusci tribe) is on the heights, the left holds the plain by the river. The auxiliaries man the Roman front supported by light troops. The second line comprises the Praetorians and 4 legions, the remaining troops form the third line while the cavalry is on the open flank. The Romans advance and the German centre charges. Germanicus orders his cavalry to turn into enemy's rear and flank. The Germans' charge only carries in the very centre where it penetrates almost to the line of bowmen. However the two German wings are in flight in contrary directions: from the river to the trees and vv. The centre is dislodged from the slopes and a general rout ensues; many killed. Arminius escapes. Romans fall back to Rhine.

Map labels: GREAT FOREST · DETACHMENTS OF 4 LEGIONS · AUXILIARIES · AUXILIARIES · 2 LEGIONS · GERMANICUS · 2 LEGIONS · ARCHERS and SLINGERS · GALLIC, BATAVIAN, GERMAN and SWISS AUXILIARIES · ARMINIUS and CHERUSCI · River Weser

Heavy troops	‖‖‖
Tribesmen	░
Light troops	░
Heavy cavalry	▲▲▲
Light cavalry	△△△

Auxiliaries of the Early Empire

As the Empire's expansion slowed and permanent borders were established, a new strategy was formulated to secure the frontiers. To the auxiliaries fell the tasks of patrolling, containing raids, and the multitudinous duties of frontier troops. (The legions were stationed within the frontiers, both to act as a strategic reserve and to intimidate potentially rebellious provinces.) The auxiliaries were organised into cohorts of infantry, *alae* (wings) of cavalry and mixed cohorts of infantry and cavalry. The infantry consisted of six centuries (80 × 6 = 480) plus officers and other supernumeraries giving a nominal 500: hence the name *cohors quingenaria*. Others consisted of ten centuries and were called *cohors milliaria* . The cavalry were similarly established as *quingenaria* and *milliaria* units, the former of sixteen *turmae* (16 × 32 = 512) plus officers and supernumeraries, the latter of twenty-four *turmae*. Some uncertainty exists over the organisation of the mixed cohorts (*cohortes equitatae*) but a likely composition was 480 infantry plus 128 cavalry (four *turmae*) and 800 infantry plus 256 cavalry for *quingenaria* and *milliaria* units respectively. In battle, the mounted portions were brigaded with the cavalry. They can be considered the counterpart of later dragoons since they were not as well mounted, nor as richly equipped as troopers of the *alae*.

Auxiliary Cavalryman (right)
This figure dates from c AD 100. He is shown equipped with the latest pattern of helmet with cruciform reinforcements on the skull. His armour is of mail, but scale armour was also worn. An oval flat shield completes his defensive equipment. His weapons are a long sword (*spatha*) derived from Celtic types, and a light spear (*lancea*) suitable for throwing or thrusting over-arm (Roman cavalry did not normally couch their spears under-arm). The historian Josephus also mentions a quiver of darts (light javelins) attached to the saddle. This is confirmed by Arrian who describes cavalry exercises in which up to twenty darts were discharged in one run.

Auxiliary Infanty (below)
The drawing (**1**) shows the normal auxiliary equipment: flat oval shield, two *lanceae* and *gladius*. **2** is a Spanish soldier of a *cohors Hispanorum scutata* with *scutum*. Both are c AD 100. **3** shows a Swiss auxiliary of a *cohors gaesatorum Raetorum* in winter dress c AD 250. He wears scale armour and carries the heavy javelin (*gaesum*) from which the unit's name derived, and the *spatha* which began to replace the *gladius* in infantry units at about this time.

1   2   3

beyond the frontier were left with no illusions about the reality of Roman strength. Claudius, in need of a military reputation, added first Mauretania, then Britain to the Empire. Roman domination was carried farther by Trajan, who annexed Armenia and temporarily occupied much of Parthia. Rome, however, was never able to impose itself finally on the Parthians.

Armed Insurrections

Apart from frontier fighting, Roman forces were on various occasions during the first century called upon to deal with local rebellions. Information at our disposal is often meagre, but such insurrections seem to have been variously motivated. It is not always easy to distinguish between local grievances and national aspirations of the peoples involved.

Rebellion might naturally be expected in a recently subdued province such as Britain. The tribe of the Catuvellauni, perhaps subjects of the Cassivellaunus dynasty which had confronted Julius Caesar, had by now extended its sway over south-east Britain. A refugee British prince, seeking aid against his father Cunobelinus (Cymbeline) had given the Emperor Gaius pretext for an invasion, but Gaius contented himself with a military demonstration on the Channel coast of Gaul and proclaimed a conquest. When a similar opportunity presented itself to the succeeding Emperor Claudius, it was taken in earnest. Caratacus*, the British prince with whom the Romans now had to contend, was defeated. He took refuge with Cartimandua, a northern British queen, who was a Roman ally, but she betrayed him and he was sent with his family as a captive to Rome. Claudius magnanimously spared his life.

Boadicea (Boudica), who revolted in the year 60, was not a member of the Cassivellaunus dynasty, but had been left queen of the Iceni at the death of her husband. The harsh and humiliating treatment of Roman administrators drove her to take up arms. The governor of Britain, Gaius Suetonius Paulinus, who had played a prominent part in the conquest of Mauretania nearly 20 years earlier, hurried back from the uncivilized regions of north-west Wales where he had been operating, and Boudica's

*The form Caractacus rests on poor authority.

Above: *Trajan's name was revered by later generations, but his victories over the Parthians were expensive and inconclusive.*

defeat and suicide followed. Meanwhile, however, Camulodunum (Colchester), London and Verulamium (St Albans) had been sacked with a massive death toll among the Romans and their British adherents.

Gnaeus Julius Agricola—even allowing for the fact that Tacitus was his son-in-law—must have been an able and energetic administrator. He had served under Paulinus in Britain, and

in other parts of the Empire as well, before his appointment as governor in 78. His military operations did much to secure Roman rule in Britain. Tacitus would have been a better military historian if he had paid closer attention to geography. He probably had no precise idea himself as to where the battle of Mons Graupius was fought or where the river Tanaus was. We are left to guess that the former site was somewhere in Scotland, and the Tanaus has been identified variously as the Tyne, Tweed, Tay or even Solway. Fortunately, archaeology has come to our aid in the tracing of Agricola's movements. At all events, he carried his victorious campaigns into the Scottish Highlands. As a demonstration of strength, he circumnavigated the whole island of Britain, and his military successes were accompanied by wise administration.

The conflict with Boudica may be traced in part to extortionate Roman financial practices: such in fact as had, under the Republic, rendered the eastern Mediterranean world sympathetic to Mithridates. Roman rapacity was a recurrent source of trouble and had in AD 21 led to a notable insurrection in Gaul, led by Julius Sacrovir. Sacrovir was a Romanized Gallic noble of the tribe of the Aedui, Julius Caesar's old allies. He was eventually defeated by the Roman

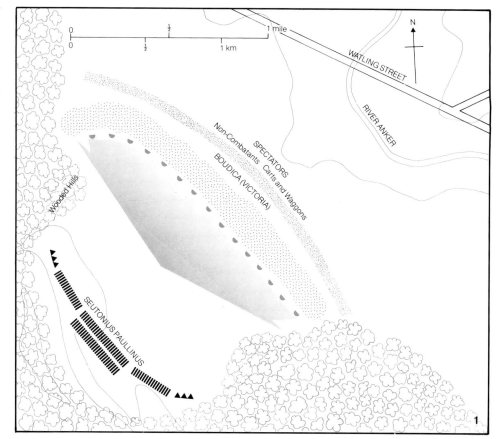

governor of the upper Rhine province (*Germania Superior*) and committed suicide. But the same record of local misgovernment continued to explain revolt. Administrators like Agricola were the exception rather than the rule. Later in the century (89), an upper Rhine governor himself, Lucius Antonius Saturninus, raised an insurrection and caused the Emperor Domitian to set out in alarm on a northwards expedition. The governor of the lower Rhine, however, remained loyal to the Emperor and Saturninus was defeated and killed, his eastward German allies having been prevented, apparently by a sudden thaw, from crossing the frozen river. The precise occasion of this revolt is uncertain, but again one would guess that finance lay at the heart of the matter.

Among serious rebellions that occurred in the first century of imperial history was the Jewish War, in which Josephus was involved. This was the product not only of economic causes but of outraged religious susceptibilities. The Romans were in general tolerant of religion, but did not know how to deal with religions which were themselves intolerant (as Judaism and Christianity were). The violence did not end when, after a horrifying siege, Jerusalem fell (AD 70) to the future Emperor Titus. Its total destruction, accompanied by appalling loss of life, provoked a series of revolts by Jewish populations in other provinces, which culminated (115-116) in insurrections throughout Syria, Cyprus, Egypt and Cyrenaica. Casualties are reported as running into hundreds of thousands. These events in turn led ultimately to repercussions in Palestine. Of Bar Kokhba's revolt, something has been learnt in recent years from the literature of the Dead Sea caves.

The Events of AD 69

Insurrections during the first century of imperial government suggest that there was often enough provincial discontent to provide ambitious leaders with a cause. They also show that there was sufficient military ability available to provide aggrieved communities with effective leadership. This was all the more inevitable in view of the fusion between Roman and local elements in the army. Sacrovir and Saturninus, and even Arminius, the destroyer of Varus' legions, were or had been Roman officers. It was only a matter of time before provincial rebellions could aim at the overthrow of the emperor himself and at the transfer of his power into hands of the rebels' choosing.

The events of the year 69 can be described more accurately in terms of civil war than of revolt, but they are the logical outcome of military and political precedents. A rebellious Romanized Gallic governor (Julius Vindex) had been defeated and killed by troops from the adjacent upper Rhine province. However, Sulpicius Galba, whose specious claims to restore the Republic he had supported, was in command of legions in Spain, and when the Praetorians at Rome proclaimed Galba as emperor, Nero, last of Augustus' dynasty, tearfully committed suicide. Galba was soon installed at Rome, but his nomination of a successor disappointed one of his military adherents, Marcus Salvius Otho, who now conspired with the Praetorian Guard. Nor did Otho long enjoy the fruits of Galba's murder, for a secret, as Tacitus observes, had been revealed by Galba's shortlived success: emperors could be created elsewhere than in Rome. Even the encouragement of the Praetorians was no longer necessary.

Otho was challenged by Aulus Vitellius, a Rhine commander. The legions of the eastern and Danube frontiers apparently supported Otho. But even if the eastern support had been sincere, it was distant, and the Danube troops were slow to move. Vitellius' officers won the crucial battle for him near Cremona, and he himself, after Otho's suicide, travelled to Rome at his convenience. The eastern legions, however, now showed their hand and proclaimed as emperor the 60-year-old general Vespasian (Titus Flavius Vespasianus). Vespasian was in a position to block the Alexandrian corn supply. But apart from that, the Danube troops favoured him. Italy was invaded. Fighting again converged on Cremona. Vitellius was prevented by his own supporters from coming to terms with Vespasian's brother in Rome, and the latter was killed in the fighting which followed. However, the victors of Cremona soon arrived at Rome. Vitellius was hunted down and dragged to his wretched death.

Vitellius had disbanded the Praetorian Guard and replaced them with Rhineland legionaries of his own. As such, they naturally supported him, but they were unable to resist the wrath of the invading provincial legions. The situation in which the legions of one province were not in accord with those of another may from this time on be regarded as familiar. To all appearances, conditions which had prevailed in the last century of the Republic had now been recreated. Until Nero's death, dynastic prestige

---

Boudica's Revolt AD 60

Romans	Boudica
Infantry	
Legionaries 5/6000	40/60000
Auxiliaries 4000	(tribesmen)
Cavalry	
1000	Unknown number
(2 *alae*)	of chariots

General situation Boudica has raised a revolt against the Roman occupying force. After sacking Camulodunum, Verulamium and Londinium, her troops move north-west along Watling Street.
1 The governor, Suetonius Paulinus, positions a hastily gathered force in a strong defensive position — a defile with wooded hills protecting the flanks and rear. The Britons, thinking an easy victory is imminent, bring their non-combatant families to watch from a large semi-circle of wagons. The Britons hurl themselves into the narrowing defile but are met by a rain of *pila* and a Roman charge — the legionaries adopting a series of wedge formations.
2 The Roman wedges compress the Britons too tightly to use their weapons. Pushed back, they are hampered by the spectators and a massacre ensues. The Romans spare none and possibly over 50000 men, women and childrer are killed while the Romans only lose 400-500. In defeat, Boudica poisons herself.

Heavy troops
Tribesmen
Heavy cavalry
Chariots
Spectators

2

had secured continuity of government, but it needed a leader of exceptional ability to establish a new dynasty. Fortunately, Vespasian was such a leader. He reigned ten years and died at the age of 70. His sons Titus (Titus Flavius Vespasianus) and Domitian (Titus Flavius Domitianus) succeeded him in turn as Emperor.

Vespasian's accession to power was marked by complications in Gaul. Julius Civilis, who commanded Batavian auxiliaries recruited from the Rhine delta, had on the request of Vespasian's officer in Italy created a diversion hostile to Vitellius. This provided Civilis with the opportunity for an independent uprising. He allied himself with a nationalist movement in Gaul, which purported to set up a Gallic Empire in place of the apparently crumbling Roman authority. The Gallic movement soon collapsed, but there was a military lesson to be learnt. Roman army units composed of foreign nationals under their own leaders could easily become an embarrassment. A trend in future policy was to post foreign troops at a distance from their home territories and to arrange where possible that auxiliary units should contain more than a single nationality. As for Civilis, we do not know what happened to him. Our manuscript sources break off at this point, tantalisingly leaving him still negotiating with an eloquent Roman commander.

Above: *A portrait of Hadrian in bronze. It may have commemorated his visit to London in AD 122.*

Right: *Hadrian's Wall. It was in fact a chain of forts and mile-castles linked by a rampart walk and extending across Britain from the Tyne to the Solway. It formed a defence against northern barbarians.*

The Stabilisation of Frontiers

The murder of Domitian in the year 96 was the outcome of domestic discord. Nevertheless, it gave great public satisfaction. Apart from his other shortcomings, the tyrant had failed to make adequate arrangements for a successor. The Senate appointed a new *princeps,* Marcus Cocceius Nerva, and Tacitus was pleased to see in this constitutional gesture a revival of Republican sentiment. Nerva was an old man at the time of his elevation. He was also childless, and after one year of power he appointed a loyal and able officer, Marcus Ulpius Traianus (Trajan), as his colleague and successor. The appointment was timely, for Nerva died early in the following year. Under Trajan, imperial expansion was renewed, and as one of Rome's greatest soldier emperors, he was shrewd enough to nominate an equally great successor. The formal nomination and adoption which usually secured

the imperial succession was much more satisfactory than the common hereditary process. It generally ensured that the successor would be a military commander, for with exceptions, one of which we have just recorded, none but a soldier could hope to survive. The Empire depended for defence and government upon military force. As for the principle of adoption itself, Roman reverence for legal forms lent it all the sanctity of a blood-tie. One may compare the relationship of patron and protégé (*cliens*), which we have already had occasion to notice.

Hadrian (Publius Aelius Hadrianus) who, as a connection by marriage, was Trajan's ward and became emperor on his death, in many ways reversed the policies of his predecessor. But this does not prove that either he or Trajan were wrong. Times were changing. The steady westward migration of peoples in Asia and Europe meant that pressure on Rome's frontiers was steadily mounting. Under Trajan, those frontiers had attained unprecedentedly wide dimensions. Hadrian saw the need for contraction and consolidation, and this policy was marked in vulnerable areas by the construction of fixed fortifications,

signal posts and entrenchments. A line of forts linked by palisades, protected the intrusive salient of territory between the upper reaches of the Rhine and the Danube. Hadrian's name is notably associated with the Roman frontier works across north Britain from the Tyne to the Solway. The line of forts and base camps, connected by a mural barrier, replaced an earlier linked chain of forts slightly to the south. "Hadrian's Wall" was initiated as the result of the Emperor's visit to Britain in AD 122; Hadrian spent a great deal of his reign in visiting outlying provinces. The Wall exemplifies the principles of Roman frontier defence as they existed in many sectors of the Empire. A chain of strongpoints was connected by a well-defined communicating road (*limes*) along which troops could move with efficiency and speed.

The dutiful Antoninus Pius (138-161), who succeeded Hadrian, presided over an epoch of comparative peace and plenty in the Mediterranean core of the Empire. But the price of social well-being was continual vigilance and preparedness on the frontiers. In Britain, Antoninus tried to advance the frontier—as he did in Germany—

AD	217	218	220	222	
	Caracalla assassinated	Accession of Elagabalus, Syrian boy priest, alleged son of Caracalla	In China, final eclipse of the Han dynasty	Elagabalus assassinated by the Praetorian Guard	Severus Alexander becomes emperor

mobility in themselves constituted a disadvantage. However, legions were withdrawn from Britain at various dates during the centuries of Roman rule, to meet pressures in other parts of the Empire, and such withdrawals, even though the legions by this time were not all first-line troops, opened the way inevitably to northern or sea-borne invaders to make incursions.

and built another wall in the form of a turf embankment on a cobblestone base, farther north, from the Forth to the Clyde. But the time came when this could no longer be defended, and after only 23 years it was decided to withdraw southwards once more and rely solely on Hadrian's stone structure for the defence of Roman Britain.

The recourse to engineering skills in order to solve manpower problems had been Julius Caesar's answer. Rome's wars against the barbarians were a continual struggle against numerical odds, and with the help of technology the Romans strove to make good what they lacked in numbers. Twenty-eight legions had been all too few for Augustus' original ambitions, and when he lost three of them in Varus' disaster, he immediately saw the need to reduce military commitments and shorten the perimeter of the imperial frontiers.

The military garrisons which manned frontier areas were (as a matter of policy on which we have already commented) not all nationally homogeneous. But they tended to form settled communities as a result of relationships with local women, and the resulting settled habits and lack of

Above: *A fort on Hadrian's Wall near Chesters in Northumberland. The illustration shows substantial ruins belonging to the fort's bath-house.*

The Task of Marcus Aurelius

Marcus Aurelius Antoninus, who succeeded to the principate at the death of Antoninus Pius in 161, was also of a quiet and philosophic disposition, but unlike his predecessor he was faced with the necessity for continual warfare. The fact that he was able to meet the challenge of military duty with energy and unbroken resolve indicates some kind of spiritual triumph over his natural temperament, at the same time making him a practising as distinct from a purely academic philosopher.

War against Parthia (162-3) was only a prelude to barbarian incursions on the Danube front (166). It was already well recognized that responsibility for imperial defence was more than a single emperor could support. An emperor's nominated successor, who now ordinarily received the title of "Caesar", was also a colleague. Marcus Aurelius was not very fortunate in his colleague Lucius Verus, whose adoption derived from a decision of Hadrian. Marcus, showing perhaps poor judgment of character, arranged

that the task of imperial government should be shared, and Verus, ruling as an equal on a collegiate basis, took command of the war against Parthia, which was won for him by his able officer Avidius Cassius.

The major cities of Parthia were captured, but this victory, like that of Trajan, though westward territories were annexed, could not lead to permanent Roman occupation of Parthia. The days were past when Romans and Parthians fought each other with characteristic national weapons and battles were a conflict of highly disciplined legionaries with incalculable swarms of mounted bowmen. Arrian, writing on military tactics in the time of Hadrian, testifies to the diversification of arms and armour and the variety of combatant methods employed by the Roman army at that epoch. Trajan's Column and other monuments tell the same story. The Romans had among their own contingents heavily mailed horsemen on the Parthian model; nor did they lack archers who could retaliate against the Parthians. If they were never able to bring the Parthian Empire within the bounds of their own, this was probably because they lacked sufficient troops to hold what had been conquered. Such vast deserts were in any case ungovernable.

Lack of numbers also told heavily against Roman defence on the Danube, and it should be stressed that Rome was now seriously on the defensive in

224
Rise of Sassanid dynasty in Persia
Ardashir overthrows Arsacid (Parthian) rulers

235
Severus Alexander assassinated

249
Decius becomes emperor and persecutes the Christians

251
Decius killed in war against the Goths

AD

197

this area. Various barbarian tribes, forced westwards and southwards by migratory pressures, crossed the Alps and reached Aquileia at the northern extremity of the Adriatic Sea. Italy was threatened as it never had been since the days of the Cimbric invasion, but the barbarians did not capture Aquileia, lacking the equipment for assaults on fortified towns. Marcus Aurelius, despite the inferior ability of his colleague, was well served by his generals on the Danube front. Lucius Verus in any case died on active service in 169, and Marcus was left in sole command.

There seems to have been a good deal of collaboration between the German tribes of the upper Danube and the Sarmatians farther east. Roman armies, relying simply on mobility and speed, had to turn abruptly from one threat to another. The invaders were defeated in a series of arduous campaigns, forced back across the Danube and reduced to quiescence. But such warfare spelt an end to current methods of frontier defence and, in years which followed, Roman strategists had to think increasingly in terms of fortified zones rather than defensible lines.

Unfortunately, the manpower problem in the time of Marcus Aurelius became all the more critical on account of a devastating plague which the army brought back from its eastern wars. Sheer lack of manpower obliged Marcus to establish a German militia, settled within the imperial frontiers, as a way of combating German threats from without. Military service was the price of the land which the settlers occupied. As the frontiers became less distinct, so also did the definition of Roman nationality. The operations of Marcus Aurelius and his officers secured the line of the Danube, but in the large frontier province of Dacia to the north of the river, which Trajan had previously annexed, a right-of-way was granted to the barbarian tribes, allowing them to preserve communications with their eastward compatriots. In some sense, the Empire was now provided with insulating zones but—to press the metaphor—this insulation could become a semi-conductor of extraneous forces.

Marcus Aurelius would probably have rendered the territory beyond the Danube more secure, but in AD 175 he had to meet the revolt of his eastern deputy Avidius Cassius. It would seem that Cassius had been deceived by a false report that Marcus was dead, and his dissident action hardly had

time to gather impetus before he was murdered by one of his own centurions. Avidius Cassius would in any case have been a preferable alternative to the Emperor's ineffective son Commodus, who eventually filled the role of official colleague and successor.

Septimius Severus and his Army

The principate of Commodus lasted 12 years, which should have been long enough to secure the succession, but Commodus did not allow the matter to trouble him. He was eventually murdered as the result of a conspiracy hatched by his Praetorian Guard commander, who had for some time shared the real power with other favourites, and at last decided that the present emperor was no longer necessary. During the next year, two emperors were proclaimed and then murdered, while the Praetorians tried to make up their minds. At last, they gave support to Septimius Severus, who commanded the Danube legions. The legions themselves, in fact, provided a firmer backing than Praetorian caprice.

Septimius had to fight for the imperial throne against other contenders, who were also supported by provincial armies. He was victorious in the ensuing struggle, partly because he commanded more troops than his adversaries and partly because he was nearer to Rome—still the key point. He temporarily came to terms with his northern rival Clodius Albinus, governor of Britain, recognizing him as a colleague. It is surprising that Albinus was deceived so easily. Septimius had time to march eastward and defeat his other opponent, Pescennius Niger, in a series of battles in Asia Minor and Syria. He was then in a position to renew hostilities against Albinus, who had advanced into Gaul and rallied the western provinces of the Empire in his favour. Perhaps Albinus also had been playing for time. The numbers engaged in the decisive battle near Lugdunum (Lyon) are reported as being equal, and the issue for long hung in the balance, but Septimius was completely victorious, deciding the battle by his use of cavalry as an independent arm.

Septimius Severus' military ability was allied to shrewd political insight. On being proclaimed emperor, he had been quick to occupy Rome and disband the Praetorian Guard. He then re-established the Praetorians to suit his own convenience. In the past, the

Above: *The frieze on Trajan's Column, which once stood over his ashes, commemorates his achievements. His men are building a campaign camp.*

Praetorian cohorts had normally been recruited from Italy, but Septimius threw membership open to all legionaries. This meant in practice that Praetorians were picked from the Illyrian legions which had supported him. They continued to serve him admirably as an imperial *corps d'élite* in the course of his eastern campaign.

Having eliminated other imperial pretenders, Septimius undertook an effective punitive expedition against the Parthians, who had given support to Niger, his eastern rival. He also had to act promptly in Britain, for the province, stripped of troops by Albinus for his continental adventure, was badly exposed to Caledonian invaders from the north. But Septimius' British campaign was incomplete and he was preparing to renew hostilities when he died at Eburacum (York) in 211.

Septimius Severus admired soldiers and believed in them, particularly in the soldiers of the Roman army. For him, their welfare was a paramount consideration, and one cannot help feeling that his attitude, despite its serious economic implications, was right. Roman civilization had come to depend completely on military power capable of defending the frontiers, and citizens who enjoyed the peace and comfort of metropolitan territories could at least be expected to support the defence effort with their tax contributions. Septimius, in fact, made sure that they did so.

Among other reforms which favoured the soldiers, he legislated that they should be able to marry legally while

AD	253	259	260	265	267
	Valerian and Galienus rule as imperial colleagues	Postumus, imperial pretender, supreme in Gaul	Valerian captured by Persians	In China, Chin dynasty established	Zenobia inherits her husband's (Odenatus) power at Palmyra

198

Above: *The outer city gate of Perge (S. Turkey) dating from the reign of Septimius Severus, AD 193-211. Perge had traditions which related it to the Trojan War but it remained an important city in Graeco-Roman times.*

on service. This facility had not previously existed, though emperors in the past had given some sort of recognition to the relations which soldiers contracted with local women and to the children which resulted. Official attitudes on this subject seem to have been in conflict. On the one hand, the serving soldier was discouraged from forming local ties which might divert him from his principal allegiance to Rome. On the other, it was desired that he should feel at home in the army. The new legislation rectified anomalies. In any case Septimius' son, colleague and successor, Marcus Aurelius Antoninus (known by the nickname of Caracalla) in subsequent years recognized the Roman citizenship of all freeborn provincials. The new constitutional enactment was not credited by an unimpressed posterity with generous motives, but regarded rather as a means of widening liability to tax. But it meant that civilians in general made a greater contribution to the defence budget. Of such a policy, Septimius would have approved.

Chaos and Recovery

In the middle decades of the third century, the Roman Empire appeared to be on the point of collapse. Barbarian attacks from without coincided with endemic discord within, and forces which were needed to resist invaders were exhausted in perennial struggles of disputed imperial succession. Between the years 238 and 253, emperors were elevated and replaced at the rate of something approaching one per year. Consuls in the old days had at least not been obliged to fight against other candidates for their yearly terms of office. The epoch has many characteristics of the Dark Age which was to descend on the western world five centuries later. Records are lacking and chronology is often hard to establish.

In the East, the situation had become particularly critical. Apart from other barbarian peoples, the Goths, who were already settled in what is now the Ukraine, carried out penetrating raids by land and sea into the interior of the Empire, plundering and destroying the cities not only of northern Asia Minor but of the Aegean coastline as far south as Ephesus. These invaders had discovered that the Roman Empire had a soft core. The frontiers were defended by troops and fortified, but once the crust of peripheral defences had been breached, an intruder had no problems. A world of unfortified cities and unarmed populations lay at his mercy.

Beyond the Euphrates, the situation had changed significantly. The Persians in their original homeland northeast of the Persian Gulf had, after the Seleucid period, survived as a Parthian vassal nation. But under the Sassanian dynasty (named from a dynastic ancestor), the Persians wrested hegemony from the Parthians and, at the beginning of the third century, became the new masters of the Parthian Empire. Nor were they slow to challenge Roman frontier positions east of the Euphrates. Very soon they captured key points and occupied territory which Rome had won from the Parthians in the course of their fiercely disputed campaigns against them.

In the year 242, a Roman financial administrator, Sabinus Aquila Timesitheus, became father-in-law of the young Emperor Gordian III and was appointed Prefect of the Praetorian Guard. In this position, he was the effective ruler of the Roman Empire, and his organizing ability was soon employed to produce excellent military results, especially on the eastern front, where Carrhae was regained from the Persians and a Roman puppet king re-established in Syria. But the death of Timesitheus brought an end to these successes. The Persian offensive was renewed. Shapur (Sapor), son of the first Sassanian king Ardashir (Artaxerxes), occupied Armenia and invaded Syria. The Roman Emperor Valerian (Publius Licinius Valerianus) conducted a campaign which ended in a disastrous attempt to relieve the Syrian city of Edessa in 260. The Emperor himself

268
Claudius II (Gothicus) becomes Roman emperor

270
Death of Claudius from plague: accession of Aurelian

273
Zenobia captured by Aurelian   Fall of Palmyra

275
Aurelian assassinated   **AD**

199

fell into Persian hands, nor is it recorded that he ever emerged from captivity. Christian writers, who attributed to him a sombre fate, were no doubt influenced by the fact that Valerian had been among the many emperors who persecuted the Christians. Christianity, however, was also persecuted by Shapur; for the new Persian Zoroastrianism was, unlike the old easy-going creed of the Achaemenids, a missionary religion, displaying all the intolerance which necessarily accompanies such a faith.

In the West, meanwhile, Gaul was overrun by the Franks and other barbarians, who penetrated into Spain and destroyed Tarraco (Tarragona). These invaders discovered, as the Goths had discovered in the East, that once the Roman frontier was breached, they need expect no further resistance. In 259, Marcus Cassianus Latinius Postumus, who was a pretender to the supreme imperial power and therefore formally at war with the Emperor Gallienus, Valerian's son, revived the "Gallic Empire", that notional establishment which had briefly struggled for existence in the days of Civilis. There was, of course, no question of Celtic nationalism, as under Vercingetorix. The independent régime simply claimed to defend Roman civilization in Gaul better than Rome could*. Neither Gallienus nor his successor, Claudius, persisted in interfering with Postumus' unquestionable service to the Roman cause. Regardless of the fact that he was usurping their authority, he amply demonstrated his power to repel the barbarians.

Thus relieved by his rival of responsibilities in Gaul, Claudius was able to concentrate his energies against Gothic enemies, who had now advanced westwards, threatening the Balkans and Italy. The Emperor's victories freed the Mediterranean from the invaders and drove them back across the Danube, with the result that he went down to history as Claudius Gothicus. But the Goths were at this time stricken by plague, and Claudius was one of the many Romans who caught it from them. He died in 270, and his cavalry commander Aurelian (Lucius Domitius Aurelianus) was acclaimed as emperor by the army.

Aurelian, though successful against a multitude of Danubian enemies, was obliged to retract frontiers in this sector, as Gallienus and Postumus had

*It is interesting to note that this is an early sign of the disintegration of the West and the decline of any central authority.

been on the Rhine. The larger perimeter was no longer capable of defence. Aurelian reigned for five years, before losing his life as a result of a local conspiracy, and under his rule the Empire had time for recovery. Like the generals who had immediately preceded him in imperial power, he had realized that the barbarians could only be expelled if the earlier static concepts of frontier defence were abandoned. Germanic tribes (originally allied contingents settled within Rome's frontiers) were ravaging Italy. Aurelian removed them after considerable vicissitudes by use of a highly mobile army, and he relied upon a cavalry force such as had already been developed by Gallienus. At the same time, the Emperor saw to it that Rome was provided, as a precaution against surprise, with strong new walls.

The Palmyrene Wars

Postumus in Gaul—attracting the allegiance both of Spanish and British provinces—had been an ostensible rebel, though in practice a very real

Later Roman Cavalry

The colour illustration shows the final development of armoured cavalry, called *clibanarii*. Fully armoured cavalry had existed in the Roman army since AD 69 when Sarmatian cavalry had been employed by Vespasian. Their numbers were increased in the second century AD. Aurelian expanded this arm c AD 275 after setbacks against rebellious Palmyran *clibanarii*. They were expanded again by Constantius II c AD 350. The reconstruction shows a *clibanarius*, c AD 275, based on horse-armour found at Dura Europos and the descriptions of Ammianus and the Emperor Julian, who notes that the rider was completely covered, with "head and face enclosed by a metal mask which makes the wearer look like a glittering statue". He further describes the extremely fine mail used to cover hands and joints. Limbs were protected by circlets of iron plates. The body armour could be constructed of scales or rectangular iron plates linked by mail. In the fourth century, helmets resembled the famous "Sutton Hoo" model and it has been suggested that this is actually a Roman helmet with barbarian embellishments.

Other Troop Types

The upper black and white drawing shows a typical Sarmatian cavalryman of the second century AD. It is based on sculpture around the base of Trajan's Column, grave *stelae* and the descriptions of Tacitus. Chiefs and nobles might be mounted on half- or fully-armoured horses. The armour was normally made of scales of iron, bronze, horn, or hardened leather. His main weapon is the *kontos*. The method of wielding this spear is shown in the colour illustration. The lower drawing shows a fourth century Roman cavalryman. The Sarmatian influence is clearly visible. The armour might be of mail or lamellar construction.

AD — 276 Probus becomes emperor — 282 Probus murdered by mutinous troops — 284 Diocletian proclaimed emperor — 286 Diocletian and Maximian, as colleagues, each assume title of Augustus — 293 Appointment of two "Caesars" to help the two Augusti —

200

ally against Rome's barbarian enemies. In the East, by contrast, Odenatus, king of Palmyra, though loyally defending the Empire against Persia, had in fact created for himself a position of independence.

The Syrian desert city of Palmyra (as the Romans called Tadmor) had for long patrolled and policed the eastward caravan routes on which its prosperity depended. This was a natural preparation for military power. In other respects also, the Semitic, semi-Hellenized Palmyrene community was well qualified to fill the role of Roman sword-bearer in the East. The Persian army relied extensively on heavy cavalry protected by scale and plate armour. The Palmyrenes, as an antidote, deployed a combination of light and heavy cavalry, archers and, where requisite, sophisticated siege equipment. In addition, Palmyra had absorbed Roman administrative techniques, while the Persians, like their predecessors the Parthians, were organized on a local feudal basis without any central control such as might have given more permanent effect to their victories.

Odenatus, a prince of Arabian stock, whose dynasty had been established by Septimius Severus, had inflicted a crushing defeat on the Persians while they were still laden with plunder from their victory over Valerian. He had subsequently suppressed over-ambitious survivors of Valerian's army, assumed command of surviving Roman troops in the area, and launched a counter-offensive in Mesopotamia, in the course of which he captured the Persian royal harem. For these exploits, he received due honour from Gallienus.

305
Diocletian and Maximian retire in favour of Constantius and Galerius

307
Constantius dies at York

312
Constantine, son of Constantius, invades Italy and wrests power from Maxentius, son of Maximian

Battle of Mulvian Bridge

316
Death of Diocletian

AD

201

In the year 267, Odenatus' beautiful and talented widow Zenobia inherited his power and ruled in the name of her young son; the king and his elder son by another wife had been assassinated in circumstances which are not fully clear. Zenobia showed herself independent of Gallienus, and Aurelian, though at first conciliatory, later felt obliged to assert his authority in the East. The Emperor's officer had recovered Alexandria from the Palmyrenes, even before Aurelian marched through Asia Minor—where Palmyrene domination had been reluctantly endured. Zenobia's general, Zabdas, wisely did not attempt to fight in mountainous country unsuited to cavalry tactics, but awaited the Roman legions in Syria. He was unable to defend Antioch, but made a second stand at Emessa (Homs). Here, the mailed Palmyrene lancers drove Aurelian's cavalry from the field, but Aurelian won the battle in their absence and dealt with them suitably when they returned in scattered units.

Only the desert, the Bedouin and the sun now defended Palmyra, whither Zenobia had fled. Not surprisingly, she made an appeal to Persia. But Aurelian bought off the Bedouin and fought off the Persians, while his army heroically maintained a siege. Zenobia, on a fast dromedary, tried to escape across the Euphrates by night, but she was overtaken and brought back to Aurelian a prisoner. Later, as we hear, she graced his triumph in golden chains, but ended her days in peace at Rome, married to a senator.

When Palmyra fell, Aurelian put to death the advisers whom Zenobia had been glad to blame, but he spared the rest of the city. After his return to the Danube, however, Roman garrisons in the East were treacherously attacked, and in a second visitation he destroyed Palmyra utterly. He must have done so with some reluctance, for the city's potential as a buffer state against Persia was considerable. But its annihilation now permitted Aurelian to impose himself on Gaul, which, after the death of Postumus, was ripe for the restitution of Roman authority.

Military and Civil Reorganization

The decade which followed Aurelian's death was marked by another sequence of shortlived emperors. The year 284, however, saw the proclamation of the Emperor Diocletian (Gaius Aurelius Valerius Diocletianus) by troops in Asia Minor. Diocletian won the war against his rival claimant and appointed Maximian (Marcus Aurelius Valerius Maximianus) as his colleague.

In 286, Diocletian permitted to Maximian the title "Augustus", which indicated possession of the supreme power. From that time on, they ruled jointly, and in 293 each "Augustus" appointed himself a colleague who bore the title of "Caesar". Four Imperial Headquarters, with their staffs, thus resulted. By regularising procedures which had proved expedient in the past, Diocletian was in fact giving recognition to the inevitability of the

Above: *Diocletian reorganized the Empire under two Imperial colleagues, each aided by an heir apparent. In AD 305 he retired to private life.*

collegiate principle. The Empire was too big for a single command. Troops might be transferred from Britain to the Danube in two months: perhaps less, if full use were made of Rhine river transport. But the Euphrates frontier was another matter. East and West were two Empires within a single civilization, and Diocletian wished to ensure that they should remain collegiate, not rival Empires. To some extent, their mutual independence was an accomplished fact which he was forced to recognise.

In re-establishing a co-optive procedure as the basis of imperial succession, Diocletian invoked another traditional expedient. Heredity— notably in the family of Septimius Severus—based simply on blood-ties, had been productive of some grotesque results. Similarly, "praetorianism", whether practised by the Guard itself or by the provincial legions, was simply an invitation to mutiny and murder. Because an emperor needed to be a soldier, it was too easily assumed that he needed to be nothing else. As in the first century AD, a blend of two principles was now expected to give best results. Co-option was confirmed by family affinities. The daughter of Diocletian and the step-daughter of Maximian married Galerius and Constantius, the two co-opted "Caesars".

It was also arranged that the two "Augusti" should retire from office after 20 years and give place to their "Caesars", who, assuming the supreme title, should appoint new "Caesars" as junior colleagues. Diocletian himself retired to his palace at Salonae (near modern Split in Jugoslavia). His choice of residence is itself significant. The imperial centre of gravity now lay in the Balkan peninsula and southeast Europe. Diocletian, like several of his imperial predecessors, had been of Balkan extraction. Rome was rapidly becoming no more than the ceremonial capital of empire. In practice, it was already merely a provincial capital, and the Senate was treated by Diocletian as if it were a body of town-councillors. He never entered Rome during the first 20 years of his reign.

With his stern eye for realities and disregard for empty forms, Diocletian also relegated the old names of Republican magistracies to purely civil functions, and increasingly used distinct titles for military appointments. Like Septimius Severus, he realized that Rome's greatest problem was one of recruiting, and he seems to have almost doubled the number of soldiers by increasing their pay. In order to do this, it was necessary to combat the monetary inflation which had long been associated with debasement of the Roman coinage. Diocletian went to the heart of the problem by exacting taxes in kind and maintaining his army with the proceeds.

Above all, Diocletian was an administrator and organizer, but it must not therefore be inferred that he was an "armchair" strategist. His reforms were worked out in the course of action and, like most Roman emperors who survived the first months of power, he had been obliged to fight for his position, suppress revolts and restrain barbarians. Maximian, his fellow "Augustus", was an ambitious man, but he knew better than to challenge Diocletian on the field of battle.

Maximian, as Emperor of the West, had in fact his own military problems. Of these, the most intractable was presented by Carausius, a rebellious admiral of the British Channel fleet. Irrepressible, Carausius was for some

AD   325
Constantine the Great
summons Council of the
Church at Nicaea

330
Byzantium is renamed
Constaninople

337
Death of Constantine

359
Shapur II of Persia
invades Mesopotamia

202

Above: *The triumphal arch of Constantine, built in AD 312. It incorporates reliefs from earlier monuments including an arch of Trajan.*

Constantine and Constantinople

Constantius died at York in 306, after a successful campaign against the barbarous Picts north of the Wall. His son Constantine was proclaimed "Augustus" by the British legions, but a period of complicated wars, negotiations, bandying of titles and dynastic marriages intervened before Constantine (known to history as "the Great") attained the supremacy which Diocletian, for all his fourfold system of government, had really enjoyed. The fourfold system was, in fact, among the less durable of Diocletian's

time endured by the two "Augusti" as a kind of supernumerary colleague in Britain and north Gaul. Eventually, Maximian's "Caesar", Constantius, drove him from Boulogne and, continuing the war against Carausius' murderer and successor, restored Britain to its former allegiance.

institutions, and its obvious vulnerability to the old maladies saddened him before his death in 316.

Constantine developed the Roman army along lines which Diocletian had laid down and which had been apparent even in Aurelian's time. Static frontier forces (*limitanei*) occupied forts in peripheral zones or manned the lines of river barriers. The best troops, however, were reserved as a mobile striking force (*comitatenses*) which could direct its energies as emergency required. The infantry units of this striking force were still termed legions, though their strength was reduced to about a third of the old Marian legion. It would seem, in fact, that the original legions had sometimes been split and apportioned between the frontier garrisons and the emperor's mobile field armies. The mobile forces, of course, had more need of a strong cavalry element, but Rome had long been accustomed to rely on the barbarians who were settled in frontier areas to supply cavalry, such forces having being classed as *numeri*. There was a natural tendency, in the interests of security, to keep the barbarians on the frontier, away from the heart of the Empire, but in view of

commitments to central mobility it could not indefinitely be upheld.

Constantine made one change which is symptomatic rather than important: he abolished the Praetorian Guard. The Praetorian cohorts were by now wholly redundant. Both their uses and abuses had been usurped by other sections of the army. The title of Praetorian Prefect was applied by Constantine to a purely civil official.

Constantine's most monumental work was, of course, his building of Constantinople, the "New Rome" and second capital of the Empire. For this role the site of the ancient Greek city of Byzantium was chosen. A glance at the map will immediately make clear the economic and strategic importance of the position selected, at the centre of land communications between Europe and Asia and of sea communications between the Mediterranean and the Black Sea. Above all, Constantinople was ideally placed as a general headquarters for operations on the all-important Danube front.

Septimius Severus, with something less than his usual foresight, had destroyed Byzantium after the city supported his eastern rival Pescennius Niger. As a result, there remained no effective base or stronghold against the Goths, who in the following generation commandeered the fleets of Greek Pontic cities and swept down in their piratical raids into the Aegean Sea. In building the walls of his new capital, Constantine was affirming his faith in fortifications in general and in the importance of fortifying this particular point. Constantine's fortifications are not those which now survive, but the position was eminently fortifiable. The barbarian invaders were never very successful in attacking fortified cities, and the walls of Constantinople withstood their attacks throughout many centuries to come.

Constantine is perhaps best known as being the first Christian emperor. In fact, he became a Christian on his death-bed, but before that date had, like other imperial pretenders of his generation, given support and encouragement to the Christians. The most immediate and tangible military effect of his attitude was the adoption of Christian battle standards. These featured a monogram compounded of the first two letters of Christ's name in Greek (XP). Constantine also had the device painted on his soldiers' shields, and it was first carried into battle when, in 312, he invaded Italy, to wrest power from Maxentius, son of Diocletian's old colleague Maximian.

361
Julian (the Apostate) becomes emperor

363
Julian's death in Persian war

379
Theodosius I proclaimed "Augustus" of the West

385
Magnus Maximus, imperial pretender, drafts troops out of Britain

AD

203

The Coming of the Barbarians

The Roman Empire in the West had virtually run its course by the end of the 5th century AD, not so much conquered as absorbed by the barbarians. In the East, Constantinople, although at times no more than a city-state, held out for more than one thousand years.

Ancient Authorities

Our knowledge of the later Roman Empire depends appreciably on Christian writers. Some of them were well placed to write with authority. Eusebius, Bishop of Caesarea, to whom we have already referred, was on familiar terms with Constantine himself. Christian accounts, in their efforts to reconcile pagan history with Biblical chronology and theology, sometimes appear tortuous, though the coincidence of Christ's birth with the Golden Age of Augustus and the foundation of the Empire suggested a providential interpretation for which no Christian writer could be blamed. In any case, we must not underestimate these ancient Christian historians by classing them with medieval chroniclers of ancient events. Jerome and Orosius, writing at the end of the fourth and beginning of the fifth century, were fully acquainted with the traditions of pagan culture and learning, which they criticized and adapted to their own purposes. They were living in a still substantially pagan world and were by no means isolated from its habits of thought.

Paganism did not, of course, end abruptly with the conversion of Constantine. A generation after his death, another pagan emperor, Flavius Claudius Julianus (Julian the Apostate) presided over the Roman world. His attempt to revive paganism can only be seen as a vain attempt to put the clock back, but his sentiments and attitudes are reflected in the work of pagan writers contemporary with him, notably in the *History* of Ammianus Marcellinus. Ammianus served under Julian both in Gaul and in the Persian campaign of 363, in which the Emperor died. Ammianus was a Greek of Antioch, but he eventually settled in Rome and wrote his *History of Rome* for Roman readers in Latin. The

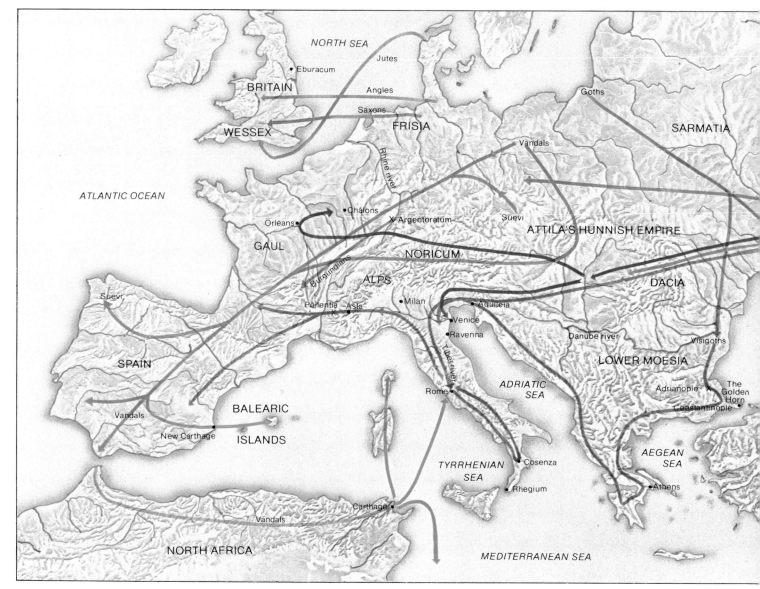

History, if it still existed in its entirety, would have begun with events of the year AD 96, where Tacitus left off. As it is, the surviving portion begins in 353 in the reign of Constantius II, the third son of Constantine the Great. The account of Julian's Persian campaign is very detailed, but it is not wholly based on personal experiences; Ammianus shares at least one important source with Zosimus, whose narrative of the campaign is also detailed.

Apart from historical accounts, mention should also be made of the work of Vegetius Renatus, a fourth century civil servant who wrote a treatise on Roman military techniques. Vegetius, however, though an important source of military information, is chronologically imprecise. Also valuable is an extant copy of the *Notitia Dignitatum,* a list of civil and military

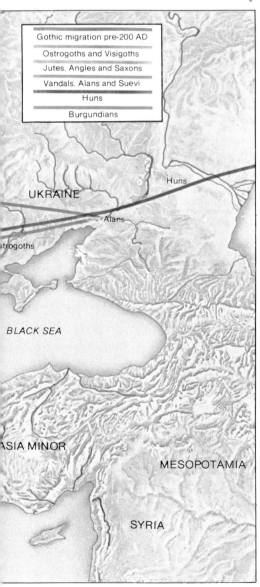

Gothic migration pre-200 AD

Ostrogoths and Visigoths

Jutes, Angles and Saxons

Vandals, Alans and Suevi

Huns

Burgundians

UKRAINE

Huns

Alans

strogoths

BLACK SEA

SIA MINOR

MESOPOTAMIA

SYRIA

appointments as they existed in the Eastern and Western partitions of the Empire at the end of the 4th century.

For later times, when Rome and the Western Empire had been transformed out of recognition by the infusion of barbarous populations, and particularly for the epoch of the great Byzantine Emperor Justinian (527-565), our main authority is the Greek historian Procopius. Procopius served in a logistic capacity on the staff of Belisarius, Justinian's invincible general, and wrote a *History of the Wars of Justinian,* which is extant. In this work, he made use both of his own contact with eyewitnesses and of earlier historical sources.

A question now arises as to the chronological limits of our enquiry. Procopius' *History* was continued by the poet Agathias. But Agathias died before he could proceed very far. For further records we have to depend on later Byzantine Greeks such as Genesius and Theophanes and a number of anonymous historians. Among the lost sources of later extant writers must be reckoned Olympiodorus and Priscus, whose diplomatic careers had brought them into close contact with the Huns.

In the West, the scholar and administrator Flavius Magnus Aurelius Cassiodorus (490-583) has left us a summary of Roman history in Latin. His *History of the Goths,* though lost, was summarized in the extant account of Jordanes, probably a Romanized Goth himself, who lived about 550. This work also contains much information about the Huns, deriving, through Cassiodorus, from Priscus.

Left: *The frontiers of the Roman Empire were increasingly put under pressure by the steady westward migration of peoples in Asia and Europe. This map shows developments between the 2nd and 5th centuries AD.*

The End of the Roman Empire

The boy Romulus Augustulus is commonly said to have been the last Roman emperor in the West. He was deposed and superseded in 476 by a German officer called Odoacer, who had served under various Roman commanders. Odoacer was content to rule as king of Italy, recognizing the suzerainty of the eastern emperor in Constantinople, and unconcerned to claim the traditional imperial titles and honours for himself. Romulus, in any case, had been a usurper, raised to power by his father's *coup d'état,* and he was not recognized by the eastern emperor. However, the abandonment of the imperial title has a symbolic significance and provides historians of ancient Rome with a pretext for closing their account.

There is no obvious valedictory date for Roman history. Any event identified as terminal must in reality be a symbolic ending. For Graeco-Roman civilization did not collapse or explode. It was simply transmuted, by a gradual process, out of recognition; in many ways its institutions, assumptions and attitudes are still with us, having survived and revived in disguised and undisguised forms during the passage of the centuries. However, it is increasingly difficult, as time advances, for any history to be a world history, and our sense of form decrees that every story should have a beginning, middle and end. Apart from Romulus Augustulus, there are various possible stopping places for the historian of ancient civilization.

In 395, the great if somewhat bigoted Christian Emperor Theodosius died, bequeathing the Roman world to his two ineffectual sons Arcadius and Honorius, the first of whom exercised imperial power in the East, the second in the West: a situation which perpetuated discord between the two halves of the Empire. The administrative distinction foreshadowed in Diocletian's arrangements gave political expression to the pre-existing cultural and linguistic difference between the Greek East and the Latin West. The difference has left its mark on ecclesiastical history. Perhaps, therefore, we might assign "the end of the Roman Empire" to the point at which it ceased to be a unity: ie, the death of Theodosius the Great.

On the other hand, the dignity and power of the Roman Empire were astonishingly restored by the conquests

397
Stilicho comes to terms with Alaric the Goth

400
Alaric resumes hostilities

403
Alaric defeated in north Italy

AD

205

of the inspired eastern Emperor Justinian, who reigned as Flavius Petrus Sabbatius Justinianus, assuming the title of "Augustus" at his coronation in 527. Justinian extended his authority into Africa, Italy and Spain, where his armies prevailed against the Vandal and Gothic invaders. He also maintained alternating war and diplomatic relations with the Persians on his eastern frontier. Justinian's services to the arts of peace were also outstanding. He initiated many works of architecture and civil engineering; his most magnificent achievement in this respect was, of course, the building of Constantinople's great cathedral Santa Sophia ("The Holy Wisdom"). Justinian has also been immortalized by his contribution to the legal faculty. His codification of Roman Law was at least as monumental a work as the building of Santa Sophia. Unfortunately, his reign, like that of many

Byzantine emperors, was troubled by theological disputes which obsessed not only the clergy but the population at large. As often in history, religious differences provided rallying points for political ambitions and aspirations. In Constantinople, opinions became war-cries, indicative of allegiance. If you backed the green charioteer in the circus, you believed certain things about the relationship of the Father to the Son and at the same time favoured one branch of the imperial family rather than another. Allegiances, on analysis, are always "package deals", but Constantinople produced a *reductio ad absurdum* of the incorrigible human tendency to faction.

After Justinian's death in 565, his far-flung Empire soon collapsed, and for a time Constantinople was well content only to defend its own walls. But again, great emperors like Heraclius (610-641) and Leo the Isaurian (717-

740) saved civilization. The last of the western provinces to survive was the "exarchate" of Ravenna. This finally fell to the Lombards (Longobards), a Germanic people who had for long occupied the north Italian territory which still bears their name. Perhaps the fall of Ravenna in 751 is another suitable terminus for Roman history. It is, of course, equally possible to propose a much earlier date, and as such, the sack of Rome by the Goths in 410 suggests itself. But this again must be regarded as a purely symbolic event. Rome at this time was not even the capital of a prefecture or its sub-division, a diocese, as the civil departments of Diocletian's and Constantine's Empire had been termed. It was certainly not a city of any military consequence. It was simply, as ancient Athens had long ago become, a venerated tourist centre, one might almost say a kind of museum.

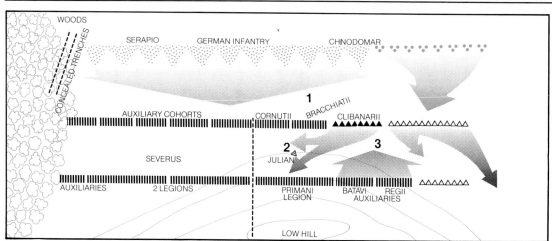

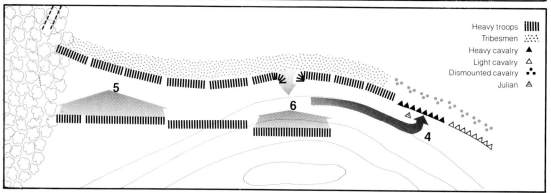

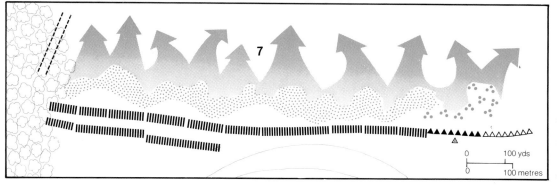

Battle of Argentoratum AD 357

Romans	Germans
Infantry*	
Palatine troops:	Tribesmen 32000
1 legion c1500	
4 cohorts of auxiliaries c2500	
Others:	
2 legions c3000	
6 cohorts of auxiliaries c3000	
Cavalry*	
Clibanarii 600	2/3000
Horse archers 600	
Light cavalry 900/1500	

*Information about some units' strength and disposition is incomplete, and so speculative.

General situation Julian is campaigning against the Germans under their king Chnodomar. He covers some 21 miles (34km) before noon on a hot August day. Julian leads his army, left wing advanced, over a hill towards the Germans. Suspecting the ambush in the woods they halt, deploy, and skirmish. The German cavalry dismounts at the insistence of the infantry who fear abandonment.
1 The Germans charge causing the Roman cavalry to panic and retreat when the *clibanarii* commander is killed (**2**). The Roman left holds. The Batavii and Regii charge to assist Cornuti and Bracchiati (**3**). The *clibanarii* retreat is blocked by the legions. Rallied by Julian they return to the fray (**4**). The Roman left pushes forward (**5**). Led by a band of nobles the Germans break through the Roman centre (**6**). They are halted by the legion of the Primani and eventually pushed back — the Romans continue to force back the Germans and they break (**7**). A slaughter ensues; many are drowned in the Rhine. Chnodomar is captured. He has lost 6000 men; Roman losses are 247 dead, 1/2000 injured.

Legend (on diagram):
Heavy troops · Tribesmen · Heavy cavalry ▲ · Light cavalry △ · Dismounted cavalry · Julian △

0 — 100 yds
0 — 100 metres

AD | 407 Military usurper from Britain (Constantine "the Tyrant") invades Gaul | 408 Stilicho put to death by Honorius | 410 Alaric sacks Rome Death of Alaric

206

The Eastern Front

Justinian was one of many emperors who would have been glad to live on terms of peaceful coexistence with the Persians—even if he had to pay for the privilege. But the Persians were not so minded. They well understood the manpower difficulties of their old adversaries, and while the eastern and western Empires were assailed by a multitude of barbarians on other frontiers, the Sassanid rulers saw fit to take their opportunity.

Since the defeat of Valerian and the retribution exacted in the name of Rome by Odenatus, the tide of war on the Euphrates frontier had ebbed and flowed recurrently. Galerius, Diocletian's faithful "Caesar", had at first suffered defeat (near Carrhae again) at the hands of the Persian king Narses. However, he amply avenged the disaster, and in the following year (298) Rome's eastern frontier was pushed still farther eastward, across Mesopotamia as far as the Tigris.

In the year 359, Shapur II, bent on restoring Persian fortunes, led his armies into Mesopotamia and captured several Roman frontier fortresses. Reacting to the eastern emergency, Constantius II was obliged to recall troops from Gaul, and the resentful army there proclaimed Julian, his "Caesar" on the western front, as "Augustus". But frontier pressures being what they were, before the imperial rivals could find leisure to fight each other, Constantius died, and Julian was left as sole emperor to vindicate Roman power and prestige in the East. He led his army along the Euphrates, assisted by river transport, and at a point some 50 miles (80 km) from Babylon, taking advantage of an ancient canal, conveyed his ships across to the Tigris. Here, however, instead of investing the Persian capital of Ctesiphon, he was lured into a further eastern march, in which lengthening lines of communication produced horrible privations for his troops. Even where the country was fertile, the enemy had devastated it. The Persians harassed him as the Parthians had harassed Roman armies in earlier times. In this campaign, Julian died of a wound, and the Persians soon recovered Mesopotamia from the inadequate officer whom his bereaved troops acclaimed as an imperial successor. Perhaps in this long story of border warfare, the Romans—or at any rate their Byzantine representatives—may be regarded as

having the last word. For the Emperor Heraclius, after a protracted series of campaigns, overcoming a formidable alliance between the Persians and the barbarian Avars north of the Black Sea (626), finally destroyed the army of the Persian king Khusru (Chosroes II) in a battle near Nineveh.

The Persian Empire was by this time thoroughly weakened and already confronted by other enemies than Rome. In 454, the Persians had to meet an invasion of the White Huns, a branch of the Central Asiatic horde which already menaced a great part of the Eurasian continent. Perhaps if the Sassanids had not squandered their energies in rather futile wars with Rome for very limited gains, they would have been better able to resist the Arabs who, early in the seventh century, fired by the message of their Prophet, defied Persian Zoroastrianism with a fanaticism greater than its own.

Above: *A cameo of the 4th century AD. The Persian king Shapur is shown capturing the Roman Emperor Valerian.*

Yet while it is possible to regard the wars of Romans and Persians as having a merely exhausting effect on both sides, these wars provided a training ground and were the source of many military lessons. The Romans

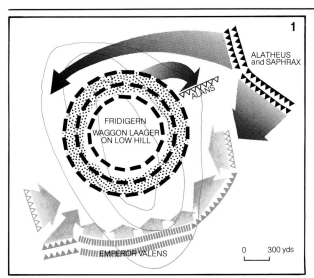

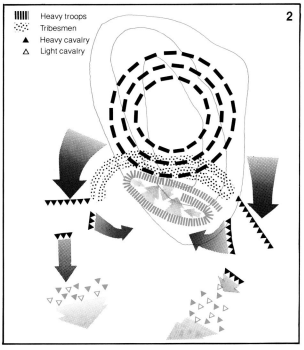

Heavy troops
Tribesmen
▲ Heavy cavalry
△ Light cavalry

0   300 yds

Battle of Adrianople AD 378

Eastern Empire Romans	Goths
*Troops**	
40000 (including perhaps 10000 cavalry)	200000 (probably only 50000 of these are combatants and 20000 may be cavalry)

*Numbers are again speculative.

General situation The Emperor Valens intends to inflict one final defeat on the barbarians in Thrace before the army of the western empire arrives to share in his victory. These include Visigoths under Alatheus and Saphrax and some Alans. Valens advances 8 miles (13km) out of Adrianople and sights a Goth waggon laager on a low hill. Valens deploys behind a screen provided by his right wing cavalry. The Ostrogoth horsemen are out of the camp foraging. Fridigern sets fire to the grass on the plain and sends out embassies to gain time. However, the Romans attack once they have deployed.
1 The Ostrogoths return, attack the Roman right flank and drive off the Roman cavalry. A dust cloud covers the field. The Roman left presses up to the laager unaware of what is happening on the right.
2 The Goths then issue from the camp and drive off the Roman left, aided by their cavalry who have circled around behind the camp. The Romans are outflanked and eventually break. Valens tries to stem the tide and shore up the rear with the Palatine legions of the Lanciarii and Mattiacii, but to no avail. As night falls the Romans are in full retreat. Valens is killed and his body never recovered. The Caesar Decius, many senior commanders and countless men also die. It is the worst defeat for Rome since Cannae.

conducted their frontier defence in the East with great sophistication, and the small fortress garrisons of the Euphrates frontier on more than one occasion showed their heroism. The Romans also learned much from Persian methods of fighting. Chain-mailed and plate-armoured horsemen, at the time when the *Notitia Dignitatum* was compiled, formed a regular part of the Roman army, a development which had started with Trajan. There seems to have been even an attempt to evolve a hybrid from the light mounted bowman and heavily armed lancer. For we learn of armoured archers on horseback (*equites sagittarii clibanarii*). There is, however, no record of their successful application in action.

Hostile and Friendly Goths

Of all the barbarian peoples who penetrated the Roman Empire in the later centuries of its history, the Goths made the deepest impression. They were a Germanic people of Scandinavian origin, who had begun their southward migration about the beginning of the Christian era. Evicted by Claudius "Gothicus" in the third century, they again exerted pressure in the fourth. Aurelian had allowed the West Goths (Visigoths) to settle north of the Danube in what had previously been the Roman province of Dacia. The East Goths (Ostrogoths), who had formed another group, had occupied the region of the Ukraine.

At the end of the fourth century, the Goths were under heavy pressure from the migratory movements of east European and Asiatic peoples, and sought the right to settle within Roman territory. The Roman Emperor Valens, then occupied in war against Persia, strove to ensure, through his commanders on the Balkan front, that the Goths should be disarmed before they were admitted as settlers, but he was unable to enforce this precaution. The unrelenting eastern pressures were driving successive waves of barbarian tribes across the Danube and the Rhine, and Valens was eventually obliged to return from the East in order to take command himself. In a violent battle near Adrianople (378) he was defeated by the immigrants and killed. His body was never recovered. Imperial prestige suffered badly. The Emperor's cavalry had fled and his infantry been annihilated.

Even after this great Roman disaster, however, the Goths did not overrun the Empire. In the first place, they were unable to capture Roman fortified points, lacking both the skill and the equipment requisite for assault on fortifications. Secondly, the Romans were saved, as often in the past, by a great general who rallied their armies when the situation seemed desperate. The saviour on this occasion was Theodosius, a gifted officer raised to the imperial power by the surviving "Augustus", Flavius Gratianus (Gratian), in order to cope with the emergency. Theodosius solved the manpower problem by enrolling friendly Christian Goths, already settled within the Empire, to resist the invaders. A treaty was at last made with the immigrants, according to which they were allowed to settle within the Empire, south of the lower Danube, as a confederate people under their own rulers, but serving under Roman officers in time of war. This was very much what they had wanted in the first place.

For Theodosius' policy of absorbing the barbarians whom he could not evict, there was an ample precedent. Such absorption was in the essence of Roman political instinct; it can be instanced in the earliest days of the Republic and in the later recognition of client kingdoms. Faced with ever-lengthening numerical odds, caused not only by migratory pressure but also by expanding barbarian populations, the Roman Emperor could hardly have

Below: *Romans versus barbarians. In the later years of the Empire, as migrant populations were increasingly absorbed, the distinction between the two groups became a legal rather than an ethnic differentiation.*

done better. It was indeed an imaginative solution. However, the point had been reached when absorption of barbarians by Romans could more appropriately be described as dilution of Romans among barbarians.

This situation, like the Persian Wars, led increasingly to the adoption of alien arms and armour by the imperial forces. In the time of Theodosius, the legionary, with his characteristic crested helmet and cuirass, was still a recognizable Roman type. But at the same time, legions were beginning to use exotic weapons such as the *spatha*—a long broadsword—which had in Tacitus' day been employed only by foreign auxiliaries in the Roman army. Instead of the *pilum*, some infantry units were now armed with the *lancea*, a lighter javelin, to which extra precision and impetus could be given by the use of an attached sling strap. The terms *spiculum* and *vericulum* also indicate new types of missile weapons. The general tendency was towards lighter kinds of throwing spears.

Goths in Revolt

In 388, with the help of a German general, Theodosius had suppressed the rebellion of Magnus Maximus, a military pretender based on Britain, who had extended his power to Gaul and Spain and finally invaded the central provinces of the Empire. Theodosius' German general then turned against him and supported another pretender in Rome, but the Emperor promptly marched from Constantinople into Italy and extinguished

AD | 443 British vainly appeal to Aëtius for military aid | 445 Attila sole ruler of the Huns | 447 Ramparts of Constantinople rebuilt after earthquake | 451 Attila defeated at the battle of Châlons

208

The Roman Army c AD 350

The Roman army had changed radically by Constantine's day. The old legions and auxiliaries were now second class border troops, greatly reduced in numbers. A mobile elite field army now existed. It consisted of cavalry units called *vexillationes palatinae* and 5 infantry *legiones palatinae* (each unit being about 1000-1500 strong) and *auxilia palatina* (10 units of 500 each). One of these auxiliaries, from a unit that was recruited in Britain is shown here. He can be identified by his shield pattern which is described in an army list in the *Notitia Dignitatum*. His belt is very like a modern "Sam Browne" belt, with attachment points for utensils. He carries a long sword *(spatha)* and *lancea.* It is uncertain to what extent armour was worn — Ammianus frequently

mentions "glittering" and "shining armour". The reconstruction is based on figures carved on the Arch of Constantine.

Other Troop Types

The light cavalryman (below) played an increasingly important part in the Roman army at this time. He belongs to a unit called *Mauri feroces* (ferocious Moors). Other light cavalry had large oval shields, like the infantry, and were called *scutarii.* The former legionary scouts were now separate units of light advanced cavalry; they wore helmets and carried small shields. All units carried javelins and *spathae* as their main weapons, but units of horse archers also existed. The drawing (below left) shows a foot soldier from a unit of Gallic and Belgic archers. He carries an axe and buckler as his secondary armament.

452	453	454	455	AD
Aquileia destroyed by Attila	Death of Attila	Persians meet invasion of White Huns	Vandals sack Rome	

209

both the Roman rival and his German supporter. Events took this course because Theodosius was a strong emperor, able to fight his own wars. Under weak or pusillanimous emperors, the real power lay with their commanders-in-chief, and the commanders-in-chief were frequently of Germanic barbarian origin.

The Goths whom Theodosius had settled south of the Danube remained loyal to him during his lifetime. But their chief, Alaric, who had commanded a Gothic contingent during the Italian campaign, aspired to a higher appointment, and after Theodosius' death he led his people in revolt. Under Alaric's leadership, the Goths from the Danube settlement (Lower Moesia), after briefly threatening the walls of Constantinople, marched southward through Thrace and ravaged Macedonia and north Greece. They were checked, however, by the very able Western commander-in-chief, Stilicho, the only officer who was able to cope with Alaric. As a result of political intrigue, the Emperor Arcadius at Constantinople ordered Stilicho off Eastern territory. Stilicho obeyed, and Alaric was then free to continue his march southwards. Athens paid the Goths to go away, but they invaded the Peloponnese. Arcadius, having had time to think again, appealed to Stilicho to come back—and

Stilicho came. He reached Corinth with his army by sea, outmanoeuvred the Goths in the Peloponnese and forced Alaric to make peace. By a new treaty, the Goths received land to the east of the Adriatic, and Alaric was proclaimed king of Illyria. It was not a solution which was expected to last, and it did not.

Alaric's attitude seems to have been in some ways ambiguous. He had at first been ambitious for promotion in the Roman army, but when disappointed had eagerly espoused the cause of nationalistic Gothic independence, which enjoyed a considerable vogue among the Balkan Visigoths over whom he ruled. The agreement which he reached with Stilicho seems temporarily to have satisfied both his Roman and his Gothic aspirations, for while recognized as king by the Gothic population, he was also granted the title of Master of the Armed Forces in Illyricum—a top Roman appointment.

"Master of the Armed Forces" was a title which had become important under Theodosius. In the time of Constantine the Great, the Master of the Horse (*Magister Equitum*) and Master of Foot (*Magister Peditum*) had been separate appointments. But Theodosius combined the two into a single command (*Magister utriusque militiae*). Officers so ranking might be attached to the emperor's staff or given

authority over specified regions, as Alaric was in Illyricum. In the West, the divided command of horse and foot persisted until a later date, but under an emperor like Theodosius' son Honorius, who was no soldier himself, the need for a unified command became imperative, and the commander-in-chief, who automatically received patrician social status on appointment, came to be known, curiously, as the Patrician. The old term *patricius*, originally applied to aristocratic members of the early Republic, had been revived by Constantine as an honorary title, but in the 5th century it was often held by successful barbarian officers and indicated supreme military command.

The Vandals

Stilicho, like Alaric, was an officer of barbarian origin. He differed in being not a Goth, but a Vandal. In the fifth century, the Vandals were a very active Germanic people, but in comparison with other barbarian nations, they were not numerous. Their earliest recorded homeland was in south Scandinavia but, migrating southwards, by the end of the second century AD they had become the restless western neighbours of Gothic settlements north of the Danube. A

Enemies of Rome

Ostrogothic Chieftain AD 350
The Ostrogoths had more cavalry than the Visigoths. They were mostly unarmoured except for chiefs such as this man.

Frankish Warrior c AD 400
A typical warrior is shown armed with a heavy throwing spear and a Frankish throwing axe. The striped tunic, shaved nape and moustache are characteristic of this nation.

Visigoth Warrior c AD 400
The Visigoths were mainly infantry. The long-sleeved tunic and odd shield are characteristic—but oval shields were also used. Captured Roman arms were frequently carried.

Sassanid Noble c AD 450
The Sassanid dynasty displaced the Parthians. This reconstruction is based on a statue of King Chosroes. *Clibanarii* were more heavily armoured, like the Roman on page 201.

AD	476 Romulus Augustulus deposed	477 Death of Gaiseric	489 Theodoric the Ostrogoth encouraged by Emperor Zeno to invade Italy

further migration was made as a result of pressure from the Huns, and in 406 the Vandals crossed the Rhine, ravaged and plundered Gaul, then made their way into Spain. In these wanderings, they were accompanied by the Alans from south Russia, but the Visigoths in Spain, acting under Roman influence, attacked them fiercely and virtually exterminated one section of their community.

In 429, under the most celebrated of their kings, Gaiseric, the Vandals, with their Alan associates, crossed into Africa. Their entire population is reported at this time to have been only 80,000 strong. Probably, not more than 30,000 of these will have been fighting men. The number is small when one remembers Ammianus Marcellinus' instance of a single German tribe which in the course of 60 years had increased its population from 6,000 to 59,000. Gaiseric soon exerted full control over north Africa. Like other Germanic nations, the Vandals had made contact with Christianity before they entered Roman imperial territory. Like many other Germans, also, they had been converted to an heretical form of Christianity (Arianism). Gaiseric was an ardent Arian and persecuted the Catholic Christians of north Africa with fanatical zeal.

The Vandals were notable as a sea-going nation. Perhaps the experience of the African immigration opened their eyes to the further possibilities of water transport. Gaiseric acquired a fleet and used it for the purpose of widespread piracy, against which the western Mediterranean, by the end of the fifth century, had absolutely no protection. It may seem surprising that a nation with a long history of overland migration should have developed in this way, but the Goths, who had similarly reached the Mediterranean in the third century, had quickly adapted themselves to maritime conditions and launched sea-borne raids on the Black Sea and further south into the Aegean.

Certainly, the seafaring habit seems to have taken deep root among the Vandals and it perhaps antedates even the Vandal occupation of Africa. At the end of the fourth century, Stilicho, adhering to the traditional methods of his compatriots, transported his army to Corinth by sea. After he had come to terms with Alaric in 397, he dispatched another sea-borne force to north Africa to quell a rebellion in that province. Clearly, Rome's great Vandal generalissimo was in undisputed command of central and western

Above: *Stilicho, the great general of Vandal descent, who defended the Western Empire against Alaric's Goths. Alaric was himself a high-ranking "Roman" officer.*

Mediterranean waters. History suggests that Stilicho and Gaiseric studied in the same strategic school.

The weakness of the Vandals, of course, lay in the paucity of their numbers, and in this they may be contrasted sharply with many other barbarian nations, who could rely on numbers to compensate for lack of military skill and sophisticated armament. For this reason, the renowned Byzantine general, Belisarius, acting on behalf of the Emperor Justinian, was able in the sixth century to cross with a fleet into Africa and crush the Vandal kingdom completely. It never revived. We should also notice, in this context, that Greek seafaring tradition in the East, given full support from Constantinople, was still able to provide a bulwark against organized piracy during centuries when the seas and shores of the West were hopelessly exposed to such attackers.

The Invasion of Italy

Stilicho, by his treaty with Alaric in Greece, had bought himself time to deal with other enemies — notably some north African rebels. Alaric, for his part, had obtained an excellent springboard for attack on Italy. In addition, Illyricum contained mines and arsenals from which his troops could be supplied. His offensive in the year 400 was well planned and had been preceded by negotiations with Ostrogothic settlers north of the Alps. As Alaric advanced round the Adriatic his allies descended from the mountains. But Stilicho was able to deflect this pincer movement, which was perhaps mistimed, and by prompt action compelled the northern enemies to retire before he confronted Alaric.

Like other barbarians, the Goths found difficulty in penetrating fortifications. Even so, the Emperor Honorius, placing little reliance on his fortress of Asta (Asti), abandoned the area of Milan and took up residence in Ravenna, where the marshes provided additional security. Stilicho, after a campaign of much manoeuvring and a fierce battle at Pollentia, inflicted a final defeat on Alaric near Verona in 403, thus securing the return of the Gothic commander and his army to Illyricum. In the following year, the Ostrogoths again attacked from the north, and on this occasion Stilicho defeated them decisively, sold many of the survivors into slavery and enrolled others in his own army.

In 407, another military usurper emerged from Britain, while the activities of Vandals and other barbarians in Gaul occupied Stilicho's attention. Alaric, alive to his opportunity, supported by fresh Danubian allies, led his people round to Noricum (Austria), north of the Alps, and received from the Emperor that territory, with a substantial payment in gold, as the price of quiescence at a difficult moment. The Emperor was closely connected by marriage with Stilicho, who virtually controlled the Western Empire during these years. But the great general suddenly fell from power, and Honorius foolishly had him executed.

There was now no commander in the West capable of placing any restraint upon Alaric, who at once asked for more gold and more land. When these were refused, he invaded Italy and marched on Rome. He raised the siege of the city when the Emperor temporized, but soon renewed it when

493
Theodoric founds Ostrogothic kingdom of Italy

c500
British victory over Saxons in Wessex

c524
The philosopher Boethius put to death by Theodoric

AD

211

The Fate of Roman Britain

In considering these years, when chaos engulfed the centre of the Empire, we may understandably feel curiosity as to the fate of Britain, situated at the circumference. In 410, answering a request for military aid against barbarian invaders, Honorius advised the Roman community of Britain to arrange for its own defence. Like other parts of the Empire, Britain was under attack, and the attackers were no longer merely the Picts (Painted-men). They were Germanic tribes from Frisia and the mouth of the Rhine. The term "Saxon" at first denoted a particular tribe; later, it was applied with little discrimination to Germanic peoples who inhabited the regions around the mouth of the Rhine and the North Sea coast.

At the end of the third century, Constantius, father of Constantine the Great, after eliminating Carausius and his successor, improved a chain of forts, which Carausius and other commanders had established, to defend the "Saxon Shore" — ie, the south and east coasts of Britain and the Channel coast of Gaul. The idea of such a defence may indeed have originated with Carausius. The Saxon-shore forts were much bigger than earlier Roman forts in Britain, and they relied upon massive masonry, not merely stone-faced earthworks. Imposing ruins are still visible and nine British forts are listed in the *Notitia Dignitatum*. Ammianus Marcellinus mentions that these defences were placed under the command of a "Count of the Saxon Shore" (*Comes litoris Saxonici*), while in the north, the Wall was the responsibility of the "Duke" (*dux*) of Britain who had his headquarters at York. In the time of Diocletian and Constantine, *dux*, that general term for a leader or guide, had become the specific title of an officer in charge of frontier defence. It was later applied to the chiefs of barbarian tribal groupings too small to qualify for rule by kings. Similarly, *comes*, meaning literally a "companion", had denoted membership of the emperor's staff. Under Constantine, it became a title applicable to high-ranking officers and officials.

In 367, Saxons, acting in collusion with Scots (who came originally from Ireland) and Picts, overran Britain. Like other barbarians, they failed to capture the strongly fortified towns, but damage done to a previously flourishing rural community was

negotiations broke down. He was thus enabled to impose an emperor of his own choosing in Rome, but quickly became disappointed with his choice and impatiently deposed the puppet. Further attempts to negotiate with Honorius at Ravenna proved fruitless, and after a third siege Alaric's men were surreptitiously admitted to Rome by some Gothic slaves within the walls. The Gothic army plundered the city for three days, but did comparatively little damage. With Stilicho gone, the sea was open to Alaric, and he aimed at north Africa. Unfortunately for his purpose, the fleet which he had assembled at Rhegium was destroyed by a storm, and he himself died soon after (410). He was buried in a river bed to ensure that his last resting place should not be disturbed.

The Gothic capture of Rome hardly amounted to a "sack". There was certainly enough booty left to reward the efforts of Gaiseric's Vandal raiders when they arrived by sea and captured the city in 455. Gaiseric carried away the Jewish temple treasures which Titus had appropriated four centuries earlier. Ships, as the Vandals well understood, were useful for the transport of moveables. The Vandal king also made prisoner the

Above: *The city walls of Constantinople, still to be seen at Istanbul. These are not the original walls of Constantine but those built later in the reign of Theosodius II.*

two daughters of the Emperor Valentinian III, one of whom he married to his son. The other, apparently not required, was sent home.

Imaginative illustrations of Rome's barbarian invaders easily leave the impression that they swept into the Empire with irresistible verve in a series of cavalry charges. Consideration of the foregoing facts, however, suggests a different view. Stilicho and Alaric, in their wars, were extremely cautious, frequently preferring manoeuvre and negotiated peace to pitched battle and bloody victory. Alaric, like Stilicho, was one of Theodosius' old officers, and his outlook on warfare was that of a professional soldier. Moreover, the people over whom he ruled, though they invaded Italy, as the legions of rebellious Roman generals had often done in the past, were not invaders of the Empire. They were simply a dissatisfied immigrant community, asserting what they considered their rights as members of the Roman world.

| 526 Death of Theodoric | 527 Coronation of Justinian as "Augustus" | 534 Belisarius, Justinian's general, overthrows the Vandals in Africa |

The Huns

The Huns were a Mongoloid nomad people who lived on the steppes of Central Asia. Around AD 370 they began to migrate, and launched a series of savage attacks on the Goths, who in turn crossed the Danube into Thrace. The Huns depended chiefly on their herds of livestock for food, clothing and their other needs. Their way of life was in many ways similar to that of the later plains Indians in America, who depended on the buffalo. They were superb horsemen—Roman writers such as Zosimus and Ammianus describe them eating, sleeping, and even performing their natural functions on horseback. The warrior shown here is fairly typical. He is dressed in woollen tunic and trousers while his jacket, leggings and cap are of goatskin. His weapons are a bow and bone-pointed arrows, a shield and captured spear, and a lariat. The Huns terrified people by their ugliness, which partly derived from their habit of ritually scarring their cheeks. His horse is of the hardy Steppe breed which still survives today. Stocky and shaggy, it could survive conditions which other breeds could not.

535
Belisarius makes war on the Ostrogoths in Italy

554
Narses, Justinian's general, drives Ostrogoths from Italy

565
Death of Justinian   Death of Belisarius

AD

213

severe, and the Duke of Britain and the Count of the Saxon Shore were both killed. The situation was restored by the valiant Roman general Theodosius (father of the Emperor Theodosius the Great), who drove out the barbarians, rebuilt fortifications, and established a valuable line of signal stations on the Yorkshire coast to give advance warning of sea-borne attack.

After two imperial pretenders, Magnus Maximus (385) and the upstart Flavius Claudius Constantinus (407) had drafted troops away from the island in support of their southward adventures, Britain was again left virtually undefended, though in the intervening period (395) Stilicho had done something to reorganize garrison forces. After Honorius' negative reaction in 410, we can rely on little but archaeological evidence for our knowledge of Roman military administration in the island.

To this obscure epoch must be assigned the exploits of the legendary King Arthur—in so far as they have any real historical basis. A Romano-British chief named Artorius perhaps resisted the Saxon invaders. Gildas, the Celtic monk, writing in Latin in the sixth century, records a great British victory in the Wessex area in about 500 AD, and Nennius, a ninth-century chronicler, associates this victory with the name of Arthur, which he gives as that of a victorious general, not a king.

The Defeat of the Huns

In 446, Roman Britain made its last known appeal for imperial help to Flavius Aëtius, the commander-in-chief (Patrician) of the Emperor Valentinian III, grandson of the great Theodosius. But Aëtius was already heavily engaged against other barbarians—who were soon to include the Huns. It was, of course, inevitable that the Huns, whose westward progress had precipitated the migration of other peoples, should sooner or later appear in their own persons. The reputation of the Huns is well known. Their cruelty was often without malice, and their malice was too terrible to contemplate. Nevertheless, in their early contacts with the Roman world, they had sometimes been enrolled in the imperial service, and Stilicho had been served by a very faithful Hunnish bodyguard.

The boastful menaces of Attila, who became sole king of the Huns in 445, suggest something of a buffoon but, far from that, he must have been a

Above: *Maiden Castle, the conspicuous hill fort near Dorchester. An important Stone Age settlement, it was later a centre of British resistance captured by Vespasian's legions.*

Right: *The Roman fort at Porchester on the Hampshire coast. This is a well preserved example of Rome's Saxon-shore defences. The Norman castle is also visible.*

commander of very shrewd ability. Under his rule, the Huns dominated and terrorized wide tracts of Europe and Asia, but their power collapsed after his death. Apart from Attila's leadership, the main strength of the Huns, as of other barbarians, lay in their immense number, swollen as it was in their case by the addition of many subject peoples. They were a Mongoloid nation of hunters and shepherds from the steppes of central Asia and, as one might expect, they extensively employed the horse and the bow for warlike as well as peaceful purposes. But the trappings of their horses were of gold and their sword hilts were inlaid with gold and precious stones. Indeed, they had an insatiable appetite for gold, and were usually willing to refrain from hostilities if offered sufficient of it. Attila had inherited from his father a royal capital "city" in Pannonia (Hungary). It was built of wood but contained a stone bath-house. From this base, Attila was able to threaten the Bosphorus. The Emperor paid him gold and ceded him territory, but though the Huns had ravaged the Eastern Empire, they could not in any case hope to prevail against the impregnable walls of Constantinople.

Meanwhile, the Western Emperor's sister, Honoria, who for her past sins had been relegated by pious relatives to a condition of perpetual chastity, for which she had no vocation, offered herself secretly to Attila, and he would have been willing to concede her the status of concubine in return for a dowry of half the Western Empire. But these terms were rejected and Attila unleashed an attack against Gaul and Western Europe.

Aëtius, the Patrician, as commander-in-chief, now formed an alliance with his old Visigothic enemies in Gaul, and halted Attila's advance at Orléans. The combined Imperial and Gothic forces then inflicted a bloody defeat upon the Huns in the "Catalaunian Plain", somewhere near Châlons. This battle has been reckoned as one of the most decisive in the world's history, but considering its violence, it decided very little. The defeated enemy was not pursued. Attila retreated to his wooden capital in Pannonia and the next year launched a major offensive into Italy. He requisitioned siege-engines with their operators, and after a three-month investment utterly destroyed Aquileia. Some fugitives escaped to the Adriatic lagoons, where their refugee settlement eventually gave rise to the city of Venice.

Attila was now met near Lake Garda by Pope Leo (the Great) who dissuaded him from marching southward against Rome. The Huns, though not Christians, tended to regard any religion with awe, and much was due to the personality of Leo, whose deterrent influence was again successfully exercised three years later when

AD | 596   St Augustine of Canterbury lands in Kent | 610   Heraclius becomes emperor | 622   Flight of Muhammed from Mecca to Medinah; Moslem era (Hegira) begins

214

Gaiseric's Vandals entered Rome. At the same time, Attila exacted a promise that Honoria and the treasure which constituted the moveable portion of her dowry should be surrendered to him, failing which, hostilities would be renewed. However, before the promise could be fully carried out, he died suddenly, having burst a blood vessel on his first night with a new concubine (453). Without their leader, the Huns ceased to be a serious menace and were soon annihilated, dispersed or expelled by the combined efforts of Goths and other Germanic barbarians who opposed them.

Aëtius, who defeated Attila in Gaul, was the son of a Count (*comes*) of Africa. In his youth, he had been a hostage among the Huns and during his sojourn among them learnt much of their customs, establishing some friendship with them. Indeed, Aëtius originally imposed his power at Ravenna with the help of Hunnish auxiliaries, and expectation that he might again need their aid explains his reluctance to pursue them after his great victory in Gaul.

Aëtius was a colourful character. History credits him, during the confused civil strife that followed Honorius' death, with having killed one of his professional rivals in single combat. He was eventually stabbed to death by his imperial master, Valentinian, whose jealousy recalls that of Honorius for Stilicho.

The Defences of Constantinople

Although the Goths and the Huns were able to exact ever-increasing payments in gold as an inducement to spare the territories of the Eastern Empire, both Alaric and Attila realized that they had little prospect of capturing Constantinople itself, and they did not waste time and effort in the attempt. We have already drawn attention to the ideal strategic position of the city. A plan of Constantinople will show it to be built on a roughly triangular promontory: the profile of a vulture-like beak, across the landward base of which a heavily fortified wall extends from the Sea of Marmara in the south to an arm of the Bosphorus (The Golden Horn) in the north.

The original wall of Constantine, damaged by an earthquake in 401, was promptly repaired by Arcadius, but during the minority of his son and successor Theodosius II, the Praetorian Prefect Anthemius demolished the old walls and built new (413). These ramparts were again ruined by an earthquake, but in the year 447 they were rebuilt in three months. Situated one mile to the west of the line traced by Constantine, Theodosius' walls (see picture on p 212) enclosed a city of double the area, and in the space between the old and the new walls the Imperial Gothic guard was stationed.

The outer face of the fortifications was protected by a broad, deep moat. An attacker who overcame this obstacle would then be confronted by a breastwork approximately equal to his own height, and some 40 feet (12m) behind this, as an inner defence, stood a chain of towers, linked by a curtain wall 26 feet (8m) high. The fourth line of defence was the main city wall itself, lying back at a further distance of 66 feet (20m), 43 feet (13m) in height, and fortified by great towers from which enfilading showers of missiles could be directed into the flanks of the assailants. Other walls of solid masonry defended the perimeter of the city where it was adjacent to the sea. These embraced the whole headland and connected with the land walls at either end. They consisted, like the land walls, of a double rampart, fortified by towers at brief intervals. The Golden Horn itself was guarded against enemy naval attack by a chain boom.

However, the walls of the capital might not have been enough to defend its inhabitants, if they had not given a high priority to naval strength. The Byzantine fleet made use mainly of light galleys (*dromones* in Greek), the equivalent of the *liburnae* used by Augustus. Clearly, with their ever-pressing need to conserve manpower, the Eastern emperors could not have afforded to develop the multireme leviathans of earlier times. The

628
Heraclius overcomes Persians and their allies
Death of Persian king Khosroes II

632
Death of Muhammed

641
Death of Heraclius

AD

215

Byzantine vessels also made considerable use of sails, and they often featured several masts, which—contrary to earlier Roman and Greek practice—were not dismounted during action. From their Arab enemies of a later date, the Byzantines also adopted the triangular lateen sail.

Relying, in the tradition of Graeco-Roman civilization, on science and technique to defeat overwhelming enemy odds, the Byzantines produced a secret weapon, which for many centuries gave them a decisive advantage. This was a type of flame missile, which was used with devastating effect against enemy ships. Many combustible mixtures employed in the Middle Ages were loosely termed "Greek Fire". The precise Byzantine compound was based on ingredients which are unknown, for it was a well-kept secret, but the characteristic of the original Greek Fire was that it ignited—or was at least not quenched—on contact with water. This suggests that quicklime was an element, and it must also be remembered that petroleum, known to the Greeks as *naphtha* (Persian *naft*), was available in surface deposits in Babylonia. The invention of Greek Fire was attributed to Callinicus, a Greek engineer from Heliopolis in Syria, who lived in the reign of the Emperor Constantine Pogonatus (668-685). Greek Fire was sometimes projected in containers in the manner of grenades, but it was also released through tubes, with which Byzantine warships were specially fitted.

Apart from the defence of Constantinople itself, the Byzantines maintained a flotilla to patrol the Danube, and behind this river frontier Justinian built a four-line system of nearly 300 fortresses and watch-towers to defend the Empire at what had for many centuries proved to be its most vulnerable point. It should be noticed that even in Justinian's day, when Constantinople was the focus of an expansionist strategy which emulated the era of the first Augustus and his immediate successors, war on some fronts remained defensive. While Africa was being won from the Vandals, Italy from the Ostrogoths, and southern Spain from the Visigoths, repeated military efforts in the East were necessary to hold the Sassanid Persians at bay. Inevitably, with the death of Justinian, the Byzantines, deprived of dynamic leadership, reverted to a defensive strategy, which in the centuries that followed was often barely enough to save the city itself from occupation by invading forces.

Above: *A map of Constantinople in 1534. The city's defences both by sea and land were virtually impregnable until breached by Turkish cannon in 1453.*

Despite Justinian's Roman sentiments and aspirations, the army which manned his defences and fought his wars was far from being Roman in character. It was not any longer primarily an army of legionary foot soldiers, but of heavily mailed cavalry on the Persian model, and the weapons on which it chiefly relied were the lance and the bow. Even in the infantry, archers and javelin-throwers predominated. Light cavalry was supplied by Huns and Arabs. There was, of course, nothing un-Roman in using barbarian auxiliaries to combat barbarian enemies. Julius Caesar had done as much. It was simply a question of degree. Indeed, many of the gradual changes in equipment may be traced back to the second century AD.

What happened in the West

No "Dark Age" closed the history of the Eastern Roman Empire. When Turkish cannon at last breached the walls of Constantinople in 1453, the traditions of the ancient world, which had until then in many ways persisted, were suddenly obliterated by the forces of medieval Islam. Historians can point to no hiatus between the continuation of antiquity and the dawn of the Middle Ages in this area. In the West, the story was quite different. Odoacer,

the first king of Italy, was a moderately enlightened ruler. But in 489, Theodoric the Ostrogothic chief, ambiguously encouraged by the Eastern Emperor Zeno, invaded Italy, besieged Ravenna for three years, came to terms with Odoacer, and then had him treacherously murdered. Theodoric, despite this, was a beneficent if illiterate ruler. He believed in the vigour of the Germanic nations and deplored their disunity. At the same time, he felt that the older inhabitants of the Empire were necessary for administrative duties. He employed the philosopher Boethius as a top civil servant and, after executing him on ill-founded suspicions, filled his place with the historian Cassiodorus. Theodoric's attitude, in so far as it divorced power from education, foreshadowed the medieval situation in which unlettered rulers employed clerics—as the word indicates—as clerks.

The Gothic kingdom of Italy fell a prey to family dissension after Theodoric's death, and Justinian had a pretext for intervention. The conquest of Italy by Belisarius was followed by a period of Gothic resurgence which lasted for about 13 years, but the Ostrogoths were finally driven out by Justinian's Armenian general Narses (553). Nobody knows where they went. Italy was now governed by one of Justinian's "exarchs" (*exarchoi*), as Byzantine provincial governors were called, and even when the briefly re-established Roman Empire had crumbled after Justinian's death, Ravenna and its adjacent territory remained under imperial control, while the Pope still acted as an imperial officer, governing the "duchy" of Rome. The Lombards, who in 568 had settled in north Italy, already aspired to dominate the whole peninsula, and for a long time the Popes, in self-defence, maintained close ties with Constantinople. However, the inevitable dispute about secular and spiritual power arose, and, after a Byzantine fleet, dispatched in 732 to reconquer Italy and effect the arrest of Pope Gregory III, had been wrecked, the Bishops of Rome, still threatened by the Lombards, found new protectors in the kings of the Franks. The Franks were northern Germanic barbarians who had remained pagan for longer than other

Right: *This mosaic of Justinian is still to be seen in the church of San Vitale at Ravenna. Ravenna replaced Rome as capital of the West, and after Justinian conquered Italy became the seat of a Byzantine governor.*

AD

651
Arabs overrun Sassanid empire

Islam replaces Zoro-astrianism

668
Accession of Constantine IV (Pogonatus)

Greek fire invented in his reign

Germanic peoples farther south. The latter, however, as Arians, were converts to an heretical form of Christianity. The Franks, when at last they became Christians, were received into the Catholic Church, in communion with Rome, and their political ties with Rome were correspondingly close. Consequently, when neither oppression nor protection was any longer to be expected from Constantinople, when Ravenna had fallen to the Lombards, and when Papal authority was assailed by strangely anachronistic revivalist movements in Rome itself, Pope Leo III, on Christmas Day, AD 800, in Rome, crowned his champion, the Frankish king Karl (Charlemagne), as Holy Roman Emperor, adding the title "Caesar Augustus". One is familiar with the observation that the Holy Roman Empire was in no sense holy, Roman, nor an Empire. Indeed, few temporal authorities can convincingly lay claim to holiness, but the remaining two-thirds of Voltaire's epigram may equally be applied to the Ravenna régime, in the years when Honorius or Valentinian III pretended to imperial sovereignty in the name of Rome.

Who, indeed, was a Roman? Not merely a citizen of that little town on the Tiber which in the sixth century BC had sided with Etruria against Latin compatriots; not, perhaps, even the Italian ally who had received Roman citizenship after the Social War in the first century BC. Again, it is hard to identify Roman nationality with the wide imperial community which had been admitted to citizenship by the enactment of Caracalla, let alone that same community when it had been permeated by barbarian invaders and immigrants.

Just as it is difficult to say who was a Roman, so it is hard to identify a Roman army, or name a date at which Roman armies ceased to exist. The "dukes" and "counts" who had been imperial officers under Constantine the Great, or under barbarian allied kings and war-lords, gradually bequeathed their titles to the hereditary aristocracies of the Middle Ages. But the old forms and the old ways of thinking died slowly. Theodoric, before his invasion of Italy, had been invested with the ranks of Patrician and consul. As late as 754, the Pope, acting in effect as an imperial officer, conferred on the Frankish king Pepin the title of Patrician.

If we choose to look back, the whole history of the Graeco-Roman world may be regarded as one long war against barbarism, in which the internecine conflicts of Greek city states, of Roman generals and imperial pretenders are merely frustrating and debilitating interludes. The Greeks and Romans sometimes saw war against barbarism as a war for liberty, yet liberty was necessarily sacrificed in order to wage it. It was, in fact, a war for literacy rather than for liberty, and were it not for the Romanized Christian clergy and the barbarian awe of religion in general, it would, in the West, have been completely lost. However, protraction of the struggle until such time as barbarism, like civilization, had been diluted, suggests a kind of victory—at any rate, a draw.

217

Glossary

Latin words are in capitals, Greek words in italic capitals.

A

ACIES Battle line.

AERARIUM Treasury. Especially, public treasury at Rome.

AGEMA An army in the field. In the Macedonian army, an élite unit.

AGGER Rampart, earthwork.

ALAE (s. ALA) Wings of the Roman army, usually formed by cavalry. Hence, cavalry units.

ANABASIS A march to the interior (literally: "a going up". The Greeks went "up" from the coast and "down" to it, whether their journey was by land or sea).

ANTESIGNANI Roman troops who fought in front of the standards.

AQUILA An eagle. The Roman legionary standard.

AQUILIFER "Eagle-bearer". Standard-bearer.

AUXILIA Auxiliary troops in the Roman army. recruited from overseas non-citizens.

B

BALLISTA Type of Roman catapult.

BENEFICARII Soldiers discharging special or orderly duties on staff of senior officers.

BRACCAE (BRACAE) Trousers, breeches.

C

CAETRATI (CETRATI) Troops armed with the CETRA, a small Spanish shield.

CALIGA (pl. CALIGAE) Heavy shoe of Roman soldier.

CATAPHRACTOI (Literally: "enclosed"). Cataphracts. A term applicable both to decked ships and mailed cavalry.

CATAPULTA (KATAPELTES, KATAPALTES) Spring-operated artillery weapon used by the Greeks and Romans.

CENTURIA Century. Company. Varying in strength from 60-80 men.

CENTURIO Centurion. "Warrant-officer" in charge of a century.

CHEIROBALLISTRA Light catapult (see illustration on page 178).

CINGULUM A belt.

CLIBANARIUS (pl. CLIBANARII) Mailed cuirassier of the later Empire. Like cataphract. (See illustration on page 201 for further details).

CLIENS Retainer. Dependant. Protégé.

COHORS A cohort. Unit of the Roman army. COHORS QUINGENARIA was c480 strong. COHORS MILLIARIA c800 strong.

COHORTES VIGILUM The night watch. Police and fire brigade at Rome.

COMES A "companion". Member of the Roman Imperial retinue. Dignitary of the late Empire. Original of the medieval "count". Thus, "Count of the Saxon Shore".

COMITATENSES (s. COMITATENSIS) "Companionate". Roman field army attached to the Emperor's person: distinct from frontier garrison troops (LIMITANEI).

CONTUBERNIUM A mess fraternity. A squad of 8 men.

CORAX A "raven". Naval grappling hook.

CORNICULARIUS Originally leader of a small unit (or wing) of troops in Roman army. Later, a military clerk.

CORVUS A "raven". Naval grappling hook. Latin for CORAX.

D

DECURIA (pl. DECURIAE) A troop of ten Roman horsemen.

DECURIO Commander of a DECURIA.

DIADOCHUS (pl. DIADOCHOI. Latinised as DIADOCHUS-I). A successor. Especially, the Successors of Alexander the Great.

DIEKPLUS (DIEKPLOUS). A Greek naval manoeuvre of breaking through the enemy line.

DILOCHITES Commander of DILOCHIA. a double LOCHOS.

DOLABRA Pickaxe. A tool used by Roman soldiers.

DRACO (Greek: DRACON) A dragon, serpent. Dragon-like military standard.

DROMONES (s. DROMON) Light galleys in Byzantine navy.

DUOVIRI NAVALES (DUUMVIRI) At Rome, 2 commissioners appointed to equip fleets.

DUX Leader. High-ranking frontier or provincial officer in late Imperial times. Origin of medieval title "duke".

E

ENOMOTIA (pl. ENOMOTIAI) Unit of the Spartan army. Literally, a group "sworn in".

EPHOROI (s. EPHOROS) Ephors. Supervisors. Magistrates at Sparta to whom the kings were responsible.

EQUITES Roman cavalrymen. Later, with social significance, cf. knights, cavaliers. But their social status was middle-class, lower than that of the senatorial families.

EQUITES SINGULARES Roman Emperor's mounted bodyguard of foreign troops.

EXARCHIA Exarchate. Province of the Byzantine Empire. Especially, the Italian province centred in Ravenna.

EXARCHOS A provincial governor of the Byzantine Empire.

EXPLORATORES Scouts or reconnaissance troops in the Roman army.

EXTRAORDINARII "Outside the ranks". COHORTES EXTRAORDINARIAE were special cohorts of Italian allies attached to a Roman general's H.Q.

F

FABRI Artificers.

FALCATA Scythe-shaped. A curved sword.

FISCUS Treasury. Especially, Roman Emperor's treasury, distinct from AERARIUM.

FRAMEA German spear or javelin (Germanic word).

G

GAESATI Troops armed with the GAESUM.

GAESUM A long Gallic javelin. (Celtic word).

GASTRAPHETES "Belly-release". Greek crossbow, supported against the user's belly.

GEROUSIA The Spartan Senate.

GERRON Wicker shield, such as Persians used.

GLADIUS Roman short cut-and-thrust sword, of Spanish origin.

GORYTUS A combined quiver and bow-case, typical of the Scythians.

H

HARPAGO (Greek: HARPAX) Naval grappling hook launched from catapult.

HASTA Spear.

HASTATI Literally "spearmen". Front line of Roman three-line battle formation.

HASTATUS POSTERIOR A title denoting status or grade of seniority among Roman centurions.

HEILOTES (HEILOS) A helot. Spartan serf

HELEPOLIS "City-taker". A giant assault-tower on wheels, used in sieges.

HEMILOCHITES Leader of a HEMILOCHIA (half-lochos).

HETAIROI "Companions". Title of Macedonian élite cavalry.

HIPPARCHIA (pl. HIPPARCHIAI) A cavalry unit.

HIPPARCHOS (pl. HIPPARCHOI) Senior cavalry commander in Greek or Macedonian army.

HIPPEIS Greek "knights": actual cavalrymen or simply of cavalier status.

HOPLITES (pl. HOPLITAI) Hoplite. Greek heavy foot soldier of the classical period.

HOPLON A weapon. Especially, the large round shield of a hoplite.

HYPASPISTAI (s. HYPASPISTES) Hypaspists. Shield-bearers. Later, special infantry corps in the Macedonian army.

I

ILE A body of men. A cavalry unit in Greek and Macedonian armies.

IMAGO (pl. IMAGINES) Picture, portrait. Roman military standards might carry IMAGINES of the emperors and other exalted persons.

IMMUNIS (pl. IMMUNES) Roman soldier excused general duties on grounds of specialist capacity.

IMPEDIMENTA The baggage of a Roman army.

IMPERATOR Roman commander-in-chief. Especially, a victor's title. Original of the title "Emperor".

K

KATAPELTES See CATAPULTA.

KOPIS Cleaver, slashing sword.

KONTOS Pike-shaft, pike.

KYKLOS Naval defensive tactical formation. Literally, a "ring" or "circle".

L

LANCEA Light spear or javelin.

LEGATUS Roman lieutenant-general. Commander-in-chief's deputy.

LIBRARII Clerks, secretaries.

LIBURNA (pl. LIBURNAE) Light, fast galley, named after an Illyrian nation.

LIMES A boundary path or balk. Especially, the Roman Imperial fortified frontier.

LIMITANEI Troops stationed on the Roman Imperial frontiers.

LINOTHORAX A linen corslet.

LITHOBOLOS Stone-throwing catapult (cf. OXYBELES arrow-shooter).

LOCHAGOS Captain of a LOCHOS.

LOCHOS Greek army unit of varying varying strength. For Spartan LOCHOS see p 46.

LORICATUS (fem. LORICATA) Clothed in a cuirass (LORICA).

M

MACHAIRA Large knife. Later, curved sword, sabre, scimitar.

MAGISTER EQUITUM Master of the Horse. The assistant or colleague of a Roman dictator. In later Empire, appointed with "master of foot" (MAGISTER PEDITUM).

MANIPULUS Maniple. Roman army unit of 2 centuries (CENTURIAE).

MILES GREGARIUS Private soldier in the Roman army.

MORA Unit of the Spartan army. A "division". See p 46.

N

NUMERI Numbers on a roll. Hence, enrolled troops. But applied especially to non-citizen troops in the later Roman army. Initially an occasional levy, they later became a permanent element.

O

ONAGER (Greek: ONAGROS) A kind of catapult. Literally "a wild ass".

OPTIO Petty officer assisting centurion (Originally at "option" of the centurion).

ORBIS A "ring": tactical formation adopted by Roman troops, especially in emergency. cf. Greek KYKLOS.

OURAGOS Man entrusted with bringing up the rear in a Greek or Macedonian army.

OXYBELES Catapult shooting arrow or bolts (cf. LITHOBOLOS stone-thrower).

P

PARABLEMA Protective screen on Greek war galley.

PARMA Light round shield.

PATRICIUS Commander-in-chief of late Roman Imperial army.

PATRONUS "Patron". Protector of a "client" (CLIENS).

PELTASTAI (s. PELTASTES) Light-armed troops, so named from their use of the PELTE (see below).

PELTE (PELTA) Light shield.

PENTECONTER Commander of a PENTECOSTYS (see below).

PENTECONTEROS (PENTECONTOROS) Pentekonter, 50-oared galley.

PENTECOSTYS Small unit of the Spartan army, nominally 50 strong.

PERIPLUS (PERIPLOUS) Circumnavigation. Greek naval manoeuvre.

PEZETAIROI Foot Companions. The Macedonian phalanx.

PHALANX Greek or Macedonian battle formation. The heavy infantry which adopted such a formation.

PHYLARCHOI Cavalry commanders at Athens.

PILUM Roman soldier's heavy javelin.

PILUM MURALE (pl. PILA MURALIA) Palisade stake, picket.

PLUMBATA (pl. PLUMBATAE) Lead-weighted dart.

POLEMARCHOS Senior army officer at Sparta and in other Greek states. Anachronistic title attaching to a political appointment in Athens.

PONTIFEX MAXIMUS Roman chief priest.

POSTSIGNANI Roman troops fighting behind the standards (in contrast with ANTESIGNANI).

PRAEFECTI Prefects. Anyone placed in charge. PRAEFECTI EQUITUM, cavalry commanders.

PRAEFECTUS CASTRORUM Roman camp commandant.

PRAETOR Roman chief magistrate. Consul. Supplementary consul.

PRAETORIUM General's headquarters in a Roman camp.

PRIMIPILUS (PRIMUS PILUS) Chief centurion of a legion.

PRINCEPS "Leader". Title adopted by Augustus and his successors.

PRINCIPES The second line in a Roman battle formation.

PRIVATUS A private individual as distinct from a magistrate.

PRODROMOI Scouts. Forward reconnaissance troops.

PROLETARII The lowest social class at Rome, who contributed to the state only by their offspring (PROLES), since they possessed no property.

PTERUGES Fringed flaps at the armpit and groin of a Greek cuirass.

PUGIO A dagger.

Q

QUAESTOR Quartermaster and purser in Roman army.

QUINQUEREMIS Quinquereme. War galley operated by five ranks of rowers on each side.

S

SAGITTARIUS Archer.

SAMBUCA Mechanical scaling ladder (called after a musical instrument).

SARCINA (pl. SARCINAE) A Roman soldier's pack.

SARISSA Long pike, as used in the Macedonian army.

SAUNION A javelin.

SCORPIO (pl. SCORPIONES) Type of catapult (Literally: "scorpion").

SCUTARII (SCUTATI) Troops armed with the SCUTUM (see below). They might be mounted or (more normally) on foot.

SCUTUM Oblong or oval Roman shield.

SIGNIFER Standard-bearer.

SIGNUM Military standard.

SOCII Allies. Especially, Italian allies who fought in the Roman army.

SOCII NAVALES Allies who served in the Roman navy.

SPATHA (Greek: SPATHE) Broad double-edged sword.

SPICULUM A "spike". Javelin or arrow.

STIMULI (Literally: "goads" or "stings") Pointed stakes or pegs planted as a defence against enemy attack.

SYNTAGMATARCHES Commander of SYNTAGMA or "regiment".

T

TAGMATARCHES Commander of a TAGMA (squadron, brigade).

TAXIARCHOS Commander of a TAXIS (similar to TAGMA).

TESSERARIUS Roman soldier responsible for distributing the TESSERA, tablet with inscribed watchword.

TETRARCHES A leader of 4 LOCHOI.

THALAMITES (pl. THALAMITAI) Rower of the lowest level on a trireme.

THRANITES (pl. THRANITAI) Rower of top level on a trireme.

TIARA Persian head-dress.

TRIARII Soldiers of the rear (third) line in Roman battle formation.

TRIBUNI MILITUM Military tribunes. Officers of the Roman army.

TRIBUNI PLEBIS People's representatives (political).

TRIBUNUS ANGUSTICLAVIUS A tribune of lower status, wearing narrow stripe.

TRIBUNUS LATICLAVIUS A tribune of higher status, wearing broad stripe.

TRIERARCHOS Captain of a trireme, citizen responsible for fitting out a trireme.

TRIERES A trireme.

TRIPLEX ACIES Three-line battle formation.

TRIUMVIRI Triumvirs. Colleagues in a three-man committee.

U

UMBO Shield boss.

V

VELITES Light-armed Roman troops.

VERICULUM Light spear used in Roman Imperial armies.

VERUTUM Javelin, dart.

VEXILLARIUS Standard-bearer. Also, VEXILLARII = legionaries serving in separate detachment under their own standard.

VEXILLUM (pl. VEXILLA) Military cloth standard or ensign.

VIA PRINCIPALIS Main street in Roman camp.

VIA QUINTANA Street in Roman camp (next to the lines of the 5th maniple).

VINEA (pl. VINEAE) Shed or penthouse for the protection of assault forces under enemy walls.

Z

ZEIRA A cloak worn by Arabs and Thracians.

ZYGITES (pl. ZYGITAI) Rower of second level on a trireme.

Picture Credits

The publisher wishes to thank the following individuals and institutions who have supplied photographs, here credited by page number. Pictures credited "British Museum" are reproduced by courtesy of the Trustees of the British Museum, London.

Endpapers: British Museum; 1: British Museum; 2-3: British Museum; 4-5: Scala; 6-7: Ronald Sheridan Photo-Library; 8-9: British Museum; 10-11: British Museum (Michael Holford Library); 12-13: British Museum (Michael Holford Library); Robert Harding Associates/Argos Museum (Photoresources); 14-15: Photoresources/Archaeological Museum, Madrid/National Museum, Athens (R.V. Schoder); 16-17: British Museum (Photoresources)/Louvre Museum/Michael Holford Library; 18-19: Ministry of Culture and Science, Athens; 20-21: Ronald Sheridan Photo-Library/National Museum, Athens (R.V. Schoder)/Sonia Halliday Photographs; 22-23: Sonia Halliday Photographs; 24-25: Ronald Sheridan Photo-Library; 26-27: Ronald Sheridan Photo-Library/Ashmolean Museum, Oxford/British Museum (Michael Holford Library)/Vatican Museum, Rome (Hirmer Fotoarchiv); 28-29: National Museum, Naples (Scala)/British Museum; 32-33: Ashmolean Museum, Oxford; 34: British Museum; 37: Ashmolean Museum, Oxford/British Museum; 39: Ronald Sheridan Photo-Library; 40: Ronald Sheridan Photo-Library/Michael Holford Library; 42-43: British Museum/Acropolis Museum, Athens (Photoresources); 45: Ashmolean Museum, Oxford; 48: British Museum; 52: Wadsworth Athenaeum; 55: British Museum; 56: Photoresources; 58: Bucharest Museum (Photoresources); 61: Photoresources; 64: R.V. Schoder; 68-69: Ronald Sheridan Photo-Library/British Museum; 70-71: National Museum, Naples (R.V. Schoder)/R.V.

Schoder; 72: Photoresources; 77: Photoresources; 83: British Museum; 87: British Museum/National Museum, Naples (R.V. Schoder); 88: Ronald Sheridan Photo-Library; 91: Photoresources; 92: Photoresources; 94: Photoresources; 97: Ashmolean Museum, Oxford; 101: National Museum, Naples (Scala); 102: Ashmolean Museum, Oxford; 104-105: Villa Giulia Museum, Rome (Scala)/British Museum; 106-107: R.V. Schoder/Photoresources; 108: Ashmolean Museum, Oxford; 113: Ashmolean Museum, Oxford; 114-115: British Museum (Michael Holford Library)/British Museum/National Museum, Naples (Scala); 116: Photoresources; 123: R.V. Schoder; 125: British Museum; 126: Ronald Sheridan Photo-Library; 128-129: British Museum/Ronald Sheridan Photo-Library; 131: R.V. Schoder; 132: Photoresources; 137: Ronald Sheridan Photo-Library; 138-139: Ronald Sheridan Photo-Library; 140-141: British Museum; 142: R.V. Schoder; 144-145: R.V. Schoder/Ronald Sheridan Photo-Library; 146-147: National Museum, Rome (Photoresources); 149: Photoresources; 150-151: British Museum/Sonia Halliday Photographs; 152: Ronald Sheridan Photo-Library; 156-157: British Museum/Photoresources; 158: Department of Manuscripts, University Library, Amsterdam; 160-161: Capitoline Museum, Rome (R.V. Schoder)/Photoresources/British Museum; 162: R.V. Schoder; 166: Bibliothèque Nationale, Paris; 168-169: British Museum/R.V. Schoder; 170: Ronald Sheridan Photo-Library; 172: British Museum; 174: Uffizi Gallery, Florence (Scala); 176-177: Prima Porta, Rome (Photoresources)/Ronald Sheridan Photo-Library; 180-181: British Museum/Ronald Sheridan Photo-Library; 184: British Museum; 188: Photoresources; 190: Louvre Museum (Ronald Sheridan Photo-Library); 192: R.V. Schoder; 194: Ronald Sheridan Photo-Library; 196-197: British Museum/Sonia Halliday Photographs; 198-199: Photoresources; 202-203: R.V. Schoder/Photoresources; 204-205: R.V. Schoder; 207: Bibliothèque Nationale, Paris; 208: R.V. Schoder; 211: Hirmer Fotoarchiv; 212: Sonia Halliday Photographs; 214-215: Director in Aerial Photography, University of Cambridge; 216-217: Sonia Halliday Photographs/San Vitale, Ravenna (R.V. Schoder).